To Joan
– helpmate for over fifty years

Social and industrial movements of far-reaching importance are now in progress, and what they portend no living man can say. The immediate responsibility for guiding their development in accordance with the welfare of the nation lies upon those to whom the country has entrusted the conduct of its business. Behind the Government is the unseen but irresistible force of public opinion; it is difficult to ascertain with any degree of precision what this opinion is, but – subject to the exigencies of party politics – the Cabinet will always endeavour to carry out what they believe to be the wishes of the Public. It is, therefore, of the utmost importance that the power which thus controls national policy, and indirectly the legislation which gives it effect, should be as fully informed as possible about the conditions upon which its opinion and its mandates are based. But our social organisation is now so complicated, and the action and reaction of forces within it so intricate and so difficult to estimate, that public opinion is apt to be formed upon a very incomplete understanding of existing facts.

Sir Arthur Clay, *Syndicalism and Labour* (1911)

CONTENTS

CONTENTS

INTRODUCTION TO THE
2002 EDITION

This book was first published in 1989, a year before Margaret Thatcher resigned as prime minister and eight years before Tony Blair won his first landslide victory for New Labour. At first sight it would seem that the political and social landscape has changed completely since then. After a frustrating delay under John Major, many hoped for the demise of Thatcherism and the triumphalist 'free market', and the resurgence of a less individualistic, more community-oriented government and society. The backlash of Thatcherism, it was hoped, would be a mere pause in the evolution of a mature professional society, with a restored balance between the public and private sector professionals and all the benefits of a mutually supportive system based on education, meritocracy, social responsibility on the part of the successful, and secure incomes and conditions of work and life for the less fortunate.

Alas, it has not turned out that way. New Labour has turned out to mean Thatcherism with a human face, even more freedom for big business to dominate the national economy and world trade, and the return of a more powerful private sector in disguise, that is, public–private partnerships with guaranteed profits to the investor and the risks carried by the taxpayer. Government, despite a half-hearted devolution to Wales, Scotland and Northern Ireland, has become even more centralized, with parliament sidelined to rubber-stamp the executive's decisions, local government all but irrelevant, and even the central administration subordinated to a power-hungry Downing Street where a presidential type of alternative government through unelected advisers prevails over cabinet ministers and civil service mandarins alike.

Paradoxically, however, the main trends of professional society, not all of them intended or beneficial, have continued to advance. These trends, road tested in a study of professional society in six major societies across the developed world published in 1996, are laid out in the following table.

THE MAJOR TRENDS OF PROFESSIONAL SOCIETY

(1) High living standards for (nearly) all

A dramatic rise in GNP per head affecting most of the population, but with an uneducated underclass of the socially excluded.

(2) The swing to services

Most workers no longer in agriculture and manufacturing but in services, some no more skilled than old manual labour but increasing numbers in professional, intellectually demanding occupations.

(3) Class into hierarchy

Broad class divisions gradually replaced by professional hierarchies, occupational ladders in diverse service occupations, increasingly employed either by the state or by large corporations.

(4) Meritocracy

Recruitment and promotion by merit, professionally trained expertise – though skewed because some can 'buy merit' more easily than others, while some have 'merit' thrust upon them.

(5) Women's equality

Professional society is the first society in history to offer women a (limited) degree of equality, based on higher education and the replacement of manual labour by mental, though at the expense of a dual burden of work.

(6) Higher education as the key profession

Higher education expands dramatically as the creator of merit, human capital, professional expertise in every major field, including bureaucracy in the government and corporate sectors.

(7) The growth of government

Professional services (education, health, welfare, defence, and law and order) all expand state administration, if not as a direct provider then as regulator and contractor. Hence the continuing rise in government expenditure, despite efforts to contain it.

(8) State welfare

The welfare state, professionally organized, an essential support of social cohesion and defence against political and economic breakdown, continues expanding although under pressure from the free market lobby.

(9) The rise of the giant corporation

Big sister to the state's big brother, the professionally managed giant corporation has become the dominant player in the national economy, with contradictory effects on its employees and customers.

(10) Globalization

The global economy is increasingly dominated by the professional executives of the TNCs (transnational corporations), the top 100 of which are richer and more powerful than three quarters of the member states of the United Nations, and use national governments as their proxies in global policies and operations.

Source: Extracted from *The Third Revolution: Professional Elites in the Modern World*, Routledge, 1996, dealing with Britain, the United States, France, the two Germanies, the Soviet Union, and Japan, since World War II.

Without changing the text below, in order to view professional society without hindsight at its level under Thatcherism, it is revealing to ask how the ten trends have fared in the dozen years since Thatcher was abandoned by the Conservative Cabinet. Surprisingly, most of the trends have continued to progress, if not always in expected ways. Average living standards in Britain have continued to rise, better than in many rival countries. In March 2002, the International Monetary Fund congratulated Britain on 'nine years of sustained non-inflationary growth, the longest such expansion in 30 years,' averaging almost 3 per cent p.a., the fastest of any developed country (*Guardian*, 8/3/02). Gross Domestic Product per head (at purchasing power parities) advanced from $12,340 in 1989 to $21,673 in 2000, a 75.6 per cent increase, amounting after inflation to 36.1 per cent – an impressive gain in living standards in a dozen years (OECD *Economic Surveys: Britain*, 1989 and 2002). Allowing for other indices of quality of life, this made Britain the fifth most prosperous country in the world (United Nations

Human Development Report, 2001). Meanwhile, the gap in disposable income between rich and poor remained much the same, though nearly one in five (18 per cent) remained below the (relative) poverty line, with less than 60 per cent of median income; while the richest 1 per cent own 23 per cent of the wealth and half the population own only 6 per cent (OECD: *Britain*, p. 65; *Social Trends*, 2002, pp. 87, 99).

The swing to services, not all professional of course, has gone still further, from 68 per cent of the workforce in 1989 to 72 per cent in 2000, reducing the share in manufacturing industry from 29.8 to 26.5 per cent, leaving consumers heavily dependent on manufactured imports from the Third World. Agriculture now accounts for less than 2 per cent of employment and even less of GDP, making Britain one of the countries most dependent on food imports. (OECD: *Britain*, Basic Statistics table).

Hierarchy has almost overwhelmed class: the trade unions have been marginalized, despite threats of strike action by rail workers, air traffic controllers, postal workers, teachers and others; and the once (predominantly) working-class Labour Party has been replaced by New Labour, a self-styled pragmatic party without the class roots of Old Labour, a worrying development for both unions and party members.

Meritocracy has been transmogrified, as merit has come to be defined in non-traditional ways, to include talents no longer dependent on higher education: pop music, fashion modelling, sport, Britart, television presenting, soap operas, and other celebrity vehicles now yield huge incomes and greater wealth than ever. Women have become yet more equal, both in higher education (up from 46 to 55 per cent of the students) and employment (up from 43 to 45 per cent of the workforce), and their hourly full-time earnings have risen from 75 to 82 per cent of men's (*Social Trends*, pp. 60, 71, 92). But recruitment and promotion have been less than feminists would like especially in the top echelons, and modest advance has been at the cost of overburdening themselves with double careers in the job market and in the domestic sphere. Higher education, the chief creator of human capital, has been broadened, largely by the upgrading of colleges and polytechnics to university status, to cater for a third or more of the student age group, although at the price of charging fees and abolishing maintenance grants which the Tories avoided but New Labour imposed at the risk of excluding the children of the least affluent.

Despite the boasted rolling back of the state, government has continued to extend its influence over civil society; control by the centre has gone further than ever before. Within government itself, where democracy has declined still more and a species of elective dictatorship, begun under Thatcher, central control has been expanded. The welfare state, victim of attack and erosion by the free market ideology, has been severely squeezed under the Major and Blair governments, to the point where public services, especially the National Health Service, education, public transport, and police and prisons, have become the main target of political complaint.

Above all, the giant corporation has become more gigantic, with mergers and takeovers increasing at a faster pace, undermining some of the most beneficial trends of professional society, notably the career ladder and secure conditions of work and retirement, now guaranteed only for the top executives. Finally, the global economy, run increasingly by the executives of the transnational corporations, has become even more dominant, extending increasingly unequal incomes and life chances across the world. This has provoked a backlash from the Third World and the anti-globalization movement, to which we should now add the threat of terrorism against the affluent West.

There are other, less healthy trends, clouds no bigger than a person's hand in the 1980s, that are now threatening the world. A by-product of affluence and economic growth, global warming, denied by the United States government and the multinational corporations, has become incontrovertible, with floods in Africa, South Asia and the United States itself, forest fires in Indonesia, California and Australia, rising sea levels in the Pacific islands and other low-lying countries, and even encephalitis-carrying mosquitoes in New York. Do-it-yourself terrorism of the Al-Qaeda kind is a serious challenge to the very notion of the nation state, and religious fundamentalism, not only by Islamists, is calling on loyalties that override patriotic nationalism. What the American government calls 'rogue states', many of them originally funded and armed by the United States during the Cold War, have begun to develop weapons of mass destruction, aimed at the West and the global economy. Both terrorists with sophisticated techniques and weapons and the scientists of 'rogue states' with nuclear, chemical and biological devices have been trained in professional institutions, often in the leading universities of the West.

All these trends, for good or ill, are at bottom driven by one single factor: human capital, or professional, educated expertise. That factor is still at work but with unexpected effects that belie the older conceptions of educated merit. The cult of celebrity and the rise of huge incomes and capital accumulations have created a new meritocracy of talent owing little to higher education in the traditional sense. Sportsmen like David Beckham and Ian Wright, pop stars like Madonna, and Paul McCartney, fashion models like Kate Moss and Naomi Campbell, artists like Damien Hirst and Tracy Emin, have become millionaires and some owners of landed estates, with success owing more to luck and media hype than to formal training. They are the exceptional beneficiaries of 'jackpot' professions in which many are called but few are chosen, but have the unlooked-for effect of giving hope to those who have missed out in the orthodox educational stakes.

On the other hand, the high road for most professionals in search of exceptional rewards has been corporate business, especially in finance and electronic services, like the vulnerable City financial traders and dot.com millionaires of the recent, now exploded, 1990s boom. These are only a special case, however, of the private sector professionals, now mostly MBAs trained in business schools, who conform to the traditional meritocratic career pattern. Like the celebrities, they are also in jackpot professions. The few who reach the top of the major corporations or law, advertising and financial firms can name their own rewards, in vast incomes and in share options, bonuses, huge pensions and golden severance pay, that bear almost no relation to success or failure.

They have had, however, a disruptive side effect on the mass of their employees, and have overturned one of the most beneficial trends of professionalism, the secure and progressive career. This has been replaced in many cases by self-employed consultancy, with bidding for uncertain work, no national insurance or pension contributions, no unemployment benefit, and no redundancy pay. These ostensibly free-lance yet virtually dependent workers have become a further layer in the hierarchy of corporate capitalism, along with shareholders, sub-contractors and franchisees, whose life chances are indirectly controlled by the executives at the head of the corporations. The giant corporations are not individual entities operating in solitary isolation but are locked into a hierarchy of institutions – from holding companies, insurance firms, banks and pension funds above to subsidiary companies, sub-contractors and franchisees below – that emulates the feudal hierarchies of barons, knights, squires, retainers, grand and petty sergeants, free-holders and serfs of the middle ages. This system, of mutual dependency and compulsory loyalty, I have called elsewhere corporate neo-feudalism (see *The Third Revolution*, Routledge, 1996, pp. 42–7).

As such it exists, in accordance with capitalist ideology, to make and extract profit from the layered dependants. Justified as long as the exchange is mutually beneficial and the reward gap not excessive, it can rapidly become exploitation. The corporate feudal lords' human capital is transformed into material wealth and fixed capital and also into power over the feudal 'tenants'. At the same time the elite have outmanoeuvred the public sector professionals, civil servants, local government officers, doctors, teachers, professors, social workers, and other public servants, in income and influence and, through the introduction of managerialism into the health service, education, social services and the rest. They have imbued the public sector with the free market view that it is a cost to the taxpayer instead of a creative investment in human capital. The one leg of the professional body politic has shrivelled at the expense of the other and almost crippled the professional ideal.

One aspect of this distortion of the ideal is the degeneration of the welfare state. The original welfare state of 1948 with its universal provision of social security, medical treatment, equal education, and pensions was gradually eroded by inflation but retained its popularity even under Thatcher. Famously she declared in 1982, 'The National Health Service is safe with us.' Her mentors in the free market lobby, however, kept up a continuous campaign against public provision with pamphlets like *Wither the Welfare State* (Institute of Economic Affairs, 1981) and *The Moral Hazard of State Benefits* (IEA, 1982) and aimed to replace it with private health insurance, education vouchers, insurance-based pensions, and the like. Although they never succeeded in abolishing it, they encouraged erosion via the stagnation of benefits and the substitution of private alternatives.

Nevertheless, they could not have expected that a New Labour government would embrace their aims with more success than the Conservatives. Prime Minister Tony Blair and Chancellor Gordon Brown began by accepting Tory limits on taxation for the first two years, which had the effect of starving the public services and limiting their growth thereafter. They 'thought the unthinkable' and made cuts where the Tories feared to tread: in payments to the disabled, in the real value of retirement pensions, grants for university students, and so on. Although they have bowed to public opinion since and allocated larger funds for them, even talking of raising and hypothecating taxes, they are only playing 'catch-up' to where they started. That a party which believed in equality of life chances and treatment should desert its founding philosophy is a measure of the decline of political credibility.

A second aspect is the extension of the Thatcherite drive towards privatization, typically, however, in disguised ways. The 'Third Way,' via private finance initiatives and public–private partnerships, is a means of partial privatization by the back door. Thatcher's programme of privatiszation, intensified by John Major, was hotly condemned by New Labour while in opposition. In office, however, it accepted the Tory privatizations, like Railtrack (the bankrupt railroad authority) and the public utilities some of which have failed and sold their assets back to the customers. It then went further and planned the partial privatization of vital public services like the London Underground, Air Traffic Control, and a number of NHS hospitals, against the wishes of their own party members and the public opinion polls.

Privatization as such is ostensibly neutral, but the effect of the Third Way has been to invite private enterprise in a one-sided bargain, by which the investors take guaranteed profits of up to 30 per cent for 30 years and the taxpayer underwrites the risk of loss. Already the system has begun to fail: in the case of Railtrack and Air Traffic Control, both operations made massive losses within months of their first crises, the Ladbroke Grove and Selby train crashes and the September 11 terrorist attack on the World Trade Center, but that did not halt the government's determination to press on with their programme for the London Underground. Meanwhile, one unintended effect has been the purchase of public utilities like water and electricity by overseas corporations, mainly American and French, that have no interest in British customers except to maximize profit. The Third Way has become a milch cow for private corporations, British and foreign.

A third distortion of the professional ideal is the subordination of British business to the global economy. In principle, the global economy is a beneficial movement, a further expansion of the market that has been going on for centuries. However, in the current acceleration of the trend, based on Anglo-American managerial or shareholder capitalism (unlike the stakeholder capitalisms of Europe and Japan) and controlled by the American-dominated World Trade Organisation, the International Monetary Fund and the World Bank, Britain and Europe and, even more so, the Third World have become dependent on rules that benefit the United States and its corporations at the expense of the rest of the world. The American government operates a double standard, insisting on free trade wherever they have the advantage, as in bananas from the Boston Fruit Company's plantations in the Caribbean or genetically modified soya or rice seeds, while slapping on protective tariffs where their own industries, like steel and textiles, cannot compete. They also demand the right to patent and copyright discoveries and inventions, even human genes and medicines vital to mankind's protection from epidemic plagues like AIDS, which ought in natural justice to be free. Such a manipulation of the otherwise benevolent global system for the benefit of one country and its big business is a derogation of the free market. That the British government, unlike the Europeans, should go along with it is a betrayal of British interests.

The final distortion of the professional ideal is the further decline of democracy adumbrated in Chapter 7 below (pp. 324–31). There it is suggested that parliamentary democracy in Britain has been inverted. Instead of the constituency party members selecting the candidates and the voters choosing between them, the MPs electing the Cabinet and the Cabinet choosing the Prime Minister, and both he and they being answerable to the Commons, the Prime Minister, once elected by the party, by a convoluted process becomes an elective dictator. He chooses the Cabinet and junior ministers, they control parliament through a draconian system of whips, and the leadership increasingly controls the list of potential constituency candidates and so the membership of the Commons majority.

New Labour has taken centralization several degrees further. The Cabinet has been marginalized by a network of special advisers centred on 10 Downing Street, where an alternative system of government has been set up that parallels and overrides the departmental ministers and civil servants. The Cabinet meets only to hear what the Prime Minister has already agreed in preemptive meetings with individual ministerial heads, often tripartite sessions involving the chief special advisers, notably information chief Alistair Campbell and chief of staff Jonathan Powell, who are far more powerful than any departmental minister. It has become a presidential system, where all decisions are made at the top and delivered as diktats to the individual ministries. The special advisers in the ministries liaise with their counterparts in No. 10, and are protected by them in any conflicts that might arise between them and the departmental civil servants. Even the election of the Chairman of the Party is not by the MPs or the paid-up members but is imposed by the Prime Minister, and is the leading enforcer of authority in the presidential structure.

Meanwhile, the House of Commons has been deprived of its role of advice and consent to the government and has become a sounding board for ministerial announcements, often already disclosed to the press, and the automatic legislator of policies determined at the autocratic centre. The House of Lords, the only element in the structure with the guts to disagree, has been filleted of its (ironically) only independent members, the hereditary peers, who are soon to be replaced by a majority of government appointees in what will become the most powerful quango in the land. This presidential model lacks, however, the safeguards of the American Constitution, the separation of powers that gives independence to the Congress and prevents the President from acting without constraint. The American system also prevents a temporary legislative majority from unilaterally changing the constitution, as in the case of reform of the House of Lords. The present incumbent, however, like Thatcher forgets one critical thing: he has overwhelming power only so long as he commands the acquiescence of the Cabinet. Absolute power corrupts absolutely, Lord Acton said; what he did not say was that absolute power sooner or later provokes rebellion. It took eleven years for Margaret Thatcher to discover that overweening pride goes before a fall. Tony Blair has yet to discover that humbling lesson, and time is fast running out.

Professional society, like every human social system before it, is subject to distortions and unintended consequences. It is Janus-faced: it has a smiling face offering material gains and cultural benefits, and an ugly one leading to exploitation, implosion and self-destruction. The hope is that its benefits will outweigh its drawbacks. It is potentially the most efficient and egalitarian system in the history of humanity for delivering affluence and disseminating happiness. Yet, like all human institutions, it is subject to the temptations of greed and corruption that clever men and women, especially those trained in professional skills without the ethics of the professional ideal, can devise. 'Be good, sweet maid, and let who can be clever,' Charles Kingsley wisely counselled. This is good advice for professionals everywhere, if professional society is to yield its unique meritocratic and egalitarian potential.

Little Venice, W2
March, 2002

PREFACE TO THE FIRST EDITION

Two decades ago I wrote a book that set out to discover *The Origins of Modern English Society* (Routledge & Kegan Paul, 1969, Ark, 1985). It found them in the more than Industrial Revolution of 1780–1880, 'a social revolution with social causes and a social process as well as profound social effects', including the demise of the old pre-industrial aristocratic society and the rise of the viable class society of mid-Victorian England. Since all history is a seamless web, it looked forward in the last paragraph, as all unfinished histories should, to the next phase of the story, the decline of Victorian class society and its replacement by the very different society of twentieth-century England. The present book, all too belatedly since most of my teaching, research and publications have fallen in between, is the long-promised sequel to that first one.

I do not regret the delay, for three principal reasons. Firstly, contemporary history, in the sense of history that stops only at the present and is still in large part remembered by people now living, is for obvious reasons the most controversial and lacks the corrective of a tranquil and healing hindsight. It therefore needs more, not less, maturity than the older kind. Secondly, a historian can never have enough experience, and the historian of contemporary society is better qualified, or less unqualified, if he has lived through a considerable part of his period. Teaching grandparents to suck eggs, never a much appreciated endeavour, is even less appreciated when done by youngsters. Thirdly, putting the first two reasons together, the delay has enabled me to see more clearly the trends which I perceived only dimly in my youthful inexperience, and indeed the years since the first book was published have brought a reaction against them which, paradoxically, has given them greater substance and reality. The owl of Minerva, Hegel shrewdly noted, flies at dusk; even if, he might have added, the twilight, optimistically speaking, turns out to be temporary.

The most important trend which I then discerned was the continuing expansion of what in the first book was called 'the forgotten middle class', the non-capitalist or professional segment of the middle class which was neglected by contemporary commentators including, most notably, the professionals themselves, who played a role in the rise of Victorian class society out of all proportion to their numbers. The professional class produced most of the social thinkers who supplied the concepts and terminology in which the three major classes, the landed aristocracy, the capitalist entrepreneurs and the manual workers, thought about themselves and achieved class consciousness. They also mounted a critique of industrial society which began, even at its height, to undermine the entrepreneurial hegemony and reform its worst excesses, in the shape of factory legislation, public health regulation, control of adulteration of food and drugs and pollution of the environment, housing by-laws, state educational provision, and the like. But the professional class was then only on the brink of the massive expansion in size and influence which was to carry it to domination in the twentieth century. Not only was it to overtake the landed and capitalist elites in numbers and importance; it was also to infiltrate all the major institutions of the modern state and modern society, from the executive government and parliament to the private capitalist corporations, and eventually to take them over.

At the same time the professional class was to transform society itself, not by replacing the plutocracy of landlords and capitalists as the ruling class, but in a much more radical and subtle way. Professionalism differed from land and capital as an organizing principle of social structure in not being confined to the few, those who owned the limited material resources of society and could charge the rest, in rent, profits or a lien on their labour, for the use of them. Based on human capital and specialized expertise, it could become as extensive as there were human beings capable of skilled and specialized service. In addition to the traditional, pre-industrial professions and the new technological and welfare ones, there could be professional managers of landed property and capitalist companies and even professionalized manual workers. The ownership of human capital was thus capable, at least in theory, of reaching much further down the social structure than the ownership of land or capital in amounts capable of supporting a ruling class, and was thus able to transform society not from the top down but from within. Instead of the horizontal layers we call classes in vertical conflict with one another, the new society would be constructed on a different principle, of professional career hierarchies rearing up alongside one another, some rising higher than the rest but each in competition to persuade society to yield as much power, prestige and income as it could win. Vertical structures, horizontal rivalries, replaced or, more accurately, overlay the horizontal structures and vertical antagonisms of class, which nevertheless, as old structures do, still survived in the 'residues' of language and, to a lesser extent, in politics.

Meanwhile, since great structural transformations reflect profound changes in mental outlook, the professional social ideal – the professionals' ideal of how society should be organized and of the ideal citizen to organize it – began to infiltrate men's minds and replace the entrepreneurial ideal on which Victorian society had been founded. The latter was an ideal based on capital as the engine of the economy, setting in motion the production of goods and services and calling forth the other factors of production, land and labour, and on competition as the fairest and most efficient way of distributing its rewards. Its ideal citizen was the self-made man, the entrepreneur who had made his way to success and fortune by his own unaided efforts. The professional ideal was based on trained expertise and selection by merit, a selection made not by the open market but by the judgment of similarly educated experts. Its ideal citizen was also a self-made man of sorts, who had risen by native ability (with a little help from his educational institutions) to mastery of a skilled service vital to his fellow citizens. The difference was that the entrepreneur proved himself by competition in the market, the professional by persuading the rest of society and ultimately the state that his service was vitally important and therefore worthy of guaranteed reward. The first called for as little state interference as possible; the second looked to the state as the ultimate guarantor of professional status.

Both ideals believed in equality of opportunity – in theory if not always in practice – but only the professional ideal had any room for equality of outcome or treatment. This was because the best guarantee of professional employment was as wide an access to professional services as possible, preferably underwritten by the state. Hence the special role of the professional ideal in the rise of the welfare state, one of the major themes of this book.

Yet this rapprochement with the state, which was in any case coming to play a much larger part in the economy and the life of society under the same pressure of demand for ever more specialized services which had expanded the professions, was to become the Achilles' heel of professionalism. The enormous expansion of state expenditure and of government employment which took place in all advanced twentieth-century societies, tolerable in Britain as long as the economy continued to expand, was to become a source of grievance and hostility when, in the 1970s and 1980s, the long-continuing relative economic decline threatened to become absolute. Along with the accustomed arrogance and condescension of the professions, the elephantiasis of the state provoked a backlash which took the form of what appeared to be, and was even claimed as such by its protagonists, a resurgence of the free market ideology of Victorian England. On closer analysis, however, it turned out to be not a revival of the entrepreneurial ideal but a reaction of one part of the professional class, the private sector managers of the great corporations and their allies, who had never felt the same degree of need for state support, against the other, the public sector professions largely employed by the state.

The bifurcation of the professional ideal reflected the splitting of the professional class into two warring factions. It also heralds the political dilemma facing contemporary Britain and by extension professional society everywhere: the unwelcome choice between the two extremes of an authoritarian state run by powerful and domineering professional bureaucrats and a more diffuse neo-feudal system of great private corporations run by equally dangerous and domineering professional managers.

Once again we stand at the threshold of what may become a great transformation of society. Which way does the future lie? This time we cannot say, 'What that society *was* to be, and how it was to evolve ..., must await another book.' What it *is* to be must await another generation and, this time, another historian.

*

Before or after he was impeached as a judge for taking bribes, Francis Bacon wrote in his posthumous *Maxims of the Law*:

> I hold every man to be a debtor to his profession, from which as men do of course seek to receive countenance and profit, so ought they to endeavour themselves, by way of amends, to be a help and an ornament thereunto.

History is a profession of debtors, if not indeed of thieves, who shamelessly borrow or steal from one another, and who in fact could not trade upon their own capital alone. To change the metaphor, we could not see even as far as we do without standing on the shoulders of our predecessors. The history of a hundred crowded years of modern English society would be impossible to write without calling on the aid of scores, if not hundreds, of scholars, by no means all of them historians, many of them friends and colleagues, most of them unknown to me except through their writings. My debts to them will be obvious from the notes to the text, and I hope that they will take each reference as a grateful thank-you for much needed help.

It would be almost impossible to list all the friends and colleagues with whom, over the years, I have discussed some of the ideas in this book, but there are a few who single themselves out by their generous encouragement and support, whether or not they agreed with me (and I fear they often did not). Among them Asa Briggs, Theo Barker, Daniel Bell, Jack Hexter, Seymour Martin Lipset, Lawrence Stone, Michael (F. M. L.) Thompson and Martin Wiener deserve more thanks than I can say. My colleagues at Lancaster and Northwestern Universities, notably Tim Breen, Eric Evans, Bill (T. W.) Heyck and Austin Woolrych, were enormously understanding and supportive. Eric Evans, Bill Heyck, Tony Morris and George Robb read and commented on part or all of the manuscript, to my gain which might have been greater but for my stubborn adherence to my views.

I must also thank Lancaster University and its History Department for the long years of camaraderie and endless conversation, the Shelby Cullom Davis Center at Princeton University for a year of gestation and research in stimulating company, the National Humanities Center for a year of research and writing at that ideal intellectual retreat in the woods of North

Carolina, and Northwestern University for welcoming a refugee from the British university system and making him feel at home in a land which still appreciates education. Finally, my warmest thanks go to my wife Joan, who gave unstintingly of her abundant enthusiasm, sympathetic criticism and effervescent personality, read the manuscript and saved me from endless slips of the pen (or the computer keys), and paid me the handsomest compliment of all by becoming a social historian herself.

Northwestern University
November 1987

Chapter 1

THE MEANING OF PROFESSIONAL SOCIETY

After the unanswerable question whether human civilization will survive for much longer or succumb to a catastrophe that may destroy all sentient life on earth, the most important question facing mankind today is: if we escape the holocaust, what sort of society will we survive to live in? What sort of society is it that has brought us to this brink, of unprecedented power both for creation and destruction? All of us now in the more economically advanced countries routinely enjoy material comforts far beyond the luxuries of Cleopatra, Kubla Khan or even Queen Victoria. We travel faster and more freely than Ariel, hear sounds and sweet airs more appealing than Prospero's, conjure living pictures out of the void at the touch of a button, have instant access to grand opera, ballet, classical and rock music, the Olympic Games and the World Cup, and all the delights that our ancestors could only dream of. And most of us live lives far longer, fuller and freer from pain than our predecessors.

At the same time we live in greater fear, not just of those old enemies famine, plague and war (the Sahel drought, the AIDS epidemic and the Gulf War show that those enemies are still with us), but of total extermination, if not by the instant horror of nuclear holocaust then by the slow attrition of the environment. In pursuit of the Nirvana of material bliss and avoidance of the Inferno of nuclear destruction we also have to choose politically, between a Western version of democracy that allows free play to competitive forces but may end in the survival of anti-democratic concentrations of economic power, and an Eastern version that claims to put human welfare first but from the outset sacrifices freedom to equality.

Increasingly Specialised

Increasingly diverse

Increasingly skilled

= Increasingly Professional

brought us to this pass? Faced with such
successes and dangers, we may well think with
'Things are in the saddle, and ride mankind.'[1] It is
that men and women working together in social
have produced these dilemmas. We ourselves,
wittingly, are the authors of our own prosperity
destruction. Whole armies of experts – scientists,
industrial managers, highly skilled workers,
hers, artists, writers, teachers, administrators and
ave contributed to our promising and perilous
situation. The world we have gained and may be about to lose is
the consequence of a myriad human activities which have only
one thing in common: they are increasingly specialized,
increasingly diverse, increasingly skilled – in a word, increasingly
professional. The twentieth is not, *pace* Franklin D. Roosevelt, the
century of the common man but of the uncommon and increasingly professional expert.

1 CLASS VERSUS HIERARCHY

We live, in fact, in an increasingly professional society. Modern
society in Britain, as elsewhere in the developed world, is made up
of career hierarchies of specialized occupations, selected by merit
and based on trained expertise. Where pre-industrial society was
based on passive property in land and industrial society on actively
managed capital, professional society is based on human capital
created by education and enhanced by strategies of closure, that is,
the exclusion of the unqualified. Landed and industrial wealth
still exerts power but is increasingly managed by corporate
professionals in property companies and business corporations.
The professional hierarchies cut across the horizontal solidarities
of class in the warp and weft of the social fabric. Both class and
hierarchy are an integral part of the fabric and neither ever quite
disappears from view. The 'great functional interests' of land,
trade and finance, each representing a vertical swathe from
landlord through farmer to labourer or merchant through putter-
out to craftsman, predominated over the latent class conflict of
eighteenth-century society.[2] The organized antagonisms of the
Anti-Corn Law League against the landlords and of the Chartists
against both landed politicians and industrial employers brought

class to the face of the cloth in Victorian society. In late twentieth-century Britain, despite the survival of class rhetoric and class-based political parties, the warp of professionalism is beginning to show through and overlay the weft of class.

A professional society is more than a society dominated by professionals. The professionals are not just another ruling class, replacing the landlords of pre-industrial society and the capitalists of industrial society as in James Burnham's *The Managerial Revolution* – though there is the ever-present danger that some of them might try to become so. Professionalism permeates society from top to bottom, in two ways. Firstly, the professional hierarchies – not all of them equal in status or rewards, or stretching as far as the top – reach much further down the social pyramid than ever landlordship or even business capital did, and embrace occupations formerly thought beyond the reach of professional aspiration. As more and more jobs become subject to specialized training and claim expertise beyond the common sense of the layman – and all professionals are laymen to the other professions – their occupants demand the status and rewards of a profession. In these days of increasingly employed professionals – close to the original model of the clergy or the military rather than medicine or the law, though even doctors and lawyers are now mostly salaried employees – this means a secure income, a rising salary scale, fringe benefits such as paid holidays and sick leave, and an occupational pension. Such professional conditions of work are increasingly within reach not merely of non-manual workers but of increasing numbers of the manual working class.

Secondly, a professional society is one permeated by the professional social ideal. A social ideal is a model of how society should be organized to suit a certain class or interest and of the ideal citizen and his contribution to it. Pre-industrial society was permeated by the aristocratic ideal based on property and patronage. Passive property, usually in land, provided the means for the ideal citizen, the leisured gentleman, to offer his unique contribution of political rule, moral leadership and encouragement of art, literature and sport. Patronage enabled him to select the recruits for those positions of power and influence not filled by property alone. Industrial society was permeated by the entrepreneurial ideal based on active capital and competition, on business investment as the engine of the economy run by the active owner-manager, ideally the self-made man who rose to wealth and influence by his own intrinsic worth and won out in open competition. The rival ideal of the working class, never achieved in practice, was the collective ideal of labour and co-operation, of labour as the sole source of wealth and co-operative endeavour as the fairest means of harnessing and rewarding it, and of the worker's right to the whole produce of labour. The professional ideal, based on trained expertise and selection by merit, differed from the other three in emphasizing human capital rather than passive or active property, highly skilled and differentiated labour rather than the simple labour theory of value, and selection by merit defined as trained and certified expertise. No more or no less than the rest did it live up to reality. Not all landlords were benevolent gentlemen, not all capitalists self-made men, not all wage earners more concerned with rising with their class rather than out of it. And not all professional men were prepared to let merit rise without help from family wealth or privileged education. Professional society is based on merit, but some acquire merit more easily than others.

The ideals compete in a wider field than the economic market for income and wealth. They compete in the societal market for income, power and status. To complicate the metaphor and make the social fabric three-dimensional, we can envisage society – any society – as an *equi-valent tetrahedron*, a three-sided pyramid, its faces labelled (with acknowledgments to Max Weber) class, power and status.[3] The faces are only three ways of looking at the same social reality, from the economic, the political, and the socio-ideological point of view. No face – *pace* Marx (or, rather, the vulgar Marxists) with the economic interpretation of society, Ralf Dahrendorf with the primacy of political authority in 'coordinated organizations' (*Herrschaftsverbanden* – derived indeed from Weber), or Weber himself with his emphasis on charisma, religious belief and morality – is more fundamental than the other two. They are *equi-valent*, of equal worth, at least until one of them wins out in the competition. Talk of economic substructure and political or cultural superstructure, as in the Marxist or *Annales* schools of historiography, is premature until one examines empirically the society in question.

Industrial society was of course based on the ownership of capital, but capital itself was based on the concept of absolute property, which was the product of law and politics. Ultimately it derived from the victory of English landlords over the peasants, the church and the crown which came to be enshrined in 12 Charles II, cap. 24, the Act of 1660 which turned feudal tenures into freeholds.[4] The capitalists, who took no part in the struggle for absolute property, were the fortuitous beneficiaries of laws enacted for the benefit of landlords. Pre-industrial society was based on landed property but ultimately on feudal conquest and the continuous struggle between landlords and kings from the Conquest to the Civil War, and thus on military force. The wealth of the medieval church, by contrast, derived from its power to persuade kings, barons and commoners to endow it with land and goods in return for spiritual services, above all prayers for their souls. When the doctrine of purgatory was rejected at the Reformation, making prayers for the dead irrelevant, half of its wealth was confiscated.

Thus wealth, power and status could derive from any face of the pyramid. For the social fabric inside the pyramid has a fourth dimension: change over time. It is not static but dynamic. The three forces, economic, political and socio-ideological, are variant forms of energy transmutable (with suitable transformers and inevitable transmission losses) into either or both of the other two. Physical force by feudal conquerors or Mafia-like, home-grown strong men is readily transmutable into wealth (land tenure) and status (lordship). Economic power is less readily transformed into status and authority because purchasing power (claims on labour) requires the pre-condition of symbolic property (currency or credit instruments), both based on pre-existing law, and also the agreement of the existing holders of power and status to honour it, by, for example, the sale of feudal land or aristocratic titles – unless, of course, these can be seized by revolution, in which case capitalism comes to rest as much on force as feudalism.

More easily forgotten is that status, or socio-ideological, cultural, intellectual or spiritual power, has often been transformed into wealth and political authority. A good case could be made (though it is unlikely to hold for all historical societies) for the primacy of the socio-ideological face. The greatest conquerors from Alexander to Napoleon and Hitler have used charisma to gather followers and inspire their armies, and industrialists like Carnegie, Ford and Nuffield have used propaganda and philanthropy to sing the benefits of capitalism. More directly, charismatic power has often been used to take over the wealth and authority of whole societies: consider the careers of Savanarola, Eva Peron or the Ayatollah Khomeini and their use of inspirational oratory to command the obedience, wealth and military force of their societies. Longer-lived political success has accrued to ideological persuasion by priests and bureaucrats: to the Aztec and Inca priest-kings who persuaded their subjects that daily human sacrifice caused the sun to rise and the seasons to return; to the Bishops of Rome whose wealth and power flowed from control of the keys of heaven; and to the Chinese imperial bureaucracy whose monopoly of administrative skill seduced wave after wave of less civilized conquerors. Socio-ideological persuasion is an enviable form of power (while it lasts, and its weakness is that it can fade as fast as the belief in it) since its devotees give freely and enthusiastically what they yield only grudgingly to military force or superior purchasing power. Political and economic elites pay it the compliment of emulation in propaganda and education.

The professions in general may not aspire to such heights of charismatic persuasion but their *modus vivendi* starts from the same face of the pyramid. They live by persuasion and propaganda, by claiming that their particular service is indispensable to the client or employer and to society and the state. By this means they hope to raise their status and through it their income, authority and psychic rewards (deference and self-respect). With luck and persistence they may turn the human capital they acquire into material wealth. In the pre-industrial past individual professionals – royal favourites (in the oldest profession) like George Villiers, Duke of Buckingham or Nell Gwyn, archbishops like Wolsey and Sumner, judges like Lords Eldon and Scott, generals like Marlborough and Wellington, and even lowly solicitors with other incomes like Sir John Hawkins or Sir Walter Scott – were able to buy land and try to found a family. In industrial society even actors and playwrights like Sheridan, Ellen Terry and Bernard Shaw turned human capital into visible wealth. But only in post-industrial society have the professions as a whole been able to establish human capital as the dominant form of wealth. Whereas a hundred years ago, according to Peter Lindert, human capital accounted for only about 15 per cent of national income, it now accounts for about 52 per cent.[5]

Property is not, as is commonly believed, an object or a credit instrument, which are just its outward signs. Leaving aside its lesser meaning as the right to immediate use of tangible objects like a car, a house or an owner-occupied farm (each of which, indeed, yields an imputed rent), property in its major meaning of power over resources, which creates relations between members of a society, is *a right to a flow of income*: rent, interest, profits, labour service, or goods in kind. It is an acknowledged and legitimated claim to other people's labour.

How could the professions transform a service into income-yielding property? Gary Becker, Pierre Bourdieu, Alvin Gouldner, Anthony Giddens and others have familiarized the concepts of human, educational, cultural and intellectual capital, by which investment in acquired knowledge and expertise yields a rate of return commensurate with that of material capital.[6] Such theories tend to assume that investment in specialized training *of itself* yields a differential return without any control of the market (other than the fortuitous economic or demographic fluctuations in supply and demand for specialized labour). Unfortunately for that analysis, specialized training of itself yields only earned income, payment for immediate services rendered, which may even fall below the cost of production if the service is oversupplied or undervalued. It cannot, except accidentally, create property in the form of vested income without some device to transform it into a scarce resource.

The transforming device is professional control of the market. When a professional occupation has, by active persuasion of the public and the state, acquired sufficient control of the market in a particular service, it creates an artificial scarcity in the supply which has the effect of yielding a rent, in the strict Ricardian sense of a payment for the use of a scarce resource. Some part of the payment, of course, will always accrue to the immediate work performed, but its value will be enhanced by an amount proportional to the scarcity of the service or skill. A natural or 'accidental' example, the fortuitous result of a unique though professionally trained voice, is that of Placido Domingo, who is paid a very large fee for each performance, most of which is rent for the use of the scarce resource, or a Henry Moore sculpture, which is a lump of stone transformed in value by his signature. Monopoly is not a *sine qua non*: scarcity may appear long before

7

outright monopoly – the landlords charged rent long before achieving a monopoly, if they ever did – and the element of rent will be larger or smaller accordingly. But *some* element of rent accrues from *any* degree of control of the market, which is why organized professions are paid more than equivalent unorganized occupations. Since the essence of property is the right to (some portion of) the flow of income from the resource owned, this professional capital, which is manifestly more tangible than stocks or shares, less destructible than many forms of material property (buildings burn more readily than people), and capable of self-renewal by means of improvement in skills and expertise, is thus in the truest sense a species of property – albeit contingent property, contingent upon the performance of the service.

The importance of such property to the professional is that it gives him what all income-yielding property provides for its possessors: independence, security, the right to criticize without fear of the consequences, and so a secure position from which to defend one's place in society or, if he so wishes, a position of leverage from which to change society or one's own corner of it. Above all, it gives him the psychic security and self-confidence to press his own social ideal, his own vision of society and how it should be organized, upon the other classes. And the gradual triumph of the professional ideal over the last hundred years, as we shall see in this book, paved the way for the hegemony of human capital and the emergence of professional society.

There was a crucial difference, however, between the hegemony of the professional ideal and that of the aristocratic or entre-preneurial ideals in earlier societies. Whereas their ideal citizen had been a limited concept, applicable to only one group in society, however many amongst the rest aspired to it – only the landed few could be leisured gentlemen, only those who acquired capital entrepreneurs – the professional ideal could in principle be extended to everyone. Every landlord and industrialist could be transformed into a professional manager, every worker into a salaried employee. Moreover, since the professional's status and income depend less on the market than on his power to persuade society to set an agreed value on his service, the ideal implied the principle of a just reward not only for the particular profession but for every occupation necessary to society's well-being.

Since, too, the ideal is justified by social efficiency and the avoidance of waste, particularly the waste of human talent, it implied a principle of social justice which extended to the whole population the right to security of income, educational opportunity, decent housing in a clean environment and, some professionals would say, the right and obligation to work. As will be argued later, the rise of the welfare state was a practical expression of the professional ideal. It was initially an attempt to extend to those as yet excluded from professional status the basic security and conditions already enjoyed by the established professions.

It is this potential extension of ideal citizenship to the whole community that differentiates professional society from its predecessors. Although the ideal embraces equality of opportunity and even equality of treatment in raising every citizen to the minimum acceptable standard of life, it is not in the final analysis an egalitarian society. To paraphrase George Orwell, all professionals are equal but some are more equal than others. It is not a class society in the traditional sense of a binary model with a small ruling class exploiting a large underclass, but a collection of parallel hierarchies of unequal height, each with its own ladder of many rungs. In this way the inequalities and rivalries of hierarchy come to predominate over those of class.

2 PROFESSIONAL RIVALRIES AND THE STATE

A professional society, therefore, is not merely the old class society fitted out with a new ruling class. It is a society structured around a different principle. The matrix of the new society is the vertical career hierarchy rather than the horizontal connection of class, and social conflict – no society being free from the struggle for income, power and status – takes the form of a competition for resources between rival interest groups. The doctors, the civil servants, the military, the social workers and administrators, the university and government scientific researchers are all manifestly in competition for public resources. The managers of private corporations are primarily concerned to limit those resources by keeping taxation down, but they are also concerned to lobby government for contracts, investment subsidies or tax breaks, favourable planning legislation, development status for their own localities of operation, tariff protection against foreign competition and, if all

9

else fails, direct government subsidies to support their invested capital and employed workforce. Even the trade unions, whose rhetoric remains proletarian and solidaristic on behalf of the whole working class, are usually more concerned in practice with demarcation disputes with rival crafts, and with maintaining employment in their own industry by keeping open plants and mines, if necessary with government subsidies.

In such a vertically structured system disputes between the interests are increasingly mediated through the state. This is inevitable, since the state, not just in Britain but in every economically advanced country, collects and disposes of an increasing share of the national income, commonly between 40 and 60 per cent of Gross Domestic Product. In Britain public expenditure grew to about 50 per cent of GDP in 1970 and to no less than 60 per cent in 1975, though more than half of this consisted of transfer payments (social security, unemployment benefit, pensions, and the like) which were returned to personal expenditure for private consumption.[7] Nonetheless, this means that about half or more of society's resources are managed by the government and are therefore open to competition by the various interests, including not only the state-funded professions and the private corporations but the Claimants' Union, the Child Poverty Action Group, Shelter and all the other lobbies representing welfare recipients.

The main struggle for society's resources, therefore, is between those who benefit directly from government expenditure and those who see themselves as the source of that expenditure. It is true that everyone pays taxes and everyone benefits from government expenditure, but they do so unequally, not only because the rich pay more individually (though not collectively) than the rest but because state employees gain more by state spending than they pay in taxes. Consequently, by far the most important division between the interest groups is between the public sector professions, those funded directly or indirectly by the state, and the private sector professions, chiefly the managers of private corporations. As the struggle between lord and peasant was the master conflict in feudal society and the struggle between capitalist and wage earner the master conflict in industrial society, so the struggle between the public and private sector professions is the master conflict of professional society.

This division leaves out a large and important group of professional occupations, namely those employed neither by the state nor by the corporations but by a host of not-for-profit organizations such as universities, churches, charitable foundations, voluntary organizations of many kinds, and so on. These non-market professionals are employed by a wide range of institutions, from those almost entirely dependent on government funding, like the universities and many research institutes, to bodies closely associated with industry, like the trade unions and employers' associations. Which side of the divide their officials will lean towards will depend on their perception of how their incomes are derived and where their interests lie. University academics have since the First World War become increasingly conscious of their dependence on public funds and have recently had a sharp reminder of the dangers of that dependence. Officials of employers' associations, on the other hand, are equally conscious of their dependence on the corporations, and would be foolish to ignore the wishes of their master. In between there is every variety of occupational interest, from those philanthropic bodies which exist principally to lobby the state for larger resources for deserving minorities, such as children in poverty, the mentally or physically handicapped, the elderly, or the veterans of past wars, to the officials of trade unions and political parties whose interests do not always chime with those of their very demanding employers. With obvious exceptions, however, the non-market professionals, not being motivated by profit, tend to lean towards the public side of the divide, partly because so many of them see the state as the resource of last resort and partly because they are perceived by the corporate sector as being the same sort of 'overhead' as government itself, and therefore as a 'cost' which the private sector has to carry. For most purposes they will be treated in this book as having more in common with the public sector professions than with the private.

The clash of interests between the public or non-market and the private sector professions helps to explain one of the most puzzling questions about modern society. Why, in the late twentieth century, in an economic system which bears little resemblance to the industrial capitalism of the Industrial Revolution, do we still talk about society in the early nineteenth-century terms of Ricardo and Marx? Modern corporate capitalism is run by professional managers who, though they control far larger capitals than Victorian entrepreneurs, are themselves for the most part salaried employees whose status and income differ only in degree, not in kind, from those of their subordinates and whose power over them ceases when they take their pensions. Other professionals, notably government bureaucrats, judges, generals, hospital consultants, town planners, trade union officials, newspaper editors and television producers, may be equally powerful in their own spheres, which may impinge unwantedly on corporate decision making. Yet most politicians, sociologists and commentators talk as if society were still divided principally into a small employing class of individual capitalists and an undifferentiated mass of wage-earning manual workers. On the right, the neo-Ricardians preach the virtues of a free market which, however appropriate to a Victorian economy of small family firms and partnerships, is wholly irrelevant to a corporate economy in which one hundred firms produce nearly half the manufacturing output and three to five firms dominate each separate industry, and the public sector employs over a quarter of the total workforce.[8] On the left, the Marxists, the antithesis of the Ricardians, attack the same free market as if it still consisted of individual capitalists extracting surplus value from a supine and unaccountably non-revolutionary proletariat. In between, the ostensibly class-based political parties, in reality large coalitions of diverse professional interests as we shall see, still pitch their appeals in class terms, with the exception (which proves the rule) that the Conservative Party has to modify its appeal to embrace a large minority of the working class.

The answer to the puzzle is that the old rhetoric of class happens to suit the protagonists of the master conflict of professional society. The ideology of the free market appeals to the professional managers of great corporations and their allies because it protects them from the accusation they most fear, that they themselves are the major threat to competition and the freedom of the citizen. By denying the incontrovertible fact that competition drives out competitors and tends towards monopoly, it enables them to present themselves as the guardians of the consumer and the deliverers of the widest choice of goods and services at the lowest prices. More significantly, by tying the concept of free choice in the market to the idea of political freedom, it enables them to claim to be the guardians of individual liberty against the tyranny of the state. The irony of their position, the poacher acting the part of gamekeeper, in no way detracts from its effectiveness. As long as the state rather than the corporations can be vilified as the major threat to freedom, then the corporate managers can pose as the defenders of the common man against the encroachments of big government.[9]

The ideology, of course, contains a contradiction. The free market itself could not exist but for the state. Without regulation to set the terms of the market, hold the ring between buyer and seller, determine the meaning and transfer of ownership, and uphold the law of contract, the market would collapse into chaos and the strong could take whatever they liked from the weak. Thus the state itself, far from being the enemy of freedom, is its source and origin. Freedom can be positive as well as negative, freedom to do and be without molestation or exploitation by other citizens as well as freedom from state intervention. Freedom from all state interference is freedom for criminals, thieves and frauds. Civil society itself exists by reason of the state, without which it would descend to a Hobbesian state of nature, the war of all against all. By denying the positive role of the state the free market ideology rests on a quicksand, a fictitious law of nature which sets up the rules of the market prior to and separate from the laws of society.

The same is true of political freedom. Without law there can be no liberty, and without the state no law. Yet the free marketeers claim that the state, which protects them and their property from depredation, has no right to set limits to competition even when it threatens to end in monopoly and the curtailment of freedom for others. They wish, in short, to have their cake and eat it, the protection of the state for themselves but not for others against themselves. It is easy to see why the rhetoric of early nineteenth-century liberalism should appeal to the private sector professionals. It promises them a heroic stance against the state while they enjoy the benefits of government.

On the other side, the class rhetoric of the left, the *doppelgänger* of the classical economists, appeals almost as strongly to the public sector professionals. The Ricardian socialists, who anticipated Marx in the theory of 'surplus value' and 'the right to the whole produce of labour' which they logically based on the Ricardian labour theory of value, diagnosed competition as the source of inequality and exploitation and saw cooperation and collectivism as the remedy. Though by no means all enamoured of the state or of violent revolution as the means to their ideal society, their socialist successors, whether Marxist or Fabian, repudiated the free market and increasingly looked to the state to redress its inequities. The motive force behind the collectivist legislation of the Victorian age restricting the rights of landlords and industrialists has been assumed to be the increasing pressure of the working-class vote, but it has been demonstrated elsewhere not only that the working-class voter showed little interest in collectivist measures until they were already in existence, but that the main challenge to the unfettered claims of property came from the professional middle class.[10]

It is not surprising, therefore, that the public sector professionals today should adopt the language of their anti-Ricardian predecessors. Richard Titmuss complained that the welfare state seemed to exist more for the professionals who administer and service it than for the recipients of welfare. The doctors, social workers, legal aid lawyers, town and country planners, professors and teachers, civil servants and local officials have a greater stake in maintaining and expanding the services than anyone else. In what Titmuss called 'the pressure group state' the most powerful of the pressure groups are the welfare professions.[11] Whatever their party politics, the most vociferous defenders of the National Health Service are the doctors, nurses and ancillary hospital workers, the Law Society defends legal aid as 'an integral part of the British system of justice',[12] social workers organize to preserve their autonomous relation with their 'clients', planners oppose free access by developers to green belts, academics lobby Parliament against cuts in university grants, teachers refuse non-classroom duties to protest against low pay and lack of resources, and public officials dispute the need for reductions in the central and local government establishment. Even such conservative government professions as the military and the police demand an ever-increasing expenditure on defence and law and order.

All this can be argued in terms of social justice for every citizen rather than the self-interest of each profession. The free market, it is asserted, has manifestly failed to produce an equitable distribution of resources or solve the social problems of (relative) poverty, maldistribution of health care, unequal educational opportunity, inadequate housing, a squalid environment, and involuntary unemployment. In a complex, interdependent society in which, it is argued, many vital services cannot be equitably or efficiently provided by the market, state provision through publicly funded professions is inescapable.[13]

The problem with such arguments, of course, is knowing where to stop. There are undoubtedly services, like defence or law and order, which are indivisible, collectively provided, and would be dangerous to turn over to private enterprise. There are others, like roads and public utilities, which are natural monopolies and, on the face of it, safer in publicly accountable hands (though the more extreme free marketeers naturally disagree). There are still others, like health and education, in which the most needy clients, the sick poor, the elderly, and most children, lack the resources to buy on the free market. And there is a final group of essential services, like poor relief cum social security and the incarceration of criminals, which, with a few disastrous exceptions like Bentham's Panopticon scheme, private enterprise does not see a profit in. The difficulty with public provision is the feedback principle: once a service becomes professionalized under public auspices the professionals discover further needs to be met and problems to be solved and a host of reasons for extending their activities. Hence the self-generating expansion of the state in all the advanced countries. This expansion is not fortuitous but the logical consequence of professionalism and the driving force behind it, the increasing complexity of modern life and the increasing division of ever more minutely skilled labour to meet its demands.

All this is not to say that all private enterprise professionals support the unfettered free market without reservation or all the public sector ones an interventionist state. There are corporate millionaires who support the Labour Party and corporate managers eager and willing to work for nationalized industries, and there are civil servants, doctors and professors dedicated to the privatization of government services, hospitals and universities. The role of a social ideal is not to determine a person's beliefs, which may indeed clash with his interests, all the more so the more independent his mind, but to provide strong motivation for inclining one way rather than another. As David Hume said two hundred years ago, 'Though men be much governed by interest;

yet even interest itself, and all human affairs, are entirely governed by *opinion*.'[14] Whether class or interest group predominates in a given society depends on how men view their situation, as allying them more with those on their own social level or with those above and below them in the same occupation or industry. The existence of 'social cranks' – men with an 'eccentric drive' who espoused the cause of a class other than their own – in the early nineteenth century, often professional men like Malthus, James Mill or Bronterre O'Brien who spoke for the landed, capitalist and working classes, helped the new class society to come to birth.[15]

The professional ideal, as we shall see, motivated many professional men to seek a new kind of society more suited to their interests and social role. Since they existed to provide services which were esoteric, evanescent and fiduciary – beyond the knowledge of the laity, not (with some partial exceptions like architects and civil engineers) productive of concrete objects, and thus having to be taken on trust – they could not accept a market valuation of their skill but demanded that society should accept their own valuation, guaranteed by exclusive education and certification. Not all achieved this enviable position but all aspired to it, and the growing numbers of employed professionals compromised by means of a negotiated salary scale and the stable lifelong career. The objective was to create a framework for the secure exploitation of human capital, defined as the investment in personal skill so as to yield not just a reward for labour but a differential return, in strict Ricardian terms a rent for the scarce resource of their esoteric skill. The size of the rent, the difference between the professional fee or salary and the price of common labour, was the measure of the success of each profession in claiming that scarcity value and establishing its status. Status rather than market valuation determined their remuneration; or, rather, their rewards were negotiated in the wider societal market of prestige and the social value placed on their service rather than by the sale of their labour in the economic market place.

This was especially true of those professions in the old class society whose services were directed to society as a whole or towards those who could not afford to pay their full cost: the clergy, the military, the public health doctors and the increasing number of private doctors who treated the poor in infirmaries and dispensaries, the teachers in voluntary aided and state schools, the academics in the less endowed university colleges, the social workers, the bureaucrats in the early welfare state such as the health and unemployment insurance divisions, and so on. It was less urgent for the slowly evolving private sector professions, whose ambitions might long be directed towards partnerships in family businesses, directorships of corporations, and emulation of traditional entrepreneurs. Nevertheless, despite the exceptional managerial tycoon, most professional managers became more dependent on a salaried career than on the windfall opportunities of capital gains and they too came to be assimilated to the stable career hierarchy. The difference was that, while the public sector professionals for the most part focused on the non-monetary rewards, on honour, fame or power rather than fortune, the prestige of rising to the head of a government department, an army, a church, an academic discipline, or a great profession, the private sector professions still tended to measure success in terms of salary and fringe benefits.

The modern bifurcation of the two rival groups of professions rests, therefore, on the concrete foundations of incompatible interests. Their divergent attitudes to the role of the state reflect their different views of it as ally or antagonist. The public sector professions see it as the origin of their incomes and resources and guarantor of their status and prestige; the private sector professionals as a threat to their incomes and capital base and a constraint on their activities. Both groups wish to capture control of government, the first to underpin and expand their work, the second to 'get government off our backs' and escape its inhibiting control. The nineteenth-century rhetoric of class conflict is for both a weapon in their competition for income and status. That rhetoric effectively disguises what is happening to modern society and the part that both groups have played in its evolution.

3 THE CULMINATION OF THE INDUSTRIAL REVOLUTION

Professional society is the culmination of the more than Industrial Revolution in which modern English society had its origins. In the earlier book to which this is the sequel that revolution, it was argued, was characterized as a revolution in men's access to the means of life, in control over their ecological environment, in their capacity to escape from the niggardliness of nature. At the material level it can be described as a rise in human productivity, industrial, agricultural and demographic, *on such a scale* that it raised, as it were, the logarithmic index of society, that is it increased by a multiple (rather than a fraction) both the number of human beings which a given area of land would support, and their standard of life, or consumption per head of goods and services ... Such a rise in scale required, involved and implied drastic changes in society itself: in the size and distribution of the population, in its social structure and organization, and in the political and administrative superstructure which they demanded and supported. It was in brief *a social revolution*: a revolution in social organization, with social causes as well as social effects.[16]

It was, after a slow evolution lasting seven or eight millennia, the logical continuation of the Neolithic Revolution, the beginnings of settled agriculture, which freed a small minority of people from the production of food to become full-time craftsmen, warriors, priests and rulers, and so to found cities and the possibility of civilization.[17] Industrialism released a majority from agriculture to work and live in industrial towns and cities, increased the population of England and Wales nearly fourfold from about 8.9 million in 1801 and 32.5 million in 1901, and quadrupled living standards per head from £12.9 per head (at mid-Victorian prices) in 1800 to £52.5 in 1900.[18] At the same time it produced a rise in the scale or organization, from workshop to factory, stage coach to railway train, sailing ship to ocean steamer, single country bank to great joint stock branch banking, village and tiny country town to great city and conurbation, and government from 16,000 'persons in public offices' in 1797 to over 100,000 civil servants in 1897. It also transformed society from a classless hierarchy of interest groups, representing the 'great functional interests' of agriculture, finance, commerce, and various manufacturers, and so on into the conflict-ridden but viable class society of mid-Victorian England.

Professional society is a logical continuation of industrial society. It has increased population still further, if more slowly, from 32.5 million in 1901 to 49.1 million in 1981, almost completely urbanized that population by bringing more than 90 per cent within reach of the amenities of a town (practically all, if we include the instant links of telephone, radio and television), and nearly trebled average living standards, from £49.9 per head (at 1913 prices) in 1900 to £142 in 1981.[19] The rise in the scale of organization has outstripped anything the Victorians could have imagined. The average factory workforce has scarcely doubled, from eighty-six workers in 1871 to 155 in 1984, but the scale of the leading plants has soared: nearly half of the manufacturing workers (47 per cent) at the later date were in establishments with over 500 workers, nearly a third (31 per cent) in those with over 1,000.[20] Since most of the large factories were owned by even larger companies, the size of firms was still larger, and becoming more so by almost continuous mergers and take-overs. The share of the largest one hundred corporations in total manufacturing output rose from 15 per cent in 1909 to 45 per cent by 1970. The 2,024 largest companies with assets of £500,000 or more in 1957 had shrunk to 1,253 by 1964; of these the largest eighty in 1957 held 53 per cent of all company assets, in 1964 no less than 62 per cent. The nationalized industries were even larger: eight public corporations in 1968 employed 2.3 million workers, 8.5 per cent of the employed population. In all, thirty-three enterprises, twenty-five private and eight public corporations each with over 50,000 employees, employed a total of 4.1 million workers, 18 per cent of the employed population.[21] The high street deposit banks were reduced from 121 in 1875 to twenty-eight in 1914 and to the 'Big Four' plus a handful of smaller ones by the 1970s.[22] The trend towards concentration was not confined to any one industry but spread right across the economy. In 1951 the three largest firms in each of forty-two industries employed on average 29.3 per cent of the workforce of each industry; by 1973 the largest three in forty industries employed 42.2 per cent.[23]

On the other side of the industrial relations fence the trade unions more than matched the employers in size and concentration. The 1,325 trade unions of 1900 had less than 2 million members (about 15 per cent of the workforce); by 1978 they had shrunk to 462 but increased their membership to 13.1 million (59 per cent). Since most of the later unions had under 50,000 members, the movement was dominated by the forty unions with more than that number, which contained 88 per cent of the membership.[24] Indeed, the whole policy of the Trades Union Congress (and of the Labour Party) could be determined by the eleven unions with over 250,000 members, which collectively disposed of 64 per cent of the total votes. Employers' associations, by contrast, were less concentrated: from forty-three federations and national associations and 810 local associations in 1900 they grew to 'some 1,350' of both kinds reported by the Donovan Commission on Trade Unions and Industrial Relations to 1970.[25] But they were no less organized and active than their trade union counterparts, and a great deal better funded.

Professional associations, although their memberships were smaller, were in many ways more successful than trade unions in uniting almost the whole of each relevant occupation. Despite their proliferation during the Industrial Revolution there were still only twenty-seven qualifying associations in 1880 (counting the four Inns of Court for Barristers and the two Royal Colleges and the Society for Apothecaries for medical doctors), but thereafter there was an enormous expansion: another twenty-one associations by 1900, a further twenty-seven by 1918, between the wars forty-six, and by 1970 another forty-six – a total of 140 since 1880.[26] In addition there were a host of non-qualifying bodies, plus forty-four white-collar unions in 1977 with some 3.3 million members. These included such obviously professional unions as the National Association of Local Government Officers with 709,000 members, the Association of Scientific, Technical and Managerial Staffs with 441,000, the National Union of Teachers with 296,000 and the various Civil Service unions with 530,000 between them.[27] These professional organizations, along with the employers' (increasingly the professional managers') associations and the trade unions, were the harbingers of the new society.

Even schools and universities, which had already risen in size during the nineteenth century, rose still further in the twentieth. In 1900 the average voluntary school had 163 pupils, nine times its eighteenth-century counterpart, and the average state school 430; by 1977 the average primary school had 210, and the average secondary school 791, and both were far more complex institutions than their predecessors.[28] In 1913 there were 26,711 students, about 1 per cent of the age group, in twenty-two universities and colleges in Britain, nearly half of them in Oxford, Cambridge and London alone, the rest in England and Wales averaging only 461 each;

by 1978 there were forty-four universities (excluding the Open University) in the United Kingdom with 296,000 full-time students, about 7 per cent of the age group, of whom over 40,000 were at London University, 14,843 at Manchester, 11,783 at Oxford, 10,978 at Cambridge, and upwards of 4,000 at each of the others. There were also 223,800 full-time advanced students at the thirty polytechnics and the colleges of higher education, a further 5 per cent of the age group.[29] Moreover, both the local education authority schools and colleges and the universities were integrated into a system financed and much more tightly controlled, directly or indirectly, by the central government.

A similar story could be told of many other institutions, such as hospitals – from voluntary hospitals and poor law infirmaries to the large integrated units of the National Health Service with their hierarchy of Regional, Area and District Hospital Boards – social work and welfare agencies, prisons, borstals and remand homes, army, air force and naval units, and so on. But this leads us on to the most significant rise in scale of all, the twentieth-century rise in the scale of government. In the past century the numbers employed by local government have risen from the 83,000 workers (including police) of 1881 to no less than 968,000 in 1979.[30] Similarly, the 107,782 civil servants (excluding industrial grades) in 1902 had increased to 547,000 by 1980 (plus 157,600 industrial staff). Altogether, the state came to employ no less than 17 per cent of the occupied population, 25 per cent if the nationalized industries are included.[31] More to the point, whereas down to the First World War most civil servants were employed in London in comparatively small central offices, and only the Customs and Excise staffs worked in the provinces, since then government offices have sprung up in every sizeable provincial town – employment exchanges (job centres), social security and supplementary benefit offices, income tax, value added tax and other taxation offices, and the like, in addition to the great decentralized headquarters such as those for Social Security at Newcastle-upon-Tyne, for DES statistics and teachers' pay and pensions at Darlington, and for vehicle and driving licences at Swansea – and they have impinged far more visibly on the lives of most citizens.

One measure of this extraordinary growth of government is the more than thirtyfold rise in national government expenditure in real terms (nearly tenfold as a proportion of national income), from £77.9 million in 1897–8 (£105.3 million at 1913 prices), about 4.9 per cent of the net National Income (at factor cost), to £66,800 million in 1978–79 (£3,389 million at 1913 prices), about 47.1 per cent of the net National Income. Of course, a great deal of this enormous increase consists of transfer payments, in pensions, social security and supplementary benefits, and the like, most of which are immediately spent again on consumption goods, and also of personal service such as medical treatment, education, housing subsidies and social work which directly benefit their consumers. But this does not detract from the point that central and local government (which spends a further £20,573 million at current prices) together handle 61.6 per cent of the net National Income or, to put it more fairly perhaps, 53.3 per cent of the Gross National Product.[32]

The rise in the scale of organization is not the cause but the effect and symptom of the rise of a much more complex, inter-dependent society. The connecting link between industrial and professional society is the familiar principle of the division of labour, which Adam Smith saw as the key to the wealth of nations in 1776. In 200 years it has transformed Britain (and a large part of the planet) from a predominantly agricultural system through an industrial mass-production economy to a post-industrial society increasingly based on services. Machines, as Smith was aware, are the by-product of the division of labour, and enable the less skilled, like car drivers and television watchers, to call up at the turn of a switch the services of skilled engineers. Telecommunications and computers have now done the same for office work, banking, entertainment, and other services. A service-based economy is admittedly ambiguous, and includes retail distribution, catering and hotel work, hospital portering, bus driving, routine office work and other low-paid jobs as well as high-paid law, medicine, finance and administration, and the post-industrial society is a good deal less upmarket than Daniel Bell's 'Knowledge rules, OK', and some critics think that many jobs are becoming 'deskilled'.[33] Nevertheless, his prediction that fewer workers would be making things and more doing things for others has turned out to be true. What Colin Clark called 'Petty's law' (after Sir William Petty, the seventeenth-century pioneer of 'political arithmetic') is still in operation: the movement of workers with economic growth from agriculture to industry to services.[34]

What is happening to industry in post-industrial society is what happened to agriculture during the Industrial Revolution. Agriculture, with the aid of fertilizers and machinery, became more, not less, efficient, and with a diminishing workforce was able to feed a majority instead of a minority of non-agrarians. Now industry is becoming so efficient, with the aid of robotics and computers, that a small minority of the population are able to produce the consumer goods for the non-manufacturing majority. (With the 'green revolution' agriculture is becoming still more efficient, and the most efficient agriculture is in the most economically advanced countries in Western Europe and North America, though not as yet in Japan.) Like the Industrial Revolution this has produced major structural changes in the economy, bringing unemployment for some as well as opportunities for others. The choice is between deindustrialization and low-grade service work on the one hand and highly automated, competitive industry and high-grade services on the other. As in the Industrial Revolution, when predominantly peasant agriculture lost out to industrial mass production, those countries which take the first road will lose out in the race for wealth and power to those which have chosen the second.

There are, however, two aspects to the division of labour, one of which Adam Smith neglected because he could take it for granted: specialization and integration. Specialization leads directly to professionalism. Specialists rapidly form guilds, associations, clubs or unions to enhance their status, protect their skills from competition, and increase their incomes. That some become organized professions and others trade unions is due to a trick of the English language, aided by English snobbery. 'Profession', as in French (or *Beruf* in German), originally meant any occupation, and the more prestigious trades were distinguished by the adjectives 'liberal' (meaning gentlemanly) and 'learned' (meaning institutionally educated) professions.[35] By dropping the epithets the more prestigious occupations, chiefly the clergy, law and medicine, laid claim to the exclusive label of 'profession', which came to mean an occupation which so effectively controlled its labour market that it never had to behave like a trade union. Trade unions, meanwhile, never quite abandoned the same aim: the Rule Book of the Amalgamated Society of Engineers in 1864 declared that the journeyman engineer had the same right to

23

protect the value of his skill as the physician. Over the years more and more occupations have made this claim, and increasingly with justice: the civil engineer whose constructions may fall down, the pharmacist whose healing drugs may kill, even the car mechanic whose slightest mistake may be lethal, can claim to be as vital to their clients' welfare and survival as any doctor or lawyer. The increasing complexity and interdependence of the modern world automatically generates specialization and organized professions.

Before specialization can complete its work, however, it has to be integrated into the finished product or service. Even Adam Smith's pin makers had to be organized to make completed pins. The ten separate operations were useless unless they came together in packets of pins ready for sale, and that required an organizer to oversee the whole enterprise. Smith refused to take the organizer's contribution seriously and argued that, even in many great works like the Carron iron foundry, his work could be left to 'some principal clerk. His wages properly express the value of this labour of inspection and direction.'[36] The more divided the labour, however, the larger the enterprise and the more complex the task of fitting all the specialized operations together.

The rise in the scale of organization was not only an effect of the increasing division of labour; it was also the cause of a further division of labour as management itself became more complex and was further divided into production, purchasing of materials, accounting, design and engineering, quality surveying and, eventually, industrial relations. Honest, competent managers outside of the owner's family and partners were hard to find, and while 'there were well-defined groups of managers in many industries: there was, by 1830, as yet hardly a managerial profession as such'.[37] Yet with the growth of large-scale undertakings like railways, steamship lines, steel, engineering and chemical works, all of which depended on large numbers of specialist workers and careful integration of their work, management became not only a profession but, with the import of Taylorism from the United States, a science.[38] The surge of defensive amalgamations, mergers and take-overs which began in the Great Depression of 1874–96 and have continued ever since made it impossible for owners to do more than a fraction of their own managing. Although it took until the new business schools of the 1960s for it to acquire its own academically certified training, company management became one of the two pivotal hierarchies of professional society.

As the business schools have discovered to their gain, management is not confined to private industry. Public administration, hospitals, universities, research establishments, the armed forces, trade unions and employers' associations, even charitable foundations, all employ diverse collections of specialists and need to be organized. The rise in the scale of their organization was, as we have seen, as much a feature of industrial society as industrial concentration itself. Post-industrial society, with its swing to services, has accelerated the trend. The enormous expansion of government has been powered by the demand for more and more specialized services, from the inspection of factories, mines, food and drugs, slum housing or financial markets' operations to the provision of pensions, social security, secondary and tertiary education, or sophisticated weapons research. Many of these professions have acquired their own self-governing associations and training, like the mine engineers, the medical officers of health, the actuaries, public accountants, social workers, public analysts, nuclear physicists, and so on. But like corporate management, public administration as such, traditionally trained on the job like any traditional craft, took until the 1960s to acquire, in the Civil Service College at Sunningdale, a recognized training of its own, and even yet few civil servants are required to attend there and most are still recruited from university graduates in classics, history, law or political science. Nevertheless, it would be naive not to recognize the administrative Civil Service as one of the key organizing professions, the central core of the public sector which forms the second pivot on which the professional society turns.

The rise of the professions to permeate and, some more than others, dominate modern society stems, then, from the logic of the division and reintegration of labour which inspired the Industrial Revolution and every large-scale development that has sprung from it. Yet how did professionalism as an organizing principle come to supersede class, and in particular supersede the plutocratic landed and capitalistic ruling class which dominated Victorian and Edwardian society? This is a long story which embraces the whole social history of the last hundred years and will occupy the rest of the book. We must begin that story by examining industrial class society at its zenith, between 1880 and the First World War.

Chapter 2

THE ZENITH OF
CLASS SOCIETY

Between 1880 and 1914 class society in Britain reached its zenith. During this period the major classes achieved their advanced capitalistic form, most clearly based on the flow of wealth from the modern industrial system and therefore on their relation to the capitalist means of production, distribution and exchange. In the process they became more sharply differentiated from one another than ever before. The rich, both great landowners and millionaire capitalists, drew together in a consolidation of that new plutocracy which was already beginning to emerge during the mid-Victorian age.[1] The middle classes, ever more graduated in income and status, came to express those finer distinctions in prosperity and social position physically, both in outward appearance, in dress, furnishings and habitations, and even in physique, and in their geographical segregation from one another and the rest of society in carefully differentiated suburbs. So too did the working classes, in part involuntarily because they could only afford what their social betters left for them but also, within that constraint, because those working-class families who could chose to differentiate themselves equally, by Sunday if not everyday dress, and by better, and better furnished, houses in marginally superior areas. Only the poorest of the poor, the 'residuum' as Charles Booth and Alfred Marshall called them, had no choice at all, and were consigned to the darkest and dreariest slums, the most segregated class of all because they and their dens were shunned by all the rest. Segregation, by income, status, appearance, physical health, speech, education, and opportunity in life, as well as by work and residential area, was the symbolic mark of class society at its highest point of development.

The distances, too, between the segregated classes were greater than before, both in physical and in economic terms. Geographical separation, a trend at work ever since the Industrial Revolution, was now reinforced by new means of transport, the horse-drawn tram and the 'people's carriage', the cheap electric tram, the suburban railway, and towards the end of the period the motor car.[2] These enabled the inhabitants of towns and still more of great cities to sort themselves out by what they could afford in terms of time and transportation as well as house rents and local rates into largely concentric rings of graded residential districts. Except in London, where some of the very rich still chose to live in the West End, the city centres were given up to the poorest, who had to live near the daily and sometimes twice-daily markets for casual labour, the unskilled but regularly employed lived a little farther out, the skilled up to a tram-ride or workmen's train ticket away, the lower middle-class clerks and the shopkeepers and smaller business men at the end of a horse-bus or short suburban railway trip, and the well-to-do middle class at the distance of a railway season ticket. Even the well-to-do were graded by ability to pay, so that Highgate and Hampstead on their salubrious hills were socially superior to Camden Town and Maida Vale, just as the Manchester suburbs of Altrincham and Alderley Edge were a cut above Wilmslow and Hale. There were exceptions, of course: inner suburban enclaves like Victoria Park, Manchester or Edgbaston, Birmingham kept their desirable status by determined private planning controls; and the circles were often eccentric, bulging on the western side and up the hills to take advantage, for those who could pay for it, of fresher air and cleaner water. But it was undoubtedly the late Victorian age which, with its trams and buses and suburban railways, began the commuter age of modern times, and with it the height of inequality between the classes.[3]

1 THE HEIGHT OF INEQUALITY

Despite the enormous rise in the national income and in average living standards during the Industrial Revolution, inequality was probably at its height between 1880 and 1914. The distribution of income was more skew and the economic distance between the classes was greater than ever before. For the beginning of the period we can still use Dudley Baxter's fairly reliable estimate of the distribution of the National Income of England and Wales in 1867, modified to take into account Sir Josiah Stamp's more accurate statistics of income taxpayers.[4] Table 2.1 shows that the upper and middle classes, under 2 per cent of all families, with upwards of £300 a year per family (nearly three times the average family income), received well over a third (36.9 per cent) of the National Income – nearly as much as the whole manual working class (39.1 per cent), who constituted three quarters of the population.

Table 2.1 Distribution of the National Income of England and Wales between families, 1867

	Families (000s)		Income (£000s)	
	Number	Percentage	Amount	Percentage
I Upper class				
1 £5,000+	4.5	0.07	111,104	16.2
2 £1,000–£5,000	25.2	0.41	69,440	10.1
II Middle class				
£300–£1,000	90.0	1.46	72,912	10.6
III Lower middle class				
1 £100–£300	510.3	8.29	93,744	13.7
2 Under £100	946.0	15.37	70,958	10.3
Upper and middle	1,576.0	25.6	418,158	60.9
IV Higher skilled	840.8	13.8	72,028	10.5
V Lower skilled	1,610.0	26.1	112,042	16.3
VI Unskilled and agricultural	1,516.8	24.6	70,659	10.3
VII Wageless families	610.4	9.9	13,466	2.0
Manual labour	4,578.0	74.4	268,195	39.1
All classes	6,154.0	100.0	686,353	100.0

Source: Dudley Baxter, *The National Income* (Macmillan, 1868), p. 15, adjusted to conform with Sir Josiah Stamp's estimates in *British Incomes and Property* (King, 1916), p. 449.

Towards the end of the period Sir Leo Chiozza Money made a similar but less detailed estimate of the distribution of the National Income of the United Kingdom for 1904, summarized in Table 2.2.

Table 2.2 Distribution of the National Income of England and Wales, 1904

| | Earners including families | | Income | |
	Number (000s)	Percentage	Amount (£000s)	Percentage
Those in:				
I Riches (£700+)	1,250	2.9	585,000	34.2
II Comfort (£160– £700)				
1 £600–£700	65	0.2	8,500	0.5
2 £500–£600	145	0.3	16,000	0.9
3 £400–£500	265	0.6	23,900	1.4
4 £160–£400	3,035	7.1	182,100	10.6
5 Other (no abatement claim or evaded tax)	240	0.5	14,500	0.8
Subtotal in comfort	3,750	8.7	245,000	14.3
III Poverty (=non-tax-payers)	38,000	88.4	880,000	51.5
Total	43,000	100.0	1,710,000	100.0

Source: L. G. Chiozza Money, *Riches and Poverty* (Methuen, 1905), pp. 41–3

He concluded that 'the United Kingdom is seen to contain a great multitude of poor people, veneered over with a thin layer of the comfortable and rich'. Those in 'riches' with over £700 a year, less than one-thirtieth (2.9 per cent) of the population, received over a third (34.2 per cent) of the National Income, those in 'comfort' with between £160 and £700 (8.7 per cent) received one-seventh (14.3 per cent), while those in 'poverty' – by which he, a Fabian banker, meant simply those below the income tax level – eight-ninths (88.4 per cent) of the population, received only just over half (51.5 per cent) of the National Income.

Baxter's and Money's figures are of course both very rough, and static, estimates and are not on a comparable basis. Sir Arthur Bowley, the distinguished pioneer of income and wage statistics, calculated that, although the wage-earning class increased their real wages between 1880 and 1913 by a third (34 per cent), their share of the National Income declined significantly, from 41.3 to 35.6 per cent. Surprisingly, so too did the share of the wealthy (the same percentage of the occupied population taxed on over £160 per annum in 1880 and over £225 per annum in 1913), from 47.1 per cent to 44.5 per cent. The reason for this divergence is that the estimated number of wage earners had shrunk from 83.3 per cent of the population to 73.4 per cent, and the slack had been taken up by the 'intermediate' class, expanding both in numbers (from 12.2 to 22.4 per cent) and in income (from 10.4 to 19.4 per cent). Allowing for this shift, which benefited those children of the working class who moved up into the lower middle class, Bowley concluded that the general increase in the National Income had been shared with remarkable equality between the classes. Although this was true relatively speaking, the absolute gap between the classes had widened considerably. While the average wage had risen from £37.8 to £50.6 per annum (prices being little different, having fallen and then risen again), the average income of his higher taxpaying group (with over £700 p.a.) had increased from £855 to £1,120 per annum, an increase equal to more than five times the average wage in 1913.[5]

Although Bowley was impressed by the constancy of the class shares, he nevertheless believed that the economic system had not produced a satisfactory livelihood for the bulk of the population. This was confirmed by the great pioneers of the poverty survey during this period, of whom Bowley himself was one. For reasons we shall see later, the late Victorians had become disturbed about the problem of poverty, as such sensational publications as the Rev. Andrew Mearns's *The Bitter Cry of Outcast London* (1883) and William Booth of the Salvation Army's *In Darkest England and the Way Out* (1890) bear witness. The concern was not new, as any number of commentators and philanthropists demonstrate, from Malthus and Thomas Chalmers in the first three decades of the century through Henry Mayhew, Charles Dickens, Baroness Burdett-Coutts, and F. D. Maurice and the Christian Socialists in the 1840s and 1850s, to Canon Barnett, Octavia Hill and the Charity Organization Society of 1869.[6]

What was new from the 1880s was determination to get at the statistical facts, to quantify the precise extent of poverty and its causes. The originator of the comprehensive social survey was Charles Booth, the Liverpool shipowner and amateur statistician, who had served his apprenticeship in the Liverpool and London Statistical Societies which, along with the Manchester Society (founded in 1833) and the Society for the Promotion of the Social Sciences (founded in 1859), were the pioneers of empirical sociology in Britain.[7] His motives in undertaking the vast survey of *Life and Labour of the People of London* in seventeen volumes, from 1889 to 1902, are still debated,[8] but his estimate that no less than 35.2 per cent of the population of the East End and 30.7 per cent of that of London as a whole were in poverty struck a chord in the hearts of contemporaries and has become accepted ever since. It seemed to be confirmed by Seebohm Rowntree's social survey of York in 1899, which found 43.4 per cent of the wage-earning population, 27.8 per cent of the total population of that much smaller city, in poverty.[9]

These were appalling figures which were, quite rightly, to have a powerful effect on contemporary perceptions and on social reform. But sympathy for the poor, however well justified, must not be allowed to obscure the meaning of the figures. By 'poverty' Booth, who thought that his results were 'not so appalling as sensational writers would have us believe', meant much the same as Bentham and his disciple Patrick Colquhoun long before in 1806: the state of 'having no surplus' and therefore having to work for one's daily bread.[10] Most of Booth's 'poor', classes C and D, 'though they would be much the better for more of everything, are not "in want". They are neither ill-nourished nor ill-clad, according to any standard that can reasonably be used. Their lives are an unending struggle and lack comfort'.[11] What we normally mean by poverty, and what many of his contemporaries took him to mean by it, he called 'want' or still worse, 'distress'. Booth himself believed therefore that only his classes A (the 'lowest class of occasional labourers, semi-criminals and loafers') and B (the 'very poor') were in what was commonly meant by poverty, and these together constituted 12.4 per cent of the East Enders and 8.4 per cent of all Londoners.[12] In other words, not 'nearly a third' but a much lower figure, one in twelve of the population, were in 'want or distress'.

Rowntree's figures were similarly misunderstood. Although his definition of poverty was more scientific than Booth's, based as it was on careful calculation of the income needed to maintain families of varying sizes in health and physically fit enough for work, his figures of 43.4 per cent of the working population and 27.8 per cent of the total population of York in poverty included 27.9 per cent and 17.9 per cent respectively in 'secondary poverty', with barely sufficient income but, because of misspending on inessentials, showing signs of undernourishment, as judged by his investigator. The proportions in 'primary poverty' – comparable with Booth's classes 'in want' and 'distress' – were 15.5 per cent of the working class and 9.9 per cent, or about one in ten of the population of York.[13]

The seemingly mathematical accuracy of the figures which so impressed contemporaries was also dubious. Booth's statistics were not of *people* at all, but of *impressions* of particular houses and whole streets extracted by his proud but inaccurate technique of 'mass interviewing' by the new school attendance officers, his 'eyes and ears'. Rowntree's statistics were also impressionistic, and collected by his anonymous (and enormously hard-working) paid investigator who called at every working-class house, inquired about the wages, earners and dependants and, where the income was deemed barely sufficient, noted the signs of 'secondary poverty'.

None of these caveats proves that poverty was negligible in late Victorian England – on the contrary, the Interdepartmental Committee on Physical Deterioration, which reported in 1904 after General Sir Frederick Maurice's complaints of the unfitness of many army recruits in the Boer War, amply confirmed the poor food, overcrowded housing and terrible living conditions, though not the alleged progressive mental and physical degeneration, amongst the slum dwellers of the great cities[14] – but they do suggest that the proportion in poverty *by the standards of the time* was smaller than Booth's and Rowntree's estimates were taken to mean.

This was confirmed by Bowley and Burnett-Hurst's much more scientific and accurate four towns survey, *Livelihood and Poverty*, though this was not published until 1915, too late to affect public opinion in the period.[15] This random sampling of working-class households in Northampton, Reading, Stanley and Warrington in 1912-13, using a new and somewhat higher poverty line, showed that an average of 16 per cent of the working class, or about 12 per cent of the total population, ranging from 4.5 per cent in Stanley (a small coalmining town) to 19 per cent in Reading, were living in (primary) poverty. It was no consolation to those actually suffering from want and distress that their suffering was shared with fewer rather than larger numbers than was commonly believed. Indeed, as today, 'relative deprivation' compared with the affluent many may lead to a greater sense of social injustice.

The causes of poverty were of three overlapping kinds. Firstly, there were the unavoidable exigencies and misfortunes of life, illness or death of the main breadwinner, old age or unemployment. Secondly came the 'life-cycle' of poverty discovered by Rowntree, in which most of the children were born into poverty brought on by their very coming and the loss of the wife's wages, most married after a brief period of prosperity into childbearing and poverty again, and then, after an interval of affluence supported by the older children's wages, sank into the poverty of old age. Thirdly, the most important at the time, was the poverty of low wages and large families. The first kind, illness, widowhood, old age and unemployment, accounted for 23 per cent of the poverty in York (of which unemployment and irregular work, in a boom year, caused 5.1 per cent), and from 13 per cent in Warrington to 31 per cent in Reading and 35 per cent in Northampton (of which unemployment and irregular work caused about 6 per cent). The second kind can best be measured by the proportion of children in poverty, far larger than the average for the whole population: 35.7 per cent of all children under 15 were in (primary or secondary) poverty in York (as compared with the population average of 27.8 per cent), and 27 per cent of the children in (primary) poverty in Bowley and Burnett-Hurst's four towns (as compared with 16 per cent overall). But by far the major cause of poverty was low wages, usually combined with large dependent families: no less than 74 per cent of those in poverty in York, and 71 per cent in the other four towns.[16] Of agricultural labourers, whose wages were the lowest of any major occupation, ranging from an average of 14s. 11d. a week in the worst county, Oxfordshire, to 22s. 6d. in the best, Durham, *most* were in poverty. According to a survey in 1913 by Rowntree and May Kendall, 'the wage paid by farmers to agricultural labourers is, in the vast majority of cases, insufficient to maintain a family of average size in a state of merely physical efficiency'[17] – and most farm labourers' families were above the

national average in size. Bowley and Burnett-Hurst concluded
from their survey:

> It is thus proved that a great part of the poverty revealed by our
> enquiries ... is not intermittent but permanent, not accidental
> or due to exceptional misfortune, but a regular feature of the
> industries of the towns concerned. It cannot be too
> emphatically stated that of all the causes of primary poverty
> which have been brought to our notice, low wages are by far
> the most important. We could go further and say that to raise
> the wages of the worst-paid workers is the most pressing social
> task with which this country is faced today.[18]

To that extent, capitalist society had succeeded in segregating
not just the immensely rich from the rest, or the middle from the
working class, but also the ordinary working class, Booth's 52 per
cent of wage earners living in comfort and indeed his 74 per cent
living above the level of want or distress, from the 'residuum', the
'outcast poor' who lived out their lives in the pariah-world of the
slums.

Nevertheless, since far more children passed through a phase of
poverty and malnutrition than lived permanently in poverty as
adults, the segregation of the classes was physiological as well as
economic and locational. Between 1880 and 1910 13-year-old
working-class boys in London and Glasgow were on the average
$2\frac{1}{2}$ inches shorter than their middle-income group contemporaries, and 4 inches shorter than upper-class boys, and there was
little evidence of much increase in average height or narrowing of
the gap between the two dates.[19] The chances of living at all were
twice as great in the highest as in the lowest class: infant mortality
rates in the upper and middle classes as late as 1911 averaged 77 per
thousand compared with 113 per thousand for skilled workers'
children and 152 per thousand for the unskilled.[20] In 1917 the
National Service Medical Boards found that only three in nine
conscripts (all born before 1900) were

> perfectly fit and healthy; two were on a definitely infirm plane
> of health and strength ...; three were incapable of undergoing
> more than a very moderate degree of physical exertion and
> could almost (in view of their age) be described with justice as
> physical wrecks; and the remaining man was a chronic invalid
> with a precarious hold on life.[21]

When class could make so much difference not merely to material possessions and cultural advantages but to the very fibre of one's being, we can truly say that class society was at its zenith.

Segregation was reinforced by growing class hostility. Although after passing through the relatively socially harmonious 'viable class society' of the mid-Victorian age, England did not return to the violent class antagonism and fear of revolution of the Regency and Chartist periods, there was in the last quarter of the nineteenth century and beyond a decided upswing in the tempo of class conflict. It took the form of an intensification of the struggle for income which showed itself, firstly, in prolonged outbursts of industrial strikes, bitter denunciations of landlords and million-aires, demands for parliamentary and local government reform, proposals for land taxes, social reform, and changes in the method of incidence of taxation, and, secondly, in challenges to the *status quo* by various kinds of socialism and incipient working-class alternatives to the existing political parties. This recrudescence of class hostility might appear surprising in a period of rising living standards for most people, including a majority of the working class, and when most of the English, including a large part of the working class, were content to keep an increasingly plutocratic Conservative Party in power for most of the time. To understand this age of contradictions we must explore the impact of the so-called 'Great Depression' of 1874–96 and the climacteric of British capitalism.

2 THE CLIMACTERIC OF BRITISH CAPITALISM

British capitalism reached its zenith in the late Victorian age in yet another sense. At some point between the 1870s and the 1890s the rate of economic growth began to slacken, first in industrial production, then in National Income, and Britain began to be overtaken in both by foreign competitors, notably the United States and Germany. The annual rate of growth of industrial production (excluding building), having reached a peak of 3.6 per cent per annum in the decade from the early 1860s to the early 1870s, slackened to 1.6 per cent per annum between the late 1870s and the late 1880s, 1.8 per cent per annum between the late 1880s and the early 1900s, and finally to 1.5 per cent per annum between the early 1900s and 1913. In per capita terms the fall was still more spectacular, from 2.4 per cent per annum in the first of those decades to 0.2–0.4 per cent per annum through most of the period and to a *negative* 0.2 per cent per annum in the last decade before the Great War, an actual decline in production per head.[22] The figures are slightly defective since they tend to exaggerate the old declining industries and understate the new expanding ones, and they do not include the new and burgeoning services like education, health, transport, and local and central government which now began to enter more largely into the National Income. Allowing for these, real National Income per head (at 1913 prices) went on growing, with occasional setbacks, fairly steadily from an index (1913–14 = 100) of 58.6 in 1880 to 80.6 in 1890 and 89.4 in 1900, before levelling out in the 1900s in the low 90s, with a final upswing to 101.6 in the boom of 1913.[23] Much of the striking improvement in average living standards in the late Victorian age, a rise of over 50 per cent in twenty years in the face of decelerating industrial production, was due to favourable terms of trade and the falling prices of imported food and raw materials.[24] Retail prices fell from an index of 96 in 1880 to 68 in 1895 before rising again to 100 in 1911–13.[25]

In the same way, much of the stagnation of production and National Income per head in the Edwardian age was due to rising prices and adverse terms of trade. The 'climacteric of the late 1890s' – the beginning of a long-term fall in the rate of growth of National Income – was partly due to this swing from falling to rising prices, especially of imports, although this only dramatized the real change in Britain's dominant economic position and leading role in world trade, which reached its apogee in the late 1890s.[26]

To contemporaries the long period of falling prices between 1873 and 1896 was known as the 'Great Depression in trade and industry'. Its existence was doubted by the great economist Alfred Marshall before the Royal Commission on the Depression in 1886, and further doubt was thrown on it by H. L. Beales in 1934, before the 'myth' was finally demolished by S. B. Saul in 1969.[27] All three were of course right in rejecting the notion of permanent depression in a period which saw not only spectacularly rising real incomes together with high and, except for a few particularly bad years like 1879, 1884–87 and 1892–95, rising employment. Yet contemporaries were not self-deluded, knew that something was amiss, and had reason to believe that their discontents, political as well as social and economic, had something to do with contemporary economic trends.

There was of course a real depression in the arable agriculture of the fertile, corn-growing south and east, as cheap grain came pouring in from North America, carried by the new bulk tramp steamers at unprecedentedly low freight rates. Cheap refrigerated meat from Australia and South America did not have the same effect, since it was shunned by all but the poorer classes (who undoubtedly benefited by it), and the pastoral farmers and landlords of the north and west did much better, particularly those who used cheap imported feeding stuffs. While Cambridgeshire farm rents, for example, fell between 1871 and 1896 by 35 per cent, Lancashire rents fell by only 1 per cent, and the Earl of Derby's Lancashire rents from farms supplying the cotton towns with milk, butter, cheese and meat actually rose by 18 per cent.[28] The falling prices hit the traditional mixed farmers and their landlords hard, however, and the majority of landowners who had no other rents from mines or urban property found themselves overtaken in income – and still more in wealth as the capital value of rural land declined even faster than rents – by their industrial and commercial rivals, and they were left standing by the great urban and mine-owning aristocrats who alone could keep up with the new millionaires.

Other industries suffered from time to time from the short slumps within the 'Great Depression', and all no doubt suffered unknowingly from the favourable terms of trade that reduced the purchasing power of Britain's overseas customers, which in turn helped to cause the downturn in British rates of industrial growth. But the real paradox of the so-called Great Depression and the cause of its discontents lay in the impact of the falling prices themselves. For falling prices have a direct effect upon the struggle for income between the classes. Just as the rising prices of the mid-Victorian period eased the struggle for income, making it easier for landlords to obtain and farmers, business men and house-holders to pay higher rents and for workers to demand and employers to grant wage increases, so the falling prices of 1873–96 exacerbated that struggle, squeezing rents, profit margins and interest rates, and making it more difficult for landlords to resist rent concessions, business men to grant wage increases, and wage earners to defend themselves against wage cuts.[29] Whereas in the middle decades of the century mild inflation made the economy seem more buoyant than it really was and the system appear to be working to everyone's advantage, so in the later decades price deflation made the system appear less successful, and people in all classes came to question whether it ought not to be modified or radically changed. Business men, farmers, and working-class leaders became interested in a revival of land reform in a variety of nostrums, from Joseph Chamberlain's 'free trade in land' through Henry Broadhurst's leasehold enfranchisement to Henry George's 'single tax' and Alfred Russel Wallace's land nationalization.[30] Some business men and landowners began to question the generation-old policy of free trade and founded the Fair Trade League in 1881. Some working men with the middle-class sympathizers began to resurrect the socialist ideas which had been so prominent in the last great price fall in 1817–48, and to found new socialist organizations like the Social Democratic Federation (1881), the Socialist League (1884) and the Fabian Society (1884). Others engaged in major strikes, most often against wage cuts, but sometimes, especially in the short recoveries within the 'Great Depression', for wage increases like the match girls', gas workers' and dockers' strikes of 1888–89. Finally, groups of working-class leaders began to challenge the old two-party political system, to say 'a plague on both your houses', and to move towards the separate parliamentary representation of the working class.

Falling prices were not of course the only factor in the increased class hostility of the late Victorian age, any more than rising prices were the only cause of the relative class harmony of the previous generation. There were, as we shall see when we come to deal with the more fundamental differences of outlook between the classes, much deeper-seated causes of conflict in the competing and incompatible class ideals which underlay the struggle for income. But the timing of the upsurge in the 1880s and 1890s was certainly affected by the swing from rising to falling prices.

Curiously enough, the return swing in the late 1890s from falling to rising prices did not have the counterbalancing ameliorative effect, and this illustrates how the underlying class antagonisms overrode the more superficial effects of price change. In the Edwardian age the economic factor which proved to be far more influential than inflation – although steepening inflation between 1910 and 1914 certainly added its quota of aggravation to an already critical situation – was the stagnation of industrial growth and of National Income per head and, most provocative of all, the decline for the first time in living memory of real wages. If anything, an inflation which fails to produce increasing money wages (and other incomes) is even more frustrating and provocative than a deflation which threatens wage (and other income) cuts. The record strike waves of 1910–14 were only partly related to the inflation of those years, as we shall see, but it certainly sharpened the bitterness of an already bitter situation.

3 THE DECLINE OF LIBERAL ENGLAND

The most far-reaching effect to which the 'Great Depression' and its associated class conflict contributed was a permanent shift in what may be called the geological structure of politics. The 'earthquake of the 1880s' – the landslip in the bedrock of politics which was epitomized by the permanent split in the Liberal Party in 1886 – was only the most dramatic of a series of movements in the social structure of politics which may be called the long decline of Liberal England. By this is meant more than the decline of the Liberal Party. Liberal England was the consensus by which a harmonious, viable class society such as existed in the mid-Victorian age could support a political system based on the assumption that all classes could be accommodated within either of the traditional parties. In practice they were unequally accommodated, and from Peel's splitting of the Conservative Party in 1846 until its recovery of a majority government under Disraeli in 1874 the 'natural governing party' to which most people looked to maintain the consensus was the Liberal Party. Its long, slow decline was the major symptom and effect of the more general decline of Liberal England. The main features of this major restructuring of British politics, which began in a small way in the 1860s and ended after the break-up of the Liberal Party in the First World War, were the drift of both the old Whig landlords and the new corporate capitalists from the Liberal to the Conservative Party and the rise of the new Labour Party which was to replace it as one of the two major governing parties.

This remarkable redrawing of the social map of politics, although abetted in its timing by the increased class antagonism of the 'Great Depression' and its Edwardian aftermath, was rooted in the logic of capitalist society at its zenith. Indeed, one of the most surprising aspects of the rise of modern class society during the Industrial Revolution is that it took so long to express itself in class-based political parties. The delay was largely due to the construction of the Liberal consensus, by the skill and success with which the English landed ruling class accommodated itself to the demands of the rising new classes, both to the emerging values of the entrepreneurial ideal and to the extremely moderate claims of the working class. But it was also due to the built-in constitutional constraints, which prevented for most of the century the formation of separate middle- or working-class political parties with any hope of effective electoral success or a parliamentary majority.

The 1880s were to undermine those constraints. The Parliament elected in 1880 was the last in which the landowners had a clear majority, that elected in 1885 the first in which they were out-numbered.[31] They could no longer afford the luxury of dividing their forces between two majoritarian parties (although the new dispensation, confused by what only gradually came to be seen as the halfway house of Liberal Unionism, took a generation to clarify itself). Meanwhile the landed majority in the Cabinet lasted down to 1905, that in the House of Lords until the inter-war period, when it ceased to matter as a force separate from the rest of the wealthy peers.[32] The lifting of the constraints on class politics – foreshadowed by the Second Reform Act of 1867 and the Ballot Act of 1872 – began a transition whose significance was much greater than it appeared to contemporaries. The most obvious landmark was the Third Reform Act of 1884 which, unlike its predecessors, gave the working-class voters for the first time the possibility of constituting a majority of the electorate. Less obvious was the accompanying Redistribution Act of 1885, whose mainly single-member constituencies allowed concentrations of working-class electors like the coalminers and textile workers to dominate particular seats and others like the cotton workers to hold the balance between the major parties. The Corrupt Practices Act of 1883, by limiting the amount per elector which each candidate could spend, had a larger effect than the Ballot Act on the independence of voters. The three acts together also brought into existence as a third force in British politics the over-whelmingly Nationalist block of eight-six Irish MPs, which was

41

perceived as a threat to property owners in Ireland and by analogy in Britain. Finally, there were the County Councils Act of 1888 and the London Government Act of 1889 which, by extending democracy to the counties (previously run by the non-elected JPs) and to London and the larger cities, gave new political groupings like London's Progressive Party and local working-class parties everywhere the opportunity to practise their skills and build up local power bases. The same could be said of the later District Councils Act of 1894, the London Government Act of 1899 which created the twenty-eight metropolitan borough councils below the LCC, and indeed of the earlier School Boards (1870) and Poor Law Guardians (1834), which now began to be targets for the new electors and their representatives. In little more than a decade (1883–94) not only the game but also the allegiance of many of the players had been completely changed.

The two most salient features of the decline of Liberal England were the drift of large and increasing numbers of landowners and business men from the Liberal to the Conservative Party and the rise of Labour as an independent political force. Neither of these developments was inevitable, and if any well-informed political observer had been told in 1880 that twentieth-century politics would be dominated by a predominantly capitalist and an ostensibly anti-capitalist party, he would have automatically assumed them to be the Liberal versus a new working-class party. The astonishing reversal by which the Conservative Party, the traditional bastion of the rural landed gentry and the Church of England, replaced the Liberal Party, the traditional home of the Great Whig, and often urban propertied and entrepreneurial, aristocracy and of the industrial middle class and the Dissenters, is only surpassed by the total replacement of the Liberal Party as the alternative governing party by the Labour Party. The astonishment is tempered, of course, by the knowledge that the stereotypes were oversimplified even in 1880, and that there had long been, particularly in London and the great ports, many traditionally Conservative merchants, bankers, brewers and government contractors, and also, particularly in the Lancashire and Yorkshire textile areas and across the south of England, those large numbers of, mainly Anglican, working-class Tories whom Disraeli had discovered 'like the angel in the marble'.[33] But the fact remains that between 1880 and 1914 the Liberal Party, which had been the 'natural party of government' for the previous half-century, lost the permanent allegiance of the landowners and many of the business men, especially the bigger, corporate capitalists, and failed to hold on to the almost automatic support of organized (as distinct from unorganized, deferential or individual ambitious) labour.

The first of these haemorrhages from Liberalism began before 1886, in the defection of individual landlords like Sir James Graham and the Duke of Argyll, of bankers like Lord Overstone, of corporate business men like Richard Potter, chairman of the Great Western Railway and the Canadian Pacific Railroad, Sir Edwin Watkin of the Midland Railway, and Sir Richard Moon of the London and North Western Railway, and of most of the great brewers, like Lord Ardilaun, the first of the Guinness peers, and Lord Hindlip of the Allsop family. As Lord Salisbury noted in the *Quarterly Review* in 1883, 'The uneasiness is greatest among those whose property consists in land,' but 'publicans, manufacturers, house-owners, railway shareholders, fundholders are painfully aware that they have all been threatened: that their most vital interests are at the mercy of some move in the game of politics.'[34] The City of London changed from rocklike Liberal to diehard Tory.[35] The metropolis as a whole changed sides: in 1865 every London parliamentary seat was held by the Liberals; by 1900 they held only eight out of seventy-two.[36] From 1886 there was a veritable flood, often via the Liberal Unionist Party like the Marquess of Hartington and his Whig followers and Joseph Chamberlain and his Midland business colleagues, but with most of them finishing their political careers in the Conservative and Unionist Party.

Peerage creations are another indication. Except for those businessmen like Lord Overstone and Edward Strutt, Baron Belper, who passed through the metamorphosis of landowner-ship, business peerages were almost unheard of before the 1880s, when Gladstone and Salisbury began to vie with each other in capitalist creations as the business class began to come into its own in status as well as wealth. Of the 200 or so non-royal peerages created between 1886 and 1914, some seventy, more than a third, represented new wealth from industry, commerce and finance. Another third represented the traditional professional routes into the peerage, chiefly via the law and the judges' bench and other service to the state of diplomacy, colonial service or the armed forces, even though such service now more rarely led to landed wealth. Only about a quarter came from that once traditional source of nobility, the landed gentry. More to the present point, although both governing parties sought to honour and gain the support of the business interests, it is significant that the Tories ennobled more of the big corporate bankers, brewers and newspaper owners, the Liberals more from traditional manufacturing industry.[37]

This tendency, for the financial and corporate interests, plus the brewers, to drift disproportionately towards the Conservative Party while more of the merchants and manufacturers stayed Liberal to the end, can be seen in the House of Commons. This period saw the greatest overlap between non-landed wealth and membership in Parliament: in 1895, for example, sixty of the 200 non-landed millionaires were MPs, and many of the rest in the House of Lords.[38] The class interests of MPs are therefore a better measure than they were before or later of the drift of the wealthy from the Liberal to the Conservative Party. The known statistics of MPs' economic interests show that, while the Liberal share of landed MPs plummeted from nearly one half in 1880 and 1885 to a quarter or less thereafter (apart from the aberration of more than half in the great Liberal landslide of 1906), the Liberal share of business MPs fell from two-thirds in 1880 and three-fifths in 1885 to less than half until the temporary recovery of 1906. Only amongst MPs from the professions did the Liberals maintain, especially when in office, an overwhelming share of the interest in the House. This becomes much clearer if we cancel out 'the swing of

Table 2.3 Liberal proportion of each interest in the House of Commons, 1868–1910

		1868	1874	1880	1885	1886	1892	1895	1900	1906	1910
Land	%	47.4	33.9	48.6	47.5	25.1	23.8	17.0	16.7	51.7	23.5
	AI	0.63	0.72	0.66	0.67	0.69	0.36	0.48	0.43	0.37	0.31
Business	%	71.8	57.3	69.7	61.1	40.9	49.9	32.0	32.3	71.6	52.5
	AI	1.73	2.05	1.58	1.22	1.39	1.15	1.09	1.03	0.93	1.11
Professions	%	72.7	61.5	77.2	68.7	45.6	56.0	40.8	44.3	82.1	57.7
	AI	2.04	2.24	2.36	1.63	1.75	1.47	1.60	1.60	1.76	1.37
Armed forces	%	44.4	24.8	41.3	28.6	11.8	14.7	7.5	11.1	40.8	24.3
	AI	0.56	0.46	0.49	0.30	0.28	0.20	0.19	0.27	0.26	0.32

the pendulum' by adjusting the raw percentages to allow for the rise and fall of party representation in the House. An associative index (AI; 1.0 = the same share of the occupation's MPs as the party's share of MPs in the Commons), as shown in Table 2.3, indicates how much greater or smaller the Liberal Party's share of each interest was than its share of the MPs of the two parties.

This shows that the Liberals maintained (with the slight and surprising exception of 1906) more than their proportionate share of the business interest among MPs, although a declining one, down to the First World War. A more refined analysis shows more clearly what was really happening. If we separate out the financiers (bankers, insurance and finance company directors) and the merchants, to represent the extremes of the rising corporate capitalists and the traditional individualists, we get the picture shown in Table 2.4.

Table 2.4 Liberal proportion of finance and merchant interests in the House of Commons, 1868–1910

		1868	1874	1880	1885	1886	1892	1895	1900	1906	1910
Finance	%	71.7	51.1	61.4	54.0	31.1	38.0	21.7	20.9	64.1	42.1
	AI	1.77	1.47	1.11	0.87	0.93	0.70	0.65	0.57	0.66	0.74
Merchants	%	82.9	72.7	81.0	77.4	57.2	66.2	46.8	39.3	87.1	66.7
	AI	3.39	3.74	2.97	2.55	2.75	2.25	2.04	1.40	2.50	2.00

Thus while the Liberals maintained an overwhelming share of the merchants, twice or more their 'proper' share, their lesser but still clear majority of the financiers down to 1885 steadily dwindled to an equally clear minority.[39]

At the electoral level the drift was reinforced by the greater geographical segregation of suburban class society. The migration of the well-to-do middle class from the industrial towns and commercial cities into the surrounding countryside had been feared by the traditionally Conservative landed gentry as a threat to their domination. In fact it proved, as far as the party if not the gentry was concerned, to be the opposite. The 'villa Toryism' of the new outer suburbanites in the county constituencies became a pillar of the Conservative Party organization, and appeared at exactly the right time to counter the newly enfranchised agricultural worker, who was claimed to have won the 1885 election for Gladstone. In the inner suburbs, too, the growth of the lower middle class of clerks, teachers and small business men, with their morbid fear of the working class, reinforced that division into Liberal/Labour inner-city islands in a suburban and county Tory sea which became the major feature of twentieth-century political geography.[40] In London the Liberals and the Fabians blamed the middle-class suburbs for wresting control of the London County Council from the 'Progressives' in 1907 and transferring it to the 'Moderates'. As Charles Masterman put it, 'In feverish hordes the suburbs swarm to the polls to vote against a turbulent proletariat.'[41]

None of this proves that the Liberal Party before the First World War was doomed to extinction. What it does suggest is that a large number of business men, and particularly the new rising plutocrats, were becoming disillusioned with traditional Liberalism and finding a more congenial home in the Conservative Party. The reasons for this have been discussed at length in my study of 'Land Reform and Class Conflict in Victorian Britain'.[42] By the 1880s the great Gladstonian Liberal Party had done its work of democratizing and reforming Britain along the lines of a purely political radicalism which could unite, for different but not yet competing reasons, the progressive forces amongst Whig landlords, Cobdenite business men and the organized working class alike.[43] From then onwards Liberalism came to represent, for all landowners and for those business men who disliked landlordism less than they feared attacks on any kind of property, a threat to property itself.

Land reform, which became an increasing obsession with 'advanced Liberals', was the link between the Irish land policies of Gladstone – and here the Third Reform Act as applied to Ireland seemed to many English property owners to have thrown the Irish landlords to the wolves – and the costly social reforms demanded not only by the radical wing of the party but also by their socialist and trade union allies outside. Some of the latter went further, to demand Henry George's 'single tax' on landed property, particularly urban or potentially urban property, and even the nationalization of mines, railways and the land itself. The threat to property will appear in its proper place, in Chapter 4. Suffice it to say here that they all represented a creeping threat to property which no longer, as in the days of Cobden and Bright, was thought to be aimed only at the irresponsible power of the landlords, leaving the business class unscathed. As Lord Salisbury so tellingly put it in 1884, 'We are on an inclined plane leading from the position of Lord Hartington to that of Mr Chamberlain and so on to the depths over which Mr Henry George rules supreme.'[44] At various points on this slippery slope most of the landowners and increasing numbers of business men chose to jump off and abandon the Liberal Party to its fate.

The fate they assumed for it was increasing domination by the 'advanced Liberals' or radicals, who were thought to be 'soft on property' whenever it clashed with the interests of the underdog, whether the underdog was Irish peasant, Scottish crofter, English slum dweller, East End docker, the 'sweated worker' in the surviving domestic trades, the elderly worker, the widow, the orphan, the unemployed, the poor generally, the colonial peoples, the ex-slaves in the West Indies, the Boers in South Africa, or the Chinese indentured labourers in the South African mines. For all of these, advanced Liberalism as it was called in the 1880s or the New Liberalism as it became in the late 1890s raised the high moral ideal of social justice for all men everywhere. This moral idealism, which some of his opponents labelled 'humbug', had been the banner under which Gladstone had created the party and passionately bound idealists of all classes to himself as 'the people's William'. In the early 1880s its destiny still seemed to be that of a great party of reform but now, if the more radical wing had its way, it would become increasingly a party of *social* reform. For the failure to maintain the momentum of reform Gladstone himself cannot be absolved from blame, perhaps more because of his opportunism in allying himself with the new Irish Nationalist balancing force than because of his well-known dislike of government intervention. From the viewpoint of Chamberlain and many radicals he chose the 'wrong' underdog for special treatment, and thus missed the opportunity of maintaining for the Liberal Party the allegiance of a large part of organized labour.

What might have happened to the Liberal Party if Gladstone had irrevocably resigned and left Chamberlain to lead it, with or without the Marques of Hartington and the Whigs, in a great programme of social reform and, perhaps, imperialism – a combination of proven appeal to the working-class voter – it is impossible to guess. It is not, however, beyond reasonable speculation that the Liberals might have become, in the fullness of time and beyond the death of Chamberlain, not very different from the twentieth-century Labour Party, a reformist coalition of middle-class intellectuals and organized labour with perhaps a social democratic instead of a socialist label to mark the difference – much indeed as the Liberal Party appeared to be in process of becoming between 1906 and 1914.

The rise of Labour and also – not by any means the same thing – of modern socialism can also be traced to the geological shift of the 1880s. Disappointment with the lost leaders, first Gladstone and then Chamberlain, and the 'wrong' directions in which they led, played a large part, along with the class antagonisms of the 'Great Depression', in the new awakenings of the 1880s, the socialist revival and the New Unionism. If this was the immediate provocation, the socialist societies of the 1880s had their roots further back, in the land reform movement, Christian Socialism, and the fugitive political socialism of the mid-Victorian period. The upsurge of land reform in the late 1860s and 1870s, which in 1880 caused the two elder statesmen John Bright and Disraeli one to welcome and the other to fear an imminent 'assault upon the constitutional position of the landed interest', belonged to that earlier phase of class conflict in which individual capitalists of the Anti-Corn Law League variety were ranged against Ricardo's monopolists of the soil.[45] It was still alive in 1885 with the founding of the Free Land League and Joseph Chamberlain and Jesse Collings's claim to have won the election for Gladstone on the cry of 'three acres and a cow' for the newly enfranchised farm labourers.[46]

What was surprising about the movement was its ability, paradoxically based on the consensus of Liberal England, to unite the middle and working classes as in 1832 and 1846 in one final attack on the landed aristocracy. This was symbolized by the founding in 1870 of the English Land Tenure Association by John Stuart Mill and his friends, together with George Odger, one of the famous trade union 'junta', and five members of the (first) International Working Men's Association (founded in 1864). It was this Association, in the persons of Helen Taylor, Mill's stepdaughter, and George Odger, which welcomed Henry George on his first tour of England in 1881.[47] His sixpenny editions of *Progress and*

Poverty, with their attack on the land monopoly and advocacy of the 'single tax', are often credited with stimulating that concern with the economic connections between wealth and poverty which led so many to socialism. If that is so, Henry George was exceedingly fortunate both in his message and in his timing. The 1870s and early 1880s were seething with attacks on landed property – Alfred Russel Wallace's Land Nationalization League of 1881 (which objected to the confiscatory nature of George's single tax), the Land Reform Union (later the English Land Restoration League) which split off from it in 1883 to organize George's second tour of Britain, the Free Land League of 1885, Henry Broadhurst's Leasehold Enfranchisement Bill of that year, and so on. The importance of land reform was that, in illustration of Lord Salisbury's 'inclined plane', it could so easily slide, via the nationalization of mines, railways and other natural monopolies, into full-blown socialism.

Christian Socialism contributed its mite to secular socialism via Stewart Headlam, founder of the Guild of St Matthew (1887), a society of Anglicans concerned with social problems, who hailed Henry George as a 'man sent from God', helped to found the Land Reform League and edit its symbolically named journal, the *Christian Socialist*, and was associated with the Fabians in such good causes at the Bryant and May match girls' strike of 1887 and the elections to the London School Board in 1888.[48]

The final mid-Victorian ingredient was Marxism itself, hardly known in England before the 1880s, which was thrown into the pot by H. M. Hyndman, the rich city man who founded the (Social) Democratic Federation in 1881, and by his friends William Morris and Marx's favourite daughter, Eleanor, who broke with Hyndman to found the Socialist League in 1884.[49] Bernard Shaw, too, and a few other Fabians were influenced by Marx, especially after the English translation of *Capital* appeared in 1887. But on the whole English socialism, as Tawney was to say, 'owed more to Methodism than to Marxism', and it was the third socialist society, the Fabian, which despite its intellectual elitism was to represent the main line of development.

Characteristically founded as 'the Fellowship of the new Life' by a group of admirers of Thomas Davidson, a charismatic itinerant philosopher, including the Quaker idealist Edward Pease, Helen Taylor of the land reform movement and the SDF, and H. H.

Champion, editor of the SDF's *Justice*, the renamed Fabian Society was soon taken over by the 'little band of prophets' led by Bernard Shaw, Sidney Webb, Sydney Olivier, and Annie Besant, who believed in a very un-Marxist evolutionary socialism to be achieved by persuasion of public opinion and 'permeation' of the two major political parties.[50] Part of their technique was to blow their own collective trumpet, to exaggerate their influence, and to claim any example, however spontaneous, of municipal or central government enterprise as a victory for Fabian 'permeation'. This was often counterproductive at the time, and has certainly given them a bad name with recent historians, but they were brilliant propagandists who undoubtedly did a great deal to question the contemporary economic system and to popularize discussion of socialist remedies.[51] Their chief drawback, from the point of view of the rising Labour movement, was their intellectual arrogance, their scarcely disguised contempt for the working-class leaders they had to deal with, and their rejection until 1900 and half-hearted acceptance thereafter of a separate working-class party in favour of their own permeation of the two parties whose possession of power they admired and wished to manipulate.[52]

All three main socialist societies had connections with organized labour and were prepared to help with speeches, advice, organizing strikes, demonstrations of the unemployed, and so on. On the face of it, the SDF, with powerful working-class orators like John Burns and Tom Mann and more experience of organizing strikes in the provinces in 1884–86 and demonstrations of unemployed in London in 1886–87, culminating in 'Blood Sunday', a fracas with the police in Trafalgar Square on 13 November 1887, was in the best position to influence the trade union movement. Yet its direct influence on the unions, who repudiated its revolutionary socialism, was as negligible as its success at the polls. Although SDF and Fabian members, including Annie Besant, Herbert Burrows, Stewart Headlam and Bernard Shaw, gave some assistance to the Bryant and May match girls' strike of 1888 which is the traditional starting point of the New Unionism, most strikes in the period were begun by the workers themselves, even when the leaders were committed members of the SDF. This was often under provocation from employers who, themselves under pressure from falling profit margins, wished to cut wages, extend hours, increase workloads, and speed up machinery. This was certainly the case with the gasworkers' strike of 1889 led by a gas stoker, Will Thorne, and the great dock strike of the same year led by Ben Tillet, also of the SDF.[53] Again and again, the strikes began spontaneously, and only then did the socialist leaders move in, often in response to appeals from the strikers. It was the struggle for income in a deflationary period, and the struggle for control of the workplace between masters and men, not the agitation of the socialists, which fomented the New Unionism, and increased the number of unionists from under 1 million in the mid-1870s to over $1\frac{1}{2}$ million by 1892, 2 million by 1900, and to 4 million by 1914.[54]

For the same reason, the poorly paid unskilled and poorly organized pioneer unions of the New Unionism could be defeated and crushed out of existence as rapidly as they had sprung up. Within twelve months of the winning of the 'dockers' tanner' Tillet's union had been squeezed out of the London docks; and the provincial dockers' and seamen's unions fared no better, as the defeat of the last great dock strike, at Hull in 1893, demonstrated. Socialist exhortation was no protection against the employers' counteroffensive in the 1890s, and most of the unskilled unions faded into insignificance. The New Unionism survived much more amongst the traditional skilled unions, the engineers, miners, textile workers, railwaymen and so on, whose unions had expanded partly in response to the new enthusiasm for industrial organization but much more in defence against the employers' counteroffensive. Its main legacy within the movement was a running battle for control of the Trades Union Congress and the larger unions, but this was as much a battle between the old and the new generations as it was between old Liberals and new socialists, between the 'old gang' of Broadhurst, Fenwick and company, and Keir Hardie, John Burns, Havelock Wilson and their allies. In 1894 this led to a pyrrhic victory by the 'old gang', a resolution excluding non-workers and nonunion officials from membership of the TUC, intended to exclude the middle-class socialists, which had the effect of expelling both Hardie and Broadhurst as non-working MPs. The same Congress excluded the more politically based trades councils (the 'local TUCs') and introduced the undemocratic block vote giving power to the big union officials.[55]

Keir Hardie and his fellows regarded the TUC as the ineffective tail of the Liberal Party, and aimed at separate working-class representation in Parliament. To this end he founded the Scottish Labour Party in 1888 and, at a meeting in Bradford in 1893 attended by delegates from the Fabians, the SDF, the Scottish Labour Party and some trade unions, the Independent Labour Party.[56] The TUC and the larger unions stood aloof. What eventually changed their minds was the employers' offensive, which in the later 1890s, in addition to the industrial conflicts which will be discussed later, also took a litigious turn. A series of court actions designed to curb the power of unions limited the right of strikers to picket and, finally, the Lords' decision in the famous Taff Vale case of 1900 made the unions liable to the extent of their whole funds for damages to employers and their customers arising from industrial disputes.[57] Even before this happened it had become clear that neither of the main political parties was willing to restore the legislative protection granted by the 1871 and 1875 Acts, and Congress in 1899 passed the resolution that, in collaboration with the ILP, the SDF and the Fabians, set up the Labour Representation Committee (1900), which after the 1906 election became the Labour Party.[58]

Thus, out of the class conflict of the later Victorian age and the intransigence of the employers and both existing major political parties, emerged the first intentionally class-based party of capitalist society. Although, with its twenty-nine MPs in 1906 and forty-two in 1910, it represented only a minute fraction of the working-class electorate, most of whom continued to vote for the traditional parties, it was nevertheless the clearest sign of the rise of a class-based party system. As such, and along with the increasingly capitalist Conservative Party, it marked the imminent decline of Liberal England.

Apart from the remaining Liberals themselves, who enjoyed a remarkable revival of their fortunes in 1906–14 but continued to agonize over their situation, caught between the devil of a seductively capitalist party on one side and the deep blue sea of labour on the other, there were few to weep over that decline. To the class-based parties it looked more like a belated acceptance at the political level of the facts of modern economic life and a clearing of the ground for the real political battle, the struggle for income between the classes. There was, however, another decline which was bound to worry everyone concerned: the threatened decline of England itself. This decline, of England's, the United Kingdom's and the British Empire's economic place at the head of the world economy and, indeed, of the military capacity of Britain as a great power, had much to do with the fragmentation of class society at its zenith. Behind this apprehension of decline lay the fear of the segregated working class, particularly of its poorer sections, and of what they might do to undermine the strength and unity of the nation.

4 THE FEAR OF THE POOR

Far more important to the rich and the middle classes even than the decline of Liberal England was the threatened decline of Britain itself as a great power and as a nation. This perception was not yet based on the fear of revolution – in the last few years before the Great War a crisis in class society was to raise alarmist fears of a collapse of industrial relations and the threat of economic break-down. It was a much more immediate fear stemming from the mere existence of a segregated working class and of poverty on a massive and nationally debilitating scale. The threat was twofold: an overt, conscious threat to Britain's competitive position in the world economy from the insistent demands of labour for a larger share of the product and for expensive social reforms paid for by the rich, and a more covert and insidious threat from poverty itself to the physical, intellectual and moral fitness of the nation. The first was a threat to profits, to investment, and ultimately to Britain's competitiveness in world markets. The second, while reinforcing the first by undermining the workers' capacity to produce, was a more direct threat to the nation's capacity to defend itself in war, and therefore to Britain's very survival. The first accounts both for the emotional intensity of the employers' counteroffensive against the new unionism in the 1890s and 1900s and also for the equally emotional alienation of the landed and capitalist classes from a Liberal Party whose cautious social reforms seemed to them to be the thin end of an enormous wedge. It was the second threat, however, which was the more powerful and effective, since it could not yet be met by mere political opposition, and it created dilemmas for the politicians and the propertied classes which split them in complex and contradictory ways.

The problem, compounded from a mixture of undoubted demographic facts, more dubious interpretations of them and still more dubious theories, notably 'Social Darwinism' as interpreted by Herbert Spencer and his followers,[59] seemed simple enough. Industrialism had created an enormous working class isolated in the smoke and dirt of the manufacturing towns and commerical cities, unhealthy, badly fed, badly housed, ill educated, often (it was believed) drunken, hedonistic and feckless, whose teeming children were likely to grow up still weaker, sicklier and more ignorant than their parents. As the sympathetic New Liberal Charles Masterman put it in 1902, 'the crowded quarters of the working classes' had produced 'a characteristic *physical* type of town dweller: stunted, narrow chested, easily wearied, yet voluble, excitable, with little ballast, stamina or endurance – seeking stimulus in drink, in betting, in any unaccustomed conflicts at home or abroad.' By 1909 he was writing about the middle-class 'suburbans' gazing darkly 'upon the huge and smoky area of tumbled tenements which stretches at [their] feet' and anticipating 'the boiling over of the cauldron.'[60]

Because the birth rate, which had been declining since 1877, was much lower amongst the undoubtedly healthier and supposedly more moral and intelligent classes above them, the poor were not only deteriorating themselves but disproportionately lowering the average physical, moral and mental capacity of the nation. In the 1890s Karl Pearson, pioneer of statistics and the eugenic movement, calculated that the poorest one-fifth to one-quarter of existing married couples would produce one-half of the next generation; by 1909 he thought that one-half would be produced by less than one in eight (12 per cent) of marriages.[61] In an increasingly competitive world in which both commercial and military success was granted to the strongest and cleverest nations, Britain, with the largest and longest-established working class most concentrated in industrial towns and cities, was the most vulnerable to stagnation and decline. Using the Social Darwinian language of the day but raising it from the Spencerian internal struggle between individuals to the external imperialist struggle between nations, Pearson wrote in 1904:

> When the extra-group struggle with inferior races abroad has run to its end; then, if not sooner, the population question will force on a severer struggle for existence between civilized communities at home. Whether this struggle takes the form of

actual warfare, or of still keener competition for trade and food-supply, that group in which unchecked internal composition has produced a vast proletariat with no limit of endurance, or with – to use a cant phrase – no 'stake in the State', will be the first to collapse.[62]

A socialist himself, he believed that this extra-group competition would force the nations of Europe in the direction of socialism, but his was only one prognosis amongst many. Almost everyone, Imperialists and Little Englanders, Conservatives and Liberals, 'Limps' (Liberal Imperialists) and Pro-Boers, individualists and socialists, Social Darwinians and religious fundamentalists, believed his diagnosis to be true.

Firstly, it rested on some undoubted facts. The birth rate had declined from a peak of 36.3 per thousand in 1876 to 28.5 in 1901 (and to about 24 on the eve of the First World War), but in the East End of London in 1901 it was still 35.6 per thousand, nearly double the 18.6 of the West End.[63] Meanwhile, foreign economic competition had been increasing, Britain was being overtaken in steel and other vital production by the United States and Germany, with some others not far behind. The struggle for markets was growing, most other industrial countries were shutting out British exports by means of high tariffs and invading Britain's traditional markets even inside the empire. The colonial and military competition was hotting up with the scramble for Africa, the partition of China, the rape of the South Pacific and other still incompletely colonized parts of the world, and Britain's control of around one-quarter of the world's land area and population was beginning to come under challenge, with French and German claims to parts of East and Southern Africa, Asia and Melanesia, and American resentment of European, especially Spanish, colonialism in the Western hemisphere, all sparking off diplomatic incidents if not actual wars. At the same time the vast, conscripted peasant armies of continental Europe compared with the tiny, volunteer army of mainly unemployed industrial workers mounted by Britain suggested a very unequal contest if it came to a great war between the powers.

These fears were confirmed by the statistics of poverty produced for London and York by Booth and Rowntree, and although, as we already have seen, their figures did not mean what they were taken to mean – the percentages in 'want and distress' and in 'primary poverty', 8.4 per cent in London and 10 per cent in York, were much lower then the overall figures of general and secondary poverty (ignoring their careful definitions), 30.5 and 27.8 per cent respectively – it was these overall figures, rounded to 'a third of the population', which were quoted sensationally in the press and widely accepted. They were put to the test in the Boer War, when large numbers of army recruits were found to be unfit for service. The Surgeon-General Sir William Taylor reported to the War Office on the 'growing deterioration of the physique of the working classes' and General Sir Frederick Maurice in articles in the *Contemporary Review* claimed that no less than three in five of those wishing to enlist were turned down on medical grounds or failed to complete their first two years of service.[64] The actual army returns for 1893–1902 showed that 34.6 per cent were rejected at the initial inspection and a further 3 per cent during the first two years of service, but the army supported Maurice's figures with the claim that the recruiting sergeants weeded out before inspection those who were likely to be rejected. In fact, nearly half of those rejected were so because they fell below the arbitrary army standards of height, weight, chest measurement and vision required. These defects may admittedly have been due in many cases to under-nourishment and lack of exercise and medical treatment, but those accepted responded wonderfully to good feeding and physical training. Even the corrected official figures were undoubtedly bad, and the belief spread that they were getting worse.

Such fears of the poor and their 'unfortunate propensity' to breed faster than was good for them or the nation were not new at the time of the Boer War. They had a much longer pedigree, going back at least to the New Poor Law of 1834 and the segregation of paupers by sex in the union workhouse 'for their own good' in an overstocked and underpaid labour market. They were given a boost by the Charity Organization Society from 1869 onwards with its demand for the revival of the principles of 1834 and its recommendation of 'labour colonies' for the adult male unemployed which would separate them from their families for as long as possible. Even such kindly and well-meaning social reformers as Canon Barnett, founder of Toynbee Hall, William Booth, creator of the Salvation Army, and Alfred Marshall, the neo-classical economist who wished to see the workers become 'gentlemen', all believed that the 'residuum' should be removed to 'labour camps' far from London.[65] Charles Booth recommended 'the entire removal of this very poor class', one-twelfth of the population of London, 'out of the daily struggle for existence' so as to free the labour market for the rest of the working class: To the rich the very poor are a sentimental interest; to the poor they are a crushing load.' He did not believe that 'the hordes of barbarians' would one day 'overwhelm modern civilization'; the barbarians were 'a handful, a small and decreasing percentage: a disgrace but not a danger'. But Booth was still a Social Darwinist and a believer in the 'invigorating influence' of 'cycles of depression': 'As to character, the effect, especially on the wage-earner, is very similar to that exercised on a population by the recurrence of winter as compared to the enervation of continued summer.'[66]

At the other extreme, even Hyndman, the Marxist leader of the Social Democratic Federation, agreed with the deteriorationists:

> Everywhere, no doubt, there is a certain percentage who are almost beyond hope of being reached at all. Crushed down into the gutter, physically and mentally, by their social surroundings, they can but die out, leaving it is hoped no progeny as a burden on a better state of things.[67]

Some of the philanthropic Fabians went further and recommended with Sydney Ball 'a process of conscious social selection by which the industrial residuum is naturally sifted and made manageable for some kind of restorative, disciplinary, or, it may be, "surgical treatment"'. The surgery required was spelled out by Bernard Shaw and H. G. Wells, who recommended 'sterilization of the failures'.[68] That such remedies for the poor of 'outcast London' were based on fear rather than simple charity can be gauged from the declaration of a self-styled philanthropist, Samuel Smith, in 1885:

> I am deeply convinced that the time is approaching when this seething mass of human misery will shake the social fabric, unless we grapple more earnestly with it than we have done ... The proletariat may strangle us unless we teach it the same virtues which have elevated the other classes of society.[69]

The difference which the economic 'climacteric' of the 1890s and the Boer War made was that they added the fear of industrial

57

decline and military defeat to fears for the social fabric. The army's complaints about the 'progressive physical deterioration' of the recruits led to the appointment in 1903 of the Interdepartmental Committee on Physical Deterioration 'to make a preliminary enquiry into the allegations concerning the deterioration of certain classes of the population', with a view to setting up a Royal Commission. This Committee of sane and sceptical bureaucrats, backed by evidence from the Royal College of Physicians and Surgeons, forced the Surgeon-General of the Army Medical Service to admit that there was no evidence of actual 'physical degeneration'. They quoted Professor D. J. Cunningham of Edinburgh University and the British Association for the Advancement of Science to the effect that, while poor food and bad housing depressed the physical standard of the individual, it did not depress the inheritance of the race, and that to restore the classes below it to the mean standard of national physique, 'all that is required is to improve the conditions of living'.[70] Dr Eicholz, Inspector of Schools to the City of London and a medical doctor, agreed. There was undoubtedly among the slum population 'a most serious condition of affairs', brought on by poor food, bad housing, overcrowding, atmospheric pollution, unhealthy conditions of work, drunkenness, and parental apathy. But this was a minority of the school population of London, which included an upper part, well-to-do and well cared for, 'not excelled by any in this country or in any other', and a majority 'consisting of the average industrial artisan population in which the breadwinners are in regular employment'. Even the slum population, 'ill-nourished, poor, ignorant, badly housed' as they were, showed little real evidence of inherited deterioration, or of 'degeneracy' which could not be reversed by removing the causes of their poverty. 'In fact, all the evidence points to *active, rapid improvement, bodily and mental, in the worst districts* so soon as they are exposed to better circumstances ...'[71]

As for the intellectual deterioration of the nation by reason of the differential fertility of 'the good and bad stocks', Karl Pearson's view in his 1903 Huxley Lecture that 'we are ceasing as a nation to breed intelligence as we did fifty to hundred years ago', and that the uneducated were outbreeding 'the intellectual classes', was dismissed by Professor Cunningham as

a pure assumption ... I do not think there is a single solid fact in support of such a view ... [I]t is stocks not classes which breed men of intellect. These intellectual stocks are found in all classes, high and low. No class can claim intellect as its special perquisite.[72]

His colleague in the anthropological survey proposed by the British Association, Mr Gray, however, thought that the concentration of population in large towns and the increase of wealth appeared to have the effect of reducing the birth rate of the superior classes and of decreasing the death rate of the inferior classes. And Sir John Gorst, the Conservative education minister, thought that, because restraints on marriage disappeared as you reach the most unfit, the race was chiefly propagated by the least fit part. The Committee reported that only a full statistical investigation could decide the issue, which was not forthcoming until the 1911 *Fertility of Marriage Census* and not published until after the war.[73]

The Report on Physical Deterioration was one of the most influential social documents of the age, and many of its recommendations, including school meals for poor children, medical inspection, physical education for both sexes, cookery and domestic science for girls in schools, tighter control of the milk supply and food adulteration, social education of mothers by midwives and health visitors, juvenile courts, and a ban on the sale of alcohol and tobacco to children, all passed into law before the war. Others, including better building regulations to prevent slums and overcrowding, town planning and garden suburbs, green belts and open spaces, and control of smoke pollution, came in more slowly. Yet even this Committee of enlightened bureaucrats could not resist the contemporary desire to put the poor out of sight in 'labour colonies on the lines of the Salvation Army at Hadleigh':

> It may be necessary, in order to complete the work of clearing overcrowded slums, for the State, acting in conjunction with the Local Authority, to take charge of the lives of those who, from whatever causes, are incapable of independent existence up to the standard of decency which it imposes.[74]

Nor were the Social Darwinians, neo-Malthusians and Social Imperialists convinced by the Committee's demolition of physical and mental deterioration. When the Fabian Society, concerned about the growing class antagonism provoked by the neo-Malthusian scare of 'race suicide', initiated its own enquiry into *The Decline of the Birth Rate* (1907), it accepted that the imprudent and the feckless, who were either poor or likely to become so, were outbreeding the rest. The author, the cautious Sidney Webb, reported, 'It looks as if the birth-rate was falling conspicuously, if not exclusively, not among the wealthy or the middle class as such, but among the sections of every class in which there is the most prudence, foresight and self-control.'[75] Francis Galton, cousin and misinterpreter of Darwin, founded the eugenics movement to give 'the more suitable races or strains of blood a better chance of prevailing speedily over the less suitable' (showing a curious lack of faith in the unaided survival of the fittest). He had already endowed a Eugenics Laboratory for Pearson in 1904, became president of the new Eugenics Education Society of 1907 (from whose 'high-strung, enthusiastic quacks' Pearson himself held aloof), and left money to endow a chair of eugenics at the University of London in 1911, which Pearson held until 1933.[76]

How widespread the fear of the teeming poor remained down to the First World War can be seen from the continuing debate in the press and the flood of books and pamphlets on differential class fertility as well as from the call for the first census of fertility in marriage in 1911. David Heron, a student of Pearson's and a fellow of the Eugenics Laboratory, in an innovative comparison between prosperous and impoverished London boroughs in 1906, found a high correlation between unchecked fertility and overcrowding, disease, mental illness and high death rates. Dr Alfred Tredgold, a neurologist and authority on feeble-mindedness, argued in 1911 from his researches that the declining birth rate was 'practically confined to the best elements; and that the worst elements, the insane, the feeble-minded, the diseased, the paupers, the thriftless, and in fact the whole parasitic class of the nation, are continuing to propagate with unabated and unrestricted vigour'. Ethel Elderton, author of an otherwise objective *Report on the English Birth-Rate* in 1914, reached the 'unassailable truth' that 'the healthy, careful and thrifty are having smaller families than the unhealthy, careless and thriftless, and the selective death rate no longer weeds out the children of the least fit'. This 'truth' was even harnessed to the hostility to Lloyd George and his progressive taxation of the rich.

Dr W. R. Inge, Dean of St Paul's, London, wrote to *The Times* in 1912 that 'the best men and women' were limiting their families in response to the growing burden of taxation to support the irresponsible, unemployed wastrels whose numbers proliferated irrespective of the economy, while another clergyman wrote to *The Daily Telegraph* in 1913 to warn on the same grounds against the mounting local taxation for their support.[77]

Those who condemned the poor for reproducing themselves were anything but unified in their remedies for the problem, which ranged from the Charity Organization Society's proposals for the revival of the workhouse test or consignment to a labour colony all the way to the Fabian and other socialist schemes for municipal socialism and nationalization. In between, in pursuit of the new working-class vote, there was every kind of proposition for social reform, as mutually incompatible as Chamberlain's 'social imperialist' tariff reform to provide funds for old age pensions and other welfare measures and Asquith and Lloyd George's budgets to tax the rich for the benefit of the old, the sick and the unemployed. Fear of the poor was not the only reason for the welfare measures of the period, as we shall see in Chapter 4, but it was the one which aroused the most intense emotions.

Meanwhile, before we come to the factors making for the decline of class society from its zenith, we must look more closely at each of the major classes, the rich and powerful, the much-divided middle classes, and the disaggregated working class, in their increasingly segregated lives.

Chapter 3

A SEGREGATED SOCIETY

Class society at its zenith was, as we saw in the last chapter, marked by a growing segregation in income, status and geographical location between the classes. What was still more striking was the segregation *within* each class. Not only did the rich, the comfortable, and the poor, in Chiozza Money's terminology, live utterly different lives (see Table 2.2 on page 30). Each of these great divisions of society was further divided by lines of cleavage which were not merely horizontal, between different layers of wealth and prestige, but also vertical. There were vertical divisions between the old rich and the new, the landed aristocracy and the new millionaires; between the business and the professional middle class and between the petty bourgeoisie and the new white-collar class, which at both levels were growing more apart; and in the working class between the 'respectable' and the 'roughs', which by no means corresponded to the difference between the skilled labour aristocracy and the lesser or unskilled. At the highest level, where landed and business wealth were drawing closer together, the rich and the powerful of both kinds were drawing away from those immediately below them. As Frank Harris, the journalist and rake who moved in the highest circles of the Marlborough House set as well as in some of the lowest of the *demi-monde*, noted, 'Snobbery is the religion of England.'[1] We shall find that to be true not only between the major social classes but within them as well.

1 THE RICH AND THE POWERFUL

The rich, the most variegated class in terms of differential wealth, power and status, were, paradoxically, becoming more unified. The most obvious effect of the 'Great Depression', especially in its agricultural aspect, and of the drift of great landowners and business millionaires from the Liberal into the Conservative Party, was to endorse and accelerate a transformation at the top end of society which would almost certainly have happened anyway as a result of the rise in the scale of organization and the top levels of wealth: the emergence of a new plutocracy. The rich and powerful amongst both the landowners and business men – together with a few exceptionally successful lawyers, engineers, architects, authors, journalists, artists and other professional men – raised themselves above the common herds of their kind and drew together in what Karl Marx and *The Queen* magazine labelled the 'upper ten thousand' and what they themselves called 'society'. This was a well-informed guess. In 1913–14 there were about 1,500 peers and baronets and another 1,700 non-hereditary knights. They overlapped with the 4,843 persons with incomes of £10,000 or more (including about 300 over £50,000 and seventy-five over £75,000), and perhaps 2,000 other members of the elite – bishops, judges, leading barristers, fashionable physicians, editors, writers, artists, academics, and so on – with the entrée to London 'society', so that there were certainly no more than 10,000 who could confidently claim to belong to the highest group in English society.[2]

London 'society' and 'the season', with its round of social engagements, balls, soirées, dinner parties, formalized social calls, and presentations at court, and the parallel annual round of social life in the counties had existed as national and local institutions for the landed aristocracy and gentry since at least the seventeenth century. It had served the enormously important functions, for them, of uniting the governing elite, providing an arena for the political struggle for power, influence and patronage at court and in parliamentary and local politics, and – by no means the least of its sociological functions – acting as a marriage market for the all-important pursuit of family alliances which were an integral part of the game of wealth and power.[3] Although there had always been rising men and women, royal favourites and mistresses, successful politicians and public servants, generals, judges, bankers and merchants – provided always that they bought the necessary ticket of entry, a landed estate – and, of course, heiresses of any variety of wealth, it was only in the late Victorian age that wealth alone rather than land and titles became the chief claim to membership of 'society'.[4]

This was because, for the first time in history, non-landed incomes and wealth had begun to overtake land alone as the main source of economic power. Between 1850 and 1880 Schedule D incomes from business and other profits of over £3,000 a year had risen from under 2,000 to over 5,000, compared with the 2,500 landowners with rentals (excluding London property) of over £3,000 in the 'New Doomsday' returns of the 1870s; business incomes of over £10,000 had grown from 338 to 987, compared with 866 landed rentals at that level; and those of over £50,000 from twenty-six to seventy-seven, compared with 76 such rental incomes.[5] By 1914 landed incomes had scarcely grown at all, so that most of the 4,843 incomes over £10,000 were from business sources. The rentals were gross, and net incomes after repairs and rates would be less in each case, but many landowners, especially the rich ones, had other sources of income, including London property, mines, stocks and shares, a few company directorships, and so on. After 1880 most landlords faced declining agricultural rents, especially in the south and east, and if they could not increase their income from other sources they faced falling rentals and even greater falls in the capital value of their land.[6] At the same time, non-landed wealth burgeoned as never before. This was the age of the millionaires. Compared with a declining number of millionaire landlords (capitalizing their landed incomes) from 118 in 1858–79 to thirty-six in 1880–99 and thirty-three in 1900–19, non-landed millionaires in the probate returns rose from twenty-seven in 1860–79 to sixty in 1880–99 and 101 in 1900–19.[7] Such immense wealth, overtaking all except the greatest landlords, could not be ignored by the aristocracy and London and county 'society'.

As Beatrice Webb, who acted as hostess for her international railway magnate father, Richard Potter, for two years in the 1880s, observed of 'this remarkable amalgam, London Society and country-house life':

> There were no fixed caste barriers; there seemed to be, in fact,
> no recognized types of exclusiveness based on birth and
> breeding, on personal riches or on personal charm; there was
> no fastidiousness about manners or morals or intellectual gifts.

Like the British Empire, London Society had made itself what it was in a fit of absentmindedness. To foreign observers it appeared all-embracing in its easy-going tolerance and superficial good nature ... But deep down in the unconscious herd instinct of the British governing class there *was* a test of fitness for membership of this most gigantic of social clubs, but a test which was seldom recognized by those who applied it, still less by those to whom it was applied, *the possession of some form of power over people.* The most obvious form of power, and the most easily measurable, was the power of wealth.

Hence any family of outstanding riches, if its members were not actually mentally deficient or morally disreputable, could hope to rise to the top, marry its daughters to Cabinet ministers and noblemen, and become in time itself ennobled.[8] And she remarked of a dinner party at Sir Julius Wernher's, the South African diamond millionaire's Bath House, 'There might as well have been a Goddess of Gold erected for overt worship – the impression of worship, in thought, feeling, and action, could hardly have been stronger.[9]

The aristocrats were equally censorious. George Russell, radical cousin and critic of the business-oriented Duke of Bedford, wrote in 1907 of the change in 'society' since 1880, the more materialism, a growing love of titles, and more ostentation: 'the rushing flood of ill-gotten gold has overflown its banks, and polluted "the crystal river of unreproved enjoyment".'[10] In 1906 Lady Dorothy Nevill (1826–1913), daughter of the (Walpole) Earl of Orford, contrasted the mid-Victorian 'Society' of her youth and middle years with the wealth-obsessed plutocracy of her old age:

In the old days Society was an assemblage of people who, either by birth, intellect or aptitude, were ladies and gentlemen in the true sense of the word. For the most part fairly, though not extravagantly, dowered with the good things of the world, it had no ulterior object beyond intelligent, cultured and dignified enjoyment, money-making being left to another class which, from time to time, supplied a select recruit for this *corps d'élite.* Now all this is changed, in fact, society (a word obsolete in its old sense) is, to use a vulgar expression, 'on the make'.[11]

We must not overstate the change, or its rapidity. Even in pre-industrial England, status followed wealth rather than wealth status, and the knowledge that anyone who made money by whatever means could buy an estate and join the landed gentry was one of the main driving forces of industrial and commercial enterprise.[12] During the Industrial Revolution itself, industrialists like the Peels, bankers like the Smiths (Lords Carrington) and adventurers like Hudson the 'railway king' had been admitted to 'society' and even to royal circles. But down to the 1880s the purchase of land with at least part of one's wealth had been the prerequisite of full admission to London and county 'society'. From the 1880s, although some of the *nouveaux riches* continued to buy country houses and landed estates, however small, for themselves, it was now a matter of choice and style, not a social necessity. Wealth by itself was enough to gain entry, not only to 'society' but to the peerage and even to the royal entourage, as financiers like Sir Ernest Cassel and chain shopkeepers like Sir Thomas Lipton became intimates of the Prince of Wales.

One reason for this change was well summed up, if somewhat exaggerated, by Lady Bracknell in Oscar Wilde's *The Importance of Being Ernest* (1895):

> What between the duties expected of one during one's lifetime, and the duties exacted from one after one's death, land has ceased to be either a profit or a pleasure. It gives one position and prevents one from keeping it up.[13]

The 'Great Depression' in agriculture had indeed reduced money rents from arable land, and land values even more steeply. Between the early 1870s and the early 1890s agricultural rents had fallen by an average of 26 per cent, still more (by 41 per cent) in arable south and east, somewhat less (by 12 per cent) in the pastoral north and west. At the same time land values fell from thirty to forty years' purchase to twenty to twenty-five years', so that an estate worth £10,000 a year in the mid-1870s whose rents fell by the average percentage (26 per cent) could fall in capital value from, say, £350,000 to £167,000 in twenty years.[14] Both rents and capital values were to rise again from about 1900 but not to the record levels of 1876. Lord Heneage remarked of his Lincolnshire neighbours in 1886 that 'landowners are in such a panic that they are letting at any price and giving 30 and 40 per cent reductions';

and a Kentish squire wrote to a neighbour about 1895, 'Land is no longer an amiable possession unless coupled with a good income from other sources.'[15] Even for the rural gentry this was somewhat exaggerated: prices were declining too, encouraging customers to buy more expensive products like meat and dairy produce, and lessening landlords' costs, including the cost of repairs and maintenance of farms and houses. But the depression and the greater competition between the rich in high living drove a larger wedge between the gentry and the greater landowners, who normally had other sources of income, particularly from mines, urban property, and increasingly, company directorships and shareholdings, not to mention greater opportunities of marrying rich heiresses, whether landed or capitalist, British or foreign.

The rich, even when in financial difficulties, certainly had greater staying power. With such huge gross incomes, there was more room for retrenchment on great houses and household expenditure, sport, horses and gamekeepers, entertaining and travel, more hope of windfalls like the death of jointured dowagers, of legacies and rich marriages, and more opportunities to sell outlying and unprofitable lands and invest in better and more exploitable ones or in business companies at home and abroad. The second Earl of Verulam, already overspending in the 1870s by about £2,000 a year, found his income fall from £17,000 to £14,000 a year by 1889. He therefore reduced his housekeeping expenses in London and St Albans from £2,300 to about £1,600, paid off his brothers' and sisters' portions with an unexpected legacy of £100,000 in 1884 thereby saving several thousand pounds a year, reduced the annual consumption of wine, champagne and brandy by hundreds of bottles, cut down his stable and game-keeping staff and gave up the hand-rearing of pheasants, increased his income from London's New River water company and from stocks and shares – and still could not live within his income. His son, the third Earl from 1895, continued his father's retrenchment, let the main house and the shooting, and not only invested in the City but took an active part in business, coming by 1913 to hold directorships in thirteen companies, from brewery, insurance and housing companies to overseas railroads, gold and tin mines, and rubber plantations. To round off the family's financial success, one of his daughters married a barrister nephew of Sir Ernest Cassel, the greater financier.[16]

The Duke of Bedford, who complained publicly in *A Great Agricultural Estate* (1897) that he was making a heavy annual loss from his agricultural estates in Cambridgeshire, Bedfordshire and Buckinghamshire, did not mention the capital gains he was making from his huge London estates in Bloomsbury, Covent Garden, St Pancras, and the East India Docks, or the profits of the sale of the Cambridgeshire Thorney estate to the tenants at mortgages which yielded far more than the rent, or (later) of Covent Garden to Sir Joseph Beecham in 1914 for £2 million![17] The Earl of Shrewsbury and Talbot, founder of the Talbot motor manufacturing company and chairman of two other companies, wrote in 1903 to his sister, 'Everyone has his Role in Life. I have taken up the commercial side & I venture to say there is no Landlord or Colliery Proprietor who knows more about his own business in their respective districts than I do.' He had his own commercial outlets in Paris, Brussels, Turin, Milan and Nice, two factories and four retail houses in London, and a company in Manchester: 'and as in London alone I had sales of Forty Thousand Pounds in July... I am not quite idle.'[18] Viscount Peel's son and heir, descendant of the cotton manufacturer and the prime minister, married Ella Williamson, daughter and heiress of 'Li'l Jimmy Williamson', Lord Ashton, linoleum maker to the world and until recently the seventh richest man in the probate returns (leaving £10.5 million in 1930).[19] Earl Peel later became a director and ultimately chairman of Williamsons of Lancaster. Of Viscount Churchill, chairman of three railways including the Great Western, his son said, 'business was his real interest... My father's associates seemed to have found out he had ability, and that as well as his name he himself was an asset.'[20] Lord Rayleigh, the Cambridge Nobel Prize physicist and a considerable landowner in Essex, was the most ingenious of landed entrepreneurs: after his Terling estate rents fell from £9,212 in 1882 to £3,091 in 1893, he opened a chain of shops in London called Lord Rayleigh's Dairies, from which by 1913 he was making a profit of £9,000 a year to add to his now more than £6,000 in rents.[21] Others married heiresses, as Lord Rosebery married Hannah Rothschild (against the wishes of both families) and the Duke of Marlborough (unhappily and not permanently) Consuelo Vanderbilt, but so did new men like Lord Leith of Fyvie whose fortune and peerage derived from his marriage to a St Louis steel heiress and from building up the great US Steel Company.[22] Others moved into business either by selling land, which became much easier under the Settled Land Acts of 1882 and 1890, and investing in stocks and shares, and/or by themselves becoming company directors.

There had long been landed business men, like the coalmining Marquesses of Londonderry, the third Duke of Buckingham, chairman of the London and North Western Railway in the 1850s, or the 7th Duke of Devonshire, principal in the development of Barrow-in-Furness and its great iron works, but these were unusual before 1880. By 1896, 167 peers, over a quarter of the peerage, held directorships, most of them in more than one company, and some in half a dozen or more; by 1920 there were no less than 232.[23] Some of these were the new industrial and commercial peers who began to be created by Gladstone and Salisbury from the 1880s: of the 200 or so new peers (excluding members of the royal family) created between 1886 and 1914, seventy, more than a third, represented new wealth derived from business, another third came from the professions, mainly law lords and other public servants in the foreign and colonial service and the armed forces, and only about a quarter from the traditional sources of the nobility, the old landed gentry.[24] But many of the business peers, like Lord Joicey and Lord Wimborne (Sir John Guest, the great iron master) were already considerable landowners, over half the new non-landed peers bought a landed estate between 1886 and 1914, and most of the rest bought 'a country house without surrounding it with property extensive enough to be called an estate'.[25]

What was important was not the invasion of 'society' by non-landed wealth or the infiltration of the business world by great landowners, but the fusion of the two in a new plutocracy of the rich and powerful. As Lady Dorothy Nevill perceptively observed in 1906:

> When this incursion first began, English Society, shrewd and far-seeing enough in its way, easily perceived that, unless it swallowed the new millionaires, the millionaires, keen-witted, pushing, clever and energetic, would engulf it in their capacious maw. So everywhere doors were flung open for Croesus to enter; his faults were overlooked, his virtues (and many a one really had virtues) lauded; historic houses passed

into his hands, whilst the original possessors besought his good offices for their sons embarking on City careers. On the whole, the result has not, perhaps, been bad, for everything must change and pass away, and there is no reason why 'Society', a relic of aristocratic days, should have proved an exception to this rule.

The new conquerors have taught their willing serfs many of the arts by which they themselves rose to wealth and power, and I am told that there are now many scions of noble houses who exhibit nearly as much shrewdness in driving bargains in the City as a South African millionaire himself; whilst, on the other hand, the sons of millionaires in several instances do not conceal their dislike for business, and lead an existence of leisured and extravagant ease, which would not compare unfavourably with that of a 'blood' of the eighteenth century.[26]

The leading historian of English landed society has confirmed this 'partial but definite transformation of the titled upper class':

The old nobility remained dominant, in numbers and in social standing if not always in wealth, but they were fused with a significant group thrown up by the new industrial England. Many of the new men, following a familiar path from fortune through land to title, rose in a single generation at a pace unprecedented since the sixteenth century. Many others disregarded the territorial foundations of the aristocratic way of life, and in their rise demonstrated in even more emphatic fashion the arrival of a monied nobility. In this way the peerage offered a reflection of the real distribution of power in society, and recorded the transition from an aristocracy of landowners not to a democracy but to an aristocracy of business and professional talents.[27]

That the great landowners were not in danger of their possessions hurrying them to the workhouse (as George Russell said of his complaining cousin, the Duke of Bedford)[28] can be seen from the wealth which they left at death, which reached a peak in real terms in the early twentieth century. The probate valuations, adjusted to include the value of their land, of the great landowners with rentals of £50,000 or more (according to Bateman in 1883), reached their highest level in the cohort who died betwen 1900 and

1919. At current prices their median estate rose from £281,500 in 1880–99 to £633,000 in 1920–39. Adjusting for the rise in retail prices, the median estate rose from £282,300 in 1900–19 to £311,300 in 1900–19 before declining to £274,000 between the wars. This may be compared with the millionaires, selected solely for their wealth at death (who overlap with both landowners and company chairmen) and with the chairmen of the 200 or so largest companies (too few to be significant before 1900). The millionaires' median estate rose at current prices from £1,283,000 in 1880–99 to £1,356,700 in 1900–19 and to £1,385,000 in 1920–29; in real terms it declined, from £1,563,300 to £1,265,300 and to £856,200 (the decline being in part the statistical effect of inflation embracing 'poorer' millionaires in smaller pounds). The great company chairmen's median estate declined in current terms from £208,600 in 1900–19 to £186,400; and in real terms from £118,300 to £79,800 (these figures were affected by the rise of new managers with less capital of their own, to which we shall return).[29] From these figures it is clear that in wealth as well as prestige the great landowners reached their zenith in this period and were more than holding their own with the business men down to the First World War and beyond.

If there was an all-too-obvious difference between the great landowners and the new millionaires it was in their social origins and education. Over 93 per cent of the great landowners came from landed families, 98 per cent from the upper class of landed, business and higher professional men. Similarly, over 96 per cent had been to private schools and most, 81 per cent in 1880–99, 73 per cent in 1900–19, to one school alone, Eton; about 18 per cent in both cohorts to other Clarendon schools (mostly to Harrow); and 36–40 per cent went on to Oxford, Cambridge or a military academy. Of the probate millionaires (who included some landowners who left that much in personalty) 71–75 per cent came from the upper class, but only 13–18 per cent from landed families, as against over 56 per cent from rich business families; 25–30 per cent were self-made men in the sense of coming from families below the upper class, as against only 2 per cent of the large landowners (presumably from the same group as the self-made millionaires). A surprising number of millionaires had been educated at public or other private schools, 53–62 per cent, of whom 25 per cent in each cohort had been to Eton and about 18 per cent to other Clarendon schools; and over 26 per cent had been to university, mostly to Oxbridge but a few (unlike the landowners) to London or the Scottish universities. The non-landed rich, if the millionaires are a typical sample, were drawn from a much wider spectrum of society than the great landowners, but still predominantly from the well-educated upper class. Despite some historians' claims that more of them came from commerce and finance than from industry, there is no sign in the probate returns that this was the case: if we include food and drink manufacturers, there were roughly as many industrialists as there were merchants, bankers and insurance underwriters.[30] The *nouveaux riches*, the South African gold and diamond mine owners, the soap and chemical manufacturers, the newspaper tycoons, the foreign-born merchant bankers, and so on, though highly visible, were less numerous than the sons and daughters of the already wealthy.

The non-landed wealth holders who now claimed their place in London and county 'society' were an extraordinary mixed group. Some represented traditional industrial and commercial wealth, like Beatrice Webb's father, Richard Potter, son of a cotton merchant and the first Lord Mayor of Manchester – the son recouped his dwindling inheritance by becoming a timber merchant, Chairman of the Great Western Railway and President of the Canadian Pacific Railroad; the Guest family Lords Wimborne, ironmasters and landowners; Samuel Cunliffe-Lister, Lord Masham of wool-combing fame; Lord Armstrong of Cragside, pioneer engineer and armaments king; John Hubbard, Lord Addington, Russia merchant and Governor of the Bank of England; the rival brewers Henry Allsop, Lord Hindlip and Michael Bass, Lord Burton, and the Guinness peers, Lords Ardilaun and Iveagh; and, to include some of the rare 'new women', Lady Hambledon, widow of W. H. Smith the bookseller, and Margot Asquith, the sharp-tongued society hostess and daughter of the Tennant family, chemical manufacturers of Glasgow. Others represented brand new wealth, some of it not very appealing to the old: the South African diamond and gold millionaires Beit, Barnato, Rhodes and Wernher; the new yellow press Lords Northcliffe and his brother Rothermere, the soap manufacturer Lord Leverhulme, Baron de Stern the merchant banker, and so on.[31]

It has been suggested that new wealth from the commerci
financial worlds, traditionally based on London and 'cleaner' and
more respectable than manufacturing industry, was socially less
distant and more readily absorbed into 'society' than industrial
wealth.[32] This view is based on a misunderstanding of the way
English society operated. It was not wealth as such which gave the
entrée but what you did with it. The two richest men of the period,
Charles Morrison, warehouseman and merchant banker, who
lived a bachelor life outside the public gaze and left £10.9 million
in 1909, and the richest of all, Sir John Ellerman, shipowner and
financier, 'as vulgar and ignorant a *nouveau-riche* as has ever
lived', who left £36.7 million in 1933, could no doubt have bought
their way into 'society' many times over, but preferred private
avarice to public display.[33] Sir Julius Wernher, on the other hand,
a brash and vulgar diamond millionaire from South Africa, who
left £10 million in Britain and untold millions abroad, made
himself instantly acceptable by purchasing Bath House, Piccadilly
and Luton Hoo, Bedfordshire 'to please his "society"-loving wife –
a hard, vainglorious woman, talkative and badly bred', as Beatrice
Webb noted in her diary, and by entertaining on a lavish scale.[34] It
can scarcely be argued that either royalty or 'society' drew a
distinction between London Jewish financiers like Lord
Rochschild or Sir Ernest Cassel and Glasgow shopkeepers and
chemical manufacturers like Sir Thomas Lipton, royal yachtsman, or the Tennant family of Margot Asquith, greatest of the
Edwardian hostesses. If intermarriage is the ultimate test of
acceptability, the Guests, the ironmaster dynasty who married
successively daughters of the Earl of Lindsay and the Duke of
Marlborough and a niece of the Duke of Westminster, were as
acceptable as Hannah Rothschild, wife of Lord Rosebery,
Gladstone's successor as prime minister. But then nineteen peers
between 1884 and 1914 married actresses, Edward VII took Lillie
Langtry to the royal bosom, and the bankrupt Earl of Rosslyn
became an actor himself.[35] It was not money but the power and
pleasure it could buy that won 'society's' heart.

This mixture of powermongering and pleasure can be savoured
from Lady Tweedsmuir's (Mrs John Buchan's) later recollection of
the ideal country house party before the First World War.

In a gathering of people selected by a really clever hostess,
there might be one or two Cabinet Ministers who welcomed

the opportunity of quiet conversation, or there might be a
Viceroy or high official from a far-off corner of the Empire,
anxious to make someone in the government of the day realize
a little more the difficulties of a particular experiment that
Britain had delegated him to carry out. These parties often
included a diplomat home on leave, a painter, and almost
certainly a musician who played to some of the company in the
evenings. Beside these eminent people there was usually a
sprinkling of women famous for their beauty or wit, or both,
who either gave the conversation a sparkling turn, or were wise
enough not to interrupt good talk, and who accordingly sat
statuesque or flowerlike.[36]

Amongst these witty and beautiful women might be royal
mistresses like Lillie Langtry, daughter of the Dean of Jersey,
turned actress to recoup her fortunes, and Lady Warwick, the
socialist countess who introduced Keir Hardie to Bertie, Prince of
Wales.

There was even a place for intellectuals, whether the aristocratic
and self-consciously brilliant 'Souls' – Arthur Balfour and his
'particular friend' Lady Elcho, Lords Curzon, Lyttleton and
Wyndham, Lady Frances Horner, Margot Asquith and her sister
Lady Ribblesdale – or those who had genuinely made their way by
their brains, like Haldane, Milner, and the Webbs, who frequently
dined with Balfour, Asquith, Sir Edward Grey, the Bertrand
Russells, and anyone else they thought they could 'permeate' with
Fabian collectivist reforms.[37] This was to give the professional
class more influence with the rich and powerful than might have
been expected from their lack of wealth, as we shall see in the next
chapter.

Meanwhile, only those were admitted who possessed either
power, political or economic, or the capacity to entertain, socially,
culturally or intellectually. Even for them there were rules to be
learned and elaborate rituals to perform. As the magazine *The
Lady* (itself a symptom of the way society was changing so as to
require printed guidance) put it in 1893:

It is a good thing for everyone that there are rules by which
Society, now that it has become so vast and complicated a
machine, is held together and enabled to work so smoothly and
easily ... it changes very fast and you must keep up with it or

you will stand out and no gentlewoman wants to attract
observation or comment or she is no gentlewoman.[38]

This was not wholly correct. The well-born, the rich and the
powerful could get away with almost anything, as the careers of
the Marlborough House set around the Prince of Wales (Edward
VII) go to show – though even there a scandalous divorce or a tiff
with the Prince could spell social disaster, as Lord Randolph
Churchill discovered. Lord Selbourne remarked of the 'smart set'
he stayed with at a house party at Cragg Hall, Cheshire that,
except for one couple, it was 'exclusively a party of wives without
husbands and husbands without wives, most characteristic of the
set', which had 'a decidedly nasty taste to me'.[39] But for more
ordinary mortals and those trying to get in, the elaborate rules
about whom you had to call on or invite and when, how to dress
for various occasions, present yourself or your daughter at court,
and so on, had to be learned. Fortunately, there were plenty of
well-connected ladies anxious to earn a little spending money,
who (anonymously) advertised their services as chaperones at as
much as £1,000 a year, to show the *nouveaux riches* the ropes and
arrange suitable introductions.[40] Without such tutoring even the
wealthiest newcomer would be lost, and might be 'cut', ostracized
and frozen out, like the vast majority of man- and womankind.

The same was true of 'county society', despite the new
democratic county councils of 1888 and parish councils of 1894.
T. H. S. Escott, one of the most perceptive observers of late
Victorian society, commented in 1893:

> Socially, 'the county' continues to exist. The wives or
> daughters of the county gentlemen who are County JPs set the
> fashion in their neighbourhood and are still regarded as
> moulded out of clay slightly superior to that of which their
> neighbours consist. But as an object of fetish worship, the
> County has in most districts disappeared. The tradesman may
> be less deferential now that he is a colleague of the squire and
> the magistrate.[41]

As it turned out, however, the tradesman was in fact *more*
deferential, he habitually elected his landed and moneyed betters
to the councils of most counties, was grateful for a condescending
nod of acknowledgment, and was still not invited to the Hunt
Ball.[42]

Counties differed greatly according to their distance from industry and the great cities, but in a county like Cheshire, near enough in the railway age for commuting to Liverpool and Manchester and with its own great chemical, textile and shipbuilding industries, the same amalgamation of the great landowners and the new capitalists was going on as in London 'society'.

> Common interests and activities soon encouraged the merger of the landed and business interests. The few landed families who had control of the politics of the shire quickly found a great deal of common ground between themselves and the new industrialists and merchants. The squires who depended for their income on small county estates were the chief members of the governing class to suffer.[43]

When the thirteen great landowners who controlled Cheshire politics included the Duke of Westminster, the Marquess of Cholmondeley, and Lords Crewe, Delamere, Combermere, Egerton of Tatton, Legh of Lyme, Stanley of Aderley, and Tollemache, and the rich business men included W. H. Lever, the soap manufacturer, Sir John Brunner and Sir Alfred Mond (later Lord Melchett), predecessors of Imperial Chemical Industries and John Laird and David MacIver, the Birkenhead shipbuilders, amalgamation on the magistrates' bench and in county and parliamentary politics was comparatively straightforward. They and their relatives at first dominated the new county borough councils of 1888 as they dominated the bench.[44] Below their level changes were going on, however, notably the rise of great suburbs and a middle-class hegemony, and eventually caused most of these 'social leaders' to leave the field to elected 'public persons'. Some, like Lord Delamere of Vale Royal and Lord Egerton of Tatton, withdrew as far as the Kenya Highlands, others, like many of the Manchester cotton men and Liverpool merchants, merely to the south of England. But this was a trend only incipient before the First World War. Until then the 'social leaders' associated with 'public persons' only in politics and on public occasions. In social life an invisible fence, marked only by the raised eyebrow or the blank stare of non-recognition, separated the rich and the powerful from the common herd even more in the country than in town.[45]

For those inside the fence it was the 'lordliest life on earth' (Rudyard Kipling), a life of 'superb ease' (Hilaire Belloc) and 'majestic leisureliness' (John Galsworthy), of 'prepared security and unconscious insolence' (Henry James), of 'careful modesty, good manners, and a kind of aristocratic humbleness, but innate superiority was the underlying assumption' (Viscount Churchill). Lady Ottoline Morrell, sister of the sixth Duke of Portland and lover of Bertrand Russell, remarked that the 'unquestioning arrogance of it all had a power of impressing itself on me as "The Thing", that it was "the supreme life" and that all other existences were simply insignificant and unimportant'. Lord Willoughby de Broke, leader of 'the diehards' who opposed the Parliament Act of 1911 which cut back the powers of the House of Lords, saw the Edwardian Age for his class as 'the high-water mark of creature comforts..... Whatever was happening to the Empire, comfort and convenience, and everything that makes for luxury, steadily increased until the outbreak of the War.'[46]

Yet that very comfort and convenience were at the expense of others, and the rich were beginning to feel themselves under attack. Charles Masterman, himself from inside the magic circle, warned in 1909 against the effects on the poor of the ostentation of the rich in their great houses, grand hotels, steam yachts, and, the most visible and aggressive toy of all, the rich man's motor car:

> Wandering machines, travelling with an incredible rate of speed, scramble and smash and shriek along all the rural ways.... You can see evidence of their activity in the dust-laden hedges of the south country roads, a grey mud colour, with no evidence of green; in the ruined cottage gardens of the south country villages.[47]

Their demand for road improvements seemed to *The Economist* in 1908 a plea to tax the many for the benefit of the few: 'Here public expenditure is calmly suggested in order to please the richest class of pleasure seekers.'[48]

The 'People's Budget' of 1909 with its supertax and special taxes on land, together with Lloyd George's attacks on dukes – 'A fully equipped Duke', he said in a speech at Newcastle in October 1909, 'costs as much to keep up as two Dreadnoughts; and Dukes are just as great a terror and they last longer' – and on the 'beerage', the new industrial and commercial peers symbolized by the ennobled brewers, supposedly triggered 'the landowners' panic'.[49] This flight from the land beginning in 1910 culminated after the First World War in the greatest permanent transfer of land since the dissolution of the monasteries.[50] In fact, as Michael Thompson has demonstrated, the landed class had consciously merged with the capitalist business world and was ready to treat land like any other investment, to hang on to it if it paid a profit and to get rid of it when it did not: 'The apparently stable Edwardian society had in fact resolved upon a social revolution, the liquidation of the landed interest, whose full accomplishment was but deferred by the First World War.'[51] This final act of abnegation by the landlords merely set the seal on the amalgamation of the rich and the powerful, at the zenith of class society, into one great capitalist plutocracy, cut off from the rest of society by the pride and arrogance of wealth itself.

2   THE RIVEN MIDDLE CLASS

Below the rich and powerful stood the serried ranks of the comfortable middle classes. By 'the comfortable' Chiozza Money meant the taxpaying families with income between £160 a year (the income tax threshold in 1905) and £700 a year.[52] This would certainly cover the vast majority of those who, while not being able to afford the troops of domestic servants demanded by a life in 'society', were known in Booth's and Rowntree's phrase as 'the servant-keeping class'. A few senior civil servants, clergymen, lawyers, doctors, local manufacturers and wholesalers, high-street shopkeepers, and so on, might rise to as much as £1,000 a year, but the average was perhaps a quarter of that figure. At the lower end the 'petty bourgeoisie', most shopkeepers, school teachers, clerks and white-collar workers, generally earned a good deal less than £160 a year but still stoutly claimed middle-class status. All who could kept servants, since in the labour-intensive Victorian middle-class home, with its still large if diminishing family, coal fires and kitchen range, heavy laundry work, and overfurnished rooms, comfort depended on service. Even clerks and commercial travellers, some of whom earned less than skilled workers, shrank from reducing their wives to 'drudgery'; there were twenty-nine servants per 100 clerks' and commercial travellers' households, compared with 103 for merchants and brokers, and only five for printers, among the best-paid of manual workers.[53] Those who could not afford a live-in servant compensated by not allowing the wife to go out to work, by hiring non-resident help, by sending out the laundry, and by 'keeping up appearances' as best they could. (The working class solved the problem by overworking the wife, and by keeping the older girls off school on washdays, when mother was sick, or a new baby arrived, and at any other time of crisis.) Since labour, especially women's labour, was still cheap and the middle class could afford to buy more of it than ever before or since, domestic service was by far the biggest single occupation, and reached a peak at this time, with about one in six of the total labour force in 1891, rising to an army of over 2 million servants in 1911.[54] This confirmed once again the widening of the gap between the classes at the zenith of class society.

The middle class as a whole was expanding, as new and more varied businesses came into existence, the rise in the scale of business and government required more managers, administrators, office workers and supervisors, and the professions and would-be professions increased in size and numbers. According to Bowley, the non-manual classes increased from 16.7 per cent of income receivers in 1880 to 26.6 per cent in 1913. Other estimates (on a different basis, allowing for more earners per family in the manual class) suggest a growth from 23 per cent of the population in 1867 to 30 per cent in 1900.[55] Within this overall expansion there were important changes: the original capitalist class of 'employers and proprietors' was nearing its peak, at 1,232,000 in 1911 or 6.7 per cent of the occupied population (nearly a fifth of them women), but was being supported by a rapidly growing class of managers and administrators, 3.4 per cent of the occupied population in 1911 (of whom a fifth were women).[56] Some of the professions, notably clergymen and lawyers, were growing much less fast than the rest of the middle class and the occupied population, but 'male professional occupations and subordinate services' grew from 2.5 to 2.7 per cent of the male occupied population, while male non-manual workers were increasing much faster than average, from 21.5 to 25 per cent of the total, in line with the swing from agriculture and industry to services, as Table 3.1 shows.[57]

Women's professional and white-collar occupations were also growing, especially elementary school teachers, clerks and other office workers, particularly typists and telephonists. By 1911 they

Table 3.1   Selected male professions, England and Wales, 1880–1911

	1880	1891	1901	1911	Percentage increase
Clergy, ministers, priests[1]	33,486	36,800	39,656	40,142	19.8
Barristers, solicitors	17,386	19,987	20,998	21,380	23.0
Physicians, surgeons[1]	15,091	18,936	22,486	24,553	62.7
Dentists	3,538	4,562	5,149	7,373	108.4
Authors, journalists[2]	5,627	7,473	9,807	12,005	113.3
Scientific pursuits	1,170	1,894	3,171	6,171	427.4
Architects[3]	6,875	7,779	10,775	11,109	61.1
Schoolmasters, lecturers	44,181	49,072	57,829	68,651	55.4
Total, eight professions	127,354	146,503	169,871	191,384	50.3
Civil service:					
officers, clerks	21,353	31,340	42,403	57,475	169.2
Local gov't, exc. police	17,993	19,710	26,337	54,257	201.5
Total, ten professions	166,700	197,553	238,611	303,116	81.8
For comparison	(000s)				
Non-manual male occupations	1,669	1,960	2,372	2,869	71.9
All male occupations	7,759	8,806	10,157	11,456	47.7
Population, both sexes	25,974	29,003	32,528	36,070	38.9

Notes: [1]Including the retired, given separately 1911
[2]Including shorthand clerks 1881
[3]Including assistants, given separately 1911

Source: H. J. Perkin, 'Middle-class education and employment in the 19th century', *Economic History Review*, vol. 14, 1961.

formed only 6 per cent of higher professionals but nearly two-thirds (62.9 per cent) of the lower professionals and technicians, over one-fifth (21.4 per cent) of the clerks, and over one-third (35.2 per cent) of the sales and shop assistants.[58] Since comparatively few of them were heads of households they do not fundamentally affect the trends in social structure in that unemancipated society. For the moment it is the enormous range in income and status of the non-manual employees which is important, not only in the class as a whole but within each subdivision and occupation.

At the top the middle class merged with the fringes of 'society', which some tried desperately to enter. At the bottom they overlapped in income, though not in lifestyle, with the prosperous working class, from which many of them had been recruited. They were in some ways more segregated and exclusive than 'society' itself, because they could not afford to be so tolerant of infiltrators and 'freeloaders'; or, rather, its various layers and segments were mutually and plurally exclusive, with minutely refined gradations of status, expressed not only in dress, style and location of house, number of servants, and possession of personal transport in the form of a riding horse, carriage and pair or pony and trap, and other visible possessions, but in the intangible rules about who spoke or bowed to, called on, dined with or intermarried with whom. As Kathleen Chorley, born in 1897, the daughter of a Manchester electrical engineer and niece of the first vice-chancellor of Manchester University, observed of the upper middle-class railway suburb of Alderley Edge:

> Snobbery was also geographical; it was almost an axiom for instance that, socially speaking, no good thing would be likely to come out of Wilmslow, the neighbouring village nearer Manchester. On the other hand, Peover, a village deeper in Cheshire than Alderley Edge, where the manager of the Manchester branch of the Bank of England lived in semi-county state, was regarded by most of our ladies with equal though different scorn as the preserve of people who like to be 'in with' the county. The people who lived round about Peover reciprocated, of course, and suspected a good many of us as we suspected the Wilmslow families. The complications were endless. Mother and Mrs Schill [a neighbour, wife of a Manchester cotton merchant], for instance, both got on admirably with 'the lower classes' because these they could meet without any fear of being drawn into or needing to draw them in to their own entourage. It was the people immediately below and immediately above that caused the trouble. The 'aboves' were as troublesome as the 'belows' for mother and Mrs Schill had twisted their sturdy self-respect into a ridiculous pattern of inverted snobbery.... I recall my mother's positive annoyance when Lady Sheffield of Alderley Park called upon her as a preliminary to an invitation to lunch.... And the social path was always a good deal wider for men than for women. Wives with the views of mother and Mrs Schill had to walk a social tight-rope.[59]

She went on to note that the social path was much wider in Didsbury and Withington, suburbs much nearer Manchester where many of the residents were younger professional men, teachers at the university, members of the Manchester bar, doctors – 'a less local and more intellectual society than ours and consequently freer'.[60] But the professions were distinguished by more than a difference in geography and income, as we shall see.

Towards the bottom end of the middle class, the demarcations and snobberies were equally divisive. On the northern, less fashionable side of Manchester Stella Davies, born in 1895, was the fourteenth of fifteen children of a mill girl's illegitimate son, who rose from warehouse boy to co-op store manager, private shop owner and, after a bankruptcy, to successful commercial traveller for a clothing firm. She recalls living in the Edwardian age in Moss Bank, an end-terrace (i.e. superior) house in Crumpsall with a large garden, a summer house and a tennis court, and their maid-of-all-work, 'Fat Ellen'. A street of working-class houses with lots of children ran the length of their garden: '*We* were not allowed to speak to *them*'. Next door lived the son of a wealthy Manchester merchant, her older brother Frank's employer, with, amongst other servants, a nursemaid in cap and apron to look after the three children: '*They* were not allowed to play with *us*'. She used to stand on the flat roof of the summer house looking at both lots of children and dream of a game of rounders.[61]

From top to bottom the middle class was riddled with such divisions and petty snobberies, not only of income and geography but also of religion – Church of England (in some country villages the Roman Catholic squire) at the top, the Quakers and Unitarians next, followed by the Congregationalists and Baptists, the Methodists, and finally, by a curious inversion, the Anglicans and the Catholics again at the bottom, mostly in the working class; of education – boarding schools at the top, followed by private day schools, and only amongst the lowest white-collar worker the non-fee paying church or local board school; and of leisure – exclusive West End or provincial city clubs (men only) and country tennis and golf clubs at the top, Sunday school teaching, men's Christian societies and mother's unions at the bottom. Every activity, from visiting the poor in Ancoats, Manchester like Kathleen Chorley's mother, with sympathy, advice or material help, or sitting in the rented pews of the church or chapel, to going to the Hallé Concerts of Miss Horniman's Repertory Theatre and avoiding the music hall and the pub, or going on holiday to Southport or Bournemouth rather than Blackpool or Skegness, was carefully graded and segregated. One spent one's time always in the company of one's equals, except of course when directing the labours of servants or workers or patronizing the city slum dwellers or the village poor. Segregation at every level and in every occupation and pastime was the hallmark of the middle class.

Yet the middle class was divided along both dimensions, vertically as well as horizontally. Running through the many layers was an important vertical barrier, not always conscious or watertight, but in some ways more significant than the division between upper and lower middle class: the division between the business and the professional classes. Marx was groping for this distinction when he recognized a middle class beneath the capitalists, without noticing that it undermined his theory that the intermediate classes would be crushed between 'the upper and nether millstones' of the bourgeoisie and the proletariat:

> What he [Ricardo] forgot to emphasize is the constantly growing number of the middle classes, those who stand between the workman on the one hand and the capitalist and the landlord on the other. The middle classes ... are a burden weighing heavily on the working base and increase the social security and power of the upper ten thousand.[62]

Matthew Arnold clearly recognized it, and brought it to the attention of the Taunton Commission on middle-class schools in 1869:

> So we have among us the spectacle of a middle class cut in two, in a way unexampled anywhere else; of a professional class brought up on the first plane, with fine and governing qualities, but without the idea of science; while that immense business class which is becoming so important a power in all countries, on which the future so much depends and which in the leading schools is, in England, brought up on the second plane, cut off from the aristocracy and the professions, and without governing qualities.[63]

This sense on the part of the professional middle class of their superiority to the business class and their close alliance with the aristocracy and gentry stemmed, for those at the upper end, from their common education at the public boarding and endowed grammar schools and, to a less extent, at Oxford and Cambridge. There the idea of moral and intellectual superiority was being linked to a new concept of the gentleman, no longer the aristocratic code of militaristic honour to be defended by duelling but the notion of a 'gentle man', educated, courteous, well-spoken, and considerate of others.[64] As a guide to professional careers had expressed it in 1857:

> The importance of the professions and the professional classes can hardly be overrated, they form the head of the great English middle class, maintain its tone of independence, keep up to the mark its standard of morality, and direct its intelligence.[65]

And as Anthony Trollope put it more cynically in *The Bartrams* (1867), a profession was 'a calling by which a gentleman, not born to the inheritance of a gentleman's allowance of good things, might ingeniously obtain the same by some exercise of his abilities'.[66] (He might also have added of his own second profession of novelist that from the experience of his mother it was one of the few callings by which a lady left with a family without means could respectably obtain the same benefits.) The sense of superiority to mere tradesmen and business men was echoed at the local level, especially in the smaller towns where big business was less dominant. In Guildford before the First World War, according to the son of a small trader, professional men were at the top, monopolizing the leading golf club, high street traders one stage lower, occupying leading positions in the chapels and local politics and meeting in the Tradesmen's Club; both excluded the smaller traders and clerks, who took to cycling and other private leisure pursuits.[67] In Woodstock, according to another:

> the professional people always held themselves a little aloof – from the trades people. And especially trades people that were uneducated ... but – if a person was well-educated and a tradesperson of course – you had the entrée into what we call the professional people.[68]

The ancient professions of the clergy, law and medicine could still obtain a gentleman's allowance of good things, though with the decline of 'Old Corruption' since the 1832 Reform Act the enormous fortunes and estates made by some bishops, judges and a few physicians serving royalty and the nobility had declined or disappeared. There were no equal successors of Lord Eldon, the Lord Chancellor, who left £707,000 plus large landed estates in 1838, or of Lord Arden, brother of prime minister Spencer Percival and a judge of the Court of Admiralty, who left £200,000 in 1827.[69] There were still successful individuals in, or perhaps from, the professions and the public service, however. The richest of all the millionaires, the shipowner and financier Sir John Ellerman, began as an accountant; W. T. Lewis, Lord Merthyr, the half-millionaire coal owner, began as estate agent to the Marquess of Bute; Lord Leith of Fyvie, the American steel millionaire, was a British naval officer who on a Royal Navy visit to San Francisco met and married the daughter of a St Louis industrialist.[70] More directly, one-fifth of the new peers of 1886–1914 came from the professions, mostly law lords like Lord Cairns, ennobled generals like Lord Roberts and Lord Kitchener, or journalists like John Morley and Lord Northcliffe.[71] But these were individual exceptions, and the professions were now rising in a different way. Firstly, as we have seen, they were growing with the accelerating expansion of service occupations during the Victorian Age. By 1911, if we add the lesser professionals and technicians to the higher ones, the professions were 4.1 per cent of the occupied population, not much short of the 4.6 per cent who were 'employers' in the census of industrial status, and if we add 'managers and administrators' the figure rises to 7.5 per cent, larger than the category of 'employers and proprietors' (6.7 per cent).[72]

More significant was the growing collective organization of the professions. To the seven qualifying associations of 1800 – four Inns of Court for barristers, two Royal Colleges and the Society of Apothecaries for medical doctors – the first eighty years of the nineteenth century had added only twenty more, for solicitors, architects, builders (not successful as a profession), pharmacists, veterinary surgeons, actuaries, surveyors, chemists, librarians, bankers (another unsuccessful attempt), accountants, and eight types of engineer. From 1880 down to the First World War there appeared no less than thirty-nine, from chartered accountants, auctioneers and estate agents, company secretaries and hospital administrators to marine, mining, water, sanitary, heating and ventilating, and locomotive design engineers, insurance brokers, sales managers, and town planners. To these we should add the non-qualifying associations, such as the National Union of Teachers, the Association of Headmasters, and the Association of Teachers in Technical Institutions, the National Association of Local Government Officers, the Civil Service Clerical Association, and the Institute of Directors, which often combined professional aspirations with something of the character of trade unions or employers' associations.[73] Since most of the non-qualifying associations represented salaried, employed professions, while the qualified still for the most part aspired to independent or self-employed status, this illustrates a critical division within the professional class which was to become increasingly important, and to which we shall return in Chapter 9.

There were also the anarchic or individualistic professions which either defied organization altogether or organized themselves for intellectual and cultural rather than professional purposes. These included what some historians and sociologists have called 'the intellectual class' which they see as coming into existence, along with the word 'intellectual' as a noun, from the 1880s.[74] It embraced three overlapping groups: what had formerly been called 'men of letters', 'men of science', and university teachers, to which we might add a fourth category, practitioners of the fine and performing arts, principally painters and sculptors, and musicians and actors. Some of these children of the free play of mind and the feelings began to seek professional ends and status at this period. The Society of Authors was founded in 1883 to defend the writer's property in his copyright.[75] The natural scientists had begun to organize as early as 1831 in the British Association for the Advancement of Science and the Royal Society began to restrict membership to active men of science in 1847, though the true professionalization of science was to take place mainly in the late Victorian age with the foundation of such bodies as the Physical Society in 1876 and the Institute of Chemistry in 1877 and the establishment (later than in London and the newer universities) of laboratories at Oxford (the Clarendon, 1872) and Cambridge (the Cavendish, 1874).[76]

The invasion of the ancient universities by natural science was an aspect of the professionalization of university teaching, which had been pioneered in the Scottish universities in the eighteenth century and in London, Durham and the new civic universities from their beginnings in the early nineteenth, but did not much affect Oxford and Cambridge until their reform and secularization by the Royal Commissions of the 1850s and 1870s. As a result the average Oxford and Cambridge don was transformed during the late Victorian age from a celibate clergyman awaiting a college living in the church on which he could marry to a career-oriented, and usually married, teacher and scholar or scientist.[77] One of the leading reformers, Mark Pattison, Rector of Lincoln College, Oxford wrote, somewhat optimistically, in 1875:

> A university is the organ of the intellectual life of the nation; it is a school of learning, the nursery of the liberal arts, the academy of the sciences, the home of letters, the retreat of the studious and the contemplative.[78]

It was also to become in the late Victorian and Edwardian age a source of new ideas on how society should be organized, preserved and reformed, and of young men eager to put those ideas into practice. Through them, as we shall see in the next chapter, the universities, particularly Oxford and Cambridge, were to become among the main articulators of the social ideal of the professional class.

Something of the social origins and economic success of a superior sample of higher professional men can be gained from the study of elites cited above in connection with the great landowners, millionaires and company chairmen.[79] The professional sample consisted not of the most financially successful but of all those who had reached the head of their profession either by being elected president of their association or institute (the Institute of Chartered Accountants, the Royal College of Physicians and of Surgeons, the Institutions of Civil and of Mechanical Engineers, the Law Society, and the Royal Institute of British Architects) or had become senior judges, vice-chancellors of universities, Clarendon school headmasters, national newspaper editors, or permanent heads of Civil Service departments. Of the professional presidents the cohorts in office in 1880–99 and 1900–19 were drawn overwhelmingly from the middle and upper classes, and more from the middle (about 18 per cent of the population) than from the upper class (about 3 per cent of the population): 64.6 per cent and 56.3 per cent respectively from the middle and 32.9 per cent and 42.5 per cent from the upper class. Most, as one would expect, came from professional families (57.0 per cent and 66.3 per cent), but slightly more from the lower than from the higher professions. Only one in each cohort, a civil engineer and an architect, came from the manual working class. This finding is confirmed by their education, which was predominantly at private schools, including at that time grammar schools (76.5 and 65.0 per cent); only a handful (14.6 and 16.7 per cent) came from elementary schools. The majority had not been to university, reflecting the apprenticeship training of most professions before the twentieth century, and of those who had (44.9 and 34.5 per cent), only a handful had been to Oxford or Cambridge, most to London and a few others to Scottish or Irish universities. Their fathers were mostly not rich (though a very few were, leaving estates up to a maximum of £180,000 and £220,100 in successive cohorts), and the median estates in the two cohorts were no more than £5,000 and £9,000, while a quarter left less than £900 and £2,700 respectively. They themselves were upwardly mobile and in financial terms modestly successful, their own median estates for the two cohorts being £47,800 and £32,000. One president of the civil engineers was a millionaire, but he was Lord Armstrong of Cragside, whose fortune came from his engineering and armament works, and one of the mechanicals was Sir Lowthian Bell the great ironmaster, who left £796,000 in 1904, each of them elected to do their Institutions honour. The average successful self-employed professional man might make a modest fortune, but scarcely enough to join the rich and powerful.

Senior judges, drawn exclusively from successful barristers, the classic 'jackpot' profession in which a few struck it rich and most did not, were in a different category. A half or more in the two successive cohorts (50 and 54.6 per cent) came from the upper class, a few were sons of landowners, and more came from the higher professions (especially the law – one-sixth and one-fifth respectively) than from business families. None was from the manual working class, and only a handful (five out of ninety in all) were the sons of white-collar workers (mostly law clerks). They were mostly educated at public or other private schools (76.5 and 75 per cent), many of them at Eton, Harrow or another of the

Clarendon schools, and all had been to university (mostly Oxford or Cambridge) and (as was essential for the bar) to one of the Inns of Court. Their fathers were somewhat wealthier than those of the professional presidents, leaving median estates of £16,000 and £11,400, and they themselves were more successful accumulators, leaving median estates in the two cohorts of £65,500 and £66,600. But then the senior judges were almost *ex officio*, like the bishops, members of 'society', and only passed through the middle class on their way up.

Vice-chancellors were at the head of the newly developing profession of university teaching, and before the First World War were mainly recruited from academics themselves. All the Oxbridge vice-chancellors, who were heads of colleges in rotation, were Oxbridge graduates, most had been to Clarendon or other private schools, most came from the upper and middle classes (83.3 and 100 per cent in the two cohorts), and only two had come from the non-manual and one from the manual working class. The more permanent vice-chancellors of the newer universities were similar in origin, mostly educated at public and private schools and at Oxford, Cambridge or London Universities, though rather more came from the upper than from the middle class (50.5 and 51.7 per cent as against 36.4 and 41.4 per cent), and only three came from the non-manual and none from the manual working class. Taken together, most vice-chancellors were the sons of modestly endowed fathers who left median estates of £6,000 and £8,000, and modestly increased the family fortunes themselves, leaving median estates of £12,700 and £15,200. One, however, was a millionaire, but he was Sir Julius Goldsmid the financier, honorific vice-chancellor of London University (which also had an executive Principal) in 1895–96, whose father left £800,000 and he himself £1,021,000.

The Clarendon school headmasters, at the head of the teaching profession, were very similar in origin to the Oxbridge vice-chancellors – not surprisingly, since at this time they were charged with the education of exactly the same narrow social group. They were overwhelmingly educated at public schools, though not necessarily at Clarendon schools, and all were Oxbridge graduates. They were all from the upper and middle classes, again more from the middle (70.6 and 76.2 per cent) than from the upper (29.4 and 23.8 per cent), though a few, like the son of Lord Lyttleton, the

Rev. Edward Lyttleton, Master of Eton in 1905-16, were of rich and noble birth. Most came from backgrounds of modest wealth, their fathers' median estates being £11,000 and £8,200, and most of those in the lower half left little or nothing; and they themselves left moderate fortunes, with median estates of £27,300 and £9,300.

National newspaper and periodical editors were leaders of one of the few professions in which a poor boy could rise from the bottom, like J. L. Garvin of the *Observer*, son of an Irish labourer, or Alfred Harmsworth, Lord Northcliffe, office boy who rose to the editor's and proprietor's chairs, but this too was rare before the First World War. Only four out of eighty-three editors came from the non-manual and seven from the manual working class. Most came from the upper and middle classes, though once again more from the middle class (55.8 and 55.1 per cent as against 32.4 and 28.6 per cent), nearly two-thirds (66.5 and 65.9 per cent) had been to public or other private schools and a sizeable group (50 and 34.1 per cent) to Clarendon schools, and most (64.8 and 51.7 per cent) had been to university, mostly Oxbridge. Their fathers were not poor, leaving median estates of £10,000 and £6,000, and nor were they themselves, leaving median estates of £23,000 and £9,300. A few were rich, like the only woman editor, Rachel Beer of *The Sunday Times*, wife of the proprietor, or Henry Labouchere, radical MP and editor of *Truth*, who left £550,000 in 1912, but then his mother was a Baring, of the banking family.[80] Newspaper editors as well as proprietors were influential figures in that society, much courted by politicians and 'society' hostesses, but since they were mostly neither rich nor, in the direct sense, powerful they can be properly placed at the top of the professional middle class.

The final profession for which we have figures is the Civil Service, represented here by the permanent heads of departments. In this period they were only just beginning to be affected by the competitive entrance examination introduced in 1870, whose effect, paradoxically, was to increase the predominance of the products of the major public schools and Oxbridge, who replaced the much more varied and haphazard beneficiaries of the old patronage system. The great majority had been to public or other private schools (87 and 80 per cent), a large if declining proportion of these to Eton or Harrow (47.8 and 20 per cent), and the share of Oxbridge graduates was increasing (from 47.5 to 57.2 per cent). At the same time, the new recruitment system gave more chance to the bright, well-educated sons of the middle class, whose share of the top jobs in executive government (rising from 26.3 to 48 per cent) caught up with that of the upper class, whose share declined sharply (from 71.9 to 48 per cent). Out of 132 top civil servants only three came from the non-manual and one from the manual working class. Overall, their fathers' wealth was on a par with most other professions, with median estates of £16,300 and £10,400, and they themselves were modestly affluent, leaving median estates of £25,900 and £14,900.

There are hints here, however, of the beginnings of a considerable change in the character of the higher Civil Service which will become clearer later, from a predominantly upper-class, major public school-educated elite to a predominantly middle-class, minor public and grammar school-educated cadre recruited typically from the sons of small business men and the lesser professions. In other words, scholarship boys (and later a very few girls) from modest backgrounds were beginning to make their way in, which accounts for the paradoxically *increasing* predominance of Oxford and Cambridge graduates. Top civil servants, though they earned only from £1,000 to £1,200 a year, mixed socially with the rich perhaps more readily then than today, and the occasional one leapt out of his sphere into imperial government and a peerage. Such a one was Frederick Milner, chairman of the Board of Inland Revenue in 1892–97, who by way of colonial government in South Africa rose to a viscountcy in 1901 and, later, membership of Lloyd George's War Cabinet.

Below the level of the elite of each profession, wealth and lifestyle were less exalted. According to Charles Booth in 1902, who was as interested in the servant-keeping class as in the poor, some London clergy (leaving aside the bishops and others amongst the rich), including a few dissenting ministers, could earn up to £1,500 a year, though curates might earn as little as £90, and a Salvation Army officer, if single, a meagre 16s.–18s. a week, and 27s. plus 1s. per child for a married couple. Barristers' earnings were notoriously chancy and could range from nothing for a briefless beginner to many thousands a year for a great QC like H. H. Asquith or F. E. Smith (Lord Birkenhead), while their clerks could earn from £200 to £400 and occasionally £800–£1,000. Booth could not give a figure for successful medical practitioners, but he found qualified resident assistants earning £60–£100 a year and non-residents £80–£150; while staff nurses earned pittances of £22–£40 a year, and even a head matron only from £70 to £150, rising to £200–£250 in a very large and rich hospital. Fleet Street journalists could earn £200–£500 a year as reporters, £400–£600 as sub-editors, and £1,000–£2,000 as editors. Local government officers in a London parish vestry (replaced by the municipal borough by the London Government Act, 1899), could earn from £110 a year for a third office clerk, or £130 a year, with uniform, for a sanitary inspector, to £450 a year for the Vestry Clerk or the Medical Officer of Health. Civil servants in the upper division could rise through three scales from £200–£600 to £1,000–£1,200 a year, in the second division through four scales from £70–£100 to £250–£350 a year. Below these there were assistant clerks on £80–£150 a year, and boy clerks on 14s. a week, rising by 1s. a week each year.[81]

How to live on such incomes – and higher ones, from £1,000 to £10,000 a year – the *Cornhill Magazine* set out to show in a series of articles in 1901.[82] Amongst those on £150–£200 a year would be found, G. S. Layard thought, bank clerks, managing clerks to solicitors, teachers in board schools, younger journalists on the best papers and senior ones on local papers, second division clerks in the Colonial, Home and India Offices, many local government officers, police inspectors, organists, curates, and certain skilled mechanics. He advised those who worked in the City or Westminster not to live in cramped accommodation nearby, but to find an inexpensive house in one of the nearer suburbs, Clapham, Forest Gate, Wandsworth, Peckham or Finsbury Park. This would be cheaper, far more healthy, and 'his neighbours will be of his own class, a matter of chiefest importance to his wife and children, the greater part of whose lives will be spent in these surroundings.' After paying the rent at 10s. a week, rates and taxes, rail fares, and 'the very considerable expenditure on dress' – since 'the bank clerk who looks needy, or the solicitor's clerk who is out-at-elbows, will find that he has little chance of retaining his position' – there was nothing for hiring domestic help, the wife had to make most of her own and the two children's clothes, to buy the food carefully and even get her husband to buy cheap New Zealand lamb or a parcel of tea in the City. Although there was money for a summer holiday, birthday and Christmas presents, newspapers, books and tobacco, there was none for alcohol or for the children's education, who were wisely sent to the public elementary school, which was 'incomparably better than any private teaching within their means'.

On £800 a year – 'to the toiling clerk it seems unbounded wealth, to the woman of fashion a poor thing in pin money' – according to G. Colmore in the next issue, 'the professional man, or the younger son with a narrow berth in the Civil Service' could make ends meet 'with comfortable success or inconvenient uncertainty'. On this a house could be taken at £130 a year in a healthy if not very fashionable street, two servants could be kept, a cook at £20 and a house parlourmaid at £18, though the wife must be willing to supervise them. £4 a week could be spent on food and washing, £30 a year on alcohol and tobacco, £70 on the husband's club and pocket expenses, and £40 on his clothes, £20 on the wife's pocket money and £50 on her clothes, £50 on holidays and travel, and £25 on entertaining, amusements and charities. 'Playgoing must be strictly limited' though 'real lovers of music can indulge their taste at little cost,' but 'a pretty home, comfortably kept, and an easy mind ... are better worth having than a large acquaintance, much entertaining, and many amusements,' since 'for most people who live on eight hundred a year these things are incompatible.' As an afterthought, 'the addition of a child, or even two children, would necessitate but little alteration in the figures.'

Even on £1,800 a year, according to Mrs Earle, economy was still necessary, and 'the young couple', apparently childless, could afford three or four servants – if the fourth were a good lady's maid who would partly pay for herself by the saving of dressmaker's bills – but personal transport (a pony carriage and groom) could be budgeted for only in the country, not in London, where cabs, buses or the Underground would be used.

On £10,000 a year (which takes us even further beyond the ken of the middle class), according to Lady Agnew, a good London house on the south side of Eaton Square (not 'an enchanting house in Grosvenor Square') could be afforded together with a medium-sized 'mansion' in the country, 'ten or twelve servants and a really good cook', and the couple could even afford three children, two boys to be sent to prep school and Eton at a cost of £3,600 over ten years and a girl who will cost £100 a year for twenty, surprisingly more expensive than her brothers. But what with moving the household twice yearly, £900 for clothes and, 'the final twist of the torture screw', £500 in rates and taxes, the poor rich family would be lucky to have a margin of £1,000 a year left over.

If the rich on £1,800 or £10,000 a year felt thus squeezed, how much more did the middle classes below them. There were constant complaints, particularly in the 'Great Depression', from the middle classes about falling profits, rising house rents, the high wages of servants, the cost of education, and so on. Yet for half the period prices were falling and those whose incomes did not fall so fast, which meant the majority, especially those on salaries which rarely if ever declined, were enjoying a rising standard of living. There were several reasons for this paradox. Many small business men and shopkeepers were not only acutely aware of the falling prices and their effect on their cash flow and profits; they were also increasingly afraid of the competition of the new large-scale firms which threatened them with bankruptcy. Shopkeepers in particular faced the competition of the large new department stores like Selfridges, Whiteleys, Maples and the Army & Navy Stores, and of the new chain stores, such as Liptons, the Maypole, Eastmans, and the ABC. What alarmed the smaller shopkeeper most of all was the rapid growth of the retail co-operative movement, which became the scapegoat for the petty bourgeoisie who were ideologically committed to private enterprise and resentful of a working-class movement which threatened to undermine their existence.[83] *The Grocer* campaigned from the 1870s to the early 1900s for a boycott of the wholesalers who supplied the co-op stores, but without success.[84] Their problems stemmed from the rise in the scale of organization in the shape of the multiples, with their economies of scale, of which the co-op stores and the Co-operative Wholesale Society, with its factories, ships and tea plantations, were only a symptom.

More important for them and the professional and salaried workers was the rising standard of living itself which increased the competition for status in every field, in dress, housing and furniture, education, leisure and entertainment, and the like. This in turn raised the costs, against the trend of prices, of keeping up appearances, of renting a good house in a better-class suburb, of educating children privately, of going to the theatre or concerts, of holiday-making, and of every effort to keep up with the ever-receding Joneses. Education became increasingly desirable and expensive as a means of fitting one's children for those expanding middle-class occupations, in professional and office work of all kinds, which required little capital but for that very reason attracted competition from bright boys and girls of the working class, now beginning to benefit from the board schools of the 1870s, the higher grade and secondary schools of the 1880s and 1890s, and the secondary schools and the scholarship ladder of the 1900s. The competition for status for oneself and even more for one's children, rather than any decline in material resources, was the major reason for the decline in the middle-class birthrate which began in the late 1870s, though its remoter origins can be traced to the decline in family size which began in the 1850s.[85] The new outlook can clearly be seen in such popular journalism as the *Cornhill* family budgets, which expected 'middle-class' couples at any level of income, from £160 right up to £10,000 a year, not to be able to 'afford' more than two or three children (though they scrupulously avoided saying how this limit was to be achieved).[86]

The final reason for the paradox of middle-class discontent in the midst of rising standards of comfort was the all-pervading sense of insecurity which was the inevitable concomitant of class society. While security based on a cushion of capital or a permanent job was the main distinction that separated them from the gross insecurity of the manual worker, most middle-class families knew how precarious that security was, and many lived in fear of bankruptcy or loss of a salaried position, of sickness of either partner or the children, or of the death of the breadwinner, any of which could plunge the family into debt or actual poverty. No amount of saving or insurance – and the family budgets from the period all show that middle-class families saved little and were underinsured – could prevent unexpected disaster, and there were endless stories of bankrupt, unemployed or widowed families falling into desperate poverty. When her husband died, Mrs Levy, the widow of a speculative builder and surveyor in Manchester before the First World War, had to give up her home, withdraw her three sons from a Margate boarding school, and open a small grocer's shop, which failed, and she was reduced to factory work.[87] For the middle-class man and still more his wife, once their main income failed, were unskilled, unfitted even for the physical work which labourers or laundry women performed, and were almost unemployable.

How much more true was this of the 'marginal men' of the

lower middle class, where insecurity was endemic. The lesser clerks, corner shopkeepers, elementary school teachers and shop assistants, many of them newly emerged from the working class, often lived in or on the margins of working-class areas and on similar incomes. They might by their dress, speech and housing be 'a cut above' the manual workers, but only they knew how precarious their position was. One of the main reasons for low-paid clerks and other white-collar workers 'keeping themselves to themselves' was that they did not want their friends and neighbours to know how modestly they had to live. The wife of a Manchester clerk told her son:

> No use being poor and seeming poor, always put on a good face outside.... She would say, I must have the windows right because more pass by than come in. We had to dress to the public.... Always give people a good impression.

The son of a Potteries insurance agent came from the social stratum of those who 'would never go out without they was dressed up'; the local working people mocked such people with the phrase 'a fur coat but no breakfast'.[88]

For the same reasons, except for those who threw themselves enthusiastically into voluntary work for the Sunday School, the Salvation Army, the Tory Party or even the Independent Labour Party, they were frustrated and lonely.[89] A Hammersmith vicar told Charles Booth about the new clerks invading his parish:

> The newcomers are quite quiet, respectable and inoffensive, but on warm evenings they will sit at their open windows in their shirt-sleeves, drinking beer out of a pot, and though they do it quite quietly it is not what I am accustomed to.[90]

That expresses perfectly the precarious position of the lower middle class; too genteel to go to the pub, not genteel enough to pass muster as 'proper' middle class.

The gulfs which separated the lower middle class from those above and below were not the only demarcations troubling them. The vertical cleavage between the business and professional men above them extended to them too. The thousands of small 'employers and proprietors' – workshop owners, small wholesalers and warehousemen, jobbing builders, shopkeepers, and garret masters in the sweated trades – were more than counterbalanced by the salaried or wage-earning clerks and foremen, salesmen and shop assistants, lower professionals such as teachers and nurses, and technicians such as draughtsmen and laboratory assistants.[91] By 1911, when the census first took into account industrial status, there were 2,618,000 white-collar workers, 14.3 per cent of the occupied population. Increasing numbers of these were women: 29.8 per cent of all white-collar workers (including management and higher professions), 21.4 per cent of the clerks, 35.2 per cent of the salesmen and shop assistants, and no less than 62.9 per cent of the lower professionals and technicians, who included school teachers and nurses.[92] Women school teachers had increased from 144,393 (out of 195,021) in 1891 to 183,298 (out of 251,968) in 1911, while women clerks had increased from 18,947 (out of 389,380) to 124,843 (out of 687,998).[93] This was a corollary of the 'service revolution',[94] which at the lower levels provided more new jobs for women than for men.

Amongst the men even more than the women it produced a distinct difference of outlook between them and the traditional, small capitalist petty bourgeoisie. If the small business man was concerned with security from competition and bankruptcy, the white-collar worker feared the loss of a regular fixed income. Richard Church, who was forced to give up an art college scholarship by his father, a Post Office sorter (then a junior Civil Service appointment) in Battersea, and become a Civil Service clerk instead, wrote of him:

> No doubt the poverty and hardship which he had known in childhood had fixed in his character an obstinacy born of hunger and degradation. He was too innocent and too lacking in intellectual self-confidence to contemplate going out to fight for himself in the open market. He had a curious belief that money making was a dirty game, something not even talked about, and all he asked was that he be assured of a regular income, no matter how small. He saw the Civil Service as the only way for himself and therefore his sons must follow him.... Like most people at that time and in that walk of life they [his parents] were grateful for small assurances: a safe job, a respectable anonymity, and local esteem.[95]

Whereas the small business man was always an individualist who thought of himself as a potential self-made man, the white-collar worker looked firstly for a secure income, secondly for a pension, and thirdly for promotion within a stable framework of employment. For some, such as the bank, insurance, and commercial clerks, the ladder might lead to branch management or even a partnership, though this was becoming increasingly rare for those without capital or connections. For others, in the large-scale environment of government, central and local, the Post Office, and large private corporations like the railways, the best to be hoped for was promotion to a modest senior clerkship or office manager. Those who identified more closely with the employer and looked to a career in the higher reaches of the middle class and those who were resigned to a future on much the same level might co-exist in the same office, the first being those with connections, ability or confidence, the second those who knew their limitations. The first tended to be commoner in small offices affording direct contact with the employer or his surrogate manager, the second in large offices or large organizations like the railways with a long chain of command.[96] The difference showed itself in their salaries and prospects of promotion. In 1909 the proportion of male clerks in the taxpaying bracket (over £160 a year) was highest in insurance (46 per cent) and banking (44 per cent), moderate in central and local government (37 and 28 per cent) and local industry and trade (23 per cent), and lowest in the railway companies (10 per cent).[97]

It also showed itself in the organizations they joined. The first kind joined the YMCA or formed semi-professional guilds like the Manchester Warehousemen and Clerks' Provident Association of 1855 or the Liverpool Clerks' Association of 1861, which provided death and sickness benefits for their members, and which led on for a militant few to a feeble and unsuccessful trade unionism. The National Union of Clerks, founded in 1890, had only 200 members by 1906, and in the upsurge of trade unionism just before the war grew from 2,350 in 1910 to 12,680 in 1914. The second kind took slowly but more solidly to trade unionism: the Railway Clerks' Association, established at Sheffield in 1897, had by 1906 recruited only 4,000 out of a possible 60,000 members, but then grew from 10,000 in 1910 to 30,000 in 1914. The National Association of Local Government Officers, founded with 5,000 members in 1905, grew to over 20,000 by 1914. In the Post Office the Postal Telegraph Clerks' Association (1881), the Provincial Postal Clerks

(1887) and others, which included women, had some 20,000 members by 1914. The woman workers, with little chance of promotion, seem to have led the way in the Civil Service, with the Civil Service Typists' Association in 1903, the Association of Women Clerks in the Board of Trade in 1911, and the Federation of Women Clerks in 1913. But with very few exceptions neither kind of clerk, male or female, showed the least interest in aligning themselves with the manual workers in the TUC or the Labour Party.[98]

The lower middle class, whether clerks and shop assistants or shopkeepers and other business men, have had a poor deal from their chroniclers. They have been mocked or patronized, from Bob Cratchett in Dickens's *A Christmas Carol* to Mr Pooter in the Grossmiths' *Diary of a Nobody* or Mr Polly in H. G. Wells's *History*. And they have been accused of being far more jingoistic in the imperialist movement of this period, climaxing in the Boer War in their precipitate volunteering for the army and their violence and bullying towards the Pro-Boers.[99] Yet they were often the backbone of the burgeoning Sunday schools and other church organizations, sports clubs, youth clubs, the YMCA, the Salvation Army, and the Boys' Brigade, the Boy Scouts and the Girl Guides, of the university extension lectures and vocational evening classes, of the new constituency organizations of both major political parties, and even of the cadres of the Fabians and the ILP.[100] They also produced probably more self-made men than the much larger working class, such as Sir Thomas Lipton, shopkeeper turned royal yachtsman, Lord Leverhulme, commercial traveller turned international soap and fats tycoon, Lord Northcliffe, office boy turned press baron, Lloyd George, solicitor's clerk turned statesman, Charles Booth, Liverpool shipping clerk turned shipowner and social investigator, Bernard Shaw, estate agent's clerk turned playwright, and H. G. Wells, pupil teacher and shop assistant turned novelist and pioneer of science fiction. At a less spectacular level, many were upwardly mobile in a more modest way. They seized every educational opportunity, formal or informal, even those intended for the working class, from the mechanics' institute to the new polytechnics like Regent Street and Woolwich, and the university tutorial classes started in 1907 by the Workers' Educational Association (one of the students in Tawney's first class at Rochdale was A. P. Wadsworth, a young journalist who was to become editor of the *Manchester Guardian*). For the lower middle class, both the self-employed petty bourgeoisie and the employed white-collar division, was the traditional first step towards higher status for the ambitious sons and, increasingly, daughters of the working class.[101]

This, paradoxically, is why they distinguished themselves so obsessively from the working class. They were, literally, trying to get away from them, in income, status, appearance, and physical residence. They did not always find it easy. Their incomes, especially in their early years, were often less than skilled workers' wages and if on the one side they had 'prospects' and more security, on the other side bankruptcy or unemployment could plunge them into poverty and unemployability more rarely experienced by the skilled manual worker. Their obsession with status, necessary for their work, often drove them to spend more on dress, rent and children's education than they could afford, sometimes to the detriment of their own and their families' health, to have smaller families than the manual workers, and to shun the overt hedonism of large sections of the working class. Most of all, it drove them to try to segregate themselves and their children, if they could, in suburbs of their own, such as Fulham, Kilburn or Ealing in London, Saughtonhall or Spring Valley in Edinburgh, Broughton or Chorltonville near Manchester, and their like. They rarely quite succeeded. Artisans, especially if there was more than one earner in the family, could often outbid them and share the same suburbs, but even there they tried to monopolize certain streets.[102] For Frederick Willis, an apprentice silk hatter, who was born in Burdock Road in a south-east London suburb, 'the working class of the neighbourhood had a great prejudice against the City swells of Burdock Road and, accordingly, the Burdock Road residents kept the rest of the district at arm's length.'[103] In mixed artisan and lower middle-class suburbs in North London, noted Charles Booth, 'We are told that contingents from different streets never mix,' and they had separate gymnasia, summer outings, and so on.[104]

It was this increasing desire for segregation and the mutual dislike of the white-collar and manual workers which reinforced at the level of the voting masses the decline of Liberal England. Gladstonian Liberalism was predicated on the assumption that all men of good will and progressive outlook would want to work together to improve the whole community, morally and socially. This belief, though with different notions of what constituted improvement, equally inspired the New Liberals and the Fabians. Liberal England foundered on the rocks of class prejudice. The Liberals could not keep the rich or the comfortable and at the same time satisfy the working class since as a rich, well-meaning but baffled Liberal, Charles Masterman, put it in 1909, 'The Rich despise the Working People; the Middle Classes fear them....'[105] On their part, the working people could scarcely be blamed for increasingly feeling the same way about the rich and the middle classes.

3 LIVES APART: THE REMAKING OF THE WORKING CLASS

As class society reached its zenith the working class, after the relative quiescence of the mid-Victorian social peace, rose once again in a resurgence of class consciousness and class conflict. The late Victorian age saw what Gareth Stedman Jones has called, echoing Edward Thompson, 'the remaking of a working class':

> The distinctiveness of a working-class way of life was enormously accentuated. Its separateness and impermeability were now reflected in a dense and inward-looking culture, whose effect was both to emphasize the distance of the working class from the classes above it and to articulate its position within an apparently permanent social hierarchy.[106]

This new or newly intensified working-class culture focused, to quote Charles Booth, not on 'trade unions and friendly societies, co-operative effort, temperance propaganda and politics (including socialism)', but on 'pleasure, amusement, hospitality and sport'.[107] It was a culture which could embrace imperialism, jingoistic music hall songs, and 'mafficking', but also comic satire of the upper and middle classes, the police, and the inevitability of the workhouse. It was 'a culture of consolation'.[108]

At the same time there was an upsurge of political and industrial unrest which culminated in the 'New Unionism' and the Labour Party, the industrial and political confrontation between the intransigent employers and the equally determined unions in the late 1890s and 1900s, and the massive wave of strikes between 1910 and 1914. At this level working-class consciousness finally achieved class-wide, permanent institutional form. Stedman Jones argues persuasively that the two levels are inter-connected: 'The rise of new unionism, the foundation of the Labour Party, even the emergence of socialist groups marked not a breach but a culmination of this defensive culture.'[109] In the sense that the working class had already come to accept capitalism and practise class conflict within the framework of a viable class society, this was undoubtedly true. The New Unionism, at least until the last few years before the First World War, was a struggle for income *within* the capitalist system (under aggressive provocation from the capitalist side, as we shall see), not an attempt to overthrow it. The Labour Party, as the political arm of the trade unions (it did not admit individual members until 1918), was an extension of the working-class culture which, Stedman Jones argues, 'accepted not only capitalism, but monarchy, Empire, aristocracy and established religion as well', and looked only for social reform, not revolution.[110]

Yet it would be a mistake to suppose that class conflict was any less real because it took place within an accepted social framework, or seemed any less threatening to the rich and middle classes because it was not overtly revolutionary. As we have seen in Chapter 2, there were reasons other than revolution to fear the poor. The struggle for income, backed by organization and numbers, might lead via industrial action to a redistribution of the product of industry in favour of the workers. Hence the employers' counterattack on the New Unionism and their resistance not only to strikes and the means of waging them (the legality of picketing and the invulnerability of union funds) but to the recognition of trade unions at the bargaining table. It might equally lead via political pressure to a redistribution of income through taxation of the rich and middle classes to pay for social reform or, still worse, to a redistribution of property through municipal socialism, confiscatory land taxes, or nationalization of land, mines, railways, and other sources of capitalist wealth. The reaction to these threats, the defence of property and the counter-attack on the unions, will be dealt with in the next chapter. A more insidious threat, as we have already seen, was that of national and imperial decline, brought on by the 'fear of the poor', as urbanization, poverty and the differential birth rate made the working class appear to be outbreeding their healthier and supposedly more moral and intelligent 'betters' and lowering the economic and military efficiency of the country. The reaction to the fear of the poor, in the shape of a demand for national efficiency and for ameliorative social welfare, will also be dealt with in Chapter 4.

For the present, the importance of these threats and fears is that they stimulated an enormous interest in what the working classes were and how they lived. From Andrews Mearns's *The Bitter Cry of Outcast London* (1883) and William Booth's *In Darkest England* (1890) through to the surveys of Charles Booth, Rowntree, and Bowley and Burnett-Hurst, from the Royal Commission on the Housing of the Working Classes (1884–85) to the Committee on Physical Deterioration (1903–04), the Board of Trade inquiry into the Cost of Living of the Working Classes in Large Towns (1905), the Royal Commission on the Poor Laws and the Relief of Distress (1905–9), and the 1911 Census of Fertility of Marriage, there was a deep concern with working-class living conditions and their implications for the health and security of the higher classes.[111] A plethora of private investigations and impressionistic accounts, like R. Howe's *How the Working People Live* (1882), Helen Bosanquet's *The Standard of Life* (1898), Lady Florence Bell's *At the Works* (1911), and Mrs Pember Reeves's *Round About a Pound a Week* (1916), described working-class life from the outside, but (until the oral historians came in recent years to let the workers, or rather their children, speak for themselves), only a handful of sources, like Arthur Morrison's *A Child of the Jago* (1904) and Robert Tressell's novel *The Ragged Trousered Philanthropists* (c. 1911, but not published till 1926), described it from the inside, from the working-class point of view. Fortunately, since the Second World War both the oral historians, led by Paul Thompson, Thea Vigne, Raphael Samuel and Elizabeth Roberts, and memorialists like Flora Thompson, Stella Davies, Robert Roberts and Mabel Ashby have opened up a veritable treasure house of new knowledge not merely about how the working class lived but how it felt to live that way.[112]

What such sources show is that the working classes lived not so much 'a life apart', to quote the evocative title used by a sensitive American, Standish Meacham, as a whole series of different *lives* apart.[113] As Robert Roberts remembers it in early twentieth-century Salford,

No view of the English working class in the first quarter of this century would be accurate if that class were shown merely as a great amalgam of artisan and labouring classes united by a common aim and culture. Life in reality was much more complex.... Inside the working class as a whole there existed, I believe, a stratified form of society whose implications and consequences have hardly been fully explored.[114]

Their world was not only segregated from that of the rich and the middle classes, it was broken up into thousands of tiny communities. In the still pre-industrial countryside, this was known and expected, given the lack of time and the cost of travel. To the rural labourers who lived in Flora Thompson's hamlet Lark Rise, little Candleford nine miles away was a great town, and Oxford twenty miles distant was a fabulous city to be seen once in a lifetime. But at the other end of the scale of urbanization the same, surprisingly, was true. Even the greatest city, from the working-class point of view, was a collection of little 'villages' in each of which everyone knew everyone else, and knew very little beyond it. Robert Roberts's 'village' in Salford, the 'classic slum', was a gridiron of some thirty streets of terraced houses bounded by two railway lines and two main roads, whose inhabitants rarely went to the twin cities' centre in neighbouring Manchester, a little over a mile away.[115] Sometimes we ought to speak of urban hamlets rather than villages, since there were differences of status between single streets or between two ends of the same street, like that between the City clerks of Frederick Willis's Burdock Road and their working-class neighbours.[116] Segregation was as strong *within* the working class as between them and those deemed to be above. In some streets, 'Every house possesses a bow-window, and every curtained bow-window a palm, and every palm emerges from the centre of a china pot. Each door glistens with varnish, at any rate for a time, and boasts an immaculate letter-box surmounted by an immaculate brass knocker.' Not far away there might be courts and alleys with earth closets and ash pits where 'very often the flags were broken and loose, and ... the clothes became bespattered with sludge' from the housewives who threw out their 'fluid refuse onto the yard floor'. In between there would be every graduation of prosperity and status: in Poplar, 'East India Road was very nice. Commercial Road began to get poor and then further along got more Jeweyfied. [West India Dock Road] got the rough part – the Chinese and all that.'[117] But it was not only in the cosmopolitan cities that the working class practised segregation. In the salubrious seaside resort of Hastings in Robert Tressell's novel, the residents were as status-conscious and hierarchical as those of Kathleen Chorley's Alderley Edge:

> Lord Street ... like most other similar neighbourhoods, supplied a striking answer to those futile theorists who prate about the equality of mankind, for the inhabitants instinctively formed themselves into groups, the more superior types drawing together, separating themselves from the inferior, and rising naturally to the top while the others gathered themselves into distinct classes, grading downwards, or else isolated themselves altogether; being refused admission to the circles they desired to enter, and in their turn refusing to associate with their inferiors.[118]

Even in the countryside, where the old feudal relationship between farmer and labourer had not completely disappeared, according to Rowntree and Kendall in their interviews of 1913, 'the conflict of interests is becoming more acute, and this is one of the causes underlying the labourer's discontent' and his flight to the town. As one old farmer put it, 'I used to take an interest in my men; but now I don't seem to care a snap about them, and I don't think they care a snap about me.'[119]

In the towns segregation was based partly, but only partly, on the economic distinctions between the skilled craftsmen, the skilled and semi-skilled factory workers, and the unskilled labourers. These counted a great deal, since the skilled worker might be paid from 50 to 100 per cent more than a labourer (25s.–40s. as against 15s.–20s.), which would put some craftsmen on equal terms with clerks and school teachers if not better, and they could afford to live, to the clerks' chagrin, in the same kind of houses. It was also a matter of status on the job:

> The craftsman always held himself aloof – sort of a little bit above the labourer. The labourer ... can only do what he's told, but the craftsman, well he's responsible for it's being turned out.... They looked up to you as somebody responsible ... they knew you had full authority.[120]

The craftsmen were more regularly employed, better fed and

clothed, and often physically larger, as John Burns noticed in 1890 of the old craft unionists at the TUC as compared with the delegates of the unskilled 'New Unionism', though he put it down to the increasing tempo of the work:

> Physically, the 'old' unionists were much bigger than the 'new'. And that no doubt is due to the greater intensity of toil during the last twenty or thirty years ... [T]he 'old' delegates differed from the new not only physically but in dress. A great number of them looked like respectable city gentlemen; wore very good coats, large watch chains and high hats – and in many cases were of such splendid build and proportions that they presented an alderman's, not to say a magisterial dignity. Amongst the new delegates not a single one wore a tall hat. They looked workmen. They were workmen.[121]

A skilled workman's average wage of 30s. a week (allowing for slack times and unemployment), according to Arthur Morrison in the *Cornhill Magazine* in 1901, would support a wife and three children living in three rooms in a humble though decent neighbourhood in London within walking distance of his work. Most of this labour aristocrat's wage went on food (12s 7½d.), clothes (2s.), and club and insurance (1s.), leaving less than 4s. for all other expenditure on pleasure and contingencies, including beer and tobacco, newspapers, travel, children's toys, education, etc.[122] Most workers were not so fortunate and had to live, often including the wife's and children's earnings, on 'round about a pound a week', in Mrs Pember Reeves's poignant phrase. In her report on the Fabian Women's Group's study of the 'ultra-respectable' families of unskilled and semi-skilled workers living in Lambeth on 18s.–30s. a week between 1909 and 1913, she shows that after paying rent, burial insurance, heating and lighting, and cleaning materials, families with two children usually (when the man was in full work) had sums from under 6s. to slightly over 10s. a week, often 3d. a day or less per head, to spend on food, much less than was allowed in the workhouse, and almost nothing except cast-offs for clothing and footwear. Their diet was a monotonous one of bread and margarine, with tiny quantities of meat, bacon or fish, mainly as a 'relish' for the father and breadwinner. Contrary to popular opinion, the men scarcely drank, smoked very little, and gave up their whole wages except for 2s.-3s. a week, out of which they often had to pay for their dinners, club or union dues, and sometimes tram fares. The LCC teachers of domestic science could not instruct girls on how to bring up a family of six on less than 28s. a week, and Mrs Reeves challenged the critics of the 'improvident poor' to show how 'providence' could stretch a pound a week to provide an adequate standard of living without a legal minimum wage or the state child's allowance which her Fabian group advocated.[123]

The farm labourers of Rowntree and Kendall's 1913 survey had to live on even less, from 10s.-18s. a week in Oxfordshire to 15s.-22s. in Yorkshire, plus occasional vegetables or milk, and in a few cases a cottage or garden worth 2s. a week. Those who had free or rented gardens to provide potatoes and green vegetables lived as well, or as badly, as the Lambeth labourers, and their children were certainly healthier. But they were all underfed, with an average protein deficiency of 24 per cent (ranging from 19 per cent for those with family earnings over 20s. to 35 per cent for those with less than 15s.) and even an average 10 per cent deficiency in calories (ranging from 5 to 42 per cent). 'On average the forty-two families investigated are receiving not much more than three-fourths of the nourishment necessary for the maintenance of physical health.'[124] And this was at the end of a generation of rising real wages for labourers and for farm labourers in particular.

It was not only a matter of income, occupational status and appearance, however. The most important distinction within the working class was that between the 'respectable' and the 'roughs'. This was not a horizontal division between the affluent and the poor; it was a diagonal frontier running right through the working class from top to bottom but taking in more at the top and progressively fewer towards the bottom. To some extent it coincided with the division between the chapel- and churchgoing (chapel for the urban working class was usually superior to church, which was for the more abject, dependent poor, and the Catholic Irish were automatically classed as rough), but this distinction was beginning to wear thin as religious attendance declined, though the children of the respectable were still sent to Sunday school. A craftsman or well-paid coalminer who drank to excess would soon place himself and his family amongst the roughs, since his spending would reduce the rent and nourishment his wife and children could afford. A labourer who abstained from alcohol, especially if his wife and children worked, might raise himself by his bootstraps to respectability, but it demanded character and willpower. As a Keighley labourer said, 'It takes something to be poor and respectable.'[125]

Most of all it depended on the character and skill of the housewife. If she was a 'manager' who could keep the house clean and tidy and cook nourishing dishes from a few bones and vegetables (and many of them could, as Elizabeth Roberts has shown)[126] and also a disciplinarian who prevented her children from playing with the 'roughs' around the corner (as one daughter put it, 'I think it's the way we were brought up.... We never got in with the rough people'; 'If I saw them outside I always spoke to them, just to say hello.... But I never went down into the street and had any connection with them'), then the family could 'keep themselves to themselves' and maintain their respectability.[127] The children of the 'roughs', on the other hand, would play on the street, mix with anybody, and sometimes terrorize the neighbourhood, for gang life and gang warfare (not always so savage as its sounds) were for many of the boys the only substitute for the supportive family life they sorely missed – though even 'rough' parents might fight over children or threaten revenge on teachers who were too ready with the cane.[128]

There were important differences between regions and between individual towns in the same region. In coalmining and other areas of heavy industry with high wages for men but little work for women, the prosperity and respectability of the family would depend not only on the sobriety of the breadwinner and the housekeeping skill of his wife but on the number of children which such patriarchal cultures tended to produce, and whether the children were still dependent or had begun to contribute to the family budget. In the textile, pottery, and other areas with much employment for women where, either by the market mechanism or simply through the employers' opportunism, men's wages tended to be too low to support a family, the family's happiness might depend more on the wife's health, the willingness of the husband to share the chores, and the availability of childminding relatives or neighbours. But as Elizabeth Roberts shows for high-wage steel-making and shipbuilding Barrow, low-wage linoleum-making Lancaster, and medium-wage cotton and engineering Preston, all in north Lancashire, you could find every kind of family pattern and household management in all three, but with more domestic and culinary skill and more home-centred family life than the working class were often given credit for. One of her Preston respondents sums it up neatly:

> My mother, their life, well they had no life. It must have been a terrible life. It was all work. It was really drudgery. But they enjoyed it. It was their family and they lived for their families. It wasn't drudgery to them.[129]

Given their fragmentation and narrow communal horizons at the zenith of class society, how, then, did it come about that the working class 'remade itself' in the institutional sense of creating afresh, or on a larger scale, class-wide institutions, such as friendly societies, working men's clubs, the co-operative trading movement, the burgeoning trade union movement and the infant political labour movement, through which to express their class-consciousness and defend their threatened interests? For the 'fear of the poor' on the part of the rich and the middle classes was returned with interest by the working class, and with good reason. For what to the employing class was merely the legitimate defence of wealth and privilege often appeared to the working class a fight for a living wage and survival.

The answer, paradoxically, is that the class-wide institutions grew directly out of the fragmented community experience of the working class. It was the local branch of the friendly society, the Oddfellows or the Ancient Foresters, the local co-op store and the quarterly meeting of its society, the local working men's club, affiliated as it was to the national Club and Institute Union, the local shop-floor trade union, and in due course the local ILP or constituency Labour Party, that drew their support and commanded their loyalty. The number of working men active in such institutions was small, the number of women even smaller, but the numbers who looked to them as the first line of defence of their 'defensive culture' and their standard of life were immense, and the loyalty they could command in a crisis, if sometimes only briefly, was fierce and tenacious.

We must be careful, with our intellectual predilections for tidy institutional history, not to take a 'top-down' view of how things happened in the working class, and try to see instead how they saw it themselves. Until they were overtaken by the trade unions during the First World War, the friendly societies were much the most numerous and well-supported working-class institutions, with a total membership approaching 4 million as early as 1872; but most were merely burial or sick clubs which, though they became crucial for survival in the crises of life, loomed in normal times no larger than the collector's weekly knock at the door for his few pence.[130] The co-operative movement was one of the great success stories of the Victorian working class, with a membership (which meant families, not individuals) rising from 350,000 in 1873 to 1,169,000 in 1893 and to 2,878,000 in 1913, and through the two wholesale societies, with its own factories, ships, overseas depots, and tea estates.[131] To most working-class wives, however, it simply meant the local store where you could buy sound, reliable goods and save money from the 'divi' at the same time, but was out of reach of the very poor because it would not give credit.

The working men's club, belonging to a national movement founded by the temperance reformer the Rev. Henry Solly in 1862 with about 900 clubs and 321,000 members by 1903, was a place, more 'your own' than the pub, where you would drink cheap, wholesome beer, play a game of cards or billiards, take your wife to hear a professional singer or comedian and, if you were really serious, listen to the occasional outside speaker.[132] A national crisis like the Boer War might produce good audiences but the clubs, once revered by Gladstone and Bradlaugh, were by then generally non-political or apathetic. Most clubs gave a hearing impartially to pro-war and pro-Boer speakers, but refused to take sides. Their striking feature was an absence of jingoism. One middle-class observer from Toynbee Hall complained in 1908 that 'certain words which had always seemed to him signified clear and worthy ideas, such as honour, patriotism, justice, either form no part of the working-man's vocabulary or are grossly and malignantly perverted from their true sense'; the mere mention of the British empire 'excites laughter as a subject to which no sincere man would dream of alluding.'[133] There were of course some Radical and Tory working men's clubs which took sides on the Boer War and imperialism as they did on other political issues, but these were for those small committed minorities who took politics seriously. Only on occasions of great national excitement, like Mafeking night or the relief of Ladysmith, did working-class jingoism break surface, and then it was an opportunity for a 'bang-up' binge of drinking and roistering as well as genuine joy at the saving of 'our boys'. Similar if somewhat more political attitudes permeated the trades councils, the 'local TUCs' of the trade union movement. Here there was great readiness to condemn the Boer War in general, but great resistance to condemning the British working-class soldier for 'the brutalities now being perpetrated in South Africa'.[134] The war, like most foreign policy issues, was a matter for 'them', the propertied and governing classes whose interests were involved; it came home to the working class when it was 'us', 'our boys', our relatives and neighbours who were being killed or, with great rejoicing, saved. The rejoicing was always greater for reliefs, retreats out of danger, or the ending of wars than for 'famous victories'. When it came to a *real* war, of course, as distinct from a colonial one far from home, working men volunteered as readily as their 'superiors', as they did in 1914.

In the same way, the great resurgence and expansion of trade unionism in this period, rising from under 759,000 members in 1888 to 1.6 million in 1892, 2 million in 1900, 2.5 million in 1910, and 4.1 million by 1914,[135] is best seen not only as a movement from below, amongst the unorganized unskilled workers (which it was only in part), but as a series of local confrontations beginning in the workplace itself, which only then led to wider organization. To take the three classic strikes which inaugurated the New Unionism in 1888-9, the London match girls, the gas stokers, and the dockers were all previously unorganized workers reacting spontaneously to intolerable conditions and wages in particular places, the Bryant and May factory in the East End, the Beckton Gasworks in East Ham, and the South West India Docks.[136] It was only when they realized they needed organizational help that they called in Annie Besant and the Fabians to form the match workers' union, Eleanor Marx, John Burns, Tom Mann and Ben Tillett of the ILP to establish the gasworkers' union, and Burns, Tillet and Mann again to organize the Dockers' Union and its street demonstrations. It is also significant that, when the excitement died down and either quiet returned to the workplace or was imposed by the employers weeding out the ringleaders, the new unskilled unions declined and very nearly, though not quite, disappeared.[137]

That the New Unionism survived and went on expanding was

due in part to the stimulus it gave to union membership in the more traditional areas of skilled craft and factory work; but it was provoked still more by the struggle for control of the work process in the workplace itself which marked industrial relations in the 1890s and 1900s.[138] The tradition amongst craftsmen and most factory workers was that they rather than the employer controlled the pace of production and, to a surprising extent, the way in which the work was done. During this period the employers tried to reimpose their control of the workplace and the work process. This was in part a reaction to what they saw as the 'insubordinate' challenge of the new or more aggressive unions, but far more important was the introduction of new machinery, new methods and new techniques of control, which speeded up the work and tried to take direct control back into the hands of management. The new machinery included, for example, new automatic gas-stoking equipment ('iron men') which did not allow the men time for rest, capstan lathes and other simplified machine tools which could be operated by less skilled engineers, new 'closing' machines in the boot and shoe industry which replaced hand workers, new printing machines which threatened the hand pressmen, new and more complex railway signalling equipment, pneumatic ship rivetting machines, and so on. The new methods included new systems of payment, piecework and output bonuses, which increased the pressure on the workers, and the new techniques of control, the time clock, supervised team work, and the beginnings of time and motion study and 'scientific management' which came to be called, after its American exponent F. W. Taylor, 'Taylorism'.[139] The 'employers' offensive' was, for obvious reasons, associated with an intensified attack on the unions, a refusal of recognition wherever possible, and a series of challenges in the law courts to established trade union rights and immunities, such as picketing and freedom from actions for restraint of trade.[140] To the employer's point of view we must return in the next chapter, in the section on the defence of property. For the moment, from the worker's point of view it looked like an attempt to wrest control of the work process for the purpose of screwing more work out of him for less pay.

Thus the industrial unrest and confrontational relations from 1889 onwards came down at the bottom to a struggle for power in the workplace. This was true of the gas stokers' strike of 1889, the unrest on the railways, and, most famous of all, the 1897–98 lock-out in the engineering industry to impose dilution by unapprenticed machine operators. It must be said that not all employers thought the new trends good in themselves or worth the cost of imposing them. Some opposed Taylorism as not worth the bad feelings, low morale and, perhaps, lost output which it provoked.[141] Many engineering employers, for example, came to value their apprentice-trained engineers and co-operated with them in supervising unskilled 'dilutees' in exchange for maintaining their higher level of wages.[142] But enough employers rushed into the fight, using blacklegs and 'free labour', to protect what they saw as the right of capital to exercise control over its property, the machinery and materials, to upset the traditional balance between craft control and employers' general oversight in the workplace. Even old craft unions like the engineers came to feel outraged and responded with militant aggression, which began in the local workplace and escalated into national disputes.

In the same way, such local guerrilla warfare led to the legal battles which finally forced the unions to accept the need for separate parliamentary representation for labour. The 'industrial offensive' in the courts, as John Saville has called it, was part of the defence of property to which we shall return. The series of actions brought by employers against unions or their members against picketing, 'intimidation', interference with contracts, and 'restraint of trade', nearly all had their origins in disputes over how the work should be carried on, with what materials, or by whom (unionists or non-unionists) – all of which the employers claimed as their prerogative. The most famous and damaging case of all, the Taff Vale judgment of 1901, grew out of an *unofficial* attempt by a group of railway workers in South Wales to improve conditions and obtain recognition of their union by the Taff Vale Railway Company.[143] It was the railway company's actions which generalized the dispute. Its suit for damages and costs for loss of trade, finally awarded at £42,000 by the House of Lords, so threatened the funds of all unions engaging in strikes that the TUC finally determined to take seriously the need, already acknowledged by the establishment of the Labour Representation Committee in 1900, for trade union MPs in Parliament. No doubt there were committed unionists and working-class politicians like Keir Hardie and Ramsay MacDonald who had been pressing for this all along, but it was not until the TUC saw the employers' forensic offensive as a threat to their very existence that they did anything concrete about it.[144]

Thus, as Stedman Jones argued though from a different standpoint, the institutional remaking of the working class was indeed compatible with the apparently localized, isolated, fragmented culture of the working class. Their lives apart, however pleasure-oriented, conservative, occasionally jingoistic and apparently inward-looking – and reservations must be made about all these epithets – were also defensive, in the strict sense that they were not left alone to enjoy their few and simple pleasures and endure their numerous burdens and sorrows but were badgered by patronizing moralists, investigators and reformers, wooed by wheedling politicians, and bullied by masterful employers and their hired strike-breakers in the workplace and the law courts. Every such encounter with the representatives of their 'betters' was a personal confrontation with the class society. As Robert Roberts perceptively observed from the depths of the classic slum,

> the upper and middle classes, self-confident to arrogance, kept two modes of address for the poor: the first was a kindly *de haut en bas* form in which each word, of usually one syllable, was clearly enunciated; the second had a loud, self-assured, hectoring note. Both seemed devised to ensure that, though the hearer might be stupid, he would know enough in general to bow at once to breeding and authority.... It was a tactic, conscious or not, that confused and 'overfaced' the simple and drove intelligent men and women in the working class to fury.[145]

Those two voices belonged not only to those obvious class antagonists, the factory manager, the Poor Law relieving officer and the magistrate, but even to the workers' self-styled friends, philanthropists like Charles Loch or Helen Bosanquet and socialists like H. M. Hyndman and Beatrice Webb.

Far from accepting (like the Labour Party, according to Stedman Jones) 'not only capitalism, but monarchy, Empire, aristocracy and established religion as well',[146] the working class had from their defensive and segregated culture learned how to react, to laugh irreverently at empire and the aristocracy, to vote with their feet against established religion, to reduce monarchy to mere sentiment for high days and holidays, and to fear and distrust capitalism to the point of challenging it head-on. They did so in enormous waves of national strikes rising to a crescendo in 1910–14, and by establishing a political labour movement which gave notice that the trade unions would either have to be taken into partnership with industry and government or would hold in reserve the vague but menacing threat of a national industrial crisis. The class-ridden society of Edwardian England was becoming less and less acceptable to a large part of the working class. One symptom was the rise of the Labour Party, especially in the localities, where it scored more victories than at Westminster; another was the resentment at the Poor Law and its callousness towards the old, the sick and the unemployed; and a third was the great wave of industrial unrest that rose to a crescendo in the last few years before the First World War. This last was the start of the crisis of class society that marked the years on either side of the war. To that crisis we must turn in Chapter 5.

First, however, we must note that there was another party to the social contract besides the property owners and the manual workers. The non-capitalist, professional middle class, patronizingly conscious of their own moral superiority to both sides, had ideas of their own about how society should be run, its benefits allocated, its disputes settled and its problems solved, and they were already beginning to bring them to bear at the very zenith of class society.

Chapter 4

CLASS SOCIETY AND THE PROFESSIONAL IDEAL

Class society in Britain, at its zenith between 1880 and 1914, already contained the seeds of its own decay. These took the form of the values and beliefs of the professional social ideal, which were beginning to infiltrate and change from within the moral outlook of the three major classes. Those classes, too, possessed their own powerful ideals of what society should be and how it should be organized to recognize and reward their own unique contribution to the welfare of the community. Each class believed that its contribution was the most vital one, and should be rewarded accordingly. The landowners and the capitalists saw themselves as providing the resources and the organizing ability which drove the economic system to provide the goods necessary both for survival and for a civilized life for the whole community. Those in the working class who thought about it saw themselves as providing the labour, the sole source of value, without which the resources and their management would be in vain. The increasing class conflict of the late Victorian and Edwardian period was the struggle for income, status and power arising out of this clash of incompatible ideals. Into this tripartite conflict came a maverick fourth class, which contributed both to the struggle and to the means of resolving it.

1 THE PROFESSIONAL SOCIAL IDEAL

This fourth class was less directly related to the struggle for a share of material production, and depended on persuading the other classes to voluntarily part with a surplus to pay for the vital, non-material services which they claimed to provide. While all

FOURTH CLASS

classes try to justify themselves by their own concept of distributive justice, the professional class can only exist by persuading the rest of society to accept a distributive justice which recognizes and rewards expert service based on selection by merit and long, arduous training. Professional people, rightly or wrongly, see themselves as above the main economic battle, at once privileged observers and benevolent neutrals since, whichever side wins, they believe that their services will still be necessary and properly rewarded. In this they may well be mistaken for, as was argued in Chapter 1, they are just as dependent on their bargaining power in the societal market for people as the richest capitalist or the most unskilled labourer. The difference with the professional is that, offering a service that is, as we have seen, esoteric, evanescent and fiduciary – beyond the layman's knowledge or judgment, impossible to pin down or fault even when it fails, and which must therefore be taken on trust – he is dependent on persuading the client to accept his valuation of the service rather than allowing it to find its own value in the marketplace. His interest, therefore, is to persuade society to set aside a secure income, or a monopolistic level of fees, to enable him to perform the service rather than jeopardize it by subjecting it to the rigours of capitalist competition in the conventional free market. It is the success of such persuasion which raises him (*when* he succeeds) above the economic battle, and gives him a stake in creating a society which plays down class conflict (in the long if not in the short term) and plays up mutual service and responsibility and the efficient use of human resources.

As long as professional men were comparatively few and depended mainly on the rich and powerful for their incomes, they tended to temper their social ideal to the values of their wealthy clients, as some of them still do. With the coming of industrial society, however, the professions proliferated, their clients multiplied and, in certain cases, for example in preventive medicine, sanitary engineering, and central and local government generally, the client became in effect the whole community. They became much freer to act as critics of society, apologists for the emerging classes of the new industrial system, and purveyors of the terminology in which people came to think about the new class society. It was this mediation of the terms and concepts in which people thought about society which gave the 'forgotten middle class' – forgotten because they left themselves out of their largely tripartite analyses of the class system – their special role in the emergence of class.

As was argued in the earlier book, professional men were the theorists, apologists and propagandists for the three major classes of the new industrial society.[1] Professors Malthus of the East India College at Marlowe and John Wilson ('Christopher North'), editor of *Blackwood's Edinburgh Magazine*, and professional authors such as Coleridge, Southey, Sir Walter Scott and Disraeli revived the moribund aristocratic ideal of paternalism and social responsibilities of property. Professor Adam Smith and public officials James Mill, J. R. McCulloch, Nassau Senior and Edwin Chadwick, among others, armed the new capitalist class with arguments against idle wealth (instead of active capital) and patronage, which they labelled 'Old Corruption' (instead of competition and selection by merit, as determined by the market or by competitive examination). And Charles Hall, medical doctor, Thomas Hodgskin, professional lecturer, Richard Carlile, radical journalist, and Bronterre O'Brien, Chartist lawyer, turned Locke's political philosophy and Ricardo's political economy, both based on the labour theory of value, upside down to forge 'the right to the whole produce of labour' which underlay the working-class ideal of co-operative labour.[2]

Yet although they 'forgot themselves' as a class, nearly all of them as individual analysts of society reserved a special place for their kind as the guides and mentors, the Platonic guardians of society: Shelley's poets as 'unacknowledged legislators of the world', Coleridge's 'clerisy' of secular intellectuals leavening every area of society, Carlyle's 'ancient guides of nations' now becoming the new 'aristocracy of talent', James Mill's 'middle rank exempt from labour, ... the chief source of all that has exalted and refined human nature', Hodgskin's 'mental labourers, *literati*, men of science' who were innocent of the charge of exploiting the manual labourer, John Stuart Mill's 'learned class' who ought to be endowed by the community for the sake of scientific discovery and speculative knowledge, and so on.[3]

Only occasionally did a professional man recognize the separate existence of his own class, and then only to emphasize its ineffable superiority. Matthew Arnold, who in 1869 divided society into the usual three classes, the barbarians, the philistines and the populace, only to criticize them for their anarchy and lack of culture, had distinguished the previous year (as we saw in Chapter 3) between 'the professional class, brought up on the first plane, with fine and governing qualities' and the 'immense business class, brought up on the second plane, cut off from the aristocracy and the professions, and without governing qualities.'[4] He was speaking before the Taunton Commission on the Endowed Schools, part of that great reform movement that, through men like his father, Thomas Arnold, at Rugby and Oxford, was in the process of converting the public schools and the ancient universities, the 'first plane' of education, into institutions designed to inculcate professional ideals and values into the sons of the aristocracy and gentry and, increasingly but not enough for the reformers, those of the business middle class

The supposedly pre-industrial, aristocratic, anti-industrial attitudes propagated by the public schools and Oxbridge, which some historians, like Martin Wiener, have blamed for the decline of the industrial spirit in England, were in fact the newly emergent social values of the reforming schoolmasters and dons whose disdain for industry and trade stemmed from their conviction that professional service was in every way superior both to endowed idleness and to what they regarded as 'money grabbing'.[5] The English landed class has never scorned profit making, whether in agriculture, mining urban development, transport undertakings such as roads, canals, railways and docks, or even in cotton mills, ironworks or brick fields whenever they could make them pay, and without their economic opportunism the Industrial Revolution could scarcely have begun when and where it did. Moreover, as we saw in Chapter 3, many of them, like the Dukes of Devonshire in Barrow steel-making and shipbuilding, the Dukes of Buckingham and Sutherland in railways, the Earl of Shrewsbury and the Hon. Charles Rolls, son of Lord Llangattock, in motor cars, not to mention the quarter of the peerage holding company directorships in 1896, were to continue to 'soil their hands' with commercial investment, whatever their public school masters and university tutors told them. It was the latter, not the aristocracy, who popularized anti-industrial values and held up the ideal of selfless public service in the professions and in government at home and in the empire, and it was the sons of the middle class, both professional and business men, who most fully imbibed these values from them. Tom Brown in Thomas Hughes's novel (1857) was upbraided by his Rugby tutor:

> You talk of 'working to get your living' and 'doing some real good in the world' in the same breath. Now you may be getting a good living in a profession, and yet not doing any good at all in the world.... Keep the latter before you as a holy object, and you will be right, whether you make a living or not; but if you dwell on the other, you'll very likely drop into mere money making.[6]

The Taunton Commission in 1868 defended the exclusive teaching of classics and mathematics, rather than more immediately useful sciences and modern languages, on the grounds of the high value assigned them in English society. The professional men and poorer gentry

> have nothing to look to but education to keep their sons on a high social level. And they would not wish to have what might be more readily converted into money, if in any degree it tended to let their children sink in the social scale.[7]

And the Clarendon Commission extolled the top nine public schools and their imitators for taking 'men of all the various classes that make up English society, destined for every profession and career' and moulding them in 'the character of English gentlemen'.[8]

Beginning in the early Victorian age through their reformation of the public schools and universities, members of the professional class deliberately set out to impose their own social ideal (which at that stage they assumed to be a national and cultural, not a class ideal) upon the sons both of the landed class and, in so far as they could reach them, of the business class as well. Their method was to start from the existing ideals of those classes, the concept of the English gentleman and the gospel of work, and to transform them into variants of their own professional ideal. Both concepts had undergone a sea change during the Industrial Revolution, that of the gentleman from the chivalrous aristocrat touchy about his honour and prepared to defend it in a duel, to the 'gentleness' of Samuel Smile's 'true gentleman', 'honest, truthful, upright, polite, temperate, courageous, self-respecting, and self-helping'.[9] Work, from being the curse of Adam to be shunned by the aristocratic leisured gentleman, had become a gospel and replaced the cult of leisure as the main justification of wealth, power and success in life, so that landed politicians like Gladstone and the Earl of Derby never stopped working, either at politics, writing or tending their estates. As Professor Alfred Marshall expressed it, 'every man, however wealthy he may be, if he be in health and a true man, does work and work hard.'[10] Both concepts had been transformed from aristocratic into middle-class concepts, and ones which sat easily with both middle classes, the professional and the business class. But from then onwards, especially in the reformed public schools and universities which formed the next generation of hard-working gentlemen, the professional and entrepreneurial ideals began to diverge. The gentleman came to be defined by his 'fine and governing qualities', his cultured education, intellectual interests and qualities of character, which rose above mere money making, while the work permissible to him was narrowed down to professional or public service to society, the state or the empire, to the exclusion of 'money-grabbing' industry and trade.

This divergence between the professional and entrepreneurial ideals within the upper- and middle-class education system found reverberations in the outside world, particularly in relation to public policy and social reform. The principles of competition, individualism and *laissez-faire*, which for the capitalist class and the early classical economists had achieved the status of laws of nature as inexorable as the law of gravity, came progressively to be questioned by professional social thinkers, civil servants and even by economists, and their restrictions and reservations found their way into legislation, over the protests of the business class. The Factory and Mines Acts from the 1830s and 1840s, the public health legislation from 1848 onwards, the Food and Drugs Adulteration and Alkali (anti-pollution) Acts of the 1860s, and the state's increasing support of education culminating in the 1870 Act, can be seen as one long campaign orchestrated by (though not confined to) the professional class against the vested interests of the propertied classes. On the radical, utilitarian side the change was symbolized by the conversion of the greatest of the Benthamite civil servants, Edwin Chadwick, to the view that *'laissez faire means letting mischief work and evils go on that do not affect ourselves'*, and by the transition in John Stuart Mill, Bentham's godson, from Benthamite individualism to Benthamite collectivism. While continuing in successive editions of *The Principles of Political Economy* to say that 'letting alone should be the general principle', he added in later ones that 'there is scarcely anything, really important to the general interest, which it may not be desirable, or even necessary, that the government should take on by itself'. He ended by claiming in his *Autobiography* (1873) that he and his wife, Harriet Taylor, had long been 'socialists'.

> While we repudiated with the greatest energy that tyranny of society over the individual which most Socialistic systems are supposed to involve, we yet look forward to a time when society will no longer be divided into the idle and the industrious; when the rule that they who do not work shall not eat, will be applied not to paupers only, but impartially to all; when the division of the produce of labour, instead of depending, as in so great a degree it now does, on the accident of birth, will be made by concert on an accepted principle of justice, and when it will no longer either be, or be thought to be, impossible for human beings to exert themselves strenuously in procuring benefits which are not exclusively their own, but to be shared with the society they belong to.[11]

Nor was the professional critique of competition and industrialism confined to the radical utilitarian wing. It was just as pronounced on the conservative idealist wing, where Coleridge's 'greatest producible sum of happiness of all men' played the same transitional role as Bentham's 'greatest happiness of the greatest number'. Carlyle, the Christian Socialists and Ruskin all attacked 'the Mammon gospel' of making money.[12] Ruskin specifically demanded that the merchant or manufacturer should have a function similar to that of the liberal professions, to 'provide for the nation':

> It is no more his function to get profit for himself out of that provision than it is a clergyman's function to get his stipend. This stipend is a necessary adjunct, but not the object of his life, if he be a true clergyman, any more than his fee (or honorarium) is the object of life to a true physician.[13]

That both the utilitarian and idealist streams of professional criticism of industrial society could converge in the socialism of the Fabians, whom Beatrice Webb recognized as spiritual descendants of Bentham and Mill, in the Christian Socialism of Stewart Headlam, and even in the Marxism of William Morris, Ruskin's most prominent disciple, the leading passion of whose life was a 'hatred of modern civilization', is no accident but a logical extension of the professional critique to the abolition of capitalist society altogether.[14]

In all its manifestations, liberal, conservative or socialist, the professional social ideal consistently applied the tests of justification by service to society and, in one form or another, of the greatest happiness of the greatest number, to the analysis and criticism of contemporary society. Down to about 1880, however, such criticisms were a disconnected series of individual correctives to the excessive materialism of the capitalist system while in no way threatening its continued existence. From the 1880s by contrast, concomitantly with the accelerated growth of professional occupations of all kinds, it began to take shape in a form that appeared to many landowners and business men to be an organized threat to the rights if not indeed to the security of private property and to the foundations of capitalist society.

2 PROFESSIONALISM AND PROPERTY

Between 1880 and 1914 the professional social ideal took a further step, from *ad hoc* criticism of capitalist society to a series of organized assaults on the concept of absolute property. Most professional men were not opposed to private property as such. On the contrary, the great majority not only accepted its existence but looked to their own expert service as in itself a property right which would in turn yield income and material property for themselves. What they were opposed to was functionless, irresponsible property, not justified by some kind of service to society. This belief in what we shall call contingent as opposed to absolute property, that is, in property rights contingent upon the performance of some justifying service, was held by thinking members of the professional class right across the whole political gamut, from the most extreme *laissez-faire* individualists to the most extreme collectivists.

At one end of the spectrum, C. S. Loch, Bernard and Helen Bosanquet, Octavia Hill and the Charity Organization Society,

who were so wedded to the individualism of the free labour market
that they proposed to revive the undiluted principles of the 1834
Poor Law and the deterrent workhouse for the undeserving poor,
those they preferred to call the 'helpless cases', stood nevertheless
for a revival in the city slums of the traditional paternalism of the
country squire. Beatrice Webb, who had begun her career in social
work as a paternalist rent collector for Octavia Hill, observed of
the COS that although 'in their opinion, modern capitalism was
the best of all possible ways of organizing industries and services,
. . . yet these devoted men and women, unlike the mass of property
owners, were yearning to spend their lives in the service of the
poor'. She praised

> the three principles upon which this organization was
> avowedly based: patient and persistent service on the part of
> the well-to-do; an acceptance of personal responsibility for the
> ulterior consequences . . . of charitable assistance; and finally,
> as the only way of carrying out this service and fulfilling the
> responsibility, the application of the scientific method to each
> separate case of a damaged body or a lost soul; so that the
> assistance given should be based on a correct forecast of what
> would actually happen, as a result of the gift, to the character
> and circumstances of the individual recipient and to the
> destitute class to which he belonged.[15]

In other words, the COS combined the paternal responsibility of
property with the professional treatment of poverty, which was to
lead on, despite their dislike of state intervention, to the
development of the professional, and eventually state-employed,
social worker.[16]

Many members of the COS and their associates in the new
university settlements of the 1880s, notably Canon Samuel Barnett,
founder of Toynbee Hall, and Arnold Toynbee himself, were
products of the reformed universities of Oxford and Cambridge,
where the professional ideal was being developed in a more
systematic, theoretical manner. At Balliol College, Oxford, from
which so many of the young residents of Toynbee Hall came, the
most influential figure was a new type of don, secular, career-
oriented, married and, and in close contact with the world outside
the ivory tower. Thomas Hill Green, the idealist philosopher, was
the first member of the university to be elected to the Oxford

CLASS SOCIETY AND THE PROFESSIONAL IDEAL

borough council. Green, who died in 1882 at the early age of 46, had an immense influence on generations of young men down to the First World War who, though ranging from extreme conservatives to advanced liberals and from high churchmen to outright atheists, nevertheless carried over his ideas into the COS, the New Liberalism, the social thinking of the church, and even, with Hobhouse and Hobson, into the Fabian Society.[17]

Green was a philosopher with a deep belief, derived from Kant and Hegel, in property as the necessary condition for the individual to realize himself and develop his individual character. For Kant, property was not, as it was for Locke, a natural right of acquisition prior to the existence of the state; it was the foundation of civil society. For Hegel it was a necessary creation of the state, since only through property and the state could the individual achieve free will and rationality. 'In his property a person exists for the first time as reason.'[18] Green's concern as a philosopher of rights was how to reconcile the conflicting claims of different citizens, particularly the claims of those with and without property. In this he belonged to the tradition of English idealism deriving from Coleridge, conduit of German philosophy, who argued against the factory owners opposed to the elder Peel's bill to protect child factory workers in 1818: 'The principle of all constitutional law is to make the claims of each as much as possible compatible with the claims of all, as individuals, and out of this adjustment the claims of the individual first become *Rights*.'[19] For Green there was no absolute freedom to do whatever one liked with one's property regardless of the harm to others. Rights were to be measured as means to a single end, the common good:

> That end is what I call freedom in the positive sense; in other words, the liberation of the powers of all men equally for contributions to a common good. No one has a right to do what he will with his own in such a way as to contravene this end. It is only through the guarantee which society gives him that he has any property at all, or, strictly speaking, any right to his possessions. This guarantee is founded on a sense of common interest.[20]

This did not mean that Green was an out-and-out state interventionist or, as some have claimed, the father of the welfare state. His notion of the state's intervention was strictly limited to correcting injustices perpetrated by property owners against the propertyless, such as child labour or the oppression of the Irish peasant:

> It is the business of the state, not indeed directly to promote moral goodness, for that, from the very nature of moral goodness, it cannot do, but to maintain the conditions without which a free exercise of the human faculties is impossible.[21]

But his considerable influence was all thrown on the side of the responsibilities of property rather than its rights, and of the duty of the community to override those rights when they conflicted with the needs of persons.

His disciples were of many political and religious persuasions, but they applied his notion of the limited rights of property in all their spheres of influence. Arnold Toynbee applied it to the Old Liberalism to justify the Irish Land Act of 1881 which overrode the rights of Irish landlords to evict Irish tenants in the name of freedom of contract, on the grounds:

> First, that where the individual rights conflict with the interests of the community, there the State ought to interfere; and, second, that where the people are unable to provide a thing for themselves, and that thing is of primary social importance, then again the State should interfere and provide it for them.[22]

The London Ethical Society was founded in 1886 by a group of Green's more rationalist or agnostic students working in and around Toynbee Hall, and came to include the Oxford idealists Edward Caird and William Wallace, the Cambridge utilitarians Henry Sidgwick, Leslie Stephen and Sir John Seeley, as well as the COS individualists C. S. Loch and Bernard Bosanquet, and the Fabians J. A. Hobson and Graham Wallas. They applied his teaching to the social problems of the day, which they regarded as moral problems concerning the duties of property.[23] The Christian Social Union, formed amongst Green's high church followers led by Charles Gore and Scott Holland after the publication in 1889 of *Lux Mundi: A Series of Studies in the Religion of the Incarnation*, applied it to the social teaching of the church. The CSU was founded, according to Bishop Gore, as 'a tardy act of repentance' by the Christian church in a situation in which 'a widespread rebellion of Labour was organizing itself against the economic slavery of the workers, and against a condition o[f ...] seemed to regard property as more sacrosanct than [...] as late as 1902, Herbert Samuel, a Balliol man an[d ...] Society for the Study of Social Ethics, was applyi[ng ...] Liberalism, and the need for the Liberals, if they w[...] nation, to regard 'men's lives and happiness of hig[her ...] than the rights of property'.[25]

That such divergent secular and religious follo[wers ...] philosophy of contingent property should expre[ss ...] such convergent terms was due less to his personal [...] after he was dead – than to his clear expression of t[he ...] ideal, which put persons and their needs before p[roperty ...] rights. Green's message of the moral responsibility of property and privilege 'spoke to the condition' of middle-class men and women brought up in Evangelical and often professional homes who, like him, were losing their religious faith and looking for an ethical substitute in the service of humanity. It reached for a wider audience through the novels of Mrs Humphry Ward, grand-daughter of Thomas and niece of Matthew Arnold, especially *Robert Elsmere* (1888) and *Marcella* (1894). *Robert Elsmere*, of which about a million copies were sold worldwide, concerns an Oxford student of 'Professor Grey' who, after becoming a country clergyman and losing his faith, goes under Grey's influence to work in the East End and, like Arnold Toynbee, wears himself out in the service of the poor. The heroine of *Marcella*, who at first bears a striking resemblance to Beatrice Webb, gives up a brilliant life in 'society' to become a social worker, joins the 'Venturists', recognizably the Fabians, and finally retires to her country estate and an idyllic marriage to do good works as a model Lady Bountiful.[26] Through such popular media Green's 'politics of conscience' had an influence far beyond Oxford and Toynbee Hall.

Nothing could be further from the organic social theory of the Oxford idealists than the rational utilitarianism which thrived unalloyed at Cambridge. Henry Sidgwick and Alfred Marshall were the self-appointed intellectual heirs of John Stuart Mill, the first in political and moral philosophy, the second in political economy. Both rejected the cloudy metaphysics, as they saw it, of the Oxford idealists, and thought Bentham's principle of utility (the 'maximum pleasure, minimum pain' principle) 'a universally applicable standard for selecting and regulating our activities'.[27] Yet utilitarianism was a deeply ambiguous theory and, as we have seen in Mill himself, could as easily justify socialism as it could individualism. The greatest happiness of the greatest number could lead as readily as Green's communal theory of rights to the notion of the 'positive freedom' of the many propertyless, to be achieved by limiting the freedom of the few property owners. From the beginning Bentham and James Mill, watchdogs of the taxpayers' property against the peculations of 'Old Corruption', had not blenched at state interference with the rights of inherited property. Bentham's doctrine of 'escheat' would, after a stated number of inheritances confined to immediate descendants, have returned land into the hands of the state (a sort of creeping nationalization), while James Mill's proposal for the taxation of the unearned increment of land values, which his son took over and made the main tenet of his Land Tenure Reform Association of 1870, anticipated Henry George's 'single tax'.[28] While Sidgwick studiously ignored or brushed aside John Stuart Mill's collectivist tendencies, attributing them to the aberrant influence of his wife Harriet Taylor, Alfred Marshall, the founder of neo-classical economics, frequently expressed sympathy for socialism but thought it impracticable; he even declared himself a socialist in so far as this meant that some of the work of social amelioration could be better performed by the state than by the individual. He merely drew the line, like Mill, at the bureaucratic tyranny which might ensue from the wholesale transfer to the state of the ownership of the means of production.[29] He was no less concerned than Green to educate his students to go forth and improve the world outside the university. As he said in his inaugural lecture in 1885:

> it will be my cherished ambition, my highest endeavour ... to increase the numbers of those, whom Cambridge, the mother of strong men, sends out into the world with cool heads and warm hearts willing to give some at least of their best powers to grappling with the social suffering around them; resolved not to rest content until they have done what in them lies to discover how far it is possible to open up to all the material means for a refined and noble life.[30]

128

His hope for the future of the working classes was in effect to professionalize them, to make their work consistent with being an industrious 'gentleman':

> The question is not whether all men will ultimately be equal – that they certainly will not – but whether progress may not go on steadily if slowly, till the official distinction between working man and gentleman has passed away; till by occupation at least, every man is a gentleman. I hold that it may, and that it will.[31]

Marshall's views of property were superficially orthodox but fundamentally radical. He believed that private gain was necessary for industrial progress, to induce men of ente[rprise] themselves to the utmost, but that the enormous [wealth] successful men now made and passed on to th[eir heirs was] counterproductive and tended to prevent human [resources] being turned to their best account. 'So far as the ri[ghts of property] have a "natural" and "indefensible" basis, the fir[st is that] attached to that property which any one has ma[de or] acquired by his own labour. But the right does no[t extend to] pass on to his heirs....' Taxes levied on the [rich, including] graduated death duties, were ethically justified, no[t to wage] war but to provide a good and varied educatio[n and] recreation for working-class children, who might d[o better in] competition than less motivated inheritors to increase the national wealth.[32] Here too we can glimpse the professional ideal of social efficiency as the test of taxation policy, and of property as contingent upon its use for socially beneficial purposes.

It is not surprising, therefore, to find Marshall's pupils, despite their apparent economic orthodoxy, proposing policies worthy of Robin Hood, robbing the rich to feed and clothe the poor. The greatest of them, John Maynard Keynes, was to turn capitalism upside down by making spending on the poor its salvation from depression and bankruptcy. But that was to be between the wars. Meanwhile, another Cambridge man with a social conscience, Charles Masterman, helped Lloyd George and Winston Churchill to prepare the People's Budget of 1909 and the National Insurance Act of 1911, as well as numerous other social reforms.[33] Finally, A. C. Pigou, Marshall's successor and the pioneer of 'welfare economics', declared in 1914:

The position from which I start is this. It is the duty of a civilized state to lay down certain minimum conditions in every department of life, below which it refuses to allow any of its free citizens to fall. There must be a minimum standard of conditions in factories, a minimum standard ... of leisure, a minimum standard of dwelling accommodation, a minimum standard of education, of medical treatment in case of illness, and of wholesome food and clothing ... The standards must be upheld all along the line, and any man or family which fails to attain independently to any one of them must be regarded as a proper subject for state action.[34]

This demand by a neo-classical economist for a 'national minimum' to be paid for out of taxes levied on the rich, with its echo of the Fabian socialist Webbs' *Industrial Democracy* (1902),[35] must have sounded to the landed and capitalist classes like a more immediate threat to the security of property than the metaphysical theorizing of Green and his idealist disciples.

The Webbs and Fabian socialism bring us to the third and by far the most conscious and deliberate attack on the concept of absolute property. The rise of socialism from the 1880s down to 1914 has usually been treated either as an autonomous development in the history of political ideas or as an aspect of the rise of labour. The extent to which it was a self-interested movement of marginal members of the professional middle class has been almost completely overlooked, except by Peter Clarke and Eric Hobsbawm.[36] With a few exceptions like H. M. Hyndman, the rentier founder of the Social Democratic Federation, and Keir Hardie, the coalmining leader of the Independent Labour Party, the great majority of the leading members of the various socialist societies of the period were professional men and women, rarely, at first at any rate, at the head of their professions: William Morris the artist-craftsman, Sidney Webb and Sydney Olivier the civil servants, Bernard Shaw and H.G. Wells the professional authors, J. A. Hobson, Graham Wallas and L. T. Hobhouse struggling academics, and so on.[37] Although they espoused the cause of the working class and in facetious moments thought of themselves in Bernard Shaw's phrase as 'intellectual proletarians', they were not motivated by the working-class ideal of a society based on egalitarian labour but by the professional ideal of an elitist society run by professional experts. All their solutions to the social problems of the day were professional and bureaucratic: industrial democracy would be a corporatist economy mediated on the management and union sides by 'equally expert negotiators, acting for corporations reasonably comparable in strategic strength', overlooked by expert representatives of the High Court of Parliament for the community as a whole; the bumbling amateurish Poor Law would be replaced by separate bureaucracies of social workers for every category of social need; municipal socialism would take care through local government officials of all local services from gas and water to public transport; grants-in-aid to the municipalities would bring them under the bureaucratic control of the central government; and the major industries like coal, the docks and the railways would be run by nationalized bureaucracies.[38] The workers were to have little or no part in the management of these concerns, since all experiments with the self-governing workshop were bound to fail because 'its essential feature, the union in the same persons of manual workers and managers, hardly ever endures'.[39] Expert managerialism was the key to success; H. G. Wells's *A Modern Utopia* (1905) was to be run by bureaucratic samurai; Bernard Shaw's future world of the Ancients in *Back to Methuselah* (1931) by the ultimate professionals, the long-lived Ancients.

Even the idealistic benevolence of the young men from the universities, like William Beveridge, R. H. Tawney, Clement Attlee and Hugh Dalton, who thronged to Samuel and Henrietta Barnett's Toynbee Hall and other university settlements, were imbued with professional ambition. As George Lansbury, the East End Labour politician, remarked of them in 1928:

> The most important result of the mixing policy of the Barnetts, has been the filling up of the bureaucracy of government and administration with men and women who went to the East End full of enthusiasm and zeal for the welfare of the masses, and discovered the advancement of their own interests and the interests of the poor were best served by leaving East London to stew in its own juice while they became members of parliament, cabinet ministers, civil servants. . . .[40]

Yet it would be cynical to imagine that the professionals were attracted to bureaucratic socialism merely by the prospect of jobs

131

for the boys. Much more importantly, it appealed to their in-built professional ideal of social efficiency and the professional concept of property. The Fabians were the first to define professional property in terms foursquare with land and capital. Sidney Webb in 1887 referred to the 'rents' of land, capital *and labour*.[41] Graham Wallas translated this into the doctrine of the three rents, 'the Rent of Land, of Capital and of Ability'. The Fabians, Wallas believed, were distinguished from the Ricardians, who recognized only the rent of land, and from the Marxists, who added the rent (profit or 'surplus value') from capital, by their perception of all three:

> We therefore came into the Society ready-made Anti-Marxists, and at once began that insistence on the Ricardian Law of Rent as applied to Capital and Ability, as well as to Land which made William Morris say 'These Fabians call their noddles their Rents of Ability.'[42]

Wallas, a sceptical socialist who eventually abandoned the Fabian Society for the New Liberalism, nevertheless consistently believed in the 'greatest happiness' principle: 'every step which leads to increased happiness, education and leisure, for our fellow-men is a step forward for our Cause.' It followed that it was the 'personal duty' of the professional man to devote his rent of ability to social purposes, though, true to professional self-interest, 'he must see that he gets his full pay.'[43] The rent of ability would of course outlast the abolition of the rents of land and capital, and the professional, bureaucratic and managerial services which yielded it would be just as necessary after the social revolution or the gradual transition to socialism as before. As H. G. Wells put it of Wallas, Morris and the Kelmscott House circle, 'They took the idea of getting a living as something by the way; a sort of living was there for them anyhow.'[44] From the point of view of land and capital, professional property was a threat precisely because it could contemplate with equanimity their abolition.[45]

The idealist, utilitarian, and socialist threats to absolute property were summed up in 1909 by J. A. Hobson, the unorthodox economist who seemed to unite in himself the idealism of Green, the welfare economics of Marshall, and the interventionism of the Fabians:

> a clear grasp of society as an economic organisation completely explodes the notion of property as an inherent individual right

for it shows that no individual can make or appropriate anything of value without the direct continuous assistance of society. So the idea of society as a political organism insists that the general will and wisdom of society, as embodied in the State, shall determine the best social use of all social property taken by taxation, without admitting any inherent right of interference on the part of the taxpayer.[46]

The threat was initially abstract and theoretical, and would become dangerous only to the extent that it took concrete form in practical proposals for legislation. Between 1880 and 1914 this is precisely what it did, in an interconnected series of movements which looked to property owners like a concerted and progressive attack on the rights of property. These were the land reform movement, the campaign for municipal socialism, and the drift towards collectivist social reform.

The land reform movement was a perfect example of the divergence of the capitalist and professional social ideals. It began as a united middle-class attack in the name of active capital and professional service on the 'idle wealth' and 'unearned rent' of the landlords, led by the two Mills and the Benthamites on one side, and by Cobden, Bright and the Anti-Corn Law League on the other.[47] After a chequered career from the 1840s to the 1860s, it reached a crescendo in the 1870s, and by 1880 Disraeli could say:

If I were asked to mention the two subjects which most occupy the thought of the country at the present moment, I should say one was the government of Ireland, and the other the principles upon which the landed property of this country should continue to be established.

The Irish question, which turned on the relations between alien landlords and Catholic peasants, was always with us, but it was his 'profound conviction – that the politics of this country . . . will probably, for the next few years, mainly consist in an assault upon the constitutional position of the landed interest'.[48] He was right. The Irish Land Act of 1881, forced on the British government by the plight of the Irish peasants under the agricultural depression and the consequent evictions and threat of violence, made the deepest breach since feudal times in the landlord's absolute right to do what he wished with his property. Its 'three F's', 'fair rent', 'fixity of tenure' and 'freedom of sale' of the tenant's interest, in effect transferred part of the beneficial ownership of the land from the landlord to the tenant. It was the first example of what may be called modern 'subinfeudation', the slotting-in of new claimants to a place in the hierarchy of permanent tenures on the lines of medieval 'subinfeudation' in the first centuries after the Norman Conquest. It was bound, as Lord Salisbury later complained, to lead to parallel demands from Scottish crofters, Welsh farmers and English tenants, all of whom suffered from falling agricultural prices and had similar grievances against their landlords, such as lack of compensation for 'unexhausted improvements' and for the game birds and animals which ate their crops.[49] The Ground Game Act of 1880 enabled British farmers to take hares and rabbits concurrently with their landlords, though the far more damaging pheasants, partridges and deer still brought the landlords a 'double rent' from the same land. Meanwhile the Agricultural Holdings Act of 1883 prevented landlords from contracting out of their obligation under the 1875 Act to compensate outgoing tenants for improvements. The Scottish highlanders gained the same security of tenure and controlled rents as the Irish peasant under the Crofters Holdings (Scotland) Act of 1886, though the Royal Commission on the Occupation of Land in Wales in 1896 was split on the method of applying the same principles to the Welsh farmers, with the result that nothing was done there.

What set the land reform movement alight, however, and drove a fire lane between its capitalist and professional middle-class versions, was the publication of Henry George's *Progress and Poverty*, in America in 1880 and in England in 1881, with its theory of rent as the sole cause of slums and poverty and its remedy of the 'single tax' on land, designed to take back for the community most of what in Ricardian theory the landlords took from the community in unearned rent. The book sold 60,000 copies in England by 1885, was eagerly read by people as diverse as H.M. Hyndman and Herbert Spencer, John Morley and Joseph Chamberlain, Charles Darwin and Alfred Russel Wallace, Arnold Toynbee and Frederic Harrison, Lord Salisbury and Tom Mann, and led the Christian Socialist Steward Headlam to talk of 'a man sent from God whose name was Henry George'.[50] He was welcomed to England on his triumphal lecture tour in 1881 by Helen Taylor, Mill's stepdaughter and co-founder of the Land Tenure Reform Association, and Alfred Russel Wallace, founder of the Land Nationalization Society. Georgism was the catalyst which transformed many moderate land reformers, believers in 'free trade in land' (the abolition of primogeniture, strict settlement, entail, and other hindrances to the free sale of land) into root and branch opponents of private property in land and, sometimes, into socialists believing in the public ownership of the mines, railways and other means of production.[51]

At the same time, Georgism was the wedge which separated those reformers who believed in the absolute sanctity of property from those who believed that the rights and needs of the community overrode those of the private proprietor. The line was a fine one, which could leave many Liberal business men, and especially urban councillors who had no doubts about the rightness of the capitalist system, to support the growing Liberal programme (from 1888 onwards) for the special taxation of land values, but it could also lead the fastidious Alfred Russel Wallace and his Land Nationalization Society to repudiate the single tax as confiscatory, whereas land nationalization respected property rights enough to pay compensation for them. This distinction led to the breakaway of the Land Reform Union (later the English Land Restoration League, the main Georgist organization) in 1883 to organize George's second lecture tour of Britain. George himself was no socialist, and his nostrum, the taxation of site values, was a method of separating the local government taxation of the ground landlord from that of the residential or business occupier. This was to become the main objective of Sir Albert Kaye Rollit, leader of the powerful Association of Municipal Corporations, who saw in it the possibility of financial independence for the towns by expanding the tax base and of an escape from the bureaucratic control of the central government.[52] At the same time, socialists like Wallace could think George's disregard for property rights too extreme for them.

Nevertheless, Georgism was seen, especially by the defenders of property, as the main slide on the slippery slope which led from the tampering with the integrity of property in Ireland, via the restrictions on the landlord's rights represented by 'free trade in land', through to outright confiscation. As Lord Salisbury put it in 1884, 'We are on an inclined plane which leads from the position of Lord Hartington to that of Mr Chamberlain and so on to the depths over which Mr Henry George reigns supreme.'[53]

It would be a gross oversimplification to suggest that only business men favoured moderate land reform and professional men the Georgist single tax and more extreme forms of expropriation of land and land-based resources. Class ideals do not operate in that mechanical manner. There were business men like Rowntree and rentiers like Josiah Wedgwood who played a leading role in the Liberal land campaigns down to the First World War and beyond, and there were professional men like W. H. Mallock, Sir Alfred Milner and Lord Chancellor Haldane who played a leading role in outwitting them, not to mention Lloyd George who characteristically played it both ways.[54] Moreover, there was one group of professional men, the conveyancing lawyers and the estate agents, who had a vested interest in maintaining the old land law and for whom reform, as the Law Society saw it, would be suicidal. Avner Offer has perceptively observed that for the legal profession the law of property itself had become a species of corporate property, which supported some scores of thousands of black-coated workers. Like any professional or other occupational group threatened with extinction they fought with fury and ingenuity against one instrument of free trade in land, the registration of title, which could have made dealing in land as cheap and simple as dealing in stocks and shares.[55] In that purpose they have substantially succeeded down to the present day.[56] This illustrates perfectly the concept of professional property based on a persuasive monopoly and the fact that its defence will always take priority over attacks on other kinds of property.

Nevertheless, there is a very real sense in which the professional concept of contingent property, legitimized by some form of service to the community, informed the land reform movement and at the same time alienated those who came to see in it the first step towards the abolition of property altogether, including the capital of the business man. *The Economist* in 1885 rebuked Chamberlain after his Birmingham speech linking land reform to social reform:

> Mr Chamberlain, of course, knows perfectly well the value of
> the institution of private property, and he is not going to
> commit political suicide by joining the movement for
> nationalization of the land, which will, sooner or later,
> incorporate among its aims the nationalization of ... capital.[57]

Lord Salisbury complained in 1894 that 'The landlord is assuming the position of the Jew of the Middle Ages or the pariah of India. He is an outcast ... who has no rights', and went on to warn business men that 'other contracts besides those of land will be subjected to the same idea'.[58] The alliance of land and capital against the common threat was institutionalized as early as 1882 in the Liberty and Property Defence League.[59] Long before Georgist taxation of land values entered into Liberal policy in 1899 and Liberal legislation with the People's Budget of 1909, many business men had begun to jump off the slippery slope and take refuge behind the safer ramparts of property in the Tory Party.[60]

'Municipalism', as the Association of Municipal Corporations called it, or 'municipal socialism', as it came to be called under the combined influence of the individualists and the Fabians, also began as a proud achievement of the united urban middle class and only gradually divided those who came to fear it as a threat to private enterprise from those who welcomed it as a step on the way to public ownership and the socialist state. As Asa Briggs has explained, the splendid town halls of the Victorian age were monuments to a civic pride which rejoiced in municipal enterprise, with borough water and sewage works, town gas and electricity supplies, municipal trams and buses, and so on.[61] Liverpool and Manchester had pioneered slum clearance and the rebuilding of working-class housing. Birmingham under Joseph Chamberlain had become a byword for efficient civic trading. For Chamberlain and his kind this was not socialism but capitalism, of the best public-spirited kind. As late as 1896 he told a Birmingham banquet of like-minded citizens:

> I have always compared the work of a great corporation like this to that of a joint-stock company, in which the directors are represented by the Councillors of the City, and in which the dividends are to be found in the increased health and wealth and happiness and education of the community.[62]

In these sentiments he was warmly supported by the Association of Municipal Corporations and its commanding president, the Conservative MP Sir Albert Kaye Rollit, who preached civic spending on welfare as the best safeguard *against* socialism.[63]

The Fabians undermined their own efforts at permeation by proclaiming the principle of trading by borough corporations a step on the way to socialism. 'Municipal socialism' seems to have been invented by W. C. Crofts, secretary of the Liberty and Property Defence League, in a pamphlet of that title in 1885, but it was the Fabians' flaunting of it as a deliberate threat to private enterprise which gave its enemies a handle. In 1890 Sidney Webb wrote, 'municipal socialism has ... the effect of absorbing in "rates" a share of the rental of the country. Our progressive municipalization of rent by increase of local rates, is clearly an unconscious form of Land Nationalization'.[64] Between them the Fabians and the individualists of the LPDL turned a bipartisan policy of encouraging the towns to do for their inhabitants what the latter could not do, or do so well, for themselves into a political threat to property and enterprise. This threat was inflamed when the Progressive Party, a combination of New Liberals and Fabians, came to dominate the London County Council in the 1890s and early 1900s and to press not merely for self-supporting municipal trading ventures but for high spending on technical education and other welfare measures. Ratepayers' associations, an old and often Cobdenite or Gladstonian Liberal device for checking municipal extravagance, were now revived, beginning with the London Ratepayers' Defence League in 1894, an offshoot of the LPDL, to oppose high spending and the taxation of ground values.[65] In London Lord Avebury of the LPDL formed the Industrial Freedom League in 1902 to combat municipal socialism, and the new right-wing Municipal Reform Society, strongly supported by the national press, wrested control of the London County Council from the Progressives in 1907. The agitation was exacerbated by the collapse of the property boom in the mid–1900s and the concurrent steep rise in London rates.[66] By 1909 the *Property Owners' Journal* was complaining of 'a depression like Egyptian Darkness', of the word 'site values' as 'a quivering shaft in the heart of ground rent owners', 'a savagery suggestive of cannibals' in medical officers of health who prosecuted house owners for breaches of 'ridiculous bye-laws', of unrentable empty houses, and of 'rates ascending to the giddy heights of Everest'.[67] George Head, a leading surveyor, responded in 1910 to the land tax clauses of the People's Budget:

Socialistic schemes are in the air which ... tinge and colour the policy of the great party with which they are most nearly allied. Some discern in the bills brought before the Houses of

Parliament by H. M. Government more than a mild flavour of socialist confiscation.[68]

By then most of the ratepayers' associations which used to be a pillar of the Old Liberalism had in their resentment of the New gone over to the Conservative side.[69] Municipal trading, once a vehicle of capitalist civic pride, had become one more example of the social service demanded of property

The tinge of socialism which Head had discovered in the Liberal welfare measures of the later Edwardian age was a reflection of that drift towards collectivism which A. V. Dicey complained of in his *Lectures on Law and Opinion* in 1905. The puzzle is why the blame for collectivism, which played an increasing, if somewhat ambivalent, role in the social legislation of both major parties from at least the 1830s onwards should have been laid, not by Dicey alone but by the propertied classes generally, at the door of the Liberal Party. Although both parties were committed to factory legislation, public health expenditure and inspection, prevention of food and drug adulteration, state education (including secondary and technical education), workmen's compensation, old age pensions, and a range of other welfare measures, the Liberals came to be more associated with high expenditure on social reform than were the Conservatives, and were therefore blamed by property owners for the 'crippling burden' on the rich and middle classes which this was held to represent. The immediate reason for this lay in the *manner* of paying for social reform. The Liberals sought increases in direct taxation of the well-to-do, by means of higher rates, taxation of land values, graduated death duties (first introduced by Harcourt in 1894) and graduated income tax (first introduced with differential rates for earned and unearned income by Asquith in 1906, and more overtly with the supertax in Lloyd George's 1909 Budget), while the Tories preferred indirect taxes, notably tariff reform, which would spread the burden more widely and regressively amongst the non-rich. Thus it was that Liberal social reform, already tarred with the brush of land reform, Georgist land value taxation and municipal socialism, as well as with their overt connections with the Lib–Labs and covert alliance with the Labour movement, came to present itself as the final step on the slippery slope to 'socialism'.

Behind this immediate cause, however, lay a more deep-seated one. It can best be described as an approach to social justice and national efficiency. Whereas the Conservatives tended to see social reform as a belated and reluctant means to social stability, the prevention of discontent and revolution, the 'ransom' which property had to pay for its security, and one of the main ramparts of property, the Liberals increasingly saw it in moral and technocratic terms, as the right of every citizen to the basic necessities of life, to protection from at least the most harmful effects of industrialism and urbanization, and even to a somewhat fairer start in life in terms of health and education, not merely for the sake of fairness but also for the sake of the economic, political and military efficiency of the nation. The actual social reforms which they passed were a pragmatic melange of many factors and compromises, as we shall see, but running through them all were the politics of conscience and the demand for social justice and efficiency.

Whence came this transition from the Old Liberalism, which stressed the political and legal equality of citizens in the free competition for income and wealth, to the New Liberalism, which concentrated on the social rights of citizens to minimum subsistence, more equal opportunity, and a fitter and more effective nation? It was in fact a paradigm of the divergence of the professional from the capitalist social ideal, the separation of the professional view that the rights of persons and the welfare of the community came before the rights of property, from the capitalist view that free and unfettered competition between political and legal equals led to prosperity for all. It was not merely that the politics of social responsibility preached by T. H. Green, Alfred Marshall, the Christian Socialists and the Fabians had more successfully infiltrated the ranks of the Liberal Party. It was also that those same principles, perceived as a threat to property, both in land and in capital, had by the Edwardian age driven out nearly all the landowners and a large proportion of the business men including, it would seem, a majority of the big corporate and financial capitalists. Who had replaced them in the domination of the party? In the 1905 Cabinet for the first time land and capital were outnumbered, and (if we count John Burns as a professional trade union leader) by a professional or at least non-propertied majority. By 1911 when, for the first time, the Conservatives chose a business man, Bonar Law, as Leader, the Liberal Cabinet was dominated by lawyers, Asquith, Haldane, Lloyd George, McKenna and Birrell. Although there were other influences still at work in Edwardian Liberalism - the fear of most merchants and some industrialists of tariff reform, the dwindling role of the Nonconformists, the need to placate and retain the Lib-Labs and to outflank the new Labour Party - the influence of the professional ideal, with its championship of social justice and efficiency and its perceived threat to property, was the most critical for its survival. We can best see this if we examine, firstly, the reactive movement for the defence of property and, secondly, the role of the professional ideal in the origins of the welfare state.

3   THE DEFENCE OF PROPERTY

The attack on absolute property was bound to provoke an energetic and spirited defence, not only from the directly threatened landlords and capitalists but also from those professional men who supported them and were still wedded to traditional ideas of property and *laissez-faire*. The defence was not simply a war of words but an organized counterattack with its own institutional armies. It was led by great landlords like the Earl of Wemyss and Earl Grey and capitalists like Sir George Livesey of the South Metropolitan Gasworks and G. A. Laws, first general manager of the Shipping Federation, both scourges of the New Unionism. Yet the heat and burden of the battle was borne by the professional men who inspired the defence or worked as organizers and propagandists for the organizations through which it was mounted. Their participation came to have a curious and paradoxical effect. Although in the short term they were effective in arresting the decline of property rights and slowing down the progress of collectivist legislation, in the long term, as we shall see, the arguments which they mounted in defence of property and against state intervention, based as they frequently were on the same professional ideal, helped almost as much as those of their professional opponents to undermine the absolute rights of property. This they did by emphasizing its responsibilities and promoting ideas of a wider distribution of property, extended social reform, and co-partnership with the wage earners, which paved the way for a new relationship between capital and labour.

The guiding spirit of the defence of property in this period was that old Bourbon of individualism, Herbert Spencer, spokesman of the undiluted entrepreneurial ideal. Spencer was an Adam Smithian rather than a Benthamite individualist, believing in the natural rather than the artificial or state-contrived harmony of interests.[70] This accounts for his shrill attack on Bentham's belief that rights, including property, were created by society, and that government therefore had the power to modify them for the benefit of the non–propertied.[71] Spencer raised the natural harmony of interests to a higher and terrifying power. By adopting a crude form of 'Social Darwinism' (strictly pre-Darwinian, Lamarckian evolution, which appeared in *Social Statics* in 1851, eight years before *The Origin of Species*), he extended 'the survival of the fittest' from the jungle of carnivores and herbivores to the civilized garden of human society, in a passage of such cold-blooded callousness that it is worth quoting at length:

> Pervading all nature we may see at work a stern discipline, which is a little cruel that it may be kind. That state of universal warfare maintained throughout the lower creation ... is at bottom the most merciful provision which the circumstances admit of.

Carnivores weed out the old, sickly and malformed among the herbivores, and so 'happiness is derived for a tribe of predatory creatures'. In the name of free competition human predators must therefore be allowed to perform the same benevolent function in civil society.

> It is in the human race that the consummation is to be accomplished. Civilization is the last stage of that accomplishment ... [T]he well-being of existing humanity and the unfolding of that perfection, are both secured by that beneficent, though severe discipline to which the animate creation at large is subject: a discipline which is pitiless in the working out of good: a felicity-producing law which never swerves for the avoidance of partial and temporary suffering. The poverty of the incapable, the distresses that come upon the imprudent, the starvation of the idle, and those shoulderings aside of the weak by the strong, which leave so many 'in shallows and in miseries', are decrees of a large, far-seeing benevolence. It seems hard that an unskilfulness which with all his efforts he can not overcome, should entail hunger upon the

artizan. It seems hard that a labourer incapacitated by sickness from competing with his stronger fellows, should have to bear the resulting privations. It seems hard that widows and orphans should be left to struggle for life and death. Nevertheless, when regarded not separately but in connection with the interests of universal humanity, these harsh fatalities are seen to be full of the highest beneficence – the same beneficence which brings to early graves the children of diseased parents, and singles out the intemperate and the debilitated as the victims of an epidemic.[72]

This far-seeing benevolence was endorsed, he claimed, by Christianity, which in Spencer's view allowed the idle poor (but not apparently the idle rich) to starve:

The command 'if any would not work neither should he eat', is simply a Christian enunciation of that universal law of Nature under which life has reached its present height – the law that a creature not energetic enough to maintain itself must die: the sole difference being that the law which in one case is to be artificially enforced, is, in the other case, a natural necessity. And yet this particular tenet of their religion which science so manifestly justifies, is the one which Christians seem least likely to accept. The current assumption is that there should be no suffering, and that society is to blame for that which exists.[73]

This curiously un-Christian view of Christianity bore little resemblance to the teachings of Christ, or even for that matter to his hero Adam Smith's well-known sympathy for the poor and unfortunate.

In the long term, it is true, Spencer believed that civilized men would develop and transmit by the Lamarckian inheritance of acquired characteristics an altruistic gratification in the pleasure of others, but in the meantime the rich were responsible for pauperizing the poor by indiscriminate charity and poor relief, which merely encouraged 'these swarms of good-for-nothings, fostered and multiplied by public and private agencies'.[74] While voluntary charity might help the deserving poor to help themselves, compulsory poor laws and indiscriminate charity only took money from the employment of the fit and deserving to expand the number of unfit and undeserving. If the state attempted to limit the operation of this law of the jungle, it could only make matters worse, by encouraging the unfit to survive and breed, thus lowering the average economic and military capacity of the nation.

In *The Man versus the State* (1884) Spencer was unrepentant – 'the lapse of a third of a century ... has brought the no reason for retreating from the position' – but more pessimistic. The old, strong, wise Liberalism, based on the regime of contract and voluntary co-operation, had been replaced *in the Liberal Party* by the 'New Toryism', based on the quasi-feudal regime of status and 'that system of compulsory co-operation which accompanied the legal inequality of classes', and was preparing the way for 'the coming slavery' of socialism.[75] By socialism he meant state intervention of any kind, from factory acts or the banning of 'coffin ships' to state education or nationalized telegraphs. Like Lord Salisbury, he saw these as the declension into the state control of everything:

> the changes made, the changes in progress, and the changes urged, will carry us not only towards State-ownership of land and dwellings and means of communication, all to be administered by State agents, but towards State-usurpation of all industries ... And so will be brought about the desired ideal of the socialists.[76]

Democratic control of the state only exacerbated the new despotism. 'All socialism involves slavery'. Slavery to the majority was worse than slavery to the few.[77] The propertied legislators who were perpetrating these 'confiscating Acts of Parliament' were preparing their own nemesis:

> For what is the tacit assumption on which such Acts proceed? It is the assumption that no man has any claim to his property, not even to that which he has earned by the sweat of his brow, save by permission of the community; and that the community may cancel the claim to any extent it thinks fit. No defence can be made for this appropriation of A's possessions for the benefit of B, save one which sets out with the postulate that society as a whole has an absolute right over the possessions of each member. And now this doctrine, which has been tacitly assumed, is being openly proclaimed. Mr George and his

friends, Mr Hyndman and his supporters, are pushing this theory to its logical issue.[78]

Spencer was not alone in his reaction to the Land Acts and the 'empirical socialism' of Gladstone's second government, or to the threats to property of Henry George, H. M. Hyndman and the Fabians. In fact, he was being pushed from behind by a group of disciples who called themselves 'individualists' and had formed an anti-collectivist pressure group, the Political Evolution Society, as early as 1873, which became the State Resistance Society in 1880.[79] This group, led by a Rugby- and Oxford-educated journalist, W. C. Crofts, who claimed to have coined the term 'individualism' in his lectures to working men's clubs in 1883, and Wordsworth Donisthorpe, a mine-owner and lawyer whose anti-statism bordered on anarchism, formed the brains of the Liberty and Property Defence League founded in 1882 by Lord Elcho (who succeeded as Earl of Wemyss and March in 1883). Originally a Tory turned Peelite and 'Liberal-Conservative', Elcho, the self-styled friend of the working class and patron of Alexander MacDonald, the miner's leader, had introduced the partial repeal of the Master and Servant Acts in 1867, which saved 10,000 workers a year from imprisonment (though not from fines) for striking without notice. Despite his belief in good relations between trade unions and employers, as a great landowner and mine owner (with a rental of £57,000 a year according to Bateman in 1880) he was an outspoken opponent of political democracy and of industrial strikes and picketing. Converted to extreme *laissez-faire* by what he saw as the Liberal, Georgist and Socialist attacks on property in the early 1880s, he set out to form an alliance of moderate Liberals and Tories, first against Gladstone's land legislation, and then, partly under the influence of the Spencerian individualists, on behalf of the whole propertied interest against 'socialism'.[80]

At a crowded inaugural meeting in 1882 the Liberty and Property Defence League attracted the support of those who saw property, both landed and capitalist, as under threat. Members came to include Earl Grey, the Duke of Somerset and over sixty other peers, Sir Edwin Watkin, Lord Brabourne, H. D. Poching and other railway magnates, Sir George Elliot for the mining engineers, and representatives of the shipowners, bankers, brewers, and other great corporate industries, besides some 210 federated trade groups and twenty London livery companies.[81] One curious group of adherents was 'the right wing of the women's rights movement', including the Personal Rights Association which grew out of Josephine Butler's campaign against the Contagious Diseases Acts, and Helen Blackburn and Jesse Boucherett's Society for Promoting the Employment of Women which, with the LPDL's help, successfully opposed Thomas Burt and the mining union's attempt to ban the employment of some 8,000 'pit-brow lasses' in 1886–87. Others were the Van Dweller's Protection Association which opposed state interference with gypsies, tinkers and other 'travelling people', and the London Association for Opposing Early Closing (of shops), which even opposed the compulsory provision of seats for women shop assistants.[82]

But the main concern of the LPDL was the purely negative defence of the absolute rights of property, opposing to the state a flat 'hands off'. In pursuit of this it acted as a parliamentary watchdog, circulating pamphlets, memoranda and weekly tables of bills to be rejected or amended on behalf of its affiliated organizations, and claiming to have opposed with 'more or less success' nearly 800 bills by 1900. Amongst these were the series of bills from 1883, held up until 1897, attempting to prevent employers from 'contracting out' of their responsibility for workmen's compensation for industrial injuries under the Act of 1880; the Shop Hours Regulation (Early Closing) bills first introduced in 1873 by Sir John Lubbock (later as Lord Avebury a pillar of the LPDL) and delayed in part until 1902; bills to restrict the employment of women in the coal industry, domestic nail and chair making, and commercial laundries, and of all factory women within a month of having a baby; Plimsoll's bills to require load lines on ships; bills restricting drinking hours and the numbers of pubs; and many more.[83]

Spencer himself, growing old, neurasthenic and reclusive, took little direct part in the League, but he supported it with donations, and he was instrumental in persuading Lord Wemyss to begin in 1894 the long crusade against municipal trading. But his ideologically committed followers, particularly the League's first secretary, W. C. Crofts, Donisthorpe the mine-owning protagonist of 'absolute philosophical anarchy' (who broke with Spencer and the LPDL in 1888 over an article of his on that theme), Thomas Mackay, historian of the poor law and ideologue of the Charity Organization Society, Frederick Millar, Crofts's successor as secretary, and the brilliant propagandist W. H. Mallock, provided an endless flow of books, pamphlets, articles, periodicals (*Jus* and the *Liberty Review*), leaflets and popular lectures, attacking state intervention in all its forms.[84] The League's most influential production was *A Plea for Liberty*, published in 1891 as an answer to *Fabian Essays in Socialism* (1889). Edited by Thomas Mackay with an introduction by Spencer himself, it contained a surprising plea by George Howell, the Lib-Lab MP and ex-Secretary of the Parliamentary Committee of the TUC, for 'Liberty for Labour'.[85]

'Free labour' was one of the main obsessions of the League, and its concern to protect non-union workers from the 'tyranny of trade-unionism' brought it into the forefront of the employers' counterattack on the New Unionism. Although William Collison, the ex-trade union leader who founded the National Free Labour Association, the main strike-breaking organization, in 1893 was not associated with the League until 1897, when it established the Free Labour Protection Association to help the Engineering Employers' Federation break the engineers' strike, the LPDL played an active role in advising employers engaged in the legal battles of the 1890s which limited trade union rights and culminated in the crippling Taff Vale judgment. Another offshoot of the League and its auxiliary, the FLPA, was the Employers' Parliamentary Council, launched in 1898 to encourage legislation restricting trade union picketing, the closed shop and sympathetic strikes, and to oppose any reversal by Parliament of anti-trade union judicial decisions. It came to play a successful role, until the return of the Liberals in 1906, in maintaining the Taff Vale decision.[86]

The final campaign of importance by the League was that launched against municipal socialism in 1899. Although Spencer had long warned against the steady growth of state ownership and control of industry through 'its local lieutenants, the municipal governments' and the enormous rise in annual local expenditure (from £36 million in 1867–68 to £63 million in 1880–81), the League had done little about it until one of its prominent members, Joseph Savory, Lord Mayor of London and a large shareholder in the City of London Electric Company which was caught out in corrupt dealings, lost a libel suit against the weekly *London*, organ of the LCC majority Progressive Party. The League's petitions 'against the dangers of municipal trading' were signed by railway, tramway, gas, engineering, electric lighting, water, etc. companies, by Chambers of Commerce, and by associations of employers, traders, property owners and ratepayers throughout the United Kingdom, [and] presented in the House of Commons by Sir John Lubbock, in the House of Lords by the Earl of Wemyss.[87]

Lubbock, created Lord Avebury in 1900, led the campaign against municipal reform and launched the Industrial Freedom League in 1902, backed by a wide range of companies headed by the Electric and General Investment Company and the British Electric Traction Company, which hoped to share in the profits from municipal electricity supply, tramways, and similar urban utilities. It found an ally in Gerald Balfour, President of the Board of Trade, nephew of the prime minister, Lord Salisbury, and brother to the next, Arthur Balfour. Unfortunately for the League and the IFL, this brought them into direct conflict with the powerful Association of Municipal Corporations headed by the rock-like Sir Albert Kaye Rollit, who fought the companies to a draw: the towns provided more electric power and tramway mileage, but 'municipal trading was blunted for a generation.'[88]

The Liberty and Property Defence League began to fade during the Liberal Government of 1906–10. By 1909 it had become no more than a token organization, and in February of that year the last issue of the *Liberty Review* appeared. Although the League outlasted Wemyss's death at the age of 96 in 1914 when he was succeeded as President by the Duke of Somerset, it had become an anachronism.[89] The reasons for this were ironical. It had come to be recognized even by the Conservative Party as too rigid and aggressive, and it was overshadowed by the more flexible and social reforming Anti-Socialist Union, founded by delegates from the London Municipal Society, the Industrial Freedom League, the Middle Classes Defence League and the (Tory) Primrose League in 1907. The chairman of the Union, Claude Lowther, an ex-Conservative MP, attacked the LPDL in 1911:

We regard the Liberty and Property Defence League as a dangerous reactionary group which engenders more socialism in one week than it prevents in a year by its wholesale opposition to all proposals which make for the people's welfare. Here is the secretary [Frederick Millar] of an organization which exists to fight socialism actually proclaiming ... a policy of negation. All logical minds must recognize that the extreme individualist is as absurd a member of the community as a pure collectivist. The latter is a socialist, the former is an anarchist.

Social reform and class reconciliation were, he claimed, more intelligent and effective ways of weaning the working class from socialism than confrontation and abuse.[90]

Within the LPDL, W. H. Mallock, its most far-sighted propagandist, had defended capitalism on the elitist grounds that the capitalists provided the incentive and managerial ability which, rather than labour, was the true source of value, and the social leadership for solving industry's and society's problems. In 1888 he recommended not only better industrial relations, high wages, and consultation between employers and workers, but also a government Labour Department to gather statistics on unemployment, state provision of public works and other help for the unavoidably unemployed, voluntary unemployment insurance, and even a statutory right to work. Instead of the 'present bickerings or smouldering war between labour and capital ... we should have a dispassionate conference between equally necessary estates.'[91] Whether consciously or not, many paternalist employers like Thomas Bushill, David Dale, Cadbury, Rowntree, George Thomson, W. H. Lever and John Lockie followed this advice and tried to create joint organizations of employers and trade unionists like the Industrial Union of Employers and Employed (1894) and the National Industrial Association (1900) which, though short-lived, were a step on the way to mutual recognition and negotiation. Others sought a way to industrial peace which they picked up from Thomas Hughes, E. V. Neale, and the Christian Socialist tradition of co-operative workshops.[92] Amongst these the most surprising experimenter was Sir George Livesey, anti-unionist and main financial support of the *Liberty Review*, who crushed Will Thorne's Gasworkers' Union at the South Metropolitan Gasworks in 1890 but became the greatest advocate amongst employers of profit sharing, as well as paid holidays, sick pay, pensions, and widows' and orphans' funds, from then until his death in 1908. In *Labour Co-partnership* in 1906 he quoted Mazzini:

Industrial workers were at one time slaves, then rising a little higher were serfs, and are now wage servants, so, still rising in position, they are destined to become partners with those who now provide the capital and directing power.[93]

Although participation in management through workers' shareholding remained 'almost negligible in all but a few cases' down to the First World War and the average bonus paid by all profit-sharing firms between 1910 and 1918 was only 5.5 per cent of wages, and although the trade unions mostly opposed such schemes as attempts to weaken their own influence with the workers, such policies represented a genuine attempt by the more enlightened employers to defend their property by means which amounted to a departure from absolute, irresponsible ownership and a movement, however small, towards its justification by good stewardship and accountability.[94]

What a minority of enlightened employers voluntarily accepted, mutual recognition and negotiation between trade unions and employers' associations, a larger number were driven to accept by growing pressure of opinion and government intervention. Given the increasing scale of organization, not only of industrial units and firms but of national employers' federations and trade unions, the whole nation came to have a vital interest in industrial disputes in such industries as coalmining and the railways. As Ramsay MacDonald, the archetypally moderate Labour Leader, expressed it in 1912:

We are too fond of imagining there are only two sides to a dispute. There is the side of capital, there is the side of labour, and there is the side of the general community: and the general community has no business to allow capital and labour, fighting their battles, to elbow them out of consideration.[95]

The government had begun to recognize this in the turbulent 1890s by setting up the Labour Department of the Board of Trade in 1892 with its succession of gifted civil servants, Llewellyn Smith, Vaughan Nash and Arthur Acland, and its growing expertise in conciliation procedures. It had further involved itself in 1907 with Lloyd George's appointment of Sir George Askwith as a roving, non-departmental conciliator, who skilfully settled the Belfast transport strike and the threatened railway strike of 1907. Lloyd George himself intervened in 1911 to force the obdurate railway companies, after long years of refusal, to recognize and negotiate with the railway unions. And prime minister Asquith personally intervened to settle the national coal strike of 1912 by offering by statute (on a regional basis) the minimum wage which the miners demanded (much to Sir George Askwith's anger at the bypassing of himself and the new National Industrial Council).[96] These interventions were reluctant and much criticized, but this does not detract from the fact that the government and its expert bureaucrats were now inexorably involved in what, with hindsight, can be seen as the beginnings of 'bargained corporatism'.[97] In this essentially bureaucratic system, the 'corporations' of employers and workers bargain not only with each other but with the bureaucratic representatives of the state, the latter at first as mere referees but increasingly as active partners (as in the Coal Mines Minimum Wage Act of 1912). At the risk of carrying the issue too far ahead of the present chapter, we may say that professional expertise and solutions based on the professional ideal were, because of the failure of other alternatives, already imposing themselves upon the relations between labour and capital before the First World War, a trend which was increasingly to dominate industrial relations down to the late twentieth century.

In a similar way, enlightened landowners came to see that a broadening of property ownership to include small freeholders was a more intelligent defence of landed property than the LPDL's negative opposition to land reform. Here again, the professional apologists of the LPDL offered a defence of property which undermined, if not its absolute character, at least its concentration in too few hands. Thomas Mackay, chief theorist of the Charity Organization Society and a firm supporter of individual property as 'a main condition of survival in civilized society', believed that a prosperity based on wage earning alone was too precarious, and should be buttressed by a wide diffusion of property amongst the working population: 'The problem of the future is the solution of this difficulty: How is the individualization of property to be brought about?'[98] The challenge of a property-owning democracy was taken up by great landowners and their professional supporters. Lord Salisbury declared in 1892:

It is rather the fashion to look upon landowners as a semi-criminal class upon which it is quite reasonable to heap every

burden you like in the shape of rates. But when we have the
alliance of those sturdy yeomen whom we hope to create we
may expect to be treated in a very different manner.[99]

This argument, deriving ultimately from Cobden and Bright's
belief in the creation of small freeholders by the effects of 'free
trade in land' upon the great estates, and carried over from the
Liberal to the Unionist Party by Joseph Chamberlain and Jesse
Collings of the 'three acres and a cow' campaign of 1885, became a
growing theme within the Tory Party from the 1880s onwards.
Henry Chaplin, Chancellor of the Duchy of Lancaster and a
leading landowner, argued in 1886, in favour of what became the
Allotment Act of 1887 (though he was against creating a class of
continental-type peasant smallholders), that 'a large increase in
the number of owners of land such as I desire is, I think, the surest
and perhaps the only safeguard against the predatory instincts of a
class whose Socialistic schemes have found such powerful
exponents in these days ...'[100] Although most Tory landowners
remained sceptical and violently opposed to compulsory provision, thus rendering ineffective the Smallholdings Act of 1892,
their leaders continued to argue in favour of peasant proprietor-
ship as the best defence of landed property as a whole. Arthur
Balfour supported the extension of state-aided purchase from
Ireland to England in 1909:

> There is no measure with which I am more proud to have been
> connected than with that of giving peasant ownership in such
> large measure to Ireland, and I hope to see a great extension of
> such ownership to England. Nothing could be more desirable
> or important.[101]

Lord Milner, in the 'landowners' panic' following the land tax
clauses of the People's Budget, summed up the argument for
buttressing large properties with small:

> There can be no manner of doubt that the institution of private
> property is seriously menaced at the present time – more
> seriously menaced perhaps in Great Britain than anywhere else
> in the world ... If the present Social Order is to endure, it is
> simply necessary, at whatever cost, to effect a great increase in
> the number of people who have a direct personal interest in the
> maintenance of private property. There is no bulwark to

communism at all equal to that provided by a large number of small property owners and especially small owners of land.[102]

By that time, however, as we have seen, 'the apparently stable Edwardian society had in fact resolved upon a social revolution, the liquidation of the landed interest.'[103] Even Walter Long, the foremost squire in the House of Commons and president of the Central Landed Association formed in 1907 to oppose the Liberal smallholdings legislation, was more interested in getting a good price for land than in saving the landed interest. He told the inaugural meeting:

Many of the amenities connected with the ownership of land have been largely reduced in value. Some have almost disappeared and there is no doubt that throughout the country there are opportunities for the transfer of land which did not exist in the days that are gone.... If we could agree upon a policy of purchase I believe that would be a very great step in the right direction for all who are concerned with our industry.[104]

The great transfers of land, chiefly to occupying tenants, delayed by the war but reaching between 6 and 8 million acres between 1918 and 1921 alone, were 'nothing less than the dissolution of the great estate system and the formation of a new race of yeomen'.[105] Ironically, the only way to defend the principle of absolute property in land, it seemed, was to sell it off altogether.

But if the number of owner-occupiers rose from 11 per cent in 1914 to 36 per cent in 1927, that still left 64 per cent who were tenant farmers and whose rights to a share in the beneficial ownership of land would be upheld by legislation during the Second World War and the post-war period, while both the owner-occupiers and tenant farmers came to achieve their security of tenure only on condition that they cultivated the land efficiently.[106] To that extent absolute property in land in 1914 still had a lot of concessions to make.

Why had the capitalists and the landlords, committed as they were to the defence of absolute property, come to give up so much of the argument by 1914? The short answer is that their hearts were no longer in it. The old, self-confident assumption that a man could do as he wished with his own had been undermined by doubts sown in their minds and concessions wrung from them by a public opinion moralized by a competing set of values. It was no longer possible for great business corporations like the railways and the coal owners to refuse to acknowledge the existence of trade unions, and the state was apt to force such recognition if they tried. Landlords were so demoralized by the prospect of diminished post-tax incomes and lost power over their land that they were selling out in droves.

Marx had observed that each new ruling class is compelled to represent its interest as the common interest of all members of society.[107] The converse was equally true, that the class which lost that battle for the mind would ultimately cease to be the ruling class. By the First World War, the propertied classes were still a long way from losing the battle, but they were already engaged, to a greater extent than they realized, in severe hand-to-hand fighting with the class which had for a generation and more been progressively undermining the concept of absolute property. As F. M. L. Thompson, English landed society's obituarist, has expressed it in relation to the peaceful demise of the landed interest:

> In the long run the old aristocratic influence could not resist the force of the intellectuals, for charm and cultivated manners were no match for reason, investigation and administrative vigour. The representatives of the old order were either too indolent to produce a coherent reasoned defence of their position or too well aware of the impossibility of justifying privilege. Instead they concentrated on the tactics of expediency and the preservation of as much as possible of the power of property for as long as possible, manipulating the machinery of political democracy through mass ignorance, prejudice and apathy to delay the spread of social equality.[108]

Similarly, as the late Sydney Checkland, historian of British public policy, observed, by 1914, 'business man was still in control', 'but he no longer had a confident rationale of what he was doing, no confirmatory theory of economy and society, and no sustaining set of religious and moral beliefs.'[109]

To see how the 'moral force of the intellectuals' and the tactics of expediency and delay could produce a compromise which was no mere deadlock but an open-ended pathway to the future, let us turn to the Edwardian origins of the welfare state.

4 THE PROFESSIONAL IDEAL AND THE ORIGINS OF THE WELFARE STATE

Like the other class ideals, the professional ideal had two strings to its bow, in its case trained expertise and selection by merit. The first, generalized as justification by service to society, was the main weapon of attack on the concept of absolute property. The second, generalized as the larger demand for social efficiency, became the leading factor in the passing of those Edwardian social reforms which we now recognize with hindsight as the origins of the welfare state. Social efficiency, in the negative form of a determined opposition to 'waste', the human and fiscal costs of *not* preventing dangers to health, economic performance and national efficiency, had long been the standard argument for state intervention in public health, factory reform, slum clearance, poor law medical treatment, state education, workmen's compensation, and the like. It had been summed up as long ago as 1859 by Edwin Chadwick, that arch-practitioner of Benthamite authoritarian intervention: *'To the questions sometimes put to me - where I would stop in the application of my principle - I am at present only prepared to answer: Where waste stops.'*[110] Before the end of the century the most important kind of waste had come to be recognized as the waste of *human* resources. As Alfred Marshall put it in 1889:

> in the world's history there has been one waste product so
> much more important than all the others, that it has a right to
> be called THE Waste Product. It is the higher abilities of many
> of the working classes; the latent, the undeveloped, the choked-
> up and wasted faculties for higher work, that for lack of
> opportunity have come to nothing.[111]

By the Edwardian age 'waste', under the influence of the Boer War and Britain's obviously declining economic and military leadership of the world, began to take on a further significance. From being a merely domestic concern to save firstly money and secondly human talent, an argument which could hope to stand up against the fiscal and moral rectitude of Gladstonian Liberalism, it now became a matter of international economic competitiveness and military survival, which the Gladstonian age had taken for granted. The naive 'internalist' Social Darwinism of Herbert Spencer, which confined itself to the survival of the fittest individuals without regard to the dangers of the unfit (who were to be weeded out) to the health and strength of the nation, was replaced by the 'externalist' Social Darwinism of Benjamin Kidd and Karl Pearson, who saw the primary struggle for survival as existing between nations, and the internal struggle between individuals as determining the nation's fitness to survive.[112]

Although Pearson was a socialist and Kidd an anti-socialist, both interpretations demanded collectivist social reform. Benjamin Kidd, a minor civil servant who published an immensely popular book on *Social Evolution* in 1894, believed that internal individual competition during the nineteenth century had served its purpose:

> Before the rivalry of life can be raised to that state of efficiency as an instrument of progress towards which it appears to be the inherent tendency of our civilization carry it, society will still have to undergo a transformation almost as marked as any through which it has passed in previous stages. We have evidence of that transformation in that trend of present-day legislation which appears so puzzling to many of the old progressive school ... It may be noticed that the character of this legislation is the increasing tendency to raise the position of the lower classes *at the expense of the wealthier classes*. All future progressive legislation must apparently have this tendency. It is almost a *conditio sine qua non* of any measure that carries us a step forward in our social development.

Since the masses had been enfranchised, Spencerian individualism had encouraged socialism by offering them nothing but exploitation and sacrifice. The answer was 'to complete the process of evolution in progress, by eventually bringing all people into the rivalry of life, not only on a footing of political equality, *but on conditions of equal social opportunities*'. What was now required as an antidote both to 'the materialistic socialism of Marx' and to the equally irreligious and materialistic individualism of Spencer was greater equality of opportunity, including the eight-hour day, the graduated income tax, and education for all, which would tend 'ultimately to place the workers more on a footing of equality in the rivalry of life with those above them.'[113]

Karl Pearson, the Cambridge and German-educated Goldsmid Professor of Mathematics at University College London from 1884 and first Galton Professor of Eugenics at London University from 1911 to 1933, was a paradoxically Marxist but anti-revolutionary socialist who believed that individualism had failed the nation:

> I believe that science will ultimately balance the individualistic and socialistic tendencies in evolution better than Haeckel and Spencer have done. The power of the individualistic formula to describe human growth has been overrated, and the evolutionary origin of the socialistic instinct has been too frequently overlooked. In the face of the severe struggle, physical and commercial, the fight for land, food, and for mineral wealth between existing nations, we have every need to strengthen by training the normally dormant socialistic spirit, if we as a nation are to be among the surviving fit. The importance of organizing society, of making the individual subservient to the whole, grows with the intensity of the struggle. We shall need all our clearness of vision, all our insight into human growth and social efficiency in order to discipline the powers of labour, to train and educate the powers of mind. This organization and this education must proceed from the state, for it is in the battle of society with society, rather than of individual with individual, that these weapons are of service.

The 'true Socialist must be superior to class interests. He must look beyond his own class to the wants and habits of society at large,' and educate himself and the governing class towards a higher social morality in which veneration for personified society, the state, would be the rational motive for conduct. In the middle of the Boer War he preached the beneficial effect of the international struggle for existence as 'the fiery crucible out of which comes the finer metal'. National survival depended not on the individual struggle for existence but on the social instincts of the herd, in which 'we must not have class differences and wealth differences so great within the community that we lose the sense of common interest.' A nation was 'an organized whole' which was 'kept up to a high pitch of external efficiency by contest, chiefly by war with inferior races, and by the struggles with equal races for trade-routes and for the sources of raw material and food supply'. Since 'you cannot get a strong and effective nation if many of its stomachs are half fed and many of its brains untrained', it was the

157

duty of the statesman 'to treat class needs and group cries from the standpoint of the efficiency of the herd at large' and 'to lessen, if not to suspend, the internal struggle, that the nation may be strong externally'. Although he would have preferred a dictator, free from the bias of class interest, to run his socialist state, the choice might prove too difficult and divisive and, though terribly cumbersome, democracy was probably the best practical solution. It followed that any reform which the democracy wanted was justified if it increased the efficiency of the nation.[114]

Not many contemporaries followed Pearson's social imperialism all the way to its proto-fascist conclusions, and Benjamin Kidd himself posthumously denounced Pearson's eugenic religion and Galton's scheme for improving the world by breeding a race of Nietzschean supermen, which could 'only be applied to the world by the methods of the German General Staff'.[115] But imperialism was rife amongst both Conservatives and Liberals, with the exception of the few pro-Boers and 'Little Englanders', and even split the Fabian Society down the middle in 1900. Anti-imperialists like Campbell-Bannerman, Lloyd George, Graham Wallas, L. T. Hobhouse, J. A. Hobson and Ramsay MacDonald, out of compassion for the poor and fear of their further deterioration, were no less in favour of social reform than the imperialists, but imperialism added power and urgency to the argument for it.[116] This came to a head in the debate on 'National Efficiency' which arose out of the Boer War. The term seems to have been coined by Sidney Webb in a famous article in the *Nineteenth Century* in 1901, 'Lord Rosebery's Escape from Houndsditch', in which he advised Rosebery to 'retailor' the Liberals into a party of National Efficiency, which would clear the slums, abolish the sweated trades, eliminate inefficiency in government, restore British commercial supremacy, adopt policies of reform in housing, sanitation, poor law, and education, together with a 'National Minimum' standard of life, all 'to insure the rearing of an Imperial race'.[117]

Rosebery was more than ready to take the bait and delivered a speech on the idea of efficiency as 'a condition of national fitness equal to the demands of our Empire – administrative, parliamentary, commercial, educational, physical, moral, naval, and military fitness – so that we should make the best of our admirable raw material'.[118] By then he and his Liberal imperialist followers, H. H. Asquith, R. B. Haldane and Sir Edward Grey, inauspiciously known as the 'Limps', had already formed the Liberal League, a party within the party, to push imperialism and social reform.[119] At the very same time Joseph Chamberlain, a more bellicose social imperialist, was concocting on the government side the policies of tariff reform and imperial preference which were designed to unify the empire and provide the money for old age pensions and other social reforms.

The Webbs attempted to bring leading imperialists of all parties together in a small dining club, the 'Coefficients', who were to represent professional 'experts' in every field of government: Haldane for law, Grey for foreign policy, H. J. Mackinder the inventor of 'geopolitics', Sir Clinton Dawkins for finance, the economist W. A. S. Hewins, Director of the new Fabian London School of Economics, Leopold Maxse, editor of *The Nation* for patriotic journalism, Carlyon Bellairs for naval questions, Leopold Amery of *The Times* for army reform, William Pember Reeves, Agent General for New Zealand, for the colonies, Sidney Webb for local government, H. G. Wells for literature, and Bertrand Russell (who was soon repelled by their imperialism) for science. They were later joined by Sir Alfred Milner, Chamberlain's chief imperialist lieutenant and patron of Amery and Mackinder.[120] H. G. Wells satirized the Coefficients as the 'Pentagram Circle' in *The New Machiavelli* (1911), but he was, if anything, even more devoted to efficient government by professional experts, foreshadowed in *Anticipations* (1902) and realized in the 'Samurai' in *A Modern Utopia* (1905). Although Chamberlain's tariff reform campaign split the Coefficients and perhaps prevented them from founding a party of national efficiency, they were an eloquent expression of the professional ideal in its social imperialist phase.

National efficiency, for all its faults and failings, had the great merit from the point of view of the professional class of appealing to the self-interest of all three major classes. To the traditional landed class and its military offshoots, worried lest an urbanized industrial society should not be able to defend itself against the vast conscript peasant armies of the continental powers, it offered an answer to the army's complaints, through General Sir Frederick Maurice, of the desperately poor physique if not the actual physical deterioration of the recruits during the Boer War.

To the capitalists, concerned about the declining competitiveness of British industry and trade and the increasing bitterness of industrial relations, it offered the prospect of fitter, healthier, better trained and educated workers, and the hope of more harmonious conditions in the workplace. To the working class it offered a larger and more rapid progress towards social improvement and a fairer society than they could have achieved by their own unaided efforts. As for the professional class – what did it offer them? Perhaps the greatest prize of all, a share in the expansion of expert services provided by or paid for by government, a higher level of remuneration guaranteed by the state and, for some of them at least, an increase in power and prestige in a system increasingly dependent for its smooth operation and success upon themselves.

Not all of these varied interests were consciously thought out and single-mindedly pursued. On the contrary, as Bentley Gilbert has noted, 'welfare legislation never figured as an electoral issue in the years before World War I'.[121] With a few exceptions like old age pensions and the graduated income tax, most of the reforms of the Edwardian period were unpremeditated and previously little discussed. As each came to be identified, however, and became an issue between the contending interests, the debate was conducted in terms which reflected the moral values raised by different protagonists of the professional ideal, and was settled by a compromise between the classes which leaned heavily towards a professional solution.

The traditionally accepted causes of the Liberal welfare measures, 'pressure from below', 'the pressure of facts', and the newly found 'intolerability' of social problems, whether or not they were adequate as explanations rather than descriptions of what was happening, all found their response in a professionally institutionalized provision of welfare.

'Pressure from below', the belated upswelling of working-class political demands after the 1867 and 1884 Reform Acts, has been questioned on the grounds that the working class 'advanced into the twentieth century with little expectation of social improvement being engineered by political means, and none at all of the "Welfare State" as we know it today.'[122] It is true that the Labour Party and the TUC passed resolutions in favour of old age pensions, free secondary education, school meals, the right to work, and so on, but comparatively few workers voted Labour before 1918, and many members of the Labour Party and the unions bitterly opposed, at first at least, some of the major Liberal social reforms, such as labour exchanges and contributory national insurance.[123] 'Pressure from below' did operate in the sense that both the Conservatives and the Liberals wooed the working-class voter with social imperialist policies of social reform which *they thought* he wanted, but the actual measures offered by strong-minded politicians like Chamberlain and Lloyd George and self-confident administrators like Sir Robert Morant and William Beveridge were based on *their* criteria, not *his*, and the Liberal reforms were made *for* him, not *by* him.

The 'pressure of facts', the impact on public opinion of the new knowledge of poverty and distress provided by Booth, Rowntree, the army recruiting figures, and the Committee on Physical Deterioration was also crucial, not so much because the facts were new – sensational reports of the condition of the poor went back to Mayhew, Chadwick and beyond – but because the 'fear of the poor' and the effect of their supposed deterioration on the survival of the nation now made the facts more urgent. Attitudes towards the political and economic implications of poverty had changed, and with them the political will to provide administrative solutions for them.

Finally, if the social problems of the age were now found to be more 'intolerable' than before, by what criteria were they judged to be so? By the professional criteria derived from the Oxford idealists, the Cambridge welfare economists, and the Fabians and other middle-class socialists, emphasizing the responsibilities of property, national efficiency, and justification by service to society. More important than the 'intolerability' of the problems, however, were the actual legislative and administrative solutions adopted for them, and these bore all the marks of the professional ideal, as we can see by examining each of the main social reforms in turn.

Old age pensions were the longest recognized social need. The capitalist view that the individual should make provision by voluntary saving for his old age was increasingly seen in the late Victorian age to be unrealistic. Canon William Blackley in 1878, prompted by the failure of the friendly societies to cater for more than a prosperous fraction of the working class and by the refusal of the 'wasteful' to 'share in the burden of natural providence', had suggested a compulsory scheme of 'national insurance'. Under this every working man between 18 and 21 would invest £10 at compound interest to provide 8s a week in sick pay and a pension of 4s. a week at age 70.[124] In the late 1880s those capitalists of conscience, Joseph Chamberlain, anxious to maintain his reputation for social reform and Charles Booth, influenced by Canon Barnett of Toynbee Hall, had taken up the question and obtained a Royal Commission in 1895 to investigate and the Rothschild Committee in 1898 to find ways of funding them. Chamberlain came to tariff reform and social imperialism at least in part as a means of funding old age pensions as well as other welfare measures. Booth's argument for direct taxation for support of the 'incapable', beginning with the elderly poor, pursued through the National Committee of Organized Labour for the Promotion of Old Age Pensions founded in 1889, was couched in terms of national efficiency:

> My idea is to make the dual system, Socialism in the arms of individualism, under which we already live, more efficient by extending somewhat the sphere of the former and making the division of function more distinct. Our Individualism fails because our Socialism is incomplete. In taking charge of the lives of the incapable, State Socialism finds its proper work, and by doing it completely, would relieve us of a serious danger ... Thorough interference on the part of the State with the lives of a small fraction of the population would tend to make it possible ultimately, to dispense with any Socialistic interference in the lives of all the rest.[125]

The non-contributory pensions provided by the 1908 Budget exactly reflected the balance of ideological forces. They made only a small breach in the capitalist ideal of self-dependence by paying 5s. a week (7s. 6d. for a married couple) at age 70 only if the applicant earned less than £26 a year, was not a pauper, lunatic or ex-convict, and had been habitually employed. In line with the aristocratic ideal, they were thus a reward for a lifetime's loyal service to the community. In line with the working-class ideal, they were a deferred instalment of the whole produce of labour. And in line with the professional ideal they were a more socially efficient means of supporting the elderly poor, who would in any case have required public support, than the repellant and arbitrary poor law. That they were not the *most* socially efficient means is shown by their replacement for most workers in 1925 by contributory pensions, which suited both the social reformers, who believed that the poor should visibly earn their pensions and receive them by right, and the Treasury officials, for whom the contributions, like national insurance, were a welcome widening of the tax base. They also suited the local civil servants (for lack of others in the localities in 1908, the Customs and Excise officers who had to administer them and the post masters who paid them) for whom they provided more work.

School meals and medical inspection in 1906 and 1907 were an obvious response to the fear of physical deterioration and the demand for national efficiency. If education, needed for the economic competition between the nations, was not to be wasted on children too hungry to learn, then it was necessary to feed them.[126] Cheap or free school dinners had been pioneered since the 1860s on humanitarian grounds by charities such as the Westminster Destitute Children's Society and since 1895 by Margaret McMillan in Bradford, but now it was generally agreed to be a matter of national survival and the only question was how to find the money.[127] The Unionist Cabinet in 1905 admitted that underfed children were 'one of the evils now generally admitted to exist', but it was brought down in December by a motion in the Commons calling for local authorities to ensure proper nourishment in elementary schools.[128] After the 1906 Election a Labour Party bill was endorsed by the Liberal majority and the local education authorities were empowered to provide facilities for school meals.

School feeding, too, reflected the balance of ideological forces. The Act made the smallest possible breach in the entrepreneurial ideal that parents should support their own children: it was permissive only, allowing Local Educational Authorities to impose a halfpenny rate, a permission taken up very sparingly by only a hundred authorities, less than a third of the total, by 1911.[129] It appealed to aristocrats like Rosebery, the Liberal imperialist, and the Duke of Devonshire, who had appointed the Committee on Physical Deterioration which recommended it, as well as to the army generals whose complaints led to that Committee.[130] It was popular for obvious reasons with the organized working class who seized on the Committee's suggestion and presented the 1906 bill.[131] And it chimed with the professional demand for social efficiency expressed by such diverse bodies as the Fabian Society, the National Union of Teachers, the Royal Colleges of Physicians and Surgeons, and the British Medical Association.[132] Most significantly of all, it eminently suited both the ideals and the interests of the civil servants who operated it, and used it as a springboard for further action in the cause of collectivist social efficiency.

The most obvious further action was school medical inspection, necessary to measure the need for school feeding and to monitor its effects, which was smuggled through Parliament in 1907 in a little-noticed bill of administrative provisions prepared by the Secretary of the Board of Education, Sir Robert Morant, at the prompting of Margaret McMillan and other local reformers, to meet another recommendation of the Physical Deterioration Committee.[133] To Morant and his colleagues, however, it was more than an information-gathering device. As a fellow civil servant, Sir Lawrence Brock, put it later:

> Morant knew ... and did not tell his Minister, that medical inspection would reveal such a mass of disease and defect that no Government subsequently would be able to resist the demand of the local Education authorities to provide treatment.[134]

This was a calculated use of the well-known governmental principle of 'feedback'. With a firm fellow-believer, George Newman, as Chief Medical Officer to the Board, Morant ensured that Circular 576 (1907) enjoining medical inspection on the LEAs was followed by Circular 596 (1908) inviting them to establish school clinics and an Act of 1909 empowering them to provide treatment from central funds.[135] By 1914 214 out of 317 LEAs were providing treatment and a further fifty-three were contracting with voluntary hospitals to provide it.[136] School medical treatment, while a logical development of the demand for national efficiency by all classes, was perhaps an early example of a social reform 'manufactured' by the state bureaucracy, with the tacit support of other professions, including the teachers and doctors, who saw in it not only a measure of justice and efficiency but an addition to their own prestige and potential employment.

The educational ladder created by the new public secondary schools under the 1902 Act and the scholarship system of 1907 was a prime example of the professional principle of selection by merit as well as of the demand for national efficiency. It had been supported by enlightened members of every political sect and party, by Arthur Balfour and Sir John Gorst for the Tories, by Lloyd George and Charles Masterman for the Liberals, by Sidney Webb and the Fabians, and by both the TUC and the Labour Representation Committee in 1905.[137] Yet it was Morant again, architect of the (Tory) Education Act of 1902 and of the (Liberal) scholarship system of 1907, who cut through the rivalries of church and dissent and of school boards and county councils to make them possible.[138] Although by 1914 only 5.6 per cent of elementary school children found their way to secondary schools, a ladder had been erected which would take larger proportions of English and still more of Welsh and Scottish working-class children on to secondary and higher education than anywhere else in inter-war Europe.[139] According to Morant, 'The purpose of the Public Elementary School is to form and strengthen the character and to develop the intelligence of the children entrusted to it.' It was only 'an important but subsidiary object of the School to discover individual children who show promise of exceptional capacity and to develop their special gifts in preparation for secondary and university education,' but the means he chose, selective grammar schools for the very brightest, were as elitist and professional as himself.[140]

The same elitist bureaucrat, forced out of Education in 1911 for his snobbish approval of his chief inspector's reference to 'vicious local inspectors' recruited from the elementary school teachers,[141] provides a link with national health insurance. On the foundations laid for Lloyd George by W. J. Braithwaite, he built up the elaborate machinery integrating the friendly societies which issued the benefits, the Post Office which collected the premiums through the sale of stamps, the local inspectors who applied and enforced the rules, the panel doctors who certified illness and prescribed treatment, and the pharmacists who supplied the drugs.[142] Rowntree had shown that sickness, invalidity and/or death of the breadwinner were, after low wages and large families, the most important cause of poverty, accounting for 20 per cent of those in poverty in York.[143] The

165

Majority Report of the Poor Law Commission (1909) recommended voluntary insurance through the friendly societies and trade unions against long-term invalidity, though the Minority demanded a 'National Minimum' paid out of taxation.[144] Lloyd George and Morant ignored both, and chose compulsory insurance for short- and long-term sickness. They cleverly bought off the opposition of the employers by hinting at heavier taxation threatened by Labour and the Minority Report; that of the friendly societies and insurance companies by employing them as agents of the scheme; that of the doctors by doubling the annual capitation fees they had received from the friendly societies; and that of the workers, over the heads of both the Labour Party and the Minority of the Poor Law Commission, by offering 'ninepence for fourpence' (3d. of the weekly 9d. stamp being paid by the employers and 2d. by the state) of the insurance premium for sick pay and free medical treatment. Lloyd George and Morant, with an eye to administrative feedback, confidently looked forward to the provision of medical treatment for workers' families, and eventual coverage of the whole population, which did come but not until 1948.[145]

Once again, national health insurance represented the balance of ideological forces. To the industrialists it meant fitter workers returning faster to work (though not all of them, especially the employers of domestic servants, saw it that way). To the workers, despite the protests of some of their representatives, it meant, for the first time for many of them, professional medical treatment and a modest income during illness. To the medical profession it meant an expanded occupation at increased renumeration for the 'panel doctors'. And to the central and local civil servants who operated the scheme it meant more employment, higher prestige, and an opportunity to practise social engineering. As Morant himself put it in 1913, 'we can make work at the Government Department the most marvellous means for true social reform that the world has ever seen.'[146]

As with health insurance by Lloyd George and Morant, state unemployment insurance was sprung on the nation by Winston Churchill and William Beveridge, but with no German precedent to call on. Unemployment, or the problem of the able-bodied poor as the Poor Law Commission Majority Report still called it, was as ancient as the Tudor poor law, but it only became an 'intolerable social problem' when the working class got the vote, when Booth and Rowntree discovered in it a major cause of poverty contributing to 20.7 per cent of the poverty in East London and (in a boom year) to 5.1 per cent of those in poverty in York, and when politicians in the 1880s like Chamberlain and Lord Randolph Churchill began to demand public measures for its relief.[147]

Yet it only became a soluble problem when William Beveridge, a young Balliol man recruited by Canon Barnett as sub-warden of Toynbee Hall, began to study the statistics produced by the Lord Mayor's Mansion House Committee on Distress and by other bodies operating under the 1905 Unemployed Workmen Act. He discovered that most unemployment was involuntary and of four distinct kinds: frictional (between jobs), seasonal (annual fluctuations in such trades as building, printing and fashion wear), cyclical (boom and slump), and structural (long-term decline of particular industries). Only a small fraction could be laid at the door, as the Charity Organization Society representatives on the Poor Law Commission believed, of the idle and incompetent. Unemployment, therefore, was in the words of the subtitle of his 1909 book, 'a problem of industry'.[148] The solution could only be a professional and administrative one: labour exchanges to fit workers to jobs as quickly as possible and unemployment insurance to tide the jobless over through bad seasons and slumps. Both the Majority and Minority Reports recommended voluntary unemployment insurance through trade unions with state subsidies, and the Minority compulsory labour exchanges. Beveridge, with Churchill's backing, turned these upside down: *voluntary* labour exchanges and *compulsory* insurance. Many of his ideas were derived from older students of the question: Percy Alden, Warden of the Mansfield House University Settlement in Canning Town and his book *Unemployment: A National Question* (1905), the radical economist J. A. Hobson, and Booth's and Rowntree's surveys of the causes of poverty.[149] But it was Beveridge, recruited by Churchill to the Board of Trade 'to formulate arguments and schemes for national Labour Exchanges with a view to getting them accepted by the Government', and the forceful Secretary to the Board, Sir Hubert Llewellyn Smith, one of Charles Booth's original investigators on the London survey, who devised the Labour Exchange Act of 1909 and the pilot scheme of unemployment insurance for 2.25 million workers in fluctuating industries included in the 1911 National Insurance Act.[150] Again, feedback was confidently expected to expand its coverage, as it did for ex-soldiers and munitions workers after the war, and for most manual and low-paid non-manual workers by 1923.[151]

Despite individualist and Fabian opposition, unemployment insurance fitted the balance of ideological forces. For the paternalist aristocrat like Churchill, it took the able-bodied poor out of the Poor Law and off the local rates. For the capitalist it carried the burden of the reserve army of labour partly at the expense of the taxpayer and the worker himself. For the worker – despite the opposition of the Webbs and the Independent Labour Party – it provided a small measure of financial security (7s. a week in return for a 2d. a week contribution), which seemed like a reasonable bargain. But the most influential contributions, and the most permanent gains, were those of the social researchers turned bureaucrats like Beveridge and Llewellyn Smith. The combination of the labour exchange and unemployment insurance was an almost perfect example of a professional solution to a problem of social engineering. Beveridge, like Morant, was no democrat but a believer in 'a strong government, a remorselessly unsentimental government' which would involve 'the extension of deliberate social action – in a word, organization – over fields hitherto left to the blind play of conflicting interests. It replaces the rule of natural law by the rule of the expert.'[152]

There were other social reforms in the Edwardian age – the Children Act of 1908, the Housing and Town Planning Act of 1909, the 1902 Midwives Act and the local infant welfare centres – to which the same analysis could be applied. But enough has been said to show how, given the current balance of ideological forces, the professional ideal could swing that balance, by selecting the social problems to be solved and by determining the nature of the solution. One final test of the process of reform remains. A welfare state, even an incipient one, which begins to provide social security, educational opportunity, and a pioneering health service involves a redistribution of income. Much of this, as with national insurance, is horizontal, from the young, healthy and employed to the same people when old, sick or jobless; but some at least had to be vertical, from the rich to the poor. Ideas of graduated taxation were, as we have seen, implicit in the professional attack on absolute property and the professional demand for justification of income by service. Although graduation did not go very far – death duties of 8 per cent on estates over £1 million in 1894 and of 15 per cent in 1909, income taxes of 1s. instead of 9d. in the pound on unearned incomes over £2,000 in 1907, and supertaxes in 1909 (over and above the standard rates of 9d.–1s. 2d.) of 6d. on incomes over £5,000 and 9d. on over £6,000 – the principle had been established which would carry maximum rates of tax to 7s. 4d. in the pound in the First World War and 19s. 6d. in the Second.[153]

At what point taxation passes from the concept of fair shares and equal burdens to that of confiscation is a matter for debate – there were many who thought that point had been passed in 1909 – but what is certain is that the principle of graduated taxation was a breach with the Gladstonian past which could not have happened unless the confidence of the rich in the inviolable sanctity of property had already been undermined. To the extent that it had, the professional ideal had triumphed in fiscal policy over the landed and capitalist by 1909.

Britain in 1914 was still undoubtedly, and would long remain, a fundamentally capitalist society. But the influence of the professional expert, with his belief in contingent property justified by service to society and in social efficiency for the benefit of the whole nation, had already begun to permeate the consciousness of the other classes and the policies and administration of government. It was in vain that Winston Churchill protested to H. G. Wells in 1902 in response to a complimentary copy of his *Anticipations of the Reaction of Mechanical and Scientific Progress upon Human Life and Thought*:

Nothing would be more fatal than for the Government of States to get in the hands of experts. Expert knowledge is limited knowledge: and the unlimited ignorance of the plain man who knows where it hurts is a safer guide than any vigorous direction of a specialized character. Why should you assume that all except doctors, engineers, etc., are drones or worse?[154]

Within a few years Churchill's and his colleagues' own actions were beginning to commit government into the hands of experts, and to ensure that the twentieth century would become the century not of the plain man who knows where it hurts but of the professional expert who 'knows best' what is good for him. Even before the Great War came to test its cohesion, class society began to go into crisis, which war appeared to mollify or postpone, but which in reality could only be surmounted by measures which challenged the system and called in the professional experts to help to provide them.

Chapter 5

THE CRISIS OF CLASS SOCIETY

Between the constitutional clash between the Lords and the Commons which provoked two general elections in 1910 and the General Strike which split the nation in 1926, class society in Britain underwent a profound crisis. The crisis was essentially to decide whether Britain was to continue along the path of increasing class conflict culminating in social breakdown or revolution or whether there was to be, not merely an accommodation between the classes of the kind which gave mid-Victorian Britain its viable class society, but something more far-reaching: a tacit co-partnership between the representatives of capital and labour in which the state would find itself increasingly involved, to the point where it became itself a partner in a relationship which transcended class society altogether.

Looking back from a later age long after the issue was decided, it is tempting to argue that the crisis was unreal, that the issue was never in doubt, that there never was a threat to the social fabric or a challenge to the established system of government.[1] This may perhaps be true in the narrow sense that, apart from a few self-consciously revolutionary syndicalists and Marxists, the British labour movement never overtly set out to challenge the elected government. Crises and revolutions, however, are rarely planned and programmed but arise out of the clash of interests and of will between threatened and frustrated social groups whose determination to gain their ends or maintain their ground can escalate without conscious intent from incompatible demands to violent contestation. In an age which saw revolutions from Ireland to China and the collapse of four great empires in continental Europe, it would be unwise to rely on 'the unique good sense of

171

the British people' to refute the possibility here. Moreover, what is important is not the mere threat and avoidance of revolution which, however improbable, appeared real enough to many contemporaries, but the transcendence of the crisis by means which were not mere temporary palliatives but the harbingers of a new social order.

The crisis was predominantly one between the classes of capital and labour, in which the government became reluctantly involved, by no means wholly on the side of capital, but it was complicated by the co-existence of three other crises, any one of which was a potentially violent challenge to the established order. It is not necessary to go all the way with George Dangerfield in *The Strange Death of Liberal England* to agree that there was *some* connection between the pre-war challenge of the Lords, the Suffragettes, the two parts of Ireland, and the striking workers, if only in the existence of a weak Liberal government unable to live up to its Liberal principles without committing suicide.[2] Connected or not, the co-existence of threats of violence from the militant women, from the Irish Nationalists if Ireland were partitioned and from the Ulstermen backed by the Tory leadership and the majority of the Lords if it were not, and from the more aggressive trade unionists, gave colour to the fear of social revolution before the war, just as the co-existence of revolutions in Russia, Germany, Austria–Hungary and Turkey as well as Ireland gave colour to the same fear after it. And just as in the early nineteenth century the fear of revolution or of a peaceful takeover from below, whether justified or not, played an essential role in the emergence of class society, so in the early twentieth the same mixture of fear and propitiation played an essential role in the crisis of class society and its incipient modification into something new.

The crisis was also complicated by the intervention of the war. In the short term the war suspended all four crises, and seemed to prove that there was a great deal more unity and cohesion in British society than many contemporaries, including the Kaiser and his ministers, had believed. It was certainly, as the social imperialists had predicted, the supreme test not only of national unity but of national efficiency. It ruthlessly laid bare the shortcomings and deficiencies of society, the economy and the political system. It confirmed the appalling effects of poverty and undernourishment on the mass armies recruited to fight it, the early weaknesses of British industry and management in producing the munitions of modern battle, and the incompetence of the minimalist state apparatus to conduct modern warfare on the grand scale. Yet in the longer term it also proved the enormous power of the modern state, when roused to accept the responsibility, to control almost every aspect of the life of society, from direct industrial production on a massive scale to the egalitarian distribution of food, the conscription of men from all classes for the armed forces, and even, by the negative pressure of scheduling reserved occupations, the tacit direction of civilian labour.

Yet the massive increase in the role of the state did not, contrary to patriotic expectations, suspend class conflict between capital and labour. On the contrary, it raised to a higher power the prestige of the labour unions and their ability, in exchange for their co-operation, to demand to be consulted and persuaded by both the employers and the state. Moreover, if in the opinion of their members their leaders sold their co-operation too cheaply, an alternative leadership thrust itself forward in the shape of the shop stewards' movement which kept alive the confrontation of capital and labour in the workplace, the comparatively rare but truculent strikes serving as a reminder that the suspension of industrial conflict was only a truce, not a cessation of hostilities. Yet the war also educated the unions, the employers and the state in the possibility of an alternative relationship, already in embryo before its outbreak, based on a tacit understanding of their underlying common interests.

The war did not end the crisis, however. With the peace, and especially with the precipitate demobilization of the troops into the old pre-war fear of low wages and unemployment, the equally precipitate dismantling of the wartime system of controls which had seemed to promise fairer shares for all, and the apparent breach of wartime promises of 'homes for heroes' and 'a fit land for heroes to live in', the crisis returned, and went through a fluctuating series of confrontations until it culminated in the anti-climactic trial of strength in 1926.

The final phase was the post-crisis settlement. Despite the vengefulness of many business men and right-wing Conservative politicians and the legend of vendetta perpetuated by the defeated labour movement, the victorious government and the leading employers did not exploit their victory to the full. Instead, they drew the trade unions into an informal, uneasy but nevertheless real triangular relationship which was an anticipation of what would later be called the 'bargained corporatism' of the 1960s. That this offended and enraged some of their constituents on all three sides – militant unionists, traditional business men, and right-wing Conservatives – merely confirms the trend, and also helps to explain it. For underlying what Keith Middlemas has called 'the corporate bias' of the emerging system was something more fundamental than a wish for industrial peace.[3] It was the professional interest of the men who ran the system – the trade union leaders, the new professional managers of the great business corporations and employers' association, and the state bureaucrats and politicians – to keep the system going without allowing it to drift too near the brink of disastrous confrontation. And beneath this system of 'crisis management'[4] lay not merely a common professional self-interest but a common philosophy, capable of embracing both their common interest in maintaining the system and their differences of outlook. That philosophy was the professional social ideal.

In this chapter we shall follow the crisis through all its stages from the massive industrial unrest aborted by the coming of the war; through the paradoxical co-existence of national unity and industrial conflict during the war; to the post-war culmination in the General Strike and its immediate aftermath. In the process we shall see how conflict and the threat of social breakdown themselves played a key role in the emergence of an alternative system of relationships.

1 THE ABORTED PRE-WAR CRISIS

In the last few years before the First World War an unprecedented upsurge of national unrest took place in Britain. The number of strikes, rarely more than 500 a year in earlier times, rose from 422 in 1909 to 521 in 1910, 872 in 1911, 834 in 1912, 1,459 in 1913 and 972 in 1914 (chiefly in the seven months before the war broke out). More to the point, these strikes were on a larger and more nationwide scale than hitherto, and the number of working man-days lost, usually 3 to 4 million a year, rose from 2.7 million in

1909 to 9.9 million in 1910, 10.2 million in 1911, 40.9 million in 1912, the year of the great coal strike, falling back to 9.8 million in 1913 and 9.9 million in 1914.[5] There had been something approaching this upsurge with the New Unionism of the early 1890s, with a record 30.4 million days lost in 1893, but there were now three times the number of union members, approaching 4 million in 1913,[6] and there was then nothing like the same threat to the industrial system and the life of the community which seemed to be inseparable from the pre-war unrest. The first nationwide strike on the railways in 1911, the dock strikes of 1911, the vast coal strike of 1912, the Dublin transport lock-out of 1913, the textile workers' strikes (in the main export industry) in 1913, culminated in the Triple Alliance of the miners, railwaymen and transport workers, which appeared to threaten a general strike in the autumn of 1914.[7]

The legend of 'the great General Strike of 1914, forestalled by the bullets at Sarajevo' has been challenged on two grounds: firstly, that the trade union leaders did not want it, that the unions concerned had either won what they wanted, like the railwaymen's forty-year objective of recognition by the employers, or were financially if not morally exhausted, like the miners and the transport workers, and secondly, that the Alliance was aimed more at controlling the militant rank and file and strengthening the power of the three federations against the other unions in their industry than at challenging the employers and the government.[8] But this does not dispose of the fears of contemporaries or of the belief on the part of even moderate union leaders that the mere threat of a nationwide strike in three vital industries would be enough to force the government to coerce the employees to surrender. There was 'the sense of an impending general clash, a civil war between capital and labour, that was strong at that time of many clashes'.[9] As Lloyd George wrote in his *War Memoirs*,

in the summer of 1914 there was every sign that the autumn would witness a series of industrial disturbances without precedent. Trouble was threatening in the railway, mining, engineering and building industries, disagreements were active not only between employers and employed, but in the internal organisation of the workers. A strong 'rank and file' movement, keenly critical of the policies and methods of the official leaders of Trade Unionism had sprung up and was rapidly gaining strength. Such was the state of the home front when the nation was plunged into war.[10]

The National Union of Railway men had given notice of a strike for 1 November. The Scottish miners were faced with a wage cut, the most resented cause of strikes even by exhausted unions, which was only averted by the owners' 'patriotic' withdrawal on the outbreak of war, and the district agreements of 1912 under the Coal Miners Minimum Wage Act were due to expire in June 1915. The London building workers were already in dispute with the London Master Builders' Association over their refusal to sign a 'memorandum' against unofficial strikes and had been locked out since January, and the National Federation of Building Trades Employers had announced a national lock-out for 15 August.[11] Any of these disputes, despite the union leaders' supposed moderation, might have provoked a confrontation which could have escalated into a much bigger clash. The most moderate of their leaders, J. H. Thomas of the NUR, believed that the Alliance was irresistible: 'I do not hesitate to say ... that we shall only use this power once. If we use it effectively, the fear of it will be sufficient for all time after.' And the more militant and syndicalist Robert Williams of the Transport Workers thought the threat powerful enough to challenge the ruling class without a strike:

> They did not want to talk too much about a strike, but they wanted to have power behind them as a final resort to put the screw upon all the governing classes of society in order to effect such demands as they might find it desirable to make.[12]

Such talk of big sticks and easy victories was like the jingoism of the belligerent nations – 'We don't want to fight, but by jingo if we do, we've got the ships, we've got the men, we've got the money too' – which led the politicians to think there would be no war in 1914, and if there were the troops would be home by Christmas. Nor does the misplaced confidence of the Triple Alliance dispose of the wider industrial unrest of the previous five years, which still represented a crisis for class society, unresolved in 1914, whether or not a general strike was imminent when the war broke out.

The causes of this pre-war upsurge of unrest have been much disputed by historians, mostly divided according to whether or not they took 'the threat of civil war' seriously. The sceptics normally point to the economic and technical factors: the steepening inflation (mild by modern standards, a rise of 13.4 per cent in the cost of living between 1903 and 1913, rising to an average of 2.3 per cent a year from 1909 to 1913); the consequent decline of real wages (money earnings rose by only 6.1 per cent, so that real earnings declined by 6.9 per cent);[13] the slower growth or even decline, as in the coal mines, of productivity, leaving less surplus to be shared between capital and labour; and the consequent refusal of employers, as on the railways where profits were further squeezed by legislative limitation of freight rates, to recognize trade unions for negotiating purposes.[14] On the other side, the believers in revolutionary working-class consciousness have pointed to more general causes of alienation and unrest: the speeding up of the pace of work by employers influenced by the new American 'scientific management' of F. W. Taylor and his disciples, responding to the slackening productivity and the fiercer international competition; the determination of many employers, notably the mine owners, railway directors, shipowners and port authorities, to discipline recalcitrant workers and curb the increasingly disruptive power of the trade unions; the struggle, emphasized above (Chapter 4), for control of the work process in the workplace itself; and, less confidently perhaps, the influence on already disgruntled workers, disappointed both with Labour and with Liberal political reforms, of syndicalist ideas of the industrial class struggle and the revolutionary general strike.[15]

All these causes certainly played a part in the crisis, but the particular economic and shopfloor grievances of individual groups of workers, perhaps excited by the electrifying political atmosphere and the belief manifested by other militants like the Suffragettes and the Irish that the threat of violence was a master card, welled up from below and forced professional trade union leaders to adopt militant postures designed to coerce the employers and the government into a confrontation which was in fact more dangerous than anyone, except a handful of theoretical revolutionary socialists and syndicalists, intended. The crisis, in other words, was a genuinely spontaneous conflagration despite the ultimately peaceful intentions of most protagonists, precisely because it brought into confrontation men who each thought their incompatible demands morally impregnable. Both sides, convinced of the rightness of their cause, moved steadily towards a clash which neither wanted, because they believed that the other side would 'see sense' and back down. That both backed down before the common danger from abroad when real war came is no warrant for thinking that the clash could have been avoided by any less dramatic means.

Whether the ultimate outcome would have been very different from the vacillations and anti-climax of the post-war denouement may well be doubted. The government would have been forced to intervene in defence of law and order and the preservation of the community from starvation and collapse in anything approaching a general strike, just as it did in 1921, 1925 and 1926, and indeed as it did in industry-wide but less than general strikes before the war. The trade unions could only have won at the expense of parliamentary democracy, and it is extremely doubtful whether any of their leaders, even the handful of syndicalists like Tom Mann, Robert Williams of the Transport Workers, or A. J. Cook of the South Wales miners, were ready with an adequate alternative. But we are concerned with the possibility not so much of violent revolution as of the escalation of confrontational class conflict on a massive scale. That was certainly a possibility in 1914, and its avoidance was entirely due to the 'luck' of the outbreak of war.

The outstanding feature of the pre-war industrial unrest was its upsurge from below, which took not only the government and employers but even the traditional trade union leaders by surprise. It was less surprising in the case of the 'New Unionists', the hitherto unorganized, or only occasionally and sporadically organized, workers like the dockers, the building workers or the Cornish clay miners. It was much more surprising amongst the old unionists, the miners, railwaymen, textile workers, and West Midlands engineering and metalworkers, who had a long tradition of organization, negotiation and, on a district or national scale, strike avoidance. Most of the strikes of the period began as 'wildcat' or unofficial strikes, often against the advice of the national union leadership. As George Askwith, the government conciliator, remarked in 1909, 'Official leaders could not maintain their authority. Often there was more difference between the men and their leaders than between the latter and the employers.'[16] The Durham miners in 1910 struck against the eight-hour day negotiated by the Mining Federation of Great Britain, over the strong opposition of the leadership, because it led to a three-shift system (in place of two day-shifts) and disruption of their home life. The South Wales coal strike in the same year sprang from a dispute about 'consideration' (additional pay) for opening a new and difficult seam at the Cambrian Combine pit at Tonypandy. The national railway strike of 1911 began as a wildcat strike at Bristol on 5 August for better pay and shorter hours which rapidly escalated into a national demand for a 2s. rise in wages and a reduction of weekly hours from sixty to fifty-four. The port workers' strikes of 1911 began with a strike of seamen and firemen of Southampton which spread by 'spontaneous combustion' to Goole, Hull, Manchester, Cardiff and London. The settlement of the great coal strike of 1912 was nearly aborted when the rank and file defeated it by 244,000 votes to 201,000, and the leadership, to get their way, had to extend a two-thirds majority rule for *starting* a strike to *settling* one. The cotton workers' lock-out of 1913 was complicated by unofficial strikes against non-unionists amongst Nelson weavers and a revolt against the official leadership amongst the Middleton spinners. The West Midlands engineering and metal workers' strikes of 1913 began with spontaneous outbreaks in Birmingham, Smethwick and West Bromwich and escalated into a district-wide demand for a minimum wage.[17]

Many of these strikes were accompanied by spontaneous local violence, sometimes involving clashes with the police and the army, which was very unwelcome to union leaders. In the summer of 1911, for example, there was rioting and looting in Tonypandy, a train was attacked at Llanelly where the troops fired and two men were killed, and there was rioting in the railway strike at Liverpool where another two strikers were killed. At Hull during the dock strike Askwith

heard a town councillor remark that he had been in Paris during the Commune and had never seen anything like this ... he had not known there were such people in Hull – women with hair streaming and half-nude, reeling through the streets, smashing and destroying.[18]

Almost anywhere, around mines, docks, railway depots and factories, violence might break out, above all where the employers tried to bring in blackleg workers past the union pickets. In London a pitched battle between dockers and blacklegs was only avoided when Winston Churchill, the Home Secretary, had the strike-breaking ship the *Lady Jocelyn*, full of blackleg labour, stopped below the port.[19]

In this seething situation, the official union leaders had to run very fast to keep up with their members. Older militants like Will Thorne, Ben Tillett, J. R. Clynes and even Tom Mann had to contend with criticism and challenges from younger ones influenced by syndicalists and revolutionary socialists from the Plebs League, breakaway students from Ruskin College, Oxford, and from the Socialist Labour Party and the British Labour Party, secessionists from the Socialist Democractic Party (which was opposed to strikes as a distraction from political action) and forerunners of the Communist Party of Great Britain of 1920.[20] Such 'agitators' would have had little influence with the rank and file, however, if ordinary union members had not already had a strong sense of grievance against the industrial system which frustrated their expectations and against their official leaders who failed to win the benefits they demanded and often seemed to be in collusion with the employers and the government to 'sell them short'.

The widening gulf between the rank and file and the union leaderships was the unavoidable result of the rise in scale of the unions which followed from their growth in size, the trend towards district and national amalgamations, and the consequent development of district and nationwide negotiations of wages and conditions which took place far from the place of work where the individual workers saw and felt the particular grievances which loomed so large in their working lives. Thus arose one of the major weaknesses of British industrial relations, the 'gap at shopfloor level' within the firm itself, which would later be filled by the shop stewards' movement, notably during the First World War.[21] But the gap was more than an incidental weakness to be remedied by better shopfloor organization. It was the inevitable prerequisite and consequence of the functional success of the trade unions. If they were to succeed in their objectives of winning a bigger share of the product of industry and better conditions of life and work for their members by means of collective bargaining, it was necessary and far more efficient that their leaders become full-time expert representatives and negotiators. This had long become obvious where the negotiations were concerned with complex conditions of remuneration or production, as in the cotton industry's Brooklands Agreement on piece rates for different grades, patterns and weaves of cloth or in the mining industry's disputes over compensation for working in 'abnormal places'.[22]

The Webbs observed and welcomed the growing professionalism of trade union leaders, and saw it as part of the wider professionalization of an increasingly corporate society. In place of individual bargaining

> we shall see the conditions of employment adjusted between equally expert negotiators, acting for corporations reasonably comparable in strategic strength, and always subject to and supplemented by the decisions of the High Court of Parliament, representing the interests of the community as a whole.[23]

In the fully developed collectivist industrial democracy

> the official of the Weavers' Union would debate questions of wages and technical training with the [Co-operative] Store or Municipality; the college of surgeons or physicians would, as at present, determine the standard and subjects of examination for the medical student and fix fees for medical attendance, subject perhaps to the democratic control of a Minister of Health. The official of the Trade Union and the official of the community would, it is true, represent the rival interests of different sections of the community. But, as members of one State the interests of their constituents are ultimately identical.[24]

In this optimistically harmonious way

> Trade Unionism adds to the long list of functions thus delegated to professional experts the settlement of the conditions on which the citizen will agree to co-operate in the national service.[25]

Meanwhile, on the other side of the fence the employer was already being replaced by a congeries of professional managers:

> in place of the single figure of the 'capitalist entrepreneur' we watch emerging in each trade a whole hierarchy of specialized professionals – inventors, designers, engineers, buyers, managers, foremen and what not – organized in their own professional associations, and standing midway between the shareholder, taxpayer, or consumer, whom they serve, and the

graded army of manual workers whom they direct ... In short, whilst Trade Unionism emphasizes the classic dictum of Adam Smith that division of labour increases material production, it carries this principle into the organization of society itself. If democracy is to mean the combination of administrative efficiency with genuine popular control, Trade Union experience points clearly to an ever-increasing differentiation between the functions of the three indispensable classes of Citizen-Electors, chosen Representatives, and expert Civil Servants.[26]

The touching faith of the Fabians in 'an elite of unassuming experts who could make no claim to superior social status' was not shared by observers of the same phenomenon to their right and left.[27] On the right Sir Arthur Clay, who saw the crisis in terms of the rise of syndicalism and collectivism and prophetically warned his contemporaries in 1912 that 'Social and industrial movements of far-reaching importance are now in progress, and what they portend no living man can say,' could understand 'the allurement of the "general strike" for uneducated and morally undisciplined men' but found it 'difficult to understand what attraction Collectivism can have for them. For wage-earners the establishment of Collectivism would mean the substitution of bureaucratic control for that of their present employers, but how would this benefit them?'

It is true that under a democratic government the Cabinet would continue to be more or less at the mercy of political parties strongly represented in the House of Commons; but if the State Socialist party are able to secure the continuance of legislative encroachment upon individual liberty now in progress until private enterprise is absorbed in the State, and Collectivism is firmly established, government 'by the people for the people' could not survive: long before this point in Collectivist development is reached, a great army of officials would have been created, linked from the highest official down to the lowest State workman by the bond of a common interest. Almost all the multitudinous and intricate functions of the daily life of a great community would be under the control of men whose position and livelihood would depend on the continuance of a system to which they owed them, and who, if

organized as they undoubtedly would be, would be in a
position to make any attempt to subvert it a hopeless
enterprise.[28]

To the Fabians' left, Fred Jowett, one of the founders of the
Independent Labour Party, opposed Cabinet government even
under a Labour administration 'because it means bureaucracy;
because it means the people are not having control'.[29] What the
Webbs welcomed and applauded, government by professional
experts, the Labour left understandably feared and suspected. How
much more then did they fear and suspect the permeation of trade
unionism itself by professional bureaucrats. Many of the
unofficial, wildcat strikes of 1910-14 displayed an instinctive fear
and suspicion by the rank and file, by no means confined to
politically conscious militants, that their union leaders were
already *too* professional, *too* bureaucratic, *too* ready to see the
employers' point of view and to respond to appeals to patriotism
and 'responsibility' by members of the Liberal government.

From the trade union officials' point of view, by contrast, they
were simply doing the professional job for which they were paid,
and negotiating the best terms that could reasonably be obtained
for their members. They could argue that they were using the
government, through the reluctant intervention of leading
politicians, to wring concessions from the employers and, even
more important for the future, to force employers to recognize the
trade unions and come to the negotiating table. Indeed, it was the
very success of this tactic of pressurizing the government which
gave them illusions of grandeur and the mistaken notion that, if
they were only united, they could coerce the government into
meeting - or into forcing the employers to meet - their demands.
As Robert Williams of the National Transport Workers'
Federation, still preaching as in 1914 the invincibility of the
united unions in the face of the government and the whole
electorate, was to express it in 1921:

When the workers are negotiating with the employers, or with
the government which invariably represents the employers,
they invariably exercise a greater influence when they speak in
terms of industrial strength and power than when they speak
politically ... Before the general strike the general election
pales in significance.[30]

In fact, nearly the opposite of this was true. Far from siding with the employers, the Liberal government had most frequently intervened to coerce them, sometimes under the threat or indeed the enactment of legislation, to recognize the unions and come to a settlement. This they did reluctantly, and would have preferred to leave such matters to the professionalism of George Askwith and the Labour Department of the Board of Trade or the new National Industrial Council of 1912.[31] But the union leaders quickly discovered that, where they could not get their way through Askwith, there was nothing to be lost by appealing over his and the employers' heads to the Cabinet itself. As Phelps Brown expressed it:

In very patient hands, conciliation proved enough to settle the disputes which, though some of them were sizeable, did not threaten to stop a basic industry throughout the country. Those that did the government tackled very differently. In the disputes on the railways in 1907 and 1911 and in the mines in 1912 what it in fact did was to coerce the employers by legislation or the threat of it. Ministers did not leave the dispute to the conciliatory service, but took it into their own hands. For its menace to the whole life of the country was felt to be intolerable ...[32]

As Lloyd George summed it up in Cabinet during the railway strike of 1911, which coincided with the Agadir crisis and the German threat of war over Morocco, 'The government are bound at all costs to protect the public from the dangers and miseries which famine and a general unrest of industry will entail.'[33] In this case Lloyd George used the patriotic, anti-German card to force the railway companies to recognize the unions and negotiate a settlement. But the unions were mistaken to draw the conclusion that the government could do no other. Asquith and Churchill were ready to fight the railway unions to a finish and to use troops, as Churchill and Baldwin did later in the general strike of 1926, to keep supplies going.[34] Yet it was Asquith himself, with tears in his eyes, who asked the House of Commons in 1912 to pass the Coal Mines Minimum Wage Act as the only way of forcing a settlement upon the mine owners.[35]

With such apparent encouragement from the politicians, it was understandable that the unions should think that they had only to threaten for the government to capitulate and coerce the employers. The employers saw the crisis the same way, and believed that the government – already suspected of favouring the unions in appointments to the conciliation service, in consultation over the trade boards and labour exchanges, and in their 'approved society' status in national insurance – was in collusion with the unions against them. Such misunderstandings and misreadings of the situation and of each other's motives were behind the mounting industrial crisis which threatened to come to a head in the autumn of 1914.

Yet, in a paradoxical way, the crisis contained the seeds of its own solution. Sir William Ashley, the leading imperialist economist, was one of the few people to recognize it at the time. He encouraged employers in 1913 to recognize and support strong trade unions: 'The weakening of unionism, paradoxical as it may sound, weakens the necessary basis for industrial peace in the only direction in which it is likely to be secured nowadays, i.e., the direction of collective agreement.'[36] And already in 1914 he saw that collective bargaining must lead, however reluctantly, to a form of corporatism:

> Society is feeling its way with painful steps, towards a corporate organisation of industry on the side alike of employers and of employed: to be then more harmoniously, let us hope, associated together, with the State alert and intelligent in the background to protect the interests of the community.[37]

This was confirmed in practice by the development in many industries of joint negotiating machinery, the price exacted and the solution imposed for the settlement of so many disputes by George Askwith and the government conciliation service. Askwith observed in July 1914, 'trade after trade was gradually being organized on a basis of good relationships *so far as the leaders on both sides were concerned*. A network of associated employers and federated trade unions was spreading over the country.'[38] But corporatism was not born, as militant unionists and recalcitrant business men believed, out of collusion between professional union leaders and their increasingly professional opponents, much as it suited their interests after the event in maintaining the stability of the system which employed them. It was born out of conflict itself and the shifts and compromises forced on reluctant participants by the logic of industrial confrontation.

If the war had not come that logic might have worked faster, either through a showdown in November 1914 or June 1915 or through the spread of collective bargaining to avert just such a mutually destructive confrontation. But the war did come, and with it a new paradox: a short cut to an enforced corporatism imposed by the state for the sake of national survival. Yet, as we shall see, wartime corporatism proved to be a bumpier ride than its patriotic participants expected, it was challenged from below by a militant rank and file who feared its embrace and, despite Lloyd George's best efforts to perpetuate it in formal corporatist institutions, it was repudiated by both employers and unions after the war with breakneck speed. Thus the crisis of 1910–14 was neither solved nor confronted, but merely aborted and postponed to the post-war period.

2   THE SUPREME TEST OF CLASS SOCIETY

The Great War, as it was called for a generation before a greater one supervened, was, as the social imperialists had forecast, the supreme test of national efficiency not only in Britain but in every one of the belligerent empires. At least four of them failed the test. Russia, Germany, Austria-Hungary and Turkey broke under the strain and their traditional military aristocracies were swept from power and destroyed. France was brought to the edge of collapse, notably in 1917 with the mutinies in the army against the terrible conditions at the front and the incompetence of the generals (by no means unique to the French). Amongst the leading industrial and military powers, leaving aside the Americans and Japanese as never fully put to the test of 'total war' affecting their home populations, Britain alone passed the test and survived without substantial threat of social collapse. This has led to the mistaken belief in historical and popular legend that Britain came through the world crisis unscathed and substantially unchanged, save for obvious benefits to national cohesion and social and political reform which arose from a successful and united struggle. In fact, as the Duke of Wellington said of Waterloo, it was 'the nearest run thing you ever saw in your life'. There were severe strains in the social fabric which came near at times to tearing it apart.

This is not to deny the very real patriotism which infused the great majority of the British people during the war, or the social and political progress which it accelerated. The outright opponents of the war, whether pacifists like Fenner Brockway, moderate socialists like Ramsay MacDonald or militant communists like John Maclean, leader of 'Red Clydeside' and 'first British consul' of the Soviet Russian government, were a tiny and much-divided minority, often counterproductive in their efforts to influence an inflamed anti-German public opinion. In the name of patriotism and national efficiency great sacrifices were called forth and freely made. Millions of men in the first seventeen months before conscription was imposed in 1916 volunteered for the armed forces. Hundreds of thousands of women, some of whom, particularly those from the middle class, had never done paid work before, volunteered for munitions and other work vital to the war effort. The whole official Labour movement, with the exception of the small and moribund Independent Labour Party, united in support of the war. Meeting in a new Joint Board on 24 August 1914 the Trades Union Congress, the General Federation of Trade Unions and the Labour Party urged both employers and workers to abandon all strikes and lock-outs for the duration and to reach amicable settlements of their outstanding differences. Despite the 'Appeal to the British Working Class' by the British Section of the Second International Working Men's Association to repudiate the war, the bulk of the Labour movement backed the call for 'a nation united behind the lads at the front'.[39]

The employers on their side dropped all threats of lock-out pending at the outbreak of war and, after a feeble attempt to regain the ground they had lost to the trade unions in the last few years by calling on the government to impose 'a sort of martial law' in civilian industry, accepted in principle an industrial truce for the duration.[40] More to the point, they came to accept a massive increase in direct government control of industry and trade which would have been completely unthinkable in peacetime. The railways were put under government control from the day the war started, though they were still managed by their old directors. Gradually British shipping and all vital supplies of food, such as sugar and wheat, and raw materials, including dyestuffs, iron ore and non-ferrous metals, were also brought under control and bulk purchase and, from Lloyd George's take-over of the Ministry of Munitions in May 1915, almost every sector of industry remotely connected with the waging of war was mobilized under government supervision. The government itself became an industrial employer on an enormous scale, with the sixteen National Factories of July 1915 rising to 250 by the war's end. Before then the coal mines, beginning with the much disturbed South Wales coalfield in December 1916, had been virtually nationalized, agricultural production was directed by the Board of Agriculture and the County War Agriculture Committees, staple foodstuffs came to be belatedly rationed, many food prices controlled, and the import of 'luxuries' such as motor cars and foreign films discouraged by a 33.3 per cent duty.[41]

The greatest government intervention of all, of course, was conscription, contemplated and prepared for with increasing apprehension, from the introduction of National Registration for men between 15 and 65 in August 1915 to final imposition in January 1916. Although direction of civilian labour, as in the Second World War, was never overtly imposed, the various devices for conserving skilled men and keeping key war workers out of the armed forces – 'badging' of munitions workers (December 1914), 'leaving certificates' (May 1915) to prevent skilled workers from leaving their jobs, 'trade cards' (November 1916) to enable selected engineers and other workers to resist the recruiting sergeant, and finally the Schedule of Protected Occupations (April 1917) – operated negatively to force men who did not wish to join the army into essential industries.[42] Thus was the whole nation mobilized for 'total war' on a scale previously undreamt of, surpassed only by the greater involvement of the civilian population in the Second World War. The concept of total war and government direction for the sake of victory was generally accepted on all sides, except for the small minorities of conscientious objectors and militant revolutionaries. The Labour Party and the TUC demanded only equal sacrifice: conscription of wealth as well as men, the graduated taxation of the rich and the prevention of profiteering by a swingeing excess profits tax, and the nationalization of any industry or activity, such as railways, shipping and the mines, deemed vital to the war effort.[43] Even the Federation of British Industries, formed to represent the employers in 1916, declared itself in favour of

nationalization ... not by the Socialist's panacea of 'appropriation' at all, but by amalgamation, by coordination and cooperation, and by bringing the state into partnership, and an increasing partnership in the big businesses that result from these amalgamations, by developing the crude beginnings of the 'controlled establishment', by the *quid pro quo* of profit-sharing and control in the national interest in exchange for the national credit and a helpful tariff.

This was a sort of 'war corporatism' which the FBI envisaged as one of the elements of post-war reconstruction.[44] During the same critical year Winston Churchill, no friend to socialism, called for all important employment to be regulated by the state, together with 'rationing tickets for everything that matters' and the fixing of prices 'so as to secure to the poorest people of this country ... the power of buying a certain modicum of food sufficient to keep up physical war-making efficiency, at prices which are not outside the scope of the wages they receive'. These things were being forced upon the government by the necessity of war. 'Why not do them now while there is time?'[45]

Churchill was right. It was the need for national efficiency which was driving the government 'inch by inch' to adopt measures of state control which it could never have considered in peacetime. And it was the civil servants responsible for running the bureaucratic war machine who saw this most clearly and planned for it. As early as September 1914 the Director of Army Contracts, U. F. Wintour, foresaw that the government would have to adopt bulk purchase to ensure supplies of essential materials. In January 1915 Sir Hubert Llewellyn Smith at the Board of Trade, responsible along with Sir George Askwith for the government's industrial relations policy on which the whole system of war production depended, forecast that 'we shall ultimately find some form of compulsion necessary in order to ensure that effective priority shall be given to Government work on existing contracts and sub-contracts'.[46] It was indeed the civil servants, the state's own representatives of expert efficiency and the professional ideal, who took the initiative in suggesting the extension of state control and in creating the machinery to carry it through: men like Sir Arthur Salter, Director of Ship Requisitioning at the Admiralty Transport Department and architect of the Ministry of Shipping, the 'whirlwind trio' E. M. H. Lloyd, E. F. Wise and U. F. Wintour at the Army Contracts Department, Sir Josiah Stamp at the Board of Inland Revenue fixing the taxes and finding the money, Llewellyn Smith, William Beveridge and Charles Rey, the group of civil servants recruited by Lloyd George from the Board of Trade to the Ministry of Munitions who broke the Clyde Workers' Committee and its revolt, and Beveridge again at the Ministry of Food who quarrelled with the Food Controller Lord Devonport's dislike of state intervention, before the latter was replaced by Lord Rhondda.[47]

A large number of business men were brought into government by Lloyd George, largely because of their expertise: Devonport, the retail grocer, as Food Controller, Joseph Maclay, the Glasgow shipowner, as 'Shipping Tsar', Lord Beaverbrook of the *Daily Express* as Minister of Information, Lord Cowdray, the engineer and oil magnate, as Air Minister, Lord Weir and Allan Smith, the engineering employers, as advisers on production, Sir Eric Geddes, the railway director, as the 'Napoleon of Transport' and then munitions chaser, and so on.[48] So too were trade unionists and Labour men, for much the same reason: Arthur Henderson and, when he resigned, G. N. Barnes in the War Cabinet were brought in to represent and reassure Labour, Barnes again as Minister of Pensions, John Hodge and G. H. Roberts as successive Ministers of Labour. There were also the professional men similarly chosen for their specific expertise: Dr Christopher Addison at the Ministry of Reconstruction preparing health and housing plans and Professor H. A. L. Fisher at the Board of Education. All these prove the rule that the war demanded professional expertise applied to specific problems, and the business men in particular showed with what alacrity professional managers could switch their talents from private to public enterprise if the incentive proved stronger than profit making.

As Sir Arthur Salter said, it was not the particular individuals who mattered but 'the logic of events and the impelling necessity of the situation',[49] but it was the bureaucratic experts who recognized the logic, defined the necessity, and created the machinery to meet it. War was the ideal environment in which to show off the paces of professional expertise and its superiority over private enterprise for 'getting things done' at breakneck speed on a massive scale. But this assumed, of course, that the experts would be given their heads and all the powers and resources to do the job, and these conditions could not, at that stage in the evolutionary process, be expected to outlast the war. Nevertheless, the lessons of state control by a few hundred senior civil servants,[50] though officially rejected by the post-war government, would not soon be forgotten or evaded. Even the Federation of British Industries, in the very act of calling for the demolition of government control of industry in October 1918, asked in the same breath for state guidance in 'the huge task' of resettling industry on a peace basis.[51] The War Cabinet concluded prophetically that 'the war has brought a transformation of the social and administrative structure of the state, much of which is bound to be permanent'.[52]

The transformation was crowned by the extension of the franchise to those who had participated so loyally and effectively in winning the war, to the working classes as a whole and, with a timidity which proved unfounded, to women but only those over 30. These two victories for democracy were, paradoxically, to justify all the fears of the pre-war Liberal government: the first ensured – together with the Liberal split between Asquith and Lloyd George from 1916 to 1926 – that the Liberals would never hold office alone again; the second, since more women than men even in the working class voted Conservative, determined along with the division of the anti-Tory vote between Liberals and Labour, that the Conservatives would hold office (including coalitions) for most of the next seventy years.[53]

Nearly universal adult suffrage was one reward for mass participation in the war, what Andrzejewski has called the 'military participation ratio', the proportion of the population drawn into the war effort.[54] In the First World War this was unprecedently high, with about 4 million men, 24 per cent of the adult male population, under arms and another 1.5 million men and women in munitions work out of a population of 42 million (or about 46 million including Ireland).[55] According to that theory such mass participation should lead to a measure of social levelling by means of progressive taxation and social reform. As Richard Titmuss expressed it after the Second World War:

> The aims and content of social policy, both in peace and war, are thus determined – at least to a substantial extent – by how far the cooperation of the masses is essential to the successful prosecution of the war. If this cooperation is thought to be essential then inequalities must be reduced and the pyramid of stratification must be flattened.[56]

Although this has been hotly disputed, at least as far as the immediate effects of the 1914–18 war are concerned,[57] it cannot be denied that such a levelling was the intention of the wartime coalition and its successor, that progressive taxation took a quantum leap during the war to a new level of 'taxable tolerance' from which it never again subsided, and that in housing policy, education and social security provision corners were turned which proved irrevocable.[58] Lloyd George had promised 'a fit land for heroes to live in', and the King's Speech to the first post-war Parliament promised even more:

The aspirations for a better social order which have been quickened in the hearts of My people by the experience of war must be encouraged by prompt and comprehensive action. Before the War, poverty, unemployment, inadequate housing, and many remediable ills were aggravated by division. But since the outbreak of the war every party and every class have worked and fought together for a great ideal ... We must continue to manifest the same spirit. We must stop at no sacrifice of interest or prejudice to stamp out unmerited poverty, to diminish unemployment and mitigate its sufferings, to provide decent homes, to improve the nation's health and to raise the standard of well-being throughout the country. We shall not achieve this end by undue tenderness towards acknowledged abuses, and it must necessarily be retarded by violence or even by disturbance. We shall succeed only by patient and untiring resolution in carrying through legislation and the administrative action which are required. It is that resolute action which I now ask you to support.[59]

Despite the almost immediate 'bonfire of wartime controls' and the onset in 1921 of mass unemployment, these promises were not so cynically disregarded as was later believed by those who expected more than the words actually said. Poverty did decline, at least in part owing to government policy, decent homes were to be provided on an unprecedented if still inadequate scale, and the nation's health and living standards did improve between the wars beyond anything expected before it. But this was not entirely due to gratitude for mass co-operation in the war effort, and at least as much to the crisis in class relations which might have lost the war and to the fear of social collapse and revolution which might have lost the peace as well.

The locus of the crisis was in industrial relations, where the combination of social harmony and patriotic fervour was by no means as uncomplicated as popular legend has it. Lloyd George, who had expected massive industrial unrest amounting to a challenge to the government if war had not intervened, saw industrial disputes as the main obstacle to a united war effort. He wrote to Ben Tillett in late August 1914:

It is very difficult to gauge what the actual effect of war under modern conditions will be upon either capital or labour, but one thing is already perfectly obvious – it must effect a revolutionary change in the relations of the state to both.[60]

In the sense that any substantial strike in an industry vital to the war effort would be a challenge to national survival and would invoke government intervention to settle or suppress it, he was more prophetic than he knew. The government, and often Lloyd George himself, were increasingly forced to take drastic action, vacillating between forcing employers to meet the workers' demands at one end of the spectrum and imprisoning or deporting strike leaders at the other. Nor was the crisis confined to workplace disputes over wages, conditions of work, excessive overtime, dilution of skilled work by unskilled men and women, and the like. Through the threat of conscription and the inefficient devices used to protect key workers, through the demand for equal sacrifice by all classes and for the 'conscription of riches' (Ben Tillett's phrase, taken up by the War Emergency Workers' National Committee),[61] through the denunciation of war-profiteering by industrialists and of exploitation by landlords of scarce housing accommodation, and through the widespread belief amongst workers that they had a right to share with management in the decisions which affected their current lives and their post-war future, the conflict escalated beyond the workplace to the main political arena. For some of their leaders at least, especially after the success of the Bolshevik revolution in Russia, the war represented the terminal crisis of capitalism and an opportunity to be exploited to the full, and if they were remarkably few they were still vociferous enough to instil into the government the fear of revolution in Britain itself.

The crisis began on what came to be known as 'Red Clydeside' where, as early as February 1915, 10,000 members of the Amalgamated Society of Engineers struck for a wage increase of 2d. an hour which stemmed from a claim made in June 1914. The strike was unofficial and as much a revolt of the rank and file against their union leaders as against the big Glasgow employers, including Sir William (later Lord) Weir, soon to be one of Lloyd George's business men in government. It was organized by the shop stewards, the unpaid local workplace officials of the union, who formed the Clyde Labour Withholding Committee. The strike, which many members of the government and even some employers thought justified by the rise in prices, was settled for 1d. an hour and an equivalent 10 per cent increase in piece rates, but the stewards went on in October 1915 to create the famous Clyde Workers' Committee which was to give the government so much trouble that it finally suppressed it and harassed its leaders. The leaders were a more diverse group than the government and employers supposed.[62] Although they all belonged to left-wing radical or revolutionary parties, the Socialist Labour Party, the British Socialist Party, or the Independent Labour Party, they included genuine if ineffectual revolutionaries like William Gallacher, Arthur MacManus and, behind the scenes, John Maclean, the Glasgow teacher whose Marxist economics evening classes drew as many as 500 trade unionists; but they also included a majority of stewards like John Muir, David Kirkwood and, again behind the scenes, the ILP journalist and publisher John Wheatley, who while bitterly opposed to the capitalist system saw little chance or benefit in violent revolution.[63] Their main unifying belief was that the official leadership of the trade unions and the Labour Party, by unconditionally supporting the war, by making the Treasury Agreement of March 1915 with Lloyd George to abandon the strike weapon, permit dilution of skilled labour and relax restrictions on overtime and Sunday working, and by accepting the Munitions of War Act of May 1915 which gave the government almost *carte blanche* control of industrial relations, had betrayed them to the employers and the politicians. The Committee's first leaflet declared:

> The support given to the Munitions Act by the officials was an act of treachery to the working classes. Those of us who have refused to be sold have organized the above Committee ... determined to retain what liberties we have, and to take the

first opportunity of repealing all the acrimonious legislation that has recently been imposed on us.[64]

They were interested in industrial unionism (one big union per industry), influenced by the syndicalism preached by the Irish trade unionist and revolutionary James Connolly, and in 'workers' control', defined as organized labour taking a 'direct share in the management down through all the departments'.[65] But their language, like that of the quasi-syndicalists before and indeed after the war, was systematically ambiguous and could be interpreted as being ultimately aimed at seizing control of the system by revolution:

> Let it be clearly understood that we make no claim to power of any kind. Our policy is simply and purely defensive; . . . multiplicity of unions spells weakness and the ultimate aim of the CWC is to weld these unions into one powerful organization that will place the workers in complete control of the industry . . . The Clyde Workers' Committee stands for Unity on the Clyde, and unity on the Clyde means freedom for the workers.[66]

The government could afford to ignore such long-term threats but it could not afford to ignore repeated strikes against dilution by key engineering workers and what it considered to be political strikes against conscription and against the Munitions Act itself. By November 1915 the government had determined that 'to obtain a reasonably smooth working of the Munitions Act, this committee should be smashed'. Dilution Commissioners were sent to Glasgow 'to convert and persuade the men in say half-a-dozen of the principal establishments to the principle of dilution', and plans were made, failing persuasion, to impose it and risk the threat of a strike. What may finally have brought Lloyd George to the end of his patience was his rough handling on a visit to Glasgow at Christmas 1915 at which his Welsh charm failed to work on the dour Scots. At a riotous meeting on Christmas Day which closed in disorder he was treated to abuse as 'the best paid munitions worker in Britain', whose 'every action has the taint of slavery about it', and to threats of a general strike against dilution and against conscription. The government suppressed the Glasgow socialist weeklies, the ILP's *Forward*, the BSP's *Vanguard* and, later, the SLP's *Worker*, arrested Gallacher, Muir

195

and Bell as the latter's publishers, which provoked strikes in all the major CWC factories except Parkhead where Kirkwood was operating his own dilution scheme.[67] Finally, in March 1916, the government ordered the arrest and deportation to Edinburgh of the main leaders of the CWC, threatened the strikers with prosecution under the Defence of the Realm Act, and actually imprisoned thirty of them. By mid-May Maclean and MacDougall of the BSP's *Vanguard*, the only genuine revolutionaries, were also in jail. The Clyde Workers' Committee, which Christopher Addison of the Ministry of Munitions suspected of 'a systematic and sinister plan' to blackmail the government into repealing the Munitions and Military Service Acts, was crushed. Although it reappeared in late 1917, and John Maclean became the (unrecognized) British consul of the revolutionary Russian government, it did not regain its threatening appearance until after the war.[68] The only substantial success the CWC claimed, and that doubtfully since it was begun by soldiers and munitions workers' wives and supported by unofficial strikes at five shipyards not controlled by the engineering CWC, was the Glasgow rent strike and the subsequent Rent Restriction Act of 1915 – though the latter had other, more national roots, as we shall see.[69]

The government's industrial strategy, in so far as it had one, was to separate the militants amongst the rank and file from the official leadership of the trade unions. In this it unconsciously justified the suspicions among the rank and file, not confined to the militants, that their leaders had sold them out. How far Lloyd George was willing to go to placate and support the official leadership is shown by his very different treatment of the coal miners who, ironically, had not signed the Treasury Agreement and considered themselves unbound by the Munitions Act. In South Wales the 1910 wage agreement was due for renewal in the summer of 1915 and, despite efforts at settlement by Askwith and Walter Runciman, President of the Board of Trade, and appeals by the Miners' Federation, the Welsh miners, seeking a permanent rather than a mere wartime wage increase, came out on unofficial strike on 15 July. Runciman, with the backing of prime minister Asquith and the Conservatives, proposed not to imprison the strikers but to fine and disenfranchise them under the Munitions Act. At this point, Clement Edwards, President of the Miners' Federation, went to Lloyd George, who immediately chartered a special train to Cardiff, taking Runciman and Henderson with him, and conceded the miners' demands.[70] Sir George Askwith considered this sort of instant capitulation made his task and that of responsible trade unionists and employers that much more difficult: 'The so-called settlement did more to cause unrest during the succeeding years than almost any other factor, and to lessen hopes of establishing a sane method for the settlement of disputes.'[71] It certainly confirmed the miners' and many other militant unionists' belief, so pregnant with misplaced confidence for the post-war crisis, that the government could not resist a resolute working class.

Meanwhile, Red Clydeside's torch, overrated in its incendiarism as it undoubtedly was, now passed to the wider, more national shop stewards' movement. This was in part due to the government's own action in dispersing the Clydeside leaders. Through the missionary travels of Arthur MacManus, who became President of the National Administrative Council of the Shop Stewards' Movement in August 1917 (and first President of the Communist Party of Great Britain in 1920), and others to Liverpool, Manchester, Barrow, Coventry, Birmingham, Derby, Sheffield, Leeds, London and other engineering centres, they became the instigators of many shop stewards' amalgamation committees.[72] But it was also a spontaneous rank and file movement by men provoked into conflict with their own union leaders, as well as with their employers and the government, above all over the question of conscription. Both the Parliamentary Labour Party (despite a Conference majority against it) and the TUC had by mid–1916 accepted the need for conscription.[73] In November 1916 the call-up of a young Sheffield engineer, Leonard Hargreaves, provoked an unofficial strike. Hargreaves worked in the same department of Vickers as J. T. Murphy, leader of the Sheffield shop stewards, a pre-war follower of Connolly and himself an ideologue of industrial unionism and workers' control, who organized a nationwide campaign for his release. The outcome was a remarkable victory for the shop stewards. Not only was Hargreaves released but the government negotiated with the Amalgamated Society of Engineers a 'trade card' scheme of military exemption certificates which was operated by the union itself.[74] A national conference of shop stewards organized by MacManus at Manchester declared, 'We will support the officials just as long as they rightly represent the workers, but we will act independently immediately they misrepresent us.'[75]

The euphoria did not last, however. In April 1917 the government, pressed by the army for more and more conscripts to staunch the bloody losses on the western front, repudiated the trade card agreement and by May provoked a massive wave of strikes throughout England (though not, significantly, on the Clyde), involving over 200,000 engineers and shipbuilders in forty-eight towns, with the loss of a million and a half working days. The government refused to meet the shop stewards and, after sending King George and Queen Mary on a tour of the affected areas to no avail, arrested the strike leaders. Finally, the Minister of Munitions agreed to meet a deputation of the shop stewards in the company of J. T. Brownlie, the secretary of the Amalgamated Society of Engineers, who agreed to call off the strike in return for the release of the leaders and further negotiations with the trade union *officials* (not the stewards). The outcome was an amended Schedule of Protected Occupations which kept many more engineers out of the army.[76]

That the shop stewards' movement was led by self-conscious revolutionaries there can be no doubt. MacManus, from the chair of a further national conference in Manchester on 5 August 1917, welcomed the Russian Revolution (not yet taken over by the Bolsheviks) and talked of the strike wave in the engineering industry as 'a symptom of the beginning of revolutionary development in this country'.[77] Six out of the eight members of the National Administrative Council elected at the 1917 Conference, including MacManus, Murphy and Gallacher, became founding members of the British Communist Party, and by 1923 MacManus, Bell, Murphy and Gallacher were all members of its Political Bureau. A further conference at Manchester in January 1918 voted to 'actively resist the manpower proposals of the government ... even though these might be agreed with the trade unions' and demanded 'that the government shall at once accept the invitation of the Russian government to consider peace'. One delegate asked, 'Who can say this conference may not start a revolution? Someone has got to make a move, and there is going to be a revolution in this country in a week or two'.[78]

But the revolutionary stewards, however few or many, could no more carry the rank and file with them than the abused officials.

Despite a growing opposition to the war, and their belief that 'a general strike in the big key industries of Europe would put an end to the war in less than a week', most stewards and workers were not willing to risk losing the war if enemy workers would not join in.[79] This was particularly true during the German spring offensive of 1918, which took the steam out of the whole movement. Lord Burnham, proprietor of the *Daily Telegraph* still believed in October 1918 that 'we cannot hope to escape some sort of revolution ... and there will be no passionate resistance from anybody', and the Soviet Russian government believed that Britain, like Germany, was ripe for revolution, but the revolution refused to happen.[80]

Some of the credit (or blame) for this must go to the clever, if opportunist, tactics of Lloyd George and his team of skilful civil servants and inducted business men and trade unionists. But most credit must go to the almost instinctive way in which the professional representatives of government, capital and labour drew together in the face of a threat not only to the survival of the country but also to the system which nourished and supported them. In one sense the militant shop stewards were correct; trade union officials did have a stake in maintaining the industrial system, but that did not mean that they had sold out to the capitalists. On the contrary, it was the *employers* who felt most aggrieved at giving up, even temporarily, what they believed had been their natural right to control their own property and discipline their own workmen, and understandably looked forward to regaining 'the right and power to manage our own businesses as soon as possible' after the war.[81] It was the professionals who ran the employers' associations who could see a new future for industrial relations in the lessons of wartime co-operation. The Federation of British Industries, as we have seen, declared in 1916 for non-socialist 'nationalization' (meaning corporatism rather than public ownership) in the form of a partnership between big business, the state and profit-sharing workers. By 1918 it was blaming 'the absence of any human touch' in industry for labour troubles and arguing that 'in future the work people would expect to be consulted on a number of questions that had previously been dealt with by employers'. Although it was bitterly criticized for its 'softness' by the tougher-minded Engineering Employers' Federation under Allan Smith, which created the rival National Confederation of Employers' Organizations in 1919, Smith and the EEF itself learned by experience to deal informally with the shop stewards' committees in the interests of industrial peace.[82] Consciously on the part of the FBI, less consciously on the part of the EEF, the officials professionally responsible for management's policy towards labour were moving towards a form of collaboration with labour – self-interested, no doubt, but no less sincere for that – despite the opposition of many, if not most, of the less far-sighted business men.

On their side, the TUC and trade unions and the labour movement as a whole enjoyed an enormous surge of power and prestige during the war which arose out of the shortage of manpower and the demonstrable indispensability of labour. The collaboration thrust upon them by the government was not wholly welcome, since it faced them with a dilemma. On the one hand, it was designed to prevent them from exploiting their advantage to the full in better wages and conditions and consultation by management, and every accommodation offered to government and the employers, on dilution, overtime, suspension of restrictive practices, and the acceptance of conscription, laid them open to the charge from their more militant members of betraying the very people they represented. On the other hand, they made enormous gains from their support of the war effort, in recognition of themselves as responsible negotiators by the employers and as a force to be considered and consulted by government. They were not taken in: they knew that if peace brought depression and a glut of labour in place of shortage, all these gains would be hotly contested. At the same time, many of them were reinforced in their pre-war belief that a united trade union movement was irresistible and that the mere threat of a general strike would produce unconditional surrender by any government.

The political wing of the labour movement gained most of all. With four Labour MPs getting their first taste of Cabinet office – two of them successively in the five-man War Cabinet – and numerous junior ministers, the Labour Party made its first real advance towards becoming a governing party. By the end of the war it had become a fully-fledged political force with a constitution, individual members and constituency parties, ready to bid against the Liberals for the role of the alternative government. Yet in some ways more significant from the present point of view was the behind-the-scenes work of the War Emergency Workers' National Committee, the body set up in August 1914 with representatives from all sections of the Labour movement:

> to protect working class interests during the War . . ., arrest existing distress, and prevent as far as possible further distress, and unemployment in the future. The Nation is only at the beginning of a crisis which demands thorough and drastic action by the State and the municipalities. Any bold, far-reaching change, which will probably be resisted by existing bureaucracy, can only be made possible by the strong pressure of well organized, well directed popular agitation.

It was not by popular agitation but by patient pressure on the government on behalf of individuals and groups oppressed, as they saw it, by bureaucracy, both civilian and military, and by property, capitalist and landed, that their most important work was done. Most of it was done, moreover, not by the ragbag Committee of 'sane patriots' like Sidney Webb and Susan Lawrence and 'superpatriots' like Hyndman, John Hodge and Havelock Wilson, of opponents of the war like Ramsay MacDonald and Robert Williams, and of 'revolutionary defeatists' like Robert Quelch or E. C. Fairchild, but by the cool and sensible Jim Middleton, Assistant Secretary of the Labour Party, who became Secretary of the Committee and brought almost the whole staff of the Labour Party with him. After a false start in urging the government to provide public works for the rapidly disappearing unemployed, the secretariat went on to press behind the scenes for most of the measures the government was later forced to adopt; more adequate war pensions, better dependants' allowances for soldiers and sailors, bulk purchase of grain and other foodstuffs, control of sugar, milk, coal and other domestic supplies, help for the special hardships of families who had lost more than one member in action, protection against eviction by landlords of soldiers' families, and so on. As Middleton put it in February 1917, 'We have made representations to Government departments almost without end. Our proposals have generally been turned down to begin with, but have been adopted in very many important particulars after inordinate and simply damnable delays'.[83]

Perhaps their most signal success – aided of course by rent strikes and protests in Glasgow, Coventry and elsewhere – was the Rent and Mortgage Interest Restriction Act of December 1915. This was based, like their pressure for higher taxation of the rich, on the principle of 'conscription of riches' to balance the conscription of men from the unrich classes, and on the professional notion that property should justify itself by service to the community, above all at this time when the working class was being forced to fight for the defence of property. The conscription of riches, Royden Harrison argues, was, through Sidney Webb who served on both the Committee and the Labour Party Executive, the real origin of Clause 4 of the 1918 Party Constitution, calling for 'the common ownership of the Means of Production, Distribution and Exchange'.[84] Although Webb and Tawney, who drafted the Constitution, needed no such source for their own belief in public ownership, the experience of the war made it more acceptable to the trade unions and the non-socialist members of the Party. But the main significance of the War Emergency Committee was its continuous experience of working behind the scenes with government, both ministers and officials, which drew the Labour movement almost unconsciously into a collaborative rather than a confrontational relationship with the state.

The third partner in the 'triangular collaboration in the industrial sphere, between government, trade unions and the business class', as Keith Middlemas has called this 'emerging corporatism', was of course the state.[85] The government's reluctant pre-war involvement in industrial relations became just as reluctant but still more inevitable during the war. If the government was bound, as Lloyd George put it, to protect the public from famine and misery in peacetime,[86] how much more was it bound to intervene to protect the country from collapse and defeat in war. The first instinct of the politicians, including Lloyd George, Churchill and Balfour, was to blame a disaffected minority of political agitators for the wartime strikes and to talk of arresting, deporting or conscripting them; but experience taught them, firstly, as Balfour admonished Churchill in Cabinet in June 1915, that coercion only created martyrs and, secondly, that agitators could work only on real grievances.[87] The eight industrial Unrest Commissioners sent to the strike-ridden areas reported that the high cost of living, the scandal of profiteering, the effects of dilution of skilled men's pay and status, conscription, and administrative incompetence were the real causes of unrest, but underlying them all:

> The want of confidence is the fundamental cause, of which many of the causes given are manifestations. It shows itself in the feeling that there has been inequality of sacrifice, that the Government have broken solemn promises, that trade union officials are no longer to be relied on, and that there is woeful uncertainty as to the future.[88]

Although the government never quite understood that the line between revolution and loyalty ran through the shop stewards' movement, not between the shop stewards and the trade union officials, they nevertheless grasped instinctively at a tacit alliance with the officials whom they saw, rightly or wrongly, as their main hope of industrial peace. By the end of the war even the bellicose Churchill was ready to argue for a powerful trade union movement and the industrialist Tory leader Bonar Law declared that 'trade union organization was the only thing between us and anarchy'. But it was civil servants responsible for industrial relations, notably men like Askwith, Llewellyn Smith and Horace Wilson at the new Ministry of Labour, who not only saw the need for 'triangular collaboration' but worked out the machinery through which it would work: the Whitley Councils for joint consultation between employers and workers in each industry on everything 'affecting the progress and well-being of the trade', the Arbitration Department of the Ministry of Labour, and over them the 'industrial parliament', the National Industrial Conference.[89]

That in the immediate post-war years the whole machinery atrophied, leaving only remnants behind, was no fault of theirs. In the nature of the case, *any* formal machinery of a corporatist character involving the professional representatives of government, employers and trade unions was bound to raise suspicion and hostility amongst their constituents. In the renewed crisis of the post-war period the lessons of the war had to be learned all over again.

3 THE CRISIS AVERTED

At the end of the war almost everyone in Britain was dedicated to the task of 'reconstruction', from the government in the King's Speech at the opening of Parliament which looked forward to 'a better social order', to those admirers of Soviet Russia who expected an immediate revolution in Britain. The War Cabinet commented, on the setting up of the Ministry of Reconstruction in 1917, that it was 'not so much a question of rebuilding society as it was before the war, but of moulding a better world out of the social and economic conditions which have come into being during the war'.[90] Nor was it a cynical piece of war propaganda to con the public into supporting the war effort, to be dismissed without remorse once victory was achieved. There is no reason to think that Lloyd George and the Coalition government did not believe in 'a fit land for heroes to live in', or that 'the hard-faced men who had done well out of the war' amongst the new MPs wished to preside over an economically depressed, socially deprived and politically discontented country.[91] No one, least of all those business men who were most determined to abolish government controls and reinstate unfettered private enterprise, wished to return to the near-anarchic industrial relations which threatened to explode into a major clash between the classes in 1914. On the contrary, the Federation of British Industries even put forward a scheme for a welfare system to be run jointly by the employers and the unions in return for concessions on overmanning and productivity, while Steel-Maitland, an industrialist and Tory Party manager, looked forward to 'a visible and automatic community of interest between masters and men, and of making the latter feel they are a corporate part of a mutually beneficent organisation'.[92] The problem, and the chief cause of the renewed crisis after the war, were the incompatible interpretations and expectations which 'reconstruction' aroused, and the consequent mutual fear on both sides of industry of what one side saw as revolution and the other as counter-revolution.

The trade unions and the Labour Party had grown in power and stature as a result of the war: trade union membership doubled from 4,145,000 in 1914 to 8,348,000 in 1920, while the Labour Party's vote had multiplied six fold, from 400,000 in 1910 to 2,374,000 in 1918, and it had replaced the Asquith Liberals as the official Opposition.[93] The Labour Party, in their manifesto

'Labour and the New Social Order', called for a brave new world which would:

> secure for the producers by hand and by brain the full fruits of their industry, and the most equitable distribution thereof that may be possible, upon the basis of the common ownership of the means of production and the best obtainable system of popular administration and control of each industry and service.

The 'Four Pillars of the House that we propose to erect' were (in the words of the 1918 manifesto, written by Sidney Webb in his capitalized Law of the Covenant style):

> The Universal Enforcement of the National Minimum;
> The Democratic Control of Industry;
> The Revolution in National Finance; and
> The Surplus Wealth for the Common Good.

This Fabian utopia meant social security, public works to maintain full employment, the nationalization of key industries including railways, coal, electric power, industrial life insurance and alcoholic drink, democratic control through Parliament rather than workers' participation, and steeply graduated taxation including a capital levy.[94] This was certainly enough to make most employers think of Soviet Russia and Lloyd George to fling the charge (in a rather odd combination of adjectives) that 'the Labour Party is being run by the extreme pacifist, Bolshevist group'.[95]

The trade union movement looked even more immediately threatening. Trade unionists, both leaders and rank and file, had gained a great deal from the war, not so much in increased money wages (which, in fact, barely kept up with prices) as in recognition and consultation and, above all, in a sense of power and self-respect which came from the manifest indispensability of labour. Yet their chief motivation at the end of the war was fear: fear of depression and unemployment and the consequent loss of bargaining power, decline of wages and worsening of conditions, and the snatching back by the employers of all the concessions they had been forced to make during the war by the shortage of labour and the pressure of a desperate government. While for the Labour Party state control and nationalization were an ultimate goal accelerated by the war, for many of the workers in the troubled industries, notably coal and the railways, they were an immediate safeguard of wages, hours and conditions which would be threatened as and when the capitalist owners took back control from the state. To this was added an urgency which stemmed from the belief that war was always followed by depression, and the knowledge that the demobilization of some 4 million troops and the closure of the munitions factories would soon flood the labour market with new competitors. For some of the more militant rank and file leaders the Russian Revolution, too, was not just an example to be admired and a model to be cautiously followed but the symptom and harbinger of a worldwide crisis of capitalism, already spreading to Germany and other parts of Industrial Europe, which had to be taken at the flood or not at all.[96] And hovering over the whole industrial scene was the mistaken belief, not only on the part of syndicalists like Robert Williams of the Transport Workers but also of moderate leaders of the Triple Alliance like J. H. Thomas of the National Union of Railwaymen, that the mere threat of a general strike was enough to bring the government and the employers to their knees.[97]

For the employers, reconstruction meant the end of state control of industry and the recovery of their power to manage their own property and workforce. As the FBI put it in October 1918, 'Among the business community there is practical unanimity of agreement that there should be as little interference as possible on the part of the State in the future Governance of industry'. Although the FBI admitted that 'some measure of national control might conceivably be a good thing in some industries', it was determined that state enterprises like the National Factories should not be allowed to compete with private enterprise in peacetime, and in January 1919 it joined with the Associated Chambers of Commerce and other manufacturers' and traders' associations to oppose the nationalization of railways.[98]

But state intervention was not the only problem. Many employers were even more concerned about the temper of the workforce and whether it was becoming alienated and potentially revolutionary. The tough Engineering Employers' Federation, which was to set up the National Confederation of Employers' Organizations in 1920 in rivalry with the 'incompetent' FBI to oppose growing labour influence in Parliament and Whitehall, was concerned not so much with 'normal' labour unrest but with revolutionary phenomena, due 'to a state of indiscipline (1) of the workpeople to their trade unions, (2) of the workpeople generally towards the government, and (3) to objections which are felt by a section of the community to the present state of society'.[99] Once again it was fear – fear of what they perceived to be a revolutionary threat to their existence – that motivated the employers.

The government too had a genuine fear of revolution and was not just playing the Bolshevik card for electioneering purposes. In the last year of the war the Cabinet had been much impressed with an analysis by its young Assistant Secretary, William Ormsby-Gore, MP, who saw connections between the shop stewards' movement, the Irish problem and the Russian Revolution:

> The essence of this movement is, of course, the new form of Marxian syndicalism, revolutionary in its aims and methods, aiming at the overthrow of the existing social and economic order by direct action; its leaders welcome unrest and strike action in any form and for whatever cause, they are the true, up-to-date revolutionaries, who seem to be appearing in every country in the world, and whether it is Petrograd, Chicago, the Belfast dock-yards, the Clyde or the West Riding of Yorkshire, it is all the same thing. It looks as if the Leaders, whether Jew or Irish, have this common feature, they are all men with dissatisfied aspirations, embittered against society and bent on using the results of the War to overthrow the existing order of things.[100]

There was plausible colour for his Cassandra-like warnings. The shop stewards' movement on the Clyde and in Sheffield and elsewhere was dominated by Irishmen, often followers of James Connolly, the syndicalist leader of the pre-war Dublin transport strike, like Arthur MacManus and J. T. Murphy, who were also members of the British Socialist Party or the Socialist Labour Party (with its connections with Daniel De Leon and the American SLP), the two main groups from which the founding members of the Communist Party of Great Britain in 1921 were to come.[101] The midwife of the British Communist Party was a Russian émigré named Theodore Rothstein, who joined the SDF in 1899, was on its Executive from 1901, dominated the breakaway British Socialist Party during the critical period between the Russian

Revolution and its transformation into the Communist Party of Great Britain, and had been a member of the Russian Communist Party (Bolshevik) since 1900.[102] Lloyd George and the government came to be well apprised of such activities through the somewhat alarmist 'Reports on Revolutionary Organisations within the United Kingdom' by Sir Basil Thomson, ex-head of MI5 and now head of the Special Branch of the Metropolitan Police, which coloured their view of the industrial labour movement.[103] They saw it as divided between the reckless 'extremists' of the shop stewards' movement and the Triple Alliance and the responsible 'moderates' of the TUC and the leadership of most of the trade unions outside the Triple Alliance. The perceived threat of revolution, albeit from a small segment of the labour movement but one which might win the battle for the minds of the rank and file against the official union leadership, helps to account for the government's strategy, which was to buy off the moderates with concessions which would strengthen their hold on the membership, isolate the extremists and, in the last resort, crush them.

As part of this strategy Lloyd George developed his 'emerging corporatism', his attempted 'contract' between government, employers and trade unions which reached its high point in the National Industrial Conference of February 1919. Whether this was as deliberate and self-conscious an attempt to set industrial relations and society at large on a new foundation as admirers of Lloyd George believe may well be doubted.[104] Lloyd George, the great extemporary prestidigitator, seduced men as he seduced women, by a dazzling combination of spontaneous charm and spur-of-the-moment promises, calculating that the same vertiginous skill would extricate him from any unfortunate and unforeseen consequences later. He grabbed at the corporatist solution because it was the only stratagem available to him in the immediate post-war crisis, and he instinctively divined that it would appeal sufficiently to the interests of the more moderate and intelligent trade union and employers' representatives to divide them from their extremists long enough to ride the crisis out. But he could not have done this if a 'corporate bias' (to use Middlemas's term) had not already been built into the instinctive responses of the union and employers' leaders, whose interests lay in gaining benefits for their constituents peacefully and with credit to themselves, with much talk indeed of threats and bluff but without the damaging industrial warfare which could only destroy their own assets – their union funds or the profits which supported employers' organizations – and thus undermine their own professional position.

What Lloyd George did not consider, and what wrecked his hopes of a formal, institutionalized corporatism, were two flaws in the scheme: firstly, the personal flaw of all philanderers, political as well as sexual, that the victims of seduction soon learn to distrust the seducer; and secondly, the more impersonal and significant fact that, if it was in the interests of the union and employers' leaders to adopt a corporate approach, it was still more in their interests not to institutionalize it. This was because an informal, tacit understanding of the kind which grows up between all negotiators (from international diplomats to police spokesmen and hijackers in hostage cases) leaves the protagonists freer to pursue their own unfettered and unstated aims, allows them personally to claim the credit for negotiating success rather than make it appear the automatic outcome of impersonal machinery, and above all protects them in both directions, from the demands of the other parties that they take responsibility for delivering their constituents' consent to agreements which may be repudiated by them, and from charges by their constituents that they have sold them out to the other side. It is against this paradoxical ambivalence of all three parties to the triangular collaboration that we must view both the immediate post-war crisis and the apparent failure of Lloyd George's instinctive formalized corporatism, and also the longer-term solution of the crisis in the informal corporate 'entente' which succeeded it.

The industrial crisis began within weeks of the armistice with a call for a general strike on the Clyde for a forty-hour week on 27 January 1919. In response to the call from a joint committee representing both the shop stewards and local trade union officials, 70,000 engineering, flour mill and transport workers stopped work, mass demonstrations were held outside St Andrews Hall, Glasgow, one of which turned into 'the battle of George Square' in which many strikers and police were injured by batons and bottles, and tanks and troops were called out to hold the deserted field. The strike was abandoned on 11 February. Twelve leaders were later arrested and two of them, Emanuel Shinwell and Willie Gallacher, were sent to prison for short terms.

Gallacher, the tactical organizer of the strike and later a Communist MP, wrote in his memoirs, 'A rising was expected. A rising should have taken place. The workers were ready and able to effect it, the leadership never thought of it.'[105] Whether revolutionary or not, the leadership failed to spread the strike beyond Glasgow, and had no idea how to deal with tanks or troops. Gallacher's rallying cry to revolution – 'Workers of Britain, the decisive hour has come. March forward, strong of heart, with the workers of Germany, the workers of Russia, the workers of all lands. March forward to the conquest of the world. Down with capitalism! Long live the Soviet Republic!'[106] – may have sounded like Lenin but it lacked Leninist vanguard leadership, tactics and ruthlessness.

Much more threatening from the government's point of view was the Miners' Federation six-to-one ballot in favour of a strike on 30 March for a six-hour underground day, a 30 per cent increase in earnings, and nationalization of the coal industry. This might have brought in their partners in the Triple Alliance, the railwaymen and the transport workers, and brought the country to a standstill. Lloyd George bought it off with the appointment of the Sankey Commission on the problems and future of the industry, whose mixed membership of coal owners, unionists, economists, engineers and Fabian intellectuals produced, as was no doubt expected, four conflicting reports, with a slight majority of members in favour of nationalization, which the government surprisingly accepted. An independent strike by the Yorkshire miners in July and August against the compromise seven-hour day and the 2s. a day earnings increase, however, gave Lloyd George a chance to retreat from his commitments, which provoked a Welsh miners' leader to declare that the miners had been 'deceived, betrayed, duped', and stored up trouble for a future when Lloyd George hoped, rightly as it turned out though not to his advantage, that conditions would be less favourable to the miners.[107] More time was bought by the Mining Industry Act of 1920, which continued government control for the time being.

Meanwhile, the government weathered mutinies in the army protesting against slow demobilization, and a second police strike (the first having been a successful wartime one for higher wages in August 1918) for union recognition in London and in Liverpool, where troops were called in to put down a riot, but which ended in the dismissal of the police strikers.[108] With the demobilization of discontented conscripts and the expulsion of the police strikers, the army and the police became more reliable, and the government, embattled in Ireland and Russia as well as on the industrial home front, was beginning to feel slightly more confident.

The nearest the labour movement came, however, to political revolution, was in the 'Hands off Russia' campaign against British intervention in defence of the Poles. Up to 350 'councils of action' drawn from the old shop stewards' movement, the local trade councils and Labour constituency parties, and a sprinkling of left-wing socialists from the BSP, the SLP and similar bodies, persuaded the TUC and the Labour Party in August 1920 to pass a resolution against this 'crime against humanity' and to threaten a political general strike. A delegation to Lloyd George failed, but the Poles' unexpected victory over the Red Army on the Vistula on 14 August saved Britain from the need for further intervention. Apart from a similar, and unsuccessful, threat to bring an end to the civil war in Ireland in July 1920, this was the only attempt to use the general strike as a political weapon.[109]

The main threat, therefore, was on the industrial front, and the government still had to face down the Triple Alliance, which was convinced that the mere threat of a general strike by the big unions which controlled the coal supply and transport could bring down any government. This the government did in three major confrontations in which its policy of divide and rule backed up by the increasing threat of counterforce successfully split the Alliance and rendered it, with the help of the onset of depression and unemployment in 1921, comparatively impotent. These were the national railway strike of September to October 1919, the miners' datum-line strike of October 1920, and the miners' lock-out of April to July 1921.

The railwaymen were the keystone of the Alliance, since a railway stoppage could have the most immediate effect on the economic life of the country, as Bonar Law had recognized in the dispute with the Railway Clerks' Association in January 1919, when he had defeated the trigger-happy Geddes brothers by reminding the Cabinet that 'trade union organization was the only thing between us and anarchy'. It had also been recognized by Sir Albert Stanley, President of the Board of Trade during the wider negotiations with the railway unions in March, who thought 'it was worthwhile paying something to avoid the threatening catastrophe'. Yet the railwaymen were much more vulnerable to the counterweapon of blackleg labour than the miners, and if these two could be split – leaving aside the much weaker third partner, the National Transport Workers' Federation with its thirty-odd loosely connected unions – then the government could face down even a railway strike, provided it was sufficiently prepared. In the event the Alliance split itself. Having failed in the summer of 1919 to force the Parliamentary Committee of the TUC to call a special national conference and threaten a general strike to coerce the government into meeting its political demands – to withdraw conscription, evacuate British troops from Russia, raise the blockade of Germany, and amnesty conscientious objectors – the three unions, led by the miners (who clung to their ballot requirement), refused to co-ordinate their strike procedures and so made it that much more difficult to synchronize strike action.[110]

In this situation the railwaymen, faced with the refusal of the employers' Railway Executive Committee to meet their demand for a generous standardized wage rate, determined to go it alone. With the concurrence of the Engineers and Firemen (ASLEF), the National Union of Railwaymen struck on 26 September without notifying its allies. This was because their Secretary J. H. Thomas, ignored his Executive Committee's order to consult the other unions, officially because it was essential to strike quickly before the government could take counter measures but actually because Thomas distrusted his vacillating allies and did not wish to widen the strike. In fact his action, while tactically successful in achieving a settlement, led to three consequences destructive of the Alliance and its weapon, the general strike. Firstly, there were bitter recriminations and abuse from the other two unions, which made the railwaymen less willing to come to their aid in later disputes. Secondly, the TUC, which had suffered greatly from the abuse and arrogance of the Alliance, set up its own General Council (replacing the ineffective Parliamentary Committee which had few powers between meetings of Congress) as a 'general staff of labour' for 'coordinating industrial action', thus rendering sectional groupings like the Triple Alliance theoretically unnecessary.[111] Thirdly, and more decisively, the government, which had mobilized at short notice 6,000 servicemen, 2,500 military lorries, and an unknown number of civilian volunteers, set up a permanent strike-breaking organization under the name of the Supply and Transport Committee. This was the body which was to help break the General Strike of 1926.[112]

It was the miners, however, who fully exposed the weakness of the Alliance before, during and after their two national disputes of October 1920 and the spring of 1921. While always quick to call for a general strike in support of themselves, they failed to support the calls of others, as for example that of the dockers in December 1919 which Robert Smillie, the miners' President, said came at 'a very inopportune time'. Worst of all, they demanded that their allies should come out in sympathy at great cost to themselves but refused them any share in the negotiations towards a settlement. The railwaymen, nevertheless, voted to support them in their 'datum-line' strike of October 1920 (against a rising scale of wages linked to 'datum lines' of national coal production) and it was the threat of a railway strike which re-opened negotiations between the prime minister and the miners' leaders and led to a settlement, barely accepted by a miners' ballot which showed a majority against it but which failed under a new rule requiring a two-thirds majority for strike action. The strike further exacerbated the mutual distrust of the allied unions, and hastened the passage of the Emergency Powers Act of the same month which gave the government its strike-breaking charter.[113]

The third and final act in the demise of the Triple Alliance (though not of the crisis) was the miners' lock-out of 1921. This was brought on by the sharp economic depression accompanied by a massive fall in the export price of coal. The government hastened the decontrol of the industry and on 31 March 1921 handed the problem back to the coal owners. The owners gave notice of massive wage cuts to match the price fall as from the date of take-over and, on the union's refusal, locked out the miners. The Alliance swung into action and gave notice of a general strike which caused the government to open negotiations with the miners and the owners. When these immediately broke down the strike call was renewed for midnight on Friday, 15 April. A meeting between the miners' leaders and a group of Coalition MPs seemed (due to a misunderstanding of some words by Frank Hodges, the union Secretary, which were interpreted as accepting the owners' demand for district rather than national wage rates) to offer grounds for a settlement, and Lloyd George invited the miners' leaders to a meeting. When, despite the urging of their allies, the miners refused to go, J. H. Thomas and Ernest Bevin, the railway and transport leaders, cancelled the strike, on what came to be known as 'Black Friday', the day the Triple Alliance broke down. The miners' strike staggered on to defeat on 1 July, mitigated by a profit-sharing agreement (17 per cent to the owners, 83 per cent to the men) and a temporary government subsidy to steady the decline in wages. But the Alliance was to all intents and purposes dead, to be replaced by the wider and more 'responsible' alliance of the TUC under its new General Council.[114]

Yet, as it turned out, the TUC was no better prepared to run a general strike than the Triple Alliance. After the failures of 1919–21, the General Strike of 1926 was no more than an epilogue to the mining disputes of 1920 and 1921, and broke down from precisely the same causes: the inability of the trade union leaders to know what to do when the government (now headed by Baldwin, Lloyd George having lost the confidence of his Conservative allies in 1922) called their bluff and challenged them to take over the country, and the miners' refusal to allow their long-suffering allies any say in the negotiations for a settlement. Once again the unions were misled – by their success in forcing the government to subsidize the coal industry to avoid a wage cut on 'Red Friday', 31 July 1925 – into thinking that a united front could coerce the state without a fight. Once again the government used the time it bought with the subsidy and a Royal Commission (the Samuel Commission) to prepare for civil war, with civil commissioners, troops and volunteers to maintain supplies and communications. Once again the unions had their bluff called and were challenged to fight or withdraw. Once again the miners refused to accept negotiations on their behalf without reserving the last word for themselves. After the fateful nine days (4–12 May 1926), in which every affiliated union except (for tactical reasons) the journalists, the sailors and firemen, and the electrical power engineers, came out on strike, the TUC backed down. The miners' strike went on to its crumbling end in December and a settlement not very different from that of 1921, except for longer hours.[115] The General Strike served only to prove that the syndicalist theory that the state could be coerced by direct industrial action without recourse to violence was false.

214

The failure of the General Strike marked the belated end of the crisis of class society in Britain, but it was not the cause of its demise. That was due to the tacit *entente* between the representatives of the unions, the employers and the state which grew up despite or, indeed, in the course of the confrontations and disputes which filled the crisis, because of the General Strike itself. Paradoxically, it also grew up despite the failure of the formal corporate machinery through which Lloyd George and his successors attempted to solve the crisis. The Whitley Councils, joint consultative bodies of employers and workers in each industry, never came to much outside government employment and a handful of small industries. The Trade Boards under the 1909 and 1918 Acts to settle wages and conditions in poorly organized trades, which expanded from eleven to sixty-three between 1918 and 1921 to cover 3 million workers, were deliberately discouraged from expanding further by the Treasury, concerned to cut expenditure and taxes so as to encourage, according to classical economic theory, private industrial investment and the creation of jobs.[116] The creation of the Arbitration Department of the new Ministry of Labour in November 1918 helped to co-ordinate the network of Conciliation Officers patiently built up by Sir George Askwith. Askwith had by now been superannuated and raised to the Lords, but his crowning ambition, the Industrial Courts Act of 1919, did not much appeal to unions and employers who, in major disputes, appealed over any lesser machinery to the Cabinet itself. And Lloyd George's grandiose symbol of corporatism, the National Industrial Conference of 400 representatives of the employers and the unions, which began in a blaze of glory in 1919, soon alienated all three constituents: the employers by recommending a forty-eight-hour week and a minimum wage, the unions by the failure to implement these, and the government by its threatening to become an 'industrial parliament' which claimed the moral right to greater authority in industrial affairs than Parliament itself. It collapsed in July 1921 when the trade union members resigned in disgust.[117]

The *entente* nevertheless survived. Both the TUC and the employers' representatives, the Federation of British Industries and the National Confederation of Employers' Organizations, came to have direct access to the government on all questions concerning industrial affairs. Whether this made them 'governing institutions' in the exclusive sense used by Middlemas there is reason to doubt. Though they undoubtedly became the most important of the interest groups continuously consulted by government, or the 'unsleeping veto groups', to use Dahrendorf's phrase,[118] they became so because they were the most striking examples of a phenomenon central to the emerging society, the almost automatic consultation by government when faced by any problem of 'social engineering' of the expert representatives in the field of action concerned. Other such bodies, like the medical doctors', the sanitary engineers' or the teachers' organizations, were consulted intermittently because their problems necessitated government intervention only occasionally, while industrial relations and economic policy came to be a continuous concern of the state.

The emerging relationship between the state, the industrialists and the trade unions is nowhere better exemplified than in the aftermath of the General Strike. While the mine owners and some right-wing Conservatives gloried in the victory (thus storing up for themselves a nemesis in which no one would come to their rescue against eventual nationalization), the majority of the government and the employers were unwilling to press their advantage over the unions at the expense of future co-operation. Baldwin declared in the House of Commons, 'I will not countenance any attack on the part of any employers to use this present occasion for trying in any way to get reductions in wages below those in force before the strike commenced or any reduction of hours.'[119] The National Confederation of Engineering Employers did indeed put pressure on the government to abolish the unique legal immunity of British trade unions under the 1906 Trade Disputes Act from civil suits for loss of trade arising out of industrial conflicts. But the 1927 Act merely banned sympathetic or insurrectionary strikes, re-emphasized the illegality of intimidation, and changed the presumption for paying the unions' political levy from 'opting out' to 'opting in', thus relying on the inertia of members to reduce, though not to abolish, financial support for the Labour Party. Despite the Labour Party's denunciations and pledge to repeal the 1927 Act, these were irritations rather than vital wounds, and the NCEO hastily backed away from the blame even for these.[120]

Meanwhile, the TUC was becoming more professional, adopting under its professional Secretary-General, Walter Citrine, a cool and pragmatic approach. The director of its new think-tank, the TUC Research Department, another shrewd professional, Milne-Bailey, argued in December 1926 that the trade union movement

> is developing its own hierarchy of government, its own civil service, its own sanctions, independently of the state; with employers it is creating codes, regulating conditions of labour … [I]t has even, at the request of the state, taken over important administrative functions.[121]

These functions would soon include formal consultation, along with the FBI and NCEO, by the government over such matters as national insurance and pensions, and in 1929 the TUC and the employers gave joint evidence to the Macmillan Committee on Finance and Industry. It was the TUC President, George Hicks, whose offer to the employers during the Edinburgh Conference led to the Mond-Turner talks in 1928 between trade unionists and progressive industrialists, and although these failed to establish another formally corporate National Industrial Council they show how far the professionals on each side had come to realize their common interest in avoiding conflict.[122]

The crisis of class society in Britain was averted not by the triumph of the government and the employers over a potentially revolutionary labour movement, which could have only been temporary, but by the common interest of professional managers, professional union leaders, and increasingly professional politicians and civil servants in keeping the system going and avoiding crises. This did not mean that they did not have their own separate, competing interests which they severally tried to foster at the expense of one another and of their constituents and the general public. On the contrary, they also had an interest in conflict, in the sense of the competitive collective bargaining which displayed their skills and made them indispensable. But their fundamental interest was in keeping the game going, for without the game they had no *raison d'être*.

Chapter 6

A HALFWAY HOUSE: SOCIETY IN WAR AND PEACE

In the development of English society in the twentieth century the two world wars mark the boundaries between three stages on the way to a more professional society. The First World War, along with the crisis of class society which straddled it, marked the end of Victorian society in its most pronounced form, a class society in which, as we have seen, social segregation and inequality reached their zenith. The Second World War, along with the demand for a brave new post-war world which accompanied it, marked the tentative beginnings of a new society in which citizenship, as T. H. Marshall observed in 1949 in his Cambridge lectures on *Citizenship and Social Class*, of itself granted claims to security of income, shelter, health and education without the humiliation which had attached to Victorian poor relief. Between these two landmarks inter-war society was in a transitional stage, a sort of halfway house in which remnants of Victorianism, such as the lingering poor law, the means test, and an intensified form of class politics, co-existed with harbingers of the future.

There were three such pointers to the future. For the first time since the Industrial Revolution there was the beginning of a shift in the distribution of income and wealth in the direction of more equality. Secondly, this shift was intensified by the deliberate action of the state in taxing the rich much more heavily than the poor, and in redistributing some small share of the revenue to the lower classes of society. It also redistributed resources horizontally, from the working class while in work to those who were for whatever reason without income. Thirdly, the state took small but significant steps towards modifying the shape of society itself, by means of sponsored mobility through the education system. All three developments, it is true, could be seen in embryo before the First World War, in the rise in real wages from 1874 onwards, in the People's Budget of 1909 and the Liberal welfare measures of 1908-11, and in the secondary school scholarships of 1907 onwards. But their full impact only began to be felt between the wars.

The transition towards a more equal society was also symbolized by changes in dress, housing, town planning and the growth of suburbs, public and private transport, leisure, and even in public morals and religious observances. In dress, that outward witness to the inner aspirations of a society, the most dramatic change took place in the sartorial history of Western civilization since the Renaissance. The shortening of women's skirts marked the approach towards greater freedom for women and more equality between the sexes, and the gradual disappearance for men of the formal morning coat, the Victorian uniform of the upper class, marked the approaching end of sartorial inequality. Henceforth, men and women of all classes would, out of working hours at least, wear much the same styles, and it would take a shrewd eye for the niceties of cut and quality to tell the difference between aristocrats at leisure in their 'lounge suits' and working-class men in their Sunday best in the same suits from the 'fifty-shilling tailors'. The transition remained incomplete, and the casual, unisex, uniclass blue jeans and T-shirts of the 1960s were still far in the future. In public architecture the plain functional slabs of modern brutalism began to replace the ornate eclecticism of Victorian civic pride, marking a change from bourgeois self-confidence to corporate anonymity and mass civilization, but as yet without the human scale and sense of fun which the best late twentieth-century building would bring. Private houses became for the most part mass-produced brick boxes regressing as it were to the mean (in both senses): the ubiquitous semi-detached house, whether privately built or council-owned, was more comfortable and convenient than either the large Victorian villa or the small working-class terraced house. With its compulsory strip of garden and occasional 'space for garage', it yet lacked many of the amenities – fitted carpets, a refrigerator and a television set – which would become the necessities of future living. Most new houses were built at much lower densities to the acre and, despite scenery-hiding ribbon development, generally separated from industrial and commercial property. Their spread was made possible by the new motor buses and private cars, a far cry from the Victorian railway suburb within walking distance of the station, but not yet designed for the highly motorized society of the late twentieth century.

In the sphere of public morals an easing of relations between the sexes could be detected, with the disappearance of chaperones at one end of society and at the other greater freedom from family control of courting hours for girls, but it was still a long, long way from the 'permissive society' of the 1960s. Perhaps the most striking change in '*mentalité*' was the steep decline in religious attendance, now absolute instead of relative, after the First World War, but most people still claimed to be Christians and were far removed in outlook from the 'post-Christian Britain' of the post-1945 generation.

The wars were also milestones in two other transitions of the greatest importance to English society and to Britain as a whole, the double helix of economic decline and rising prosperity. The first, descending spiral was the onset of economic decline, relative rather than absolute, in comparison with other advanced industrial countries, which increasingly began to overtake Britain in production, foreign trade and living standards. This relative decline had begun before the First World War when Britain had already been overtaken in heavy industry, though not in foreign trade and overseas investments, by the United States and Germany, but it did not become glaringly obvious until well after the Second World War. Only in the late 1960s did Britain come to be decisively overtaken in production per head and average living standards by most of Western Europe and in the 1970s by Japan. Between the wars the decline was still shielded from public view by a cushion of past investment and by very favourable terms of trade which still enabled Britain to pay its way in the world in the 1920s, sliding not very far into the red only in the 1930s. There was nonetheless a sense of nostalgia for lost economic hegemony and the golden age of free trade, and a touching faith in its restoration which bedevilled economic policy.

The second helix was the obverse of the first. Relative decline was accompanied by an absolute advance in production and productivity at a pace not seen since the height of the Industrial Revolution. This made possible, along with the favourable terms of trade, a rise in living standards which benefited all classes, not least the working class. Many of the poorest were raised out of the harsh, grinding poverty which had been their lot in Victorian society. The improvement was modest and fell short of the comparative affluence of the second half of the twentieth century, but it was real enough to lead social surveyors to invent, in fact if not by name, the concept of relative poverty which would be used to question that later affluence.

This conjunction of political and economic progress and decline is the supreme paradox of Britain's history in the twentieth century. The descending spiral of Britain as a world and imperial power and as the leader in world trade and the ascending spiral of individual prosperity and public welfare were intimately intertwined. It was surprising but true that the country which had at the beginning of the century been the head of the world's largest empire and the world's leading exporter of manufactured goods should progressively lose those positions and yet should find itself both richer than ever before in terms of public and private affluence and more powerful in terms of its ability to destroy its enemies – at the cost, it goes without saying, of destroying itself. The paradox is easily enough explained: the decline was relative, the rise in affluence absolute. While Britain was making progress in the production of goods and services at rates unparalleled since the Industrial Revolution, other countries, many but not all with far larger resources, were advancing still faster and would eventually, though not until the late 1960s and 1970s, decisively overtake it. Just as in the nineteenth century Britain taught the world the hard lesson that military and economic power followed industrial hegemony, so in the twentieth Britain had to learn the hard lesson that relative failure in the industrial race meant loss of military and commercial leadership.

The two world wars contributed to it directly with the loss of overseas investments, small in the first but much larger in the second, and, more importantly, the loss of export markets. Britain's share of world trade in manufactures fell from 30.9 per cent in 1913 to 21.3 per cent in 1937 and, after a temporary recovery to 25.3 per cent in 1950, to 16.5 per cent in 1960. Even if world trade as a whole was growing, by 27 per cent to 1929 though declining by 11 per cent in 1929-37, Britain's share lagged behind by 19 per cent in the 1920s and by 20 per cent in the 1930s, and in volume terms UK exports scarcely reached three-quarters of their

1913 level in the 1920s, or three-fifths in the 1930s.[1] The immediate cause of the decline was Britain's failure to adjust her production to the new patterns of world trade. British industry continued to concentrate on the old nineteenth-century staples, cotton, coal, shipbuilding, heavy chemicals and heavy engineering, when world demand was turning increasingly to new lighter products, cars, man-made fibres, and consumer goods of all kinds. Britain, it is true, did begin to invest in these new industries, but not enough to replace the decline in the older ones, either in production or in the employment of labour and capital. In the 1920s the decline was masked by the invisible earnings from the overseas trade balances of the pre-war period and by the very favourable terms of trade which enabled British exports to buy larger quantities of food and raw materials from the primary producers, but by the 1930s even this windfall failed to fill the developing gap in visible trade.

The origins of this revolution in Britain's world role go back to the falling rate of economic growth in the generation before the First World War but they were not recognized until afterwards, and only dimly then. As late as 1925 a Conservative government believed that it could wish Britain back to pre-war prosperity simply by restoring the gold standard at pre-war parity. The Labour government of 1929–31 had no better idea how to cope with the new world of declining trade and unemployment. It took the financial crash of 1929 and the Great Depression of the 1930s to convince the National government that the world had changed. Even then, if it abandoned free trade only to find that the resulting retaliation acted to reduce trade all round, it continued to apply the nineteenth century shibboleths of retrenchment and a balanced budget. Only a few individuals, J. A. Hobson, John Maynard Keynes and Ernest Bevin, put the alternative view that balanced budgets were not the answer but operated to make the situation worse by discouraging both spending and investment. What the Americans in the New Deal and the Germans under Hitler worked out for themselves, that government spending need not be a drag on enterprise but the starter motor that set the machine in motion, British governments of both parties refused to contemplate. Only the belated and half-hearted Special Areas legislation of 1934 and 1937 tried to stimulate enterprise in the depressed areas, and this created less than 50,000 jobs in areas where in 1935 over 360,000 workers were registered as unemployed.

All told, unemployment rarely fell below 10 per cent of the insured population in the 1920s and averaged 17 per cent in 1929–36, and in 1932 it peaked at nearly 3 million, 23 per cent of all insured workers. It was far worse in the old industrial areas of the north and Wales, where it averaged 23 per cent throughout the 1930s, and 29.5 per cent in 1932.[2] What finally helped to solve the problem, besides subsidized house building and transport construction, was government spending on rearmament from 1936 onwards, and even then there were still over a million and a half unemployed at the outbreak of war in 1939. But the war itself only confirmed Britain's decline, selling off the last remnants of overseas investments and further depleting export markets. After a short-lived recovery in the immediate post-war reconstruction boom, Britain's relative decline continued without abatement, and by 1966 it had been overtaken in per capita income, not only by the older competitors, the United States and Scandinavia, but by the six countries of the new European Common Market, and would shortly be overtaken by Japan.

To the reasons for the decline in competitiveness – lack of sufficient investment, still more lack of an adequate return on what investment there was, due to unimaginative management, recalcitrant trade unions fearful of redundancy, low trust industrial relations, and the like – we must return later, in Chapter 9. Meanwhile, the picture was by no means as gloomy as it might appear. On the contrary, production was, surprisingly, growing faster than before the war, faster than at any time since the Industrial Revolution, while national income per head was growing faster than Edwardian rates and almost as fast as Victorian. Although economic historians differ as to the exact figures, Gross Domestic Product seems to have grown between 1924 and 1937 by about 2.3 per cent per annum, compared with 2.0 per cent per annum in 1856–99 and 1.1 per cent in 1899–1913. National income per head in real terms (at constant, 1913 prices) grew even faster (thanks mainly to the favourable terms of trade), at 2.6 per cent per annum, the same rate as between 1856 and 1913, much better than the 1.1 per cent in 1899–1913 but somewhat slower than the 2.9 per cent in 1856–99. Thus average annual real incomes rose by about 29 per cent between 1913 and 1938, while average real annual wage earnings for those in work rose by slightly more.[3]

This improvement could be seen everywhere, even to some extent in the depressed areas, in the new houses, both private and municipal, with their gas cookers, electric light, and better furnishings and appliances, in the better clothing and shoes of the working class – children in rags and without shoes, commonplace before the war, were now a rarity – and in the new shops, cinemas, dance halls, greyhound tracks, and all the appurtenances of a somewhat more leisured and affluent society. Even the unemployed were, with the exception of those with large families, better off than the average unskilled worker before the war, while poverty of the harsh, grinding kind documented by Booth and Rowntree had been halved, as we shall see. All this is not to say, of course, that the so-called affluent society (with all its ambiguities) of the later twentieth century had already arrived. Far from it: poverty was still rife by current standards, as social surveyors like Rowntree argued when he raised his poverty line to take account of 'human needs'. But the fact that the line could be raised in this way argues that the average standard of living was rising.

Before we come to the effects of these contradictory changes on society and the various classes within it, however, we must consider the impact of the First World War, that great divide between the Victorian and Edwardian world and the new world of the twentieth century.

1   THE GREAT DIVIDE, 1914–18

The Great War came to be seen by those who looked back from the inter-war period to the lost world of Victorian and Edwardian England as a great divide between two quite different societies. For the nostalgic rich and powerful, who felt they had lost so much, that earlier society inhabited an Indian summer of gracious living, the whirl of the London 'season' and country house parties, an endless round of pleasure based on low taxes, cheap servants and the self-confidence which went with unquestioned status. At the opposite pole, the poor and their professional surveyors looked back on a world in which life for the great majority was one long struggle to survive, in which a labourer's wage in full work was insufficient to maintain a moderate family of two or three children above a very low poverty line, and in which a majority of the working class passed through a period of malnutrition at some time in their lives. For the middle class, who were the first to feel the decline of personal service and its increasing cost, life had lost some of its accustomed amenities, though it had brought new ones in compensation. For all classes, the war was a major watershed, a mountain range between two climatic zones, a bourne of no return that proclaimed that, for good or ill, things would never be the same again.

For this reason the First World War has often been credited or blamed for a series of major social changes which, it has been countered, would probably have happened sooner or later anyway. Although it inaugurated very little, the war certainly accelerated most of the major trends which were already in operation in pre-war England. To the extent that it dramatized the transition, it marked a boundary between two significantly different societies. We have already seen its role as the supreme test of a class society which was already in crisis when war broke out in 1914, and how at one and the same time it postponed and intensified the crisis until it came to a head, and a delayed dénouement, after the war. Now we must consider its effects on the long-term social trends: changes in the direction of economic growth, in living standards and the distribution of income and wealth; changes in the position of women; changes in the hopes and expectations of education; and the more ethereal but no less significant changes in religious belief and moral conduct.

What dramatized the war most of all as a great historical divide was its unprecedented cost, in life and limb, in money and material resources, in lost trade and overseas earnings, and in Britain's power and economic position in the world. The cost in human life was horrific: 745,000 men were killed (plus another 200,000 from the empire) and 1,600,000 wounded out of the more than 4 million who served in the armed forces – nearly three in five of all British men of military age.[4] The dead, nearly one in seven of those who served and nearly one in ten of those of military age, constituted the 'lost generation' whom contemporaries came to see as the missing political and business leaders, and the missing husbands and fathers, of the inter-war years. Even though some of the survivors, like Clement Attlee and Harold Macmillan, were as capable as their predecessors, and the decline of mass emigration, always more men than women, from its pre-war peak probably meant that there were more potential husbands than before, there was the sense of a stunning loss which could never be replaced. The civilian population too was more affected by this first total war than by any previous conflict, and although less than 1,500 people were killed in air raids (compared with 60,000 in the Second World War), most of the occupied population, including unprecedented numbers of women, came to be engaged in 'war work', either in the forces or in industries essential to the war. The sense of having participated in a great struggle to save the nation from destruction was almost universal.

The cost in money and material resources was also immense: about £12 billion by 1920 to the British Exchequer, less than half of which had been raised by taxation, the rest by internal borrowing.[5] The National Debt rose elevenfold, from £706 million to £7,876 million and debt interest came to absorb up to 40 per cent of state expenditure between the wars. Income tax rose dramatically, and permanently, to a new plateau, from 1s. 2d. (6 per cent) in the £ in 1913 to 6s. (30 per cent) in 1918, and never fell below 4s. (20 per cent) again, while supertax on higher incomes jumped from 6d. in the £ to 6s. in 1918 and to 8s. 3d. from 1931 onwards. More strikingly, the numbers swept into the income tax net jumped from about 1 million to 8 million, over 40 per cent of the occupied population. Thus the taxable capacity of the population was raised to a higher plane, and the modern trend towards big government accelerated. Public expenditure rose from 12 to 52 per cent in 1918 and, after falling back to 24 per cent in 1929, reached 35 per cent in 1939 (and a huge 74 per cent in 1943), this displacement effect massively increasing the power of the state to intervene in the life of society.[6]

The war and its consequences were less costly in lost foreign investments and repudiated foreign debts. Sales of private assets to pay for essential imports, mostly to the Americans, exceeded overseas investments by £300 million, but this was less than a tenth of the nearly £4 billion held by Britain in 1913.[7] Inter-government lending lost a similar amount: Britain lent £1,825 million, mainly to European allies, and borrowed £1,340 million from the American, Dominion and colonial governments, but when the new Russian and some South American governments defaulted there was a small net loss.[8]

The normal revival of trade would soon have recouped these losses, but British exports failed to regain their old levels and the biggest economic loss was in foreign markets. After a short burst of success in the 1920s, the British balance of payments in the 1930s became negative, briefly, for the first time since Waterloo. Thus in the economic field there was 'a radical change in Britain's position *vis-à-vis* the rest of the world', which many contemporaries attributed to the capture of traditional markets by allies less involved in the war like America and Japan, and by neutrals who had been forced to supply themselves.[9] In fact it was mainly due to British industrialists and traders persisting with products like coal, ships, heavy engineering and textiles for which world demand was shrinking, and not investing enough in the new consumer goods like motor cars, radios and electrical appliances for which demand was rising. But to the hard-pressed business men and unemployed workers of the day it seemed that the pattern of world trade had changed and that the war had changed it. This was undoubtedly true: the British had simply failed to change with it; or, rather, they had not changed enough. They did indeed invest in the new and expanding industries, motor cars, light engineering, 'artificial silk' (rayon), and so on, so that a large part of the inter-war unemployment could be attributed to the high productivity in these new industries, which therefore failed to absorb enough redundant workers from the old. But unemployment of both labour and capital was the principal problem of the inter-war period, and undoubtedly reached a new scale after the 1914–18 war and seemed in some obscure way to be connected with it.

The war too was credited with the end of *laissez-faire* and the beginnings of state collectivism in the shape of government control of war production. While pre-war thinkers and politicians had only discussed socialism and nationalization, the wartime government had put them into practice. It had not set out to do so but was forced by degrees not only to take over the munitions industry but to control the production, transport and distribution of every commodity, including food and fuel, remotely connected with the war effort. As Sidney Pollard has put it:

> What appeared at first as a specific need or shortage often
> quickly became a symptom of a much wider alteration in
> supply and demand relationships. Some relatively minor
> control, to deal with an immediate issue, often had
> repercussions which required Government intervention further

227

and further back, until the State found itself directing a major part of the country's industries, and controlling or licensing most of the remainder. Thus a sudden demand for blankets would set up an immediate rise in price and lead to the hoarding of wool tops, which would affect other sectors of the woollen and worsted industries; and this, in turn, might affect British agriculture or imports from Australia, and so on in unending progression.[10]

This led on inexorably to state control of most manufacturing industry, transport, mines, and ultimately to food rationing and the control of labour. The official war history noted:

The final step was to assume responsibility for all visible supplies, to control all private importation and distribute material to non-munitions as well as munitions trades, thereby virtually bringing the industries connected with munitions supply, and all the industries using munitions materials, including private as well as munitions trading, under the control of the [Army Contracts] Department.[11]

By the end of the war the twenty clerks of the Contracts Department in August 1914 had grown to 65,000 officials in the mighty Ministry of Munitions set up under Lloyd George in 1915, which came to control 2 million workers in 250 government factories, mines and quarries, and another 1.4 million in 20,000 controlled establishments.

Beyond the munitions industry state control came to be symbolized by six Controllers, of shipping, labour, food, food production, coal and national service. They were all 'experts', drawn from the industries or interests concerned, and though some of them, like Food Controller Lord Devonport of the grocery chain Kearley and Tonge, were anything but competent, they were formidable dictators of large areas of economic life.

The mobilization of labour followed the same reluctant pattern. When the first 2.5 million volunteers for the army proved insufficient, Lord Derby's National Registration Scheme of October 1915 tried to get men to 'attest' voluntarily for what proved to be compulsory service, and only when the 2.25 million attesters were called up did the government resort to conscription, of single men in January 1916 and of married men in May. Meanwhile, workers in reserved occupations were in effect directed into essential work and held there by devices such as the notorious 'leaving certificates' and 'trade cards' which the shop stewards, if not the trade union leaders, considered the badge of slavery. Food rationing was avoided until the last few months of the war, preceded by appeals for voluntary self-denial, meatless days, rules against 'flaunting' luxury foodstuffs, and even a Royal Proclamation on saving grain read in places of worship, before the U-boat campaign finally forced it on the whole country in April 1918.

State control was not without its advocates, some old nationalizers like Sir Leo Chiozza Money who saw it as a foretaste of socialism to come, some new converts like Winston Churchill who wished the government to accept wholeheartedly the path of necessity, while some cautious pragmatists like *The Times* agitated for 'mobilizing the whole nation' and the *Manchester Guardian* urged the control of profits under what it called 'war socialism'.[12] The war certainly proved that state control and even nationalization could be made to work, for some purposes, more productively than private enterprise. It encouraged many people, like R. H. Tawney, Sidney Webb, Chiozza Money and the three trade union representatives on the Sankey Commission on the Coal Industry in 1919, together with Lord Sankey himself, to think that nationalization of a key industry could work in peacetime.[13] As J. M. Keynes said in 1924:

> War experience in the organization of socialized production
> has left some near observers optimistically anxious to repeat it
> in peace conditions. War socialism unquestionably achieved a
> production of wealth far greater than we ever knew in Peace,
> for though the goods and services delivered were destined for
> immediate and fruitless extinction, none the less they were
> wealth. Nevertheless, the dissipation of effort was also
> prodigious, and the atmosphere of waste and not counting the
> cost was disgusting to any thrifty or provident spirit.[14]

Whether the efficiency of state production could have overcome the atmosphere of waste was never given a trial, however, since the predominantly Conservative Coalition of 1918-22, full of what Stanley Baldwin called the 'hard-faced men who looked as though they had done well out of the war',[15] was in no mood to continue war socialism a moment longer than was militarily necessary. It made 'a bonfire of controls' in a bid 'to go back as far as possible to the social and industrial situation as it existed at the outbreak of the war'.[16]

Even the one breach with *laissez-faire* which most Conservative business men now favoured, tariff reform to protect their own particular industries in the shape of the McKenna duties of 33.3 per cent on 'luxury' imports to save shipping in 1915, failed to make more than a dent in the Cobdenite orthodoxy of free trade. Though they were continued after the war, and 'key industries' were ineffectually 'safeguarded' in 1921, a full-blown protectionist platform lost Baldwin the election in 1923, and it took the Depression and a National Coalition in 1931 to bring back protection.

On the other hand, no coalition, however powerful, could bring back the pre-war social and industrial situation, which for the great majority was a very good thing. A golden age it may have seemed in retrospect for the rich, but for the working class, especially the unskilled, it represented the bad old days to be avoided at all cost. Reconstruction for them meant a new start and an attempt to build a better society. That they were frustrated in their hopes by the failure of social reform in 1918–20, by the onset of mass unemployment in 1921, and by the 'Geddes axe' laid to the root of public spending – the first of those cycles of economic depression and deflationary public expenditure cuts which dominated the 1920s and 1930s – must not be allowed to conceal the very real changes in distribution of income and living standards which also characterized the inter-war period.

The most dramatic change was in the living standards of the working class. Robert Roberts, the child of a corner shop in Salford, the 'classic slum', called the war 'the Great Release'. 'The first world war cracked the form of English lower-class life and began an erosion of its socio-economic layers that has continued to this day ... "Things", people repeatedly told one another, "will never be the same again." '[17] Although the troops themselves were miserably paid, many of them were never so well fed and clothed, and at home labour of all kinds, including women's, was in such demand that wages rose sharply, especially for munitions and engineering workers: 'Some of the poorest in the land began to prosper as never before.'[18] Money wages had nearly trebled by 1920 but much of the gain was eroded by inflation and real wages rose

230

on average no more than 10 per cent. The money improvement was crucial, however, since in the steep price fall of the early 1920s wage earners were able to hold on to most of the gains, so that real earnings levelled out by the 1930s at about 30 per cent above those of 1913.[19] As John Burnett, historian of the cost of living, has put it, 'If the Great Depression [of 1874–96] marks the first important step by the working classes of England towards material comfort, the First World War, for all its horrors and miseries, marks the second.'[20]

Equally important for the poorest workers was the narrowing of differentials which lifted the floor on which the unskilled labourer stood. In 1913 unskilled labourers' wages in most industries were between one-half and two-thirds of skilled men's; by 1919 they were between three-quarters and five-sixths. The effect of this, together with the trend towards smaller families, was to lift the average unskilled labourer and his family, provided he were in work, out of the harsh, grinding, absolute poverty of the pre-war period. Sir Arthur Bowley, who during the war had argued on the basis of his pre-war study of five industrial towns that 'to raise the wages of the worst-paid workers is the most pressing social task with which this country is faced today', went on to say in his repeat study in 1925, 'It has needed a war to do it, but that task has been accomplished, so far as rates of wages are concerned, though employment has not yet been permanently possible at all those rates.'[21] Poverty in his five towns had been more than halved, indeed had been cut by two-thirds (from 12.6 to 3.5 per cent) for those in work on full wages, and this improvement was confirmed by other social surveys, of London, York, and Bristol.[22] Even the unemployed, though more numerous, were as well off on their new insurance benefits as the unskilled wage earners in full work before the war, although that still left those with very large families in poverty.

The narrowing of differentials also operated between the working class and those above it. In 1924 Bowley and Stamp found a modest shift of 1 per cent of the National Income before tax from the higher income groups to wages since 1911 (from 43 to 44 per cent), despite the smaller size and shorter hours of the working class, and this was increased by old age pensions and employers' national insurance contributions.[23] After income tax, which had quadrupled since before the war and was not paid until the Second

World War by most working men, the shift in income distribution, modest enough in all conscience, was still keenly felt by the taxpaying classes, who pined for the palmy days before the war. At the bottom end the lowest middle-class taxpayer in 1913 paid about 6 per cent of his income in tax, in 1919 about 13 per cent; at the top end, the man with an unearned income of £10,000 in 1913 paid 15 per cent, in 1919 over 50 per cent.[24] The rich could not but look back at the war as the beginning of their decline in lifestyle and prosperity.

One reason why taxation did not return to the old levels after the war is that Britain for the first time had become a (nearly) complete democracy. Only in 1918 did every man over 21 get the right to vote, along with every woman over 30, and the electorate trebled to over 18 million. Universal adult suffrage (completed when women between 21 and 30 finally got the vote in 1928) was meant to be a reward to working-class men and to women of all classes for their enthusiastic and patriotic participation in the war effort, as the Speaker's Conference on the franchise bill declared in 1917. No doubt manhood suffrage and certainly votes for women were on the verge of attainment in 1914. But it was the war which finally brought it about, and with it a profound change in the structure of politics, albeit in an unexpected direction. Far from putting into more or less permanent power one or other of the 'progressive' parties, the working-class vote divided unevenly between them, indeed between all three major parties, and the Conservative Party was effectively in power, if not always in office, until 1945.

The question whether this would have happened if the Liberal Party had not split over the conduct of the war in 1916 or if it had managed to come together again sooner after it ended will no doubt divide political historians for ever – though as we have seen there were much older and deeper sociological causes behind the decline of Liberal England. The war, however, changed both the teams and the nature of the game. The rise of the Labour Party from a pressure group to official Opposition and alternative government was enormously accelerated by the war and the participation of Labour ministers in the cabinet. The rise of the Labour vote from 0.5 million in 1910 to 2.4 million in 1918, 5.5 million in 1924 and to 8.4 million in 1929 ensured that the Tories would have to woo the working-class voter even more assiduously than before the war. Though they were to offer reforms which they thought the working class wanted, provided these did not endanger the main social and economic fabric they existed to conserve, they soon learned that to take away gains which had already been granted was to court electoral defeat. If the proportional representation recommended by the Speaker's Conference in 1917 had been accepted by Parliament, the structure and the story of British politics in the twentieth century would no doubt have been very different. In its absence the Conservative Party was able to cling to office, mostly with a minority of the popular vote, for fifty of the next seventy years, through its success in capturing at least a third of the working-class vote. It was to be that third, voting across class lines, which was to determine the shape of British politics.

According to the late Philip Abrams, 'The one group in English society to which the war brought a significant extension of social and political privilege was middle-aged, propertied women.'[25] Such women, like those leaders of the militant Suffragettes and the non-militant Suffragists Emmeline Pankhurst and Millicent Fawcett, had seen the war as an opportunity to show what women could do and threw themselves enthusiastically into the war effort.[26] Others, like Beatrice Webb, one of fourteen well-to-do women who served on the eighteen-member social affairs committee of the Ministry of Reconstruction, seized the opportunity to exercise their undoubted talents for administration and policy making.[27] Thousands of middle-class ladies rushed to 'do their bit' as nurses, VADs (Volunteer Aid Detachments), officers in the women's auxiliary forces, industrial welfare workers, and so on, and many more substituted for men in government offices, business and the professions. For most women, however, the call was not to glamorous jobs in the public eye but to arduous ones in the munitions factories, engineering workshops, bus conducting, even garbage collecting, any occupation in fact where they could release men for service in the army. For some it offered escape from the drudgery of domestic service, dressmaking or shopwork, but winning the vote and other women's rights was probably the last thing on their minds. Probably the second factor after the need to win the war was the added earning power and the increased self-confidence which a well-paid job brought with it. As Robert Roberts noted:

233

Women grew in social stature and gained an authority they have never lost since ... But whatever war did to women in home, field, service or factory, it undoubtedly snapped strings that had bound them in so many ways to the Victorian age. Even we, the young, noticed their new self-confidence. Wives in the shop no longer talked about 'my boss' or 'my master' ... She discovered her own rights. The pre-1914 movements for her political emancipation, bourgeois in origin and function, meant very little to the lower-working class woman. In the end the consequences of war, not the legal acquisition of female rights, released her from bondage.[28]

Women's employment in the war effort was at the base of both kinds of emancipation, personal and official. The 'munitions girls', including the yellow-skinned 'canaries' filling shells with TNT, were the most obvious, increasing from 212,000 in 1914 to over 900,000 by the war's end, and enjoying their few years of economic independence with riotous spending on fur coats, jewellery, boiled ham high teas and the cinema. In industry as a whole women's employment increased from 2,179,000 to 2,971,000, in transport from 18,000 to 117,000, in commerce (mainly office work) from 505,000 to 934,000, in national and local government (including school teaching) from 262,000 to 460,000.[29] Many were recruited from domestic service, which shrank from 1,658,000 to 1,258,000 but refused to disappear. The *New Statesman* reported of the new women workers in 1917:

> They appear more alert, more critical of the conditions under which they work, more ready to make a stand against injustice than their pre-war selves or their prototypes. They have a keener appetite for experience and pleasure and a tendency quite new to their class to protest against wrongs even before they become 'intolerable'.[30]

Some doughty women led unaccustomed street protests: riots and looting of German shops in London and Manchester, food riots in the mining towns of West Cumberland, rent strikes in Glasgow.[31] If none of these were new to historians of an older Britain, they shocked contemporaries with a different image of womanly behaviour.

Women's participation and newfound confidence found their reward in the long-delayed vote, in the Sex Disqualification

(Removal) Act of 1919, and in the opening of Parliament itself to women, with Lady Astor the first to take her seat in 1919. Yet many of these gains were nullified soon after the war by the pressure to force women out of jobs to make way for demobilized troops, by the massive increase in unemployment, worse for women than for men, by the tacit acceptance of unequal pay for women and by the new or reimposed rule in the Civil Service, teaching and many other occupations that women must resign on marriage. The number of women workers declined rapidly with the peace: in 1921 there were relatively fewer at work (33.7 against 35.3 per cent) than in 1911. Yet 'things were never the same again'. Women in the professions and white-blouse occupations had increased in number, those in factory work and domestic service had decreased, as more middle-class (or aspiring) women demanded more jobs and many working-class women, emulating the old aspiration of the skilled working class, responded to higher living standards by electing to stay at home to look after their children, a luxury many could not previously afford.

The new self-confidence expressed itself in two highly symbolic ways, one in the most private and intimate of emancipations, the other in the most public and visible. The first was in the practice of birth control, which had indeed begun amongst the middle class in the late Victorian age but now spread throughout society, reaching for the first time a majority of the working class. Its progress can be measured by the fall in family size: women marrying between 1900 and 1909 had an average of 3.5 children, those marrying between 1920 and 1924 2.4.[32] The fall was greater, since middle-class families were already small, amongst the working class. Professional families shrank by a quarter, manual and agricultural wage earners' families by a third (though unskilled labourers' families, still with larger families than the rest, only by a quarter).[33] Clerks and textile workers were the pioneers, followed last of all and more slowly by the miners and agricultural labourers. The statistics say nothing about the causes, however. Just as the decline of the middle-class birth rate from the late 1870s was naively attributed to the Bradlaugh-Besant trial, so the post-war decline of the working-class birth rate was put down to mechanical causes like the 'prophylactics' (condoms) against venereal disease issued to the troops from 1917 and Marie Stopes's *Married Love and Planned Parenthood* published in 1919. Such arguments ignore the fact that most working-class couples who took precautions, according to the Royal Commission on Population, 1949, practised *coitus interruptus*, and that Stopes said little about contraception and coyly recommended only an ineffective vinegar and water douche or quinine solution pessary.[34] This confirms that, as with the middle class, it was the motivation rather than the means that mattered.

One of the few historians to ask working-class mothers of the period how they limited their families, Diana Gittins, found that they learned nothing from Maries Stopes, from their doctors, or even from their own mothers. Enlightenment came from their own age mates in the factories and offices.[35] It was therefore the expansion of women's employment during the war that probably had most effect on the spread of contraceptive information. As for the motivation, it did not need middle-class propaganda to teach the possibility of escape from the cycle of poverty, that having fewer children would speed the rise in living standards. Thus the war played a double role, by increasing both the motive for limiting family size and the knowledge of how to bring it about. Whatever the reason, it had the effect of dramatically decelerating population growth. From the first census in 1801 down to the 1911 census the rate of growth was never less than 10 per cent per decade; after 1911 it was never more than 5.5 per cent.

The second, more visible emancipation of women was in the realm of dress. Clothing has been an expression of the values and ideals of society since civilization began, and the dramatic change in women's fashions which came in during the war expressed the most profound transition in attitudes to women and in women's belief in themselves since Anglo-Saxon times (the last age, according to Lady Stenton, in which women approached equality with men, and both sexes wore long skirts).[36] The shorter skirts of the war years, like the trousers of the 'munitions girls', have been explained by their greater practicability for factory and other traditionally masculine occupations. But women had worked in factories ever since they were invented without departing from traditional dress, and their refusal to abandon short skirts or even, at least for casual and leisure wear, trousers in the post-war period shows that deeper change in women's psychology and men's appreciation of it was in progress. The demand for equality had led in the Victorian age to experiments in freer dress by *avant-*

garde ladies like Mrs Bloomer and the pre-Raphaelites, but it was only in the First World War that enough free spirits came together to make the experiment stick. No doubt the change would eventually have come anyway, and there were hints of shorter skirts on the way from about 1912, but it took the war, with its self-confident and self-assertive women workers, to impose this unprecedented change in women's dress and the feminine psyche.

For some, both the pruriently scandalized and the hopefully libertine, shorter skirts meant looser morals, and within nine months of the outbreak the popular press was running a campaign about illegitimate 'war babies'. In fact, illegitimate births were fewer in 1915, and although by the end of the war they were 30 per cent higher than pre-war, they fell in the early 1920s to the lowest rates ever recorded.[37] No doubt the war presented greater opportunities for casual sex amongst soldiers and 'munitions girls' far from home as well as encouraged stronger emotions between men going to the front and women wishing to be 'kind' to them. More significant, perhaps, was the increase in the number of marriages: how many illegitimate babies were the fruit of planned marriages frustrated by death or injury at the front? Any notion of a permanent change towards sexual permissiveness was undermined, on both sides, by the swift return after the war to traditionally strict public standards of premarital conduct in the middle and upper working classes (whatever the private behaviour behind it), and by the traditionally loose behaviour long before the war at the two extremes of society, amongst the notorious libertines of high society and the notoriously feckless 'roughs'. Not until the permissive 1960s did 'free love' and premarital cohabitation become overtly acceptable, and whatever dent the war made in public morals in the conventional sense was quickly repaired. Morality concerns more than sexual behaviour, however, and the twentieth century was to be in some respects a more moral society than any before, as we shall see.

For contemporary feminists the war marked the end of Victorianism. As the historian of the women's movement, Mrs Ray Strachey, summed up in 1928:

> No woman of today would go back if she could to the
> conditions which her grandmother endured. No girl would
> submit to the clothing and the restraints of 1837, no wife
> would be content to merge her whole legal and financial

existence in that of her husband; no matron would agree to put
on her cap and retire from life at thirty-five. And even if
women would do these things, men would not approve! ...
neither sex would now, even if it could, turn back the hands of
the clock.[38]

If women's liberation still had a long way to go, it had already
come a long way since Victoria's day.

Even children participated in the war and benefited from that
participation, both in the imprudent short term and in the
enlightened long term. According to H. A. L. Fisher, the first
educationist to be minister of education, by 1917 600,000 children
had left school prematurely – at 13 years of age or less – to work,
most of them in well-paid but dead-end jobs either connected with
the war effort or releasing adults for it. Many of them lost out
permanently in missed education and apprenticeships, and in his
proposal in 1917 for a post-war Education Act Fisher said that it
was

> prompted by deficiencies which had been revealed by the War; it
> is framed to repair the intellectual wastage which has been
> caused by the War; and should it pass into law before peace is
> struck it will put a prompt end to an evil which has grown to
> alarming proportions during the past three years – I allude to
> the industrial pressure upon the child life of this country – and
> it will greatly facilitate the solution of many problems of
> juvenile employment, which will certainly be affected by the
> transition from a basis of war to a basis of peace.[39]

What worried many observers even more was the evidence the
war produced of the physical wastage of peacetime. As in the Boer
War when they had led to the Committee on Physical
Deterioration being set up, the recruitment statistics of the Great
War showed on a much more massive scale the low standard of
physical health and fitness produced by a society which brought
up more than half of its children in poverty. Of the 2.5 million
recruits examined in 1917–18 only 36 per cent were passed as fit for
full military duties, and 41 per cent were graded as unable 'to
undergo physical exertion' or 'totally or permanently unfit for
military service'.[40] That nearly two-thirds were below the standard
for front-line service was an indictment of the low-grade food and
living conditions in which most of them had been reared, and

fully justified the pre-war campaign for national efficiency. As the new minister of health, Christopher Addison, himself a medical doctor, pointed out in 1919, 'the armies of children who are physically defective' in the elementary schools had become

> the hundreds of thousands of men who were physically unfit and could not pass the very moderate standard of physical fitness which the army required. Then it was revealed as a source of national weakness, which is very great in time of emergency, but it is just as much a source of national weakness in time of peace.[41]

Such incontrovertible facts gave added point to Fisher's argument that conscription meant 'that the boundaries of citizenship are not determined by wealth and that the same logic which leads us to desire an extension of the franchise points also to an extension of education'.[42]

The 1918 Education Act, much amputated in its passage, was intended to be a children's charter: universal compulsory schooling to 14, part-time day continuation schools from 14 to 18, abolition of fees in public elementary schools, physical training for all, improved standards in the higher school classes, special provision for handicapped children, and nursery school places for all who wanted them. Some of these gains fell to the post-war Geddes axe, notably the day continuation schools, but, together with the expansion of the 11-plus scholarships and 'free places' in the grammar schools and from 1920 the few hundred state scholarships to the universities, they had breached the class barriers to more egalitarian education. It was a far cry from *The Times Educational Supplement*'s opposition in 1910 to 'so large a proportion as 25 per cent of "free placers", ex hypothesi boys and girls from working-class homes, in an average Secondary school to which middle-class parents send their children' on the grounds that 'in an old country like England, whose lines of social distinction are sharply drawn, they cannot be set aside in practice' since 'the parents of paying pupils will hold aloof'.[43] Where men of all classes had shared the same trenches and thousands of officers had risen from the ranks, such sentiments no longer went unchallenged. By contrast the Report of the Departmental Committee on Scholarships and Free Places in 1920 had the same fear of middle-class withdrawal but talked instead of 'an undesirable segregation of social classes'[44] – a significant change of focus.

The war proved to be a turning point in religious observance. Considering the support given by the churches to the war to end war, the pathetic faith of some of the troops about to 'go over the top', and the naive belief in miracles like 'the angel of Mons', it might have been expected that the war would increase the power of religion or at least arrest the relative decline in church attendance which had persisted since the 1851 Religious Census. In fact, quite the opposite occurred. Whereas 'in all the major Churches organizational expansion continued to the eve of the First World War' in terms of absolute if not of proportional church attendance, 'All the Churches lost ground substantially during World War I.'[45] Despite a revival in the 1920s from the low point of 1917, the war marked the beginning of the steep decline in the number of church attenders; in York, for example it declined, from about a third of the adult population in the Edwardian age to a sixth between the wars and only a tenth after the Second World War.[46] The immediate reasons for the change can be found in soldiers' diaries and letters from the front. One soldier wrote just before he was killed, 'Any faith in religion I ever had is most frightfully shaken by the things I've seen.'[47] The longer-term factors were more complex: 'if supportive social and political causes had been operating in favour of organized Protestantism in the Victorian and Edwardian eras, their significance waned with the First World War.'[48] If religion is defined by its modern historians as 'the attempt to effect certain ends either in this world or in other worlds by means wholly or partially supernatural',[49] then the war put it to a test which many contemporaries thought it had failed.

It also failed a less obvious test. It could no longer claim to be, as even Victorian doubters like Matthew Arnold and George Eliot believed, the sole foundation of morality. The passionate unity and social cohesion of wartime, though never quite so complete as unthinking patriots believed, proved that law and order at least could rest on other foundations. If criminal statistics are any guide to general conduct, then the population was no worse behaved after than before the war. The proportion of offences per 100,000 was almost the same in 1921 (273) as in 1911 (269), and serious crimes declined by a third. Drunkenness in terms both of what could be commonly observed on Saturday nights and of drink-related arrests declined dramatically. Murders and other crimes of violence reached record lows, and Britain between the wars became a less violent society than ever before – or since.[50] Although, unlike church attendance, crime in general was to rise again, moderately in the 1930s, steeply in more recent times, the grim fate the Victorians feared for a post-Christian Britain did not materialize. Indeed, if true morality is caring for one's neighbour, the twentieth century was to become a more truly moral age than its predecessor.

In all these ways, in economic progress and decline, in social structure and living standards, in the onset of full democracy, in the status of women, in the size of the average family, in the social aims of education, in the decline of religion and the rise of a more caring morality, the First World War marked the great divide between the society created by the Industrial Revolution and the one which created the welfare state. Though it did not originate that transition, which was foreshadowed long before the war, it accelerated and dramatized the change, which was far from complete. To this extent it marks the boundary between Victorian class society at its zenith and the halfway house between the wars.

2 SOCIAL CHANGE BETWEEN THE WARS

Britain between the wars was a halfway house, not between a grossly unequal class society and some mythical egalitarian society of the future, but between one unequal society and a somewhat less unequal one in which the state intervened to redistribute income and, to a lesser extent, wealth and opportunities among its citizens. The reasons why this transition came about, the change from a purely class-based, market-oriented society to a more corporate one based on the status of citizenship, will be addressed in the next chapter. Here we shall be concerned with the changes themselves and their effects on the different levels of society emerging from the First World War. To catch the transition on the wing we shall have to look for comparison backward and forward, before the First World War and after the Second.

The three major pointers to the future, we saw at the opening of this chapter, were (1) the beginnings of a shift in the original distribution of income and wealth in the direction of more equality, or of less inequality; (2) the intervention by the state to bring about a further redistribution of income from the rich to the poor, and from the working class while in work to those without income either temporarily or permanently; and (3) the small beginnings of state-sponsored social mobility via education. All three began in embryo before the First World War, but they certainly had little opportunity of changing society in any visible way before 1914. Before the war any pre-tax shift in income and wealth was at best minimal. Significantly graduated taxation began only with the People's Budget in 1909, old age pensions for a small minority of the very elderly only the same year, national health insurance for most workers and unemployment insurance for a few were only implemented in 1913, and between 1907 and 1914 comparatively few working-class children benefited from the new grammar school scholarships. No one at the time thought of these exiguous beginnings as social engineering by the state, and it was only between the wars that they reached a scale to deserve that label.

In the history of inequality, according to the careful revision of historical national income estimates by Peter Lindert and Jeffrey Williamson, '1867 looks like a watershed. Sometime around this mid-Victorian benchmark an episodic shift took place. It now appears that income inequality declined for at least a century after 1867.' If so, the trend was barely perceptible before the First World War. In 1867, based on Dudley Baxter's figures quoted above (Chapter 2, Table 2.1), the top 10 per cent of income earners received about 50.6 per cent of the national income; by 1913 they still received 49.8 per cent – a decline, given the uncertainty of the sources, well within the margin of error.[51] The decline in inequality, most economic historians agree, became perceptible only between the wars. Lee Soltow concluded that long-run inequality continued down to the end of the nineteenth century: 'Only since the First World War has there been a decrease, and this decrease is substantial.'[52] This has been confirmed by the Diamond Commission on the Distribution of Income and Wealth of the 1970s, which found that the top 10 per cent of earners received 40.5 per cent of total personal income (before tax) in 1938 and 32.1 per cent in 1949 (see Table 6.1).

It will be noticed: (1) that the decline of the top 1 per cent of earners before tax was much steeper before and after the Second

Table 6.1   Distribution of personal income before and after tax, United Kingdom, 1938–39 and 1949–50

'Tax units'	1938–39		1949–50	
	Before tax	After tax	Before tax	After tax
Top 1%	17.1	11.7	10.6	5.8
Next 2–5%	14.4	13.6	12.5	10.9
6–10%	9.0	9.3	9.0	9.0
Top 10%	40.5	34.6	32.1	25.7
11–30%	20.7	22.3	23.6	24.8
Bottom 70%	38.7	43.1	44.2	49.4
	100.0	100.0	100.0	100.0

Source: Royal Commission on the Distribution of Income and Wealth (Chairman: Lord Diamond), *Report no. 1: Initial Report on the Standing Reference* (HMSO, Cmnd. 6171, 1975), Table 10, p. 36. 'Tax units' = married couples filing jointly and single earners, omitting those earners below the exemption limit, £135 per annum in 1938–39 and £250 in 1949–50

World War than for the top 10 per cent; (2) that the incomes of the next 20 per cent, roughly the prosperous middle class, remained much the same; and (3) that the bottom 70 per cent, the working class and some low-paid non-manuals, made only modest gains. This was of course before taxation and the social benefits mainly to the lower-paid, which will be dealt with below.

Wealth has always been more concentrated than income, for the obvious reason that unearned incomes from property have always gone to the few who drew them ultimately from the many, whether tenants, outworkers or employees, but even wealth has seen some redistribution since the First World War. Peter Lindert concludes from his long-term survey:

As far as the data can reveal, wealth inequality remained steady from 1740 until 1911–13, subject to what are now wide confidence bounds. The pronounced levelling of wealth inequality within this century has left us with a distribution in the 1970s and 1980s that is clearly less unequal than any now documented for the past.[53]

Even before that, according to the Diamond Commission, the share of total personal wealth held by the top 1 per cent of adults (aged 25 years and over) declined from 69 per cent in 1911–1913 to 62 per cent in 1924–30, 56 per cent in 1936–38, and to 43 per cent in 1954. At the same time the share of the top 10 per cent declined somewhat less, from 92 per cent in 1911–13 to 91 per cent in 1924–30, 88 per cent in 1936, and to 79 per cent in 1954.[54] These figures, however, are based on probate returns, and exclude small estates below the exemption limit, the real value of most people's cars, furniture and consumer durables and, more importantly, the capital value of pension rights, including the state pension rights which, since 1925, have accrued to wage-earners and their widows and, since 1948, to most adults. When these are allowed for, the share of the top 10 per cent in 1972 was reduced according to the Diamond Commission from 69 to 45.7 per cent and the share of the bottom 80 per cent increased from 15.6 to 40.7 per cent.[55]

The statistical trend towards the more equal distribution of income and wealth *before tax* has been challenged by left-wing critics, who believe that modern capitalism inevitably widens the gap between rich and poor, and that the rich understate their income and possessions so as to avoid taxation and rearrange their resources between their relatives: 'the redistribution of wealth over this century has not been between the rich and the poor, but between successive generations of the same family.'[56] The figures have also been challenged by right-wing critics, who believe that they present 'a deformed picture of British society ... which makes it easier for politicians and commentators to invoke the feelings of envy present in most societies at most times', and complain that 'the statistics on which popular discussion rest are too weak for the purpose to which they are put'.[57] Such critics tend to think that the trend towards equality has gone too far, and that Britain's relative economic decline is due to the discouragement of enterprise and capital accumulation by punitive income taxes and death duties or capital transfer tax.

Be that as it may, there can be little doubt that the period since the First World War has seen a remarkable change in the patterns of income and wealth. As a judicious summary of these complex changes by W. D. Rubinstein concludes:

> Broad trends in wealth and income distribution, and gains in living standards and property ownership, seem to indicate growing and, in some respects, unprecedented degrees of equality (with bastions of privilege remaining), while those who perceived the existence of a class-based economic elite see little or no evidence of its passing.[58]

Leaving aside the changing nature of that economic elite, which it is one purpose of this book not to deny but to explore, the unprecedented decline in inequality which began in the inter-war period was but the first step on the way to a further turn of the egalitarian screw by the intervention of the state.

To some extent the change in the original, pre-tax distribution of income and wealth was due to the introduction of graduated death duties in 1894 at 8 per cent on estates of £1 million-plus and to their successive raising to 15 per cent in 1909 and to 40 per cent between the wars. Despite the common belief, in the words of *Burke's Landed Gentry*, that 'death duties are a voluntary tax', the probate returns show that the rich still volunteer to pay them, partly because of the increasing taxation of gifts *inter vivos* but mostly because of the 'King Lear syndrome', the fear of losing control and even independence along with their wealth if they pass it on to relatives. Those who doubt their efficacy have only to ask what would have been the distribution of income and wealth in the absence of death duties. They are, however, only a prologue, as it were, to the second pointer to the future, the direct action of the state in bringing about a far larger change in the distribution of income and wealth since the First World War.

State intervention took two forms, graduated taxation and the payment of social benefits to those in need. The effect of graduated income tax, scarcely known before 1909 except in the form of the lower exemption limit and abatements for smaller incomes, can be seen from Table 6.1. In 1938 the share of personal income received by the top 1 per cent of income receivers was reduced by nearly one-third, from 17.1 per cent before tax to 11.7 per cent after tax; the share of the top 10 per cent by nearly one-sixth, from 40.5 to 34.6 per cent. By 1949 the reduction was still steeper, for the top 1 per cent of income receivers by nearly half, from 10.6 to 5.8 per cent and for the top 10 per cent by one-fifth, from 32.1 to 25.7 per cent. While the share of those in the middle (including, surprisingly, the moderately rich between 5 and 10 per cent of income earners as well as the next 20 per cent) changed little, the share of the bottom 70 per cent was increased by 1938 by nearly half, from 38.7 to 56.8 per cent, and in 1949 by much less, about one-ninth, from 44.2 to 49.4 per cent.

The aggregate figures, however, give little notion of what they meant in terms of individual incomes. A rich man earning £10,000 a year paid 8 per cent in tax in 1914, 42.5 per cent in 1919, 37.1 per cent in 1924 and 39.1 per cent in 1938. There were nearly 5,000 such incomes in 1914 and 9,200 in 1925; but while after tax there were 4,000 in 1914 there were still only 4,120 in 1925. Moreover, as Sir Arthur Bowley pointed out at the time, because of inflation the equivalent of £10,000 in 1914 was £18,000 by 1925, and to receive the same purchasing power after tax required a gross income of £30,000. The number of rich people with the spending power represented by £10,000 a year in 1914 had therefore declined from 4,000 to 1,300. Bowley commented:

> The general result of the whole system of taxation, wage adjustments, and social expenditure has been a very marked redistribution of the National Income ... The very rich have less than half their pre-war income (allowing for taxes and changes of prices); the least well off of the working class have gained most.[59]

Redistribution by taxation was only the first part of this unprecedented social engineering. The second was the rise of transfer payments to the poor by means of social benefits. There had of course been statutory poor relief since Tudor times, and the Liberal government of 1906–14 had begun old age pensions and national insurance before the war. But the poor law had been deliberately deterrent to minimize the cost, old age pensions were confined to people over 70 with incomes under £26 a year, and health insurance benefits for most of the working class and unemployment insurance for a small minority were paid only from January 1913. Only from 1923 was unemployment insurance extended to most workers and their dependents, and contributory old age, widows and orphans' pensions to most wage earners and their families from 1925. These social benefits and others in kind, including medical treatment for the insured (though not for their families), maternity and child welfare clinics, tuberculosis sanatoria, school medical treatment, state secondary education for some, housing subsidies, and the like, totalling only £89 million in 1910 (4.2 per cent of GNP), amounted to £412 million in 1920 (6.8 per cent of GNP), £596 million in 1938 (11.3 per cent of GNP), and £2,094 million (18 per cent of GNP) by 1950.[60]

They were not all paid for out of ordinary taxation, and the insurance benefits in particular represented in large part a horizontal transfer from the wage earners while in work to the same people when they were sick, unemployed or too old to work. Nonetheless, these were valuable rights which could be viewed as the equivalent of property. John Hilton, a shrewd egalitarian observer, estimated in 1938 that the old age pension capitalized as an annuity at age 65 was worth between £250 and £350, up to twice a year's wage for the average worker; unemployment insurance was worth a capital sum of over £500, and education, school milk, medical and dental treatment between £100 and £500 depending on the number of children.[61] In sum, according to one estimate, whereas in 1913-14 the working classes contributed 20 per cent more in taxes than they received in social benefits, by 1925-26 they received 15 per cent more than they contributed (a gain of £45 million); by 1935-36 they received 21 per cent (a gain of £91 million). Altogether, it was calculated that in 1937-38 there was a transfer of £386 million from the rich to the poor (8.8 per cent of the National Income) and in 1948-49 a transfer of £1,260 million (13.1 per cent).[62] Thus the state had operated to bring about what T. H. Marshall was to call 'the compression, at both ends, of the scale of income distribution'.[63]

The third and final pointer to the future was even less intentional than the other two, the incipient role of the state in sponsoring social mobility. This had been mooted from the turn of the century by such would-be social engineers as Sidney Webb and Sir Robert Morant, more in terms of 'national efficiency' and saving the waste of talent in the lower reaches of society than of creating a meritocracy. Between the wars the creation of an educational ladder, narrow enough in all conscience, from the elementary school through the grammar school to college and university was a measure of social justice rather than a deliberate piece of social engineering. Nevertheless, while graduated taxation and social benefits merely levelled up and levelled down the extremes of income inequality, educational mobility was the only means by which the state could directly modify the social structure, as distinct from encouraging spontaneous mobility via the market for people. As a result, while Britain still had one of the smallest percentages of university entrants in the developed world, it came to have the largest percentage of working-class students within its university population.[64]

Not that education became the only or indeed the chief means of social mobility. Far from it: privileged education did not prevent many members of the upper middle class sliding down into the lower middle or even into the working class; and the old, well-worn paths of upward mobility taken by self-made men of energy and enterprise continued in use and sometimes went further and higher than the educational route. From Lord Nuffield of Morris Motors to Lord Stokes of British Leyland there were spectacular examples of self-made men who would have been positively handicapped by higher education. Indeed, university education could be described as a process by which potential tycoons are turned into civil servants and academics. Be that as it may, the inter-war period saw the beginnings of an institutionalized machinery of state-sponsored social mobility via the educational system which reversed the Victorian belief in education as the buttress of class society. Or rather, education came to reinforce the social structure in a different way, by upgrading men (rarely women before the Second World War) of talent and training into the professional and managerial classes.

Here we must make a sharp distinction between intentions and consequences. The expansion of secondary and higher education since the First World War has certainly increased the absolute numbers of children from the working classes going to secondary school and university, but it has relatively benefited the middle classes even more, so that the percentage of university students coming from the working class has hardly changed since the 1920s. This is because the middle classes, and especially the professional and managerial classes, have a livelier appreciation of the value of education and of the opportunities for obtaining it than the working class, and in any movement towards a more meritocratic society will be more assiduous in acquiring the necessary merit.

All this is borne out by the two major social mobility studies in England and Wales in this century, the London School of Economics survey led by David Glass in 1949–53 and the Oxford Social Mobility Project directed by A. H. Halsey and John Goldthorpe in the early 1970s.[65] The Oxford survey was more detailed and sophisticated but, since only part of their earliest cohort, born between 1913 and 1922, came of age between the wars, has little bearing on inter-war society, and will become more relevant in Chapter 9 on post-1945 society. The LSE study 'yields a picture of the achievement up to the outbreak of World War I . . . of the English system of public education.' It showed that, while the proportions of working-class children (from their social categories 5, 6 and 7) achieving a secondary education over the period 1900–40 nearly trebled, a middle-class boy (from categories 1, 2 and 3) still had more than four times the chance of one from the skilled working class (category 5) of getting a grammar school education, and more than five times the chance of one from the semi- or unskilled working class (categories 6 and 7). There was even more disparity for girls, with a middle-class girl having three and seven times the chance respectively of a skilled and lower working-class girl.[66]

As might be expected, the chances of going on to university were even more unequal. Boys from the professional and managerial classes (categories 1 and 2), whether born before 1910 or in 1910–29, had thirteen times as great a chance of going to university as a working-class boy (categories 5–7), and a middle-class girl no less than sixty times the chance of a working-class girl. Yet all this must be seen in the perspective of a society in transition from one in which education was the consequence of status rather than its cause to one in which it was becoming a significant factor in placing recruits in positions of influence and authority. The proportions attaining a secondary education, though still a minority in all classes, increased by about 40 per cent in the middle class and more than doubled in the working class. The numbers of middle-class boys going to university nearly doubled, from 4.4 to 8.5 per cent, between those born before and those born after 1910, and the same at a lower level of participation for girls, from 2.1 to 4 per cent. The proportion of working-class boys going to university grew from 0.9 to 1.4 per cent, of girls from 0.1 to 0.2 per cent.[67]

What is striking about these figures is not merely the disparities between the classes but the tiny proportions even of middle-class men who even at the end of the expansion achieved secondary education (less than two in five) and a university degree (one in twelve). The surveyors could nevertheless conclude that the traditional routes of upward mobility, via training on the job or the working up of a small concern into a large one, were now overshadowed by the acquisition of formal educational and professional qualifications. In other words, the scholarship boy had overtaken the self-made man.[68]

Since this was a halfway house between a wholly class-based and a partially meritocratic society, there was still a strong tendency for sons to follow fathers in the same occupation. One study within the LSE survey of Cambridge graduates in teaching, medicine, the church and the law showed that over the previous half-century the proportion following their fathers into these four professions had fallen only from 45 per cent to 36 per cent, while even in democratic Scotland about one in seven sons in the same four professions had followed in the footsteps of their fathers.[69] This was not very different from the social classes generally, where a large minority but rarely a majority of each category except, surprisingly, for skilled workers, followed their fathers in the same class. Even in the top professional and managerial middle classes (categories 1 and 2), most of those born after 1890 came from families below that level, though very few from the working class. There was surprisingly little change over time, however, which suggests that education was not so much expanding opportunities for upward mobility as replacing old, less formal ones.[70] The self-made entrepreneur was being replaced by the professional and the salaried manager.

Amongst the elite groups at the heads of the various key institutions in society there were only small signs of this trend before the Second World War, for the very good reason that it takes a generation or more to rise to such positions. An exception was the Civil Service, where entry by competitive examination began in 1871, and there was a steep decline in the number of heads of department coming from upper-class families and educational backgrounds. The proportion with fathers in the top class of the elites survey (large landowners, big business men and higher professional men) declined from 72 per cent in 1880–99 to 45 per cent in 1920–39; and the proportion educated at the eleven major public schools declined similarly from 71 per cent to 41 per cent – those from Eton alone from 44 per cent to 10 per cent. Only the number educated at Oxford and Cambridge increased, since the new men coming up from below were mainly lower middle-class scholarship boys at those two universities. On the surface there seemed to be little change at the top of other professions, senior judges, vice-chancellors of universities, and the presidents of the leading professional institutes, but if we turn to family wealth, especially in real terms (at 1913 prices), we shall find (in Section 4) the beginnings of a decline in the median wealth of their fathers as measured by their probate returns. Even the chairmen of the 200 largest companies, a wealthy and conservative group, came from families whose median income in real terms had been halved since the late Victorian age – a measure of the extent to which they were being infiltrated by the career manager without inherited wealth.[71]

These were early days in the transition towards a different sort of elite structure, and the great landowners, Conservative Cabinet ministers, and (partly because of inflation) the increasing number of millionaires still held on to their wealth and came, on the whole, from the highest echelons of society. But even they felt that the old order was threatened by the egalitarian forces at work in inter-war society, as we shall see next. In the next four sections we shall consider how these changes in the inter-war period, in the original distribution of income and wealth, in the role of the state in the redistribution of income through taxation and transfer payments, and in state-sponsored and other forms of social mobility, affected the rich and powerful, the elites whose position did not depend on wealth, the middle classes, and the working class.

3   THE OLD ORDER CHANGETH

'The old order is doomed,' wrote the Duke of Marlborough in 1919 when death duties were raised to 40 per cent, a rate he claimed was deliberately aimed at preventing the inheritance of great houses. 'These fortresses of territorial influence it is proposed to raze in the name of social equality,' *The Times* lamented; 'England is changing hands' and 'the stately homes of England' were being turned into schools and other institutions. The *Estates Gazette* estimated in 1921 that a quarter of England had been put on the market. The patrician Liberal Charles Masterman claimed in 1922, 'There is taking place the greatest change in the history of the land of England since the days of the Norman Conquest; with the possible exception of the gigantic robberies of the Reformation.' F. M. L. Thompson, noting the sale of 6 to 8 million acres between 1918 and 1921, much of it to sitting tenants, and the consequent increase in owner-occupiers from about 11 per cent of all farmers in 1914 to 36 per cent in 1927, has called it 'a startling revolution in the countryside, nothing less than the dissolution of a large part of the great estate system and the formation of a new race of yeomen.'[72]

By no means all the sales were to the tenants and other small owners. There were still big business men willing to buy status and prestige, like the soap manufacturer Joseph Watson who bought Lord Willoughby de Broke's Compton Verney in 1921 and was created Lord Manton, the brewer Newall-Cain who bought Lord Melbourne's Brockett Hall (from an intervening owner) and became Lord Brockett in 1933, or the self-made financier and shipowner Sir John Ellerman, already a great landowner with over 100,000 acres, who bought Great Portland Street from Lord Howard de Walden in 1925.[73] But the old aristocratic round of the London season and the country house party was no longer what it was. The Duke of Portland complained in 1937 that:

> large estates ... have been and are still being broken up, and the houses attached to them sold to individuals, most of whom have little or no connexion with the land ... When I first lived at Wellbeck the great neighbouring houses, such as Clumber, Thoresby, and Rufford, were all inhabited by their owners. ... Now not one ... is so occupied, except for a few days in the year.

In the old days, he went on, the great town houses 'were thrown open every season for large social gatherings', including Hertford, Grosvenor, Dorchester, Lansdowne, Devonshire, Spencer, Chesterfield, Stafford, and Montague Houses. 'At present, only Londonderry, Apsley, Bridgewater and Holland Houses remain as private residences.'[74]

The country gentry, entirely dependent on agricultural rents which in the 1930s reached their lowest point since 1870, suffered most. Thompson estimated that only a third of the gentry families of Essex, Oxfordshire and Shropshire of the 1870s remained in residence by 1952.[75] Many of their houses simply disappeared, or were let or sold to farmers, wealthy commuters, or institutions. In face of the competition of cheap food from overseas, agriculture declined between the wars, arable land tumbled down to grass, fields became derelict, weeds multiplied, ditches were choked, gates and fences fell into disrepair, roads left unmade, buildings decayed, and the landscape assumed a neglected and unkempt appearance.[76] Even sitting tenants stopped buying, and the number of owner-occupiers stagnated until after the Second World War.

The great urban landowners too were selling off parts of their holdings. In 1919 the Duke of Bedford, Lords Portman, Camden, Cadogan and Northampton sold off parcels of their London estates, Berkeley Square and estate were sold in 1922 for £2 million, Devonshire House the same year, and even part of the Duke of Westminster's Belgravia in the late 1920s. At the seaside, the Haldons had already liquidated their Torquay holdings by 1914, Lord Radnor began to dispose of his land at Folkestone in 1920, at Bournemouth Sir George Tapps-Gervis-Meyrick got rid of his ground rents in 1921 and the Earl of Malmesbury of his in 1923, and the Scarisbricks and Heskeths of theirs in Southport in 1926. In the industrial areas, that 'leviathan of wealth' the Duke of Sutherland gave Trentham Park to the City of Stoke-on-Trent in 1912, the Ramsdens sold their entire Huddersfield estate to the Corporation for £1.3 million in 1920, Lord Derby began selling his Liverpool ground rents, Lord Calthorpe sold the outlying parts of his Birmingham estates, the Dudleys their Black Country properties, Lord Fitzwilliam his Eccleshall estate in Sheffield, the Marquess of Bute his Cardiff building property and docks, and Lord Shaftesbury abandoned his Belfast connections and gave the castle to the city. David Cannadine concluded, 'in the towns as in the countryside, the period from the 1870s until the outbreak of the Second World War saw the aristocracy under attack and in retreat.'[77]

The old order was not yet doomed, however, it was simply changing and 'yielding place to new'. Like Mark Twain's, the reports of the great landowners' demise were exaggerated. Despite the much resented death duties (which were levied at only half-rates on agricultural land), the great landowners still held on to most of their wealth, as measured by their probate returns. Their median estate (with land) at death actually rose from £287,500 in 1880–99 to £633,000 in 1920–39, and retained most of its value in real terms (from £282,300 to £274,700 at 1913 prices) (see Table 6.2.6 on page 263) while over a quarter of them, more than in the late Victorian age, died millionaires. Many were still amongst the wealthiest men in Britain. Of the 177 millionaires dying in the 1920s and 1930s, twenty-four of them were principally landowners, to whom another five should be added for settled land excluded from probate before 1925. Four out of eight decedants leaving over £3 million in the 1940s (including the Dowager Countess Peel, heiress of Lord Ashton, whose wealth was partly in linoleum manufacture) were landowners. The richest of the ten, the eleventh Duke of Bedford, left £4.7 million in 1940, yet his son the twelfth Duke, after paying duty at 75 per cent, could still leave £5.8 million thirteen years later.[78]

The new order was, of course, that amalgamation of old and new wealth in a new plutocracy which was already emerging in the generation before the First World War. Now, however, the assimilation process was reversed. The great landlords were becoming great corporate business men rather than the business men landed aristocrats. The successful landowners who continued to increase their wealth and vie with the great business tycoons were those like the Dukes of Bedford and Westminster and Lords Derby and Cadogan who formed companies or trusts to manage their estates, treated land as only one form of investment amongst many, sold unprofitable parcels and bought higher yielding stocks and shares with the proceeds, accepted directorships in other companies, especially banks and insurance companies rather than industrial corporations, and generally behaved like financial tycoons rather than landed grandees.

Even their lifestyle changed, though not as much as they complained. Many used their non-landed income to keep up the traditional style – the Calthorpes re-equipped Elvetham, the Berkeleys restored their Gloucestershire castle, Waldorf and Nancy Astor still kept open house at Cliveden, and the Devonshires continued their itinerant life between their five or six houses – and despite the rising costs of servants, the lack of suitable neighbours, and the preference for a more private, comfortable existence made possible by modern amenities and consumer goods, some were able to keep up their old extravagant way of life down to the Second World War. As Gathorne-Hardy put it in relation to domestic service and the decline of the British nanny, 'It is 1939 that is the significant divide, not 1914.' Nevertheless, the old way of life had lost its savour for many, and led them to live near to other plutocrats in London's West End, with a *pied à terre* in the country in part of their old mansions. The old landlords did not die, and indeed were to enjoy a great revival in their fortunes after the Second World War, but the glamorous way of life they once dominated began to fade into the preferred anonymity of the twentieth-century plutocracy.

This self-effacement was reflected in politics. It has been argued that a quarter of the Conservative Cabinet ministers between 1916 and 1955 were 'aristocrats', but this was by the peculiar definition of anyone with a titled grandparent.[79] It is clear that most of the leading aristocratic politicians of the inter-war period, such as Churchill, Sir Anthony Eden, or Lord Halifax, were either scions of noble houses removed from the main line or minor landlords not in the league of the great magnates. In the 1935 Cabinet only the Marquess of Londonderry, in the honorific office of Lord Privy Seal, was a great landowner of the Duke of Omnium type which had dominated Victorian politics. The leading members were business men or rentiers like Stanley Baldwin and Neville Chamberlain, Sir John Simon, barrister son of a small farmer and builder, Sir Samuel Hoare of the Norfolk landed banking family, Sir Godfrey Collins, the Scottish publisher, Sir Kingsley Wood, solicitor son of a Wesleyan minister, Walter Runciman, Methodist shipowner and insurer, and, curiously, three sons of the working class, Ramsay MacDonald, illegitimate child of a ploughman and a servant girl, his son Malcolm MacDonald (working-class at one remove), and J. H. Thomas, the railway unionist always cartooned in his dress suit. Apart from Londonderry, Halifax and Eden, the leading landed members were Sir Philip Cunliffe-Lister, who had married into the woolcombing inventor's family and its coal mines, W. Ormsby-Gore, plutocratic son of Lord Harlech and chairman of the Midland Bank, and two offshoots of great houses, Oliver Stanley, younger son of the Earl of Derby, and Lord Eustace Percy, younger son of the Duke of Northumberland. Their presence attested that members of the old aristocracy still had advantages in politics if they wanted them; the question was, did they still want them? To the extent that they did, the halfway house of inter-war politics still had its foundations in the old, pre-war order.

Nor yet were the great landed politicians replaced by plutocrats. The business tycoons and millionaires took even less part in politics, unless behind the scenes, than they did before the war. The notorious Victorian bosses of the industrial towns, like Lord Ashton, the 'linoleum king' of Lancaster, the Hornby family of Blackburn, the Woods and Sidebottoms of Glossop, and the Peases of Middlesbrough, now sold out to great combines or left their firms to be run by professional managers, leaving local government to small business men, shopkeepers and trade unionists. Only the odd really big business man, like Lord Weir, the Glasgow engineer brought in as 'munitions Czar' in the First World War, pioneer of the electric power National Grid and 'architect of air power' for the Second World War, Sir Alfred Mond, Lord Melchett, first head of the chemical giant ICI and protagonist of the Mond-Turner talks between big business and the TUC, or the newspaper tycoons Northcliffe and Beaverbrook with their own political axes to grind, played a continuous if often backstage role at the national level. By far the largest group of Conservative ministers between 1916 and 1955 were the forty-three professionals (including ex-civil servants and public administrators), followed by nineteen landowners, sixteen rentiers, and sixteen business men (out of 100). On the Labour side the twenty-five professionals were second only to the twenty-eight union officials (out of sixty-five ministers), who were in effect a special kind of professional. Amongst Tory MPs professionals were in a clear majority (52 per cent) in the inter-war Parliaments and the largest group (24 per cent) of Labour MPs apart from the manual workers (72 per cent), most of whom were trade union officials.[80] Politics was already more than halfway towards becoming a professional occupation, in both senses.

What is more difficult to discover is the extent to which business itself was becoming professionalized. The rise of the giant corporation, as we shall see in the next chapter, was a special feature of the 1920s, and as the vehicle for the mergers and amalgamations of scores of family businesses it automatically replaced the owner-managing entrepreneur by the professional manager who controlled far more capital than he owned. Even when the family business owner became the new corporate manager, he had to learn a new and unfamiliar behaviour pattern, less autocratic and paternalistic, more bureaucratic and consultative, which many found intolerable, or intolerant of themselves. In this way Lord Leverhulme was not succeeded in the chair of Unilever as he wished at his death by his son but by Francis D'Arcy Cooper, a professional accountant. Lord Nuffield was eased out of day-to-day management of Morris Motors to concentrate on his philanthropic works and go on his endless world cruises. At ICI

Lord Melchett was succeeded at his death in 1930 by Sir Harry McGowan, the career manager who had put together the chemical giant.[81] Indeed, only fifty-two out of over 500 chairmen of the largest companies in the period 1905–39 were wealth holders of the traditional kind (leaving over £500,000 at death).[82] Since the capitals of these companies ran into millions of pounds (the fiftieth in 1930 had a market volume of £6.3 million), 90 per cent of the chairmen were in effect professional controllers of other people's capital. This fact may not have come home to many family business men absorbed by big corporations who continued to behave like old-fashioned entrepreneurs but they were, perhaps even more than the career managers who were beginning to replace them, vehicles of the transition to managerial capitalism.

Recent research on the very wealthy in Britain has emphasized their concentration in the non-manufacturing sectors of the economy, commerce and finance, and especially in the City of London.[83] Much of this has been misconceived. It assumes, firstly, that large individual fortunes are somehow more important to the economy than the relative weight of the various sectors in the generation of aggregate income and employment. Agriculture, mining and manufacturing have always employed more workers and produced more wealth than commerce and finance, and still do, despite the rise of a 'service economy'.[84] Secondly, it confounds commerce and finance, and assumes that the manipulation of money by the City is closer to the distribution of goods by merchants and retailers than the latter is to production. The Morrisons, Sainsburys, and Marks and Spencers are bracketed with the Rothschilds, Samuels and Slaters rather than the Lords Leverhulme, Bearsted and Nuffield who were also commercial distributors of the soap, petrol and cars they manufactured. Finally, it manipulates the figures even in its own terms by refusing to count as manufacturing the food, drink and tobacco industries, which produced more millionaires than any other 'standard industrial category', because 'these trades are not normally thought of as part of the Industrial Revolution.'[85] The inclusion of food, drink and tobacco gives manufacturing in the late Victorian age (1880–99) 62 per cent of the probated millionaires as against 38 per cent for commerce and finance, 46 per cent as against 58 per cent in 1900–19, and 55 per cent as against 40 per cent in 1920–39. If commerce is excluded, finance (banking, insurance, stockbroking, and 'other finance') accounts for only 21, 31 and 17 per cent of millionaires dying in the three successive periods.[86] So much for the supposed domination of wealth by the City of London. The whole argument, however, becomes irrelevant when set against the accelerated rise of corporate capitalism between the wars, when the managers of giant corporations, with interlocking boards of directors and shareholdings, did not ask each other what category they belonged to. They increasingly invested in diversified enterprises, producing either goods or services, as long as they were profitable. This curious attempt to divide the new plutocracy, at last amalgamating into a single economic elite, thus falls to the ground. What remains of it is the increasing centralization of the British economy, both commerce and manufacturing, in managerial corporations based in London.

Yet society between the wars was no longer run by the same kind of ruling class that dominated Victorian England. Despite the merging of great landed and business wealth into a new plutocracy, there was also a greater fragmentation of the competing elites into separate hierarchies which, unlike the old days of patronage and absorption of new men into London society, were no longer part of a unified ruling elite. To understand this we must turn to the changes which were taking place in recruitment to the other elites.

4 'MONEY ISN'T EVERYTHING'

For the other elites, developing independently, money was not the sole source of their prestige and power. They were not as rich or economically powerful as the great landowners and business tycoons, but they were increasingly important within their own spheres as decision makers and opinion leaders: politicians, high civil servants, judges, vice-chancellors of universities, national newspaper editors, leading accountants, architects, physicians and surgeons, engineers, and even trade union leaders, who were becoming what Robert Taylor has called 'the fifth estate'. Except for the last, much has been made of their supposed recruitment from a narrow segment of society, largely from middle-class families via a small number of public schools and, to a lesser extent, the unversities of Oxford and Cambridge. This widely accepted notion stems from a number of sociological studies based on easily accessible sources of information on elite figures' education and, occasionally, fathers' occupation. It is founded on the fallacy that education at a public school and/or a father in the Registrar-General's social classes 1 and 2 (higher professional and managerial occupations) are sufficient guarantee of a wealthy and privileged origin.

In fact, there is a far greater range of income, wealth and status within those schools and classes than between them and the state schools and the classes below. Classes 1 and 2 may include great landowners, millionaire business men and rich judges but they also embrace farmers, shopkeepers, poor clergymen and mere professors. The so-called public schools have always catered for the same wide range of families, from aristocrats and big business men to the poorer clergy and the lesser professions. Even the great Clarendon schools, except perhaps for Eton, never had a majority of boys from the gentry and aristocracy. At Winchester from 1820 to 1922 a quarter of the pupils came from the landed elite, only 11 per cent were from business families and the rest were sons of the clergy and the other professions, many of whom made sacrifices to send them to public school.[87] No more than 15 per cent of Harrovians entering the school in 1840, 1870 and 1895–1900 had elite fathers. Even at Eton there was an immense range of family income, from princely to genteel poverty, from the £200,000-plus per annum of the Marquess of Hartington's father, the Duke of Devonshire, to the £438 10s. pension of the retired Indian civil servant father of Eric Blair, better known as George Orwell, who recalled the Etonian son of a Russian *émigré* boasting that his father had 200 times as much income as Blair senior.[88]

It was to test this dubious notion of the narrowness and uniformity of elite recruitment that the Social Science Research Council in the 1970s funded the only study to date which considered the family wealth as well as the education and fathers' occupations of elites in British society since 1880. The study examined the probate returns of both the fathers and, where deceased, of the elite figures themselves. It also extracted the father's occupation, where necessary, from the elite person's birth certificate, a more reliable source than the published directories. The full results of the survey have been deposited with the British Library Lending Division and are available to researchers, and the material has been used in various publications by myself and more especially by my then research associate, Dr W. D. Rubinstein, whose labours produced the information in 3,227 incumbents of 4,484 elite positions between 1880 and 1970 on which the more than 500 tables were based.[89]

At the halfway stage in this history of English society since 1880, looking before and after, this information on the recruitment of elites becomes particularly relevant, and a summary of the main results is given here in Tables 6.2.1–6.2.6.

The tables show that, apart from the trade union leaders and the Labour Cabinet ministers, the university vice-chancellors and national newspaper editors, the elites were recruited to a large extent from the upper and middle classes, that is, from families constituting 3.3 per cent and 18.8 per cent of the occupied population as defined by the Registrar-General's classes 1 and 2 in the census of 1951. They were also educated predominantly at public schools and to a disproportionate extent at the eleven major public schools (Eton, Harrow, Winchester, Westminster, Rugby, St Paul's, Charterhouse, Merchant Taylors', Shrewsbury, Marl-

Table 6.2   Elites in British society, 1880–1970, by cohort

Table 6.2.1   Children of the upper class (about 3 per cent of the occupied population) (%)

	1880–99	1900–19	1920–39	1940–59	1960–70
Conservative Cabinet	88.5	73.1	76.3	71.0	63.4
Liberal Cabinet	62.4	60.5	33.4	–	–
Labour Cabinet	–	–	28.0	28.4	28.6
Newly created peers	85.0	71.3	61.8	62.4	51.1
Top civil servants	70.2	48.0	44.7	36.8	39.2
Large landowners	98.1	98.0	99.0	98.3	98.8
Big company chairmen	75.0	77.5	73.2	69.3	68.5
Presidents of professions	32.3	38.6	45.0	45.3	45.2
Trade unions leaders	–	–	–	–	–
Senior judges	50.0	54.2	46.0	61.4	75.0
Oxbridge vice-chancellors	38.8	29.4	22.2	36.8	18.1
Other vice-chancellors	54.6	51.7	31.3	20.6	22.6
Heads of nationalized industries	–	–	–	32.6	44.9
Newspaper editors	32.4	28.6	33.3	34.4	39.3
Millionaires	70.6	75.4	70.1	79.1	67.6

Table 6.2.2   Children of the working class (including non-manual) (over 70 per cent of occupied population) (%)

	1880–99	1900–19	1920–39	1940–59	1960–70
Conservative Cabinet	–	1.9	–	1.3	–
Liberal Cabinet	–	2.3	6.7		
Labour Cabinet		100.0	24.0	35.3	31.4
Newly created peers	0.8	2.1	6.5	14.7	17.2
Top civil servants	1.8	4.0	10.7	11.2	19.0
Large landowners	–	–	–	–	–
Big company chairmen	6.3	7.3	6.1	6.9	9.9
Presidents of professions	2.1	1.3	8.3	10.3	12.3
Trade union leaders	100.0	94.7	76.0	83.8	74.9
Senior judges	4.8	6.3	6.0	–	4.2
Oxbridge vice-chancellors	16.6	–	16.7	5.3	18.2
Other vice-chancellors	–	6.9	6.3	15.4	32.1
Heads of nationalized industries				25.5	16.3
Newspaper editors	8.8	16.3	18.8	18.8	19.6
Millionaires	2.9	2.6	7.0	5.8	16.2

Table 6.2.3   Educated at (eleven) major public schools (about 2.5 per cent of 14-year-old boys in 1967) (%)

	1880–99	1900–19	1920–39	1940–59	1960–70
Conservative Cabinet	77.5	67.4	64.4	51.5	57.5
Liberal Cabinet	44.4	34.9	13.4		
Labour Cabinet			10.8	22.8	24.0
Newly created peers	69.3	42.9	43.1	36.9	27.1
Top civil servants	71.1	47.2	40.6	31.1	25.3
Large landowners	94.5	91.4	95.3	90.1	89.2
Big company chairmen	45.5	42.6	42.1	38.0	45.3
Presidents of professions	26.5	22.5	30.6	26.0	27.7
Trade union leaders	–	–	–	–	–
Senior judges	38.2	26.7	34.0	39.3	48.0
Oxbridge vice-chancellors	35.3	22.2	16.8	28.0	15.4
Other vice-chancellors	20.0	25.0	21.0	5.4	14.0
Heads of nationalized industries				23.7	21.7
Newspaper editors	50.0	34.1	28.6	32.1	30.7
Millionaires	43.5	43.3	48.8	50.7	48.9

Table 6.2.4 Educated at state schools (92.8 per cent of 14-year-old boys in 1967) (%)

	1880–99	1900–19	1920–39	1940–59	1960–70
Conservative Cabinet	3.2	6.1	7.1	11.5	15.0
Liberal Cabinet	7.4	14.0	33.3		
Labour Cabinet			57.1	57.1	63.0
Newly created peers	9.1	10.1	12.8	25.9	36.9
Top civil servants	–	12.9	15.8	14.7	25.2
Large landowners	–	–	–	–	–
Big company chairmen	9.1	11.1	9.1	14.8	14.7
Presidents of professions	17.6	16.3	14.3	15.6	20.0
Trade union leaders	100.0	100.0	96.3	100.0	100.0
Senior judges	20.6	15.5	10.0	8.9	10.4
Oxbridge vice-chancellors	17.6	22.2	27.7	16.7	15.4
Other vice-chancellors	10.0	8.3	23.7	40.5	48.0
Heads of nationalized industries				39.5	30.3
Newspaper editors	23.4	20.4	26.9	23.2	25.0
Millionaires	34.4	15.8	12.8	10.4	19.6

Table 6.2.5 Fathers' median estate at 1913 prices (including land where appropriate) in thousands of pounds

	1880–99	1900–19	1920–39	1940–59	1960–70
Conservative cabinet	80.4	52.4	58.6	31.4	7.3
Liberal Cabinet	18.9	25.5	7.3		
Labour Cabinet			3.6	0.8	0.3
Newly created peers	39.3	30.0	18.2	6.3	2.3
Top civil servants	14.8	11.7	3.9	1.7	1.3
Large landowners	102.4	129.6	189.1	206.8	94.4
Big company chairmen	108.1	72.8	49.5	30.9	8.8
Presidents of professions	5.3	9.2	7.7	5.2	2.2
Trade union leaders	–	–	0.1	–	–
Senior judges	17.4	12.4	7.8	12.9	7.6
Oxbridge vice-chancellors	5.3	10.3	2.3	6.4	0.7
Other vice-chancellors	0.4	8.7	2.6	1.3	0.9
Heads of nationalized industries				1.1	1.4
Newspaper editors	9.8	4.9	4.9	1.4	1.7
Millionaires	59.4	109.4	201.6	232.8	93.7

Table 6.2.6 Median own estate at 1913 prices (including land where appropriate) in thousand of pounds

	1880–99	*1900–19*	*1920–39*	*1940–59*	*1960–70*
Conservative Cabinet	136.8	59.5	44.0	18.7	*
Liberal Cabinet	108.1	53.7	6.2		
Labour Cabinet			5.3	4.4	*
Newly created peers	119.1	69.4	56.0	10.4	6.1
Top civil servants	19.7	8.4	5.2	4.1	*
Large landowners	282.3	311.3	274.7	102.7	22.2
Big company chairmen	572.3	118.3	79.8	36.1	14.8
Presidents of professions	41.2	22.3	15.2	8.3	4.8
Trade union leaders	–	1.1	0.7	0.5	*
Senior judges	79.9	48.3	25.9	12.8	6.1
Oxbridge vice-chancellors	10.7	10.7	8.0	6.9	*
Other vice-chancellors	17.4	8.8	7.0	4.5	*
Heads of nationalized industries				4.6	*
Newspaper editors	15.5	5.1	5.0	3.8	*
Millionaires	1563.3	1263.3	856.2	516.5	306.4

*Number too small for comparison
Source of Table 6.2: Harold Perkin, *The Economic Worth of Elites in British Society since 1880* (Report to the SSRC 1977, deposited in the British Library Lending Division, Boston Spa), where definitions and numbers of each elite will be found.

borough and Wellington). Yet when we turn to family wealth as measured by father's estate at death or (where deceased) the elite person's own probate return, the picture changes dramatically. Only the median returns are given here, which means that half of each elite and of their fathers left less than the amounts shown, and in many cases nothing at all. There was, first of all, an immense difference between the elites defined by their wealth, the millionaires, great landowners and, to a lesser extent, the big company chairmen, and the elites not defined by ownership of property. Between the wars, no elite amongst the latter except the Conservative Cabinet ministers and the newly created peers had fathers who left median estates reaching five figures at 1913 prices, and only the senior judges left (slightly) more than £10,000. Neither at the outset nor at the end of their careers were most of the elites rich in any sense acceptable to the plutocracy. Not one of them, for example, on average, could have lived more than modestly on the interest of their father's wealth, supposing it could have been realized. Compared with the plutocracy they were on average poor men without the economic power to buy large amounts of the labour of others. And yet in their own spheres they were extremely powerful, making decisions which had important implications for the lives and careers of many of their fellow citizens.

The modesty of their backgrounds can be confirmed in individual cases. The Archbishops of Canterbury, the most powerful men in the Church of England (not in the original study but surveyed later by Rubinstein), were all technically from Class 1 and all except one (Cosmo Lang of Park School, Glasgow) educated at elite schools, yet only one archbishop between 1880 and 1945 was not from a comparatively modest home, and he a 'second generation' archbishop. Archbishop Archibald Tait (served 1868-82) was the son of a small Scottish landowner who 'ruined himself by unremunerative agricultural experiments and had to sell his estate', leaving nothing at his death; Edmund Benson (1883-96), was the son of a Birmingham chemical manufacturer in 'reduced circumstances', who also left nothing; Frederick Temple (1896-1902), the son of an army major who rose to be Governor of Sierra Leone but died when Frederick was 13, leaving a widow and fifteen children 'in narrow circumstances'; Randall Davidson (1903-28), the son of a small Edinburgh merchant who left £4,145; and Cosmo Lang (1928-42), the son of a Scottish Presbyterian minister and Principal of Aberdeen University, who left £3,866. Only William Temple (1942-45), son of Frederick, was born in the purple as the son of an elite father, and he was a rare episcopal socialist.[90]

High civil servants were becoming an increasingly powerful elite, yet one of them, H. E. Dale, asked in 1941:

What kind of young man enters the Home Civil Service? He is nearly sure to possess both ability and industry above the average of his contemporaries at school and the University. Secondly, many of the entrants are poor and without family influence - the sons of country parsons or small tradesmen or widows living on tiny incomes who for years have made sacrifices in order that their clever boys may not be robbed of a university career and the chances it offers. A young man of this origin must earn his living from the moment he leaves the University.... In any case [his family] can do nothing for him and he knows it.[91]

This inside assessment is borne out by the backgrounds of three literally average heads of departments, the median cases in terms of father's probate valuation in the cohorts 1920–39, 1940–59 and 1960–70 (all in post at some level in the inter-war period). The father of Sir Maurice Holmes, Permanent Under-Secretary for Education (1937–45), was an inspector of elementary schools who rose to be chief inspector and left £1,781 in 1936. The father of Sir Frank Lee, PUS at the Ministry of Food, the Board of Trade and the Treasury between 1949 and 1962, was a schoolmaster at Brentwood, Essex who left £2,125 in 1928. And the father of Sir Douglas Haddow, PUS at the Scottish Office from 1965, was a schoolmaster in Lanarkshire who died in 1919 when his son was 6, leaving £2,375.[92]

Vice-chancellors of universities, especially Oxford and Cambridge, were from more modest backgrounds. Benjamin Jowett's father was a Fleet Street printer, while others included the sons of a druggist, a naval surgeon, a tea dealer and, in more recent years, a stone mason, a chauffeur and a Post Office sorter. Only just over one-quarter came from upper-class families, mostly professional. Their fathers left median estates of £2,600 (at 1913 prices) and they themselves £7,100. Even the heads of the professional institutes, arguably the most successful practitioners of their kind, who came almost equally from upper and middle-class families and were overwhelmingly educated at public schools, had fathers who left on average £7,700 (at 1913 prices) and themselves left no more on average than £15,200.

Thus the professional as distinct from the landed and business elites between the wars, even when they came from the upper reaches of society via privileged education, were often born into families of modest wealth and, though they tended to outdo their fathers in accumulating property, left only modest estates themselves. What is more telling, however, especially considering the rise in real National Income per head (which approximately doubled between 1880 and 1939 and doubled again by 1980), is the steady decline in average wealth both of their families of origin and of the incumbents themselves. In real terms, only the fathers of millionaires, great landowners and (in the inter-war period only) Conservative Cabinet ministers made gains down to and beyond the Second World War, when even they began to lose out. Meanwhile, in terms of their own median probate valuations, every elite group without exception endured an unrelenting diminution in real wealth throughout the period from 1880 to 1970.[93] In this respect the inter-war period was halfway down the slide, at the end of a steady glissade and before the steep plunge of the post-war era.

This pattern of decline in elite family wealth is compatible with the transition from the unequal class society of Victorian to the more professional and meritocratic society emerging in the twentieth century, in three demonstrable ways. Firstly, the opening up of the elites to entrants of modest background, mainly from the middle and lower middle class rather than the working class, was reflected in the decline in their fathers' median estates. Secondly, the decline in incumbents' median estates reflected the narrowing differential incomes of the middle classes, both propertied and professional, over the wage earners, and the effect of graduated taxation on their ability to accumulate capital. It may also have reflected, thirdly, the swing towards pensionable salaries and, for some, self-funded pension plans, which absorbed savings but expired at death and left no trace in the probate returns – another symptom of a more professional society. Against all three must be set the growth in owner-occupation of houses, especially in the middle class, which would tend to raise the probate return, though not enough apparently to stem the decline. All told, there can be little doubt that, for the non-wealthy elites as well as for the plutocracy, the inter-war period was the middle stage of the transition.

5   SPIRALISTS AND BURGESSES

One effect of the rise of large-scale business and of the more interventionist state in the twentieth century is what might be called the 'nationalization' of the middle class. As local industrialists sold out to or merged with giant, nationwide corporations and the central government began to open local offices in every sizeable town, a new kind of cosmopolitan or rootless middle class of managers and administrators began to appear, different from the local business and professional men who constituted the traditional middle class. This was particularly noticeable after the First World War, when many of the old town bosses in the industrialist areas, like Lord Ashton, the 'linoleum king' of Lancaster, the Woods and Sidebottoms of Glossop, the Peases of Darlington, and the Palmers of Jarrow, abdicated and left their once paternalistic domains to face the rigours of depression with only the local 'shopocracy' and trade union leaders at the helm. The new managers and civil servants had no roots in the town and looked elsewhere for promotion or career advancement. This led one sociologist in the 1950s, William Watson (based largely on a social and political survey of Glossop), to distinguish between the 'spiralists', the career professionals who would move up by moving round, and the 'burgesses', the traditional local business and self-employed professional men – traders, builders, doctors and solicitors, and the like – whose whole careers would be spent in the locality.[94]

There was often tension and mutual disdain between the locals and the 'offcomers' (as they were called in the north), because of differences in outlook, values, horizons, and even speech. The old middle class, educated at the local grammar school and dominating the local Rotary Club, the Freemasons, and the Conservative and Liberal Associations, were fiercely loyal and defensive about the local community and involved in its politics, while the newcomers tended to be detached, aloof from local squabbles, with their eyes on their next promotion to a 'better' (usually a bigger) place.

The newcomers also tended to speak differently. Whereas the burgesses clove to an educated version of the local accent, the spiralists, even if they came from the same or similar backgrounds, had 'corrected' their accents at public school or university and aspired to a version of the 'received standard English' being put out by BBC radio. They did not perhaps go all the way with the stilted, braying, arrogant tones then affected by BBC announcers and newsreel commentators – an affectation which when played back now only provokes disbelieving laughter – but they eschewed the regional accents spoken by their neighbours. 'Received standard English' was not the speech of the aristocracy, who spoke in a much gruffer, clipped, down-to-earth, less pretentious manner. It was the speech of a new, aspiring middle class who believed themselves to belong to a nationwide elite. Its affectations can still be heard in repeats of Neville Chamberlain's 1939 'We are at war' broadcast, so nervous, tinny and insincere compared with Churchill's rousing, aristocratic prose. Only the educated Scots and Welsh were immune from it: Ramsay MacDonald and, ironically, Sir John Reith, Director-General of the plummy-voiced BBC, Lloyd George and Thomas Jones, Secretary of the Cabinet. It was not, as many believed, hallowed by tradition – few Victorians spoke like that – but a new invention, created in the reformed public schools and the southern grammar schools and now imposed on the new middle class by the BBC.

In the large cities as distinct from the smaller industrial towns it became the speech of the 'posher' suburbs – the Surrey commuter belt, Birmingham's Edgbaston, Manchester's Wilmslow and Altrincham, Edinburgh's 'refained' Kelvinside. For the real social division between the wars was not between the prosperous south and the depressed north but between the inner cities and industrial towns and the new outer suburbs of housing estates and by-passes. J. B. Priestley in his *English Journey* in 1933 noticed that, in addition to the old, romantic, idealized, rustic pre-industrial England of the posters and picture books and the dirty, depressed and depressing nineteenth-century industrial England of the dole queues and belching chimneys, there was a third England of chromium and glass, art deco and functional architecture:

> This is the England of arterial and by-pass roads, of filling stations and factories that look like exhibition buildings, of giant cinemas and dance halls and cafés, bungalows with tiny garages, cocktail bars, Woolworth's, motor coaches, wireless, hiking, factory girls looking like actresses, greyhound racing and dirt tracks, swimming pools, and everything given away for cigarette coupons.

This newer England was a 'large-scale mass production job, with cut prices', cheap and accessible, without privilege or deference, in which the young people at least

> do not play chorus in an opera in which their social superiors are the principals; they do not live vicariously, enjoy life at second hand . . .; they get on with their own lives. If they must have heroes and heroines, they choose them for themselves, from the ranks of film stars and sportsmen and the like.

It was 'as near to a classless society as we have got yet'.[95]

But it was not yet a classless society. On the contrary, suburban

England was more visibly graded into discrete social layers than either the old, traditional countryside, in which the rich at least knew the poor, or the nineteenth-century industrial towns, in which the boss lived up the hill, overlooking the crowded cottages of his workers. The explosion of urban expansion brought about between the wars by the motor car, the motor bus and the delivery van was much more dispersive than the railway and the tramcar. It almost doubled the amount of land under bricks and mortar and concrete in a generation, from 6 to 11 per cent of the total acreage. Nearly 4 million houses were built between the wars, over 1 million by local authorities, most of them on suburban housing estates.[96] The new suburbs sprawled outwards from the cities, filling in the green spaces between the railway suburbs, flooding the gaps between the towns, and bringing in an ugly new word for an ugly new concept, the conurbation. The suburbs were only classless in the sense that each catered only for the class that could afford that price of house and no more, or that level of rent on a council estate. The classes and subclasses sorted themselves out more neatly than ever before into single-class enclaves which did not know or speak to each other. The life of the 'stockbroker belt' with its big cars and detached houses and private infant schools was more remote from the white-collar semi-detached private estate than ever the squire was from the village almshouses or the cotton spinner from his operatives' cottages.

Yet this new social geography fitted the life of the spiralist much better than the old. As he moved up, whether in the same city or a different one, he could move unnoticed from one anonymous suburb to a slightly better one, acquiring the accoutrements of the better life – a 'modern semi', a detached house, a car, a telephone, a refrigerator, and so on – as he went, without his co-workers even knowing, much less remarking. The burgess had always lived in the eye of the community. The spiralist lived anonymously.

The middle class as a whole has expanded in the twentieth century, from about 25 per cent in 1911 to 31 per cent in 1931, 41 per cent in 1951, and 43 per cent in 1971. Much of this, it is true, was due to the huge expansion of office jobs for women, and male white-collar jobs rose only from 26 to 29 and 32 per cent. But it was still sufficient to increase the chances of upward mobility significantly beyond what they would otherwise have been. As the Oxford social mobility project noted:

The increasing 'room at the top' created by the growth of professional, higher technical, administrative, and managerial positions could provide the occasion ... for inequalities of life chances to be reduced, but without the members of any class having to become less advantaged than before in absolute terms.[97]

What has been less noticed, however, is the changeover within the higher middle class, from a predominance of owner-managing business men to one of professionals, managers and administrators. Employers and proprietors shrank from 7 7 per cent of the male occupied population in 1911 and 1921 to 7.6 per cent in 1931, 5.7 per cent in 1951 and to 5.2 per cent in 1971. Meanwhile, higher professionals (both salaried and self-employed) and administrators and managers grew from 5.4 per cent in 1911 and 5.9 per cent in 1921 to 6.2 per cent in 1931, 9.6 per cent in 1951 and to 16 per cent in 1971. To put it another and more appropriate way, Guy Routh has shown that, while the *self-employed* employers and (higher and lower) professionals shrank from 1,459,000 (7.5 per cent of the occupied population) in 1921, to 1,248,000 (5.5 per cent) in 1951, the *salaried* professionals, managers and administrators grew from 1,438,000 (7.4 per cent) to 2,609,000 (11.6 per cent). Between 1921 and 1951 the ratio of the salaried professionals and managers to the employers and self-employed increased from near equality to about 2:1.[98] While the change proceeded more slowly between the wars than later, the trend was undoubtedly from an entrepreneurial towards a salaried professional and managerial society.

Yet, curiously enough, middle-class incomes were not keeping up commensurately with the expansion. Annual average money wages rose 103 per cent between 1911–13 and 1938, average annual salaries by only 71 per cent, while prices rose by 56 per cent. According to Routh, the average money earnings of a typical group of higher professionals (lawyers, doctors, dentists, the clergy, army officers, engineers and chemists) rose between 1913–14 and 1935–37 by 93 per cent, compared with 97 per cent for skilled workers and 105 per cent for unskilled. Public administrators were still more depressed, and the typical first division civil servant (principal grade) suffered a nearly 50 per cent decline in real income. Only business managers gained substantially, with a rise of 120 per cent. In general, the differentials between the classes were narrowing somewhat, in line

270

with the trend towards greater equality. Higher professional earnings for men, 4.1 times the average for all occupations (male and female) in 1913-14, were only 3.9 times in 1935-36 and 2.9 times in 1955-56. Managerial salaries, on the other hand, were gaining, rising from 2.5 times the average in 1913-14 to 2.7 times in 1935-36 and 2.8 times by 1955-56.[99]

What was happening was that management, once very much second best to owner-enterprise, was becoming more professional and becoming professionally paid. Meanwhile, certain traditionally high professions, once paid at aristocratic levels, were falling in real income and pulling down the average. Bishops' average incomes fell from £3,400 in 1913-14 to £2,700 in 1924, a fall of 55 per cent in real terms; high court judges' and senior Cabinet ministers' remained at £5,000 till after the Second World War, a fall in real terms of 36 per cent by 1938 and 74 per cent by 1955.[100]

Routh explains the rigidity of the national pay structure, together with the tendency of low-paid workers to more than keep up despite their weak position in the labour market, by socio-psychological causes, the conservatism of all social classes in the face of change and, more especially, the quasi-medieval belief in a 'just wage'. Every occupational group, he quotes Elliott Jacques, had an intuitive knowledge of what they ought to be paid, and struggles hard to defend it and to restore it whenever it is undermined. Unfortunately, it does not mesh with what others intuitively feel *they* ought to be paid, and they struggle just as hard to restore differentials, thus perpetuating an unstable and constantly changing equilibrium. In certain situations, like the inter-war period, when there is sympathy for the underdog, flat-rate increases become the norm for some trade unions, and the pay 'floor' is raised by general agreement.[101]

This theory fits the experience of an incipient professional society in which there is a stronger sense of the justice (equity rather than equality) of rewards. Each profession, including business management, believes that its remuneration should be linked to its social function rather than to its fluctuating values in the labour market. At the one end, the unskilled should not be allowed to sink to their almost negative value in an overloaded free market. At the other, outrageously high traditional salaries for judges, bishops and politicians should not be raised in line with inflation but allowed to fall to 'reasonable' levels. To anticipate

Chapter 8, we may say that the revival of the 'just wage' is an aspect of the professional social ideal of a functional society based on the just reward of merit and service. The 'moralization of incomes' was already beginning to express itself between the wars in pulling down the mighty and raising up the meek.

Spiralists and burgesses could also be found expanding and contracting at lower levels of the middle class. On the one hand, small business men, shopkeepers, local builders, workshop manufacturers and self-employed craftsmen were shrinking in numbers as the multiple stores, big construction contractors and great corporations outcompeted them. On the other, there was a huge expansion of clerical workers, minor civil servants and local government employees, school teachers, technicians, inspectors, supervisors and foremen.

Clerical workers were the fastest expanding occupational group in the first half of the twentieth century, growing from 887,000, 4.8 per cent of the workforce, in 1911 to 1,465,000, 7 per cent in 1931 and 2,404,000, 10.7 per cent in 1951. Most of this expansion, it is true, was among women office workers, who increased from 179,000, 3.3 per cent of women workers, in 1911, to 648,000, 10.3 per cent in 1931, and 1,413,000, 20.3 per cent in 1951, but this was partly due to the greater (and no doubt discriminatory) promotion of male clerks to administration and management.[102] Office workers of both sexes were often paid no more than skilled manual workers – in 1935 Civil Service clerks earned almost exactly the same as engine drivers – but in outlook, dress and even speech (due to grammar school education) were often very different.

They were also treated differently by their employers. As one candid employer noted in 1947:

By a process of usage the workers in this country have been divided into two classes:
(a) those who are expected to work something under forty hours a week and are, in general, trusted by the community and their employers to put in a reasonable amount of work during their working day; and
(b) those who are expected to work about forty-eight hours per week and also are, in general, not trusted by their employers.
As a result they are paid strictly according to the hours spent at their place of work.[103]

The first group, the office workers, often had holidays with pay, paid sick leave and even pensions, besides cleaner and safer conditions of work and closer relations with the boss, and many repaid the trust by rarely forming trade unions, except in large-scale offices like the Civil Service and the railways. The second, the manual workers, as we shall see, retaliated with the same lack of trust, which led to what Alan Fox has called the 'low-trust industrial relations' which have bedevilled British industry and contributed to its decline.[104]

The office workers were not immune, however, from the rise in the scale of organization. Already before the First World War the large groups of clerks in the Civil Service, local government, the Post Office and the railways, without the personal employer and paternalism of the small family business, had begun to organize white-collar unions. Between the wars, the rise of the large corporation 'created the monster office in which vast numbers of clerks are herded together for their daily work, just as the concentration of capital herded the former craftsmen or cottage workers in the factory.'[105] As a result, clerks began to join unions in larger numbers, which increased to 204,000 members in the new white-collar section of the TUC in 1946.[106]

Meanwhile, the office workers and the lesser professions like the teachers, nurses and technicians acted out the spiralist dream at the lower levels of the middle class, pursuing safe jobs with pensions and promotion up the career ladder by changing jobs and homes, while the lesser burgesses, the small business men and shopkeepers, strove to keep afloat against the competition of the growing corporations. But whatever the mutual disdain between them, their common bond of middle classness was their conscious-ness of superiority, in appearance, status and education, to what was still the great majority, the manual working class.

6 THE ROAD FROM WIGAN PIER

In the Preface to George Tomlinson's autobiographical *Coal-Miner*, published in 1933, Sir Arthur Bryant, the upper middle-class historian, takes to task George Orwell's *The Road to Wigan Pier*:

It was written by a young literary man of refined tastes who at some apparent inconvenience to himself has 'roughed it' for a few weeks at Wigan and Sheffield. The impression left by the first part of the book is that Wigan and Sheffield are Hell: the corollary worked out with great skill in the second part, that every decent-hearted man and woman, sooner than allow such conditions to endure a day longer, should at once enrol in the ranks of those who are seeking change by revolutionary methods . . .

But there is an even more fatal weakness in the premises, for though Wigan and Sheffield may perhaps genuinely seem Hell to a super-sensitive novelist paying them a casual visit, they do not seem Hell to the vast majority of people who live there.[107]

This passage gives an insight into the two most common attitudes to the working class held by those upper middle-class observers who bothered to notice in the 1930s. Both assumed that the working class were 'all the same', but one believed that they lived in pig-sties and liked it that way while the other thought that pig-sties ought to be abolished. Even the sympathetic George Orwell, an old Etonian from a very modest middle-class family, could not realize how insulting his picture of the filth and squalor of the lumpenproletariat slums of Wigan was to the average respectable working man, while Bryant's belief that they actually liked it because they knew no better was degrading.

What both, like most of their class, lacked was discrimination. The inter-war working class even more than its Victorian predecessors had a prickly sensitivity to the nuances of status more refined than *The Tatler* or *Country Life*. It was not just the traditional distinction between the 'roughs' and the 'respectables' reported by Margaret Stacey in her study of Banbury. There was a finely graded social value attached to each district, every street, even two ends of the same street. It was of course an intensely local feeling. Richard Hoggart found in Hunslet, an inner suburb of Leeds, in the 1930s the same kind of urban village that Robert Roberts described in Salford before the war: 'The more we look at working-class life the more surely does it appear that the core is a sense of the personal, the concrete, the local: it is embodied in the idea of, first, the family and, second, the neighbourhood.' The obverse of this was that the world outside the family and the neighbourhood was often strange and hostile, and the working class were just as undiscriminating about the classes above as vice versa. Society was divided into 'Them' (with a capital T) and 'Us':

'They' are 'the people at the top', 'the higher ups', the people who give you the dole, call you up, tell you to go to war, fine you, made you split your family in the thirties to avoid a reduction in the Means Test allowance, 'get yer in the end', 'aren't really to be trusted', 'talk posh', 'are all twisters really', 'never tell yer owt' (e.g. about a relative in hospital), 'clap yer in clink', 'will do y' down if they can', 'summons yer', 'are all in a click [clique] together', 'treat you like muck'.[108]

'They' were represented by the local authority figures, the doctor, the clergyman, the relieving officer, the magistrate, and their minions and surrogates, the policeman, the Labour Exchange clerk and the rent collector. George Tomlinson, the Nottinghamshire miner, equated them with the local Conservative Party:

All that the ordinary miner understands about Conservatism is that local jumped-up people, with a small car and an equally small mind, and who live in the residential part of town, as they love to call it, are Conservatives (or pretend to be). They who have made their money by selling him bacon, pit boots, and insurance policies, are now able to sit back in comfort and write to the local press pointing out how the miner is wrong on each and every occasion, but who never in their lives entered a miner's home in order to get a proper understanding of him and his problems.[109]

The miners, whether of Wigan or Nottingham or of Scotland, Wales, Yorkshire and elsewhere, once part of the high-paid labour aristocracy, were the hardest hit by the inter-war depression, with unemployment rates running at 18 and 22 per cent in the good years 1929 and 1938 and no less than 42 per cent in 1932. Their plight epitomized the experience of the long-term unemployed. A Rhondda miner spoke to investigators of the feeling of being spied upon by officials from the Labour Exchange: 'To men who had worked in the only industry they had known for anything from fifteen to fifty years, this was a new experience, of the most humiliating and degrading kind.'[110]

Other skilled workers, too, in the Lancashire cotton and engineering industries of Walter Greenwood's *Love on the Dole*

(1935), the unemployed shipbuilders of Ellen Wilkinson's Jarrow, *The Town that was Murdered* (1939), or in the distressed areas generally in the Pilgrim's Trust's *Men Without Work* (1938), suffered unwonted privation and degradation in the 1930s. At the bottom of the depression in 1932 when unemployment averaged 22.9 per cent, it was only 13.1 per cent in London and the south-east but 26.3 per cent in the north-west (cotton and engineering), 29 per cent in Scotland (coal, engineering and shipbuilding), 30.6 per cent in the north-east (wool, coal and shipbuilding), and 38.1 per cent in Wales (coal and tinplate).[111] The despair and deprivation of the distressed areas rightly became a legend, which helps to explain both the enthusiasm during the Second World War for rebuilding a better world with full employment and also the Labour victory of 1945.

But *Wigan Pier* was not the whole truth about the working class between the wars. As David Lockwood has observed:

> the working class which suffered disproportionately from poverty and unemployment was the working class of the communities of the older, declining heavy industry. What is lacking is a description of the remainder of the working class, particularly that not inconsiderable part of it that was relatively secure in its employment, working in the slowly expanding new light industries, living in better homes and less cohesive communities, enjoying stable real incomes and limiting its family size.[112]

These were the workers in the brand new car factories of Birmingham, Coventry, Oxford and Luton, the radio, vacuum cleaner and cigarette factories of West London, the aircraft factories of Bristol, Yeovil and Preston, and in many others making cosmetics, pharmaceuticals, petro-chemicals, rayon, electrical components and household consumer goods in many parts of the country. There were also thousands of car mechanics and home appliance repairmen, building workers erecting houses in every region including the depressed areas, shop assistants and delivery men distributing the new consumer goods, gas fitters and electricians installing cookers, wiring and meters, and bus operators and utilities men serving the new suburbs. These new, expanding industries were thicker in the Midlands and the south, but by no means confined to them. New shops, new bus networks, new house building and new services were found everywhere, electric power and radios, for example, increased as fast in Liverpool and Cardiff as in Birmingham or Portsmouth, and expenditure on football pools and cigarettes may have been greater there.[113]

Despite the high rates of unemployment, averaging 10.6 per cent in the 1920s and 16.1 per cent in the 1930s, the great majority of the working class were employed throughout the inter-war period, and only a small minority were unemployed for more than twelve months. Surprisingly, apart from coalmining, wages did not fall except temporarily in the early 1930s even in the worst hit industries, and on average money wages in both the old industries and the new were rising moderately and real wages considerably between the wars, in 1938 by 30 per cent over 1913 and 18 per cent over 1920.[114] Most of this gain was due to increased productivity in the new industries and, surprisingly, even in the old as outworn, inefficient factories and plants were closed down, and also to the cheaper food and raw materials imported with the improved terms of trade between manufacturing and primary producing countries. Both of these gains were, in a sense, paid for by the unemployed: increased productivity meant that the new industries employed fewer workers than they might have done (though without it they might have priced themselves out of world markets altogether); and improved terms of trade meant that overseas customers could buy fewer British exports, thus reducing employment in the export industries. But for most of the working class they meant falling prices and rising spending power.

In addition to the rise in real wages there was, as we have seen, an increase in the social income going mainly to the working class, in the form of insurance benefits and pensions, medical treatment, education, and the like, totalling £596 million or 11.3 per cent of GNP on 1938. In individual terms this averaged £12.5 per head in 1938, or about £46 per household.[115] Since most of it went to the working class, this added the equivalent of about £1 a week per family to an average wage of only £2.5 per week. Or, rather, it added more than that to those families who needed it, in sickness, unemployment, widowhood, old age, and so on. Although the working class contributed part of that sum – in addition to insurance contributions, no less than two-thirds of all indirect taxation, as opposed to income tax, was paid by the 88 per cent earning less than £250 a year – they were net gainers, paying only 79 per cent of what they received. All told, the effect was to raise the incomes of the working class by 8–14 per cent in cash terms, plus the value of the various social and educational services in kind.[116]

Finally, this increased income had to support a smaller average family. The decrease in the average number of children from 3.4 to 2.2, collectively dependent on their parents for only about two-thirds as long, and the decline of the average household from 4.4 persons in 1911 to 3.7 in 1931 (and to 3.2 in 1951), meant that the wage now had to support 20 per cent fewer people. Adding all these gains together, the average family may have been about two-thirds better off in 1938 than before the war.[117]

The raising of the average, still more of the floor of unskilled wages, helps to explain the lifting of about half of the very poor, and most of those in work, out of the harsh, grinding poverty of the pre-war surveys. In a repetition of his five towns survey in 1924, Sir Arthur Bowley found that:

> The improvement since 1913 is very striking. Even on the assumption that all the families suffering from unemployment in a particular week had no adequate reserves and that their unemployment was chronic, the proportion in poverty in 1924 was little more than half that in 1913 [6.5 per cent against 12.6 per cent]. If there had been no unemployment the proportion of families in poverty in the towns taken together would have fallen to one-third (3.6 per cent against 11 per cent) and of persons to little over a quarter (3.5 per cent against 12.6 per cent). All the towns except Stanley [a Lancashire coal mining town] show an improvement in nearly the same ratio; and it is also found for both sexes and all ages.[118]

Other surveys confirmed Bowley's finding. *A New Survey of London Life and Labour* by a team led by Sir Hubert Llewellyn Smith, the great civil servant who began as one of Charles Booth's assistants, found that nearly 10 per cent were in poverty compared with 31 per cent in Booth's late Victorian survey. A Bristol survey in 1937 found 10.7 per cent of the working class (perhaps 7.5 per cent of the whole population) in poverty, and surveys of Merseyside and Southampton during the Depression found 17.3 and 20 per cent of the working class (about 13 and 15 per cent of the whole population) below their poverty lines. The most comparable study, Rowntree's second survey of York, found that 'primary' poverty had fallen from 9.9 per cent of the city's population in 1899 to 4.2 per cent in 1936.[119]

Here we come upon the paradox of rising standards, however. As conditions improve and the worst kind of poverty diminishes, the minimum acceptable level at which people can be expected to live also rises. Rowntree was not content to accept that the 1899 standard was applicable to the poor in a more prosperous and hopefully more humane society, and so he applied to the same data a new 'Human needs' standard, allowing not merely for the maintenance of 'physical efficiency' but also for an improved diet (based on the British Medical Association's recommendations), slightly more for clothes, housing, heating and lighting, insurance and trade union subscriptions, travel to work, and even 'luxuries' like newspapers, writing paper and stamps, a radio licence, beer, tobacco, books and holidays. By this new standard Rowntree found that 17.8 per cent of the population of York (31.1 per cent of the working class) were now in poverty.[120]

What Rowntree had done, without naming it, was to invent the concept of relative poverty, which would be rediscovered in the 1960s by Peter Townsend and Brian Abel Smith.[121] As applied by them it would, as we shall see, become a 'Catch-22' both for the poor and for the welfare state: every time the state raised its standard of provision (as measured by the minimum standard of social security) it would thrust more people down into poverty. But the fact that it was necessary for Rowntree to raise his poverty line in 1936 is a measure of the improvement that had occurred and of the possibility of further reform.

None of this means that the affluent society had already arrived or that large numbers of working people were not suffering from hunger, bad housing, and ill-health. Sir John Boyd Orr in 1936 claimed that only 40 per cent of the population were well fed, and 10 per cent (including 20 per cent of the nation's children) badly fed, leaving the rest, half the population, to some extent undernourished – though he later reduced this to one-third.[122] Despite the building of over 4 million houses between the wars, nearly 4 per cent of working-class houses in England and Wales and no less than 23 per cent in Scotland were found to be overcrowded in 1936.[123] On the new council estates, because of the higher rents, Dr M'Gonigle found in Stockton-on-Tees that the new tenants might be worse fed than in the old slums.[124] Despite the fall in the (standardized) death rate, from 13.8 per thousand in 1913 to 9.3 in 1937, there was still a great deal of ill-health, especially amongst working-class women (wives and children of insured workers were not covered by national insurance for medical treatment). In one 1930s survey less than one-third of working-class wives were found to be in good health, more than one-fifth in 'indifferent health', and the rest, nearly one-half, in 'bad' or 'very grave' condition.[125] Despite the steep fall in infant mortality, from 154 per thousand live births in 1900 and 110 in 1910 to 57 in 1935, it was still two-thirds higher in the unskilled working class than in the professional and managerial classes.[126] Despite the enormous reduction in infectious diseases like scarlet fever, diphtheria, measles and whooping cough, they still killed far more children of the poor than of the rich, and child deaths in the slums could be relatively twice as numerous as in the better-class suburbs.[127] And despite the increase in the average height of children aged 10–14 by one inch per decade since 1900, there was still a marked difference between boys at public schools and those at state elementary schools.[128]

Nevertheless, despite the depression, the signs of improvement could be seen everywhere, even in the distressed areas. It was now rare to see children, even in the slums, with wizened, old men's faces, in rags and without shoes.[129] In the Sunday school anniversary processions each spring many working-class children turned out with new clothes and shoes, and their parents went to church or chapel for that once. Rowntree found at York that while religious attendance had halved since 1899, from 36 to 18 per cent of the population, attendance at the pub had also declined: 'One may walk through working-class streets every evening for weeks and not see a drunken person.'[130] National beer consumption had dropped from 34 million barrels a year in 1910–13 to 20 million in 1930 and even to 13 million in 1933 during the Great Depression.[131] Mass Observation noted that while in a typical industrial town like Bolton 'the pub had more buildings, holds more people, takes more of their time and money, than church, cinema, dance-hall, and political organizations put together', only one-third of the voting population were regular pub-goers.[132] One at least of Rowntree's causes of secondary poverty had steeply declined.

On the other hand, his two other major causes, tobacco and gambling, had enormously increased. Cigarettes, popularized by the 'sophistication' of movie stars and by free gifts and cigarette cards, became chic for all classes, and tobacco consumption almost doubled between 1914 and 1938. Gambling, so far as it could be measured, on horse racing and the new crazes of greyhound racing and the football pools, more than trebled, from £63 million in 1920 to £221 million in 1938, a large part of it by the working class. Over sixteen times as many people gambled on football as paid to watch it, and some 5 to 7 million people a year spent over £30 million on the pools. The cinema became the most popular of entertainments, with nearly 1 billion attendances in 1938, nearly twice as many as all other forms of paid public entertainment (including the theatre, racing, football and cricket) put together; about 40 per cent of the population went to the 'flicks' once a week, and 25 per cent went twice. At home over 9 million households bought radio licences by 1939, and 95 per cent of the population could listen to the BBC or, for lighter fare, to Radio Luxembourg or Frecamp, and many working-class families could afford a gramophone as well.[133]

Working hours were shorter, about forty-eight hours a week instead of fifty-four before the war, and so other inexpensive forms of leisure became popular. Dancing to the big bands at the 'palais' and to the gramophone in youth clubs, even those attached to churches and chapels, became all the rage. Hiking was enshrined in popular song. Cycling, once confined to the middle class, became a universal pastime. Reading was transformed by the new cheap paperbacks and expanded public libraries, and book sales increased to 7 million by 1939, while public library loans more than quadrupled from 54 million in 1911 to 247 million in 1939. Gardening was brought within reach of the masses by the allotments movement and the new private semi-detached housing and council estates. Only the car, except for a favoured few skilled workers often with working wives, remained a middle-class passport to trips to the country and the seaside – with the cheapest Ford at £100, nine months' wages, and petrol at 1s. 9d. a gallon, nearly two hours' earnings for an average worker, motoring, except perhaps by motorcycle or the family motor bike and sidecar, was still an expensive hobby.[134]

Holidays, however, were coming more within reach of the

working class. Holidays with pay, except for white-collar workers before the 1930s, were stimulated by the 1938 Act and increased from about 4 million (out of the 18.5 million workers earning less than £250 per annum) in 1937 to 11 million in 1939. Already in 1937 about 15 million people took holidays away from home, many taking advantage of the new motor coaches at about half the cost of the railway, and still more took cheap day excursions by bus or rail. Holiday camps were pioneered by Cunningham's for young men in the Isle of Man from 1935 and Butlin's for the whole family at Skegness from 1937. Only a third of the population, however, could afford to holiday away from home, and in this too the inter-war period was still in unfinished transition.[135]

In more basic ways standards of comfort were rising, and the working class were getting an increasing share of amenities. By 1939 one family in three was living in a house built since the war, many of them working-class. Most houses, both old and new, came to have gas and/or electricity, and all the new housing estates including those for the working class had hot water, fixed baths and indoor lavatories, and usually a small patch of garden back and front. Expenditure on furniture rose by half between 1924 and 1935, and on electrical appliances nearly trebled.[136] Home, even for the working class, was becoming a place of comfort and relaxation.

Despite votes for women in 1918 and 1928 and the Sex Disqualification (Removal) Act in 1919, home was still the sphere of most married women, especially in the working class. Women office workers might be increasing and a few more women making their way into the professions, but there were relatively fewer women at work between the wars than before or since – barely a third of those of working age. Most married women workers went back home after the frenetic activity of wartime, many driven out of jobs by male hostility, and scarcely one in ten remained at work. The traditional skilled working-class ideal of keeping the wife at home to look after the house and children spread downwards to the less skilled, and male chauvinism, always strong in the working class, was little dented before the Second World War. Many poorer families made ends meet by the wife taking in lodgers or washing or doing part-time work unknown to the census enumerators, but only the poorest of mothers, except in the traditional strongholds of women's factory work like Lancashire and the Potteries, faced the indignity of going out to work full-time. Those who did so were ill-paid, often accused by the male-dominated trade unions of taking men's jobs away, and were the first to be dismissed when work was short. Only domestic service, still the largest occupation for women despite its relative decline, kept up its numbers, and there were more servants in 1931 than in 1911. These were mostly single women, and for most working-class girls in service or in industry the height of ambition remained a husband and family not too far removed from the home of their mothers who, in a culture still marked by separate spheres and different leisure activities for husbands and wives, gave the emotional and material support they needed in a tediously narrow and solitary life.

Much has been made, especially since the Second World War, by nostalgic scholarship boys like Richard Hoggart and middle-class sociologists like Michael Young and Peter Wilmott of the supposed decline of the working-class community and the comforting nearness of 'our Mam', both in the old inner cities like Leeds with the incursion of mass-produced culture and on the new housing estates with the move from cosy, integrated urban villages like Bethnal Green to the featureless anonymity of the suburbs like Greenleigh, nearly twenty miles away.[137] Such judgments, by the upwardly mobile and romantic outsiders, underestimate the resilience and social inventiveness of the working class. The spirit which had created the rich Victorian culture of working-class institutions of the supposedly 'insensate industrial towns' – the trade unions, co-operative stores, friendly societies, building societies, working men's clubs, and church and chapel bible classes, mothers' meetings and youth clubs, brass bands, tonic-sol-fa choirs, dog- and pigeon-fanciers' societies, gardening clubs, football and cricket teams, and even the public house darts, domino and bowling matches – was still alive and thriving between the wars, even on the new housing estates. As James Cronin has observed on the 'class blindness' of middle-class surveyors:

> It is possible, however, to read the apparent impenetrability of working-class life in quite a different way, as proof not of the paucity of friendships and institutions but of their richness. It is clear, after all, that by about 1920, British workers had elaborated a broad array of institutions – unions, cooperatives,

local political parties, working-men's clubs and a plethora of groups devoted to sports and hobbies – running through the neighbourhoods and factories and centred upon the family, the pub or the place of work. It is unlikely that this culture disappeared during the inter-war period, but it does appear to have become less aggressive and self-confident.[138]

Self-confident or not, it certainly did not disappear. If anything, it was reinforced by the rise of the Labour Party to major electoral status, not only at the national level but in the industrial towns and inner cities and even in a few counties like Durham and Glamorgan where it came to dominate local government, and it was able to improve educational opportunities and encourage youth clubs, old people's clubs and homes, and music and the arts. Even on the new council estates like Dagenham, where sociologists lamented that 'by removing families from tenement buildings they have destroyed that compulsory neighbourliness which was a feature of the old system',[139] the evidence showed the opposite. On the London County Council estate at Becontree near the Ford Works at Dagenham, which grew from 2,000 residents in 1922 to over 100,000 ten years later, Terence Young reported in 1934 that the newcomers quickly founded tenants' associations, Labour and Conservative Party branches, consumer co-operative societies, working men's clubs, two Salvation Army halls, seven churches, four pubs (owned like the houses by the London County Council), three co-operative guild branches, two Independent Labour Party branches, and the Dagenham Trades Council representing all the local trade unions.[140] On a similar estate, Ruth Durant found in 1939:

> Today Watling is still distinguished by its successful social activities. It appears that even now, although local unity has been lost, there is more neighbourliness, more corporate life on the Estate than in adjacent suburbs or in the parent town. In London's inner suburbs clubs have been established for the people; the community centre at Watling was planned and is run by the people themselves.

While some inveterate Cockneys would 'sooner be back in London', most liked their new homes, with their bathrooms and gardens.[141] A Mass Observation report on twelve old and new communities in the same year showed that a larger majority of the new suburban residents than of their old neighbours in the parent towns were satisfied with their homes and neighbourhoods.[142]

It seems likely, in fact, that the working-class suburbs were more community-minded and more socially alive than the more affluent suburbs, where the middle classes, despite their Conservative, Rotary, bridge, golf and tennis clubs, lived a more private life, more wary of contamination by neighbours 'not quite like us'. Nevertheless, as rising incomes gave more freedom to choose leisure pursuits and friends and less economic dependence on neighbours and relatives, the prosperous working class, naturally and without conscious emulation, began to aspire to that more home-centred, privatized life which had long been a feature of the suburban middle class. In social life, the inter-war working class looked both ways, backward to the solidarity of Victorian class society and forward to the affluent society of the post-war world. For an increasing number of them the road was not towards but away from Wigan Pier.

That new world, little noticed by them, was already being created all around them, in the new corporate economy and society which were beginning to emerge between the wars, and which was to affect the lives of all classes more profoundly than any development since the Industrial Revolution.

Chapter 7

TOWARDS A CORPORATE SOCIETY

The crisis of class society which culminated in the General Strike owed its demise, we saw in Chapter 5, to the tacit *entente* between the employers, the trade unions and the state which later commentators on politics, the economy and society have come to call corporatism. Corporatism is an extremely ambiguous concept with unhappy associations with Mediterranean fascism (though not with German Nazism), and has since been variously applied to regimes as different as Mussolini's Italy and Swedish social democracy. In essence the concept is an attempt to describe an ordering of society, economy and the state which cuts across the structures of class, individual capitalism and parliamentary democracy. On the continent it had its origins in nineteenth-century Catholicism's reaction against liberal democracy and reached its most formal expression in the statutory representation of the 'corporations' of employers, trade unions and the professions in Franco's Spain or contemporary Austria. In more recent discussion it has been called by Pahl and Winkler 'fascism with a human face' and by Colin Crouch, who applied it to industrial relations in contemporary Britain, a 'bargained corporatism' in which employers' representatives, trade union leaders, and representatives of the state negotiate with one another outside the channels of parliamentary democracy.[1]

Most definitions of corporatism have been as nebulous as the concept itself. Philippe Schmitter, the political scientist who revived interest in it in 1974, defined it as:

a system of interest representation in which the constituent units are organized into a limited number of singular, compulsory, non-competitive, hierarchically ordered and functionally differentiated categories, recognized or licensed (if not created) by the state and granted a deliberate representational monopoly within their respective categories in exchange for observing certain controls on their selection of leaders and articulation of demands and supports.[2]

Colin Crouch reduced this drastically to:

the operation of putatively representative organizations as the intermediaries regulating their own membership within a wider system of order[3]

with the implication that the system of order involved the state. Pahl and Winkler, whose approach was through the sociology of the mixed economy, saw it as:

a comprehensive economic system under which the state intensively channels predominantly privately-owned business towards four goals ... Order, Unity, Nationalism and 'Success'.[4]

Keith Middlemas, a historian more alive to its empirical failures in Britain than to its theoretical niceties, talked rather of 'the corporate bias' of the triangular relation between big business, trade unions, and the government, all three of which preferred informal, backstairs bargaining to institutionalized procedures.[5]

The unifying strand running through all these definitions is the representation of organized interest groups – particular occupations, industries and professions – rather than individuals or classes. This has a curious echo of the 'virtual representation' of the 'great functional interests' which lobbied government in eighteenth-century England not for a share of power but for patronage of their group needs and desires.[6] That echo is not fortuitous, since modern English society is beginning to recapitulate the structure of its pre-industrial origins, to re-emphasize the vertical threads of interest in its social fabric, so long obscured by the horizontal threads of class. The interest groups of contemporary society, however, though they bear some resemblance to eighteenth-century functional interests like the General Chamber of Manufacturers or the landed and East India interests, differ from them in one important respect: they are fundamentally bureaucratic career hierarchies with leaders whose interests overlap but do not wholly jibe with the interests of those they profess to represent. The leaders are primarily career professionals of an increasingly – which is not to say completely – meritocratic stripe, motivated as much by their need to justify their existence and that of their organization as by their role as spokesmen for a particular interest group. This applies equally to the trade union officials representing their members and to the professional managers representing their shareholders – not to mention a whole range of representatives of particular professions, voluntary organizations, local government and the other lobbies – as it does to the government ministers and civil servants with whom they deal. For that reason corporatism can best be regarded as the institutional framework of professional society.

It is only, however, the institutional framework, not the driving force which propels it in the direction of increasing corporate organization nor the spirit which animates it. The driving force is the collective self-interest of professional hierarchies seeking to expand their status and span of control. The animating spirit is the professional social ideal which defends and justifies their collective self-interest in terms of the service performed for society by each professional hierarchy and the principle of social justice which it upholds.

Such a claim to superior social service and exclusive moral rectitude does not prove that professionalism is in fact a superior principle of social organization, any more than similar claims by other social groups. *All* classes, *all* interest groups, *all* social groupings make such claims. What matters in any particular society is which social grouping manages to impose, by persuasion, bribery or brute force, its own principle of organization and social ideal upon the rest. In pre-industrial society it was the landed elite which imposed its own structure of property and ideal of the leisured gentleman upon the rest. In Victorian industrial society it was the entrepreneur, the individual owner-managing capitalist, who imposed his belief in the competitive free market and in the moral superiority of self-help and active labour on both landlord and labourer. In post-industrial corporate society, it is the professional bureaucrat, private and public, who increasingly seeks to impose his principle of social organization – *la carrière ouverte aux talents*, the stable career hierarchy, and management by experts – and his social ideal – a functional society efficiently organized to distribute rewards according to personal merit professionally defined – upon old-fashioned individual capitalist and proletarian worker alike. Just as in industrial society the capitalist saw no necessary function for the landlord, so in post-industrial society the professional bureaucrat, not least in corporate business, sees no necessity for the individual capitalist, who is simply an irritant, a quixotic element, an unpredictable maverick in an otherwise stable system of bureaucratic imperialism. Likewise, the traditional, insecure, wage-earning proletarian, without career expectations, staff status or pension rights, is an evolutionary throwback, to be gradually transformed into a professionalized worker with statutory rights and responsibilities.

If, in the midst of a neo-Ricardian backlash against public bureaucracy, state intervention and welfarism, the professional ideal seems to be temporarily losing ground, that is perhaps because it has already gained so much ground to lose, and the ebbing tide has taken back much less than at first sight appears. Privatization of nationalized industries, for example, has merely transferred control from public to private bureaucrats or, more commonly, relabelled the same managers private instead of public functionaries, no longer responsible to government but to shareholders too scattered and numerous to control them. The welfare state has not been dismantled so much as subjected to a larger measure of selectivity, which only gives more work and power to social administrators. And the much-vaunted attack on public expenditure since 1979 has only led to a larger percentage of GNP flowing though the sluicegates of the state, leading to higher taxation for all but a small percentage of the population.[7]

Why this paradox should occur we must examine in the final chapter. Here it must suffice to say that the professional hierarchy has already imposed itself so firmly on contemporary society that, like the stricken whale, every effort to throw off the harpoon merely serves to make its barbed grip the stronger. Or, rather, the struggle is not about *whether* but about *which* professionalism will triumph, the public, the private or the quasi-private variant, the last being that of the non-profit-making corporations, neither corporate capitalist nor corporate state, such as the universities, the leading charities, and the professional bodies themselves.

But this is to anticipate. In this chapter we shall be concerned with the three dimensions along which corporatism, the institutional vehicle of professional society, has advanced since the inter-war period. First in logic and chronology is the rise of the corporate economy, which has not only made British industry and business the most concentrated in the post-industrial world but has transformed its structure from an individual capitalist to a professional, managerial model. Here we shall be dealing with the 'true' corporation, the original from which the rest have been plagiarized, but we shall take it beyond the usual structural concerns of the business historian to what may be called the professionalization of management and, still more remote from them, the professionalization of the working class.

The second dimension is the rise of the corporate state, not in the formal sense of the institutionalization in Britain of anything approaching the replacement of parliamentary democracy by a structure of corporate representation, but in the sense of the informal involvement of powerful interest groups in government decision making. These include not only the professional representatives of the major employers and trade unions but also those of other interest groups and lobbies spanning the whole breadth of British society. Here we shall be primarily concerned with the special interests of the professional representatives themselves, with their increasingly separate interests from those they represent, and with the paradox that, while they have their *raison d'être* in the corporate relationship, they stand to lose by formalizing that relationship and making it visible and therefore vulnerable to their constituents.

The third dimension, at once concrete and nebulous, may be called the rise of corporate society itself. In its concrete form it is encapsulated in the rise of the welfare state. By this is not meant the Whiggish notion of inevitable progress towards a more caring society but the struggle both to achieve a more efficient functional society and to create a field in which rival professional empires compete for control and domination. In its more nebulous form it can be seen as the effort to impose on Britain the professional ideal of a society based on human capital and personal merit rather than on material property or idealized labour. Here we shall be concerned with the part played by intellectual and welfare professionals in the rise of the welfare state, and with the concept of social citizenship, or what it means to be a member of society under a professional regime.

All three dimensions necessarily overlap and interpenetrate as economy, politics and society necessarily overlap and interpenetrate in every community. All three are increasingly suffused by the professional ideal as it struggles, sometimes consciously, more often unconsciously, to oust and replace both the once dominant ideal of the individual capitalist and its rival ideal of the potentially socialist worker. The irony of the struggle is that the evolution of both capitalism and socialism, in their corporate and statist forms, were paving the way for the triumph of the man at the helm of each, the professional manager and the state or union bureaucrat whose interest would inevitably come to be different from that of the owners of capital, the electors and the sellers of labour power who had placed him in control. To this extent the triumph of the professional man and his ideal was prepared by the very opponents over whom he triumphed.

1 THE CORPORATE ECONOMY

The rise in the scale of organization, especially but by no means exclusively the organization of industry, was one of the central features of the Industrial Revolution.[8] Its most obvious form was the transition from the small domestic workshop to the large factory, but even greater rises in scale took place in transport from the stagecoach or wagon to the national railway network, in banking from the local country bank to the nationwide joint-stock branch banking system, in insurance from the self-dissolving tontine to the giants of industrial life assurance, in trade unionism from the tiny trade club to the national amalgamations, and in the scale of the community itself in which most people lived, from village and tiny town to great city and suburb, metropolis and conurbation. No aspect of life was untouched by it. Church and chapel, school and university, friendly society and social club, retail shop and public house, organized sport and entertainment, all were affected by the drive towards large-scale headquarters and branch, regionally or nationally organized institutions. The rise in scale was a logical increase in size and wealth but it was not the *cause* of the Industrial Revolution. Rather it was the effect of an explosion of collective but increasingly specialized human energy which, in unleashing what Marx called the enormous forces of production slumbering in the lap of social labour,[9] demanded a new and larger framework of institutions to harness and contain them.

(1) Concentration in British industry

When that apparently once-for-all revolution in social organization had taken place, few Victorians could imagine that in a competitive system any further increase in scale was necessary or desirable. John Stuart Mill thought that the contemporary joint-stock company had reached the limit of acceptable size under private enterprise and that any further advance would require the substitution of state management. Only Alfred Marshall could see no limit to the growth of joint-stock organization: under free market competition and increasing returns to scale there was almost 'nothing to prevent the concentration in the hands of a single firm of the whole production of the world'.[10]

Yet the rise in the scale of economic organization in the twentieth century was to leave that of Victorian Britain far behind. In 1880, when joint-stock organization was still in its infancy, the hundred largest firms in Britain probably accounted for less than 10 per cent of national production.[11] In 1909, after the first great wave of industrial mergers which so impressed Alfred Marshall, the hundred largest industrial firms accounted for about 15 per cent of manufacturing output. By 1930 at the end of the second wave the largest hundred firms accounted for 26 per cent. Falling back to 21 per cent in 1948, the hundred largest firms by 1970 after the third great wave of mergers produced no less than 45 per cent of total output.[12]

Some of these firms became gigantic concerns. In 1919 the forty-eight largest companies each had a market value on the stock exchange of over £4 million, eleven of them over £10 million, and the largest, the cotton thread manufacturers, J. and P. Coats, £45 million. By 1930 the top eleven were valued at over £20 million each and the two largest, Unilever and Imperial Tobacco, at over £130 million. That meant that a mere handful of large firms already dominated each major industry. By 1930 five firms in each major industrial group accounted for more than half the production, except in drink (49 per cent) and metal manufacture (46 per cent). In building materials (83 per cent), chemicals (86 per cent), metal goods (87 per cent), shipbuilding (90 per cent), and tobacco (no less than 99.7 per cent) it rose to five-sixths or more.[13] After a pause during the Depression of the 1930s and the Second World War the trend towards industrial concentration was resumed. The share in capital assets (book valuation) of the largest hundred companies increased from 60 per cent in 1957 to 75 per cent in 1969, and (on another measure, market valuation of the equity) from 79 per cent in 1969 to no less than 91 per cent in 1976. Over much the same period the share of total assets held by the ten largest firms in 1969 exceeded 65 per cent in each major industry except non-electrical engineering (32 per cent), and in all but five industries out of fourteen exceeded 75 per cent.[14] By 1985 the top fifty industrial corporations each had a stock market valuation of over £800 million, and of these sixteen were valued at over £2 billion.[15] At the same time Britain came to have the lowest proportion of small manufacturing firms in any advanced country: the 27,000 firms with less than ten employees each in 1963 accounted for only 2 per cent of the workforce.[16] Concentration in private industry could hardly go further without becoming outright monopoly.

Concentration was not of course confined to industry. It was still more marked in banking, where the major London clearing banks were reduced to no more than four by 1968; in insurance, where a mere handful of companies like the Prudential and Guardian Royal Exchange out of the 500 operating in Britain dominated the field; in property and shipping, where giant mergers such as Trafalgar House-Cunard and P. and O.-Bovis exploited the tax advantages of setting off ship depreciation against capital gains on office blocks; and in retail trading where department stores, chain stores and supermarkets with familiar names came to dominate every high street.[17] In coal mining, transport, and communications, energy supplies and public utilities concentration reached its ultimate form of monopoly in the shape of nationalization, a monopoly which the recent privatization of Cable and Wireless, British Telecom, Britoil, and the rest has done nothing to diminish. In single-industry terms the scale of organization could go no further.

Although part of the trend towards fewer and bigger firms was due to the technical economies of scale from larger plants, vertical integration, central purchasing, or national distribution, the overwhelming cause was the amalgamation of firms by purchase and merger. The first large amalgamations began in the late Victorian 'Great Depression' of 1874–96 as defensive measures against the rigours of competition at a time of falling profit margins. Some of these, like United Alkali or the Calico Printers Association, were large, loosely integrated combines of no great profitability. By the 1920s, however, came the day of the huge 'efficiency combines' like Unilever and Imperial Chemical Industries, nursing their reputations for innovation, good employment practices, concern for the consumer, and public responsibility. By the 1960s and 1970s mergers were being midwifed by government, even by a Labour government in the case of the General Electric Company, British Leyland and International Computers Ltd, as the supposedly best strategy for technological innovation and national economic growth, even though the economic arguments and practical results remained in doubt and in some cases were disastrous. Only a small number of giant firms, like Ford, Courtaulds and Rank-Xerox, grew primarily by the classic model of reinvestment and internal expansion, though even they swallowed many rival firms.

The driving force behind the trend of both internal and external growth, it appears, was not technological necessity or competitive economic advantage. It was, rather, something in the structure of the business corporation itself which drove it on to become even bigger, either by ploughing back profits or, more commonly, by swallowing more and more of its competitors whole. That something was no impersonal, abstract feature of the corporate structure, but the very human collective self-interest of the managers in the process of professionalization.

(2) The professionalization of management

The trend towards what was in the early stages very properly called monopoly capitalism began with the ambition of traditional capitalists to dominate their respective industries and eliminate competitors. Business men like W. H. Lever who tried to monopolize the soap trade in 1906 or Sir Alfred Mond (Lord Melchett), founder of ICI, who in 1926 was accused by the press of trying to amalgamate everything in sight, were playing the traditional game of capitalist competition.[18] In the Social Darwinian survival of the fittest the free market was bound to lead

294

to fewer and larger survivors. What the owners did not bargain for was that the vast enterprises they came to preside over would become literally unmanageable without the aid of a new breed of men who specialized in the management of corporations. Far more than important than Mond, Brunner, or Nobel to the chain of mergers, ultimately of 600 companies, which culminated in the creation of ICI was Sir Harry McGowan, the career manager of obscure Glaswegian origin in Nobel's Explosives, who had learned how to midwife large-scale amalgamations by consolidating into one enterprise in 1911 the whole explosives industry of Canada.[19]

As Deputy to Sir Alfred Mond and later Chairmen of ICI, McGowan represented the new professional career manager without substantial capital who rose by sheer ability through the ranks to control giant corporations far beyond the dreams of Victorian entrepreneurs. His like became increasingly familiar in the figures of Sir Josiah Stamp, the economist and civil servant who became chairman of the largest inter-war railway, the London, Midland and Scottish, Sir Paul Chambers, the Inland Revenue official who ended as Chairman of ICI, Lord Stokes, the Leyland mechanic who created British Leyland (now the Rover Group), Lord Kearton, son of a bricklayer who became Chairman of Courtaulds, the British Oil Corporation and the British Enterprise Board, and Lord Armstrong, son of a Salvation Army officer, who rose to be head of the Civil Service and Chairman of the Midland Bank.

More significant than the superstars of career management was the professionalization of management itself. The 'divorce between responsibility and ownership' noted by the Liberal Industrial Inquiry in 1928 and the separation of ownership from control analysed by Berle and Means in America in 1932 did not in itself abolish capitalism or lessen the concentration of wealth in comparatively few hands. As Berle remarked in 1954, 'The capital is there and so is capitalism. The waning factor is the capitalist.'[20] What it did do was to transform the structure of business and increasingly transfer day-to-day control over vast capitals owned by other people to career managers in bureaucratic hierarchies. Although individual capitalists or families continued to own immense wealth – between 1911–13 and 1960 the share of personal wealth held by the top 10 per cent of the adult population declined only from 92 per cent to 83 per cent – the average shareholding in 1928 was only £301, and it soon became unusual for any single family to own a majority of the shares of any large company.[21] The very process of growth by amalgamation militated against individual ownership and control. Multiple mergers obviously diluted family holdings in the ensuing holding company or combine, and although with a fragmented equity a minority of 25 per cent, or even 5 per cent of the shares if skilfully managed, could give ultimate control, this could only be achieved by the owners becoming themselves in effect professional managers of other people's assets. A few chose that path, and there are still Van Den Berghs at the helm of Unilever, Fords in command at Ford, a Pilkington (admittedly related to the main family fourteen generations back) recently retired as chairman of Pilkington's Glass, Sainsburys in control of the Sainsbury chain stores, not to mention the new self-made tycoons of the post-war retailing, property and merchant banking booms at Tesco, Grand Metropolitan, Trafalgar House, Hill Samuel, and Slater Walker. But the great majority of giant corporations are now managed by career managers with very little capital of their own. In 1969 the chairmen of the top hundred British industrial companies owned only 2.5 per cent, and their entire boards of directors only 7.5 per cent, of the equity of their companies.[22]

Furthermore, the largest holdings in the biggest companies were increasingly held not by individuals but by other institutions, notably insurance companies, pension funds and trade unions. In 1982 individuals owned only one-third of all equities quoted on the Stock Exchange. The rest, over £100 billion, were held by institutional investors. The pension funds alone held £40 billion, including those of great nationalized industries such as the Post Office and the National Coal Board, each with over £4 billion. The Prudential Insurance Company held shares worth over £10 billion in 600 companies, including £259 million in GEC, £221 million in ICI, £158 million in RTZ and £125 million in Shell. The men who controlled these vast investments were all salaried career managers, often without a single share of their own: Ronald Artus, son of an aircraft fitter, chief investment manager of the Prudential with £3 million a day to invest; Ralph Quartano, of Sherborne School and Cambridge, chief executive of the Post Office Staff Superannuation Fund; and Hugh Jenkins, Llanelli

Grammar School and no college education, controller of the NCB pension fund. The power of veto such men wield, when they wish to exercise it, over the companies they invest in is final. In 1982 Quartano blocked the Thames Television tycoon Lord Grade's attempt to give a 'golden handshake' worth about £1 million to a retiring executive; in 1978 Jenkins forced Allied Breweries, and by extension all public corporations, to ballot the shareholders before making or accepting a take-over bid; and in 1956 Kenneth Usherwood, an earlier 'man from the Pru', which held 5 per cent of the equity of Birmingham Small Arms which in turn owned 25 per cent of the Daimler car company, fired Sir Bernard Docker, flamboyant Chairman of Daimler and husband of the incorrigibly extravagant Lady Docker of the gold-plated Daimler car.[23] The rise of the institutions, whose funds derive not from capitalist investors but from the insurance premiums and pension contributions of millions of non-shareholders, symbolizes the emancipation of the professional manager from capitalist control.

Once in command of the vehicle of control and expansion, the large corporation, the professional manager had every incentive to expand his empire. Although called into existence as the main prop and support of the capitalist and even more dedicated to making a profit, his ultimate interest was by no means the same. Profits were important not for their own sake but as a test of managerial success and as the means to further expansion of managerial power. The First World War, in which capitalists like Lord Devonport, food retailer turned government food controller, Sir Eric Geddes, railway director turned inspector-general of war transport, and Sir William Weir, engineering employer turned director of Scottish munitions and controller of British aeronautical supplies, were drawn into 'war socialism' for their managerial experience, showed that there were other objectives of production than profit.[24] Efficiency, maximum production and the skilful avoidance of strikes and other labour troubles, all for the sake of winning the war, came first.

In the changed economic conditions of the inter-war period, with increased foreign competition in the 1920s and world depression in the 1930s, even the capitalists lost faith in the doctrine of free enterprise and began to look to cartels, price rings and mergers to put an end to wasteful internecine competition. As early as 1919 John Maynard Keynes wrote of 'an extraordinary weakness on the part of the great capitalist class, which has emerged from the industrial triumphs of the nineteenth century':

> The terror and personal timidity of the individuals of this class is now so great, their confidence in their place in society and in their necessity to the social organism so diminished, that they are the easy victims of intimidation. This was not so in England twenty-five years ago, any more than it is now in the United States. Then the capitalists believed in themselves, in their value to society, in the propriety of their continued existence in the full enjoyment of their riches and the unlimited exercise of their power. Now, ... they allow themselves to be ruined and altogether undone by their own instruments, governments of their own making, and a Press of which they are the proprietors.[25]

The survival of British capitalism and its salvation from socialism came to be seen to depend on the new organizers of large-scale industry, the professional managers. Their watchwords were 'rationalization' and 'scientific management'. Rationalization meant the pursuit of efficiency by the reduction of 'wasteful', 'unfair', 'destructive' or 'ruinous' competition, by mergers and amalgamations, often with government encouragement and support, to buy out and close down 'overcapacity', and the cutting of costs, which often meant in the last resort the cutting of wages.[26] Rationalization has a bad name because of its association with the rationalization of the coal industry which led to the General Strike, of the cotton industry and the closing of scores of cotton mills, and of the shipbuilding industry and the closing of yards like Palmer's at Jarrow, 'the town that was murdered'. But its undoubted successes, particularly in the new mass-produced consumer goods industries of the Midlands and the south-east, were a triumph for the new managerial approach and were responsible for the not inconsiderable creation of new jobs and rising living standards in the inter-war period.

Scientific management, stemming from the Americans F. W. Taylor and F. B. Gilbreth before the First World War, also earned a bad name with the workers for its emphasis on time and motion study and the speed-up of assembly lines, but from the point of view of the new managers it was the symbol of their new professionalism. What expertise could the line manager, as distinct from the specialist accountant, company lawyer or works engineer, claim if not the scientific application of means to ends, the marriage of finance, administration, technology and labour to the efficient production of goods and services? Scientific management:

> provided for some businessmen an ideology to replace the doctrine of competitive free enterprise, whose ethical foundations and claims to be a gospel of human freedom were being undermined by socialism, a rival doctrine which in some respects overlapped the ideology of rationalization.[27]

As Lyndall Urwick, doyen of managerial theory in the inter-war years, put it, rational scientific management 'is intellectually possible; it is in line with our tradition; it is materially profitable; it will save our economic system from disaster.'[28] It represented the substitution of intelligent planning within the large corporation for the vagaries of the external competition of the free market.

It was for that reason, as well as the overwhelming competition of the big corporations, that many private business men, owner-managing capitalists of the traditional sort, deeply suspected the rationalization and scientific management movements. For *The Economist* in 1924 one aim of rationalization was 'the enhancement of profits by the elimination of competition'.[29] An accountant involved in many mergers noted in 1926:

> Men who have been accustomed to personal domination almost amounting to dictatorship in their own businesses do not take kindly to a change of circumstances whereunder they themselves become members of a Board of Directors, and may find themselves subject ... to the control of others.[30]

Sargant Florence, who talked to many of them, recorded in 1930 how they preferred power in their own small works to a share in a large amalgamation, how they relished the game of competition, cherished a *petit bourgeois* attitude to property, and clung to their own little business with a dynastic desire to hand it on to their family.[31] They were, perhaps instinctively, engaged in a battle of ideologies, between the entrepreneurial ideal of the owner-managing capitalist dominant in the Victorian age and the professional ideal of managerial expertise applied regardless of family sentiment or loyalty to twentieth-century mass production.

It was a losing battle, not merely because their ideal was obsolescent but because the very competition which was its main principle and justification had been too successful and was in process of evolving them out.

The battle was long drawn out, however, and even affected the structure of the new enlarged corporation. In most cases down to and beyond the Second World War, unlike most American examples, it took the form of a loose grouping of subsidiary companies under a holding company concerned primarily with financial, especially investment policy. This was a structure that suited the ex-owning family managers of the constituent units, who could enjoy the benefits of scale, increased financial security and reduced competition, while pretending that nothing had changed. It also discouraged the new professional managers from reaching their full potential, since the small holding company headquarters did not have the resources to measure their performance and pull them up to the mark. Apart from a few giant concerns like ICI and Unilever which were forced by the diversity of their constituent parts or their geographical spread to operate from the start with separate divisions, only the American companies operating in Britain, like Ford, General Motors, or IBM, adopted a multi-divisional structure before the Second World War.[32] The unitary holding company tended to operate along functional lines, with specialist managers at central headquarters in finance, production, marketing, industrial relations, and so on, leaving the subsidiaries little autonomy or scope to innovate. The multi-divisional type was not only more efficient, with the divisional managers allowed more opportunity to develop new ideas and products and even to compete against one another, but was also more purely managerial in that the multiple bureaucracies needed to run it finally did away with the individual capitalist altogether, except in a very few cases where an owning family member became assimilated to the ethos of professional management.

Only after the Second World War did the major British industrial corporations adopt the multi-divisional structure, chiefly under American example and advice – no less than twenty-two of the hundred largest companies employed the American consultants McKinsey and Company.[33] In 1950 only eight of the top hundred firms were multi-divisional; by 1970 seventy-two of them had adopted that structure, and all but six had diversified their production to some degree in that direction.[34] They had learned that the American firms operating in Britain were simply more professional: more profitable, more capital-intensive, paying more attention to sales and marketing, more concerned with the academic and technical qualifications of their managers, and planning their operations more professionally:

> First, and perhaps most important, US firms in Britain have access to more *knowledge* and *expertise*. . . . Second, they tend to use such knowledge and expertise as is available . . . more effectively. These two considerations give them the *power* to be more efficient. Third, US subsidiaries would appear to have a more dynamic and professional attitude to management and decision taking. They are usually under considerable pressure from their parent companies which encourage a spirit of competitiveness among their offshoots. This is reflected in their greater *will* to be efficient.[35]

By contrast, British management cherished a cultivated amateurism. The average British director in the late 1960s at the end of the managerial revolution has been described by a management survey as '56 years old, not particularly mobile, most likely educated at a public school and, having only a 50 per cent chance of a university education, most likely graduated from Oxford or Cambridge'. Only 9 per cent of the sample had received any business education other than professional training, mainly in accountancy. Yet they were nevertheless overwhelmingly professional employees rather than owners of the enterprises. Only 15 per cent had family connections with important shareholders, and the great majority owned few or no shares in the companies they managed. Their main reward was in the form of salary, perquisites were few, and stock options, common in America, were almost unknown.[36]

Britain's industrial managers, in brief, had undergone a revolution, but a reluctant one. As compared with the self-confident Americans (before the Japanese undermined *their* confidence), they were defensive about their status and even about their commitment to their profession. They have been accused, along with their predecessors back to the late Victorian age, of being responsible for 'the decline of the industrial spirit' and therefore for much of Britain's economic decline. Martin Wiener has attributed this *trahison des clercs* to the influence of British elite education in pre-industrial aristocratic values at the public schools and Oxford and Cambridge,[37] but we shall see in the next chapter that the values taught there were modern professional rather than traditional aristocratic.

However reluctant, the management revolution was real enough nonetheless. For good or ill, the controllers of twentieth-century business in Britain have ceased for the most part to be individual owner-managing entrepreneurs in the Victorian mould and have become professional managers owning little capital other than the human capital derived from their abilities, education and experience. Their human capital, like that of other professions, gave them material gains in the form of a continuing flow of income, a high degree of security of employment or compensation for dismissal, substantial pension rights, and even some material wealth in the shape of cars, houses and, sometimes, a small but significant share in the corporate equity. Amongst occupational elites, career managers were more successful in amassing personal wealth than any other, except for those defined by mainly inherited properly, the great landowners and the millionaires. The managerial revolution (in the narrow sense of the control of industry) is reflected in the sharp decline in median wealth left at death by the chairmen of the largest 200 companies: in real terms at 1913 prices, from £572,300 in the 1880s and 1890s to £226,000 between the wars and to a meagre £14,800 (£76,400 in current terms) in the 1960s. Yet at the end of the decline their median wealth at death was still nearly three times that of other leading professional men in the same survey, which was only £4,800 in real terms (£26,500 in current terms).[38] In their case human capital acquired a material value which carried beyond the grave.

The professionalization of management had implications for the workers as well as for traditional capitalists. Managerialism as a theory has always been resisted by Marxist intellectuals because they fear that it undermines their interpretation of the exploitive nature of industrial capitalism and the egalitarianism of post-revolutionary society. So it does, but not in quite the way they suppose. It certainly changes the exploiters, from the owners of the means of production to the controllers of the corporate bureaucracies. To the workers, however, there is no particular gain in being exploited by professional managers rather than by old-fashioned capitalists, and indeed there may well be loss. Successful capitalists could often afford the luxury of paternalism, as evidenced by a well attested tradition of benevolence stretching from Samuel Greg and Robert Owen down to the Cadburys and Rowntrees, whereas professional managers were paid to maximize profits by cutting wage costs and overheads. Some professional managers, nevertheless, like some paternalist owners, had a longer-term vision of profitability as it was affected by industrial relations, and believed that loyal, contented workers were more productive and therefore more profitable.

This approach, often associated with the American 'human relations' school of Elton Mayo and his 'Hawthorne experiments' at the Western Electric factory near Chicago in 1927–32, began in Britain before the First World War. As the leading historian of management thought, John Child, has put it, 'By the early twentieth century a few British employers, dismissed as sentimentalists by most of their peers, were challenging the practical and moral bases of laissez-faire.'[39] Benevolent firms like Lever Brothers, Hans Renold, Mather & Platt, and Cadburys pioneered enlightened labour management policies which emphasized high wages, shorter hours, improved communications between management and workers, joint consultation, and employee counselling. Edward Cadbury believed that 'business efficiency and the welfare of the employees are but different sides of the same problem', and, although other paternalist employers often pursued this line in order to outflank the trade unions, he conceded the workers' right to a dual allegiance:

> The test of any scheme of factory organization is the extent to which it creates and fosters the atmosphere and spirit of cooperation and good-will, without in any sense lessening the loyalty of the worker to his own class and its organizations.[40]

The First World War, with its manifold problems of evoking the co-operation of the industrial workers in the war effort, proved him right, and led to the far-reaching schemes of industrial consultation embodied in the Whitley Councils. Although these failed to survive in peacetime in most industries, with the significant exception of the Civil Service, the war had a profound effect on management thought. This was summed up by John Lee, the Director of the London Telegraph and Telephone Centre, in his pioneering book *Management: A Study of Industrial Organization* in 1921. Industrial managers, he argued:

are an expert professional group, and the new science of industrial management is coming to recognize them as that factor in industry which is calling for study and consideration. This evolution of a separate management ... brings experience and special training to bear on the work of management in a way which was never possible to the old-fashioned owner who 'could do what he liked with his own'.

He looked forward to university-based management education in a 'synthesis of the sciences' and in ethics for 'a trained body of administrators, proud of their calling as professional men ..., themselves reasonably paid but not personally benefiting from the profits'.[41] In *The Social Implications of Christianity* he argued for 'a priesthood in industry, just as there is a priesthood in worship', who would encourage worker participation and eschew autocracy but would nevertheless exercise tight control by imposing an 'intelligent subordination'.[42] In this way Lee foreshadowed the professionalization of management and its separation from both capital and labour over the next forty years, down to the founding of the business schools of the 1960s.

Management thought between the wars was dominated by the pursuit of two not always compatible goals, industrial harmony and rationalization. Management spokesmen came to argue that industrial unrest was due to outmoded conflict between capital and labour which could be resolved by the 'third factor in industry', the 'dispassionately free' managers who 'hold the balance and see fair play'. On the other hand, they emphasized the role of scientific management in the rational reorganization of industry, which often meant loss of jobs through labour-saving investment and industrial concentration at a time of high unemployment, and ignored or rejected the role of the trade unions in the productive process, particularly after their defeat in the General Strike.[43] During the 1930s, under the leadership of Lyndall Urwick, much influenced by F. W. Taylor's scientific management, industrial administration became a technical study in which the 'human factor' was merely one aspect of 'a pure theory of organization' applicable equally to 'governments, churches, or armies' as well as to production. At the same time, British management thought came to incorporate the Harvard human relations school of Elton Mayo, Mary Parker Follett and T. N. Whitehead and their belief that 'the contentment of the individual is the greatest single factor in efficient production'.[44]

It would be a mistake to think that most managers avidly read and imbibed such ideas, any more than most Victorian capitalists had read Ricardo, Samuel Smiles or Herbert Spencer. Very few belonged to the various management associations, the Institute of Personnel Management (1946, founded as the Welfare Workers' Association in 1913), the British Institute of Management (1947, founded as the Institute of Industrial Administration in 1920), or the Works Managers' Association (1931).[45] As late as 1948 only about 20,000 managers out of more than 400,000 in Britain belonged to management institutes. The BIM still had only 19,000 members in 1963.[46] But all managers were increasingly forced to pay attention to the detrimental effects of bad industrial relations. In particular, the stresses and demands of the Second World War and the subsequent period of full employment forced on managers a growing realization that autocratic or coercive management was no longer effective and that skilled personnel management was not peripheral but central to production.

Much of this new approach may have been self-interested or manipulative, but that only underlined the need for professionalism in organizing their collective enlightened self-interest. The post-war difficulties of the British economy and the alarming gap between British and American levels of productivity revealed by visiting delegations of managers and trade unionists made British managers more open to American influence and example, and it was at this stage that the ideas and practices of the American business schools began to have an impact in Britain, culminating in the movement for management education in the 1960s.

Management theory, the basis of the new professionalism, did not come into its own in Britain until the founding of the new business schools in the universities and polytechnics of the 1960s. Even then it was looked on with suspicion by many, if not most, practising business men, who regarded management as an art to be learned on the job rather than a science based on intellectual theory. When one of the first management schools, cautiously called the Administrative Staff College, invited an academic sociologist to provide them with a text on 'management and the social sciences', the Principal recorded:

> We needed to overcome in the minds of members attending the College's courses the distrust which many of them felt for the social sciences; this was not always easy to accomplish, especially where managers had behind them a successful record of management in human terms.

Five years later, in 1972, he continued, 'the problem of distrust is markedly less' but 'has not been removed entirely.'[47] Nevertheless, the creation of the London and Manchester Business Schools as full university institutions with special government funding marked the arrival of management as a distinct profession with its own body of expert knowledge and formal means of acquiring it.

By that time the change was so familiar that it had even come to be recognized by the Labour Party. While only the revisionists agreed with Anthony Crosland that 'Britain had, in all essentials, ceased to be a capitalist country', the party as a whole recognized, in *Industry and Society*, part of Hugh Gaitskell's attempt to modernize the party's attitude to the mixed economy in 1957, that a new class of managers had replaced 'power-hungry' capitalists:

> as companies grow larger and their affairs more complex, management becomes increasingly important, increasingly hierarchical, increasingly specialist, and increasingly professional. More and more it assumes a life of its own. In the large companies, it is the managers who now undertake the functions once performed by capitalist owners.[48]

However much management's pretensions to intellectual autonomy were doubted by sceptics, its claim to professional status was founded, no less than that of other professions, on the creation of human capital, and on that test it was supremely successful. The professionalization of management and the bureaucratization of industry were the necessary concomitant of the corporate economy.

(3) The professionalization of the working class

More relevant than management theory to the actual experience of workers under the new system was the practice of managers striving to get more work and profit out of them. On the one hand, most British managers looked on trade unions with distaste as at best a necessary evil. On the other, in so far as they themselves were employees who were justified by their work rather than their ownership of the means of production, they were open to the moral pressure of their own professional ideal, that other employees too who loyally served the corporate purpose were deserving, not indeed of equal treatment but of rewards and privileges graduated according to their worth. Such rewards and privileges came to include holidays with pay, pension rights, paid sick leave, and security of earnings and employment.

After the managers themselves, such rewards and privileges were accorded first, naturally enough, to the 'staff', the office workers with whom the managers worked most closely and on whom they depended for the carrying out of their primary functions. As early as 1916 *The Clerk*, the organ of the National Union of Clerical Workers, could claim:

It should be remembered that, although by reason of their unorganized state, clerks suffer many economic disabilities, yet they have a great many economic advantages not enjoyed by manual workers. Among them may be cited permanency of employment, periodical increases of salary, payment of salary during sickness and holidays, comparatively reasonable hours of work, and in certain sections superannuation. These advantages, chiefly matters of custom and usage, constitute a powerful common interest among clerks, and should be an equally strong reason for protective organization.[49]

'Custom and usage' in this early plea for quasi-professionalization underlines the fact that the largely unorganized clerks had not gained their advantages by trade union pressure but by the enlightened self-interest of their employers, anxious to bind these managerial auxiliaries to willing service. Though some had achieved them at the whim of individual capitalists, they had been institutionalized first in the larger companies of the late Victorian age and early twentieth century, notably the railway companies, banks, insurance houses, and such consciously paternalist industrial companies as Courtaulds, Brunner Mond, and Pilkingtons, and the large-scale public employments like the Civil

Service, the Post Office and the co-operative societies.[50] In the new enlarged corporations, public and private, bureaucratic rules easily turned concessions into permanent rights, especially for the permanent staff of white-collar workers.

For long the gulf between white-collar and manual workers remained unbridgeable, however, and it was with the greatest reluctance that, except for a handful of *ex gratia* concessions of paid holidays, paid sick leave or tiny pensions to particularly loyal and long-serving workers on an individual basis, employers extended such privileges to ordinary wage earners. Nor were such gains demanded by the trade unions, who long showed a marked lack of interest in fringe benefits, preferring to concentrate their efforts almost exclusively on improving wages and hours of work. Thus most improvements in fringe benefits for manual workers until well after the Second World War were concessions by management, usually designed to improve workers' morale and productivity, especially in periods of labour shortage.

Before the First World War holidays with pay were rare for manual workers, but between the wars they became the norm. In 1920 the Ministry of Labour reported that paid holidays were enjoyed by about 2 million workers. During the sittings of the Amulree Committee on Holidays with Pay in 1938 they spread to nearly 8 million, 42 per cent of those earning less than £250 per annum, two-thirds of whom were manual, shop and domestic workers; and the numbers increased to over 11 million after the Holidays with Pay Act, 1938.[51] After the Second World War two weeks' paid holiday became standard for most full-time workers until the early 1970s, when Britain's impending entry into the Common Market led to a further round of increases, to three or four weeks in most cases.[52] More significant was the increasing demand by manual workers, often ahead of their unions, for 'single status', equality with the non-manual workers not only in the amount of time off but in all other conditions of work.

A similar but later pattern was followed with regard to occupational pensions, sick pay, and security of earnings and tenure. Pension schemes for non-manual workers were pioneered by the Civil Service in 1834, by the local police forces as they came into existence in the mid-nineteenth century, the larger railway companies in the 1870s, local government from 1895, and by the more paternalist private companies like Courtaulds and Pilkingtons, often on an *ex gratia* basis, in the last years of the century, but they were almost unknown for manual workers. For them the main expansion, led by the newly nationalized industries and larger private corporations, came after the Second World War. By the late 1950s nearly 9 million workers, over a third of the workforce and more than half of them manual, belonged to occupational pension schemes. By 1975 the total had risen to 11.5 million, about half the workforce, two-thirds of them in the private sector, and nearly half of them, 5.2 million, manual workers. Most of the latter were in the public sector and those industries like chemicals, transport and communications dominated by giant corporations.[53] The manual trade unions continued to prefer adequate state pensions to occupational ones, which they suspected as devices of management control, but their own members began to press for more equality with the non-manuals and for company pensions as a normal right to be negotiated.[54] It would appear therefore that until recently, mainly since the non-manual unions led by imaginative officials like Clive Jenkins became influential in the TUC, occupational pensions evolved more as a management strategy for retaining employee loyalty than under pressure from the trade unions.

Contributory sick pay schemes, in which the workers paid most of the cost through deductions from their wages, were pioneered in the eighteenth century by benevolent employers like Ambrose Crowley in coalmining, Arkwright & Strutt in cotton, Boulton & Watt in engineering, and John Christian Curwen the Cumberland land and coal owner, who unsuccessfully introduced a national insurance scheme, based on the practice at his Workington mines, in Parliament in 1816.[55] Most workers who could afford to preferred to pioneer their own friendly societies, which became much the largest working-class institutions of the nineteenth century and which formed the model for Lloyd George's national health insurance in 1911. Paid sick leave as a right, not based on contributions, came first for non-manual workers and was only recently extended to manual workers. According to the Ministry of Labour in 1964, industry-wide schemes existed in only three small industries and none of the larger ones before the Second World War. During that war eleven more such schemes were introduced and between 1947 and 1963 a further twenty-three, by which time nearly a million workers were covered by them, in addition to more local and non-manual arrangements which brought the total up to 57 per cent of the male labour force. By 1970 three-quarters of adult male and two-thirds of women workers were so covered, including 90 per cent of non-manuals, 65 per cent of male manuals and 48 per cent of women manual workers.[56] The trade unions played little part in this development, at least until recently, and once again it seems to have been motivated primarily by the managerial desire for employee loyalty during the post-war period of full employment.

The sharpest distinction between manual and white-collar workers in Britain has always been, and still remains, their differential security of earnings and employment. Managers and other professional people, and indeed most office workers, enjoy a career, that is, a planned course of employment in which income is not only secure but rises by annual increments, formal or customary, and tenure is protected by long periods of notice and/or compensation for redundancy. Most manual workers, by contrast, have traditionally been paid hourly or weekly wages, fixed according to 'the rate for the job', and have been dismissable at a week's notice or sometimes less. Insecurity, the ever-present threat of unemployment and cessation of earnings, has been the habitual lot of the manual worker. This accounts more profoundly than lower income or inferior working conditions for the collective psychology of the British working class, their constant fear of change, suspicion of management, restrictive practices, and opposition to any kind of labour-saving innovation. Unlike America, where there was nearly always the possibility of moving on to other jobs or opportunities, and unlike Japan, where the large corporations which dominate the economy provide life-long employment and rising pay scales even for manual workers, Britain has never solved the problem of insecurity of earnings and employment for the working class. This may indeed be the most important cause of its economic decline and industrial malaise.

Nevertheless, from an early date the demands of industrial efficiency made it impracticable to dismiss all the workers whenever orders fell of and there was always a need to preserve a core of skilled men, along with the office staff, against a recovery of trade. There was also the problem of piece work, introduced for the benefit of managerial control and productivity, but requiring incentives to retain the workers during slack times by guaranteeing a minimum wage. Attempts to deal with such problems go back to the Industrial Revolution and the depression after the Napoleonic Wars, but apart from a few redundancy payment schemes in paternalist firms like Cadburys and Pilkingtons between the wars, little formal provision was made for guaranteed earnings or compensation for dismissal until the Second World War. The Essential Works Order, 1941 guaranteed war workers a 'normal' week's earnings to discourage absenteeism and high labour turnover. After the war the guaranteed week was extended by the mid-1950s to cover the engineering industry, transport and communications, agriculture and forestry, mining and quarrying, pottery, chemicals, food and drink, catering, distribution, and public administration. The guaranteed annual wage, however, which became widespread in the United States under union pressure, never made much headway in Britain, except for one or two American subsidiaries like Ford or Thomas Hedley, but greater security of earnings, or at least of a percentage of basic rates, was enshrined in the Conservative Party's Code of Industrial Relations Practice of 1971 and endorsed by the Labour government in 1974.[57]

The British approach to security of employment has not been through negotiation of annual guaranteed wages but through compensation for redundancy. Compensation for loss of office (the 'golden handshake') has long been normal practice in the case of directors and other high managerial staff, which underlines the concept of human capital invested in the corporation by the managers. Office workers, too, have long been protected by long periods of notice or payment in lieu. For manual workers, however, despite isolated examples at Kenrick's hardware in 1891 or the resettlement scheme in flour milling in 1931, redundancy pay was almost unheard of before the Second World War.[58] Redundancy only became a problem with the full employment of the post-war period, when efforts to reduce overmanning in old industries and switch labour to new ones led to schemes in mining, gas, railways, engineering, vehicle manufacture, chemicals, textiles, and shipbuilding to pay workers to go elsewhere. By 1962 over 5 million workers were covered by redundancy agreements.[59] The trade unions resisted redundancy on principle, so that severance pay was a managerial device for overcoming

311

worker resistance to productive efficiency. This was backed up by the Labour government between 1964 and 1970 which, having set out to encourage employers to 'shake out' labour by such devices as the selective employment tax, passed the Redundancy Payments Act, 1965 which enshrined the principle of a property right in the job. This right, together with compensation for unfair dismissal, was reinforced by the Conservative and Labour Industrial Relations Acts of 1971 and 1974, and by the Labour and Conservative consolidating Employment Protection Acts of 1978 and 1980. Although the amount of compensation was small, one week's pay after two years for each year of service (two weeks' pay for each year over fifteen), the principle of human capital and compensation for its loss was extended from the managerial to the working class. The cause was not pressure from below but the pursuit of managerial efficiency: it was 'part of an overall manpower policy aimed at securing a greater acceptance by the workers of the need for economic and technological change'.[60]

The direction of all these trends, in holidays with pay, occupational pension rights, paid sick leave, and security of earnings and employment, was towards 'single status' for manual and non-manual workers.[61] Equality of fringe benefits did not guarantee equality of status, and the non-manual unions fought for their customary differentials in these as in hours and pay or at least for compensation for their loss.[62] Nevertheless, the trend went beyond fringe benefits to the treatment of workers on the job, in such matters as hours of work and 'clocking on', canteen and toilet facilities, method of payment (by monthly cheque rather than weekly pay packet), and so on. An investigation by the Industrial Society in 1966 showed that 180 firms had a policy of progressively equalizing the terms and conditions of employment of manual and non-manual workers. Two surveys by the British Institute of Management in the 1970s showed that the policy was being put into practice by more and more firms.[63] To some extent this was due to the belated demand of manual workers, often ahead of their unions, for an end to class divisions at work, an aspect of 'embourgeoisement', the ambition of some workers for middle-class status. But the conclusion of the most thorough study of the subject is that 'the introduction of staff grade or single status schemes is an interesting example of change in manual workers' status initiated from above', based on the managerial belief that equal treatment was not merely just but also the best policy for increasing worker co-operation and productivity.[64]

Indeed, the whole movement towards the assimilation of both kinds of worker to a common status can be regarded as a spin-off from the professionalization of management. It is part of the philosophy of modern management that, as the 1971 Code of Industrial Relations Practice expressed it:

> Differences in the conditions of employment and status of different categories of employee and in the facilities available to them should be based on the requirements of the job. The aim should be progressively to reduce, and ultimately to remove, differences which are not so based.[65]

The Industrial Society in 1966 saw it as a radical advance from an earlier philosophy. Traditional distinctions, it said:

> are frequently illogical and unsupportable by any evidence. Too often they are relics of an outworn social and industrial system. Their removal would do much to remove the petty disagreements and resentments that bedevil industry and would help strengthen the responsibility, loyalty and unity of purpose in industrial undertakings of all sizes.

Whether such sentiments will be powerful enough to overcome the most important remaining distinction between 'staff' and 'shopfloor' occupations, Alan Fox's division between 'high-trust, high-discretion' and 'low-trust, low-discretion' jobs, remains to be seen.[66] Pessimists argue that the trend is in the other direction, towards reducing discretion and increasing managerial control amongst routine non-manual workers and reducing them to the same low-trust, discretionless situation as most manual workers. But fringe benefits have become both a customary expectation for most workers and a useful instrument of managerial policy, so that their rapid demise would seem to be unlikely even under the current swing towards greater managerial authority.

In the virtual absence until recently of trade union interest, 'most types of fringe benefits seem to have spread from causes other than collective bargaining or union efforts.'[67] Amongst those causes was the desire by the larger and more successful firms, especially in conditions of full employment, to attract and retain better workers while not appearing to break tacit understandings on wage competition, their wish for the same reason to enhance their reputation as 'good employers', their belief that such benefits would facilitate 'a change in manual worker attitudes and make them a valuable asset to the company', and 'possibly even a reduction in industrial strife'.[68] Whatever the ulterior motivation, there can be little doubt that the underlying philosophy is based on the needs of professional management and the belief that an extension of managerial values to the manual workers will facilitate the work of management and increase the efficiency and profitability of industry. To that extent managerial self-interest is the main factor in the professionalization of manual work.

The professionalization of the working class as a whole must be set in a wider context. In so far as most manual workers in Britain, despite the efforts of the larger corporations, have not yet achieved professional status in the sense of a career with security of tenure, rising scales of pay, and the customary white-collar fringe benefits, they have increasingly looked to the state to provide them with the basic security that the professional middle class take for granted. If, as Engels and later Marxists have argued, the failure of the proletariat to pursue social revolution is to be explained by their emulation of bourgeois values, it is manifestly not the traditional capitalist bourgeoisie whom they have emulated, with their insecure and fluctuating profits, but the career-oriented, employed, professional middle class, with their security of income, control of their own work schedules, and occupational pensions. From one point of view the welfare state, however inadequate to the task, is an attempt to provide for the working class some of the same conditions of work and life that the professional middle class have achieved for themselves. That aspect of the professionalization of the working class, however, takes us beyond the corporate economy to the rise of the corporate society, and will be dealt with in Section 3 of this chapter.

Meanwhile, the professionalization of industry, both managers and workers, was the main, if unintended, consequence of the corporate economy, and in turn it had major implications for corporatism itself, in the triangular relationship between employers, trade unions and the state. Though the corporate state is much wider than that narrow triangle, it cannot be gainsaid that without the involvement of the professional managers and employers' representatives, the professional trade union officials, and the professional politicians and civil servants, it surely could not exist.

2 THE CORPORATE STATE

Large-scale enterprise in industry and commerce, in the trade unions and in most other institutions of twentieth-century Britain was more than matched by the rise in the scale of government. Government expenditure as a proportion of Gross National Product rose from 12.7 per cent in 1910 to 26.1 per cent in 1930, to 39 per cent in 1950, and to 49.3 per cent in 1974. Including transfer payments such as social security and the capital investments of the nationalized industries, it increased from about 45 per cent in 1950 to no less than 60 per cent by 1975.[69] A large part of this expenditure, of course, consisted of transfer payments in the form of national insurance benefits, old age pensions, and the increasing interest on the National Debt, but even allowing for these the role of the state in the direct production of goods and services had enormously increased. By 1961 the nationalized industries alone employed nearly one in ten of the labour force. Altogether, government employment rose from 6.9 per cent of the total workforce in 1931 to 24.9 per cent in 1950 and, after a slight decline to 23.5 per cent in 1961, to 26.2 per cent in 1973.[70]

At the same time, in order to pay for this expansion, there was a matching increase in taxation to levels inconceivable to the Victorians. It was not a uniform rise but took place in sudden steps, during the two world wars and their preceding rearmament phases. The standard rate of income tax (only a partial measure of taxability) rose from less than 1 shilling in the £ (5 per cent) in 1901 and 1s.2d. (6 per cent) in 1910 after the 'People's Budget' to 6s. (30 per cent) in 1919. After falling back between the wars, but only to 4s. (20 per cent) in 1926–30, it rose during the 1930s rearmament to 5s.6d. (27.5 per cent) and then during the Second World War to 10s. (50 per cent). From 1909 onwards 'supertax' on higher incomes also increased, from 6d. in the £ to 9s.6d. at the end of the Second World War, making a top rate of 19s.6d. (97.5 per cent). The standard rate fell back by the 1970s to 33 pence in the new decimal £, with a top rate on high incomes of 83 per cent.[71] Since 1979 the standard rate has fallen still further, to 27 per cent, and the marginal rates for high earned and unearned incomes to 60 per cent and 75 per cent, but the decline has been more than counterbalanced by increases in value added tax and social security contributions.[72] More to the point for most people, the proportion of the active population paying income tax at all – very few wage earners paid income tax until the Second World War – has risen from about one in nine (11 per cent) in 1904 to over 90 per cent during and after the Second World War.[73]

Whether or not this rise in the state's direct provision of goods and services and redistribution of income through taxation and social security was an inevitable accompaniment of post-industrial welfarism or the fortuitous result of a particular conjunction of political and social forces – and the parallel rise of state expenditure in other advanced countries suggests that it is the former – the effect has been to expand the scale of government and the involvement of the state in every aspect of the national life. Not only has the state come to provide the incomes of a large and increasing section of the population, from the government bureaucracy and the workforce of the nationalized industries to the changing beneficiaries of the welfare state, but it has become increasingly involved in guiding and subsidizing private industry and in controlling through fiscal and monetary devices the whole economic system. However reluctantly, governments of every political hue have been drawn into an intimate relationship with business and other institutions of social and economic life far beyond the classic concerns of the nineteenth-century ideal of the minimal state. Above all, they have been unable to ignore the conflicts between increasingly powerful groups in society whose threats of non-co-operation can in a complex, interdependent system bring the economy to a halt. The most powerful of these groups were, of course, the great corporations which came to employ a majority of the workforce and the institutions representing most of that corporate labour, the trade unions.

(1) Informal corporatism

The expansionist twentieth-century state, as it impinged upon wider and wider areas of social and economic life, found itself having to treat with a widening range of organized groups, like the professional bodies representing the medical doctors, the social workers and the teachers, and the voluntary associations representing philanthropic activities of every kind, from the protection of consumers to the protection of the environment. From the beginning, however, the core concern of the state was inevitably with the groups at the centre of the economy, the industrial corporations and the trade unions. The triangular relationship which developed between the government, the employers and the trade unions so came to dominate the thinking of those concerned about the way modern society was going that the term corporatism came to mean that relationship alone. As the inheritors of the intense class conflict between capital and labour which, indeed, precipitated the government's involvement in the 'corporate triangle', the corporate business men and the trade union leaders were bound to loom large in both the practice and the theory of corporatism, and they will do so here.

The corporate state, however, while embracing this triangular relationship, is a much wider concept. As a leading American student of British political institutions has expressed it, the producers' organizations are but a part of 'a vast, untidy system of functional representation that has grown up alongside the older system of parliamentary representation'.[74] Where the state controls so large a proportion of society's resources and the environment in which they are deployed, self-interest impels almost every group to organize collectively to lobby the state for a larger share of what it has to hand out. The late Richard Titmuss's complaint about 'the growth of a "Pressure Group State" generated by more massive concentrations of interlocking economic, managerial and self-regarding professional power' was provoked more by the welfare professions, the doctors who wanted bigger capitation fees for health service patients, the teachers who wanted higher salaries and fewer responsibilities outside the classroom, and the social workers who wanted *carte blanche* to deal with *their* 'clients', than by the industrial producers.[75] Representatives of consumers of social welfare like the National Federation of Old Age Pensioners Associations, the Claimants' Union, Shelter, the Child Poverty Action Group, and the organizations of the unemployed, must also organize to make their demands heard. All interest groups in a society in which the state pays so many pipers must compete to have their tunes noticed and rewarded.

The interest groups, nevertheless, with the strongest and most continuous need to influence the managerial state are the corporate employers and the large trade unions. The state, too, needs to influence them, since failure to obtain the co-operation of management and/or labour can lead to social and economic breakdown or even to military defeat. This had become obvious before the First World War, when prime minister Asquith and the ubiquitous Lloyd George had felt impelled to intervene personally in 1911 and 1912 to defuse national coal and railway strikes at a time of increasing international tension. The ensuing war had forced the state to take both sides of industry into partnership, by no means an always equal or harmonious partnership, as state managers of war industry on one side and as procurers of labour co-operation on the other. Wartime collaboration did not survive the post-war renewal of class conflict, and Lloyd George's attempt to introduce a formal corporatism in the shape of the National Industrial Conference of 1919 was a failure. The ensuing crisis of class society culminated in the General Strike of 1926.

The General Strike played a key, if paradoxical, role in the rise of the corporate state. The origins of the triangular relationship between government, unions and employers lay in the efforts to construct a *modus vivendi* out of the ruinous industrial relations left behind by the strike. Ignoring their Bourbon extremists, moderate men on both sides of industry and in government, like Walter Citrine and Milne-Bailey of the TUC, Lord Weir of the National Confederation of Employers' Organizations, and Steel-Maitland, Conservative minister of labour, realized that a peaceful industrial future required some sort of *entente* between the combatants about the limits beyond which conflict should not be pushed. There was some attempt to institutionalize this *entente* in the Mond-Turner talks between representatives of the TUC and the NCEO in 1928, but these foundered on the militant opposition of class warriors like A. J. Cook of the Mining Federation of Great Britain and Allan Smith of the Engineering Employers' Federation. Instead, the NCEO, the Federation of British Industries and the TUC began informal meetings in 1929 which grew into a permanent joint sub-committee to discuss common interests, including industrial legislation, unemployment and national economic policy. Through this machinery they gave joint evidence to the Macmillan Committee on Trade and Industry in 1930, to the Imperial Conference in 1931, and to the Imperial Economic Conference at Ottawa in 1932.[76]

In the process of collaboration the tripartite representatives learned from one another the central problem of a corporatist structure, the fear and suspicion on the part of their constituents that they would become 'incorporated' in the system and sell them out. There was a growing gap between the increasingly professional officials of the employers' associations and trade unions and their constituent firms and worker members, still wider between the 'peak organizations', the TUC, FBI and NCEO, and their respective affiliates. This gulf was what continually undermined any high-level institutionalization of corporate relations, which worked best when the contacts were informal, low-key and addressed to the solution of immediate practical problems.

What Keith Middlemas has called the 'corporate bias' of British industrial politics is in effect a description of the informal corporatism which grew out of the need of professional representatives – including professional politicians and civil servants – to cover their flanks against the barbs of hostile constituents. Their predicament was a delicate if familiar one. Employed to negotiate with one another and increasingly skilled in that art, they came to understand one another too well and to share a common interest in finding peaceful solutions to potentially disruptive problems. Yet their professional interest did not lie in a fully institutionalized corporate structure, which would have taken the mystery out of their art and exposed them even more patently to the charge of conspiring with the other two sides of the triangle. To the contrary, what Walter Citrine, General Secretary of the TUC, called 'a friendly intimacy and a confident relationship without sacrifice of principles by any of the parties or any interference with the autonomy of the respective constituents'[77] was precisely the formula suited to their professional interests. To their purist critics, the militant unionists, the unabashed free marketeers, and the more partisan politicians on either side, even this degree of intimacy equalled betrayal. In their own terms the critics were right: the professional negotiators did have a separate interest. It was not that they were in some way wiser or more far-sighted than their opponents, only that their objectives were different. Class war was less likely to sustain their position and perpetuate their status and rewards than the quiet pursuit of accommodation. The particular form that corporatism took in Britain owed more to the professional self-interest of its protagonists than to any theory of corporatism.

Corporatist theory there was in plenty between the wars, but it had little influence on developing practice. Most of the theorists were convinced that parliamentary democracy had somehow failed to understand or represent the economic forces in actual or potential conflict in society and that some alternative institution was needed to represent those economic interests alongside or instead of Parliament. They were mainly divided between those who were concerned to save industry from democracy and those who wished to make it more democratic. The first group, the authoritarian Tories, had begun by admiring Mussolini, though they were soon disillusioned by Mosley and Hitler, whose authoritarianism left little room for any corporation other than the state. Their aim was to solve industry's problems on managerial terms, by an appeal for co-operation between management and labour on the basis of a new moral order, national unity and voluntary self-discipline. They included Lord Melchett of ICI, better known as Sir Alfred Mond of the Mond-Turner talks, Sir Basil Blackett, Governor of the Bank of England, Sir Arthur Salter, archetype of financial civil servants, the Tory imperialists Leo Amery, Hugh Sellon and Lord Eustace Percy, and Roy Glenday, economic adviser to the FBI.[78] In 1934 Melchett introduced a bill in the House of Lords, drafted by the new research organization Political and Economic Planning and backed by his new Industrial Reorganization League, to permit industries to reorganize themselves for more efficient production, but it was blocked by the FBI's fear of formal corporatism.[79] Right-wing corporatists looked back to a mythical traditional England free from class conflict and aimed to embrace labour in a paternalist framework which would make such conflict well-nigh impossible. If they had any influence it was through some of their number, like Melchett and Glenday, engaging in the informal dialogue with the trade unions which was emerging anyway.

The second group were a handful of Tory democrats valiantly striving to keep alive the natural alliance of patricians and people so successfully preached by Disraeli. In 1927 a quartet of Conservative MPs from depressed northern constituencies connected with the *Weekend Review*, Harold Macmillan, Robert Boothby, Oliver Stanley and John Loder, published a corporatist symposium, *Industry and the State,* which questioned the free market's ability to correct its own errors and imbalances. During the ensuing decade they put forward schemes for self-governing industries each guided by a Planning Council, the whole economy guided by a National Planning Commission or even an Industrial Parliament, though without executive powers.[80] Although the group had some success in softening the hard-faced image of Conservatism in the 1930s, its major influence lay in the future when these young turks came of age, and it came to full fruition only in Macmillan's national Economic Development Council in 1961.

In *The Next Five Years* (1935) Macmillan was joined by a third group, not of Tories but of moderate socialists who also looked for a less class-ridden and more harmonious society, though on a rather different basis. These men, including the MacDonaldite renegades from the Labour Party Clifford Allen and Allen Young, who became Macmillan's secretary, drew their inspiration from a deep if eccentric spring, G. D. H. Cole's guild socialism.[81] But mainstream Labour passed by on the other side. Like the FBI and the NCEO, the TUC toyed in the early 1930s with the idea of a National Industrial Council, but backed down under the attacks of Harold Laski and the Labour Party National Executive who preferred the informal corporatism which rearmament evoked from a government desperately in need of the co-operation of the trade unions.[82] As the Chairman of the Conservative Party told a recalcitrant right-winger in 1938:

> It may seem strange to you, with your right-wing views, that we have to tolerate such a position that we cannot defend the nation against the will of the trade unions, but there it is. It is part of the price that we have to pay for this alleged democracy.[83]

Once again it was the dual self-interest of the corporate representatives, on the one side their need for willing co-operation and on the other for an 'arms-length' approach to it, that made informal corporatism the obvious response to their ambivalent situation.

(2) The triple entente at war

The Second World War, much more than the first, was a triumph for the triple entente between government, employers and workers, at least after the politically unacceptable and militarily incompetent Chamberlain had been ditched as the price of Labour and TUC co-operation. This was partly due to the unity of the country against the fear of Nazi invasion, more to the need for Labour's involvement in the Churchill Coalition to ensure the co-operation of the working class, most of all to the lessons of the First World War and the informal corporatism of the 1930s. Ernest Bevin, who as Coalition minister of labour made himself the apex of the triangle, persuaded the trade unions at a delegate meeting in May 1940:

> virtually to place yourselves at the disposal of the state. We are Socialists and this is the test of our Socialism.... If our movement and our class rise with all our energy now and save the people of this country from disaster, the country will always turn with confidence to the people who saved them.[84]

Since labour rather than capital was the scarce resource of wartime production, Bevin was able to set up a new tripartite Production Council and impose on the War Cabinet, the Treasury, and the supply and service departments his demands for his own ministry's control of conscription and direction of labour, for a 100 per cent excess profits tax, higher wages for low-paid workers in agriculture and the railways, and a host of industrial relations improvements, including the appointment in war industries of medical, welfare and personnel staffs.[85] Though he could not, any more than other corporate operators, always deliver the full co-operation of his constituents, the war workers, he was able to extend on more equal terms the tacit social contract that had been emerging before the war. Speaking for the War Cabinet, he told the tripartite National Joint Council, representing the government, the TUC and the British Employers Confederation (as the NCEO had now become):

> We came to the conclusion that, with the goodwill of the TUC and the unions, and the Employers' Federation, a little less democracy and a little more trust, in these difficulties we could maintain to a very large extent the peace-time arrangements, merely adjusting them to these extraordinary circumstances.[86]

As an earnest of that trust, the National Joint Council was replaced by a seven-a-side Joint Consultative Council meeting twice-monthly under Bevin's chairmanship, which became the main instrument of government industrial policy. It successfully opposed a Treasury proposal for a wage freeze, and upheld collective bargaining, banned strikes and lock-outs, negotiated dilution of skilled labour and, with a combination of food subsidies, rationing, price controls and moderate wage increases, kept the cost of living down and real wages gently rising throughout the war.[87] Compared with the industrial unrest of the First World War, the Second was, except for a small amount of militancy in the coal mines, a time of industrial peace. Continuous co-operation between both sides of industry and the government was ensured through the formal corporate institutions, both at the top and in the revived Whitley Councils for individual industries covering over 15 million workers. As a leading historian of trade unionism expressed it, 'the records of the [TUC] General Council begin to read like the records of some special government department, responsible for co-ordinating policy in the social and industrial spheres,' and, Middlemas comments, that was equally valid for the British Employers' Confederation.[88]

On the employers' side, leading spokesmen like Sir Cecil Weir of the BEC began to accept the principles of collective bargaining and joint consultation, and even to acquiesce in the inevitability of nationalization of some industries:

> Public ownership was not of itself the bogey which it had been. We had to ask whether a particular enterprise would work better under public or private ownership and it was also clear that there were cases where the former could not be avoided.

The only, significantly professional, condition was that 'the control, administration and management should not be bureaucratic, and should be recruited from the right sources, under terms of remuneration which would attract the best men'.[89] The new managerial elite had arrived, and were prepared to abandon their capitalist masters provided only that their own power, status and rewards were to be safeguarded.

Yet no more than the trade union leaders could the managerial spokesmen deliver their constituents' consent to repudiate conflict when the 'extraordinary circumstances' of the war came to an end.

Even before victory ended the desperate need for collaboration, the employers and the trade unions began to prepare for a post-war world in which, despite the euphoria of Reconstruction, they expected a recrudescence of depression, unemployment, low profits and a consequent struggle over diminishing returns. The reluctance of Churchill and the Conservatives to commit themselves whole-heartedly either to the Beveridge Report or to Keynesian full employment determined the rank and file of the Labour Party and the TUC to force their leaders to abandon the Coalition government as soon as the war in Europe ended. The return to party politics and the landslide Labour victory marked the limits of wartime corporatism, but they by no means spelled its end. On the contrary, it was to be the post-war evolution of party politics and its paradoxical effect on democracy that were to make the corporate state all the more necessary and inevitable.

(3) The decline of democracy

The Second World War was fought by the Western powers to save parliamentary democracy from plebiscitary dictatorship. Yet in Britain there has since the war been a decline in the power of Parliament over the executive. Politics has become (despite the rise of the Alliance in the 1980s) largely a contest between two major parties whose members constitute small and shrinking minorities of the electorate, controlled by even smaller oligarchies of activists. The aim of the parties is to obtain a 'mandate' from the electorate to enable a tiny group of professional politicians to carry out a set of policies for up to five years with little or no further reference to the people or even, except in the last resort, to the people's representatives in Parliament. The party caucuses completely control voting in the House of Commons so that, through its party majority, the government controls Parliament rather than Parliament the government. This amounts to a system of plebiscitary democracy in which the people make a very occasional choice between two groups of leaders, one of which then imposes its will on the other without hindrance from a complacent majority in the legislature. When, as has been the case in every election since the war, the governing party attracts the votes of a minority of the electors and even of those actually voting, and the combined share of the electorate voting for the two major parties has fallen from 77 per cent in 1951 to 55 per cent in 1974 and 61 per cent in 1979,[90] the result can hardly be said to be democracy at all.

Not surprisingly, the decline of parliamentary influence over governmental decision making has been accompanied by a decline in the quality of the MPs. In contrast to the Victorian age or even the inter-war period, few leading figures in other walks of life have been attracted to a parliamentary career (except for those who crown a successful non-political career with a seat, since 1958 normally a life peerage, in the House of Lords). In particular, leading business men and trade unionists, and indeed leading professional people of all kinds, have increasingly shunned party politics, with the result that the House of Commons no longer directly represents the great functional interests of the country, least of all the two sides of industry. In contrast to the Baldwins and Bevins of the inter-war parliaments, the large industrial corporations and trade unions have preferred to sponsor second rankers as candidates, who increasingly become professional politicians dedicated to a full-time career in politics rather than in business or the trade unions. The last active major business man in the Cabinet (aside from employers' association officials like John Davies of the Confederation of British Industry, secretary of trade and industry in the Heath government of the early 1970s) was Lord Mills, minister of fuel and power in 1957–59, and the last major trade union leader Frank Cousins, minister of technology in 1965–66. Both had to be provided with *ad hoc* seats, Mills in the Lords and Cousins at a specially created parliamentary by-election. Both failed as ministers and chose early resignation.[91]

Paradoxically, this avoidance of Parliament by leading professionals was largely due to the professionalization of politics itself. As not only management and union administration but also politics became full-time careers, the former two became too busy and the latter too demanding to combine them. Only a few occupations with 'unstructured time' like law and journalism could accommodate the increasing demands of parliamentary attendance and constituency duties. It is significant that in a class-based party system in which Conservative voters are more bourgeois and Labour voters more working-class than in any other country, business men have never been a majority of Conservative MPs and current workers never since the war a

325

majority of Labour ones. In both parliamentary parties the largest single occupational group has increasingly come from the professions, particularly from those professions like law, journalism and teaching which earn their living by talk and argument. By 1974 and 1979 worker MPs had shrunk to 14 per cent of the House and business MPs to 19 per cent and 22 per cent.[92] Apart from a few landlords and farmers, nearly all the rest were professionals of one kind or another.

It was not their professional provenance, however, that made them a separate profession. Increasingly an MP's life cut him off from his previous career or reduced his chances of returning to a high place on its ladder, at least until he could retire from high government office. His ambition was transferred not to Parliament but to ministerial office, for which service in the Commons was almost (except for the 'slip road' through the Lords) the sole avenue. Politics became, like the bar, a 'jackpot profession' in which a few win all the prizes and the rest trudge on with mediocre reward. Without government office an MP is mere 'lobby fodder', voting not according to his conscience or his constituents' interests but to the dictates of the government or the shadow cabinet. Unlike Edmund Burke's independent representative or the American 'pork barrel' senator, the British MP has become a machine politician, and the machine that pulls his levers is the party.

The decline of democracy in fact begins at the grass roots in the constituency parties, where a parallel system of intermittent elections, at annual general meetings attended by small minorities of the membership, of a local executive committee ensures that a small oligarchy controls the selection of the parliamentary candidate. In the Labour Party, for example, where a typical constituency management committee consists of thirty members, a caucus of sixteen can impose its candidate, often on a constituency with a safe Labour majority. This system has so disillusioned ordinary party members that membership of both major parties slumped during the 1970s – the Conservative Party from about 2 million to about 1 million, the Labour Party from 1.3 million to 600,000 – thus enabling even tinier minorities of determined activists to take over constituency parties. Since activists tend to be more extreme than the ordinary members, still more than the habitual voters, the opting out of involvement in the annual election of executive committees accounts for the take-over of many Labour parties by the Bennites in their various guises and of Conservative parties by Powellites, later after Enoch Powell's defection to be transformed into Thatcherites. In this way the constituencies, which should be the bulwarks of democracy at the grassroots level, have become the instruments of factions of the central parties and, when one faction wins control, of the national party itself. The hijacking of both major parties in the 1970s – of the Conservative Party by Sir Keith Joseph and his friends to the benefit of Margaret Thatcher and of the Labour Party by Tony Benn and the disaffected left to the (temporary) benefit of Michael Foot – was made possible by the capture of the constituency parties by the right- and left-wing activists of the two parties, many of them new to the parties and with allegiances to more extreme bodies outside. The ultimate threat to a would-be independent-minded MP is to withdraw the party whip, which will almost automatically ensure that he loses his seat at the next election. Thus the national leadership controls the MPs, not the MPs the leadership, and democracy is converted into oligarchy. And through control of patronage, notably access to the highest offices of state and still more the threat of dismissal, the prime minister controls the national leadership, thus accelerating the trend towards prime-ministerial dictatorship.

The final phase of the corporate state owed its development to the decline of parliamentary democracy. Since at least the 1920s both sides of industry have been convinced that Parliament is out of touch with the real world of business. In 1926 Milne-Bailey of the TUC secretariat argued that 'inadequate knowledge is very real and constitutes a genuine defect in any parliament elected on a territorial basis'. He proposed an Economic Council, less grandiose than the Tory corporatists' Industrial Parliament, which 'merely seeks to do well what parliament at present does badly, and in so doing achieves the full recognition, by the community, of the claims of vocational groups.' Through such an Economic Council the trade union movement 'would exercise far greater influence on the economic and industrial affairs of the nation than they can possibly do at present.'[93]

It was not only with the rise of the oligarchic party system since the war, however, that the vocational interests were forced to by-pass Parliament and take their grievances, demands and threats of non-co-operation direct to the government. The House of

Commons became a theatre for the presentation of government policy and legislation, and for belated and usually ineffectual criticism by the Opposition, only after discussion behind the scenes between ministers and civil servants and the functional interests concerned. The real decisions were agreed on behind closed doors by 'unassuming experts', as Sidney Webb called his ideal Fabian rulers, on both sides of the table.

The only officially published clue to this process was the endless stream of reports from parliamentary committees and royal commissions on particular services and occupations issuing from the Stationery Office: on the Civil Service, the police, the press, the National Health Service, doctors' and dentists' remuneration, electricity supply, port transport, public libraries, higher education, the aircraft and shipbuilding industries, and so on.[94] Far more important than these exceptional problems needing official inquiry were the almost continuous and rarely documented meetings at particular ministries with representatives of interests lobbying the government for aid, protection, exclusive privileges, changes in taxation, in the social services, in the publicly funded infrastructure (especially roads, airports and dock facilities), and the like. One enormously expanding area involved the government as employer (after the war) of up to a quarter of the occupied population in the growing public sector, where ministers and civil servants came to negotiate incomes and resource provision directly, in the National Health Service, school and higher education, the armed forces, and the Post Office (until it became a public corporation), and indirectly, through the state-appointed managements of the nationalized industries.

Conversely, the increasing involvement of the state in the management of the economy, its responsibility (until recently) for maintaining full employment, containing inflation, safeguarding the balance of payments, upholding the value of sterling, and encouraging national economic growth, forced it in turn to seek the co-operation of the major economic interests, notably the corporate employers and the trade unions, and in effect to take them into partnership. The TUC, for example, was represented by 1958 on no less than 850 tripartite committees alongside representatives of the government and the employers, culminating at the top in the National Production Advisory Council on Industry and the various economic planning boards.[95] The triple partnership was crowned by the creation in 1961, under the premiership of the inter-war corporatist Harold Macmillan, of the National Economic Development Council. With its own secretariat and its dependent 'little Neddies' for particular industries, this was a landmark in the public recognition that a planned economy required a corporate structure. As Andrew Shonfield remarked:

> All planning of the modern capitalist type implies the acceptance of some measure of corporatism in political organization: that follows from basing the conduct of economic affairs on the deliberate decisions of organized groups of producers, instead of leaving the outcome to the clash between individual competitors in the market.

The NEDC, representing the TUC, the CBI and the government and normally chaired by the Chancellor of the Exchequer, Shonfield regarded as 'a second parliament with a corporatist character', and it would seem to justify Middlemas's description of the two industrial partners as 'governing institutions'.[96]

There were limits to formal corporatism, however. The NEDC was not and never became an industrial parliament. It had no legislative or executive powers, it could only advise on relatively marginal matters of policy, and it was not involved in what became the most contentious issue of tripartite relations in the 1960s and 1970s, prices and incomes policy. The various attempts by governments of both parties between 1959 and 1979, through such bodies as the (Conservative) National Incomes Commission and the (Labour) National Board for Prices and Incomes, to pursue competitive economic growth while restraining inflation tested the triangular relationship almost to destruction.[97] The resultant cycle of pay pauses followed by pay explosions and runaway inflation nearly wrecked the understandings between the trade unions and both Labour and Conservative governments and helped to bring down the Heath ministry in 1974 and the Callaghan ministry in 1979. This breakdown of the tripartite understanding led to the popular belief that Britain had become ungovernable, in the sense that the government could no longer impose its will on what Dahrendorf called 'the unsleeping veto groups'.[98] It led to the unsuccessful attempts by both the first Wilson and the Heath government to 'tame the trade unions' by coercive legislation, followed by a government dedicated to neo-Ricardian free market economics and the confrontational politics of the 1980s. As we shall see later, the Thatcher government, though contemptuously opposed to corporatism, was to practise it covertly, if selectively, as assiduously as its predecessors.

Meanwhile, the breakdown of formal corporatism did not end the need for informal co-operation between government and the functional interests. Indeed, Britain's economic decline relative to the other advanced nations has been due less to a lack of innovative ideas and skills than to the mutual frustration of the distrustful partners in the triangular relationship. Much of the failure stemmed from the inability of the professional representatives of the interest groups to 'deliver the goods'. While this failure occurs daily in industrial relations on the shop floor, where trade union officials cannot guarantee acceptance by their members of productivity deals, the most spectacular example was the 'Social Contract' signed by the Labour Party and the TUC in 1973, which committed the next Labour government to specific measures of social and industrial reform in return for voluntary wage restraint.[99] Against the background of the world-wide oil crisis and the consequent 'stagflation' (the unprecedented coincidence of recession and inflation), the TUC could not hold wage claims in check. Record wage increases and inflation reached a peak in 1975, and militant rank and file dissatisfaction culminated in the 'winter of discontent' in 1978–79, which helped to bring down the Callaghan government in the May election.

Even so, informal corporatism had not been without some success. The TUC under Jack Jones and Vic Feather had helped to bring the wage explosion under control and the CBI had obtained for the employers important modifications of the Industry Act, 1975, concerned with state investment in private industry through the National Enterprise Board.[100] Even the revival of free market policies in the 1980s was not, as we shall see, brought about by old-fashioned individual capitalists but by professional spokesmen for corporate business, for whom free enterprise meant freedom for professional managers like themselves. Just as the trade union corner of the triangle had come to mean not the workers but the professional officials, so the business corner had come to mean not the shareholders but the managers of the great corporations and the officials of the employers' associations. To them the rhetoric of socialism and capitalism, public and private enterprise, nationalization and privatization had come to represent the very real interests, in power, status and rewards, of the public and private sector professionals who ran the tripartite institutions of the corporate state.

Meanwhile, much of the content of the tripartite dialogue between government, unions and employers, like much of the equally corporatist interaction between government and the publicly employed professionals in the health service, education, the social services, and the like, was concerned as much with social as with economic matters. This concern might be called the moral distribution of resources in society, the allocation of income and services not determined by the market but ultimately by political decisions about the moral claims of vital services and their clients upon the state. Viewed in this way, the welfare state becomes an outgrowth of the corporate state, an expression of the bargaining between different social interest groups, the taxpayers, the welfare professions, and the potential beneficiaries. Beneath the struggle for public resources it comes down to conflicting moral assessments of competing claims upon the community, of the rights and responsibilities of different members of society, of what it means to be a citizen. In this sense we can talk, next, of the rise of a corporate society.

3 THE CORPORATE SOCIETY

Before the rise of modern social science the commonest way to describe society was as the body politic.[101] Men and women were members, unequal members to be sure, of a common entity, the community or commonwealth. All members were recognized as interdependent and could not survive without one another's help, although the extent of that help and of one man's right to call upon another for it might be debatable. Only with the triumph of the market and of an individualist philosophy in the eighteenth century could mutual service be left to the cash nexus and the self-interest of the individual. Even then, Adam Smith believed that the survival of the body politic overrode other considerations and that, since 'defence is of much more importance than opulence', the Navigation Acts, for example, should take precedence over the free market.[102]

The rise of the corporate society, which if it were not for the intervening age of individualism would come close to being a tautology, is in a sense the return of the body politic. During the twentieth century we have all, officially as it were, become members one of another. At the risk of taking a somewhat Whiggish view of social policy – which will be amply redressed later – we can say that we have in a single lifetime expanded the concept of 'Who is my neighbour?' from the parochial (or poor law union) level to that of the whole nation. This development has best been expressed by T. H. Marshall in a famous essay, 'Citizenship and Social Class', published in 1950. He saw the newly completed welfare state as the culmination of a centuries-old concept of expanding citizenship: 'the modern drive towards social equality is, I believe, the latest phase of an evolution of citizenship which has been in continuous progress for some 250 years.' The seventeenth and eighteenth centuries had seen the rise of civil or legal citizenship: 'liberty of the person, freedom of speech, thought and faith, the right to own property and conclude valid contracts, and the right to justice'. The nineteenth and early twentieth centuries had added political citizenship: the universal right to vote for elected representatives in central and local government and thus participate in political decision making.[103] These legal and political equalities in an age of competitive individualism, however, had increased the possibility of becoming more unequal. 'Differential status, associated with class, function and family, was replaced by a single uniform status of citizenship, which provided the foundation of equality on which the structure of inequality could be built.'[104] It had been left to the twentieth century to reverse what Sir Henry Maine had called the movement of progressive societies from status to contract[105] by adding social rights to the legal and political ones. Thus was created a single status of citizen which guaranteed a civilized social life for every member of society.

In practical terms social citizenship meant guaranteed rights to a minimum income in time of need, to decent housing, medical treatment, education suited to ability and needs and, via a full employment policy, to a job for all those who needed one. This combination of minimum rights was provided for the first time on a comprehensive basis by the welfare state. It was neither socialism nor the pursuit of an egalitarian society, but primarily a species of 'class abatement', a way of mitigating the inequities of the free market by ensuring a minimum 'social income' to all those in need.[106] It did not cure inequalities of income and wealth except in the sense of raising the 'floor' below which people were not allowed to fall, but by making money income less relevant to the services they could call on it made them more equal in real terms. 'The unified civilisation which makes social inequalities acceptable, and threatens to make them economically functionless, is achieved by a progressive divorce between real and money incomes.' In the major social services like health and education, in grammar school and university scholarships, in legal aid, in rent controls with security of tenure, and with (then contemporary) food rationing, food subsidies and price controls, 'The advantages obtained by having a larger money income do not disappear, but they are confined to a limited area of consumption.'[107]

To his colleague Lionel Robbins's objection that by mixing the free market based on money incomes with an egalitarian real income system we were getting the worst of both worlds, Marshall replied that, far from being illogical, the apparent inconsistencies were in fact a source of stability and sprang 'from the very roots of our social order in the present phase of the development of democratic citizenship'.[108] In other words, in modern society people wanted both the chance to earn more than the next man and the assurance that failure to achieve that would not undermine their ability to survive the contingencies of life. It was a subtle compromise dictated by social not by economic logic, and the best guarantee of social peace and a civilized social life.

Marshall's analysis is justly famous, but no one seems to have asked why he came to make it. It became so self-evidently part of the common sense of twentieth-century social thought – even when that common sense is under attack – that its provenance went unquestioned. Marshall was in fact a spokesman for the professional ideal as it applied to social policy. His analysis perfectly combined the elements of that ideal: a belief in the inequality of monetary rewards based on personal merit and effort modified by an underlying equality of 'real income' in services based on mere membership of society. He was not of course the only spokesman. Half a century before, large numbers of New Liberals, Fabian socialists and even Tory and Liberal imperialists had been groping towards a concept of fairer shares and more equal opportunities for all, in pursuit not so much of greater equality as of 'National Efficiency' and 'the rearing of an imperial race'.[109]

After the First World War such thinking did not die away, despite the disillusionment of many intellectuals with war and empire. On the contrary, the double bite of international competition and economic depression, in a world in which socialist revolution had been transformed from a future dream or nightmare into a present threat or promise, made the integration of society an urgent necessity. In such an atmosphere both those who wished to defend the status quo by pre-emptive reform and those who wished to change it in the direction of non-revolutionary socialism sought ways of mitigating the most glaring inequalities and injustices of the society they had inherited. The solutions they found to the social problems they discovered and defined involved increasing state intervention and increased numbers of professional purveyors of social services. These in turn soon found opportunities to expand their services and make themselves indispensable, so that the snowball of welfare provision acquired an additional momentum from within. Finally, the beneficiaries of state welfare, primarily but by no means exclusively the working class, came to regard legislative expedients as rights contingent upon membership of society. This sense of a right to minimum standards of provision of social security, medical treatment, education, housing and, ultimately, full employment, was reinforced by the Second World War, when the need for an integrated society overrode all other considerations. By then the theoretical, practical and democratic origins of the corporate society all converged to make the completion of a comprehensive welfare state irresistible. To see how this consensus was arrived at we need to look in turn at the intellectual, the administrative and the socio-political origins of the corporate society.

(1) The intellectuals and the welfare state

The welfare state is commonly supposed, like Topsy, to have 'just growed'. According to one recent historian of its 'shaping', 'There has ... been little welfare state philosophy, like those associated with socialist or fascist structures; not even a body of ideas like those surrounding the nineteenth-century capitalist state in its heyday.'[110] In fact, a complete blueprint not only for the welfare state but also for the corporate society can be found in the writings of R. H. Tawney, co-author with Sidney Webb of the Labour Party constitution of 1918. Tawney, from the impeccably professional background of an Indian Educational Service family, united in himself all three great streams of social thought inherited by the twentieth century from the nineteenth: the Idealism of Thomas Arnold's Rugby and Edward Caird's Balliol College, Oxford and its practical application at Toynbee Hall in the East End of London; the Cambridge neo-classical and Fabian tradition of the London School of Economics; and the moral socialism of William Morris, Keir Hardie and the early Labour Party.[111]

In his lectures on *Equality* published in 1931 Tawney anticipated in a much less Whiggish way his junior LSE colleague Marshall's thesis on the evolution of social citizenship. The third lecture on 'The Historical Background' traces how the legal privileges of feudal society were succeeded by the civil and political liberties of capitalism, which 'condemned the inequalities of the feudal past; it blessed the inequalities of the capitalist future'. Equality now meant 'not the absence of violent contrasts of income and condition, but equal opportunities of becoming more unequal'. Equality of opportunity, in a famous passage, was the 'tadpole philosophy', the idea that, although most of them will live and die as tadpoles, a few of them can hop nimbly on to the land and croak the virtues of a system which can turn any tadpole into a frog.[112]

The alternative was not just a fairer start and a wider diffusion of opportunity to rise or the redistribution of monetary income from the rich to the poor but the creation of 'a social income, received in the form, not of money, but of increased well-being':

> What is important is not that all men should receive the same pecuniary income. It is that the surplus resources of society should be so husbanded and applied that it is a matter of minor significance whether they receive it or not.

The social income would take the form of public provision: for health, especially that of infants, children and expectant mothers; for housing, one of the major causes of ill-health; for equal education, not just equality of educational opportunity; and for the contingencies of life – sickness, invalidity, unemployment and old age – 'to mitigate the insecurity which is the most characteristic of the wage earner's disabilities'. Such social provision, growing since the Edwardian period, 'Dr [Hugh] Dalton has happily called income from civil rights', which 'has an effect in mitigating disparities of income out of all proportion to the expenditure involved'.[113]

Tawney had already gone beyond social income from civil rights, the intellectual cornerstone of the yet unnamed welfare state, to the concept of 'industry as a social function'. By this he meant industry no longer controlled by functionless owners but by salaried managers and workers, preferably under public owner-ship.[114] This was the theme of his earlier book, *The Acquisitive Society* (1920), the most powerful indictment of capitalist society since Marx, which advocated a 'functional society' in which every industry and occupation would be rewarded according to its service to the community:

> the organization of society on the basis of function, instead of on that of rights, implies three things. It means, first, that proprietary rights shall be maintained when they are accompanied by the performance of service and abolished when they are not. It means, second, that the producers shall stand in direct relation to the community for whom production is carried on, so that their responsibility to it may be obvious and unmistakable, not lost, as at present, through their immediate subordination to shareholders whose interest is not service but gain. It means, in the third place, that the obligation for maintenance of the service shall rest upon the professional organizations of those who perform it, and that, subject to the supervision and criticism of the consumer, those organizations shall exercise so much voice in the government of industry as may be needed to secure that the obligation is discharged.[115]

This passage encapsulates his concept of a professional society, in which the redundant capitalist is replaced by professional managers and professionalized workers.

Yet if Tawney was the prophet of professional society, it does not follow that he was the cause of it. His brand of Fabian, gradualist socialism did indeed permeate the Labour Party, more so than the communism of Karl Marx, and was one of the inspirations of the legislative programme of the Labour government of 1945–51; but the welfare state was evolving long before that, and mostly under governments which owed little or nothing to his influence. The idea of government intervention to maintain individual income was a principle advocated before the First World War both by Fabian socialists like the Webbs, a generation older than Tawney, and by neo-classical economists like Alfred Marshall's pupil and successor at Cambridge, A. C. Pigou.[116] Between the wars it was accepted by intellectuals in all three parties, by the Webbs and their disciples in the Labour Party, by the Liberals Beveridge and Keynes, and by corporatists like Harold Macmillan in the Conservative Party.[117] The social ideal uniting these political rivals, most of whom belonged to the professional middle class, was, whether consciously or not, the ideal of a society which tried to avoid the waste and inefficiency which they saw in traditional capitalism and which pursued a policy of professional efficiency and social unity.

The Webbs' contribution to the evolution of the welfare state, much trumpeted by them and their admirers, was a largely negative one, 'the break-up of the poor law'. Apart from the Wheatley Housing Act of 1924, which expanded the provision of public housing, the two minority Labour governments of 1924 and 1929–31 in which Sidney Webb served (as Lord Passfield) were powerless to make fundamental changes in social policy, and most of the advances in welfare were made by their opponents: notably Neville Chamberlain's old age, widows' and orphans' pensions in 1925, based on the insurance principle which the Webbs rejected, and his replacement of the poor law in 1929 by public assistance, the very scheme which the Webbs had fought against in 1909.[118] For the provenance of national insurance, the main pillar of the emerging welfare state, we must turn elsewhere.

As we have seen, the last Liberal government had grasped at insurance as a means of extending the resources available to the state without extending the income tax further down the social scale or breaching the (to them) sacrosanct principle of free trade. Lloyd George had learned 'the magic of averages'[119] from the Victorian friendly societies which pioneered sickness and burial insurance. Churchill had learned it from the trade unions which paid unemployment benefit, via William Beveridge whom he had met through the Webbs in 1908 and soon recruited to the Board of Trade to advise on labour exchanges and unemployment insurance. Beveridge came from precisely the same background as Tawney. Son of an Indian Civil Service judge, educated at Charterhouse and Balliol, drawn into social service at Toynbee Hall which he used as a base for scientific investigation into the causes of unemployment, he was more strongly convinced than the ever-modest Tawney of the unquestionable superiority of the professional expert.[120] He became the embodiment of the strong-willed reforming civil servant in the classic mould of Edwin Chadwick, John Simon or Robert Morant.[121] Lacking Tawney's empathy with the working class, he saw himself as the quintessential social engineer, designing a social policy which would be proof against both the temptations and the demoralization of the old poor law. National insurance fitted his specification perfectly: it forced the working man to save against the inevitable rainy day so that when it came he could receive his benefit not as a charitable dole but as an earned but deferred right.[122] Thus the Victorian virtues of independence and self-respect were preserved and, equally important, the social system was saved intact at minimal cost.

Beveridge lived to see this clever principle extended to cover, first, unemployed returning veterans (1920), then the whole manual working class and their dependants (1923, 1936), old age, widows' and orphans' pensions (1925), and, finally, as the result of his phenomenally popular Report on *Social Insurance and Allied Services* (1942), to the whole population (1948).[123] But by that time the insurance principle was already an anachronism. Between the wars mass unemployment had undermined the capacity of insurance contributions to carry the burden. A disillusioned Beveridge criticized the Labour government of 1924 for indefinitely extending 'uncovenanted benefit' to the long-term unemployed, and the Conservative government of 1927 for divorcing the claim to benefit from payment of contributions.[124] He complained bitterly to the Royal Commission on Unemployment Insurance in 1931:

The present system bears no resemblance to the practice of trade unions or to the scheme of 1911 that was meant as an extension of it. Every important idea in either has gone by the board. The benefit has been made unlimited in time and

338

practically divorced from the payment of contributions: it has become neither insurance nor a spreading of wages, out-relief financed mainly by a tax on employment.[125]

This 'insupportable tax' led to the cutting of the benefit in 1931, which split the Labour Party and brought down the government, and to the introduction in 1934 of the means test for those on 'uncovenanted benefit'.

Beveridge was equally perturbed after 1948 when inflation eroded the real value of the benefits he had proposed, and the National Assistance Board was transformed from a safety net for those few expected to fall through the system into a permanent support providing 'supplementary benefit' to old age pensioners and other claimants who could not live on the basic scales.[126] But the problem was inherent in any insurance-based system of social security: some members of society would inevitably fail to pay enough qualifying contributions, while others would have needs which no insurance scheme could meet. Thus Beveridgean social insurance could never be more than a halfway house towards a fully corporate society in which membership alone was sufficient qualification for an adequate social income from civil rights. That only arrived by the back door in the 1970s when social security, as a matter of administrative practice rather than legislative policy, began to be paid to almost anyone who could show need, whether or not they had paid the insurance contributions.

In some respects Beveridge did go beyond the principle of insurance. His 1942 Report on *Social Insurance* laid down three essential assumptions: a comprehensive health service provided mainly out of taxation, a tax-based scheme of family allowances for second and subsequent children, and a policy of full employment without which unemployment could undermine any system of insurance as it had done between the wars.[127] This last assumption was a startling departure from the free market which could not have been made without the contribution of another great Liberal civil servant, John Maynard Keynes. Keynes too came from an impeccably professional background. Son of a Cambridge don and, after a brief apprenticeship at the India Office, a Cambridge don himself, he was drawn back into public service by the urgent demands of the First World War.[128] At the Treasury he brilliantly managed the wartime foreign exchange policy, before becoming Lloyd George's chief financial adviser at

Versailles and chief critic of the resultant peace treaty and its unrealistic German war reparations.[129] Like Beveridge an incorrigible elitist and defender of traditional social structure, he derived from his mentor Alfred Marshall, the founder of Cambridge economics, as Beveridge had derived from the Balliol Idealists, that hatred of social injustice and belief in the duty of public service which Oxford and Cambridge then taught to the best of their sons. 'He was keenly alive to great social evils and sensitive to suffering. He was by nature a progressive and reformer. He believed that by thought and resolution things could be made much better, and that quickly'.[130] Neither an egalitarian nor a socialist, he was enough of a capitalist to have made half a million pounds on the stock exchange and to have restored the finances of King's College, Cambridge by shrewd investment. His mission was to rescue capitalism from its own vices by teaching it how to prevent the alternating evils of unemployment and inflation. To achieve this, 'I bring in the State; I abandon *laissez-faire* ... not enthusiastically, not from contempt for that good old doctrine, but because, whether we like it or not, the conditions for its success have disappeared.'[131]

In his lecture on *The End of Laissez-Faire* in 1924 he declared, 'The important thing for the Government is not to do things which individuals are doing already, and to do them a little better or a little worse; but to do those things which at present are not done at all.' These included actively managing the economy so as to encourage saving and investment along the most actively productive channels. The aim should be the full employment of both capital and labour to achieve optimal production without either unemployment or inflation. Thus capitalism could be preserved but only by transforming it into a professionally operated system:

> For my part, I think that Capitalism, wisely managed, can probably be made more efficient for attaining economic ends than any alternative system yet in sight, but that in itself it is in many ways extremely objectionable. Our problem is to work out a social organization which shall be as efficient as possible without offending our notions of a satisfactory way of life.[132]

This social organization was to be neither socialist nor capitalist, at least in their Marxist or Ricardian senses. As he told Bernard

Shaw in 1935, 'I believe myself to be writing a book on economic theory which will largely revolutionise ... the way the world thinks about economic problems.' The final upshot, not immediately but in the course of the next ten years, would be that 'there will be a great change, and, in particular, the Ricardian foundations of Marxism will be knocked away'.[133]

The book, *The General Theory of Employment, Interest and Money* (1936) – long foreshadowed by his earlier writings and by his evidence to the Macmillan Committee on Finance and Industry in 1930-31 – solved (to Keynes's satisfaction and that of the first post-1945 generation of economic policy makers) the economic riddle of the Sphinx, how to achieve full employment without national bankruptcy or raging inflation.[134] The solution involved the government in stimulating spending and investment during depressions and – an aspect underplayed at the time and neglected since the war – damping them down during booms. Thus the state and its professional advisers would become continuously responsible for monitoring and managing the economy.

The Keynesian revolution, resisted by the government in the 1930s (though already beginning to percolate through the back corridors of the Treasury) took hold during the war, when Keynes himself was called back to the Treasury to perform the same service as in the First World War. Afterwards, 'the Keynesian ideology' swept all before it, until the failure of what some latter-day Keynesians like John Eatwell claim to be a bastard form of the master's theory was attacked by the revival of the free market ideology in the stagflation of the 1970s.[135] Meanwhile the belief that unemployment could be cured by the professional manipulation of the economy was the prerequisite of the Beveridgean welfare state and of the new professional organization of society. Although anti-Keynesians do not agree, it is still arguable that the long secular boom for a quarter century after 1945, in contrast to the two decades of depression after 1920, can be credited to Keynesian demand management and the management of the world's currency which he negotiated at Bretton Woods in 1944, and that the return to an unregulated world economy has manifestly failed to maintain the same degree of prosperity.[136]

The third and final stream of social thought contributing to the corporate society was, surprisingly, that of Conservative intellectuals. A strain of paternalism had run through Conservative thinking from Peel and Disraeli through Salisbury and Balfour down to Churchill and Macmillan. It saw in the protection of the poor the best hope of social cohesion and the defence of property. Between the wars it was best represented at the intellectual level by Harold Macmillan and the small group of MPs from depressed industrial constituencies who contributed to the corporatist symposium *Industry and the State* (1927), mentioned above. Macmillan was already edging towards Beveridgean and Keynesian solutions. Recalling his reaction to the hunger marches of the 1930s, he declared:

> There was, of course, national, local, individual relief and assistance, on a scale unequalled in the history of this or any other country. But charity, whether of the nation as a whole or from their neighbours, was not what the men wanted. They wanted work.[137]

There were also other Conservative voices, deriving not from the paternalist tradition but from its opposite, the Liberal *laissez-faire* tradition of Ricardo, Cobden and Bright, which had infiltrated the Conservative Party along with the renegade Liberal Unionists of the 1880s and the various National Liberals and Liberal Conservatives of the inter-war period. They found expression in anti-statist polemics like Hilaire Belloc's *The Servile State* (1911), Lord Chief Justice Hewart's *The New Despotism* (1929), and Friedrich von Hayek's *The Road to Serfdom* (1944). Hayek, part of the 'white immigration' from Hitler's Europe which was nearly as anti-communist as Hitler himself, bore witness in 1935 to the decline of *laissez-faire* and the rise of the corporate state:

> For more than half a century, the belief that deliberate regulation of all social affairs must necessarily be more successful than the apparently haphazard interplay of interdependent individuals has continuously gained ground until today there is hardly a political group anywhere in the world which does not want central direction of most human activities in the service of one aim or another.[138]

For the time being they were muted or disregarded, but continued to work below the surface towards their revival in the more favourable conditions of the 1970s. Their very despair at this time is evidence of the success of their opponents' philosophy.

Since most of the inter-war evolution of the welfare state was enacted by Conservative statesmen who belonged to neither of these extremes of the party and who, like the architect of all the key changes in welfare provision from 1925 until the war, Neville Chamberlain, were anything but intellectuals, we are left with a paradox and a puzzle. If overt social thought counts for so little in the acts of practical politicians, what part, if any, did it play in the legislative rise of the welfare state? The answer lies in the extent to which social thought defines both the problems needing to be tackled and the range of solutions which can be seriously contemplated. In establishing contributory pensions in 1925, abolishing the poor law and replacing it by public assistance, local authority hospitals and municipal child care in 1929, and transferring responsibility for the long-term unemployed to the central government in 1934, Chamberlain was consciously pursuing 'the full circle of security for the worker' accepted as an objective on all sides.[139] Clement Attlee observed to Harold Laski in 1944 before the great Labour welfare programme of 1945–51:

> I count our progress much more by the extent to which what we cried in the wilderness five and thirty years ago has now become part of the assumptions of the ordinary man and woman. The acceptance of these assumptions has its effect both in legislation and administration, but its gradualness tends to hide our appreciation of the facts.[140]

But legislation and administration did not merely reflect or absorb increasingly professional thought. They also interacted with increasingly professional administrative practice.

(2) The welfare professions and the welfare state

In 1958 an American student of the British welfare state observed of British socialism, 'Utilitarianism and the managerial aspects of Fabianism have gradually triumphed over utopian socialism, revolutionary socialism and Christian socialism'.[141] All three socialisms, however, believed in managerialism in the sense of control by expert elites, whether the Webbs' 'co-efficients', H. G. Wells's 'new samurai', Lenin's 'inner party democracy', Tawney's professional functionaries, or indeed Beveridge's explicit 'rule of the expert'.[142] What they perhaps did not bargain for was the extent to which the welfare state would come to exist as much for the welfare professions as for their 'clients', the ostensible beneficiaries. In his *Essays on 'The Welfare State'* (1958) one of the pioneers of the academic study of social administration, Richard Titmuss, asked whether the social services were 'being artificially developed by the professional, administrative and technical interests upon whose skills the services depend':

> What, to put it crudely, are we getting for our money? Is it an increasing proportion of the cost going, first, to those who do the welfare and, second, for treating at a higher standard the symptoms of need rather than in curing or preventing the causes of need?

He instanced the huge total of future expenditure mortgaged to fund the retirement pensions of some 1,500,000 professional and technical workers and administrators in the Health Service.[143] He foresaw in the drift towards professional control the threat of irresponsible power:

> As the social services become more complex, more specialized and subject to a finer division of labour they become less intelligible to the lay councillor or public representative. A possible consequence is that, collectively, more power may come to reside in the hands of these interests. The question that needs to be asked of professional associations is whether they are prepared to assume greater responsibilities to match their added knowledge and the power that accompanies it.[144]

The knife cut both ways of course, and most welfare professions claimed that they wished to increase their power and responsibilities precisely in order to provide a more caring and efficient service. Either way, the welfare professions were not passive spectators of the rise of the welfare state: they were active partners whose influence on the kind, pace and structure of provision was often crucial, if not indeed decisive.

Nowhere was this partnership more clearly seen than in the evolution of the National Health Service. Of all the caring professions the doctors have always been regarded as the most indispensable and therefore the most powerful, whenever they were united. Their power was manifested in 1911 when the British Medical Association forced Lloyd George to modify his health insurance scheme and increase the capitation fee per patient paid to the panel doctors as the price of their co-operation.[145] Between the wars, however, when the foundations of the NHS were laid, the doctors were not united but split between three rival interests, each of whom hoped to dominate the emerging service: the voluntary hospitals, the insurance-based panel doctor system, and the local authority health services including the newly transferred poor law hospitals.[146] After 1929 the voluntary hospitals, ancient, venerable and staffed by the leaders of the medical profession (usually on an honorary, part-time basis), began to lose ground to the old poor law infirmaries, now operated by the city and county councils with public funds and full-time staffs. The local authorities, with their other responsibilities for preventive public health, tuberculosis, venereal diseases, and school, child and natal clinics, bid fair to become 'a state medical service by instalments, almost by stealth'.[147] The panel doctors feared they were on the way to extinction, but were given a boost by the Dawson Report of the new Ministry of Health's Consultative Council on Medical and Allied Services in 1920, which called for the grouping of general practitioners into 'primary health centres' as the first line of medical care.[148]

The Dawson Report is an excellent example of the influence of a leading professional on policy in his own field. During the war Sir Bertrand Dawson (from 1920 Lord Dawson of Penn), physician to King George V, had become the major-general responsible for organizing army medical services in Europe, where his experience had taught him the need for the detailed co-ordination of health care. Although far from socialist, his ideas were naturally taken up by the socialist State Medical Service Association and the Labour Party, but his own outlook was simply professional: the 'increasing conviction that the best means of maintaining health and curing disease should be made available to all citizens'.[149] Dawson's 'utopian picture' went too far for most general practitioners, who feared the loss of their autonomy and the right to sell their practices on retirement, then their only source of superannuation. The BMA's Report on *A General Medical Service for the Nation* in 1938 – a further example of welfare policy making by the profession, though a defensive one – concentrated

345

on extending health insurance treatment to cover workers' families, and on making the 'family doctor' the centrepiece of a co-ordinated national health system, controlling access to the consultant and specialist services.[150]

Meanwhile, many working-class families were deserting the general practitioner for the cheaper outpatient departments of the hospitals, both voluntary and public, and for the many specialized services of the local authorities, including the school, child and antenatal clinics. In the hospital sector, the local authority institutions in the 1930s rapidly overtook the voluntary hospitals in numbers of beds, medical technology and range of services. They were backed by the Ministry of Health, where the Chief Medical Officer of Health in the late 1930s, Sir Arthur MacNalty, aimed at the 'growth of the National Health Service ... provided by local authorities for all classes of the population'. Their speed of advance took the voluntary hospitals by surprise, and in 1939 the latter belatedly set up the Nuffield Provincial Hospitals Trust to pursue the co-ordination on a regional basis of hospital services.[151]

By the time the Second World War arrived, with its imperative demand for an integrated hospital system to cope with the expected massive casualties from air attacks, the need for a national health service was universally accepted, but the three rival interests had fought one another almost to a standstill over who should administer it. The BMA for the GPs and consultants set up a Medical Planning Commission which reported in 1942 in favour of a planned service but opposed anything which stood in the way of autonomy for the individual doctor and the voluntary hospital.[152] The Ministry looked to a public salaried service based on health centres and the local authorities. Yet such was the power of the rival factions of the profession that the resultant National Health Service was itself fragmented into three independent sectors, the hospital service, the general practitioner service, and the personal and public services of the local authorities.[153]

The National Health Service Act of 1946 has been described as 'a "doctor's measure" much more than a "patient's measure"; that is to say, it was intended to correct certain desperately serious faults in the organization and quality of the British medical services rather than in their class distribution.'[154] As in 1911 so in 1948 the BMA got its way in negotiations with the minister, now Aneurin

346

Bevan, over scales and methods of payment.[155] It was also a doctor's measure in the sense of ensuring that at every level of organization, from the Ministry through the Regional Hospital Boards down to the Local Medical Committees for general practice, the profession was represented and was generally deferred to by the lay members. In an astonishing example of reluctant corporatism the minister promised to submit all draft regulations to the BMA before promulgating them.[156] Harry Eckstein, the American historian of the NHS, concluded:

> What the BMA had been denied during the drafting of the NHS Bill, it got immediately after its enactment.... What was granted, in effect, was the right to argue a case rather than merely to present it, and an assurance that agreement with the profession would be earnestly sought, not just that its views would be taken into consideration.[157]

According to Brian Abel Smith, historian of the nursing profession, the power and privilege of the doctors were now entrenched because 'ministers did not dare to challenge a profession which had by now too high a standing in the eyes of public opinion'.[158]

This verdict has been amply borne out by the subsequent history of the NHS. In the allocation of resources the doctors' priorities override the patients' needs. Hospital medicine predominates over primary care; high technology medicine such as cardiology and transplant surgery takes priority over mental health or geriatrics; under the 1959 Mental Health Act doctors have absolute power to incarcerate patients indefinitely; and under the 1967 Abortion Act this 'great social responsibility is placed firmly on the shoulders of the medical profession' by law.[159] Despite the increase in malpractice suits and criminal cases in which the General Medical Council has usually failed to act until forced to by court decisions, an official Committee of Inquiry into the Regulation of the Medical Profession in 1975 concluded that 'the medical profession should be largely self-regulated' because 'the most effective safeguard of the public is the self-respect of the profession'.[160] Even though a survey in 1977 showed that most 'improvements' in the doctor-patient relationship were for the benefit of the doctor rather than the patient, the BMA in 1979 was still seeking payments for services beyond a narrowly defined norm, which in effect redefined and limited the responsibility of the GP to the patient.[161] Above all, a doctor-dominated service had turned health care from a broad social concern with the whole lifestyle, conditions of work and the environment of the population into a narrow concern with the sick individual.[162]

Nevertheless, despite the cynical criticism of the 'disabling profession' by Illich and others,[163] this had been done in all good faith: every profession defines its problems in terms of the solutions it is qualified to offer and the service it believes in. A health service defined and dominated by treatment specialists was bound to be a sickness-oriented system rather than a programme for positive health.

What applies to the health service applies equally to the other social services. One observer wrote in 1965:

> Over the past fifty years the treatment of social problems has been dropped into the professional lap and has been held on to tightly. The propaganda about the professional's exclusive right to treat social problems has reached its high mark. The professionals, the public and even patients are firmly convinced that the only 'bona fide' treatments and 'cures' available come from 'legitimate professionals' with the right set of degrees.[164]

Most of the social services have been organized around professional skills rather than client needs, for the obvious reason that the professionals came with the rise of public welfare to control access to the service and allocation of its resources at the point of provision. The key role of the caring professions in the rise of the welfare state can be illustrated in relation to social work, education, and town planning.

Professional social work was invented by social workers. The attempt by the Charity Organization Society in late Victorian England to discriminate between the 'deserving' and the 'undeserving' poor – later softened to the helpable versus the hopeless cases – led to a training course for 'case workers' at Southwark from 1892 which, transferred to the new London School of Economics in 1912, was the foundation of the profession at the heart of both voluntary charity and the growing social services of local government.[165] Between the wars it tended to fragment into the specialisms dealing with the elderly, the sick and convalescent, the mentally ill, the handicapped of various kinds, children in need of care, delinquents of all ages, 'problem families', and so on. The classic process of 'feedback' came into operation, with every extension of welfare legislation serving to reveal still more social problems requiring treatment. Titmuss's remark in 1965 could have applied to any part of the twentieth century: 'during the last twenty years, whenever the British people have identified and investigated a social problem there has followed a national call for more social work and more trained social workers.'[166] This *ad hoc* method of growth led to a proliferation of officials treating individuals rather than the families in which the problems originated, and the Seebohm Committee on Personal Social Services in 1968 recommended an integrated profession with a single generic training.[167] A Fabian critic commented, 'A citizen reading the report might indeed conclude that it had more to do with the work satisfaction and career structure of the professional social worker than it had to do with his own needs or rights in the modern welfare state.'[168] Another professor of social administration remarked, 'Each additional social worker appointed revealed the need for two more.'[169] The unintended consequence was a further expansion and bureaucratization of the system, with more administrators and fewer field workers in contact with the public. The ensuing 1970 Act was 'a charter for social workers', who became in effect a court without appeal in the disbursement of relief in money or kind to emergency applicants, in decisions to take children into care, and in preparing social inquiry reports on convicted delinquents for sentencing purposes. Although social workers do not have the prestige or the rewards of doctors – they are known to the public for their failures rather than for their successes – they have to a large extent taken control of the lives and fate of large and vulnerable sections of the public. To society at large they have become the most visible representatives of the welfare state, so that the profession and the system have come to appear identical.

Teachers are a much less successful profession than doctors or social workers, but they have nevertheless had considerable influence on the development of education under the welfare state. Much of that influence, however, has been self-frustrating, because of the fragmentation of the profession into quarrelling factions reflecting the divisions of the English education system by social class and educational level. The National Union of Teachers, founded by the elementary teachers in 1878, came to represent the bulk of non-degreed teachers in the state elementary schools (until 1944 for most children to age 14) and, since 1944, in the primary and secondary modern schools, most of them underpaid women, while the grammar and public boarding school teachers tended to join the Assistant Masters' and Assistant Mistresses' Associations, or the (until recently) single-sex Association of School Masters.[170] At the higher education level there was a similar division between the university teachers in the Association of University Teachers and the other college lecturers, represented by the Association of Teachers in Technical Institutions and its predecessors, and more recently by the new Association of Polytechnic Lecturers.[171] These entrenched bodies helped to perpetuate the institutional divisions, so that it became almost automatic for the 1944 Education Act, for example, to be interpreted, despite its neutral language, as laying down a tripartite division of state secondary education into grammar, technical and secondary modern schools.

The transition to the supposedly classless comprehensive school in the 1960s and 1970s, opposed by many grammar school teachers but pushed through by the NUT and its allies in the Labour Party, was partially thwarted by the teachers' practice of 'streaming', which had the same self-fulfilling effects on the children's performance as the old tripartite schools.[172] This was possible because, more than in any other advanced country, it was the teachers who decided how and what should be taught. As a Chief Education Officer said in the 1970s, 'Within reasonable limits the headmaster and his staff are free to run the school as they think best.'[173] In few other countries do parents have so little knowledge or influence over what is done to their children inside school or have the teachers been so successful at resisting parental demands for involvement or change (a position now under challenge by education secretary Kenneth Baker and the Thatcher government).[174] The NUT were able to emasculate the Plowden Committee's 1967 proposals for educational priority areas with greater resources in inner cities, and A. H. Halsey's 1977 proposals for parental participation in pre-school nursery centres.[175]

Nevertheless, the teaching profession has never been able to achieve the same autonomy as the more prestigious professions. They were able to exclude untrained (including degreed) teachers from state schools only in the late 1960s when a prominent NUT member, Edward Short, became Secretary of State for Education, but his support for a Teachers' Registration Council on the lines of the General Medical Council failed to overcome the divided views of the teachers' organizations.[176] Their problem was not merely that the profession was fragmented but, paradoxically, that it was too enthusiastic for its own good about the value of the service it provided. In pressing governments to expand education, unlike the medical, legal and other professions which limited entry in order to control the labour market, the teachers recurrently overproduced themselves, thus overstocking the market and reducing their own employability.[177] The profession nevertheless played a vital role in the welfare state and in the reproduction of professional society.

Town planners, a much more recently established profession stemming from the 1947 Town and Country Planning Act, have achieved even less autonomy than the teaching profession. Yet they have collectively become one of the most powerful of professions, since their decisions in the post-war period have had a visible effect on the largest numbers of people. Given their traditionally narrow view of their function as concerned primarily to control mixed land use and to end overcrowding and urban sprawl by planned dispersal to suburbs and new towns, their ability to overwhelm the public and their elected councillors with technical expertise, and the enormous impact their decisions had on property values, they were able to reshape whole communities according to their vision of the future. They certainly had the most influence on the development of further planning legislation, since only they understood the technical complexities of the law and its administration.[178]

Unfortunately, the consequences were not as benign as their intentions. Not only did planned dispersal of the population intensify the class segregation which had from the beginning been a feature of industrial society, yielding amorphous public and private housings estates with ever more finely graded social strata, but the condition aptly called 'planners' blight' came to infect the inner cities, where slum clearance and zoning laws caused large areas to fall into decay.[179] Whether or not the criticism was wholly deserved – and the inner zones of many unplanned American cities like Houston and Los Angeles could be equally blighted – town

351

planners by the 1970s became the most bitterly attacked of all the public service professions. Their alienation of both the powerful propertied interests and the general populace underlined the leading role they had played in the expansion of the interventionist state.

The doctors, social workers, teachers and town planners amply illustrate the way in which the welfare professions contributed directly, both in policy making and in day-to-day practice, to the development of the welfare state. As Titmuss put it in 1965, 'In the modern world, the professions are increasingly the arbiters of our welfare fate; they are the key holders to equality of outcome; they help to determine the pattern of redistribution in social policy.'[180] They were able to use their strategic position at the point of decision making and delivery of vital services to increase their power, status and rewards. They could not have done so, however, unless their services had been perceived as indispensable and as contributing directly to the needs of the citizen of the increasingly corporate society. They therefore needed the faith and support of the public, the beneficiaries of the welfare state, and to the role of the latter in its evolution we must finally turn.

(3) Citizenship and the corporate society

T. H. Marshall's concept of social citizenship was a brilliant distillation, after the fact, of half a century of developing moral claims upon the state on behalf of all its members. As we have seen, the welfare state represented a moral revolution, a widening of the notion of 'my neighbour' from the extended family, the parish, the poor law union, and the county and county borough, to the whole national community. From this point of view it was more than a patchwork of devices to secure the unfortunate against the exigencies of life in the mature capitalist economy, or even to buy off the discontent of capitalism's victims. It was an integral part of the growing corporate society, in which 'we are all members one of another' and each has a claim upon all the rest to a minimum social income, access to educational opportunity, health care, decent housing and a clean environment, and even (until recently) to full employment, all in the name of citizenship itself. Thus corporate society restored, as an ideal if not always in practice, the 'body politic' of pre-industrial tradition, now informed by an egalitarian rather than a patriarchal spirit. Interdependence between its organically related parts came to replace the atomic individualism of the intervening period of industrialism. In the eyes of its protagonists the moral ideal of mutual responsibility had replaced the enlightened self-interest of free market capitalism.

Of course, it is worth repeating, *all* classes, *all* interest groups, *all* social groupings of whatever kind claim a moral superiority to all their rivals, based on the belief that their particular contribution to society's well-being and survival is superior to all others' and that what is good for themselves is good for all the rest. The principle of social justice upheld by the welfare professions differed from other such principles only in its marriage of a comprehensive acceptance of the claims of social citizenship with the self-interest of the professionals who existed to meet them. As in pre-industrial society dominated by the landed aristocracy and in industrial society dominated by the owner-managing capitalist, so in post-industrial professional society the moral ideal of the dominant elite came out on top – or, rather, the interest which could impose its ideal upon the rest became the dominant elite. It was, as we shall see in the next chapter, the professional belief that human capital in the shape of educated professional expertise devoted to society's needs and functions was morally superior both to the passive property of traditional landlords and rentiers and to the active capital of the owner-managing business men that underlay the rise of professional society.

It would be tempting to think that this revival of the body politic, of a more cohesive, organic model of society, was the direct result of pressure from the welfare professions' clients, of the demand of an increasingly democratic electorate for the care and support of all citizens who fell into difficulties beyond their own means to avert. Yet Bentley Gilbert's observation that 'welfare legislation never figured as an electoral issue in the years before World War I'[181] might be extended down to the Second World War, in the sense that no *new* initiative in social legislation was put before the electorate before it was introduced. It was not until the 1945 election that a general programme of welfare legislation was voted on by the electors – by which time all parties claimed to support it so that there was in effect no choice. Before that the role of the voters, where it impinged on the growth of the welfare state at all, was to defend rights already granted, as in the call for the restoration of unemployment benefit cuts and the rejection of the means test in the 1930s.

This reflects a surprising paradox, that although the mass of the people were often indifferent if not opposed to the introduction of welfare measures such as national insurance or a raised school-leaving age, they almost always vehemently resisted the withdrawal of such gains. There was, and indeed still is, a sort of ratchet effect (frequently complained of by the free market lobby) by which the level of welfare provision was steadily and easily notched up but was only painfully, and usually temporarily, pushed down again. What Tawney called the social income was not demanded beforehand or even welcomed when it came, but once it was in place any attempt to reduce it was bitterly opposed.

The reason for this paradox is simple enough. As we have seen, social problems might be keenly felt but were not intellectually realized until they were articulated by social reformers and the increasingly professional bureaucrats who succeeded them, and the choice of solutions depended on the way they were defined. The definitions and possible solutions were offered by what may be called professional solutionmongers: self-appointed reformers like the Fabians, the Family Welfare Association (the old Charity Organization Society), or the Child Poverty Action Group, elected politicians like Lloyd George, Churchill or Aneurin Bevan, and masterful civil servants like Morant, Llewellyn Smith or Beveridge. Whichever solution was chosen for enactment from among those on offer – and many of them, like that of the Webbs versus Churchill and Beveridge's solution for unemployment, were diametrically incompatible – rapidly became the benchmark from which there must be no falling back. What had often been a mere *ad hoc* solution soon became an established right of citizenship.

Not everyone, of course, would accept this view of the growth of social citizenship as a reluctant but self-reinforcing moral revolution. The radical New Right, led by Hayek, Milton Friedman and the free marketeers, have seen it as the road to statism and economic ruin brought about by well-meaning but misguided liberals and social democrats.[182] The Marxist New Left, on the other hand, have seen it as a subtle attempt to legitimate capitalism and ensure its survival. The neo-Marxist Claus Offe has gone further and argued that ever since capitalism began welfare institutions have been a precondition of its existence: 'under modern capitalist conditions, a supportive framework of non-commodified institutions [i.e. services not sold on the market] is necessary for an economic system that utilizes labour power as if it were a commodity.'[183] Neither the free marketeers nor the Marxists, however, can explain, except by the machinations of a supposed conspiracy of their enemies, how so popular yet unsolicited a framework came into existence, or why after the recent period of unprecedented right-wing reaction in Britain and the United States the welfare state not only survives but continues to grow in terms of public expenditure. The hostilities of both New Right and New Left to 'welfare socialism' cancel each other out and are evidence against both conspiracies. Some other explanation must be sought.

The true explanation is the growing role of professionalism in modern society and the growing influence of the professional social ideal. The seemingly *ad hoc* solutions to social problems which went into the making of the welfare state had a cumulative effect because there was a coherent social philosophy underlying them. That philosophy was neither capitalist nor anti-capitalist but different from both. It was the philosophy of a functional society based on expertise and the avoidance of waste, especially waste of the most valuable asset in a complex, highly specialized economy: human resources.

Curiously enough, both the New Right and the New Left subscribe, unwittingly, to this philosophy. The neo-Ricardians justify the free market by its efficient allocation of resources and its fair distribution of rewards to those who perform most efficiently the functions that society needs to survive and prosper. The neo-Marxists are incensed that the free market does not function efficiently but is shot through with self-defeating inefficiencies or, in their terminology, 'contradictions', which will bring about its inevitable downfall. Although they disagree diametrically as to the organization of their alternative societies, they both claim to apply the same criteria, functional efficiency and the fairest distribution of rewards. If we allow, as we must given the nature of the corporate economy and the corporate state, that the two sides speak for the private sector and the public sector respectively, we can understand why the first should argue for a free market (that is, a *free corporate* market) and the second for a statist bureaucratic (that is, a *state corporate*) solution to the problem of social organization. In each case their chosen solution would maximize their own power, status and rewards.

Returning from the two extremes of professional casuistry to the middle ground inhabited by most British opinion, we have already seen something of the role played by professionals in the intellectual theory and practical development of the welfare state. What connected the *ad hoc* and often disparate remedies adopted for the solution of social problems was not so much any ready-made theory as a common set of assumptions about how a social problem was defined and what constituted a tolerable solution to it. A social problem was a situation which was intolerable not merely because it offended against humanitarian sentiment but because it created avoidable waste and militated against social efficiency. Thus poverty, overcrowded slums, and unemployment became social problems only when they came to be seen as avoidable and as creating idle, sickly families with underfed children who made poor workers and unfit soldiers and so undermined national efficiency in world trade and the defence of the country. The costs of ill-health, including childish ailments, tuberculosis and venereal disease, in lost wages, foregone production and belated and therefore more expensive medical treatment, were higher than those of school clinics, sanatoria and VD treatment centres, and national health insurance was cheaper than supporting a poverty-stricken and broken-down workforce. Neglect of education, beginning with the lack of secondary education for the intelligent children of the poor, was a waste of human resources and an encouragement to the bright and able young to use their talents anti-socially. Even old age pensions could be justified as a cheaper as well as a morally more defensible system of support for the elderly than the universally dreaded workhouse.

Such arguments were not new but at least as old as Edwin Chadwick's belief that sanitary reform was a cheaper and more efficient preventive of ill-health and poverty than urban neglect. What was new in the twentieth century was the belief that most social problems, not just the obvious public ones like sanitation and water supply, were the products of social organization rather than individual inadequacy. Unemployment, in Beveridge's subtitle, was 'a problem of industry' rather than individual fecklessness. Poverty, according to Booth, Rowntree, Bowley and Burnett-Hurst, was caused by low wages, sickness or death of the breadwinner, unemployment or old age, much more than by drink or gambling. Slums and urban squalor, according to expert witnesses before the Committee on Physical Deterioration (1904), were caused by inadequate town planning and the side effects of the casual labour market. Problems thus defined as institutional and societal rather than moral and individual cried out for collective, professional solutions rather than moral discipline or exhortation. And once the legislative and administrative treatment began, the process of professionalization and feedback set in, by which the welfare professionals uncovered new problems which demanded further legislative and administrative solutions and the recruitment of still more welfare professionals.

The process, however, went deeper than the self-interested empire building of the welfare professions and their supporting bureaucracies. It entailed the application of a new mode of thought, or the wider-ranging extension of an old one. Over against the social ideals of the three major Victorian classes – the aristocratic belief in the sanctity of property and privilege, the capitalist belief in active capital and competition, and the working-class belief in labour as the sole source of wealth and the primacy of solidarity – the welfare professions set up their own professional ideal of justification by expertise and functional service. Like all class ideals it represented a challenge and a threat to the other classes. Just as the original capitalist ideal had been a moral reproach to the idleness and corruption of the landed aristocracy and the working-class ideal had been a moral protest against the confiscation of 'surplus labour' (a pre-Marxist concept) by both capitalist and landlord, so the professional ideal, at least in its public sector form, was a moral condemnation of the social irresponsibility and functional inefficiency of the unregulated free market which it accused of producing most of the problems of industrial society.

After a century of hegemony (to use Gramsci's neo-Marxist terminology), the entrepreneurial ideal was by the mid-twentieth century in retreat. Its principal tenet that the individual standing alone could solve all his own problems was manifestly inappropriate to a corporate economy in which the individual business man was everywhere yielding to the corporate leviathan, and to a corporate society in which social problems were held to be structural and organizational. To the professional ideal capitalist individualism was disingenuous – corporate capitalism no longer practised competition either within the corporation or in the market place. Where it stood in the way of 'obviously needed' reforms, such as wartime rent controls, slum clearance or social security, it had to be converted, coerced or pushed aside. Not that the entrepreneurial ideal was defeated overnight or harried out of existence. On the contrary, a struggle between the ideals ensued which is still going on, in which capitalism in a sea-changed form is currently making a determined counter attack. If we wish to understand the transformation of modern society from an individualist to a corporate basis, from an individual capitalist to a corporate professional society, we must now turn to the struggle between the class ideals and the triumph of the professional ideal.

Social conflict, of which class conflict is a special case, I argued in the earlier book, is at bottom a struggle for income, status and power.[1] Crude material self-interest, however, is neither very flattering to the ego nor very persuasive of the rest of society. Any group seeking to improve its position in the societal market for people will present a conscious image of its ideal self and the ideal society to which it aspires. The group whose ideal image most permeates what may be called the texture of social thought – not so much conscious, academic social philosophy as the terminology, the concepts and criteria, above all the unquestioned assumptions in which everyday talk about society is carried on – will itself dominate society and enjoy the highest status and rewards. In pre-industrial times the aristocratic ideal of the leisured gentleman and his hierarchical society, based on the unearned income from passive property and on selection by patronage, justified the hegemony of landed gentry who, to the admiration of Malthus, 'consumed more than they produced.' Industrial society was dominated by the individual owner-managing entrepreneur, whose ideal was a society based on active capital, the engine which drove the whole machine, and on free market competition, which selected the fittest to survive and provided goods and services at lowest cost. The entrepreneurial ideal challenged its aristocratic precursor as immoral and corrupt: passive property was considered idle wealth and patronage was labelled 'Old Corruption'.

Both ideals were challenged by the working-class ideal based on labour as the source of all wealth, and on co-operation as the alternative to competition, in the shape of either small-scale Owenite socialism or state collectivism. In terms of that ideal both landlord and capitalist were parasites, living on the surpluses, rent and profit, extracted from the working class with the aid of the monopoly of land and the unequal competition of the labour market. Although the working-class ideal never succeeded in dominating society, it was not altogether without effect: its claims were, very partially, met by the collectivist legislation which restricted the rights of property owners and factory masters and recognized the bargaining position of trade unions.

The history of nineteenth-century England can largely be written in terms of the struggle between these three ideals, in which the entrepreneurial ideal came out on top but the other two survived to continue the fight. Yet it cannot be fully understood without the contribution of a further class and its ideal. In the earlier book I called the professional or non-business class the 'forgotten middle class' of Victorian England not only because it was then largely ignored *as a class* by contemporaries, but because, although it provided most of the social theorists and commentators of the age, it 'forgot itself' in the social theories it invented and popularized.[2] John Stuart Mill, one of the more sceptical, said of the political economists:

> They revolve in their eternal circle of landlords, capitalists, and labourers, until they seem to think of the distinction of society into those three classes as if it were one of God's ordinances, not man's, and as little under human control as the division of day and night.[3]

The political economists were not alone. All the professional thinkers of the day thought about society in tripartite terms: Carlyle's 'Workers, Master Workers, and Master Unworkers', F. D. Maurice's 'the aristocracy, the trading classes, and the working classes', Karl Marx's landowners, bourgeoisie and proletariat, Matthew Arnold's 'Barbarians, Philistines, and Populace'.[4] Only the last, in an obscure place, his report on continental education to the Taunton Commission on middle-class schools in 1868, found it necessary to distinguish between the two parts of the middle class, the professional class 'with fine and governing qualities, but without the idea of service' and 'the immense business class which is becoming so important a power in all countries' but which in England was cut off from the aristocracy and the professions, and 'without governing qualities'.[5]

Yet this self-neglect did not prevent the Victorian professional class from having a social ideal and a role in the development of society. Even when providing ideals for the other classes and considering themselves as individuals raised above the economic battle, they referred to their own kind in flattering terms: James Mill's middle rank exempt from labour, 'the chief source of all that has exalted and refined human nature'; Coleridge's 'clerisy' in charge of 'all the so-called arts and sciences, the possession and application of which constitute the civilization of a country'; John Stuart Mill's 'learned class' which ought to be endowed by the state; Carlyle's 'Aristocracy of Talent'; and so on down to the

Webb's 'Co-efficients', H. G. Wells' 'new samurai' and Beveridge's 'rule of the expert', noted above.[6]

What all these images had in common was the ideal of educated talent in the service of society. In nineteenth-century terms this was a very radical ideal. It was just as hostile to 'Old Corruption' as the entrepreneurial ideal, and indeed helped to undermine and replace it by the selection of public officials by examination; it also became critical of its main ally, the business ideal, and helped to curb the excesses of the free market in the realms of public health, factory reform, food and drug adulteration, and so on.[7] In the process, what had appeared to be a unified bourgeois ideal became bifurcated and turned against itself. The anti-industrial spirit which Martin Wiener has discerned in English culture since 1850 is, as we shall see next, nothing less than the triumph of the professional ideal.

1 THE PROFESSIONAL IDEAL AND THE DECLINE OF THE INDUSTRIAL SPIRIT

In a deservedly famous book, Martin Wiener attributes the relative economic decline of Britain since 1850 to 'the decline of the industrial spirit'.[8] Since the Industrial Revolution when inventors and entrepreneurs were the cultural heroes of popular works like Samuel Smiles's *Self-Help* and *Lives of the Engineers* and the Great Exhibition of 1851 was a celebration of Britain's technological leadership, the educated elite, according to Wiener, has become increasingly anti-industrial, increasingly ashamed of the materialism and money-grubbing of dirty-handed industry, increasingly hostile to technological progress and economic growth. The educated young took to industrial employment only as a last resort, if they failed to find employment in the Civil Service, the army or the church, the liberal professions, or the government of the empire. A climate of opinion developed amongst the upper and middle classes which looked back to an old, pre-industrial, agricultural and craft-based countryside as the 'real' England, and regarded the industrial towns in which most people came to live as an aberration, a 'city of dreadful night' through which the nation must pass from a bright, 'natural', moral past to a hopefully post-industrial future of leafy housing estates and garden cities. This rustic, folksy myth was not confined to conservative, nostalgic paternalists like Richard Jeffries or Stanley Baldwin, but constituted the 'English dream' of radical critics like John Ruskin and William Morris:

> Forget six counties overhung with smoke,
> Forget the snorting steam and piston stroke,
> Forget the spreading of the hideous town;
> Think rather of the pack-horse on the down,
> And dream of London, small, and white, and clean.[9]

(Filthy, smelly, disease-ridden medieval London would have been much flattered by Morris's vision of a Utopia that never was.) Wiener continues:

> In consequence of this anti-industrial myth, England became an industrial society led by men who were deeply opposed to what they saw as the industrial ethos with all its effects and ideas. Business men increasingly shunned the role of entrepreneur for the more socially rewarding role of gentleman.... Gentry values, and the gentry myth of England, domesticated industrialism in political thought and action as they did in the wider culture, separating the 'acceptable' from the 'unacceptable' face of industrial capitalism. There was, as a result, little commitment by political leaders to the whole-hearted pursuit of economic expansion.[10]

Leading industrialists, like Samuel Courtauld in 1942, came to believe that 'the worship of material values is the fatal disease from which our age is suffering'; and the president of the Institute of Industrial Management told his members the following year that 'the old conception of industry was based on the amount of money to be made out of it, and he suggested that the proper outlook was how much happiness sprang from it.'[11] Many British business men thought of themselves either as gentlemen-farmers more concerned with their milk yields than their industrial investment capital/output ratio, or as public servants skilfully maintaining the *status quo*.[12] Their leisurely, gentlemanly attitude to business, which viewed the too avid pursuit of profit as sordid, ended in the relative stagnation of the British economy, which by the 1960s had been overtaken not only by the Americans but by the West Europeans and the Japanese.

The Wiener thesis has been much criticized by economic

historians, who have pointed out that it is the actual behaviour of business men, not the brave, benevolent face they put on it in public relations exercises, that determines economic growth; that the rate of British economic growth, although declining since the 1870s, was as fast as the country's resources warranted; that a nation as small as Britain could not indefinitely continue as the workshop of the world; that the pace of growth for a generation after 1945 was faster than in any period since the Industrial Revolution; and that in the same period, in which Britain was overtaken in production and national income per head, the overtaking countries, notably West Germany and Japan, were not burdened with heavy defence costs and a declining empire.[13] Others have pointed out that the public schools and universities, especially Oxford and Cambridge, which Wiener blamed for their lack of interest in science and technology, began to introduce those subjects and to send more of their graduates into industry and commerce at precisely the period, the generation before the First World War, when Britain's relative industrial decline began.[14]

Whether or not there are other causes of Britain's economic decline, there is still enough truth in Wiener's description of the anti-industrial outlook of the British to warrant investigation. Two problems, however, arise with his aetiology. Wiener puts down the nostalgic, conservative, gentlemanly attitudes of British business men to the survival of pre-industrial aristocratic values in a country which never experienced the overthrow of the aristocracy by war or revolution. These values were absorbed by the new industrialists both directly, through emulation by business men themselves buying land and setting themselves up as country gentlemen, and indirectly, through the education of their sons in the public schools and the older universities. The problems with this explanation are, firstly, that it assumes that aristocratic values were in fact anti-industrial and, secondly, that they were the values taught in the new and reformed public schools and universities of the Victorian age.

Contrary to the first of these assumptions, the aristocracy and gentry before and during the Industrial Revolution were the most economically progressive and profit-oriented ruling class in Europe. They invested eagerly in agricultural improvement and enclosure, in trading ventures, mining, roads, river navigations and canals, docks, early railways, urban development and even, where circumstances permitted, in manufacturing such as brick-making, iron-founding, and textiles.[15] It is true that they preferred not to manage such enterprises in person but through managers or leaseholders, but so little did they despise wealth from whatever source that they would marry anyone for her money. It was the smaller gentry on the fringes of the landed class, like some of Jane Austen's characters, who felt threatened by *nouveaux riches* 'tradesmen from Birmingham', but the self-confident aristocracy felt no such insecurity.

Curiously enough, the emulation of the landed class which Wiener blames for the 'gentrification of the bourgeoisie' was one of the driving forces of the Industrial Revolution, leading inventors and entrepreneurs alike striving to join the ruling elite and 'found a family'. While this *might* have diverted their energies and capital away from industry, as it had for generations of new men before them (only to be replaced by others coming up behind), the solid permanent nature of the new fixed industrial capital made the break increasingly difficult, while the increasing scale and wealth of the late Victorian company made it perfectly possible to unite a landed estate and country house with a permanent base in industry. Sir Julius Wernher, Sir John Guest (Lord Wimborne), W. H. Smith and Lord Leverhulme were only the best known of the newcomers, who bought land without giving up business and were welcomed by London 'society' at the highest level. Meanwhile, the great landlords drew an increasing proportion of their wealth from mines, docks, railways and urban property, far outdistancing their agrarian country cousins suffering from the agricultural depression in the south and east, and were not averse to investing their surpluses and even themselves in business itself.[16] In 1896 167 noblemen, a quarter of the active peerage, held directorships of companies.[17] Far from despising one another, the wealthier landowners and the neo-corporate capitalists joined together in a new plutocracy.[18] If at the very time that Britain's relative economic decline was supposed to have begun the most prosperous and successful landowners were throwing in their lot with big business, that decline could hardly be due to the anti-industrial influence of the aristocracy.

Contrary to the second assumption, that the anti-industrial values taught in the public schools and older universities were the surviving aristocratic values of an earlier epoch, the schools and colleges of the Victorian age were newly reformed institutions consciously reacting against the old, pre-industrial society. From the point of view of the new society, imbued with middle-class values both entrepreneurial and professional, the Oxford and Cambridge colleges and the old endowed schools were nests of vice, idleness and inefficiency.[19] If they were to serve the needs of a new, more serious and progressive age they had to be reformed, their vice and corruption suppressed, and their indolent fellows and masters turned into hard-working career professionals with a mission to educate efficient, responsible Christian gentlemen rather than effete aristocratic rakes and loungers. They even transformed the idea of a gentleman, from a man of good birth and prickly military honour into a 'gentle man', honest, upright, considerate and dedicated to the service of his fellows and his country.[20] Bertrand Russell grasped the wrong end of the stick when he said that 'the concept of the gentleman was invented by the aristocracy to keep the middle classes in order'.[21] Its modern version was invented by the Victorian middle classes to keep the aristocracy up to the new moral mark and incidentally end the adolescent practice of duelling, and was imposed by the reformed public schools and universities.

The reforms were at first chiefly moral and disciplinary, the introduction of Thomas Arnold's system of forming 'Christian men, for Christian boys I can scarcely hope to make': 'What we must look for here is, first, religious and moral principles; secondly, gentlemanly conduct; thirdly, intellectual ability'.[22] Arnold has been given too much credit for the whole revolution, and there were other reforming headmasters, Vaughan at Harrow, Cotton at Marlborough, Irving at Uppingham, and many more, but the moral reaction against the Hogarthian education of the old society was the same everywhere. Traditional bullying was to be sublimated into the responsibility of senior boys as monitors or prefects for discipline, including corporal punishment. The spontaneous savagery of the old free-for-all playing fields was replaced by organized games, which fostered team spirit and loyalty to the house and school as well as individual prowess. Daily chapel, three times on Sundays, inculcated a serious unaristocratic attitude to religion which emphasized duty to God and man. The study of the classics, formerly a pointless 'mental discipline' and a source of Latin tags for church sermons and parliamentary speeches, was transformed into an education in the history, literature, philosophy and politics of the model ruling elites of the ancient world. The whole system came to be aimed not at socializing a leisured class for a life of cultured idleness and aristocratic field sports (the individual sports of hunting, shooting and fishing), but at forming an active, responsible, physically fit, self-disciplined elite of professional men and administrators for public service in church and state, the empire and the liberal professions.

The system spread rapidly to the older public boarding schools and the new model ones which were being founded on all sides. Contrary to popular opinion and their own snobbish propaganda, most of them catered for middle-class boys rather than the aristocracy and gentry. At Winchester, for example, the most intellectual of the nine great Clarendon schools, the overwhelming majority of the boys from 1830 to 1914 came from families in the church, the law, the armed forces, and other professions – admirers, no doubt, of the aristocracy but in process of becoming rather a different class. Only about one in five or six of their fathers were 'gentlemen of leisure', and fewer still, one in twenty rising to one in seven, were in business.[23] The new and reformed schools were not just a middle-class but a professional-class phenomenon. The aristocracy sent their sons overwhelmingly to Eton, with a small minority – less than 10 per cent – to other Clarendon schools. The gentry were perforce more catholic in their choice, but wherever they went were rarely more than a minority. Business men until the last decades of the nineteenth century rarely sent their sons to boarding schools at all unless, like Sir Robert Peel or W. E. Gladstone, they were intended for public life rather than the family business.

For the professional middle class the new schools were attractive because of their economy. They were a cheap and affordable means of obtaining what was claimed to be an upper-class education at middle-class prices. Not every school was a Dotheboys Hall, but the poor food, hard beds, unheated rooms and inadequate plumbing universally reported kept down the cost. The original, pre-industrial aristocratic form of education had been by private tutor, culminating in the frighteningly expensive and morally dangerous grand tour of Europe, for which 'schooling in public with a mob of boys' was a poor substitute reluctantly resorted to, especially during the Great French Wars. The railways of the Victorian age, together with the system of boarding pupils in masters' houses, often to take advantage of the cheap, endowed teaching at ancient grammar schools, brought the new and reformed schools within geographical and financial reach of a burgeoning professional middle class more dependent than their business counterparts on education and paper qualifications for their careers.

The careers followed by public school alumni were as strikingly professional as their fathers', with some adjustment for generational changes in fashion. Whereas clerical fathers of Wykehamists declined from nearly half at mid-century to one in seven by the end, their clerical sons declined from a third to one-twentieth or less; but the professions as a whole, including government service and the armed forces, continued to take about three out of every four Wykehamists.[24] If Winchester is typical – and lesser public schools took even fewer sons of the aristocracy and gentry and no more of the business class until the twentieth century – the reformed public schools of Victorian England were overwhelmingly staffed by professional men educating the sons of professional families for professional careers.

The same is true, if to a lesser degree, of the ancient universities. Reformed from without by the pressure of largely middle-class public opinion, led by James Heywood, the Manchester Unitarian banker, and the Benthamite partisans of the *Westminster Review*; and from within by Thomas Arnold (after his elevation in 1841 to the Oxford chair of history), Mark Pattison and Benjamin Jowett at Oxford and Adam Sedgwick, Henry Sidgwick and the elder Baden Powell at Cambridge, the two universities were transformed in a generation from clerical-run seminars for the Anglican clergy and finishing schools for leisured gentlemen into professionalized institutions. They were operated by career dons for the sons of the landed and professional classes preparing for careers in the public service, including politics, the home and Indian Civil Services, colonial government, and the liberal professions.[25] They still retained a place for 'gilded youth', from the 'heavy swells' of Victorian Oxbridge to the 'bright young things' of the *Brideshead Revisited* period between the wars, but they were more a decorative excrescence than a predominant feature. Two-thirds of the undergraduates at Sidney Sussex

College, Cambridge from 1843 to 1914 whose backgrounds are known came from professional homes, and no less than 94 per cent of the graduates of Balliol College, Oxford between 1832 and 1914 went into government service or the learned professions. Only sixty-five out of 983 Sidney Sussex men came from the landed gentry, 153 from the business classes, and fifty-one from the working class; all the rest were from the professional middle class. Only twenty-nine of the Balliol men went into business, none into industry but all twenty-nine into banking and land agency.[26] If Sidney Sussex and Balliol were typical, Victorian Oxbridge, like the public schools, was a professional-class phenomenon.

What, then, were the values taught in the public schools and ancient universities of Victorian and Edwardian England? They were the values of the men who reformed and ran them, the new breed of career professional masters and dons. They were only incidentally anti-industrial; their positive aspect, far more important than the negative, was the belief in education for the public service. In contemporary terms this meant service of the public in politics, the home Civil Service, administration of the empire, and the liberal professions including, not least, the teaching profession in the public schools and universities. We have seen in Chapter 4 how great Oxford and Cambridge tutors like T. H. Green, Arnold Toynbee, Alfred Marshall and A. C. Pigou aimed to send out into the world, in Marshall's words, strong men with cool heads and warm hearts to grapple with the social problems of their age. T. W. Heyck has argued that 'the ideal of disinterested public service' began with the landed gentry, and 'noblesse oblige' was certainly a part of their ideal.[27] Yet for them it was optional, and under 'Old Corruption' it was rarely completely disinterested. For the professional middle class, on the other hand, it was the heart of their ideal, since their status depended on persuading the public that they had a disinterested service to offer. Social and educational work at Toynbee Hall and other university settlements in the slums was only one way of serving the public. More could be done by occupying positions of power and influence, as Beveridge did at the Board of Trade and Keynes at the Treasury. It was not that such service could not be performed at all in industry – as Rowntree pioneered social surveying from his base in the chocolate factory; it was simply that in the opinion of men so educated industry offered less scope, less excitement, less sense of moving the world in a morally progressive direction and, not least, less psychic reward in the shape of visible prestige and invisible self-respect.

The great African administrator Frederick Lugard expressed it well when, as a young product of Rossall School, he was offered in 1875 a job in his brother-in-law's sugar refinery. He wrote to his sister:

> If I go in for this I have to throw overboard the ICS [Indian Civil Service] which if I passed it would be an infinitely better thing besides being a thoroughly gentlemanly occupation, and look at it how I may, I can't bring myself to think that an Assistant in a Sugar Factory is such. Of course, a gentleman is still a gentleman wherever he is, but still the Lugards have been in the Army and the Church, good servants of God and the Queen, but few if any have been tradesmen.[28]

Lugard failed the ICS examination and went to Sandhurst, the army college, and after service in India, Uganda and Burma became colonial Governor of Nigeria and Hong Kong. Wiener reads this as an example of aristocratic values in action, but nowhere did Lugard hint at the leisured life of the landed gentleman. On the contrary, he sought and achieved the strenuous life of a great public servant.

The links between the public schools and Oxbridge and the public service were strengthened by the competitive examinations for the Indian Civil Service from 1858 and for the home Civil Service from 1870, by the Cardwell reforms in the army in 1871, the continuing expansion of the empire, and by the growth and increasing formalization of the professions. Professional-class education and the public service were a perfect match: the schools and ancient universities consciously prepared their students for a life of service, and the public service provided appropriate employment for young men with high-grade education but little or no capital. As a later colonial administrator in Lord Cromer's crack Sudan service put it:

> My schooling was an excellent preparation for my career in the Sudan Political Service. From an early age one was taught to be self-reliant and to accept responsibility. The virtues of self discipline and physical fitness, both essential elements in

371

public school training, were to prove of estimable value as also was the exercising which one gains from being a house and subsequently a school monitor.[29]

The public schools and ancient universities were not intended to educate business men or their sons and, far from setting out to convert them to the public service ideal, did what they could to keep them out and to embarrass them with contempt for 'trade' when they insisted on coming. Between 1752 and 1886 only 0.1 per cent of Oxford entrants and rather more but still only 9.4 per cent of Cambridge students came from business families.[30] University men were the academic elite of the schools, intent on professional careers. The schools themselves took rather more business men's sons but still only 11 per cent of Wykehamists born between 1820 and 1922 came from business families, increasing to a peak of 15 per cent for those born between 1900 and 1910. Winchester actually sent more boys into business – an average of 16.4 per cent, increasing to a peak of 27.9 per cent in 1900–14 – than it took from there.[31] Even Oxford and Cambridge, especially after the establishment of Appointments Committees in 1892 and 1901 to encourage recruitment to industry, began to send graduates into business. By 1913 nearly 20 per cent of Oxford graduates and by 1903–07 24 per cent of Cambridge pass men (those without honours degrees or much hope of passing public entrance examinations) went into business careers.[32]

Since the First World War and more particularly since the Second the public schools and Oxbridge have attracted increasing numbers of business men's sons (and, latterly, daughters) and sent more of them into business. Of boys at Winchester born between 1900 and 1909 and between 1910 and 1919 and at school (mostly) between the wars, 14 per cent and 15 per cent came from business families and 28 per cent and 19 per cent went into business.[33] The Oxford and Cambridge University Appointments Boards strengthened the links with industry, particularly with the larger corporations coming into existence like ICI, Courtaulds, Unilever, and their kind, to the distaste of many dons and students who, like Sir Ernest Barker, thought that the university should be 'a stronghold of pure learning' and of 'long time values against the demands of material progress'.[34] Statistics are hard to come by and the Royal Commission on Public Schools in 1968 muddied the issue by compounding the professional and business classes: 'Over ninety per cent of boarding pupils in boys' public schools (excluding children of armed forces personnel who are not allocated to any social class in the official classifications) had parents in the professional or managerial classes'.[35] By that time, however, the professionalization of management had gone so far as to assimilate the managerial to the professional class, so that the public schools were catering for much the same sort of people.

The Commission gave no statistics of careers in general but its survey of 'Who gets to the top?' showed that over 70 per cent of the 'directors of prominent firms' and of the Bank of England came from public schools (which catered for 2.6 per cent of 14-year-old boys) and most of the rest from the other independent and direct grant schools (which catered for another 4.8 per cent). At the same time it showed that the public schools provided over a third (and the other independent and direct grant schools nearly another third) of the students at Oxford and Cambridge, over two-fifths of entrants to the Administrative Class of the Civil Service, nearly two-thirds of the entrants to the Foreign Service, a third of the vice-chancellors, heads of Oxbridge colleges and university professors, a fifth of the Labour MPs and two-fifths of the 1967 Labour Cabinet, over three-quarters of the Conservative MPs and nine-tenths of the 1963 Tory Cabinet, over half of the admirals, generals and air marshals in the armed forces, two-thirds of the physicians and surgeons at the London teaching hospitals and on the General Medical Council, three-quarters of the Anglican bishops, four-fifths of the judges and QCs, and a quarter of the Fellows of the Royal Society.[36] By that time the public school men were dominating the commanding heights of all the major professional and managerial hierarchies, and it was no longer true that they neglected business. The most that could be claimed was that they showed a marked preference for the City – banking, insurance, stockbroking, investment companies, and the commodity and currency markets – and for the larger commercial corporations over traditional manufacturing industry. In this they displayed a keen sense of the drift of the modern economy away from manufacturing and towards finance and commerce.

This realistic adjustment was in line with the traditional flexibility of elites in English society. In recent years, especially since the generational revolt of the 1960s, there has been what a progressive headmaster, John Rae of Westminster School, has called a 'public school revolution'.[37] On the academic side Latin has become optional, Greek has almost disappeared, mathematics and science, economics and computing have come to the fore, and current affairs and general studies have taken a more formal place in the curriculum. Compulsory chapel and compulsory games have been much reduced or abolished, and individual sports like tennis, squash and golf are offered as alternatives to cricket and rugby. Fagging for prefects and official beating of younger by senior boys have practically disappeared. Beginning with Marlborough in 1969, girls have been admitted to the sixth form in many boarding schools and to the lower school in a few (much to the chagrin of the headmistresses of competing girls' schools). Restrictions on contact with the extra-mural world, including the female sex, have been eased though not abolished, and community service (such as helping old people and deprived children) has become a prominent feature of spare-time activities. The unisex youth culture of the post-1960 generation has invaded the schools, bringing with it anti-authoritarian attitudes, pressure group politics like the environmental and anti-nuclear movements, pop music, drink and drugs. Exclusiveness remains, but the over-confident 'effortless superiority' of public school boys of the past towards their age mates has been somewhat dented, especially when scholarship boys and girls from state schools often get better degrees at Oxford and Cambridge, still more when young pop stars with working-class accents have shown how to make fortunes larger than those of dukes, merchant bankers and, certainly, of most professional men. Above all, in a world of career hierarchies in both business and the professions there is no more prejudice against business amongst public school boys and Oxbridge graduates than in society at large. Indeed, there may well be less, since the higher rewards of the City and big business are more within their grasp.

What, then, remains of the Wiener thesis? Paradoxically, a great deal. The professional ideal of public service, a sense that service to the community should come before the pursuit of profit, has permeated society far beyond the public schools and older universities and has infiltrated business itself. What Wiener called the gentrification of the industrialist is really his professionalization. When the director-general of the Institute of Directors said that 'directors are a kind of aristocracy: they should be men of parts, and they should have interests outside their business', he meant an educated aristocracy, with an ideal of service to the world outside. ICI executives compared themselves not to leisured aristocrats but to the prestigious professions. 'We think of ourselves as being a university with a purpose,' said one, and another, 'We are very similar to the Administrative Class of the Civil Service.' According to W. J. Reader, the social structure of ICI's predecessor Brunner Mond's management at Winnington, Cheshire 'reproduced the split in the English middle classes between "the professions" and "trade".' 'Technical men of graduate standing' could take election to the Winnington Hall Club for granted; no one else could, least of all engineers (not normally at that time graduates) and commercial men.[38] Since the 1920s more and more managers and technical men have been to public school or become graduates: a survey of 400 managers in 1956 showed that while only 7 per cent of those born before 1895 were from public schools, 38 per cent of those born after 1925 were old boys; and while only 7 per cent of the oldest cohort had degrees, 58 per cent of the youngest group were graduates.[39] The proportion has steadily increased since then. Professionalization has meant more than an increase in qualifications: it has meant the importation into business of the professional principles of a stable, progressive career, security of tenure, and the tradition (if not always the reality) of public responsibility.

To be sure, there has been a reaction against this weakening of the profit motive by free marketeers of the 'Selsdon man' and 'Grantham woman' variety, but these have often been politicians and propagandists rather than business men themselves, and their very stridency is evidence of their exasperation with the uncapitalistic attitudes of traditional British business managers. Perhaps the best evidence of the permeation of British capitalism by the professional ideal comes from traditional self-made men who succeeded without the aid of elite education or professional training. William Morris, Lord Nuffield (the Henry Ford of the British motor industry), Isaac Wolfson of Great Universal Stores, and Sir David Robinson (pioneer of rental television), all crowned their careers by founding Oxbridge colleges.[40] There bright young men like themselves would be syphoned off from making entrepreneurial fortunes into the public service, the professions or managerial careers in established corporations. To this extent even the most entrepreneurial of business men came to be imbued with the professional ideal.

The decline of the industrial spirit, then, was in reality the retreat of the entrepreneurial ideal before the incursions of professionalism. Business itself became permeated with the professional ideal, in two ways: firstly, through the professionalization of management, which attracted a different kind of business man educated, often at public school and/or university, in the tradition of public service; and secondly, through the conversion of traditional business men not so educated to an ideal of public responsibility which manifested itself in handsome gifts to universities and other public charities. There were of course exceptions to this idealistic picture, and there were still traditional capitalists who pursued ruthless efficiency and naked competition in the old-fashioned way. But it is striking how many of them began as outsiders to the British system, men like the Scottish American Ian McGregor of the British Steel Corporation and the National Coal Board, central European Arnold Weinstock of the General Electric Company, the Australians Sir Michael Edwardes of British Leyland and Rupert Murdoch of *The Times* and *Sun* Newspapers, and Czechoslovak Robert Maxwell of the *Mirror* group, and they have found few imitators among native British business men. Noel Annan, himself a pillar of the intellectual aristocracy whose influence he has pointed to in Victorian England, correctly diagnosed that the one common assumption shared by the whole spectrum of opinion makers in modern Britain, 'that the career of money-making, industry, business, profits or efficiency is a despicable life in which no sane and enlightened person should be engaged', became 'the accepted gospel of the country' through 'the propaganda of the intelligentsia'.[41] The success of that propaganda was in effect the triumph of the professional ideal.

The professional ideal, however, penetrated much deeper than the career preferences of public school boys and university graduates or the inferiority complexes of business men. It went to the very heart of the concept of property. As we shall see next, it transformed property from the absolute concept created by pre-industrial English landlords and inherited by industrial capitalists into the more contingent form appropriate to the professional society of the late twentieth century.

2 PROFESSIONALISM AND HUMAN CAPITAL

All societies turn on their concept of property.[42] Where one man, as in Pharaoh's Egypt, owns all the property, there the structure of society is monolithic and all power and resources flow to the centre. Where nature's goods are free or held in common, as amongst the Australian aborigines before Captain Cook, there power is diffuse and resources are distributed, if not equally, then according to the daily efforts made to appropriate them. Coming nearer home, medieval society in England was based on the feudal concept of contingent property, held directly or indirectly from the king in return for service, military, spiritual or servile, and (in theory at least) forfeited on failure to perform the service. Between the Black Death and the Civil War this was replaced by the concept of absolute property, by means of which the English landlords turned lordship into ownership and defeated the claims of crown, church and tenants to service, loyalty and protection. This same concept of absolute property was seized on by the incipient capitalists of pre-industrial England as the basis of contract and the free market, and laid the foundations of industrialism, under which those who owned the resources absolutely could buy the labour of those who did not. The concept of property, enshrined in custom and law, determined the relationships between the members of society and decided who got what, when and where.

The protean nature of the concept, its ability to change its shape and nature from one society or one period to another, is due to its infinite flexibility. Best conceived not as the ownership of things fixed and immovable but as the right to a flow of income from a scarce resource, that flow is capable of being divided and diverted into a myriad channels and can therefore sustain an infinitely variable congeries of relationships. Even at its most absolute, property still had to yield taxes to the king, tithes to the church, rates to the poor, repairs to the highways, and contributions to the local defence of the country. It varied also according to the nature of the scarce resource. Absolute property in land yielded rent, an unearned income which supported an elite of leisured gentlemen, free to do what they liked, including governing the localities and the country. Absolute property in industrial capital demanded active management, so that capitalists were less free to govern and often had to employ others to do it for them, as in the end they came to employ others to run their businesses. Passive landowner-

377

ship and active capital thus produced competing elites and contrasting social structures. For much of the nineteenth century many business men attacked the landlords for their 'idleness' and 'corruption' and supported schemes of land reform designed to clip their wings and make them conform to their own entre-preneurial ideal. Only when more extreme reformers, demanding confiscatory taxation of land or outright land nationalization, began to threaten the principle of absolute property itself did both kinds of property owner rally to the common defence. These more extreme land reformers, I have argued elsewhere, were led by men from the professional middle class like John Stuart Mill and Alfred Russel Wallace, who were opposed to completely absolute property, and helped lay the foundations of the professional approach to the concept.[43]

The professional concept rests as much on a scarce resource as the landed or capitalist, but instead of controlling land or capital it sets out to control the supply of expertise. Human capital may at first sight seem to be more evanescent than land or machines, but in practice it is the only form of property capable of enlarging itself and, in the last resort, of self-reproduction. Human capital theorists have generally assumed that investment in education *of itself* yields a differential flow of income, and great ingenuity has been applied to calculating the additional increment produced by different levels of qualification – usually with disappointing results.[44] What such calculations have ignored has been the element of scarcity of the resource. Some kinds of expertise may be scarce by their very nature, like that of a Kiri Te Kanawa or a Barbara Hepworth, for which the famous opera singer or sculptor may charge a rent. But most professional expertise does not enjoy a natural scarcity, and its value has to be protected and raised, first by persuading the public of the vital importance of the service and then by controlling the market for it. That is why the organized professional bodies are, as much as trade unions, institutions for educating the public and for closing the market, and operate 'strategies of closure' including control of entry, training and qualification, and seek a monopoly of the name and the practice. Even the 'unqualified' professions like the Civil Service, journalism and the theatre try to make early entry and practical experience stand in for qualification.

When such devices succeed, they create an artificial scarcity of the resource, the particular expertise, and produce a flow of income in the form of a rent, in the true Ricardian sense of a payment for the use of a scarce resource. Scarcity may appear long before a complete monopoly is attained (the landed class never had a complete monopoly of the land) and the element of rent may be larger or smaller accordingly; but some element of rent accrues from *any* degree of control of the market, which is why organized professions are paid more than unorganized occupations. Since the essence of property is a right to (some portion of) the flow of income from the resource owned, professional capital – which is manifestly more tangible than corporate shareholdings, less destructible than buildings and machinery, and capable of self-renewal and improvement – is thus a species of property in the truest sense.

It is, nevertheless, not an absolute but a contingent form of property, contingent, that is, upon the performance of a service. It is this principle of justification by service that lies behind the professional right to property and the professional social ideal. It is also the foundation of the claim to moral superiority which, like other classes before them, the professional class make over their rivals. Just as the landed aristocracy claimed superiority for their monopoly of the leisure in which to guide society and pursue the high culture of 'civilization', and the business class claimed superiority over the idle rich for the productive use of wealth, so the professional class claimed superiority over both for their provision of expert services without which society could not thrive or even survive. It is not necessary to take sides in this invidious moral competition to see that, in the increasingly complex society of twentieth-century England in which a vast and increasing range of expert services are necessary to social survival and well-being, the professional ideal of justification by service has the edge over justification by wealth, whether active or leisured. The very defence offered by landlords and business men, that they too provide a social service in the shape of conservation of the land and the most efficient provision of goods, bears witness to the professionals' assumption of superiority.

The importance of property in this sense to the professional man went beyond moral self-confidence and self-respect. It gave him independence, security of tenure, a firm base from which to criticize without fear of the consequences, a secure position of leverage from which to move society, or his own particular corner of it, in the direction of change and reform. Above all, it gave him the psychic security to press his own class ideal, his own view of what society should be and how it should be organized upon the rest of society. The ideal as it emerged in the nineteenth century was based on the primacy of expert service and selection by merit, measured no longer by aristocratic opinion, the competition of the market or popular vote but by the judgment of the qualified expert. As such it challenged the aristocratic ideal of the primacy of passive property as being idle wealth and patronage as favouritism and corruption. It challenged the working-class ideal of the right to the whole produce of labour and co-operation in place of competition as not distinguishing between more and less qualified labour or between equality of opportunity and equality regardless of merit. And it came to challenge its old ally, the capitalist ideal of active property and the survival of the most meritorious through competition, as putting profits before social responsibility and the blind selection of the market before the expert assessment of true merit. After beginning in harness with the capitalist ideal in attacking the abuse of aristocratic power in government (parliamentary, financial and administrative reform), taxation (the corn laws and other hindrances on free trade), and religion (tithes, church rates, control of education), it rapidly turned against the abuse of capitalist power in children's employment, unsafe factories and mines, insanitary housing, adulteration of food and drugs, pollution of the environment, and so on. The collectivist legislation of the Victorian age can be read as one long assault on the irresponsibility of capital and competition by a public opinion moralized by the professional social ideal.

The logical outcome of that assault, as was pointed out in Chapter 1, was an attack on the concept of capital itself. This has occupied most of the twentieth century and, although the struggle is not yet concluded and is indeed subject to the backlash we shall explore in Chapter 10, the professional concept of property has made sufficient inroads into the absolute concept to have modified it beyond recognition. Since the concept of contingent property based on professional service is an echo of the feudal concept based on military, spiritual or labour service, we can think of this process as a species of 'subinfeudation', the slotting in of new 'tenants' in the hierarchy of property holders or of intermediate claimants on the flow of income from a scarce resource. The process of subinfeudation can be discerned in relation to six different kinds of property, notably rented houses, leaseholds, farms, land generally, property in jobs and, finally, industrial capital itself.

Most privately rented house property in Britain has been subject to rent control since 1915, when it was introduced under threat of rent strikes beginning in Glasgow to protect soldiers' wives and munitions workers from exploitation by profiteering landlords during the wartime housing shortage. It was maintained, often reluctantly, for the majority of rented houses between the wars, when every attempt to reduce or abolish it was met by the argument that this would cause hardship to a great number of tenants, and that people must come before profits. Rent control and tenant security were extended to nearly all unfurnished houses during the Second World War and more recently to furnished lettings (other than short-term holiday accommodation and the like).[45] Even those free marketeers who disliked the policy could only plead for a wider distribution of home ownership, with the implication that until there were sufficient homes to go around at low enough prices the system of rent controls was unavoidable.[46] The unintended consequences were the withdrawal of the private landlord whenever he could from the housing market, which meant when controlled tenants with security of tenure died or voluntarily removed, so that privately rented accommodation shrank from 91 per cent in 1914 to 53 per cent in 1957 and 11 per cent in 1984, and a consequent upsurge of owner-occupation, from about 9 per cent of the housing stock in 1914 to 29 per cent in 1951 and 61 per cent in 1984. The difference was made up by the supply of public housing by the local authorities, negligible in 1914, rising to 18 per cent of the housing stock in 1951 and 32 per cent in 1978, a measure of the failure of the policy to solve the housing shortage.[47]

The result has been that not only the remaining 'statutory tenants' of private houses and flats have come to share the beneficial ownership with the landlord but even the council tenants of the new towns and local authorities have (less formally) acquired the same share of the property rights. When a privately owned house is sold to the sitting tenant the price is normally about half the value on the open market. The same applies as official policy to the sale of council housing under current (1988) government schemes, which also provide for subsidized mortgages at below market interest rates. Thus the tenant has acquired approximately half the value of the property and has become a 'subinfeudated' tenant sharing the benefits of ownership with the landlord, whether public or private. It may of course be argued that under the pressure of the market and under current government policy, both private and public housing stocks are decreasing, to be replaced by owner-occupation, but the principle of the protected tenant sharing ownership with the landlord remains and has actually been perpetuated by the Housing Act, 1980, which provides for a new type of protected shorthold tenancy, albeit for a limited duration of from one to five years.[48] It is significant that even a Conservative government committed to the free market did not feel strong enough to restore in full the absolute property rights of housing landlords. What it will do in its third term remains to be seen.

Under the Leasehold Enfranchisement Act, 1967 the ground landlord of residential property in London and elsewhere, who used at the end of the lease to possess the building even where it was built by the tenant, is obliged to sell the freehold of a house (not as yet of a flat) or grant an extended lease to the lessee at the latter's option, at an arbitrated price or rent based on the current market value of the ground rent.[49] This makes the purchasing or continuing leaseholder co-parcener of the beneficial ownership with the ground landlord and, in effect, a subinfeudated tenant.

Tenant farms in Britain have been subject to rent control with security of tenure since their introduction during the Second World War to safeguard the production of food, subject to eviction for bad farming by the County War Agricultural Committee. They were continued at the behest of the National Farmers' Union – a good example of corporatism at work – by the Agricultural Holdings Act, 1948. The surviving wartime disciplinary power of eviction for bad farming was transferred from the County Agricultural Committees to the Agricultural Land Tribunals by the Agriculture Act, 1958, under which and subsequent Acts in 1963, 1968 and 1970 the tenant could defeat a notice to quit by a counter-notice invoking the protection of the tribunal, which could also fix the rent by arbitration.[50] Thus the good farm tenant was nearly as secure as the house tenant, and similarly shared the beneficial ownership with the landlord and with a similar result, that tenant farms have shrunk from about two-thirds of the holdings at mid-century to about 41 per cent in 1981. It is surprising that, both under Labour governments which gained little political support from farmers and under Conservative governments traditionally tender to landlords, the absolute property rights of agricultural landlords have been thus whittled away. An unintended consequence is that many new owner-occupiers have sold out to large 'agro-business' corporations which now farm an increasing proportion of the available land and are assimilating agriculture to the corporate structure of industry.

Formerly, landlords would have been able to recoup their losses by selling or leasing part of their land for development for industrial, commercial or residential purposes, even at the cost of bribing farm tenants with a share of the capital gains. But since the Conservative Town and Country Planning Act, 1932, all land has been increasingly subject to planning controls by local and central government and, since the Labour Town and Country Planning Act, 1947, to a fluctuating series of development charges and similar taxes on the incremental gains from changes in land use which have had the effect of syphoning off from the landlord part of the benefits of ownership.[51]

The history of land and property policy in twentieth-century Britain is exceptionally tangled. It is not, as is often thought, a straightforward conflict between a Conservative Party dedicated to the defence of property and opposition parties bent on clipping the wings of property owners. All three major parties have been divided. The Liberals, who became concerned in the late Victorian age with the problems of the unearned increment and variants of the single tax but feared outright land nationalization, lost the landlords and many of the business men to the Tories without gaining the working-class voters, and consequently lost also their hopes of office.[52] The Conservatives represented not only the landowners but also the developers, the construction industry, and the advocates of a property-owning democracy, all of whom felt threatened by the landlords' absolute right to withhold land from the market or charge a monopoly price for releasing it. The Labour Party was divided between the protagonists of land nationalization and the pragmatists who saw the best hope of solving the housing shortage and winning a fair share of the capital gains created by the community in a judicious combination of planning regulation, compulsory purchase, and taxation of betterment. Unfortunately, all three parties pursued their vacillating policies with little regard to the constraints of the market and the powerful interest groups which could defeat government pressure by withholding land or development funds or construction skills in what amounted to a strike of capital. Those interests could also respond to relaxation of pressure by commercial property booms in the 1950s and 1970s which not only made a killing for property speculators but diverted funds from productive to unproductive investment.[53]

Despite the consequent twists and turns of policy, the principle has been established that landowners do not have the absolute right to do what they would with their property and to unlimited capital gains arising therefrom. They have not been fully compensated for loss of betterment for denial of planning permission or for 'worsenment' arising from development on neighbouring properties, and they have been forced to share the capital gains arising from development with the community. As freeholders they have watched their mineral rights disappear (under a Conservative government in 1939) as well as their ownership of the air space above them. Although they have not been constrained or penalized nearly as much as some of their critics desired or opponents threatened, there can be no doubt that the absolute property rights which landowners enjoyed for upwards of three centuries have been severely curtailed in the twentieth.

In certain parts of the country they have been curtailed even more and shared more directly with the community. In the National Parks and Areas of Outstanding Natural Beauty planning legislation has restricted development within the narrowest bounds and opened up large tracts of the countryside to access by the public. Where landlords and their tenant farmers can no longer exclude the public from their land, their exclusive enjoyment of their property has been reduced to a mere stewardship for the community.[54] Even where public access is restricted, the principle that the government, on behalf of society, can invade to flood land for reservoirs, build motorways, lay gas pipes, erect power lines, sterilize land for military purposes, and in other ways interfere so deeply with the rights of property means that the concept is no longer absolute.

The absolute rights of industrial capital have been undermined from a different direction. Interference with the industrialist's right to do what he liked with his property began in the nineteenth century with the Factory Acts, the Mining Acts, the Alkali Acts, and the Workmen's Compensation Acts. Even his right to control the distribution of his gross income, subject to contracts of employment with his workers, began to be limited before the First World War, with the originating measures of the welfare state. He was forced to insure privately against industrial injuries in 1897, and to pay his share of National Insurance for health and, in certain cases, for unemployment in 1911. These compulsory levies were extended in 1920, 1925 and 1936 to cover health and unemployment insurance for the great majority of workers and old age, widows' and orphans' pensions for workers and their families, and from 1948 for the whole employed population and their dependants.[55] It has been argued that employers' national insurance contributions are a tax on employment which falls ultimately on the worker, but this is not the experience of trade union negotiators in this country nor of the more expensive schemes in the continental Common Market countries.[56] In practice the state has established the right to determine for certain, admittedly limited, purposes the distribution of the product of industry between employer and worker.

That principle has been extended much further by incomes policy and dividend restriction, which have been in intermittent, if hotly debated, operation since the war (1948–51, 1961–62, 1966–72, 1973–74, 1975–76, and 1977–79).[57] Whatever the political arguments for and against such policies – and most governments up to 1979 have tried the case both ways – no one disputes the right, as distinct from the wisdom, of the state to limit increases in earnings and dividends and thus to determine in large measure the distribution of the flow of income from business.

Taxation policy has moved in a similar direction. Below a certain threshold taxes do not encroach on the concept of property; above that threshold they do, as witness the deliberately confiscatory nature of Henry George's 'single tax' or the intention of the highest rates of modern death duties.[58] Victorian governments set their face against 'progressive taxation', except to relieve low-income earners altogether, and believed that in principle everyone should contribute an equal proportion to the expenses of the state. Since 1894 death duties have risen from 8 per cent at the maximum to 80 per cent, and if Burke's *Landed Gentry* has characterized death duty as 'a voluntary tax' it is surprising how many millionaires and great landowners still volunteer to pay it.[59] Though no doubt ingenious ways are found to avoid the new capital transfer tax which has replaced it, that does not detract from the acknowledged right of the state to tax capital at confiscatory rates. Similarly, graduated income tax has increased since 1909 from 8.8 per cent to 97.5 per cent at the highest marginal rate during and after the Second World War, falling back to 83 per cent before 1979, and then to 75 per cent on unearned and 60 per cent on earned income in the 1980s. Though there has not been a vast redistribution of wealth between individuals, mainly because governments continue to use capital windfalls as current income, there has been a large redistribution from individuals to the state.[60] Thus the state has become the final arbiter of the division of the product of industry to an extent which would make most Victorians turn in their graves.

All this may be dismissed as restricting the absolute rights of capital rather than transforming them. The same cannot be said of recent employment legislation, which has eaten more deeply into those rights. The whole trend of employment law in the 1960s and 1970s was, under both political parties, towards the 'subinfeudation' of industrial property itself. The 'statutory employee', as we may call him, has come to share in the ownership of his job in the same way as the statutory tenant of his house. As Lord Denning, Master of the Rolls, said in a case in 1969:

> a worker of long standing now has an accrued right in his job; and his rights gain value with the years. So much so, that if the job is shut down, he is entitled to compensation for loss of a job – just as a director gets compensation for loss of office.

Still more explicitly, the Norwich Industrial Tribunal in 1968, chaired by the President of the Industrial Tribunals of England and Wales, declared:

> A redundancy payment is compensation for the loss of a right which a long term employee has in his job. Just as a property

owner has a right in his property and when he is deprived he is entitled to compensation, so a long term employee is considered to have a right analogous to a right of property in his job, he has a right to security and his rights gain value with the years....[61]

This was the position under the Redundancy Payments Act, 1965. Since then the principle of compensation has been extended to cover unfair dismissal under the Conservative Industrial Relations Act, 1971 and the Labour Trade Union and Labour Relations Act, 1974. The Employment Protection Acts, 1975 and 1978 confirmed the employee's proprietary right in his job: full-time workers declared redundant after two years in the job must be paid compensation according to their length of service. It is true that the compensation is not enormous – one week's salary for each year of service, rising to two weeks for each year over fifteen – and that the courts have developed fairly sophisticated limitations on entitlement. But the principle remains that the state has taken it upon itself to make the claims of labour a first charge (after tax debts) upon industrial capital in cases of redundancy or bankruptcy, and has thus eaten deeply into the absolute rights of capital.

The final inroad – short of nationalization – will come if and when the British government implements the famous Fifth Directive of the European Economic Community, which enjoins industrial democracy upon the member states. Under this the workers would share with management and shareholders direct control of industry itself. In 1976 the Labour government, in response to that directive, appointed the Bullock Committee of Inquiry on Industrial Democracy. Its report recommended a form of controlling board for each large corporation – '2x + y', i.e. two equal groups of worker and management representatives with a balancing group of independents, 'little Lord Bullocks' – which would have allowed the management side, representing the legal owners, the shareholders, to be outvoted. The Wilson government was not prepared to go so far, and its White Paper substituted the EEC's preferred German system, under which a supervisory board with a minority of employees' representatives oversees an exclusively managerial executive.[62] Under the Thatcher government all such schemes have lapsed but many Conservatives and business men still believe in worker participation and, in whatever form industrial democracy eventually comes, it will be a long step towards sharing the control, and to that extent the effective ownership, of industrial capital between the nominal owners and the workers.

Meanwhile, the concept of absolute ownership of capital is being undermined in a more direct and subtle way. The decomposition of capital, in Dahrendorf's telling phrase, the familiar separation of ownership and control identified by Berle and Means and advocated by Tawney half a century ago, is in daily and increasing operation.[63] The rise in the scale of the modern business corporation discussed in the last chapter inevitably increases the distance between the multiple share-holders and the executive directors, whose span of control over resources far exceeds their nominal ownership of the corporate enterprise. In 1969, as we have seen, the directors of the hundred largest British companies owned only one-thirteenth of the equity.[64] Every take-over bid, merger and amalgamation increases the number and impersonality of the shareholders, for whom their shares become no more than negotiable paper, traded at fluctuating values in a market as far removed from productive industry as the reflecting moon from the sun. Moreover, individuals in 1982 constituted only one-third of all shareholders of companies quoted on the Stock Exchange. Two-thirds of shares were owned by institutions: banks, insurance companies, pension funds, unit trusts, trade unions, holding companies, and the like.[65] The resulting fragmentation of ownership meant that, through these institutions, the ultimate owners or beneficiaries of the flow of income from capital were the bank depositors, insurance policy holders, pensioners and pension fund contributors, unit trust holders, trade union members, and so on situated at the end of the channels of flow, who had no notion whence their anonymous dividends ultimately derived. Those who did know, the professional intermediaries who made the investments, were by no means passive conduits but active controllers of the flow, wielding power in proportion to the funds they manipulated. They were in a real sense the archetypal subinfeudated tenants of the whole quasi-feudal system. Having inserted themselves at key points in the hierarchy of ownership, they potentially represent the new feudal lords and knights whose power and status rest on the indispensable function they perform.

Thus the decomposition of capital is the result of the professionalization of management, and specifically of investment management. The absolute ownership of the flow of income has been literally fragmented into a myriad irrigation channels, but the controllers of the sluice gates retain the power to alter the flow, to fertilize one area and dry up another, according to the advantage they can see for themselves and their institutions. Any one controller may have limited autonomy, and a mistaken investment policy can leave him high and dry or drown him in unprofitable liquidity. But there are nodal points in the system where a few large-scale investors make decisions which can make or break whole industries or towns or occupations. It is conceivable that these key controllers, the barons of the system, may abuse their power to make their fortunes at the expense of the other beneficiaries, as some of them already do, by 'insider trading', dealing on their own account, and so on.[66] The main hope is that professional office will limit their tenure of exploitation and impose institutional discipline within it. Beyond that the only hope is eternal vigilance, and the policing of the financial institutions by the countervailing professional hierarchies, notably those of the state in the shape of security and exchange commissions and the like. Unless this is done effectively and conscientiously, we may end at the mercy of the robber barons of this new version of bastard feudalism.

Be that as it may, the twentieth century has seen the dissolution of the concept of absolute property invented by English landlords between the Black Death and the Civil War and exploited by English capitalists from then down to the early twentieth century. It has been replaced by a contingent concept of property based on professional service, which has fragmented the flow of income and other benefits from land and capital, and inserted a series of intermediate subinfeudated tenants or beneficiaries into the hierarchy of ownership. This quasi-feudal system is in danger, like the original feudal system, of lapsing into a further round of exploitation by would-be absolute owners if they are allowed to turn their human capital into large-scale material capital, but meanwhile it offers at least the opportunity of a wider dissemination of the benefits of ownership than any previous system and of a higher moral justification of property by functional service.

As with all previous classes which rose to dominance, however, the success of the professional class in imposing its own ideal and its version of property upon the rest could easily spill over into a species of arrogance or 'effortless superiority'. In the final section of this chapter we must deal with the chief drawback of professionalism, its condescension towards the rest of society, including other professions.

3 THE CONDESCENSION OF PROFESSIONALISM

The superiority claimed by the professional social ideal, much more than the other class ideals, was apt when it expressed itself in individual rather than collective ways to border on arrogance and condescension. This stemmed from the structural character of professionalism which based itself on human rather than material capital and on trained intellectual rather than manual labour. The professional *had* to assert the high quality and scarcity value of the service he provided or forgo the status and rewards that went with it. And since that service took a personal form it could not be detached from the superior person who provided it. This indeed was the Achilles' heel of professionalism, through which entered the spears of individual arrogance, collective condescension towards the laity, and mutual disdain between the different professions. On all three levels professionalism was weakened by its own vanity and elitism, which often infuriated other individuals, classes, and rival professions. Above all, it prevented the professionals from dominating the new society *as a class.* Instead, professionalism contrived to restructure society on a different principle from class as traditionally understood, in a new vertical structure of rival career hierarchies, a fragmented society of competing elites in which a single dominant elite or ruling class was hard to find. At the same time, the arrogant assumption of superiority was to produce a backlash against professionalism, not only from those who claimed to speak for the traditional classes of capital and labour but, by an internal division within professionalism itself, by recrimination from within between two warring factions which each claimed superiority over the other. These two warring factions were, roughly speaking, the public sector and the private sector professions. In this section we shall deal with the provocative condescension of the professions, and only touch on the backlash against and between them, leaving their bifurcation to the next chapter and the backlash to the final chapter of the book.

The individual critics of traditional society drew on a long legacy of social criticism of industrialism going back to Coleridge, Carlyle, Matthew Arnold, Ruskin, William Morris, and beyond. Like their Victorian predecessors they were 'a sort of classless class, relatively detached from the everyday struggles of the market-place', who thought of themselves as lone intellectuals raised above the crowd by their talent for perception. In fact, this very detachment was one of the chief identifiers of the professional class, which, as we shall see, was marked by fragmentation and mutual competition between professions.[67] Intellectuals in particular, though drawn almost exclusively from the professional middle class, tended to think of themselves as free-floating mental operators set apart from their social origins. Some intellectuals, like the Bloomsbury group, were in fact Victorians of a familiar rebellious kind but saw themselves as raised above the common herd by their revolt against their parents' generation. Their attitudes and behaviour, especially in sexual matters, were all too Victorian, at least at the leisured aristocratic level to which they aspired.[68] They were all convinced of their superiority to the money-grubbing business men and benighted workers outside the magic circle of the arts and literature. Virginia Woolf, for all her empathy for poorer women, realized that between 'my comfortably capitalistic hand' and the working-class women of the Co-operative Guild she met in Newcastle in 1913, 'the barrier is impassable.'[69] J. M. Keynes, who did more for the working class than any other capitalist economist, could not join the Labour Party because it was a 'class party, and the class is not my class. . . . I can be influenced by what seems to me to be Justice and good sense; but the class war will find me on the side of the educated *bourgeoisie*'.[70] But the real disdain of Bloomsbury for the productive classes is summed up by one of its lesser lights, Clive Bell, who pleaded in *Civilization* (1928) for an unconsciously Marxist extraction of surplus value from the many for the support of the civilized few:

> Civilization requires the existence of a leisured class, and a leisured class requires the existence of slaves – of people . . . who give some part of their surplus time and energy to the

support of others. . . . The trade unionist is as good as the profiteer; and the profiteer is as good as the trade unionist. Both are silly, vulgar, good-natured, sentimental, greedy and insensitive; and as both are very well pleased to be what they are neither is likely to become anything better. A will to civilization may exist among the Veddahs of Ceylon or the Mege of the Gold Coast, but no sign of it appears on the Stock Exchange or in the Trade Union Congress.[71]

A similar condescension towards the industrial classes can be found amongst most of the fashionable writers of the inter-war period. T. S. Eliot warned against 'the pagan society' with its strange gods of 'Compound Interest and Maintenance of Dividends' on one side and 'an illiterate and uncritical mob' on the other.[72] Using Coleridge's terminology, he looked towards the clerisy of intellectuals like himself 'both to maintain inherited ideas, and alter the sensibility of their time':

> . . . one of the chief merits of the clerical elite is that it is an
> influence for change. To some extent, therefore, there is, and I
> think there should be, a conflict between class and clerical
> elite. On the one hand, the clerical elite is dependent on
> whatever is the dominant class of its time; on the other hand, it
> is apt to be critical of, and subversive of, the class in power.

But they are not united in their ideas or criticisms:

> It is not the business of clerics to agree with each other; they
> are driven to each others' company by their common
> dissimilarity from everybody else, and by the fact that they find
> each other the most profitable people to disagree with, as well
> as to agree with. They differ from a class in having very
> different backgrounds from each other, and by not being
> united by prejudices and habits. They are apt to share a
> discontent with things as they are, but the ways in which they
> want to change them will be various and often completely
> opposed to each other.

They are, however, united on one significant object: 'They have at least one common interest – an interest in the survival of the clerisy.'[73]

His fellow clerics went beyond their mere survival. W. B. Yeats advocated 'the despotic rule of the educated class', while D. H. Lawrence preached the need for a governing elite to control and raise the cultural standards of the masses from which he himself originated.[74] Wyndham Lewis saw an inevitable separation 'between creative man and his backward fellow', between 'those who decide for the active intelligent life, and those who decide (without any stigma attaching to the choice) for the "lower" or animal life'.[75] Bertrand Russell attacked both 'the error of aristocracy' and 'the error of democracy' and called for what amounted to a meritocracy, a world ruled by the best brains drawn from all classes.[76] Aldous Huxley in *Brave New World* (1932) satirized the meritocratic divisions of a materialistic, Ford-worshipping society into clever, professional 'alphas', obedient executive 'betas', and happy-go-lucky hard-working 'gammas'.[77] The Marxist writers of the 1930s, Christopher Caudwell, John Strachey, Stephen Spender and company, had, to match their disillusionment with the capitalist bourgeoisie, an almost Leninist conviction that the proletariat was incapable of knowing its own destiny unless led and guided by the 'active intellectuals'.[78] Even George Orwell, despite his sympathy for the unemployed of the depressed areas, could hardly suppress his disgust for the lifestyle of his Wigan slum host dispensing the tripe with an unwashed thumb, or his disdain both for the educated southerner who goes north 'with the vague inferiority-complex of a civilized man venturing among savages' and for the northerner who 'comes to London in the spirit of a barbarian out for loot'.[79]

Less scornful intellectuals, more concerned with practical democracy and economic justice like the predominantly liberal 'Next Five Years Group' of 1935, including J. A. Hobson, Ernest Barker, A. D. Lindsay, Norman Angell and H. G. Wells, advocated purely professional solutions to the social problems of the day; while committed socialist reformers like Harold Laski, Douglas Jay and Barbara Wootton assumed that democratic socialism could only be operated by professionals.[80] In Laski's words,

> Any system of government, upon the modern scale, involves a body of experts working to satisfy vast populations who judge by the result and are careless of, even uninterested in, the processes by which these results are attained.... A democracy in other words must, if it is to work, be an aristocracy by delegation.[81]

And, as we have seen, the doyen of Labour intellectuals, R. H. Tawney, specifically advocated a professional society in which industry, as well as all other economic functions, would be run by professional managers and professionally organized workers.[82]

These attitudes were reinforced by the influx of continental intellectuals, characterized by Perry Anderson in a now famous essay as 'the White emigration' [sic]: Friedrich von Hayek in economics, Lewis Namier in history, Karl Popper in social philosophy, Isaiah Berlin in political science, Hans Eysenck in psychology, Karl Mannheim in sociology, Bronislaw Malinowski in anthropology, Ludwig Wittgenstein in philosophy, and so on, who came to dominate English intellectual culture in the twentieth century.[83] It was almost as if the English establishment, having lost confidence in the aristocratic and capitalist ideals which had so long supported it, had run out of ideas and of the intellectuals who had traditionally supplied them, and were forced to turn to the new wave of intellectuals fleeing from Hitler's Europe to fill the vacuum. There were, of course, left-wing as well as right-wing immigrants – Isaac Deutscher, Nicholas Kaldor, Thomas Balogh, Eric Hobsbawm, Sidney Pollard – but for the most part the left-wingers, like Marcuse, Adorno, Horkheimer and Fromm, passed on to the United States where, paradoxically, the academic free market gave them greater opportunities for self-expression, in New York's New School of Social Research ('Frankfurt on the Hudson') and elsewhere. Meanwhile, their counterparts in Britain were taken to the bosom of the establishment, which expressed its gratitude in a shower of university chairs, fellowships and knighthoods. The white immigrants had an even greater, continental conviction of the superiority of academics and intellectuals, combined with a healthy respect for the power of the state, which they knew how to manipulate even as they warned against it. In their own way they represented the condescension of the professional elite even more than their British rivals.

Eliot, himself a white immigrant though in a reverse direction, had made a distinction between the employed and the unemployed clerisy, between those who were paid to pursue intellectual careers and those who had to earn their living, like himself, by other means (such as banking or publishing) or by 'the sale of their clerical produce (books, pictures)'.[84] With the decline since the

Victorian age of unearned incomes and of the rewards of freelance authorship and art, more of the clerisy had come to concentrate in the universities where clerical disdain for the unintellectual laity could thrive in segregation.[85] Thus began the paradoxical role of the modern university, at once increasingly the gatekeeper to the career hierarchies of modern professional society and the hermetically sealed preserve of the professional specialist. One profession after another, from medicine in 1858, through engineering, law, accounting, architecture, estate management, social work, and finally down to business management itself in the 1960s, transferred the bulk of its training from apprenticeship on the job and/or privately provided vocational courses into the ambit of the university. In a more specialized world it was cheaper and more efficient, especially after the establishment of the University Grants Committee in 1919 when the state began to subsidize university education on a larger scale, to get the universities to take over the training function of most professional bodies. Meanwhile, the professions endeavoured to keep as much control over entry as before by recognizing university courses, offering exemption from their qualifying examinations and, where they could as with the medical schools, obtaining formal representation on university bodies. In this way, university teaching became the key profession which educated for, controlled access to, and did much of the research for the other professions.[86]

There was another, more detrimental aspect of this development. In order to preserve their separate function and existence, it became necessary for the university disciplines to emphasize their separation from the professions they served outside the walls and also, inside the walls, from the other university disciplines. All professions use strategies of closure to segregate themselves from the laity and from one another – control of entry, training and examination, use of a privileged title or nomenclature, state monopoly of the name or practice, and so on. University disciplines have come to use more rigorous devices: access to research, an esoteric jargon, the possession of a PhD, scholarly publication, a national or international reputation within a narrowly defined field, and the like. Segregation has become all the more attractive and necessary in those fields whose subject matter is most accessible to the laity, that is, in the humanities and social studies.

Perhaps the best example is the study of English literature, which only became a university discipline in the early twentieth century, but has since tried to become *the* humane discipline, the modern substitute for theology and philosophy. In the hands of F. R. Leavis and the Cambridge English School it became (in their own opinion) the exclusive guardian of 'high culture', the preserver of 'the great tradition', the defender of humane values from the 'technological-Benthamite' horrors of industrial society, mass production and Americanization. Leavis and his followers looked back to a golden age before 'the dissociation of sensibility' when people of all classes responded to a unified culture.[87] The difficulty was that they found it in different ages: Leavis himself before Milton, his wife Queenie in the pre-industrial eighteenth century, Richard Hoggart in the working-class culture of his boyhood before the depredations of the modern popular press, and so on.[88] Leavis objected to the word elitism – 'a product of ignorance, prejudice and unintelligence' – but not to the idea of an elite, especially the second or educated elite which was responsible for checking and controlling the first, the political or ruling elite. Culture, narrowed to a rarefied great tradition of the 'picked experience of ages', was in their keeping: 'In any period it is upon a small minority that the discerning appreciation of art and literature depends: it is (apart from cases of the simple and familiar) only a few who are capable of unprompted, first-hand judgement.' All literature and art, indeed all human experience, outside the authenticated stream of pure high culture belonged to the 'muddled mass-society' which, by definition, was beneath consideration.[89] Small wonder that 'good literature' in the twentieth century has become a minority cult, written by the few *cognoscenti* for the discerning few.

Most other university disciplines, some like nuclear physics or genetic engineering with more justification, some like structural linguistics or philosophy less so, have gone the esoteric way of English literature and become almost inaccessible to what Leavis saw as the defunct common reader. Peter Scott, editor of *The Times Higher Education Supplement,* has chronicled in *The Crisis of the University* (1984), the decline of the traditional university which stood for a broad education in a unified and unifying culture and its replacement by the modern university, plagued by 'academicism' and 'instrumentalism', i.e. by fragmentation into increasingly hermetic and esoteric specialities on one side and by self-absorbed professional training and industrially commissioned research on the other. The 'visible college' of the academic community, sharing a common language and values and passing them on to the next generation of concerned citizens under their care, has been fractured into a myriad 'invisible colleges' of the ever more splintered disciplines, each determined to hold its ground against all-comers by means of an exclusive jargon and mind-set or to corner the market in an enclosed and lucrative career. Having rejected communication with one another outside their narrowing specialisms, they have totally lost the capacity to reach, educate and persuade the public on whose financial and moral support they depend. An unintelligible intelligentsia, according to Scott, retreats from reality into a self-indulgent world of verbal disputation, while a professional technocracy pursues its amoral, mechanistic philosophy of scientific progress oblivious of its implications for mankind.

Beneath this intellectual failure, Scott believes, lies a deeper, moral one. It is nothing less than the prospect of 'the repeal of modern society', the unravelling of its political, intellectual and moral fabric. In this the university is both victim and accomplice: victim because the hostility of modern politicians of both right and left has singled it out as a threat either to the social order or to fundamental reform; accomplice because it has frivolously cut itself off from the popular sources of its support. The task of higher education, at which in Britain it has clearly failed, is to recreate in each generation an intellectual culture accessible to the common man and woman and a moral order that is a guarantee of both freedom and social progress.[90]

Scott's indictment is a portent of the backlash against professionalism to which we shall return. For the moment, it points to a symptom of that collective condescension of the professions for what they perceive as the uncomprehending masses incapable of understanding their message. This was the real *trahison des clercs*, the treason of the intellectuals, against which the masses were right to revolt.[91] But, more in Britain than elsewhere, the professionals within the university and without are not content to disdain only the non-professional laity, who cannot aspire to professional status. In the fragmented world of university disciplines as amongst the disparate career hierarchies outside, the rival professions come to disdain one another. To adapt the aphorism of Bernard Shaw about Englishmen in general, one professional cannot open his mouth without being despised by another one. Far from standing together against the world, each profession sees every other as outside the pale, part of the uninitiated mass banned from the mysteries of its own exclusive altar. Lawyers and doctors respect one another only if they maintain respectful distance, and have recently clashed over their respective responsibility for the increase in medical malpractice suits. Academics from different parts of the 'hard–soft' spectrum suspect one another's competence: 'Physics is fundamental knowledge; chemistry is only applied physics'; 'natural science is science; social science is organized prejudice'; 'economists deal in facts; political scientists think the plural of anecdote is data'; 'social science produces testable theories; history is mindless empiricism' – and so on down the line. The mutual incomprehension between the 'two cultures' was proverbial before C. P. Snow discovered it and was chastised by Leavis. Within the humane sciences historians are at odds with both sociologists and literary critics dealing with the same period. As for the fine arts, academics 'in the lump' are no more and no less philistine than the man in the street, who tends to think that abstract painting and twelve-tone music are bad cases of the emperor's new clothes.

All this of course is to say no more than that all professions justify their existence by claiming superiority in their chosen field of expertise over all others. But the implications for a society based on human capital and specialized expertise are profound and surprising. Far from working together to consolidate their leverage on the rest of society, as landlords, capitalists and even workers, less successfully through their trade unions, have tried to do, the professions, despite abortive attempts in the early 1970s, have never managed to unite in the professional equivalent of the Confederation of British Industry or the Trades Union Congress. For that reason, although their ideal, operating through individuals and collective interests, has achieved much in shaping professional society, they have failed to become a ruling class or a unified elite. Instead, modern society is becoming a congeries of parallel career hierarchies. Some of the hierarchies are indeed higher and more powerful than others, but none has yet become the master interest overbearing all others. It is possible, of course, that the state bureaucracy or the corporate managers might try to usurp control over all the rest, and the pendulum seems to swing towards first one and then the other, but neither has yet been able to assert exclusive mastery. Nor does it seem to be in the nature of rival specialisms, each claiming superiority over all others, to accept such a single master interest. Although still half-obscured by the horizontal solidarities of class, the new society has a different architecture from the old. It is not so much a layered pyramid rising to a needle point, more a giant's causeway, its obsidian columns rising indeed to different heights but all vertical, parallel and discrete.

Even in a giant's causeway some vertical planes are more gapingly obvious than others. The sharpest discontinuity by far is not the traditional one between the employed and the self-employed professions, which still has some importance, though more between members of the *same* profession such as law, medicine or accountancy than between distinct professions. It is *within* the employed or salaried professions, now far outnumbering the self-employed, between those who perform a public service, paid for out of taxation or voluntary contributions not derived from their immediate clients, and those employed by private corporations. At the risk of some oversimplification, we may call these the public sector and private sector professionals respectively. The public sector includes not only the Civil Service and local government officers, the employees of the various welfare services from health to state education, the nationalized industries, and the armed forces, but also the quasi-independent, non-profit making public institutions such as the universities, the BBC, the charitable foundations, and the officials of the trade unions. The private sector, of course, includes the managers and other professional employees of the private corporations in industry and finance, the manufacturing companies, the banks, insurance and investment companies, the newspapers and independent television companies, the private airlines and shipping companies, and also their collective representatives in the trade associations, the Confederation of British Industry, the British Institute of Management and the specialized managerial associations, and so on.

The line between public and private is a shifting one, as

industries and services are nationalized or privatized, or are commercially or philanthropically oriented, and it obviously differs from country to country. Medicine, for example, is predominantly a public service in Britain but predominantly a private one in the United States, which makes for a profound difference in the outlook of British and American doctors. Higher education is almost wholly a public service in Britain but almost equally divided between public and private in America and Japan, though with different apportionments of prestige between state and private universities in the last two countries. Broadcasting is divided between public and private corporations in Britain, wholly public in France and almost wholly private in the United States, with consequent differences in self-perception on the part of the broadcasters. This is not to say, of course, that the attitudes of professionals are wholly determined by their employers or their terms of employment. Their loyalty to their profession and its ethic normally come first. But as with all social roles, the structure of their rewards, their source of income, job opportunities and chances of promotion are bound to influence their outlook and performance, whether or not their employers overtly pressure them in specific directions. By and large, the public sector professions in Britain have emphasized the need for expansion of the services they provide, at whatever expense to the taxpayer or voluntary contributor, while conversely the private sector professions have emphasized freedom from taxation and from state interference with their operations.

This dichotomy between their interests *vis-à-vis* the state has set up the sharpest tension within professional society. Superficially, it parallels the traditional battle between the competitive individualism and the collectivism of Victorian class society, which is why it can be fought out in the obsolete terms of the Ricardian free market versus Marxist or Fabian socialism. Yet at a deeper level it is clearly a struggle between professionals providing essentially the same services – management, medicine, education, broadcasting – over how those services are to be provided and whether professionals gain more by controlling a state service and presenting the bill to the community or by selling their services privately to those who can best afford to pay for them. The answer is not predetermined for the individual professional by his current position on one side of the line. It is perfectly possible for a private doctor to think he would have more security and higher pay in a public health service or conversely for a public doctor to hope for bigger rewards in a private system, and for a manager in a nationalized enterprise to hope for more freedom of decision and stock option bonuses from privatization. Human nature being subject to inertia, however, there is a strong tendency for professionals to opt for the devil they know, and to press for enhanced prestige and reward within the institutional framework in which they find themselves. Doctors in the British National Health Service press for more state resources; American doctors lobby against 'socialized medicine'. British professors complain of cuts in government grants to universities and research councils; American professors in state universities do much the same, while in the private universities they solicit charitable donations and lobby for federal research grants and contracts. British corporate managers bitterly oppose nationalization but, once they are nationalized, immediately behave like public servants; when they are privatized they revert instantly to corporation type.

What the rivalry is *not* about is old-fashioned free enterprise versus socialism. Free competition of the Ricardian kind was between individual capitalists so numerous that no one or small group of them was in a position to corner the market. The modern market is dominated by at most 200 great corporations, which means that most industries are dominated by three to five giant corporations which can if they wish determine the volume, price and quantity of the product or service. Overseas competition helps to keep oligopoly within bounds, but also ensures that new internal capitalist interlopers, except perhaps in very new products or services for a short period of time, have next to no chance to compete. The cry for less state intervention is therefore a cry for more freedom for giant corporations, or rather for the professional managers who run them. It is just as much a case of professional special pleading as the demand of public sector professionals for more state resources. The main difference depends on which side of the public/private sector they stand.

In professional society, therefore, the old ideological conflicts between small-scale capitalism and state socialism are obsolescent – though not always recognized as such – and overtaken by the rivalries of the professions, and specifically by the opposition between the public sector and private sector professionals. What both sides want are much the same things: autonomous control of a particular service and the status and rewards which flow from it. The difference lies in their strategies for achieving them. While the public sector professional starts from the belief that his service is so essential to society that it must be provided *gratis* (or nearly so) and society must pick up the bill, the private sector professional starts from the belief that his service is so attractive that the customer will willingly pay. Problems arise at the margin, where some customers cannot afford to pay for a service which society deems essential, like health or education, while others demand the right to pay for a higher quality of service, especially for 'positional goods' which confer advantages which by definition cannot be open to all. There is therefore no agreed line between public and private provision, and the struggle pushes it back and forth according to the success of the public and private sector professionals in persuading the community to prefer their particular approach.

Yet both equally represent the professional social ideal, of a society which distributes rewards according to desert and social justice. The difference turns on their approach to social justice. Both believe in a basic equality among citizens, but the public sector professionals tend to seek greater equality of outcome, basing their case on the right of everyone to a reasonable share of society's resources to be guaranteed by people like themselves, while the private sector professionals stress equality of opportunity, not only to reward the merit in which they themselves excel but also to enlarge the total resources to be shared by everybody. Given that the welfare state as it had evolved was ambivalent and had never clearly distinguished which of the two equalities deserved priority, it is easy to see how they could agree to support it, though for different reasons. One side concentrated on raising the floor of inequality for the underprivileged, the other on the opportunity for some of them to make themselves 'more unequal' than the rest. It was to be an uneasy compromise, but for a generation after the Second World War there was to be sufficient agreement to maintain a mutually suspicious consensus. When economic growth decelerated and prosperity declined in the 1970s and 1980s, consensus broke down and confrontation ensued.

For twenty-five years after the Second World War, however, a reasonable equilibrium was reached between the two sides, under the name of the 'mixed economy' or 'Butskellism' (from the supposed consensus between the two opposing Chancellors of the Exchequer of the early 1950s, R. A. Butler and Hugh Gaitskell). This compromise was immensely successful both politically, in gaining substantial support from all parties, and economically, in supporting an unprecedented rate of economic growth with moderate inflation and full employment. Unfortunately, that rate of economic growth, though neck and neck with the benchmark country, the United States, was inadequate when compared with other competitors, notably the six original partners of the European Economic Community and Japan, and seemed to threaten not merely relative but ultimately absolute failure and decline. The threat, flagged by increasingly frequent balance of payments crises, became acute when, with the oil crises of 1973 and 1979, world depression exposed the lack of competitiveness of the British economy. The compromise of the mixed economy had never been accepted by the extremists on the fringes of both major parties, the committed nationalizers on the left of the Labour Party and the committed free marketeers on the right of the Conservative. As disillusion with the old Butskellite compromise grew in the 1970s and with it disillusion with traditional party politics, the extremists seized their chance and began to move towards control of their parties. They did so in the name of the nostalgic ideologies inherited from Victorian class society, Ricardian free enterprise and its *alter ego*, Marxian state capitalism.

This backlash against the mixed economy was also, at bottom, a backlash against professional society itself. It was a protest by the self-styled champions of that threatened species the private entrepreneur, the small owner-managing capitalist superseded by the giant corporation, and by the equally self-appointed champions of the proletariat, the supposedly revolutionary working class which, they complained paradoxically, was in process of being incorporated within the corporate economy and society. At the same time, the backlash derived its energy from the clash between the two professional sectors: the private sector professionals rallied to the cry that *they* supplied the material wealth which the public sector 'squandered', while the public sector professionals resented the social costs which the private sector shouldered on to the public. It was, therefore, the mutual hostility of the public and private sector professions which fuelled the political struggle of the 1970s and 1980s. But first we need to look at the social changes since the Second World War, which transformed not only the terrain of the battlefield but also the nature of the armies locked in combat.

Chapter 9

THE PLATEAU OF
PROFESSIONAL SOCIETY

Between 1945 and the early 1970s professional society reached a plateau of attainment. This did not mean a utopia based entirely on merit, social efficiency and social justice. It meant, rather, a society which accepted in principle that ability and expertise were the only respectable justification for recruitment to positions of authority and responsibility and in which every citizen had the right to a minimum income in times of distress, to medical treatment during sickness, decent housing in a healthy environment, and an education appropriate to his or her abilities. No society has ever lived up to its ideal – neither the aristocratic society of pre-industrial England to its ideal of the leisured gentleman practising paternalism nor the industrial society of Victorian England to its ideal of the self-made man practising fair competition – and professional society was no exception. Selection by merit was still distorted by inherited wealth and privileged education for the few. Social security was eroded by inflation and the failure of national insurance to prevent an unfortunate minority from falling into poverty. There remained gross disparities in medical treatment between different classes and different regions under the National Health Service. Decent housing and a healthy environment were limited by scarce resources and the obstruction of vested property and industrial interests. And education remained the main source of unequal life chances between those who could pay for it or obtain the best of state education and those who could not.

Nevertheless, if societies can be categorized by their ideals, by their self-imposed objectives and their criteria for success in attaining them, post-war British society differed from pre-industrial aristocratic and Victorian entrepreneurial society in consciously pursuing the ideal of a welfare state, in which society accepted responsibility for the minimum support, health, accommodation, environmental cleanliness, education, and even employment for every member. As the first official handbook on Britain in 1949 and its annual editions for many years declared:

> In Britain the State is now responsible for a range of services covering subsistence for the needy, education and health services for all, housing, employment or maintenance, the care of the aged and the handicapped and the nutrition of mothers and children, besides sickness and industrial injuries benefits, widows' and retirement pensions, and children's allowances.
>
> None of these services has been imposed by the State upon an unwilling public. All of them are the result of cooperative effort between successive governments and the people whom they governed.[1]

The very fact that there was disagreement on how best successive governments should carry out their responsibilities and what precisely the ideal meant proves that the ideal was taken seriously. Constant criticism from one side that the state was not doing enough to achieve the ideal and from the other that it was undermining the means, social efficiency and economic growth, of achieving it, shows that the ideal was accepted in principle, however inadequate the practice. And the struggle between the two versions of the ideal, the one stressing public intervention to ensure as much equality of outcome as possible, the other stressing individual initiative to evoke as much equality of opportunity as could be, guaranteed that the ideal would remain at the forefront of public discussion. To that extent the professional ideal was the organizing principle of post-war society.

It would remain so for as long as that society remained prosperous and moderately proof against the strains of economic depression and unemployment, as it did with increasing difficulty down to the early 1970s. With the oil crisis of 1973 and the subsequent world recession the consensus on ends gave way to increasing confrontation, until 1979 brought to power a government pledged to destroy the consensus and put the clock back to the enterprise society of an earlier age. There is reason to doubt, as we shall see in the final chapter, whether its expressed ideal was truly entrepreneurial or did not mask an exaggerated version of one form of the professional ideal – that of the corporate professional masquerading as old-fashioned owner-manager – trying not to put the clock back but to swing the contemporary pendulum further its own way. But that is to anticipate a wider question, whether the plateau reached in the quarter-century after the Second World War led on to an escarpment plunging down to a renewed trough of capitalist enterprise and devil-take-the-hindmost competition, or whether it was the upland approach to a still higher range of professional society. Was it, to push the geographical exploration metaphor perhaps too far, the Alleghenies leading to the Mississippi basin or the High Plains leading to the Rocky Mountains? Judging by the further increase in the 1980s in public spending and the failure to dismantle the welfare state, it was at least as likely to be the latter as the former.

Before we climb to the plateau, however, and explore its further side, it will be necessary to approach it through the dark valley of the Second World War and the revolution in expectations which pointed the way.

1 THE SECOND WORLD WAR AND THE REVOLUTION IN EXPECTATIONS

The Second World War was an even greater turning point for Britain than the First. Although it was much less destructive of life – the British came off lightly, with only 305,000 killed in the forces and the merchant navy plus about 60,000 civilians killed in the air raids (less than half the dead of the First World War) compared with over 25 million lives lost by other belligerents – it was a much more total war involving the whole population, and much more completely changed the course of history. Britain put more man- and womanpower in proportion to population into the war effort than Germany or any other belligerent except Russia. Nearly 8 million people were in the armed forces by the last year of the war, every man between 18 and 60 was either called up or directed into the war industries, and every unmarried woman between the same ages. Government expenditure increased sixfold, from £1 billion in 1938–39 to £6.2 billion in 1944–45, 83 per cent of which was spent on defence. The Civil Service nearly doubled, from 388,000 to 705,000, not counting 'industrials', as government tried to control every aspect of life from war supplies and the direction of labour to food and fuel rationing and the design and quality of 'utility' furniture and clothing.[2]

The war cost £28 billion in taxes and domestic borrowing (repaid only years later in much smaller pounds), nearly twice the real cost of the First World War, plus massive loans from the United States, Canada and the Sterling Area (the empire and Commonwealth which supplied much of the resources for the war outside Europe, as India did in the Burmese campaign against Japan). Overseas debts multiplied sevenfold, from under £500 million to £3,500 million, and nearly all the gold and dollar reserves and foreign investments disappeared.[3] Practically all the export markets went, either taken over by the Americans and Canadians or supplied perforce by the old importing countries themselves. In addition to about 4 million houses damaged, nearly half of them destroyed, much of the industrial base – factories, mines, railways, power stations, gasworks, and so on – had either been bombed or was worn out and needed replacement. In short, Britain was transformed overnight from a first-rate (if no longer the largest) military, political and economic power to a near-bankrupt nation completely outclassed by the United States and Soviet Russia.

It is true that other countries, including Russia, Germany, France, Italy and Japan, had suffered more and faced a harder task of recovery. Yet in a sense Britain had fallen further, from a world imperial role which would never be recovered. The costs in men, money and military equipment of hanging on to that role, down to the final withdrawal from East of Suez (except for Hong Kong) in the early 1970s, were to divert resources from reconstruction and recovery while other countries, including the ex-enemies West Germany and Japan with exiguous defence spending, forged ahead in economic growth. There were other and more deep-seated reasons why Britain, after the first American-aided recuperation and export boom, failed to keep up with the leaders in post-war recovery. The war can be blamed for too much. But whether or not it was the cost and destruction of the war or the way in which the war transformed the world political and economic context to Britain's detriment, there can be no doubt that it closed one chapter of history in which Britain was a world-class power and opened another in which decline to a middle-range European power, and by no means the strongest or most prosperous, seemed inevitable.

There was another side to the story, however, and that was how the war prepared the way for a more state-interventionist, more equal and caring society after it ended. It produced a revolution in expectations, about what the nation could do when roused to meet a common threat, about how far the state could go in organizing people for a common purpose, about the capacity of government to organize large-scale production and distribution, about what the community owed its members in times of emergency and distress, and about the possibility of planning for a fairer, less wasteful, more productive world in the future. Many of these expectations, as we have seen, had been growing between the wars and, like 'homes for heroes' and the nationalization of the coal mines, had even been unsuccessfully anticipated in the First World War. The Second World War gave an even stronger practical demonstration that state intervention and mutual responsibility between citizens on a large scale could work and that the war could not have been won without them.

State intervention in production and distribution was planned from the first, unlike the First World War when it was only gradually and reluctantly forced upon the government. Aside from the massive expansion of Royal Ordnance Factories, engineering, aircraft, motor vehicles, shipbuilding, coal, iron and steel, gas and electricity, railways, road transport, and construction were all brought under government control as essential war industries. All other industries were subordinated to the war effort. Textiles, clothing, furniture, domestic utensils, and so on, essential to the civilian population as well as to the armed forces, were subjected to the closest controls, to limit their use of manpower and raw materials and keep them only to essential production.[4]

Food production was given the highest priority since every extra ton of food produced was a ton of cargo space saved on the transatlantic convoys. Every available acre was ploughed, old grassland turned into wheat and potato fields, and the arable fields climbed up the Downs and the Pennines to heights not ploughed since the Middle Ages. County War Agricultural Committees ensured that inefficient farmers either improved or ceased to farm. The Women's Land Army - whose down-to-earth motto was 'Backs to the Land' - took over part of the work, and with government subsidies 6 million more acres were brought under the plough. Increased grain and potato production was at the expense of the livestock, especially pigs and poultry, which drove down the meat and egg ration even further. Despite the demands of war the number of agricultural workers grew from about 600,000 to 750,000, including 80,000 Land Girls and 40,000 prisoners of war, and tractors increased almost fourfold from 56,000 to 203,000. Even industrial workers became 'farmers'; under the 'Dig for Victory' campaign garden allotments grew from 815,000 to 1,400,000, and there were hundreds of thousands of domestic poultry keepers and pig club members.[5]

Food rationing had been planned in 1938 and January 1940, bringing a sense of equal sacrifice to the most sensitive area of consumption. The rich could still spend up to 5 shillings (half a day's average manual wage) on a hotel or restaurant meal, but the government soon introduced cheap meals for most school children and 'British Restaurants' where anybody could get a good, plain, three-course meal for little more than a shilling. The weekly rations fluctuated, but from August 1942 were down to 1s. 2d. worth of meat, 4oz. of bacon, 8oz. of butter, fats and margarine, 8oz. of cheese, one egg, 8oz. of sugar, and (over a month) 16oz. of soap, 8oz. of sweets and 16oz. of jam or other preserves. A 'points' system allowed for a monthly choice of canned goods, such as salmon, fruit or vegetables. Orange juice and cod liver oil, free to poor families, were provided for expectant mothers and young children. Bread and potatoes were off ration until 1946, when the dollar shortage forced bread rationing for the first time. The whole dietary system was designed by the scientific expertise of Sir Jack Drummond, who calculated the protein and vitamins required by adults and children (with extras for miners and other heavy workers), with carbohydrate 'fillers' like bread and potatoes *ad lib*, so that a large part of the population was better fed than before the war. 'The biggest shop in the world', with 50 million customers, a £600 million turnover and 50,000 civil servants by 1943, the Ministry of Food became the sole importer of basic foodstuffs, and purchaser of most domestic food supplies. Under Lord Woolton, career manager of a chain of department stores, it was also responsible for keeping the black market within bounds.[6] The feeding of the nation, so vital to morale, was one of the success stories of the war and helped to give state intervention a good name.

Recruitment to the armed forces and the direction of civilian labour was also far better organized than in the First World War. Conscription was planned before war began and the first 21-year-olds were called up on 1 September 1939. The age of conscription was gradually extended downwards to 18 and upwards to 51. From December 1941 unmarried women between 18 and 25 were conscripted too, for non-combatant though often dangerous duties in the Auxiliary Territorial Service, the Women's Auxiliary Air Force, and the Women's Royal Navy Service; far more women of all ages were directed into munitions and other vital industries. Direction of labour was introduced in the crisis month of June 1940, when France fell and the bulk of the British Expeditionary Force was evacuated from Dunkirk, and gave Ernest Bevin, the redoubtable union boss who became minister of labour, power to direct any person to perform any service he thought fit and to set the pay, hours and conditions of the job. As the Labour leader, Clement Attlee, now deputy prime minister to Winston Churchill, explained, 'It is necessary that the Government should be given complete control over persons and property, not just some persons of some particular class of the community, but of all persons, rich and poor, man or woman, and of all property.' It was often unnecessary, since men and women sought patriotic (and high-paid) work, and many married men with children were only too anxious to work in reserved occupations. Only about 1.1 million directives had to be issued in 1940–45, only 88,000 of them to women. It had to be extended, late in 1943, to the most unpopular work of all, in the coal mines where some 21,000 'Bevin boys', including some appalled middle-class youths, were sent in 1944–45, mainly to work on underground haulage and maintenance.[7] Conscription threw men and women of different classes into the melting pot of war together, and though their military ranks often, though not always, reflected the civilian structure it gave a consciousness of all being in it together.

Evacuation of some 3.5 million children and mothers of infants from London and the large cities in 1939–41 and again in 1944–45 during the V-weapon attacks also threw the classes together, in closer proximity than some of them liked. Although great efforts were made to match socially children and hosts, some middle-class foster parents were shocked at the poor health, inadequate clothing, and what they took to be the slovenly speech and bad

411

habits of some working-class children – and the children were often equally appalled at the stern discipline and, sometimes, the unappetizing food of their hosts. Some mothers and children could not stand it and repatriated themselves back to their bomb-threatened homes, but for most the enforced cohabitation was an illuminating experience on both sides.[8]

It was also mutually illuminating for the adults, chiefly women, who volunteered or were directed to the armaments factories of the Midlands and the north and for their hosts and neighbours. In many cases easy-going 'roughs' from city slums came into close contact for the first time with the puritanical 'respectables' of the industrial working class, and the mutual horror surpassed anything experienced by the innocent middle-class foster parents of evacuees. The upper working-class locals were amazed and fascinated by the personal (and sexual) habits of the newcomers, and the neighbourhoods buzzed with gossip about them.[9]

Both sides worked enormously long hours, as in the First World War, at dangerous work for unprecedentedly high wages, which they began to make the most of in their short leisure time, especially from 1942 when the American GIs began to arrive. Dancing, particularly the new jive and jitterbug, had never been so popular, nor the pub or the cinema. There was a renaissance in light entertainment and in classical music and the performing arts as two state-supported organizations, ENSA (the Entertainments National Service Association), which brought popular comedians and singers, and CEMA (the Council for Education in Music and the Arts), which brought classical music and art exhibitions to the munitions workers and the troops.[10] For the people at home – and until the North African landings of late 1942 most of the troops were not overseas but in Britain preparing for the Second Front – there was a remarkable camaraderie which took in grumbling at the black-out and rationing, a gritty determination to 'see it through', and an increasing belief that so much work and sacrifice deserved to be rewarded.

At what point the expectations of a better post-war world took over from the mere hope of national survival is difficult to determine. The initiative certainly did not come from the government. Churchill made no secret of his belief that Lloyd George in the First World War had made promises he could not fulfil, and that the blood, sweat, toil and tears he offered had no other reward than escape from Nazi enslavement. In a speech in March 1943, he envisaged expansion of national insurance for all classes for 'all purposes from cradle to grave', a national health service, 'broader and more liberal education', and alongside 'a widespread healthy and vigorous private enterprise ... a broadening field for state ownership and enterprise, especially in relation to monopolies of all kinds', but he warned against 'attempts to overpersuade or even to coerce his Majesty's Government to bind themselves or their unknown successors ... to impose great new expenditure on the state'.[11] The Queen caught the spirit as early as October 1940, in a letter to her mother-in-law Queen Mary towards the end of the Battle of Britain: 'The destruction is so awful, the people so *wonderful* – they deserve a better world.'[12]

The one area in which people could not afford to wait for a better world was in the social services. At the beginning of the war the government expected fearsome casualties from air attack: at least one quarter of a million casualties in the first fourteen days.[13] They also expected – surprisingly, as it turned out – increased unemployment from industrial dislocation and a massive increase in destitution. The government was therefore driven to emergency measures: in addition to evacuation, a take-over of the hospitals, both voluntary and local government, in the name of co-ordination and the provision of subsistence without strings to the expected victims of bombing and industrial distress. The Unemployment Assistance Board became plain Assistance Board with responsibility for everyone in need without application of the means test (finally abolished in 1941). As Richard Titmuss, then a civil servant concerned with the emergency hospital service, came to observe:

> by the end of the Second World War the Government had, through the agency of newly established or existing services, assumed and developed a measure of direct concern for the health and well-being of the population which, by contrast with the role of the Government in the nineteen-thirties, was little short of remarkable. No longer did concern rest on the belief that, in respect to many social needs, it was proper to intervene only to assist the poor and those who were unable to pay for services of one kind and another. Instead, it was increasingly regarded as a proper function of Government to

ward off distress and strain among not only the poor but almost all classes of society.[14]

Long before that, however, planning for a future in which there would be 'no more distressed areas, no more vast armies of unemployed, no more slums, no vast denial of equality of opportunity', as Harold Laski put it in 1940,[15] had become the chief way of boosting morale and making the struggle seem worthwhile. PEP (Political and Economic Planning), which had published a report on *The British Social Services* in 1937, set up a Post-War Aims Group even before the war began, and by July 1942 had produced a pamphlet, *Planning for Social Security*, which anticipated the post-war legislation. G. D. H. Cole got Treasury backing for the Nuffield College Reconstruction Survey, one of many planning groups set up by professional interests, including the British Medical Association, the Town and Country Planning Association, the three main political parties, and a general pressure group under the chairmanship of J. B. Priestley, then a popular broadcaster and morale booster (much disliked for his socialist views by part of the government, which persuaded the BBC in 1940 to stop his weekly broadcasts).[16] Priestley's group went public on 4 January 1941 with a special issue of *Picture Post* devoted to *A Plan for Britain*, with articles by Thomas Balogh the economist on 'Work for All', A. D. K. Owen, a political scientist, on 'Social Security', Maxwell Fry the architect and town planner on 'The New Britain Must Be Planned', A. D. Lindsay, Master of Balliol College, Oxford on 'A Plan for Education', Julian Huxley the biologist on 'Health for All', Dr Maurice Newfield on 'A Real Medical Service', and Priestley himself on holidays and leisure.[17] It was a professional blueprint for a professional society.

Arthur Greenwood, Labour minister of health, was connected with these groups and sympathetic to their aims. Responding to the TUC's request for better coverage of health insurance, he persuaded the government to set up in June 1941 an inter-departmental committee of civil servants under Sir William Beveridge, a pioneer with Churchill of national insurance, on the first prerequisite of any plan, social security. Beveridge was an elitist, self-important, rather humourless man, who did not welcome the job and wrote to his sister, 'I am Chairman also of a Reconstruction Committee on the Social Services: but I'm not doing much about that while I can do anything about the war.'[18]

He offended his civil servant colleagues on the Committee by circulating without consultation a memorandum laying down his dogmatic proposals, derived from his long-held beliefs on national insurance, and the Cabinet decided that the report, still thought of as internal technical advice, should be in the Chairman's name alone. Fortunately, the Committee had a secretary, D. N. Chester, a temporary civil servant from a working-class background recruited from Manchester University and later to be Warden of Nuffield College, Oxford, who understood the importance of the subject to the working class and its morale.

The report, its publication delayed by government doubts, came out in November 1942 under the driest of titles, *Social Insurance and Allied Services*. It was an instant best-seller, selling along with its shorter summary 635,000 copies. Within two weeks, a Gallup poll found that nineteen people out of twenty had heard of it, and nine out of ten believed that its proposals should be adopted. It declared roundly that 'a revolutionary moment in the world's history is a time for revolutions, not for patching'. Social insurance was one part only of a comprehensive policy of social progress, and all 'five giants on the road to reconstruction', Want, Disease, Ignorance, Squalor and Idleness, should be tackled together. It noted that the state already made provision in the exigencies of life for most of the population, but that there were obvious gaps in the coverage, such as medical treatment for workers' families, and maternity and death benefits. Want could be finally abolished by a comprehensive system of social security on the insurance principle, everyone contributing and everyone receiving benefits as of right in the exigencies of life, sickness, unemployment, widowhood and old age. The state scheme would provide for a national minimum; it should leave room and encouragement for individuals to provide more than the minimum for themselves and their families. There were three assumptions without which the scheme would fall short of its aims: children's allowances for all after the first (to solve the old problem of large families in poverty); a comprehensive health and rehabilitation service for all citizens, not just for the insured workers; and a plan for the maintenance of full employment, to prevent mass unemployment from bankrupting the system. The whole scheme would be funded by a single weekly stamp, paid for jointly by the worker and the employer (or by the self-employed

415

person alone), and the benefits should be adequate and proof against inflation. The aim of the plan was 'to abolish want by ensuring that every citizen willing to serve according to his powers has at all times an income sufficient to meet his responsibilities'.[19]

The excitement and acclamation with which the Beveridge Report was received can only be understood in the context of the time. It came at 'the turning of the tide', just after the battles of El Alamein and Stalingrad. As Churchill put it with understandable simplification, 'Before Alamein we never had a victory. After Alamein we never had a defeat'.[20] People, already oriented to post-war reconstruction by the public discussion of planning, were looking for light at the end of the tunnel, and Beveridge seemed to shine that light. Archbishop Temple in broadcasts had popularized the term 'welfare state' to contrast Allied governments, who supposedly put the welfare of their people in a very general sense before military might, with the 'warfare states' of the Axis Powers (in fact the Germans put proportionately less effort into warfare than Britain until the closing stages of the war).[21] The term instantly attached itself to the Beveridge proposals, and 'the welfare state' became a shorthand way of referring to the whole programme, including social security, a national health service, educational opportunity, and full employment. Any politician who promised these was for the welfare state; any who dragged his feet was against it.

Churchill, unfortunately for the Tory Party and its hopes of winning the post-war election, was perceived as dragging his feet, although some of the younger, more perceptive Conservatives, led by Quintin Hogg, saw it as 'a flag to nail to the mast, a symbol, a rallying point for men of good will – above all, an opportunity to re-establish a social conscience in the Tory Party'.[22] The war minister even refused to allow ABCA (the Army Bureau of Current Affairs) to distribute a summary of the report to the troops because it was too controversial. The Labour Party, the TUC, the Liberal Party, and the British Council of Churches enthusiastically endorsed it. In the parliamentary debate on the report in February 1943 the government, led on the domestic side by the poker-faced ex-civil servant Sir John Anderson and the penny-pinching Chancellor of the Exchequer Sir Kingsley Wood, half-heartedly endorsed about half of it and, at Churchill's insistence, left the necessary legislation to a post-war government. They provoked a revolt of 119 Coalition MPs, ninety-seven of them Labour, and led the mining MP, James Griffiths, the future minister of national insurance, to remark that 'This makes the return of the Labour Party to power at the next election an absolute certainty'.[23] Churchill and the Tory leadership had misread the mood of the people.

To some extent the enthusiasm was misplaced. The Beveridge Plan looked backward rather than forward, to the Edwardian conception of national insurance as a provision for the deserving poor who had paid their dues rather than to society itself as one great family responsible for all its members. It left many loopholes through which non-contributors could fall into distress, and the safety net, the old (Unemployment) Assistance Board transformed into the National Assistance Board in 1948, was to apply the old means test and even, unintended by Beveridge, to prop up the inadequate insurance benefits with supplementary benefits. Nevertheless, the report contributed greatly to the revolution in expectations which seized hold of the British people in the midst of this most total of wars and prepared them to demand a new kind of society when it ended.

The Labour Party gained most from these expectations. As in the First World War, it benefited enormously from its entry into the Coalition government in 1940 and particularly from the increased stature of Clement Attlee as deputy premier, Ernest Bevin as minister of labour and Arthur Greenwood as minister of health, who between them dominated the control of manpower and the social services. The trade unions gained, too, from the shortage of labour, growing from 6.3 million members and 31 per cent of the eligible workforce in 1939 to 8.8 million and 43 per cent in 1946,[24] and from the further growth of corporatism as the government and employers were forced to seek their co-operation. By 1941 Pit Production Committees in the coal mines and Yard Committees in shipbuilding were established, and by 1942 even the reluctant Engineering Employers' Federation, under pressure from the government, signed an agreement with the Amalgamated Engineering Union to establish Joint Production Committees in works with over 150 workers. Even the Ford Company, after a brief strike early in 1941, was forced to recognize the union at their Manchester works, and at the main works at Dagenham two and a half years later. Outside the mines there were relatively few strikes during the war, and nothing like the Red Clydeside and other labour unrest of the First World War. The shop stewards were as anxious to keep up production to defeat the Nazis as the union leaders and the government, and even the Communist Party gave up their agitation against a capitalist war after Russia was invaded in July 1941. As James Cronin has expressed it, 'With Bevin formulating state policy ... the unions were accorded a status and a dignity scarcely imaginable before 1939,' and both they and the Labour leadership 'emerged from the war stronger and more self-confident.'[25]

The Labour Party and the working class were not the only ones looking for a better post-war world. Opinion polls showed that the middle classes, too, supported the Beveridge Plan and a Gallup poll in April 1945 even showed a majority of them in favour of the nationalization of key industries.[26] Civil servants, teachers and other public employees had suffered pay cuts during the inter-war Depression, and the salaried middle class was united with the manual workers in not wanting to return to the 1930s. Despite the Coalition government's Education Act and the White Paper on Employment of 1944 committing the government to 'the maintenance of a high and stable level of employment after the war', the Conservative Party became tarred with the brush of depression, cuts in social services and, of course, Munich and Appeasement. Even the army, in North Africa, Italy and, finally, France and Germany, was caught by the passion for social reform. In June 1945 the revolution in expectations swept the Labour Party into power with a landslide majority, and (though the atomic bomb did not end the war against Japan until August) the post-war world began.

2 'MOST OF OUR PEOPLE HAVE NEVER HAD IT SO GOOD'

The quarter-century after the Second World War saw the culmination of all the trends leading to professional society: the rise of an affluent, permissive, more homogeneous society with greater equality between the classes, the sexes and the generations, the completion of the welfare state run by professional administrators and experts, and the creation of a mixed economy controlled on both sides by professional managers. Affluence was the most obvious trend. After the immediate post-war austerity, Gross Domestic Product rose by 2.6 per cent per annum in the 1950s and 2.8 per cent in the 1960s, enabling living standards per head to double in real terms between 1946 and 1973.[27] In 1954 the Chancellor of the Exchequer, R. A. Butler, forecast that the standard of living would double in twenty-five years. During the 1959 election campaign, Harold Macmillan, the flamboyant prime minister, was able to claim, in a much misquoted phrase, 'Most of our people have never had it so good.'[28]

Material progress was only marred by the knowledge that other industrial countries, including the recent enemies West Germany and Japan, were experiencing even faster growth. The original six members of the European Economic Community achieved an annual rate of growth of 4.9 per cent between 1950 and 1973, but it was not until the late 1960s that they shot into the lead, so that British complacency remained unshaken until then.[29]

Success was also marred by the decline of Britain as a world power and by the retreat from empire. Yet this too was not taken too seriously at first. Political and military decline was cushioned by the consciousness of victory in war, the rapid acquisition of the nuclear deterrent as one of only three and then five nuclear powers, by permanent membership of the Security Council of the United Nations, high standing in the world financial system, and by the 'special relationship' with the heir to British hegemony, the United States. The retreat from empire was disguised as the long-planned evolution of self-governing colonies and their transformation into autonomous dominions on the pattern of Canada, Australia, New Zealand and, less happily, South Africa. The expanded Commonwealth of Nations was heralded as a pattern of international co-operation and mutual aid for the future of the world. The independence of India, Pakistan, Ceylon and Burma in 1947 was hailed as a triumph of good sense and statesmanship which would in due but not overhasty course be extended to the rest of the larger deserving colonies and federations, like the West Indies and the Rhodesias. Colonial guerrilla wars in Malaya, Cyprus, Kenya and elsewhere came gradually to be seen as sorting out inter-communal strife preparatory to emancipation. The Suez fiasco in 1956 was a cold douche of reality in the face of Britain's diminished power, but merely accelerated the evolution of empire into commonwealth as 'the wind of change' blew most of the remaining colonies into independence in the 1960s and Britain retreated to its home base.[30]

The main legacy of empire, apart from a fund of goodwill in parts of the Third World and a number of almost insoluble political problems in Palestine, Rhodesia, South Africa, Guyana and elsewhere, was a sudden influx of immigrants from the old colonies and new dominions, who added to the variety of what was coming to be seen as a more open and mobile British society. Non-white immigrants from Asia and the West Indies, some of them escaping from a post-colonial situation they found uncomfortable, more of them merely seeking jobs and a better life, were at first encouraged by British governments and employers seeking cheap labour in the post-war reconstruction boom. The welcome turned to alarm when race riots, beginning in Notting Hill in 1958, spread to many cities where the non-whites congregated and were treated with suspicion and hostility by a society which, except for the easily assimilated Scots, Irish and Jews, had experienced little in the way of alien cultures for the last nine centuries. Whether the English were more xenophobic than the French towards their Algerian, the Germans towards their Turkish and Yugoslav, or even the Swiss towards their Spanish and Portuguese 'guestworkers', none of whom, unlike the British immigrants, were granted full citizenship, may well be doubted, but Britain acquired a race problem which took it by surprise.[31]

In some areas of London, Birmingham, and the textile towns of Yorkshire, Lancashire and the East Midlands, race replaced class as the main source of tension. Although still powerful as a cause of difference and antagonism, class was loosening its grip on the old rigid divisions of English society. There were still great inequalities of income, wealth, education, speech and dress, and most people had to work for their livings while others belonged to what one of them called 'that reservoir of persons economically free and used to responsibility from an early age'.[32] There were still major differences in people's relations to the means of production, though even they were becoming more alike in the sense of more dependent on paid employment. With the spread of affluence, the decline of domestic service and deference and, to a lesser extent, the growth of educational opportunity, the classes were becoming more alike in dress, in expectations of material comfort and personal services, in leisure and holidays, and in lifestyle generally. At one end of the scale it was no longer possible for the rich to maintain vast houses with troops of servants totally insulated from the rest of society: as we have seen, the Second World War saw the end of all that. At the other more and more people came to own their own house, with modern amenities better than the Victorian aristocracy enjoyed, consumer durables like television sets, refrigerators and washing machines, a garden, the mobility afforded by a car, more time for a variety of leisure activities, longer holidays away from home, many of them abroad, and so on.

There came into being a kind of average lifestyle, home-centred, family-oriented, servantless, with leisure time devoted to home-based activities, television watching, gardening, do-it-yourself decorating and home improvement, with weekend car trips to the country or the seaside, and annual holidays in Britain or abroad, a lifestyle which encompassed a growing majority of the population. By 1971 over half of all families owned their own home (and two-thirds of the rest lived on secure tenures in low-rent public housing), over half had a car (and 7 per cent more than one), two-thirds had a refrigerator and/or a washing machine, and over 95 per cent had television. Most adult male manual workers worked forty to forty-five hours a week, non-manual workers slightly less, and two-thirds had three weeks' annual holiday or more (only 28 per cent had less than two weeks). At least 95 per cent of the members of every class spent a large part of their free time watching television, two-thirds (except for the less skilled working class, where it was half) spent some time gardening, and half or more in home decorating, car cleaning, and playing with children. Taking a drive in the car, socializing in the pub, and going for a walk were popular activities with half or more of every class, while the only participatory sport with more than a 10 per cent following was swimming, with 22 per cent.[33] Although there were differences of taste in programmes viewed, music listened to, books and newspapers read, age and size of car, destination of car rides and holidays, and so on, there was an astonishing similarity between the way of life of all classes, which would only become more similar with time. By 1984, for example, 95 per cent of manual workers would have four weeks' holiday or more, two-thirds of every class except the poorest (44 per cent) took a holiday away from home, and from 89 to 94 per cent of every class took day trips in the summer.[34]

421

Much of this convergence was due to the tendency towards single status for manual and non-manual workers, in matters such as hours of work, holidays, sick pay, occupational pensions, and conditions of work, which was subsumed under the professionalization of the working class in Chapter 7. It also owed much to the rise of the so-called 'affluent worker', to which we shall return, pursuing the same comforts and amenities already enjoyed by the middle class. It was reinforced by upward mobility from the manual to the non-manual class, especially by women workers, an increasing proportion of whom were married. Non-manual male workers increased from 32 per cent of those occupied in 1951 to 41 per cent in 1971, non-manual women workers from 46 to 57 per cent, and the proportion of married women working, manual and non-manual, from 22 to 42 per cent.[35]

Meanwhile, entrepreneurs continued to decline in numbers, male employers and proprietors from 5.7 to 5.2 per cent of the occupied population, and females from 3.2 to 2.9 per cent, while professional administrators and managers increased, males from 12.6 to 21.5 per cent and females from 11.6 to 15.5 per cent, thus reinforcing the change within the non-manual sector towards professional and largely salaried occupations.[36] This came to be one of the major reasons for the steady increase in upward social mobility without an equivalent downward flow over the previous few decades which the Oxford Social Mobility Project observed in 1972. John Goldthorpe and his colleagues found that, amongst men born in ten-year cohorts from 1908–17 to 1938–47, increasing numbers were making their way from below into what they called the 'service class', the professional, administrative and managerial Class I, and its 'cadet' or subaltern level, Class II. Indeed, a clear majority of each of these classes was recruited from below, 54.3 per cent of Class I and 57.6 per cent of Class II (plus 19.1 per cent into Class II from Class I). Because these classes were small, 14.3 per cent and 12.2 per cent of the total population, this still left the majority of the working class (Classes V, VI, and VII) where they were, so that while the top classes were more open the lower classes were relatively closed and becoming more so. The authors argued, however, that *if* the division of labour had not changed, producing more jobs at the professional and managerial level, there would have been little or no increase in upward mobility, and the *relative* chance of a working-class boy rising into the top class would have remained much the same.[37] Against this it can be said that it was the expansion of service-class jobs produced by professional society that brought about the undoubted *absolute* increase in upward mobility. For the generation that came to maturity in post-war Britain this represented at least a once-for-all increase in occupational opportunity.

How unequal opportunity still was is made clear by the other half of the Oxford Social Mobility Project, on educational mobility. A. H. Halsey and his colleagues, using slightly different ten-year birth cohorts from 1913–22 to 1943–52, found that in the first three cohorts at least there had been a large expansion of state selective education for first-generation grammar school boys, which 'gave "superior" education to vast numbers of boys from "uneducated" homes'. But because of much greater drop-out rates for those from less advantaged backgrounds in terms of income, 'family climate' and 'cultural capital', their life chances were improved much less than they might have been: 'the proportion of working-class boys reaching A-Level, and *pari passu* securing places at university, could comfortably be doubled without any lowering of standards.' Moreover, boys from the service class had a much greater share of public school and other private education and consequently a much better chance of a university education (though ultimate success owed more to social background than to type of school). Only 5.1 per cent of all the men in the survey had a university education, and a further 1.4 per cent went to a college of education to train as teachers. Part-time further education accounted for 45.1 per cent more, so that more than half the sample had some form of training beyond school. The university students were very unevenly distributed. One in five of the boys from Classes I and II went to university, compared with one in twenty-two of those from the lower non-manual and highly skilled working Classes III–V, and one in fifty-six of those from the less skilled working Classes VI–VIII. This meant that a boy from the service class had a four times greater chance of a university education than one from the intermediate classes, and eleven times greater than one from the working class. When they reached the university, because of the large difference in size between the classes, working-class boys constituted one-fifth of all students, intermediate-class boys over a quarter, and service-class boys over half.

By the last cohort, born in 1943–52, the chances for all classes had more than trebled compared with the first: 8.5 per cent (instead of 1.8 per cent) of the age group now attended, including over one in four of the service class sons, nearly one in twelve of the intermediate group, and one in thirty of the working class. Meanwhile, the gap between the top and the bottom classes had slightly increased: for those born in 1913–22 it was 8 : 1, for those born in 1943–52, 8.5 : 1. Yet in terms of merit as measured by IQ scores (an admittedly dubious measuring rod), the service class only achieved 14 per cent more university places than its estimated (58 per cent) meritocratic share, while the working class lost only 4 per cent of its 'proper' (28 per cent) share. The 4 per cent misallocation represented about 6,000 working-class boys *every year* who were denied their meritocratic due, hardly a trivial figure, and the absolute gains of expansion to the service class were massive compared with those to the working class. Nevertheless, expansion meant that large numbers of 'first-generation' students from all the classes, including 88 per cent from the service class whose parents had not experienced university education, gained access to higher education for the first time, showing how much more they now depended on the education system for success, and the working class found a ladder which, however narrow, was far wider than any previously provided.[38] In other words, educational opportunity in post-war Britain was still very unequal but much nearer to a meritocracy than it had ever been before.

There was also an increasing similarity of incomes. 'The compression, at both ends, of the scale of income distribution' after taxes paid and benefits received, which T. H. Marshall found in 1950, came to be sharply questioned in the 1960s, as we shall see. But there can be little doubt that the poor would have been much poorer and the rich much richer if it had not been for the welfare state and the graduated income tax. The Diamond Commission on the Distribution of Income and Wealth shows that the top 1 per cent of income earners received after tax in 1949–50 less than six times the average income and by 1972 no more than four times – not enough to employ a household of servants on the Victorian scale.[39] Even the poverty surveyors who challenged that finding could only show that, allowing for every kind of fringe benefit and income in kind, the top 1 per cent had a final income about eight times the median, and the marginally rich (the second 5 per cent, i.e. the sixth to tenth percentiles) about three times the median and less than four and a half times the average income of the poor household on supplementary benefit.[40] We must return to the controversial question of the distribution of income and the incidence of poverty later, but meanwhile it is clear that by the standards of any previous age the rich were less rich in terms of the amount of labour of the poor they could buy, and to that extent there was more equality.

The working class was also more affluent, certainly in absolute terms and probably also relative to the middle class. Average weekly earnings for adult male manual workers rose from £8.30 in 1951 to £30.93 in 1971, a rise in real terms of 68 per cent. For manual women they rose from £4.50 to £15.80, a real rise of only 58 per cent, compared with about a 60 per cent rise in real salaries for both non-manual men and women.[41] With more dual-income couples, more working-class families were able to live like the middle class. Journalists and sociologists began to talk about the affluent worker and his 'embourgeoisement', his emulation of the middle-class way of life. In so far as this meant any more than the acquisition of material possessions and advantages such as more leisure and holidays once thought to be the privilege of the middle class, it seemed to imply that workers as they became more affluent would become less class-conscious, less attached to their trade unions and the Labour Party, more individualistic in seeking promotion for themselves and education for their children, and more inclined to accept the capitalist economic system and its political support in the Conservative Party.[42] A team of sociologists who studied a group of affluent workers in the motor, ball bearing and chemical industries in the then thriving town of Luton in the 1960s found that, on the contrary, despite their enjoyment of material gains such as house and car ownership and foreign holidays, they were just as solidaristic in support of the trade unions and Labour as more traditional workers. They had a more 'instrumental' attitude to work, i.e. they viewed it simply as a means to making money to support a better lifestyle, and were just as alienated from boring work on the assembly line as before. Yet the investigators also found that they were more individualistic in the sense of having ambitions for their families and pursuing them in a relatively purposive and planned fashion, in marked contrast to the fatalistic social philosophy which they associated with the traditional working class, and that they practised a more 'bourgeois' family life, with more 'companionate' relations between husband and wife and closer relations between parents and children.[43] Whether or not this amounted to *'embourgeoise-ment'* or was merely 'convergence' (from both directions) towards the average or common lifestyle we saw developing above, it presaged a narrowing of the differences between the classes and their enjoyment of life.

In absolute terms the poor too 'had never had it so good.' Rowntree's third survey of York in 1950 showed that poverty in the old harsh Victorian sense had all but disappeared. Even by the 'human needs standard' of 1936 he found only 1.7 per cent of the population (2.8 per cent of the working class) below the poverty line.[44] Applying the same standard to the national Family Expenditure Survey of 1953–54, Brian Abel Smith and Peter Townsend found over twice as many, 4.1 per cent of the population, in poverty, but still far less than between the wars.[45]

Poverty, however, is not so easily exorcized, and from the late 1960s a powerful lobby argued that poverty was not an absolute but a relative concept, and that anyone who lacked the resources to participate in the activities, customs and diets commonly approved by society was relatively deprived and therefore in poverty by the standards of the time.[46] There were various ways of measuring relative poverty – by a percentage, commonly 50 per cent of the average income, or by a scale of relative deprivation including such criteria as not having four basic household amenities (indoor flush toilet, sink and tap, fixed bath, gas or electric cooker) or not having a holiday away from home in the last twelve months – but the most plausible was the state's own standard, the social security level of national assistance or supplementary benefit. By the latter standard, Abel Smith and Townsend in a large sample survey in 1968–69 estimated that 3.5 million people, 6.4 per cent of the population, were living in relative poverty. At a higher standard, 40 per cent above the supplementary benefit line, they found 11.7 million, 21.5 per cent of the population, living 'on the margins of poverty'.[47]

The problem with relative poverty is that it does not measure poverty in the ordinary sense of lacking adequate means of existence, but inequality, which is a fluctuating concept. Worse still, it contains a paradox: the more generous the welfare state

426

becomes, the more people it thrusts into poverty. Unless the state is able to ensure that everyone below the line knows how to claim and actually receives supplementary benefit, the concept ensures that the poor will always be with us and that nothing short of a massive redistribution of income can cure it. It is thus in danger of becoming counterproductive by leading people to despair of the welfare state and consequently to reject it. The real project of the poverty surveyors, therefore, was not merely to abolish poverty but to set narrower limits to inequality. Hence their attack on the unfair shares of the rich, and on the official statistics which seemed to show that they were getting poorer, both before and after tax. They disputed the findings of the Diamond Commission on the Distribution of Income and Wealth that the original share of personal income of the top 1 per cent of income receivers had been cut by over a third by taxation and that their post-tax income had declined from 5.8 per cent in 1949–50 to 4 per cent in 1972–73. Taking account of all their resources including fringe benefits, social services and private income in kind, and (much the largest and most controversial item since some assets were unrealizable and others double-counted since they yielded interest or dividends in the original income) the 'annuitized value of assets', the survey *increased* their estimated share from 5.4 per cent (before tax) to 6.7 per cent. Similarly, it increased the post-tax share of the top 10 per cent (which the Diamond Commission found had declined less dramatically) from 24.9 to 27.5 per cent.[48]

At first sight this left plenty of room for further redistribution, but on a closer view the rich were not so very rich compared with earlier times. The top 1 per cent had less than seven times the average pre-tax income and perhaps four and a half times after tax – unequal indeed, but not the fabulous wealth which enabled their rich ancestors to buy vast amounts of the labour of the poor. The marginally rich, meanwhile, reached far down into the middle class. The average non-asset income of the second 5 per cent (6–10 per cent) was only £2,103, less than half the salary in 1969 of a university professor. Put more graphically, to lift every household in the bottom 40 per cent receiving less than £777 (79 per cent of the mean, the line of marginal poverty, supplementary benefit plus 40 per cent) up to that level would have taken nearly twice the whole pre-tax income of the top 1 per cent or over two-fifths of the pre-tax income of top 10 per cent.[49] Whether such a draconian (gross, not marginal) rate of tax would have been politically viable or administratively collectable is questionable, leaving aside its effects on investment and the future creation of wealth.

What is beyond question is that the poor would have been in a far sorrier position but for the welfare state. If we look at the redistribution of income after all taxes, direct and indirect, paid and all benefits in cash and kind received, we can take some measure of how far the state helped the lower paid. In 1970 all those earning less than £905 (70 per cent of average male manual earnings) received more than they paid; those earning £620 received on average £189, 30 per cent more than their original income; those earning less than £260 received £431, or 625 per cent of their original income of £69. In short, all those earning less than 58 per cent of the median income (70 per cent of average male manual earnings) received substantially more than they contributed. To that, perhaps inadequate, extent the welfare state pursued the principle of equality of outcome.

There was a further factor operating in the direction of equality, and that was the increasing importance of human capital. Human capital is as important to professional society as land was to pre-industrial society and industrial capital to industrial society. It can be defined as the capitalized return to human skills, or the skill differential over unskilled labour multiplied by the number of years' purchase for other property (e.g. for land, twenty years' purchase for a rent yielding 5 per cent on capital) and discounted for depreciation or 'wastage'. Peter Lindert has observed that the classical economists, obsessed with rent, profits and wages, were able to ignore this factor because 'The relative neglect of human capital differences as a basis for inequality was less serious in a world in which they accounted for only about 15 per cent of national income as compared with about 52 per cent today'. Whereas 'in 1867 the returns to skilled labour accounted for between 5% and 25% of the national income', a century later they amounted to 46-58 per cent of pre-tax household income. More important, by the early 1970s 'the economic ranks had been homogenized as far as the three factors [land, profits, and labour earnings] are concerned', and the top decile received very little of its income from land, little more from other property incomes than the other 90 per cent, and most of its income (78-90 per cent, compared with 84-97 per cent for the rest) from personal earnings.[50] This is another way of saying that in a professional society the dominant form of income comes from personal skill and expertise, acquired by education and training.

The same applies to the distribution of wealth. The Diamond Commission did not attempt to include human capital in its distribution of wealth but it did elaborate its estimates to include one element created largely by human capital, namely accrued pension rights. The estate duty method of estimation (series B, assuming that those not covered by the returns had no wealth) showed that the top 1 per cent of the adult population owned 56 per cent of all personal wealth in 1936–38, 43 per cent in 1954, and 30 per cent in 1972 (and the top 10 per cent at the same dates 88, 79 and 72 per cent). The inclusion of occupational pension rights reduced the share of the top 1 per cent in 1972 from 29.9 to 25.6 per cent (and of the top 10 per cent from 72 to 64 per cent). The poverty surveyors attacked the Commission for making further estimates taking account of state pension rights, on the grounds that the knowledge that the accrued rights of 55–59-year-old women were worth £8,577 in 1975 'would be news indeed to middle-aged working-class women'; but since their state pension rights were usually the most valuable thing they owned it would be good news which made the prospect of old age a lot brighter than without. Taking these estimates into account reduced the share of the top 1 per cent to 17.4 per cent of the total wealth (and of the top 10 per cent to 45.7 per cent).[51] The inclusion of pension rights, an easily measurable fraction of human capital, considerably reduced the degree of wealth inequality. The inclusion of human capital *as a whole*, according to Lindert, would have made the distribution of wealth essentially the same as the distribution of income, which is to say a great deal less unequal.[52]

The way in which the elderly are treated is a good test of a professional society. Since pensions are deferred income or accumulated human capital, they measure the proportion of the population enabled to acquire it in this form. By 1970 75 per cent of non-manual men and 47 per cent of non-manual women workers were in occupational pension schemes, and 46 per cent of manual men but only 18 per cent of manual women workers. (By 1982 64 per cent of all married pensioners were receiving occupational pensions, though only 54 per cent of single men and 33 per cent of single women pensioners.) State pensions meanwhile came to provide for the whole retired population, and increased from 4.1 million (17.5 per cent of the adult population) in 1951 to 7.8 million (21.5 per cent) in 1971. (By 1987 there would be 8.5 million, 23 per cent of the adult population). Over that period the value of the state pension for a married couple increased from 30 to 37 per cent of average male manual earnings (and to 50 per cent by 1981).[53] Though more human capital accrued to professional and managerial men than to their women colleagues or to manual workers of both sexes, the professional principle of pensions as deferred career earnings was being gradually extended to the whole population.

In relations within the family, between the sexes and the generations, there was less inequality. More women were marrying (four out of five in the 1960s compared with three out of five in the 1930s) and were marrying younger but were having no more children (even in the short-lived 'baby booms' of the late 1940s and early 1960s families were no larger, the high birth rate being due to more mothers of childbearing age) and, as we have seen, far more married women were going out to work. This led some sociologists to talk of the 'symmetrical family', with both parents working and helping with childrearing and housework. Husbands in all classes were helping more in the house, though least at top and bottom in company directors' and unskilled manual workers' families, and there was still much sexual division of labour, with the wife cooking and caring for the children and the husband washing the dishes, gardening, home decorating, and doing some of the housework.[54] But women who went out to work out of interest, to pursue a career or simply to earn money to make ends meet or improve the family's living standard, soon found that they had liberated themselves into a double burden of work, and that most of the cares of home and children fell on them.

It did, however, give them more financial and psychological independence, and the women's emancipation movement of the 1960s, which followed rather than caused the expansion of employment, was pioneered by professional career women who felt the injustice of this new version of the double standard. Women's liberation owed more to the professional social ideal than meets the eye. In a society predicated on reward according to merit it was morally impossible to deny to women who had proved their worth by intellectual ability and practical competence recognition of their merit – or, if perversely denied, it became a challenge for women to demand their rights.[55] The triumphs of the movement – the Divorce Reform Act of 1969 which made irretrievable breakdown of marriage the sole ground; the Matrimonial Property Act of 1970 which made the wife's contribution to the marriage, in money or in kind, an equal claim on the marital property; the Equal Pay Act of the same year which aimed at equal reward for equal work by the end of 1975, and the Sex Discrimination Act of 1975, which set up the Equal Opportunities Commission to even up job and promotion chances – were all expressions of the principle of equal reward for equal merit. Ideals can of course be frustrated in practice, and ways were found by employers to evade the last two acts, but the legislative acceptance of the principle was a revolution in the relations between the sexes.

Teenagers were liberated too from traditional parental controls, by affluence, possession of more disposable income than any other age group, and the shortage of teenage labour, reinforced by the trend for more children to stay on at school and enter higher education, where universal student grants from 1959 based on parental income provided adequate maintenance. With far more money to spend on clothes, pop records, consumer durables like 'hi-fi' equipment and motorbikes, and on leisure activities, a burgeoning youth culture developed. Its cult heroes ranged from Bill Haley and the Comets, a transatlantic import of the 1950s, through the lovable Beatles and the rebellious Rolling Stones of the 1960s, to the 'unisex' David Bowie and Boy George of the 1970s and 1980s. It was expressed in youth fashions, from the nostalgic 'Teddy boys' of the 1950s through the 'mods and rockers' to the 'flower people' and the (less handsome and more racist) 'skinheads' and 'punks' of the 1960s and 1970s. It was exploited by big business, both legitimate in the shape of pop concert promoters and record companies and illicit in the shape of drug racketeers, but it successfully demanded a more colourful, cosmopolitan and hedonistic life for the young.[56] The significance of the youth culture, especially by the 1960s, was not only that it was almost classless, so that public school pop groups like the Hollies had to fake a working-class accent to become acceptable, but that it reversed the sociologists' 'principle of stratified diffusion' (the theory that trends in dress, music, entertainment,

431

and lifestyle always begin at the top and work their way down through society).[57] If it had ever been wholly true – and the past history of the upward trajectory of trousers, the lounge suit, and casual wear generally, not to mention American jazz and the blues, or the decline of church attendance, suggest otherwise – the 1960s turned it upside down, with the young of the middle and upper classes emulating the denizens of Liverpool and the East End of London.

In nothing did the new fashionable classlessness manifest itself more than in dress. If the inter-war period saw the first real revolution in costume since the fashion cycle began, with skirts above the knee and 'beach pyjamas' for women, the 1960s saw the second, not so much the mini-skirt and 'hot-pants' as the 'unisex' jeans and T-shirts which spread right across the world from San Francisco via London to Hong Kong. This was a perfect example of upward diffusion: blue jeans (the fustian of the Victorian working class) had been the working dress of the American farmer and the 'overalls' of the British working man. They became the uniform of the (largely middle-class) student revolt in the universities of the late 1960s and early 1970s. Their adoption by the middle-class young, even with designer labels by Gloria Vanderbilt or Jordache, was the symbol – not much accepted by their still class-ridden elders – of the classless young.

The 1960s was the pivotal decade, too, for the so-called 'permissive society', the final kick of revolt against Victorianism itself. There had always been 'permissive behaviour' at the highest and lowest levels of society, amongst the Victorian Prince of Wales's Marlborough House set and the 'roughs' and amongst the inter-war Prince of Wales's Fort Belvedere set and the low-class 'monkey runs' of the industrial towns. Yet Geoffrey Gorer in the early 1950s found that the great majority of respondents to his newspaper questionnaire disapproved of sex before marriage and still more of sex outside it.[58] As the Hungarian immigrant humorist George Mikes explained, 'Continentals have sex; the English have hot water bottles.'[59] Although their behaviour did not quite measure up to their ideals, the British, especially of the lower middle and upper working class, were both inhibited and censorious. Most of them remained so throughout the 'permissive revolution', which affected the young far more than the middle-aged. Contrary to popular belief, it began before the contraceptive pill liberated women – *some* women, since it was used only by a minority, and most of them within marriage – from the more obvious consequences of free love. The main effects were a more general acceptance of monogamous unmarried couples living together and a small rise in the rate of illegitimate births, from 4.8 per thousand live births in 1931 and 1951 to 8 per thousand live births in 1971, while the rate of premarital conceptions scarcely rose at all. They did, it is true, more than double in the next fourteen years, but that was because of the rise of 'informal' marriage between couples living together, and two-thirds of illegitimate infants were registered in the names of both parents.[60]

There was nonetheless a vast change in public attitudes towards sexual behaviour and the discussion of it in private conversation and the media, which found expression in changes in legislation. This more intellectual aspect – sex in the head, as it were – owed something to the professional ideal of rational discourse and opposition to ancient taboos and moral obfuscation. It began perhaps with the 'Angry Young Men' of the mid-1950s, John Osborne, Alan Sillitoe, Kenneth Tynan and company, protesting against the fusty nostalgia and moral hypocrisy of the English. It was taken up by enlightened professionals like Richard Hoggart, Roy Jenkins and Lord Wolfenden, who represented a cooler and more rational challenge to traditional puritanism. The Wolfenden Committee in 1957 recommended greater tolerance for homosexuals. Professional experts like Richard Hoggart queued up to defend D. H. Lawrence's *Lady Chatterley's Lover* at the 1960 obscenity trial which determined that pornography was legal as long as it was art, thus precipitating the gold rush of girlie magazines from *Playboy* to *Hustler*. Roy Jenkins as Home Secretary in the late 1960s sponsored a raft of 'permissive' legislation: the Abortion Act and the Family Planning Act of 1967 which allowed abortion for medical and psychiatric reasons and free contraceptive advice through the National Health Service; the Sexual Offences Act of the same year which decriminalized homosexual activity between consenting adults in private; the Divorce Reform Act of 1969, mentioned above; and the abolition of the Lord Chamberlain's censorship of the theatre in 1968, which led to Kenneth Tynan's 'Oh, Calcutta!', 'No Sex Please, We're British', the longest-running comedy of all time, and other thespian masterpieces.

Permissiveness was not without its critics, who called it promiscuity and pornography. The redoubtable Mary White-house, Birmingham housewife and self-appointed moralist to the nation, extended her 1964 campaign against rude words on BBC radio and naughty scenes on television into a general war against vice and pornography, aided by Lord Longford, the Labour ex-minister who subjected himself to harrowing sessions of X-film viewing in the cause of morality. Like-minded politicians had passed the Street Offences Act of 1959, which was designed to banish prostitution but instead simply drove it underground. There was also unsuccessful religious and moral opposition to free abortion and socialized contraception, and even to freer divorce by Dr Shirley Summerskill, MP who called it a 'Casanova's charter'.[61] Some naive moralists even condemned mini-skirts for encourag-ing instant sex, not realizing what every Victorian seducer knew, that long skirts and split draws (or none) gave much readier access than tights. Despite all their efforts, by 1972 the official handbook on Britain could say with bureaucratic understatement:

> In the past twenty years the traditional pattern of life in Britain
> has undergone considerable change. Not only have distinctions
> of class and social habit become less rigid, but subjects
> formerly taboo in public discussion are now openly considered
> in books, plays and films and in ordinary conversation. A more
> informed tolerance of behaviour which deviates from the usual
> pattern is reflected, for instance, in the growing popular
> sympathy for the difficulties of the unmarried mother. The
> passing of new laws on such matters as abortion, divorce, and
> homosexuality, though disliked by many people (particularly
> of the older generation), is nevertheless indicative of public
> unwillingness to penalize individuals with particular social
> problems.[62]

Behind the rise of this essentially secular morality lay the decline of religious belief. Church attendance, which had been declining relatively during and since the Victorian age and absolutely since the First World War, now reached diminutive proportions. In 1966 the major Protestant and Roman Catholic churches claimed in membership only 21 per cent of the population, compared with 26 per cent in 1901. In 1967 it was estimated that only 15 per cent of the English attended religious worship on an average Sunday.

Including these, one in four claimed to attend once a month, but one in five attended only for weddings, baptisms and funerals, and 35 per cent never attended at all. By 1974 Anglican attendance had declined by a further 12 per cent and Roman catholic attendance at Sunday mass by a further 16 per cent. Geoffrey Gorer found in 1950 that, although three-quarters of his respondents claimed a religious affiliation and over half sent their children to Sunday school, less than one in six were regular attenders, and only 14 per cent of the men and 11 per cent of the women believed in an after-life.[63] Much of the decline was due to apathy rather than active disbelief, and the distractions of the increasingly secularized Sunday, with television, gardening, car cleaning, car drives, the cinema and other leisure pursuits taking precedence over church attendance. But none of these diversions would have counted if religion still had the emotional and intellectual power to command belief – as the success of the more millennial and transcendental religions such as the Mormons, the Jehovah's Witnesses, the Seventh-Day Adventists, and a levitation of Indian mystics demonstrated – and the ultimate cause must be laid at the door of secular science. Science had been undermining religion since Darwin and Huxley, and scientific theology had been doing the same since George Eliot's translation of Strauss's *Leben Jesu* and the Tübingen school of biblical criticism. On the one hand, the common man felt that in a scientific world he had 'no need of that hypothesis'. On the other, the uncommon intellectual, steeped in theologians like Bultman, Bonhoeffer and Tillich, looked for a 'religionless Christianity', a God-like life force, which culminated in Bishop Robinson of Woolwich announcing 'the death of God' in 1963. He would be followed later by Don Cupitt, a Cambridge College dean, in a famous iconoclastic television series, and by Bishop Jenkins of Durham whose induction it was popularly believed caused York Minister to be struck by lightning.[64] When the clergy themselves abolished an anthropomorphic god, people began to suspect that their own profession was killing religion – and was about to commit suicide.

Yet in a deeper sense professionalism created a more moral society. If the core of the Christian message without God is to love one's neighbour as oneself, then the twentieth-century welfare state could claim to be more Christian and certainly more moral than Victorian England, since it had expanded the concept of neighbour beyond the parish and poor law union to the whole nation. The concept had been evolving, we have seen, since the Edwardian age, and by 1942 the Beveridge Report could claim that provision was made for most people against most of the exigencies of life. The Labour government of 1945–51, building on the revolution in expectations during the war, extended it to the whole population. Certain items, notably family allowances for second and subsequent children and the Butler Education Act of 1944 providing secondary education for all, were enacted before the war finally ended, but the Attlee government implemented them and passed the great series of acts – the National Insurance, Industrial Injuries Insurance, and National Health Service Acts of 1946, the Town and Country Planning Act of 1947, and the Children Act and National Assistance Act of 1948 – which completed the universal coverage of the system. The date 5 July 1948 became 'the vesting day of the welfare state'.

Thereafter, in principle if less so in practice, the state was ultimately responsible for the welfare of every citizen 'from the cradle to the grave', 'from the womb to the tomb' or, as the troops irreverently put it, 'from the erection to the resurrection'. There was to be much debate about the adequacy of the coverage and about the principles, of 'universalism' versus 'selectivity', on which provision should be made, but there was almost complete consensus between politicians and the public on the need for a welfare state. As we shall see, the welfare state was to put the professional social ideal to the test, and even help to split it in two – not on the question of its existence but on the meaning of citizenship and the claims of social justice. Nationalization was to split it too, not so much over the merits of socialism versus capitalism but over which professional bureaucracy, that of the state or the private corporation, was best fitted to run large-scale industry. This brings us, however, to the most important development in post-war professional society, the bifurcation of the professional ideal.

3 THE BIFURCATION OF THE PROFESSIONAL IDEAL

Every society contains the seeds of its own decay. Just as in Victorian England the entrepreneurial ideal which attacked the aristocratic ideal of pre-industrial society split away from and was in turn attacked by the professional ideal, so in post-1945 society the professional ideal split into two rival camps which then began to attack each other. They fought under the banners of the free market versus collectivism inherited from that earlier, Victorian conflict, but just as society had changed out of all recognition so the conflict too was different. That earlier society had been dominated by thousands of comparatively small owner-managing capitalists whose greed and self-interest could be held in check by competition as well as by minimal, if expanding, state regulation. The task of the professional ideal had been to moralize a potentially amoral competition and to set limits to the exploitation of workers, victims of adulteration and pollution in all classes, and of society at large by fraud, embezzlement and tax evasion.

Twentieth-century society, by contrast, was increasingly dominated by large-scale organizations, not only giant private corporations run by professional managers but also still larger state corporations and the vast administrative organs of the welfare state, run by very similar people. In private industry the share of the largest 200 firms in manufacturing production rose from 73 per cent in 1957 to 86 per cent in 1969. In the public sector the share of the occupied population employed by government rose from 8 per cent in 1950 to 17 per cent in 1971, and to 27 per cent if the nationalized industries are included.[65]

The professional managers and administrators on both sides and the professional experts of various kinds they employed were for the most part salaried employees carrying out much the same tasks in much the same manner. They were certainly sufficiently similar in social background, education and training, income, lifestyle, conditions of work, social attitudes and motivations to represent the same social ideal, of a society based on selection by merit and dedicated to social efficiency and social justice.

On closer inspection, however, their relations to the system of production were subtly different, and their structure of rewards, not merely material but psychological, led them in different directions. Each professional occupation or group might have a different structure of rewards and so a different outlook and motivation, which might also change from time to time. For example, medical doctors in the private sector catering for rich or insured patients would view themselves and their interests differently from salaried consultants or general practitioners in the

National Health Service. Scientists working in private industry had a different outlook, more geared to foreseeable returns, from those in the universities or the Civil Service. Managers in a private corporation performing exactly the same work and receiving much the same salaries as those in a nationalized industry might still have different ambitions and see greater opportunities of enhancing their rewards. The main line of cleavage, therefore, ran between those employed by the private or profit-oriented sector and the public sector, including the non-profit-making institutions such as universities, churches and charitable foundations.

This is not, of course, to say that all those on one side of the line automatically and inevitably supported one version of the ideal and vice versa. The explanatory value of an ideal is that it allows people to choose a position different from their purely material interest, which is what makes social and political discussion and conflict so intriguing and unpredictable. Opinion makers and political leaders in particular often take stances which superficially contradict their economic interests, millionaires like Lord Samuel or Robert Maxwell who support the Labour Party, social reformers like Michael Young or Peter Townsend whose policies would raise their own taxes, or academics like Friedrich von Hayek or Lord Beloff who extol extreme versions of the free market which might undermine state support for universities. In the earlier book I called such mavericks 'social cranks', meaning people with eccentric drives, since in a class society they espoused the interests of a different class. I argued that 'there was in the professional middle class a whole ready-made class of potential social cranks', since at that time professional men could so easily consider themselves to be above the main economic battle between the landlords, capitalists and labourers, and could ignore it or take sides as they chose. It was obvious even then that the interests of particular cranks might be more self-serving than they appeared: Malthus's apologia for landlords could be linked to his connections with the old patronage system; James Mill's for capitalists to his hopes of employment by the East India Company; and Feargus O'Connor's championship of the workers to an outsider's hopes of political power. And the professional class as a whole had an interest in promoting a civilized society which would honour their exclusive privileges and guarantee their rewards.[66]

As time went on and professions proliferated, however, more of them were forced to enter the political and economic arena to press their claims and defend their privileges. The human capital they lived by was not, *pace* the economists, a more or less automatic function of their education and training but had to be nurtured by persuading the public, ultimately through the state, to let them control the market for their service by excluding the uneducated and unqualified. What turned human capital into property was, as with land or industrial capital, the rent it could be made to yield, the payment for a scarce resource over and above the immediate labour performed, the differential value between common and highly skilled labour for which a client, an employer or the state was willing to pay a premium. Specialized training of itself only yielded earned income which, if it could be offered by anyone, would soon descend to the competitive, marginal level. To turn it into property yielding a scarcity premium or differential rent required some device to transform it into a scarce resource.

The device was closure, the restriction of access to the profession by means of expensive or selective training, education and qualification, better still by the grant of a state monopoly of the service. That is why, in an increasingly specialized society, the expanding service occupations so avidly sought professional organization and control of the market for their services. The vast expansion of the qualifying associations since 1800 was an attempt to consolidate the financial and psychic rewards accruing from the monopoly of certain kinds of human capital. After 1880 they came in an accelerating procession: twenty by 1900, another twenty-seven by 1918, forty-six between the wars, and another forty-six by 1970. To these should be added a host of aspiring professions and semi-professions, who failed (until very recently in some cases) to establish a monopoly of the service: from the National Union of Teachers (1878) or the British Dental Association (1880) through the Association of Hospital and Welfare Administration (1898) or the Royal College of Nursing (1916) to the Advertising Managers' Association (1932) and the British Nuclear Energy Society (1962).[67]

Some of the most important professions, however, had never been self-employed and did not need that form of organization, notably the clergy, the officer corps of the armed forces, the Civil Service, local government officers, university teachers, and, more recently, professional business managers. As their numbers expanded, and as more of the qualified professionals became employed either by other professionals or by corporations public or private, they too began to feel the need for defensive organization. Because of their claim to high status professional associations did not, until recently at least, like to call themselves trade unions – although the most successful like the British Medical Association or the Law Society might be described as trade unions which so successfully controlled the labour market that they did not need to strike – but in the more corporate climate of post-war society it became necessary for even the most gentlemanly to organize more effectively to deal with their corporate or state employers. White-collar unions affiliated to the TUC grew from 745,000 members in 1957 to 3.3 million in 1977, 4.6 million if white-collar workers in manual unions are included, and there were many others outside the TUC. Trade union density (membership as a percentage of all employees) grew amongst male non-manual workers from 34 per cent in 1948 to 43 per cent in 1970, while it declined from 64 to 61 per cent amongst male manual workers.[68] More remarkable were the undoubtedly professional unions joining the TUC, the National Association of Local Government Officers in 1964, the Society of Civil Servants in 1973, the Association of University Teachers and the Institution of Professional Civil Servants in 1976, and the top civil servants of the First Division Association in 1977. ASTMS (the Association of Scientific, Technical and Managerial Staffs), the most dynamic of professional unions, began to recruit not only industrial technicians and research scientists but clergymen and airline pilots. Even managers, who had long shunned unions as incompatible with their status, began to form staff associations, especially when their industries were nationalized, as in British Steel in 1968, Rolls Royce in 1973, and shipbuilding in 1977.[69] The salaried professions were coming to recognize their need for collective negotiation with the giant corporations, both public and private.

Nationalization brought the dichotomy between the public and private sector professionals to a head. Their managers were forced to confront the question of whether their interests lay with the traditional free market outlook of corporate management or with the public service outlook of the civil servants and other state-employed professions. The 'Morrisonian' principle on which the

Attlee government had set them up (Herbert Morrison, Leader of the Commons, had organized the London Passenger Transport Board in 1934 as a public corporation answerable to government and not to the workers or the consumers) modelled the nationalized industries on private corporations, but responsible through a minister to Parliament instead of to an annual general meeting of shareholders. In all other respects (to the dismay of Aneurin Bevan and the Labour left who hoped for some form of workers' control and a 'social service' function for the consumers) they were capitalist organizations, expected to make a profit or at least to break even.[70] Their managers were, inevitably in the early stages, recruited from private industry and there was considerable overlap on the controlling boards. In 1956 106 of the 272 members of the national and regional boards of the eight leading nationalized industries were directors of private companies, and a further seventy-one were professional managers and technicians whose careers began in private industry.[71] The Bank Rate Tribunal in 1957, an early inquiry into 'insider dealing', revealed a chain of common membership (and considerable kinship links) between the boards of the nationalized Bank of England, the 'Big Five' clearing banks and the City merchant banks.[72] A career manager like Frank Kearton, Chairman of Courtaulds, might find himself on the boards of several nationalized industries and part-time Chairman of the government Industrial Reorganization Corporation (midwifing private corporate mergers) in 1966–68 before becoming Chairman of the state-owned British National Oil Corporation in 1976. International corporate executives like the Australian Michael Edwardes of the multinational Chloride Group and Ian McGregor of Lazard Frères of New York could be called in as 'profit doctors' for nationalized industries like British Leyland, British Steel and the National Coal Board before returning to private business. With such constant interchange between public and private industry, it is not perhaps surprising that Conservative governments down to 1974 accepted nationali-zation in principle and that most public corporation managers thought and behaved like private sector ones. The mixed economy was very mixed indeed.

On the other side of this two-way managerial fence, the traditional owner-managing capitalist was rapidly disappearing and being replaced by career managers and corporate representatives of financial institutions. Although there were still Pilkingtons at Pilkington's Glass, Cadburys at Bourneville, Sainsburys in the high street stores, Ferrantis at Ferranti's and so on, by 1963 less than a third (29 per cent) of the largest 116 companies were controlled by traditional tycoons or family business men, a third (32 per cent) by professional career managers, and the rest (39 per cent) by 'coordinator controllers' representing banks, insurance and other financial corporations (as in the case of Shell, British Petroleum, and Vickers).[73] The last group represented the increasingly interlocking structure of the corporate economy, with the investment managers of a comparatively few financial institutions in control of immense investment capital and, where they wished to exercise it, of the power to hire and fire company boards. Where about 100 corporations accounted for three-quarters of manufacturing production and employment, which meant that three to five companies dominated each industry, the power to administer prices (by 'price leadership' if not by collusion), negotiate national across-the-board wages (often through 'joint employers' negotiating machinery), and thus to predetermine profits was concentrated in very few hands.[74] The only restraint on this power (apart from the trade unions' ability to negotiate above-average pay settlements) was exercised by exactly similar professional managers, either by corporate raiders, take-over bidders, asset strippers and the like who, manipulating huge sums of borrowed money or paper securities ('junk bonds'), threatened managements with dismissal, 'greenmail' pay-offs in aborted take-overs, or defensive efficiency drives, or by foreign corporations outcompeting them. The object of the game was not so much profits for their own sake, since few of the players owned more than a fraction of the vast shareholdings involved, but, at the lowest level of success, autonomy for the management of each corporation and, at the highest, continual expansion of the corporate enterprise and the span of managerial control.

It is obvious, therefore, why the rhetoric of the free market should be attractive to the private sector professionals. Although designed for the comparatively small-scale Victorian capitalist and a much more competitive economy, it could be readily adapted to the world of collaborative giant corporations because of its appeal to empire-building professional managers. Free enterprise now meant freedom for career managers to climb to the top of large corporations and make them still larger, by internal growth (ploughing back the profits) or colonization (swallowing up other corporations by friendly mergers or hostile take-overs). Since they claimed that they did this by professional ability in the name of economic efficiency and the common good of the whole community, they could still hold to the professional ideal but with a particular emphasis, on equality of opportunity. Just as the Victorian entrepreneur, whether self-made or not, had justified himself by the myth of the self-made man, so the corporate manager, whether born in the purple of the bourgeoisie or risen from the ranks, justified himself by belief in the deserved reward for merit.

The contention between the private and public sector professionals, therefore, was at bottom a dispute about equality. The first believed in equality of opportunity, on the grounds that rewarding merit was the most effective way of ensuring economic growth and a larger national product to share out amongst the community, while the second gave priority to equality of outcome, as the only sure way to achieve fair shares for all. This is of course a crude dichotomy, since the first (with a few extreme exceptions) did not altogether abandon equalizing income tax or welfare for the poor, and the second (save for a few utopian socialists) believed in equality of opportunity for aspiring professionals like themselves and thought of real equality of incomes as a desirable but distant dream. Nevertheless, the two approaches to equality ran through the propaganda of each side as the organizing threads on which all their criteria of the good society were hung.

The dichotomy was the main dispute dividing the major political parties. Although both parties were still largely class-based, the Conservatives winning a majority of the votes of the middle classes, rising to an overwhelming share at the top, and Labour increasing their share down the scale to a less overwhelming majority of the working class, they were both increasingly led by professional men (and very few women). Professional MPs outnumbered business men and farmers on the Tory side of the House of Commons in 1951 by 45 to 43 per cent, in 1979 by 55 to 40 per cent. On the Labour side they outnumbered manual workers in 1951 by 46 to 37 per cent and in 1979 by 49 to 35 per cent – and, since most of the worker MPs were professional trade union officials, by far more than that. As befits a professional society, they were also increasingly university-educated, 41 per cent of Labour MPs in 1951 and 57 per cent by 1979, 65 and 68 per cent of the Conservative MPs, most on both sides from Oxbridge. (The few Liberal MPs were even more professional and university-educated.)[75] The chief difference was in secondary schooling, three-quarters of the Conservatives being ex-public school boys compared with about a fifth of the Labour MPs.

Not surprisingly, the party programmes were expressed in professional terms. Quintin Hogg (later Lord Hailsham), advocating a property-owning democracy in 1947, defended private property because 'the desire to obtain it provides an incentive for work which is morally legitimate, and at the same time sufficiently material to operate on natures which in most of us contain certain elements not entirely spiritual or unself-seeking'.[76] Iain Macleod in 1958 thought that 'Opportunity versus Equality' would be the battle cry of the next election: 'On our banners we will put "Opportunity", an equal opportunity for men to make themselves unequal.'[77] Timothy Raison in 1964 claimed that we were breaking away from the fundamental injustice of class which could deprive a man of the right to make the most of his talents:

> The sons of the poor are coming slowly into their own in industry and learning – and they do so not by overthrowing the old order but by being incorporated in the particular community, whether it be boardroom or high table. . . . One sometimes gets the impression that Professor Titmuss and his disciples are more interested in making the rich miserable than in making the poor happy.[78]

On the other side, equality of opportunity was equated with Tawney's satire on 'the tadpole philosophy' by which the tadpoles in the pond were asked to rejoice in the exceptional frog who made it to dry land.[79] Aneurin Bevan warned in 1952 against 'the managerial society' in which the citizen might become 'the passive creature of a class of supposed supermen, even though these present themselves in the guise of public servants'.[80] In 1959 Hugh Gaitskell's seven basic principles of socialism included: concern for the worst-off, 'social justice, and equitable distribution of wealth and income', a classless society without snobbery or privilege, equality of all races and peoples, belief in human relations 'based not on ruthless self-regarding rivalry but on fellowship and co-operation', precedence for public over private interest, and freedom and democratic self-government.[81] The revisionist Anthony Crosland in 1956 held, with Tawney, that 'socialism is about equality' not public ownership, although the centre left, including Richard Crossman, thought that equality was impossible without 'a true national resources budget' in which 'the public dominates over the private sector', while the far left believed that 'the equality of man' could only be achieved 'through public expenditure, public controls, and public ownership'.[82] Crosland was still arguing in 1975 that 'Socialism ... describes a set of values, of aspirations, of principles which socialists wish to see embodied in the organization of society'. These were essentially 'an overriding concern for the poor', 'strict control over the environment', and

a belief in equality. By equality we mean more than a meritocratic society of equal opportunities, in which unequal rewards would be distributed to those most fortunate in their genetic endowment or family background. We also mean more than a simple redistribution of income. We mean a wider social equality embracing the distribution of property, the educational system, social class relationships, power and privilege in industry – indeed all that is enshrined in the age old dream of a 'classless' society.[83]

Although both parties continued to uphold the welfare state they approached it from opposite directions. The Labour Party believed in 'universalism', the universal provision of comprehensive services, so that all should be eligible for the same benefits in social security, health, education, and so on. For example, large families could best be helped by child allowances paid to the mother for all children, and then taxed to 'claw back' the cost from richer fathers. The Conservatives, by contrast, believed in 'selectivity', concentrating welfare benefits and services on those who needed them and leaving the rest to provide additional support for themselves. In their view large families in poverty because of the breadwinner's low pay should receive family income supplement, introduced by the Heath government in 1971. The egalitarian retort was that the poor and disadvantaged rarely knew their rights and that only about half of those qualifying for FIS actually claimed it.[84]

The welfare state was a compromise between these two approaches. While Beveridge had intended that social security should be 'universalist', covering the whole population, with flat-rate contributions and benefits adequate enough to raise the recipients out of poverty, he had also argued that 'in establishing a national minimum, [the state] should leave room and encouragement for voluntary action by each individual to provide more than that minimum for himself and his family'.[85] In practice it became still more of a compromise. The benefits were eroded by inflation and, in the view of the egalitarians, by the rise of living standards which left increasing numbers in relative poverty and needing additional help. National assistance, intended as a safety net for the unfortunate and diminishing few, became the regular support of an increasing minority of old age pensioners and other state insurance beneficiaries. The poverty surveyors estimated that in 1968, while 3,995,000 people (including dependants) were receiving supplementary benefit, 2,430,000 (including 1,315,000 elderly people over 65 and 410,000 children) were eligible for but not receiving it.[86] To the egalitarian poverty surveyors this seemed to be intentional. Titmuss in *The Irresponsible Society* (1960) attacked the myth of the 'welfare state' (which he always placed in quotation marks):

> Reinforced by the ideologies of enterprise and opportunity it has led to the assumption that most – if not all – of any social problems have been – or soon will be – solved. Those few that remain will, it is thought, be automatically remedied by rising incomes and minor adjustments of one kind or another. In short, it is coming to be assumed that there is little to divide the nation on home affairs except the dreary *minutiae* of social reform, the patronage of the arts, the parking of cars and the effectiveness of corporal punishment.

He claimed, to the contrary, that 'universality' had failed to bring about economic egalitarianism: 'Those who have benefited most are those who needed it least,' especially in education where the middle class got most of the grammar school and university places, in the National Health Service where the poorest third of the nation got the worst medical treatment, and in housing where

446

the subsidies to council tenants were more than matched by mortgage tax relief to the better-off. His main targets, however, were the 'fringe-welfare' and stock options distributed by great corporations to their senior managers, 'as the great feudal lords distributed estates in the Middle Ages', the power of the insurance companies which were coming to dominate the 'pressure group state' and the 'massive concentrations of interlocking economic, managerial and self-regarding professional power' which acted as 'accelerators of inequality; inequalities in the distribution of income and wealth, educational opportunity, vocational choice, pension expectations, and in the right to change one's job [discouraged by tied pension rights], to work in old age, and in other spheres of individual and family need'.[87]

On the other side, while 'few Conservatives would doubt that the social services for the most part are here to stay', according to a member of the progressive Bow Group, Geoffrey Howe, 'even in a prosperous society necessary claims on public expenditure can only be met if the social services ... are drastically refashioned, so that their claims are diminished.' And he attacked Sir Keith Joseph, later known as a hard-line monetarist, who continued to seek 'scope for sensible men to provide additional protection and amenity for their families and themselves *on top of* the State provision'.[88] Neither side was consistent. Crossman as Labour Minister of Health in 1969 proposed income-related benefits and pensions which increased inequality between middle- and working-class pensioners, and the Heath government enacted a similar scheme, thus breaking the Tory principle that additions to state benefits should be left to the private sector. It could be argued, nevertheless, that by making the social security system less dependent on insurance, so that *anyone* in need regardless of contribution entitlement – including for example middle-class students on summer vacation – could claim subsistence, both parties had by 1970 come to accept the principle of social citizenship, that mere membership of society gave an indefeasible right to maintenance when income ceased.

The continuing struggle was over whether such maintenance should aim at a more equal distribution of income for the sake of a basic equality or at the prevention of poverty so as to give everyone a more equal start in the race for opportunity. The radical programme of the public sector professionals began with the

447

abolition of excessive wealth and income and the imposition of an equitable distribution of income and other resources by the state and proceeded to the reorganization of employment by means of public ownership and industrial democracy and the limitation of professional and managerial autonomy.[89] They assumed that society as a whole 'owned' the national income and could distribute it as the majority pleased. Their ideal society implied a massive bureaucracy of professionals like themselves to administer incomes and employment and prevent cheating. On the other side, the radical programme of progressive private sector managerialists was for a meritocracy with great social mobility and equal opportunity for all, by no means incompatible with considerable inequality in rewards, but providing concentrated welfare services 'to alleviate the patches of real hardship which still exist'.[90] They held that individuals 'owned' their own incomes and, deducting only what they democratically agreed to allow to the state for common purposes, could do whatever they wished with their own. Their ideal society implied freedom for professionals like themselves to become as rich and powerful as they could without feeling guilty about it. Both sides aimed at 'national regeneration', the first by building an egalitarian utopia, the second by dynamic economic growth to provide enough wealth for all.

The conflict crystallized, naturally enough, in the sphere of education. There 'parity of esteem' versus equality of opportunity in secondary education had been in contention since the Hadow Report of 1926. The Education Act of 1944 which had introduced 'secondary education for all' appropriate to their 'needs' and 'aptitudes' had not specified how this should be done but had been interpreted to mean a tripartite system of selective education. This divided all children in the state sector at age 11 into those with academic, technical and other kinds of potential, catered for in grammar, technical and secondary modern schools. The 'eleven-plus' selection was based on the theory of the educational psychologist Cyril Burt, later proved to be founded on false evidence, that intelligence was a fixed genetic endowment (IQ = intelligence quotient, measured as a percentage of the median score of all those tested) which could be measured infallibly at 10 years of age and used to separate the academic sheep scientifically from the non-academic goats. Curiously, the principle was not applied to the private schools where, above a low qualifying standard, children of all abilities were educated together. The problem with the system was that it operated a self-fulfilling prophecy: those selected for grammar school received academic training and learned how to pass examinations; the rest accepted their second- or third-class status, were taught and examined less, and became 'failures'. The dilemma for reformers was that any unselective alternative might widen the gap between the state and the private schools and reduce equality of opportunity.

At first hailed as a victory for egalitarianism which gave opportunities to bright working-class children, the system came under increasing fire in the 1950s from educationists like Professors Robin Pedley and John Vaisey who persuaded the Labour Party to back comprehensive education in unified state secondary schools.[91] Educational selection was brilliantly satirized by Michael Young's *The Rise of the Meritocracy* (1958) which warned of the dire consequences of applying the principle 'Merit = IQ + Effort' and ended in a revolution by the uneducated proles against the meritocratic elite in 2034.[92] Michael Shanks on the other hand argued in 1961 that 'a ruling class based exclusively on merit would be less likely than any other sort to lose touch with the mass of the people, from whose ranks it would be continually drawing fresh recruits'.[93] The Wilson government of 1964–70 increased the number of comprehensive schools tenfold, which then catered for about a third of secondary school children. The next development was surprising: middle-class parents who had opposed the comprehensives came to appreciate them as subjecting their children to less strain than selection while still leaving the ladder of opportunity in place (enhanced by streaming for perceived ability in some schools, which often favoured middle-class children). By 1974 under Margaret Thatcher at the Department of Education and Science comprehensive education had doubled again, to cater for two-thirds of the age group. This was aided by the geographical segregation of the classes, so that inner-city schools were predominantly working-class and suburban ones middle-class.

The struggle for both kinds of equality, meanwhile, shifted to the much more intractable frontier between state and private education. Anthony Crosland in 1956 had attacked British education as 'divisive, unjust and wasteful', owing to 'the appallingly low quality of parts of the state system'. Even if these were improved, we shall still not have equality of opportunity as long as we maintain a system of superior private schools, open to the wealthier classes, but out of reach of poorer children however talented and deserving. This is much the most flagrant inequality of opportunity, as it is the cause of class inequality generally, in our educational system; and I have never been able to understand why socialists have been so obsessed with the question of the grammar schools, and so indifferent to the much more glaring injustice of the independent schools.[94]

John Vaisey in 1962 blamed the stagnation of the British economy on the shortage of skilled manpower at one end of the educational system and the monopoly of elite positions by the products of the public schools at the other. Since about a fifth of Labour MPs and a third or more of Labour Cabinet ministers had been to public schools, Vaisey, a grammar school boy from a working-class background, was one of the few prominent Labour men to propose drastic reform. He suggested that the 100–150 Headmasters' Conference schools be put under an Educational Trust charged with maintaining their existing religious or occupational character but accepting without fees only boys and girls at least 15 years old from a socially and intellectually representative pool nominated by all the other secondary schools in the country.[95] Even the Labour-appointed Commission on the Public Schools of 1968–70 could suggest nothing more than a socially mixed entry, and its recommendations were ignored by both the Conservative and Labour governments of the 1970s.[96] However, the Oxford Social Mobility Project found that 'differences between types of school turn out to be very largely a consequence of their differing social composition'. Boys of the same social background achieved much the same public examination results whether they were in public, private, state grammar or comprehensive schools.[97] The only result of Labour's campaign against privileged education was the cessation in 1974 of government funding of the direct grant schools, the old, prestigious, endowed day grammar schools, which were forced to choose between the public and private sectors and mostly chose the latter, thus (except for the remaining scholarships) cutting off one more ladder of opportunity for those who could not afford to pay.

The most obvious advantage of a public school education was easier access to the universities where the privately educated, about

4.5 per cent of the age group, constituted nearly a quarter of the students, and especially to Oxford and Cambridge where they formed nearly one half.[98] Since in a professional society the universities were the gatekeepers to the most prestigious and lucrative occupations, higher education became the focus of the dispute over equality of opportunity. Both professional ideals could agree that equal opportunity should be encouraged for the very able, and as a result of the Anderson Committee of 1956 on student support Britain became the first western country to provide grants covering both fees and (on a parental means test) maintenance for all undergraduates accepted by a university. The penalty for this generous policy at a later stage, however, was that Britain came to have one of the smallest proportions of students relative to the age group in Europe and, despite that, was the first country actually to cut back student numbers in the 1980s.[99]

Meanwhile, in the late 1950s and 1960s the need of a professional society for educated manpower expressed itself in a demand for a great expansion of higher education. Since the rise of professional society was a worldwide phenomenon generated by the application of scientific expertise not only to industry but to all the activities of society, the expansion of the universities, the powerhouses of research and ideas as well as the producers of professional experts, was equally international. Britain always had fewer students relative to population than most advanced industrial countries but had kept up as fast a rate of growth from 1956 to 1970, though it began to lag behind in the 1970s.[100] What came to be known as the Robbins era in Britain saw an explosive growth of higher education. The number of university institutions nearly doubled, from twenty-six in 1950 to forty-four in 1970, and full-time student numbers more than quintupled, from 85,000 to 460,000 (plus a further 24,000 part-time students).[101] The expansion began before the Robbins Committee on Higher Education reported in 1963, with an attempt to meet the 'bulge' and the 'trend', the post-war bulge in the birth rate which would hit the universities in the 1960s and the increasing trend to stay on at school and qualify for university entrance. The University Grants Committee had already in 1959 invited bids from local communities for the founding of seven new universities, which eventually grew to ten, plus the upgrading of a dozen university colleges and colleges of advanced technology.[102] The Robbins

Committee was an effect of the expansion rather than its cause.

It was also the first inquiry into the whole of higher education, including the growing local authority sector of technical, art and further education colleges and the mixed sector of teacher education colleges owned by local government and the churches. The report recommended a massive expansion of higher education, in universities from 130,000 students in 1962 to 219,000 in 1973 and to 346,000 in 1980, and in both sectors together from 216,000 in 1962 to 392,000 in 1973 and 558,000 in 1980.[103] In fact, the short-range predictions were surpassed, with 247,000 full-time university students and 482,000 advanced students in higher education by 1973 (though the longer-term, 1980 figures fell short at 273,000 and 482,000, plus 53,000 foreign students from outside the European Economic Community).[104] The Robbins Report based its recommendations on the principle of equality of opportunity, that everyone who was qualified and wished to enter higher education should be provided with a place. Equality of opportunity also applied to institutions: every college which could justify its academic claim to become a university should be granted that status, beginning with the immediate upgrading of the ten colleges of advanced technology, and every department in a non-university college could qualify for the grant of degrees through the new Council for National Academic Awards. In the run-up to the 1964 election both political parties accepted the report with acclamation, and all seemed set fair for a smooth, if elitist, escalator of opportunity.

At this point the Labour Party won the 1964 election, on the professional platform of 'a new deal for the scientist and technologist in higher education, a new status for scientists in government, and a new role for government-sponsored science in industrial development'.[105] A new egalitarian Secretary of State for Education, Anthony Crosland, was persuaded by his civil servants that the Robbins approach was too elitist and would lead to 'academic drift', the process by which local authority colleges escaped from state control into the 'private sector', as they called the independently chartered but largely state-funded universities. He therefore announced in 1965 the 'binary policy', a sort of educational apartheid of separate but equal development by which the public sector colleges would provide further and higher education right up to degree level for those students who did not qualify or wish to go to the university. Degrees under the CNAA could be granted all the way up the system and at the highest level would be taught in thirty polytechnics (upgraded technical colleges), intended to be local people's universities analogous to comprehensive schools.[106]

The outcome in fact was very different. Instead of concentrating on science and technology courses for local students, the polytechnics, unable to attract enough science students because of the overprovision of places in the new universities and ex-CATs, found themselves catering for large numbers of social science and humanities students unable to get into the universities, often living away from home like most university students. Although they took a large share of the expansion, especially when the universities had their numbers cut back in the 1980s, they became in effect second-class universities with little research activity and large teaching loads, unable to change their status, and catering not for the masses but for the less qualified half of the 13–15 per cent of the age group who entered higher education. Equality of outcome had foundered on the rock of a half-hearted equality of opportunity.

Meanwhile, the universities were drawn more firmly into the public sector. Because of their increasing dependence on government funding, which rose over tenfold from £20 million in 1952 to £235 million (plus £79 million in capital grants and £67 in student fees and maintenance) in 1970,[107] the state was bound to tighten its control. In 1964 responsibility for the University Grants Committee was transferred from the light yoke of the Treasury to the professionally expert Department of Education and Science, and in 1968 the universities were made subject to the parliamentary Comptroller and Auditor General.[108] These changes meant that the universities became more directly controlled by the government, which through the UGC came increasingly to determine capital investment, academic development, faculty and other staff salaries, and student numbers. It was perhaps inevitable that in a professional society the state should attempt to control the key profession which educated the other professions. The irony was that in Britain where the universities had always prided themselves on their autonomy, state control was to become by the 1980s under a 'free enterprise' government even heavier than elsewhere.

Universities had a special role in professional society, not only because they housed the key profession but because they increasingly provided the ammunition for the two versions of the professional ideal. Many of the spokesmen for the two ideals were professors who had the expertise and the research time to develop them. This was most obvious on the public sector side, where professors like Titmuss, Abel Smith, Townsend, Pedley and Vaisey developed the evidence and the arguments for equality of outcome in distribution of income, welfare policy and education. It was less obvious on the private sector side but nonetheless crucial, as the disciples of Professors Friedrich von Hayek and Milton Friedman began to colonize university economics departments and the new business schools. Alan Peacock of Buckingham University College, Sir Alan Walters of the LSE and Johns Hopkins University, Sir James Ball of the London Business School and Baroness Cox of East London Polytechnic were to become advisers to the new radical leadership of the Conservative Party. Ironically, the radical right affected to believe that the universities and polytechnics were full of left-wing egalitarians who despised free enterprise and economic growth, while at the same time recruiting authors and advisers from them in large numbers.

The two academic camps certainly disliked each other. Since social ideals are moral systems, each thought the other outside the moral pale. To the protagonists of the private sector the egalitarian academics were freeloaders on the productive system, moralizing critics who opposed enterprise and economic growth, 'bleeding-heart liberals' who bit the hand that fed them and, at the extreme, would-be dictators in the name of the proletariat. To the pro-public sector academics the supporters of the free market were callous and morally irresponsible, indifferent to the sufferings of the poor, defenders of wealth and privilege and, at the extreme, paid retainers and consultants who had prostituted themselves to powerful corporations. In the clash of two moral systems opponents are held to have no moral ground to stand on. In the last resort equality of outcome and equality of opportunity were incompatible principles. The antagonists, frozen in two separate ethical dimensions, talked past each other. In the 1970s and 1980s they were to come near to breaking off relations altogether.

4 THE PERSISTENCE OF CLASS

As with previous societies, aristocratic and entrepreneurial, a considerable distance lay between the ideal and reality of professional society. Other social groups, however much incorporated into the dominant structure, did not give up their ideals altogether, and the professional ideal itself failed to live up to its promise in either of its forms. Complete equality of outcome or condition, it goes without saying, was never within sight of being achieved, and equality of opportunity was systematically distorted by the privileged access to education and employment open to wealth and family influence. The principle that society's resources should be distributed according to desert, whether defined as intellectual or technical merit or as the right of citizenship, was the moral ideal meant to justify the structure of rewards but, as with the ideal of the leisured gentleman in pre-industrial England or the self-made man in Victorian society, it was only a rough approximation to reality. Although the vertical warp of professional career hierarchies increasingly overlay the horizontal weft of class, the social fabric still consisted of both elements, and class conflict thrust itself to the surface stubbornly and repeatedly. Indeed, by the late 1960s and 1970s, there was to all appearances a resurgence of class conflict.

The language of class certainly persisted. Social and political surveys never failed to elicit a response to the question, 'What class would you say you belong to?' even if some respondents were clearly pulling the investigator's leg. National Opinion Polls in 1972 reported that 91 per cent of their sample believed in the existence of social classes and that 95 per cent identified themselves with a particular class: 82 per cent of the top two 'objective' classes (by occupation) called themselves 'middle-class' (and 13 per cent 'working-class'), as did 73 per cent of the lower middle class (24 per cent calling themselves 'working-class'), while 53 per cent of the skilled workers and 59 per cent of the less skilled called themselves 'working-class' (though no less than 43 and 35 per cent described themselves as 'middle-class').[109] There was enough correspondence and disjunction here to confirm Margaret Stacey's finding in her second survey of Banbury: 'tap the social images which Banbury people had in their minds, [and] weak and confused conceptions of social class emerged.'[110] Her respondents, however, were in no doubt who was too high up the social ladder to speak to them and who was too low to be spoken to; for the colonel's wife, for example, only three other families in her village existed.

For English snobbery, the essence of class in the popular sense, was very much a matter of speech. It was still true, as Professor Higgins had put it in Shaw's *Pygmalion*, that 'it is impossible for an Englishman to open his mouth without making some other Englishman despise him'. The sociolinguists and educational psychologists of the post-war period confirmed this: A. S. C. Ross in 1955 with his 'U' and 'non-U' English usage (popularized by Nancy Mitford, a genuine U-speaker, who called a mirror a looking glass, a dessert a pudding and a lavatory a loo, simply because the rest of her tiny tribe despised those who did not), and Basil Bernstein in 1970 with his 'restricted' working-class and 'elaborated' middle-class codes.[111] Even the humorists fell into their own trap, like the upper middle-class Jilly Cooper, who was equally uncomfortable with the upper-crust 'Harry Stow-Crats' and the working-class 'Mr and Mrs Definitely Disgusting', not to mention the upstart 'Nouveau-Richards'.[112] Like most observers, Anthony Crosland in 1956 attributed such differences of speech, prestige and style of life to the divisive education system, the segregation of children into public schools, grammar schools and secondary modern schools marking them indelibly for life. For whatever reason, the English certainly had the reputation for being the most class-conscious nation in the world.[113] Whether they were in fact more snobbish than the French with their *grands bourgeois* and *grandes écoles*, the Americans with their Social Registers and alumni loyalty to prestigious universities, or even the socialist Scandinavians with their snobbish use of occupational titles, the English obsession with class and 'received standard English pronunciation' versus regional accents made them seem so.

In strict usage these were not differences of class, of economic relation to the means of production, but of status, of ranking in the hierarchy of prestige. The two were naturally connected, but class was a much more serious matter. Hierarchy was bound to persist in a professional society, especially in the opportunity version, and even in its egalitarian form prestige and differences of lifestyle as well as income (perhaps in a narrower range) would remain, if only to determine who was to manage the redistribution of resources. In practice, while professionalism in the first sense of the career hierarchy applied only to a growing minority – a much larger minority than landlords in aristocratic or entrepreneurs in industrial society – and even in the second sense of extending professional ambitions and conditions of work to the rest was still restricted, class differences in the traditional form of landlords, owner-managing capitalists, and manual wage earners with few or no professional 'perks' were still powerful.

The major lines of cleavage remaining amongst the employed members of society were between those with reasonable job security and long periods of notice and those without, and between those on rising salary and promotion scales and those on more or less fixed or fluctuating wages. In a more fully professionalized society like Japan where, in the large corporations at least, the manual workers too had lifelong employment and rising scales of pay, these lines were disappearing, but in Britain they were still firmly in place.[114] While managers, engineers, technologists, university academics, school teachers and other professional groups were on one to six months' notice and on salary scales which peaked in the 50-60 age group, manual workers, sales assistants and routine office workers were on one to four weeks' notice and earnings which peaked in their thirties and thereafter slowly declined.[115] (For male as distinct from female technicians, office workers and sales people this pattern was more often broken by promotion to the managerial ladder.) These patterns of job security and remuneration continued to influence differences in outlook between the classes, their different reactions to inflation, depression, labour-saving innovation, the threat of redundancy, incomes policy, and so on.

They also led to measurable differences in the demographic experiences and material circumstances of the groups above and below the manual/non-manual line. Professional people still married later, had fewer babies, lost fewer by stillbirths and infant mortality, had taller offspring with better health (less eye defect and tooth decay), used the health services more, had less illness and lived longer, suffered less unemployment, more usually bought their own houses, and had more years of schooling. Much of this was related to income differences, as one would expect, though these were becoming narrower: by 1973 median weekly income for households with professional and technical heads was £64.60, for clerical workers' households £50, and for manual workers' £48.50; moreover, because the last more often had more than one income, the top third of manual households had higher incomes than the bottom third of professional households.[116] Indeed, the whole question of distribution of income was becoming skewed not only by working wives who lifted their 'tax unit' (married couple) into a higher bracket but also by what was coming to be called the 'feminization of poverty', as larger numbers of unmarried, separated, divorced, and widowed women came to head one-parent families with much lower incomes than the average households. In 1971 there were 620,000 such families with over 1 million children, five-sixths of them headed by women, many of them from the more divorced middle class.[117] These aside, it is obvious that the security and rising incomes of the career professionals gave material advantages apart from size of income over the wage earner, in terms of buying a house and other durable consumer goods, educating children beyond the compulsory age, and generally planning expenditure further ahead. Higher income alone could not compensate the manual worker for lack of these advantages.

Income and wealth were still the main source of inequality, nevertheless. Richard Crossman, a Labour minister who was enough of a 'social crank' to vote for a socialist policy which might take more of the profits of his farm, expressed the non-material advantages of the rich very neatly in his 1967 diary: 'Anne and I have a facility of freedom and an amplitude of life here which cuts us off from the vast mass of people.'[118] There were still plenty of wealthy families much richer and more cut off than the Crossmans. Between 1945 and 1970 twenty-eight people died leaving more than £3 million each. They included eight landowning peers (two Dukes of Westminster, the Duke of Bedford, the Earls of Derby, Radnor and Sefton, Viscount Portman, and Dowager Countess Peel, whose wealth also came from linoleum), twelve industrialists (eight in engineering, two in tobacco and two in the drink trade), four property developers, and three from banking families.[119] These amply confirmed that the old wealth from landowning and manufacturing was still alive and well, though the property developers and motor manufacturers pointed to new ways of making large fortunes.[120] What the probate returns did not show were the very newest ways: the purest forms of human capital were in the arts, entertainment and sporting fields, where superstars like the Beatles, Richard Branson (pop records and air travel) or Steve Davis (the snooker player) could make fortunes which put ordinary millionaires in the shade. By 1984, for example, Paul McCartney would be a quarter-billionaire. He was outshone, however, by the Queen and the Duke of Westminster, the Vesteys, the Sainsburys, Sir James Goldsmith and Garfield Weston (all the last four in food distribution), the Cayzer family (Lord Rotherwick) in shipping, and Gerald Ronson in property.[121]

Superstars apart, even the great landowners and millionaires as a group were becoming poorer: in real terms (at 1913 prices) the great landowners' median estate at death, £275,000 between the wars, declined to £103,000 in 1940–59 and to a mere £22,000 in the 1960s, while the millionaires' median estate (defined of course in shrinking pounds) scarcely rose at all in current terms, and in real terms declined from about £856,000 to £517,000 and to £306,000.[122] No doubt some of the landed decline was due to avoidance of death duties, notably by creating companies to run the estate and spreading the shares around the family. Some, like the Duke of Bedford and the Marquess of Bath, made a remarkable recovery by turning their homes and grounds into living museums, pleasure gardens and safari parks. Others, like the Earl of Derby and Lord Harlech, chairmen of television companies, went into fashionable, up-to-the-minute business. Still others, like Lord Lichfield the photographer or Humphrey Lyttleton the trumpet player, made their own way into the glamorous worlds of fashion and pop music. Furthermore, the property boom of the late 1960s and 1970s and the spectacular rise in agricultural land prices, too late to affect the probate returns yet, have restored the fortunes of many landed families, and turned even gentlemen farmers with 1,800 acres into millionaires.

One cannot escape the impression, nonetheless, that the movers and shakers of the corporate economy were not the inherited wealth holders but the corporate managers, men like Sir Paul Chambers, an LSE graduate and ex-tax inspector who rose to be chairman of ICI (1962–68), his successor Alexander (Lord) Fleck, who started as a lab boy at 14, or a more recent chairman, Sir John Harvey-Jones, who left the navy at 33 and worked his way up from trainee work study officer to the top job; Arnold Weinstock, the career manager who rebuilt GEC; Donald (Lord) Stokes, the apprentice mechanic at Leyland Motors who merged most of the British-owned vehicle industry into British Leyland; Frank (Lord) Kearton, the Oxford scholarship boy who headed Courtaulds and British National Oil, or Kenneth Usherwood, the Cambridge scholarship boy who rose to command Prudential Assurance and a vast investment in British industry.[123] Such men leave substantial but still modest fortunes, but their power while in office outshines that of most dukes and millionaires. Along with the pop stars and sporting heroes, they demonstrate the extraordinary material potential of human capital.

While the rich deprecated the continued existence of class – Macmillan told the Queen in 1959 that 'the most encouraging feature of the Election ... is the strong impression I have formed that Your Majesty's subjects do not wish to allow themselves to be divided into warring classes or tribes filled with hereditary animosity against each other'[124] – the middle classes continued to acknowledge it, either by sending their sons to public schools and buying as much privilege as possible or by deprecating it as loudly as they could, and sometimes both. The great feature of the period was the decline of the small owner-managing business man and the rise of the salariat. While male 'employers and proprietors' declined from 888,000 in 1951 to 812,000 in 1971, higher and lower professionals and administrators and managers had increased by 70 per cent from 1,964,000 to 3,355,000 and now constituted more than one in five of the male occupied population. Professional women had increased by 69 per cent from 804,000 to 1,358,000, though more in the lower professions like teaching and nursing than the higher ones.[125] There were many kinds of salaried professional. Beyond the distinction between those employed by the public and the private sectors there were significant differences between the individual professions, each with its own claim to status and importance. After company chairmen, directors and top managers of corporations with median salaries of £66.50 and £69.60 per week in 1971, medical doctors and lawyers, whether independent or employed, claimed the highest status and incomes, and top civil servants and academics were not far behind, with median salaries of £58 a week or more. Architects and planners, accountants, engineers, scientists and technologists, college lecturers, and a range of middle managers were significantly below them, with weekly salaries from £41 to £53. School teachers, technicians and draughtsmen, welfare workers, office supervisors, works foremen, senior clerks and sales representatives were all clearly a grade below, with weekly salaries in the £30s. All were clearly above the manual and routine office workers, with weekly earnings in the £20s.[126] These income differentials were reflected in the size of house, the sort of neighbourhood, the make of car, the kinds of holiday, the type of children's schooling and so on which each occupational group could afford, and they still segregated themselves by town, suburb and village to emphasize their differences, even though those differences were less spectacular than before.

The chief difference distinguishing the salariat from the working class was the psychological one that flowed from greater job security and rising scales of pay. They found it easier to plan for the future, to obtain mortgages and loans for buying cars and consumer goods, to invest in their own and their children's education, to commit savings to holidays and leisure pursuits. In these ways they had the edge on the traditional small business man, who had no job security, automatically rising income, built-in occupational pension, or state unemployment or sick pay, and often lived in fear of depression or bankruptcy. They were also separated from one another. While the civil servants, academics, school teachers, welfare workers, NHS doctors and nurses, and other public employees had little or no access to fringe benefits, such as company cars, help with school fees, low-interest housing loans and the like, these were becoming commoner in the private sector as a way of overcoming high income taxes, particularly during periods of government pay restraint. On the other side, public sector professions often had greater job security, longer holidays and, from the 1970s, inflation-proof pensions, so that each side could envy the other. Such mutual resentments were aggravated by the sense of the public employees that they were better educated, or at least better qualified, than most company managers, 58 per cent of whom according to a 1971 study came from below the middle class, and only 40 per cent of whom were graduates.[127] Both could rejoice in their belief in equality of opportunity, but by different routes, via education and by climbing the corporate ladder. The growing gap in their ideological outlook owed something to this difference in provenance – though at the very top the two tended to converge in educational and social background.

The overwhelming sense, however, was of a middle level of society increasingly fragmented into discrete career hierarchies, each to some extent in competition with the rest for resources. The major split might be between those who saw each other as controlling two rival cornucopias, one drawing its flow of resources from the bounty of the taxpayer, the other from the spending of the consumer, but each profession was to some extent in competition for resources with every other. Government expenditure was not boundless, and what one public sector profession took another could not have. Defence, health, education, social welfare, roads and the environment, even the nationalized industries seeking investment, all dipped into the same pool, which against taxpayer resistance could not be endlessly enlarged. At the same time, private sector managers and specialists were engaged in not one but several competitions for resources, between themselves and between their corporations and divisions, and also with the state over taxation, investment grants and credits, and even subsidies. Although the struggle for income between the classes, particularly with the manual wage earners, was still sharp, for the middle-class salariat the struggle was increasingly between the different specialisms. That is why the 'rebellious salariat', as Clive Jenkins and Barrie Sherman called them, came to organize more effectively to pursue that struggle through the state and the private corporations. The public professions in particular became caught up in the corporate game of persuading the state to allocate more expenditure to defence or school education or the universities or the Health Service or the social services or such traditional and basic services as the police and firemen. Increasingly, they found themselves threatening 'non-co-operation' (a polite term for strikes or go-slows) in, for example, the schools, the universities or the hospitals if they did not get the salary scales and conditions of work they wanted.

What, indeed, was the difference between this kind of activity at the professional level and the demand from the dockers, the railwaymen, the gas workers, the steel workers or the coal miners for increased public resources for investment and, ultimately subsidized wages in the nationalized industries? And how, for that matter, did that in turn differ from the demands of the managers of private industries such as Upper Clyde shipbuilders, the Harland & Wolff shipyards, the car makers British Leyland and Chrysler, Rolls Royce aero-engines, or the machine tool makers Alfred Herbert for subsidies or rescue from imminent bankruptcy? Admittedly, some of these corporate crises finally came to a head only in the economically troubled 1970s, but the logic of a corporate economy, in which the great private corporations were as vital to the prosperity and stability of society as the nationalized industries, was already leading in that direction. By then government, the corporations, both public and private, and the trade unions and professional associations were so inextricably enmeshed in the machinery of the corporate state that no party to the competition for resources could afford to ignore it.

At first sight the working class seem to have been excluded from professional society. Leaving aside the 'professionalization of the working class' in the shape of professional conditions of work and remuneration, such as single status, sick pay, paid holidays and company pensions, discussed in Chapter 7, and the welfare state itself as compensation for those left out, most labour history has concentrated on their class consciousness and potential either for revolution or at least for radical reform of the capitalist system, and on the reasons for their failure to achieve one or the other. In recent years a more sophisticated approach has taken over, which emphasizes the distance between the workplace where, especially in Britain, a continual struggle for control of the production process was taking place, and the official or institutional labour movement, where trade union officials and Labour politicians repeatedly lost touch with their members and became 'incorporated' in the capitalist system.[128] For the more left-wing historians this represented a 'betrayal' of the working class and the proletarian revolution. For the less committed it was an almost inevitable compromise with the short-term realities of working-class life, in which the need to get the best possible pay and conditions *now* had to take precedence over the ultimate goal of a socialist society and the abolition of capitalism. Either way, the result was a *pis aller*, a failure of the working class to achieve its historic goal, due primarily to its lack of unity around a single class consciousness and to the shortcomings of the political and industrial leaderships.

If, however, we do not start from this eschatological scenario but simply ask what ordinary workers, including the militant and discontented, wanted from their admittedly underprivileged situation, we get a rather different picture. The evidence suggests that most industrial disputes began at the grass roots, over some particular grievance in the workplace amongst a section of the workforce, and only then escalated, if at all, to the level of the plant, the firm and, very occasionally, the whole industry. This was especially true in Britain after the Second World War when, in conditions of full employment and with the welfare state buttressed by the tacit corporatism of the unions, the employers and the government, most disputes were spontaneous outbreaks, increasingly labelled 'wildcat' strikes, deplored by the official union leaders as much as by the employers and the politicians.

Intense localism was reinforced by the trend towards plant and shop floor bargaining. By 1951 it was reported that 'the centre of gravity in the engineering unions has moved more and more to the shop stewards', and the same could be said for the docks, the mines, and a growing list of other industries.[129] Wiser employers met the demand for local bargaining part way, and a system of 'local corporatism' developed that quickly settled most disputes, which were usually over modest demands for improved pay and working conditions. Even the strike wave of 1957–62, initially provoked by the income restraint imposed by the government in 1956, and composed of small-scale workplace actions, revealed how 'the aims and expectations of working people were stable and restrained'.[130] Surveys showed that most workers were concerned with immediate issues affecting the job, and not with management policy, pricing, profits, or the ownership of capitalist property. Conflict was no less sharp for that, and intense heat could be generated over 'custom and practice' governing the work process, the settling of piece rates, benchmarks for 'measured day work', overtime bonuses and, above all, differential rates of pay and demarcation (who does what?) disputes between different occupational groups. By the mid-1960s nearly half of all strikes were over 'working arrangements, rules and discipline' or managerial control issues.[131] Turner, Clack and Roberts in 1967 found there were two central motivations for industrial disputes in a period of full employment: the demand that wages should be 'fair' in comparison with other workers, and the claim that workers had property rights in a particular job, both as against other workers and, under threat of redundancy, against the employer.[132]

The remarkable thing about these objectives is how closely they paralleled those of the salaried professions. Demarcation disputes between occupations and issues of differential pay between more and less skilled workers mirrored professional demands for the monopoly of a particular service and for payment commensurate with its superior value. The manual worker's opposition to redundancy without adequate notice and compensation for the worker's property in the job was the precise equivalent of the professional's demand for protection of his human capital. Control over the work process was what every self-respecting professional demanded as of right. The local corporatism by which 'workers are participating more deeply in a wider range of managerial decisions' and 'the growing, if not yet clearly articulated, demand for greater personal participation'[133] were the basic conditions which every profession expected. If such 'restrictive practices' were recognized as inevitable by the Donovan Commission on Industrial Relations in 1968, or condemned by employers and politicians for resisting innovation, holding down productivity and defeating economic growth, how did they differ from the restrictive practices of certain professions examined by the Monopolies Commission in 1970?[134]

Sir Otto Kahn-Freund, an Anglophile immigrant, in his 'thank-offering to Britain lecture' in 1979 saw 'restrictive labour practices as part of a general pattern of attitudes especially characteristic of British society':

> Anyone coming to this country from the Continent – perhaps also coming from America – is puzzled beyond words by the careful and rigid division of professional and commercial activities in Britain. This, he feels, must be a nation riddled with demarcation lines, and with professional taboos and rituals.

The demarcation enforced in the name of the public interest by the barrister and the solicitor, the architect and the builder, the optician and the ophthalmic surgeon, were species of the same genus as those enforced by trade unionists on the shop floor, the building site, or in the shipyard:

All these specializations may be damaging and beneficial at the same time, they are all part of a national heritage, they may all be a danger to efficiency and conducive to waste of resources. What should not be overlooked is that this – to some extent – pre-capitalist basis of contemporary British society engenders what is in the strict sense an ideology: it is the ideology of conservatism – in the non-party political sense – an attitude which is shared by many adherents of all political parties, right and left.... It is an ideology nurtured by a rational desire for self-preservation and by irrational vicarious corporate selfishness....[135]

The British working class, in other words, was imbued, for good or ill, with precisely the same outlook on the terms and conditions of work as the professional middle class. Even the most class-conscious of industrial disputes had a 'professional' dimension to them. Most strikes for increased pay, like the renewed strike wave of 1968–72 after the pay pause of 1967, were 'catch-up' disputes demanding parity with similar workers or the restoration of traditional differentials over the supposedly less skilled. The troubles over decasualization of dock labour settled by the Devlin Inquiry were exacerbated by disputes over the handling of cargo by different gangs. The Jones-Aldington Report of 1972 on containerization showed the dockers' union and the dock employers, old sparring partners, surprisingly coming together to safeguard their industry against interlopers, even where the container packers belonged to the same union (the Transport and General Workers).[136] Even that most militant of unions, the National Union of Mineworkers, which claimed, debatably, to have brought down the Heath government in 1974 with its flying pickets and the state-imposed three-day working week, was concerned not to wring a larger share of surplus value from a capitalist employer (since this was a nationalized industry making no profit) but, like any public sector profession, to obtain a larger slice of public expenditure out of the taxpayer.[137] The miners' complaint that the TUC and the other unions failed to rally the working class behind them was due to an ironic recognition by the rest that the miners' was a sectional cause which, if successful, would have imposed costs on all of them through higher taxes and prices.[138] Indeed, with the exception of the Ford strike of 1971, significantly concerned with national parity between car workers, most of the major strikes of the early 1970s were in nationalized industries – electricity in 1971, mines and docks in 1972, mines, railways and electricity in 1973 – and had the same objective of gaining a larger share of public funds from a government determined to cut public expenditure.[139]

Given the fragmentation of the industrial labour movement, historically more divided in Britain between craft, industrial and general unions than elsewhere, it is not surprising that sectionalism (what Lenin called 'trade union consciousness') was more powerful than working-class solidarity ('revolutionary class consciousness'). That helps to explain the paradox that, while the labour movement was so powerful in the workplace that it appeared to have a veto over innovation and change, at the national level it was often so weak and ineffective. Opinion polls increasingly showed that trade unions were unpopular with many unionists themselves or, rather, that while many unionists supported their own particular union they were deeply suspicious of other people's unions – a very 'professional' attitude indeed.[140] It also helps to explain why a third or more of the working class increasingly voted for parties other than Labour. Some political observers began to talk of 'class dealignment' and the decline of class voting as class support for both major parties began to shrink between 1964 and 1974.[141] During the 1970s the share of the working-class vote going to the Labour Party, still 69 per cent in 1964, shrank from 58 to 50 per cent, and by 1983 it was down to 38 per cent.[142] To explain this, as some labour historians do, by the failure of the Labour Party to be more class-conscious or revolutionary seems a strange twist of logic: a vote for the Tories or the Liberals was hardly the way to hasten the socialist dawn.

There was, nonetheless, some truth in the critics' allegation that many trade union leaders and Labour politicians had become incorporated into the corporate system. That indeed had become their function. In the 1960s corporatism had become institutionalized with Macmillan's establishment of the tripartite National Economic Development Council in 1961, the Wilson government's ill-fated National Plan in 1965, and the Industrial Reorganization Corporation in 1966 to encourage large-scale mergers in private industry, such as British Leyland and GEC. In all these developments trade union leaders and, when in office, Labour politicians were intimately involved with the employers' representatives and the civil servants. The system was to reach its zenith in the 'social contract' between the Labour Party and the TUC in 1973, whereby the next Labour government exchanged welfare measures, such as price controls, food subsidies and frozen council rents, for support and co-operation in wage restraint. Such corporatist bargains were bound to be seen by the militant rank and file as an unwarranted restraint on free collective bargaining, but that was not the same as a defeat for the working class. Free collective bargaining itself was not a socialist but a capitalist, free labour market principle, a relic of the late Victorian economy, endorsed by the trade union legislation of the 1870s. It is not self-evident that those demanding it in the 1970s were more progressive or revolutionary than the corporatists who were trying to improve by centralized bargaining the real wages and political clout of the working class. By different sorts of bargaining the corporatists and their critics were both playing the professional game of 'talking up' the share of society's resources going to their own occupational group. The dispute was paradoxically the ultimate proof that the working class had joined the professional society.

This was not how it appeared, however, to those involved in the increasing industrial unrest of 1968–74. To many on both sides of industry and politics, faced with the growing evidence of the failure of the British economy to compete in the modern world and blaming that failure on Britain's 'low trust' industrial relations and the mutual frustration of management and labour, it seemed that the country was plagued far more than others by a resurgence of sheer bloody-minded class conflict. Each side blamed the other for the failure of corporate planning to solve the problem of sustained economic growth. Every attempt to 'dash for growth' by stimulating investment evoked a short-lived consumer boom which sucked in imports and provoked a balance of payments crisis, followed by severe deflation, government-enforced pay restraint and, as soon as it was relaxed, a further explosive round of pay increases. Many employers and right-wing politicians began to complain that full employment gave the unions too much power and that the only way to break the cycle of boom and bust, inflation and deflation, was a return to the classic discipline of the free labour market – in other words, 'a dose of unemployment'. Many on the Labour side came to believe that corporatist planning was simply a device for holding down wages when the market favoured labour, and vied with their most extreme opponents in demanding a return to collective bargaining in the free labour market.

Economic recession and balance of payments crises brought out the old class warriors on both sides. The radical right, who had been crying in the wilderness throughout the Keynesian consensus, began to revive and publicize the ideas of Friedrich von Hayek and Milton Friedman of the Chicago School of free market economics, and through Enoch Powell and his disciples to infiltrate the grass roots of the Conservative Party. The radical left, long marginalized in the Labour movement by the power of right-wing union barons like Ernest Bevin and Arthur Deakin, recovered its strength through a generation change to barons of the left like Frank Cousins, Jack Jones and Hugh Scanlon and, with their help in the Labour Party, through Anthony Wedgwood Benn and the leftward drift in the constituency Labour parties. An exasperated Harold Wilson blamed the seamen's strike which 'blew the Government off-course' in 1966 on 'a small body of politically motivated men' intent on furthering Marxist revolution. He was almost certainly wrong – there were such men but they spectacularly failed to stir up trouble except when the ordinary workers felt a strong particular grievance – but it all added to the increasing belief in the resurgence of class conflict. Both the Wilson government of 1964–70 and the Tory Opposition led by Edward Heath exacerbated this belief. The failure of the National Plan and the balance of payments crisis and devaluation of 1967 convinced the Labour government that exhortation was not enough to break the cycle of boom and bust and it determined to use more coercive methods, on two fronts. Firstly, it introduced what the radical right was already advocating, a system of monetary controls which would in theory limit the money supply that fuelled both pay increases and price inflation. Secondly, it set out to reform the system of industrial relations. Disappointed at the Donovan Commission's voluntarist remedies for wildcat disputes, a group of ministers led by Wilson, Barbara Castle, Crossman and Crosland determined on penal sanctions against premature and ill-considered strikes. The White Paper *In Place of Strife* (1969) proposed government-enforced settlement of demarcation disputes, a compulsory twenty-eight-day cooling-off period and a government-supervised ballot of union members before an official strike. The proposals split the government and the parliamentary party, were opposed by the National Executive Committee and the TUC, and had to be abandoned in favour of an informal corporatist 'solemn and binding undertaking' that the member unions would observe the TUC's guidelines on unofficial strikes. Though the attempt at regulation failed, it not only strained relations between the government and the unions and between the leadership of the movement and the rank and file but encouraged the view that there was a vast upwelling of working-class discontent which had to be contained.

The same view was held by the Tories, who welcomed *In Place of Strife* and began to develop coercive proposals of their own. In preparation for the 1970 election the Shadow Cabinet met at the Selsdon Park Hotel in Croydon to draft a right-wing programme – promptly labelled 'Selsdon Man' dug up from the Victorian past – to 'roll back the frontiers of government', exchange Keynesian economic policies for monetarist controls, reduce direct taxes, increase the police force, and introduce a coercive Industrial Relations Bill. The Bill would enforce collective agreements, make trade union rights including protection of union funds dependent on obeying a code of good behaviour, regulate the closed shop, limit peaceful picketing to providing information only and ban intimidation and secondary picketing (of premises other than the primary employer's) altogether, and allow the government to proscribe strikes it deemed injurious to the national economy. Enacted in the Industrial Relations Act of 1971, this was to lead to the greatest head-on collision between government and unions since 1926, to confrontation with the whole labour movement, the imprisonment of striking dockers (released on the intervention of the Official Solicitor), four national emergencies leading up to the 1973 miners' dispute and the Heath government's fall, and to the belief that, because of the supposed veto of the unions over any government economic policy which they vehemently opposed, Britain was becoming 'ungovernable'.[143]

Both *In Place of Strife* and 'Selsdon Man' were symptoms of the crumbling of the Keynesian-Beveridgean consensus on full employment and the welfare state and harbingers of a backlash against professional society in general. The backlash was precipitated by the increasingly obvious failure of Britain to sustain rates of economic growth commensurable with its rivals in Europe, North America and the Pacific fringe, and by the fear of impending economic decline, which became acute with the onset of the world oil crisis in 1973. It took several forms. There was rising criticism of the individual professions and their pretensions and privileges, including some of the most ancient and venerable like the medicine and the law. There was increasing resistance to the expansion of the welfare state and its mounting cost in public expenditure and taxation. And there was a parallel reaction against corporatism and the apparent sharing of power with the lobbies and pressure groups of management, unions, the professions, and the growing profusion of 'single-issue' special interest groups, such as the poverty lobby and the environmentalists. Finally, there was a repudiation of consensus itself as an ideal and its replacement by the politics of confrontation, between revived versions of the traditional war parties of socialism and the free market. As we shall see in the final chapter, however, the backlash was not quite what it seemed but, paradoxically, a confrontation between the two rival factions of the professional ideal.

Chapter 10

THE BACKLASH AGAINST PROFESSIONAL SOCIETY

Professional society thrived for over a quarter of a century after the Second World War, that is, for as long as full employment and a booming economy allowed it to meet all reasonable demands upon it for rising living standards and welfare services. For twenty-eight years it achieved a positive sum game, with almost everyone, including most of the poor in absolute if not relative terms, gaining, and very few losing. Such economic decline as there was was relative, and could only be perceived in comparison with the more rapidly growing economies of Western Europe, Canada and Japan. Governments worried over the failure of Britain's economy to grow more rapidly had tried various measures, including Keynesian demand management and, from the early 1960s, some indicative planning of the French type to try to break through to higher rates of expansion. But as long as 'most of our people had never had it so good' there was no desire for fundamental change in the policies which were producing un-precedented material progress. Only with the return of hard times and world recession in the 1970s and 1980s did politicians and commentators of all shades of political opinion begin to question the basic tenets of the system. As so often before, in the 1830s–40s, the 1870s–80s, and the 1920s–30s, adverse economic trends brought a new questioning and rethinking of attitudes and policies, and old doubts and critiques which had long been suppressed or ignored came flooding back to the surface.

The reaction was not confined to economic policy, although that formed the cutting edge. Underlying it was a much more general backlash against professional society in all its aspects. At the first and most obvious level there was a reaction against the

472

power, privileges and pretensions of the special interest groups of all kinds, but especially against the organized professions. The state-supported professions, including the Civil Service, the university academics, school teachers and social workers, came in for particular attack, since they came to be seen as unproductive occupations parasitic upon the wealth-creating private sector. Disillusion with the 'caring professions' led to the attack on the welfare state and the attempts to reform it, with mixed success. At the second, related level, the reaction was against the seemingly unstoppable growth of 'big government', with the attempt to 'roll back the state' by cutting public expenditure and privatizing nationalized industries. At the third and final level the target was corporatism, the involvement of the special interest groups, above all employers and trade unions, in the framing of government policy. The 'unsleeping veto groups' were blamed for the unseemly scramble for national resources in the shape of government grants, subsidies and pay claims which stoked inflation and undermined economic growth. At all three levels the backlash turned out to be not a return to an earlier form of society but a reaction of professional society upon itself, or of one set of professionals against the rest.

This triple backlash against professionalism and the corporate state it inspired, the subjects of Sections 1 and 2 of this chapter, presented a marvellous opportunity for a movement of social and economic protest which for a generation or more existed only in the muffled form of rumbling discontent but now reappeared as the resurgence of the old, nineteenth-century ideology of the free market. It had the advantage of appearing to offer a positive, coherent alternative to the corporate, high-spending welfare state and to the Keynesian management of the economy which it claimed had failed. In fact, as we shall see in Section 3, the resurgence was not quite what it seemed. It was not a reaction *against* professional society but a rounding of the private sector professionals who ran the great corporations and their academic and journalistic supporters upon the public sector professionals. The former saw the latter as a burden upon the private sector in two senses, as consumers of the wealth which it produced and as controllers and regulators of its managers' freedom of action. Allied to the undoubted failure of the old policies to solve the new economic problems of the 1970s, they were able to undermine confidence in the Keynesian-Beveridgean consensus amongst leading politicians in both major political parties and, more significantly, to win a dedicated following in the group of right-wing Conservatives who 'hi-jacked the party' in 1975. They claimed to have a complete answer to Britain's economic decline, in monetarist control of inflation, the reining in of the runaway welfare state, the privatization of nationalized industries, and the stimulation of private enterprise by the reduction of taxation and government regulation. These remedies they proceeded to apply when they won office, on a minority of the popular vote, in 1979.

As we shall see in Section 4, Britain's economic decline is a much more deep-seated problem than the naive analyses of the two extremes, the free marketeers and the advocates of comprehensive nationalization, suggest. It is rooted in professional society itself, at least in the transitional form it has taken in Britain. The clash between the public sector professionals, with their ideal of a benevolent state caring for every citizen, and the private sector professionals, with their ideal of freedom for the enterprising, wealth-creating managers of the great corporations, is a distorted echo of the old clash between the individual capitalist and proletarian workers of Victorian society. As such it encourages the perpetuation of obsolete class attitudes by unreconstructed class warriors who are more concerned with winning old battles than with solving the problems of contemporary society. Worse still, the prospect of a victory for either extreme presents Britain with a dilemma. A triumphant public sector solution would bring with it the risk of an authoritarian state, eager to control every aspect of the individual's life. A victorious private sector solution would import the more insidious threat of a corporate neo-feudalism, in which the multinational barons of conglomerate capitalism would control the destinies of everyone else. The dilemma is more acute in Britain than elsewhere because of the rigid political structure and the decline of democracy, which enable extremist minorities to capture the vehicles of power and impose their nostrums upon the majority. Unless we can expose this false dilemma and achieve a sensible balance of co-operation between the state and society we shall continue to swing between the two poles of the dedicated and dangerously naive 'true believers' of right and left.

1 PROFESSIONALISM UNDER FIRE

The condescension of professionalism, the suspicion of individual professions as conspiracies against the laity, and the rivalry and mutual disdain which many professions felt for one another, all suggest that a reaction against the pretensions of professionalism was sooner or later inevitable. There had always been an under-current of scepticism about the professions from Bernard Shaw's (or even Molière's) time onwards, and this was compounded in the 1970s by the writings of iconoclasts like Ivan Illich, with titles like *Deschooling Society* (1974), *Medical Nemesis* (1975) and *Disabling Professions* (1977).[1] But it is patently difficult to distinguish the buzzings of perennial gadflies, easily brushed aside, from a sustained backlash by an effective body of hostile opinion. The most obvious source of such a backlash was the revival of the free market ideology to be dealt with in Section 3. Professional organiz-ation was in its nature, as Magali Larson has shown, the antithesis of the free market and meant to exclude unqualified competitors from the service monopolized by the qualified.[2] The free market-eers displayed particular animus against certain professional monopolies, such as the solicitors' exclusive right of conveyancing property or the opticians' grip on the sale of eye glasses.[3] Yet in many ways they were already riding a tide of popular displeasure at the pretensions and privileges of individual professions. It was in the nature of professional society to set up rivalries between different occupations competing for power and resources, and it was easy for criticism of particular professions to spill over into criticism of professionalism in general.

Surprisingly, some of the earliest and most effective criticism came from the left rather than the right. Richard Titmuss, the somewhat reluctant champion of the welfare state, attacked 'the Pressure Group State' as early as 1960 for the self-interest of the professional groups battening upon what he called 'the irrespon-sible society'. What aroused his ire even more than the professional managers who awarded themselves handsome 'perks' over and above their already large salaries were the welfare professionals who seemed to put their own convenience and rewards before their patients and clients.[4] Out of frustration at the inadequacies of the welfare state, this criticism of the purveyors of state services became a common theme with the poverty lobby, down to and

475

including Paul Wilding's *Professional Power and Social Welfare* (1982).[5] It did not occur to them that their attacks, meant to divert more resources from the providers to the beneficiaries, would be taken literally and used to condemn state welfare altogether.

Meanwhile, there were increasing numbers of spontaneous attacks on what Margaret Thatcher was to call traditionally 'immune targets',[6] including the three ancient professions of law, medicine and the clergy. Lawyers were criticized not only for the solicitors' monopoly of easy but expensive procedures like conveyancing and divorce – the Law Society was hotly condemned for its alarmist advertisement in 1979 showing a child being 'split down the middle' by a 'do-it-yourself' divorce – but also for the unique British division between barristers and solicitors (not to mention the further division of the bar into 'silks' and 'juniors') which doubled the fees levied by the profession.[7] It was alleged that lawyers were so entrenched in Parliament, the Inns of Court and the Law Society that it was impossible to reform the law or for a wronged client to obtain redress. In one widely reported case of a former member of the Law Society council who allegedly helped a defendant company to defeat his own client and then charged the latter £198,000 for his services (later reduced to £67,000 by the courts), the Law Society found the complaint 'unsubstantiated', and a judge decided that his court had no jurisdiction over the Society.[8] The law itself came in for increasing criticism. In 1974 Sir Leslie (later Lord) Scarman in his Hamlyn lectures asserted that the Common Law was no longer a sufficient protector of the individual. It was incapable of protecting human rights in a manner consistent with Britain's international obligations. It was ill equipped to resolve conflicts within the vast and complex field of welfare rights. It was inadequate for the protection of the environment. And it had demonstrated its incapacity in the field of industrial relations. Scarman called for a modern Bill of Rights or, later, for the incorporation in British law of the European Convention on Human Rights. The latter was already binding on the British government but ignored by British courts unless and until appeals were made to the European Court in Strasbourg. In consequence of the conservatism of British justice Britain had provided more successful appeals to Strasbourg than any other member country, including those for such basic rights as trade union membership for civil servants and *habeas corpus* for mental patients.[9]

The legal profession obstinately refused to reform itself or the law. In 1968 the Home Secretary, Roy Jenkins, declaring that 'much of our criminal law is obscure, confused and uncertain', set up a Law Commission to consider its codification. After seventeen years' work it published a code, but with little hope of its adoption. Professor J. C. Smith, head of the drafting team, feared that 'no amount of abstract argument as to the virtues of codification is going to overcome the conservatism, inertia and actual hostility which will have to be faced if the code is to become a reality'.[10] Even the judiciary is no longer above criticism. When in 1984 the Centre for Criminological Research at Oxford University issued a report on the sentencing practices of judges, Hugo Young commented in the *Guardian*, 'the Lord Chief Justice, Lord Lane, backed by Lord Chancellor Hailsham, has issued one of the most philistine diktats ever handed down by a man in his position,' and had forbidden further research. 'Lord Lane', he continued, 'has enshrined ignorance as a judicial virtue, and intellectual privacy as the hallmark of the priesthood over which he presides.'[11] The almost universal ridicule of the law lords' decision to forbid newspaper publication of excerpts from Peter Wright's book *Spycatcher*, already published in Australia, the United States and Hong Kong, in July 1987 showed to what depths respect for the judicial process had shrunk. The majesty of the law no longer guaranteed acceptance of the infallibility of the judiciary.

The medical profession, too, was no longer immune. Although not so deeply under suspicion of overcharging, recommending unnecessary 'elective surgery', and frequent malpractice as the American profession (partly because of their different structure of rewards which did not charge patients directly or encourage 'make-work'), British doctors were no longer the god-like functionaries, beyond questioning much less criticism, they had once been. A spate of malpractice suits in which doctors would rarely give evidence against medical colleagues, a number of widely publicized drug cases involving GPs, and at least one notorious case of a forensic pathologist convicted of rigging the evidence against a long series of men accused of murder, contributed to a clouding of the profession's image in the public eye.[12] Like the lawyers, too, the doctors stubbornly resisted reform. In 1974 the Davies Committee drew up a code of practice for dealing with patients' complaints about hospitals, and in 1978 a House of Commons Select

Committee recommended that the Health Ombudsman should be empowered to investigate these. The British Medical Association responded that any doctor who acted as a medical assessor to the Ombudsman would 'forfeit the confidence of his professional colleagues'. The Ombudsman was precluded from investigating about a third of all the complaints reaching him each year because they touched on clinical judgment, and the complainants' only recourse was to the law courts where it was almost impossible to get a doctor to testify on their side.[13] The final blow to the prestige of the profession was their work to rule and threat of strikes in the 1970s against the National Health Service, aggravated by actual strikes by nurses and ancillary staff.[14] Although part of a general wave of unrest amongst the employed professions as accelerating inflation eroded salaries, it was felt to be particularly heinous for the leading life-and-death profession to appear to betray its Hippocratic oath.

The clergy's prestige, and especially that of the Church of England, had been progressively undermined by the decline of religious belief. The highly publicized 'agnostic' theology of Bishop John Robinson of Woolwich, Dean Don Cupitt of Cambridge University and Bishop David Jenkins of Durham, trumpeting the 'death of God', the irrelevance of the Trinity and the virgin birth, and their replacement by a non-anthropomorphic life force, contributed not so much to existing unbelief as to the questioning of the integrity of an endowed priesthood that did not believe in God.[15] In compensation for its weakening theology, the church came to emphasize its moral and social responsibilities. As a result it suffered a curious inversion in its political image. Once 'the Conservative Party at prayer', it now came to be associated with the defence of the welfare state, criticism of government policy on unemployment, the inner cities, and the miners' strike of 1984–85, and support for popular liberation movements in the Third World. While by no means socialist but rather benevolent liberal or Tory paternalist, it naturally aroused the ire of the free marketeers. Typical of their response was a collection of essays published in 1985 by the Social Affairs Unit of the Institute of Economic Affairs entitled *The Kindness that Kills: The Churches Simplistic Response to Complex Social Issues*. Mrs Thatcher's more forthright comment was that the church leaders were 'cuckoos'. A government spokesman even described a report on *Life in the City*

(1985) by the Archbishop of Canterbury's committee as 'Marxist'.[16] Such predictably intolerant reactions may bear witness to the humanity and independence of the church, but they do not increase respect for the clergy in the eyes of the public.

Other professions came under increasing attack for not living up to their self-acclaimed standards of behaviour. The Monopolies Commission, set up to investigate monopolistic behaviour amongst business corporations, extended its investigations to restrictive practices in a range of professions in the late 1960s, but its 1970 report had little effect.[17] The Director General of Fair Trading, Sir Gordon Borrie, could still in 1983 attack 'the unacceptable face of the professions', singling out solicitors, accountants, veterinary surgeons and opticians for restricting competition and charging clients more than was strictly justified for their services.[18] Professions often demanded self-regulation and then refused to implement their own codes against erring members. The Royal Institution of Chartered Surveyors, the senior association of estate agents, met stiff resistance from its own members in 1975 when it proposed to police its rule against conflict of interest by setting up a register of their holdings in property companies. The Financial Intermediaries, Managers and Brokers Regulatory Association, established in the early 1980s in response to investigations by the Securities and Exchange Commission into insider dealing in the City, admitted that, while 'it enables the honest firm to stay in business even though it made an honest mistake', it could do little to prevent deliberate fraud.[19]

Perhaps the most surprising fall from grace was the decline in the trust originally given without stint to those high priests of the future, the scientific community. Once regarded as the saviours of mankind from want, ignorance and all the ills that flesh is heir to, scientists came to be looked upon with suspicion as the manufacturers of side effects, including pollution of the atmosphere and the oceans with toxic chemicals and radioactive materials, which may make the planet uninhabitable. Every great scientific advance seemed to bring with it a corresponding cost, such as the erosion of the ozone layer which protects human beings, animals and crops from cosmic radiation or the degradation of the oxygen-replenishing powers of the biosphere which make the earth a life-enhancing system. James Lovelock's 'Gaia hypothesis' by which life itself continually renews the means of life in a perpetual cycle of

harmony may no longer work in a world where massive technological intervention in the environment can overwhelm the self-
recuperative forces of nature.[20]

The Campaign for Nuclear Disarmament began in 1958 in
protest at the enormity of the scientists' bomb and its threat to
human life. For a few years CND had a tremendous impact on the
conscience of the nation, with thousands joining in its annual
Aldermaston march each Easter, converging on the great mass
meeting in Trafalgar Square. It faded as it became clear that
Britain was no longer the moral leader of world opinion, and after
1965 it became swamped in the general protest against the Viet-
nam war. Nonetheless, it helped to highlight the threat of nuclear
holocaust and the irresponsibility of the scientists who had made
possible the destruction of the planet.[21]

In the same year as the first Aldermaston march John Kenneth
Galbraith drew attention to the 'private affluence, public squalor'
which resulted from unregulated economic growth, and two years
later E. J. Mishan questioned 'the basic unwritten premise of
economic science ... that economic development is a good
thing.... [T]he thorny path of industrialisation leads, after all,
only to the wasteland of Subtopia.' His later books attacked technological development not only for its threat to the quality of life but
for the big government needed to control it and for the individual
alienation, social disintegration and spiritual imbalance that
accompanied it. Even the scientists' boasted search for truth came
under his fire:

> the disinterested pursuit of knowledge saps the spiritual
> sustenance of men. It destroys also the myths that shore up
> their morale, the bonds that hold them together, their ideas of
> kith and kin, their pride in their history and their folk heroes –
> beliefs that one by one are doomed to be shattered by troops of
> eager young historians in search of professional recognition.
> There is, in short, much knowledge that we should be happy
> to live without.[22]

Rachel Carson's *Silent Spring* on the destruction of wild life by
pesticides, published in Britain in 1963 and earnestly debated in
Parliament the same year, began a movement for ecological conservation which swelled into a general attack on what science, technology and unlimited economic development were doing to the

environment and the quality of life. Paul Ehrlich in 1968 warned about *The Population Bomb* which would nearly double world population and add 20 million people to Britain's numbers by the year 2000, and the Club of Rome in 1972 issued its famous report on *The Limits to Growth* which questioned whether unlimited expansion was worth the human and environmental costs. The same year Edward Goldsmith, founder of the environmental journal *The Ecologist,* attacked most scientists as the 'priest-hood of industrial society' who were in process of destabilizing the 'natural system', in which men worked to keep their families, women stayed home and raised children, infant mortality should be allowed to do its work of keeping the population within bounds, and normal racial prejudice allowed to keep out un-wanted foreign elements. All these critiques of headlong, self-destructive expansion – the anti-nuclear movement, the economic steady-state or no-growth movement, the ecological movement, and the back to nature movement (though not zero population) – were drawn together in 1973 in E. F. Schumacher's *Small is Beautiful: Economics as if People Mattered,* a radical rejection of the whole direction of scientific, technological and economic development since the Second World War. The book had an enor-mous success among the mainly middle-class, non-market pro-fessional groups who were the backbone of all these movements, and for a time it looked as if they would have a permanent effect on the direction of British politics. The victory of Thatcherism in 1979, however, undermined their success and set many of them to defend themselves and their often public sector careers against the new brutalism of the free market.[23]

Professional scientists, technologists and orthodox economists, nevertheless, would never again enjoy the complacent self-confi-dence they took for granted down to the mid-twentieth century. They could not escape the accusation that, if the world ends not with a whimper but a big bang, it will be the scientists and tech-nologists and their political and economic backers who have brought us to that Armageddon. Great hopes are still centred on science's capacity for solving the world's problems but more and more people are asking: at what horrifying cost and with what destructive side effects? The time when science was the beneficent angel pointing the way to the future has gone, and now Lucifer, the most intelligent of all the angels, is seen by many as about to

481

fall from the heavens in a shower of thunderbolts.

Scientists and technologists are to be found on both sides of the public/private sector divide, and it is a moot point whether the private sector technologists or the government, especially the military, scientists are the more dangerous. The private sector professions in general, as we have seen, are not immune from the popular backlash against the privileges and pretensions of professionalism, and indeed may have greater opportunities for peculation and self-aggrandizement than the rest. The main brunt of the reaction has been borne in recent years, however, by the public sector professions. This is because higher standards have come to be demanded of those professions supported by the state and funded by the taxpayer, which do not generate immediate income and are therefore seen as a cost to society rather than as creators of wealth.[24] As we have seen, this crude simplification into 'productive' and 'non-productive' occupations, a hangover from the Ricardian and Marxist labour theories of value, and its equation with the division between the public and private sectors, does not stand up to logical analysis: candy floss or fruit machine manufacture in the private sector is not obviously more productive than antenatal care producing future workers or education producing human capital in the public sector. But the perception persists, fostered by a very active lobby, that the private sector produces the wealth that the public sector consumes or, in their emotive language, 'squanders'. Since everyone pays taxes everyone, quite rightly, feels entitled to demand value for money from those professions whose remuneration and fringe benefits are compulsorily levied by the state. But they do not ask the same question of those private sector professionals who simply help themselves at the expense of a hidden tax on the consumer.

While most people seem unconcerned, for example, by the 'golden handshakes' and large single-premium pension contributions handed out to retiring company directors, the inflation-proof pensions negotiated in the 1970s for civil servants, Health Service employees, local government workers, and others in the public sector have been constantly attacked, even though an inquiry appointed by Mrs Thatcher recommended that the principle be extended to private sector pensions, where indeed it already operated in forty-nine schemes.[25]

Architects and town planners, who like scientists span both

sectors, came in for increasing criticism for the high-rise council estates which arose around the inner cities in the 1960s and within a few years deteriorated into the vandalized and soulless slums depicted in Anthony Burgess's *A Clockwork Orange*. In this case the backlash took a positive form in the community architecture movement which involved local residents in the rehabilitation of derelict areas. For once, under the patronage of the Prince of Wales, the profession reformed itself, and in 1986 Rod Hackney, the inspiration of the movement, became President of the Royal Institute of British Architects.

No professionals have been more exactingly criticized or resented when they failed to come up to expectations than the so-called 'caring professions', the social workers, nurses and hospital auxiliaries, teachers and youth workers, and the vast range of health visitors, counsellors, home helps, foster parents, and so on maintained by the modern welfare state. Even so compassionate a journalist as Katharine Whitehorn in 1979, exasperated by the teachers' and social workers' strikes and the doctors' work-to-rule, attacked 'the overblown fake figure of the Caring Professional' and characterized them all as 'mercenaries of care'.[26] Such disputes hit working mothers particularly hard and set up a climate of opinion which encouraged disillusion at both ends of the political spectrum, amongst those who wanted more and better welfare and those who believed that welfare provision should be reduced or privatized. They particularly encouraged those who wished, in the words of one Institute of Economic Affairs pamphlet, to *Wither the Welfare State*, to challenge the Health Service, to offer 'choice' in education by providing vouchers expendable at private or public schools, and to question whether the welfare state existed for the rich or for the poor.[27] But the attack on the welfare state was only one aspect of the larger attempt to push back the growing incursion of the state in the life of society.

2 ROLLING BACK THE STATE?

The backlash against individual professions, especially those employed by the state, began to merge with the second wave of the backlash, the attack on government welfare in general and on the growth of government spending in proportion to the economy.

Paradoxically, this too began on the left. The poverty lobby led by Professors Titmuss, Townsend and Abel Smith had long attacked the inadequacy of the welfare benefits to cure poverty, and had demonstrated that in 1968–69 6.4 per cent of the population, 3.5 million people, were in relative poverty, that is, below the supplementary benefit line, and 21.5 per cent, 11.7 million, were living 'on the margins of poverty', within 40 per cent of that line.[28] During the 1970 election they claimed that in relative terms the conditions of the poor had worsened under the Labour government of 1964–70, and Peter Townsend's television appearances during the campaign may have contributed to the surprise defeat of the Wilson government. Townsend came to despair of the capacity of parliamentary socialism to eliminate poverty and produce radical social change and concluded that 'the question left unanswered by Labour's rule is whether democratic socialism can be effective'.[29] A younger generation of egalitarians began to question whether some welfare programmes, such as student grants for higher education, mortgage taxation relief for home owners, and subsidies for commuter rail services, did not benefit the well-to-do more than the poor: 'in some cases it is likely that there would be greater equality if there was not public expenditure on the service concerned.'[30] Marxist writers further left never had much faith in the welfare state, which could only postpone the inevitable decline of capitalism by buying off revolt, at the same time squeezing profits and slowing up the rate of capital accumulation to pay for welfare.[31] No doubt neither the soft nor the hard left meant to help the right-wing attack on the welfare state, but the unintended consequence of their criticisms was to encourage the view that public expenditure on welfare was futile.

There had long been an undercurrent of distaste for state welfare in the Conservative Party, but this had normally taken the form of a demand not for its abolition but for minimizing its expense by strict economy, selective provision, and the encouragement of private alternatives such as medical insurance, independent education, and company pensions. Down to the early 1970s the bipartisan consensus on the welfare state held firm, and only those prepared to 'think the unthinkable', as the Institute of Economic Affairs put it, dreamed of challenging it root and branch. Even Ralph Harris, Director General of the IEA, appalled by the apparent rise of government spending from 15 per cent of the national income in 1900 and 30 per cent in 1930 to 50 per cent in the 1970s and 53 per cent in 1982, did not oppose some state provision of welfare: 'We could all agree that no-one should be allowed to fall below what we judge an acceptable poverty level,' though he held that 'the disincentive cost of the British welfare state has now become the major obstacle to spreading prosperity through the more effective operation of vigorous competitive enterprise'.[32]

With the deadly combination of world recession and raging inflation of the mid-1970s, however, all Western European governments found the costs of social security, health and pensions soaring, and all of them were forced to try to economize and slow down, since they could not stop, the rise in public spending. In Britain expenditure on social welfare, which had risen from 14.7 per cent of GDP in 1963 to 17.9 per cent in 1973,[33] accelerated alarmingly, and gave a new edge to the arguments of the extreme right. Sir Keith Joseph who in 1973, on the eve of the oil crisis, introduced a new and more generous earnings-related state pension scheme, was suddenly moved in 1974 to set up the Centre for Policy Studies, with Margaret Thatcher as President, to question official Conservative Party policy on the consensus of the mixed economy and the welfare state. Their unexpected success in capturing the leadership of the party for Margaret Thatcher in 1975 brought to the fore hitherto 'unthinkable' ideas of the balance between state activity and the free market. They set out to redress the balance in favour of the private sector, to cut welfare provision back to the basics, concentrate resources on the genuinely poor and needy, discontinue the 'frills' above and beyond bare necessity such as earnings-related unemployment and sickness benefits, and to encourage as many people as possible to 'stand on their own feet'. This was part of a general plan to 'roll back the state', which would go far beyond the reduction of spending on welfare.

Strangely enough, once in office, the New Right increased spending on welfare rather than reducing it. Much of the increase was unintended and due to the more than doubling of unemployment to 3.5 million caused by the government's tight money policy, to the trebling of those among the unemployed seeking supplementary benefit (over and above insurance benefit) from 350,000 to 1.1 million, and to the increased use of the Health Service which usually accompanies unemployment. There was also an increase in the number of retirement pensioners, partly for demographic reasons and partly due to earlier retirement (down to the minimum pension ages of 60 for women and 65 for men) by redundant workers. Despite efforts to economize, by discontinuing earnings-related benefits for unemployment, sickness, widow-hood, and so on in 1981 and the taxing of all benefits for those with other income from 1983, expenditure on social security increased by a third in real terms between 1978–79 and 1985–86, and expenditure on the Health Service by a fifth. Spending by the Department of Employment, chiefly on job stimulation schemes, increased by two-thirds. Only spending on education stagnated, and that disguised an increase for schools balanced by steep cuts in spending on colleges and universities.[34]

Far from trumpeting the demise of the welfare state, government ministers began to boast, at the next two elections in 1983 and 1987, about increased public expenditure on hospitals, schools, pensions, and the employment services. Reasons for this turn-around can perhaps be found in the public opinion polls. Gallup found that the percentages of respondents believing that 'govern-ment services such as health, education and welfare should be extended, even if it means some increase in taxes' increased steadily from 34 per cent in 1979 to 49 per cent in 1981, 1982 and 1983, and to 59 per cent in 1985; those favouring tax cuts, even if it meant some reduction in such services, shrank from 34 per cent to 20–23 per cent and to 16 per cent.[35] The aspect of professional society that centred on the social rights of citizenship had survived the onslaught of the New Right and seemed to be entrenched in the national psyche.

The New Right had more success in rolling back other advances by the state. Margaret Thatcher and her allies made no secret of their dislike for state employees (with the notable exceptions of the police and fire services and the armed forces) and of all those occupations dependent for their incomes on the taxpayer rather than the market. They believed them to be parasitic upon the creators of wealth and, undisciplined by market forces, almost by definition inefficient if not actually incompetent. Mrs Thatcher particularly disliked civil servants and academics (though she made good use of some of them), whom she bracketed with the clergy as representing the 'anti-industrial spirit' which she deplored: 'nowhere is this attitude [suspicion of making money] more marked than in the cloister and the common room. What these critics apparently can't stomach is that wealth creators have a tendency to acquire wealth in the process of creating it for others.' By contrast, the new entrepreneurs whom she admired 'didn't speak with Oxford accents. They hadn't got what people call the "right connections", they had just one thing in common. They were men of action.'[36] There could be no clearer expression of the dichotomy in perception between the public and the private sector professionals.

Her government set about cutting the public services down to size and taming their functionaries. They abolished the Civil Service Department in 1981 and brought civil servants' careers back under the direct control of the Treasury. They reduced the diplomatic establishment of the Foreign Office. They forbade the civil servants at GCHQ, the secret telecommunications head-quarters at Cheltenham, to belong to a trade union, despite the European Court's ruling that their human rights had been violated. And the Attorney-General mercilessly pursued through the courts civil servants like Sarah Tisdall and Clive Ponting accused of leaking government secrets to the press (though not those from 10 Downing Street who leaked a letter from the Solici-tor-General, to both his embarrassment and that of two of her ministers forced to resign over the Westland Helicopter affair). The universities – despite the fact that she has used more academic economists as advisors than any previous prime minister – have learned the harsh lesson of dependence on the state from the cuts in student numbers and the forced redundancy or early retirement of one in six of the academic staff scheduled in 1980 – with more cuts still to come. The unintended consequence has been not only a gap in the academic generations which may never be repaired but a brain drain of some of the best scholars and scientists, principally to the United States and Australia, rivalling that from Hitler's Germany. School teachers, striking or working to rule to maintain their lagging incomes, have had their salary negotiating machinery withdrawn and have been invited to make 'no strike' agreements as a condition of its restoration. By 1985 all the public sector occupations from top civil servants and hospital doctors to nurses and train drivers – except for police and firemen (average real earnings up 9.9 per cent and 10.8 per cent) – had lost income in real terms since 1981 (an average decline of about 5 per cent), compared with an average rise in real income for non-manual men in the private sector of 11.1 per cent and for non-manual women of 15.3 per cent.[37] This was in part the unintended consequence of the government's anti-inflationary policy, which it could impose directly on its own employees but only indirectly through monetary policy on other occupations, but it chimed well with its animus against the public sector.

The government could roll back the public sector most directly by privatizing nationalized industries, and this it did, cautiously at first but with increasing enthusiasm as the policy succeeded both in raising large sums of capital (used to offset the public sector borrowing requirement) and in attracting private investors (adding to the voters with a stake in preventing the return of a renationalizing Labour government). Nationalization of 'the commanding heights of the economy' by the Attlee government of 1945–51 had become part of the post-war consensus, accepted by both major parties and a large majority of the electorate down to 1979 (and indeed down to 1983 and beyond). But support for *more* nationalization, always a minority, declined sharply in the 1970s, from 32 per cent in 1974 to 17 per cent in 1979 (and 18 per cent in 1983), while support for privatization rose dramatically, from 22 per cent in 1974 to 40 per cent in 1979 and 42 per cent in 1983.[38] Encouraged by public opinion, its own free market ideology, and by increased losses and worsening labour relations in such industries as coal, steel, British Shipbuilders and British Leyland, the Thatcher government sold off shares in British Petroleum in 1979, 1981, 1983 and 1987, in British Aerospace, British Sugar, and Cable & Wireless in 1981, Amersham International (radiochemicals), the National Freight Company (road haulage), and British North Sea Oil in 1982, Associated British Ports (1983 and 1984), British Gas onshore oil operations, Sealink ferries, and Jaguar Cars (part of British Leyland), and (one of the largest corporations in the world, worth £4 billion) British Telecom in 1984, and subsequently British Airways, the National Bus Company, Shorts of Belfast, Unipart (part of British Leyland), Rolls-Royce (aero-engines), the remaining Royal Ordnance Factories, the British Airports Authority, and British Gas.[39] All this was done in the name of competition but, as Lord Weinstock of the General Electric Company, one of the biggest suppliers to such nationalized industries as electricity, telephones and railways, remarked in 1983, the sale of British Telecom merely turned a public monopoly into a private monopoly. Since then, British Telecom has turned in record profits, but a MORI poll commissioned by the National Consumer Council reported in July 1987 that consumer dissatisfaction had increased since privatization and was worse than for any other utility service.[40] As for welcoming competition, one of the first acts of the newly privatized British Airways was to make a take-over bid in July 1987 for its main rival, British Caledonian, to gain a 90 per cent monopoly of British air routes.

State enterprise was thus rolled back. Employment in the nationalized industries fell from 1,849,000 in 1979 to 1,034,000 in 1986, and from 7.3 to 4.2 per cent of the employed workforce. Surprisingly, this made only a slight dent in the public sector: other government employment fell by only 37,000 to 5,347,000, and the proportion of all public sector employment to the total workforce only from 29.3 per cent to 26.4 per cent.[41] If we were to add the unemployed at both dates as a special kind of state 'employees', we should find that public sector 'employment' had actually risen, from about 36 per cent to about 39 per cent.

As a well-informed political scientist, Dennis Kavanagh, observed in 1987:

> This writer's expectation is that there will be a new 'consensus' on social and economic policy, though it may be more difficult to obtain on the former, and that the new policy mix will include most of the social and welfare elements of the old one and some of the economic thinking of Thatcherism. But rather than 'rolling back the state' the post-Thatcher era will have more to do with holding the line on state provision of welfare and government intervention in industry.[42]

Wherever the division lay between the public and private sectors, professional society required expert functionaries on both sides of the line. Government policy might marginally shift the line, but it was completely unable to reduce the dependence of the state and society on the services of the professionals.

The third and final wave of the backlash against professional society was the attack on corporatism. This too was a form of rolling back the state, away from its close involvement with the professional groups on each side of industry. The aspect of corporatism most resented by the radical right was that of the corporate state, committed to central planning in consultation with the major special interests, notably the employers and the trade union leaders. As we saw in Chapter 7, informal corporatism of this kind was inherent in the nature of professional society. The competition of rival professional occupations for larger shares in society's resources led naturally to the lobbying of government by organized interest groups, not merely (where appropriate) for larger salaries, budgets, grants or subsidies but also for privileges and legislation to bolster their position in the wider competition of society. Thus rising professions sought self-regulation, control of training and a monopoly of an occupational title or function, trade unions wanted exemption from civil suits arising out of industrial disputes and legislation in favour of employment protection or the closed shop, and corporate managers lobbied for favourable taxation, trading rights and industrial relations law. All the interests had come to expect to be consulted by ministers and civil servants before policy was finalized or legislation passed affecting their own industry or service.

To some extent consultation between the members of the 'corporate triangle', the employers' organizations and the trade unions, had been formalized in the National Economic Development Council and the regional 'little Neddies' set up by the Macmillan government in 1961 to discuss the whole field of economic policy. Whether this amounted to the central planning to which the New Right so violently objected is doubtful. Central planning, even of the non-compulsory, indicative kind practised for example by the French, has only been tried once in Britain and that was in the short-lived National Plan developed by George Brown's Department of Economic Affairs, aborted by the balance of payments crisis of 1966 and the devaluation of 1967. Such planning was supplementary to the market, not alternative to it, and fell far short of the command economies of the Soviet bloc. The New Right, nevertheless, saw any interference with the free market as the thin edge of a totalitarian wedge. Hayek, their prophet, claimed that there was no compromise between 'the commercial and the military-type society'. The 'efforts of policy to alter prices and incomes in the interest of what is called "social justice"', whether or not in consultation with employers and workers, were doomed to failure, and could only result in inflation on the one side and the unemployment of overpriced workers on the other. Collective bargaining, a form of interference with the individual market in labour, was the ultimate cause of inflation.[43] Collective bargaining through the state in the form of corporatism was even more dangerous. The fault lay in majoritarian democracy itself. Hayek's disciple Ralph Harris observed that politicians of all parties were prone to buy votes from large or powerful groups such as trade unionists, farmers, old age pensioners, tenants, owner-occupiers, and other significant minorities. Their method was to pass laws conferring privileges or immunities on enough special interest groups to build up a winning coalition of votes. The only solution was a written constitution with built-in safeguards against democratic tampering with the market.[44] It is one of the ironies of the libertarian right that its instincts often seem to come out against democracy.

As prime minister, Edward Heath tried to apply the revived free market philosophy, nicknamed 'Selsdon man' after the Croydon hotel where the new Conservative policy was hammered out, in his first two years of office in 1970–72, but was soon forced by inflation and other economic difficulties to make his famous U-turn and reintroduce prices and incomes policy. The Labour Party raised corporatism to a higher level in the 'Social Contract' of 1973 with the trade unions whereby the next Labour government would exchange a range of social reforms and benefits for wage restraint, but in government the massive inflation of 1974–76, the balance of payments crisis of 1976, and the deteriorating industrial relations culminating in the 1978–79 'winter of discontent' seemed to prove the critics of corporatism right. The Thatcher government therefore came into office on a wave of disillusion with corporate bargaining, determined to abolish prices and incomes policy and let the market operate without any interference by the state save the disciplinary control of the money supply. They clung to their anti-corporatist line through the worst recession of the post-war period, while unemployment rose to 3.5 million and manufacturing output fell by more than a fifth, much of it permanently. The theory of the market was tested to the brink of destruction.

The attack on corporatism, however, was very selective. It was the public sector professions which found themselves pushed out in the cold and their services, particularly health, education and local government, subjected to new directions and financial cuts without consultation. The Clegg Commission on public sector pay, with its principle of comparability which had committed the

491

government during the election campaign to heavy pay increases, was abolished in 1980. Nationalized industries were privatized with little consultation with their workers, and major plant closings took place in the railways, steel and the coal mines with no consultation at all. The trade unions in both sectors ceased to be 'governing institutions', if they ever were. Employment Acts in 1980 and 1982 restricted lawful picketing to the strikers' place of work (thus banning 'flying pickets' and secondary picketing of other employers), removed the unions' immunity from civil action in the courts (thus making them liable for damages to employers arising from unlawful disputes), required that new closed chops should be approved by four-fifths of the workers and existing ones by a clear majority, and provided compensation for workers excluded or expelled from a union in a closed shop. A further Act in 1984 required the re-election of union officials within five years and ballots on the political levy, provided government funds for postal votes, and made a pre-strike ballot compulsory if the union was to be free from civil suits arising out of the strike. Unlike its predecessors, the government refused to intervene in major strikes, even those in the public sector like the miners' strike against pit closures in 1984–85, preferring to leave negotiations to the management. The days of 'beer and sandwiches at no. 10' for union leaders were over. To a surprising extent the 'taming of the unions' succeeded, union membership fell from over 12 million in 1980 to under 10 million in 1985 – although due more to unemployment and the decline of manufacturing than to defections – and the number of strike days lost (apart from the coal industry) declined.

Far from undermining corporatism, however, these measures proved how tenacious it was. The government's efforts to 'roll back the state' and to 'bring the trade unions under the law' were avidly supported by the institutions representing business and the employers. The Confederation of British Industry with some caution, the Institute of Directors with much less, Aims of Industry, the Adam Smith Institute, and a long tail of employers' associations, local chambers of commerce and ratepayers' associations with enthusiasm, continued to press for a restoration of what they saw as the natural scheme of things. Under the latter, private enterprise would carry on business under a benevolent, minimalist state, management would be 'free to manage' without too much interference by the state or the trade unions, and the burden of taxation would be reduced and shifted away from the corporations and the managers, and towards the individual consumer. All this was advocated in the name of freedom of the individual and the free market, but as the patron saint of the market, Adam Smith, had cynically remarked:

> People of the same trade seldom meet together, even for merriment or diversion, but the conversation ends in a conspiracy against the public, or in some contrivance to raise prices. It is impossible indeed to prevent such meetings, by any law which could either be executed, or would be consistent with liberty and justice.[45]

Formal corporatism was hardly necessary for the views of management to reach and influence a sympathetic government. The multiple channels through which business men and politicians normally communicate were reinforced by publicity and educational campaigns by the Institute of Economic Affairs and its Social Affairs Unit, Aims of Industry, the National Association of Freedom, and various ratepayers' groups, and the national press was heavily weighted on their side. Such dissident voices as Lord Weinstock, Lord Kearton, the Sainsbury family, or Robert Maxwell of the *Mirror* group were 'filtered out'. Corporatism was not dead but reverted to its natural, informal mode in which, under a right-wing government, business interests were automatically more influential than those of the public sector professions, the manual workers or the consumers.

Perhaps the best example of this influence, apart from the industrial relations legislation already noted, was taxation policy. The business interests pressed long and hard for the reduction of taxation, especially of the higher levels of income tax, on the grounds that these were disincentives which discouraged managers and entrepreneurs from working harder. They asserted that Britain was heavily taxed compared with other countries, and British business men penalized in comparison with their competitors. In fact, international surveys showed that Britain was about halfway down the tax league table of OECD countries, with the Netherlands, Scandinavia, France and West Germany well above and Italy, Japan and the United States slightly below. In 1987 'marginal tax rates on average wages' were 43.9 per cent in the UK, compared with 40.9 per cent in the United States, 51.2 per cent in

France and 62.7 per cent in West Germany. Britain's top rate of 60 per cent, compared with West Germany's 56 per cent, Italy's 65 per cent and Japan's 76.5 per cent; the US figure, then 37.5 per cent, embraced federal tax only and left out state and local taxes and the near-compulsory private medical insurance covered by taxation in Western Europe, which together would lift the top rate nearer to 50 per cent.[46]

Responding to this well cultivated myth of overtaxation, the Thatcher government in 1979 immediately reduced the standard rate of income tax from 33 to 30 per cent and the top marginal rate from 75 to 60 per cent, and shifted the burden to indirect taxation by raising the Value Added Tax from 8 to 15 per cent. Since then standard income tax has been steadily reduced to 27 per cent and compensating increases made in national insurance premiums and the like. The result of this redistribution of the (increasing) tax burden, was that, taking all direct and indirect taxes together over the first six years of the Thatcher tax changes, only the highest 6 per cent of income earners had gained while 87 per cent were worse off, the hardest hit being the poorest households with gross earnings below £35 a week, which included most families on unemployment or supplementary benefit.[47] As John Kenneth Galbraith commented in another context, such 'incentive' taxation policies assume that the rich work harder if they are paid more, while the poor work harder if they are paid less.

The most recent success of the private sector lobby is the proposed replacement of local government rates on property by the 'community charge', a poll tax on residents. Although business properties will still pay 25 per cent of the costs in property-based rates, the main burden will shift from the 18 million ratepayers to 35 million adult residents.[48] The unintended consequence will probably be massive evasion, which will take the form of non-registration leading indirectly, as in the old poll-taxed American South, to the disfranchisement of the poor and underprivileged. This will be a victory for those who, with Friedrich von Hayek, believe that public spending should not be voted by those 'without a stake in the community'.

Thus the attempt to roll back the state was at best a stand-off, at worst a take-over by one set of professionals of the powers of the state for their own purposes. The attack on corporatism, like those on the public sector professions, the welfare state and 'big government', was paradoxically a further example of professional society turning upon itself. The backlash was primarily an assault by the private sector professions upon their public sector counterparts, whom they held responsible for the excessive expansion of welfare services, the uncontrollable growth of government, the accelerating inflation and, ultimately, for Britain's uncompetitive economy and incipient economic decline. The unifying theme running through all three waves of the backlash was an appeal to the libertarian doctrine of the free market, which enjoyed a remarkable revival from the 1970s onwards. It is now time to analyse that Victorian doctrine and account for its extraordinary revival in an age which, in economic structure and social values, would appear to have long outgrown it.

3 THE RESURGENCE OF THE FREE MARKET IDEOLOGY

All three aspects of the backlash against professional society came together in the resurgence of the ideology of the free market. That ideology had never been completely abandoned either by the Conservative Party at its most Butskellite or even by the Labour Party, which continued to accept the mixed economy. But in its extreme nineteenth-century form, unmitigated by the professional ideal, the welfare state and corporatism, it had increasingly since the First World War become an isolated cult with a dwindling set of devotees. Their guru from the 1930s was that most un-English of economic philosophers Friedrich von Hayek, an Austrian 'white immigrant' who had been through the hyperinflation of the 1920s and the rise of Nazism and, understandably, had never lost his horror of both. His obsession with inflation as the cause of all economic woes and opener of the floodgates of totalitarianism informed all of his voluminous writings, including his influential and powerfully argued *The Road to Serfdom* published at the height of the Nazi menace in 1944.[49] They all exuded the Austrian school of economics's gospel of the free market not only as the fairest and most perfect allocator of society's resources but also as the sole guarantor of individual liberty against the ever-encroaching state. This equation of the market with political freedom was one of those naive strokes of genius out of which proselytizing religions are made. Its powerful seduction attracted a tiny band of devoted disciples amongst his students and colleagues at the London School of Economics in the 1930s, some of whom, including Lionel Robbins, T. W. Hutchison, Arthur Seldon and Lord Croham, were to achieve great influence in a later generation and help to overwhelm the by then established economic gospel of his rival guru and *bête noire*, John Maynard Keynes.

Hayek's rivalry with Keynes, a clash of two powerful, egotistical personalities who met in Cambridge when the LSE was evacuated there during the war, is a clue to his compulsive crusading. Keynes's glamorous, cultured, effortless superiority, so much at ease in the great world of international statesmen, literary lions, and stars of the performing arts, must have sorely tried the obscure continental scholar's patience, coming as he did from an intellectual background where only deep scholarship and the power of esoteric ideas gave any just claim to fame. Keynes, although a charming host and brilliant conversationalist, seemed to Hayek to possess a deeply flawed intellect which seized upon stop-gap solutions to immediate problems without thinking through the consequences.[50] His most famous 'discovery', that the market could not achieve equilibrium at full employment without the active intervention of the state to manage aggregate demand, damping it down when the economy overheated and stimulating it by deficit spending when depression threatened, appeared to Hayek an irresponsible interference with the self-correcting mechanisms of the market which could only end in disaster. Demand management at the macro-level, given the power of special interests, especially the trade unions, to influence government policy, could only work in one direction, to stimulate inflation. It set up a ratchet effect by which inflation accelerated with every crisis but refused to go down again afterwards, and became more and more difficult to cure. It ignored the relative price effect at the micro-level, by which new industries and services attracted capital and labour away from the old and declining ones so as to encourage innovation and general growth. Central planning of any kind merely distorted the workings of the market and, since no bureaucrat could anticipate people's needs as well as they did themselves through market choice, served mainly to perpetuate the stagnating *status quo*. Keynes, 'the illustrious man, whose name I believe will go down in history as the grave digger of the British economy',[51] was therefore the main cause of the slow economic growth and gradually accelerating inflation which were to bring the long post-war boom to a foreboding close in the 'stagflation' of the 1970s.

Keynes's influence was all the more galling because he, like Hayek and his disciples, believed in the power of ideas. They never tired of quoting the famous passage from *The General Theory* in which Keynes attributed the origins of government policy to thinkers like himself:

> the ideas of economists and philosophers, both when they are right and when they are wrong, are more powerful than is commonly understood. Indeed the world is ruled by little else. Practical men, who believe themselves to be quite exempt from any intellectual influences, are usually the slaves of some defunct economist. Madmen in authority, who hear voices in the air, are distilling their frenzy from some academic scribbler of a few years back. I am sure that the power of vested interests is greatly exaggerated compared with the gradual encroachment of ideas. Not, indeed, immediately, but after a certain interval; for in the field of economic and political philosophy there are not many who are influenced by new theories after they are twenty-five or thirty years of age, so that the ideas which civil servants and politicians and even agitators apply to current events are not likely to be the newest. But, soon or late, it is ideas, not vested interests, which are dangerous for good or evil.[52]

Hayek and his followers saw Keynes as the 'defunct economist' whose ideas, for evil rather than good, dominated not only British government policy but, through the adoption by the Americans at the Bretton Woods conference in 1944 of the fixed exchange rates which bedevilled the free market until 1971, the whole world economy for the next three decades.

It is not surprising, therefore, that they set about out-Keynesing the Keynesians and, surprisingly late, in the mid-1950s established their own institution to educate the public in what they considered to be the only true, original principles of classical economics. The idea of a research organization to influence intellectual economic opinion came from Hayek himself, who laid in the mind of Antony Fisher, founder of Buxted Chickens, the egg which hatched a decade later in the Institute of Economic Affairs. With Ralph Harris as General Director from 1957, Arthur Seldon as Editorial Director from 1959, and an Advisory Council including the ex-Fabians Colin Clark and Graham Hutton, the Liberals Sir Oscar Hobson and Lord Grantchester and the Conservative George Schwartz, it began a programme of publications which stretched to over 200 books and pamphlets over the next twenty years.[53] They covered a vast range of topics, from economic policy, taxation and the right to property, to pensions, house rents, education and the welfare state, but the thrust of the programme, to quote two American admirers, was 'the market alternative works.... Try the market or, even more concisely,... privatise.'[54] Competition, Adam Smith's benevolent 'invisible hand', was the panacea which would allocate income and wealth more equitably, encourage more enterprise and stimulate greater economic growth than any possible alternative to the capitalist system. It was above all the cure for inflation, the evil of evils, which was caused by the government printing money, and could only be ended by the state restricting the money supply to the amount warranted by the available goods and services. Employers could then no longer meet the inflationary wage claims of the trade unions by raising prices. Monetarism, a wonderful all-purpose tool of economic policy, might cause short-term unemployment but in the end competition would force both prices and wages down to their natural level at which both capital and labour would enjoy full employment. Inflation gone, the self-correcting mechanisms of the market would restore and maintain equilibrium and continuing healthy economic growth.

The free marketeers did not, of course, reject all state intervention. Hayek recognized that the market required for its operation a framework of rules enforced by the state, to prevent theft and fraud and keep the peace, and that there were 'public goods', such as defence, law and order, and free use of the roads, which were indivisible and must be collectively provided and enjoyed. Beyond that minimal role, however, all state provision was likely to do more harm than good. Sacred cows like state education, medical treatment and pensions were cheerfully slaughtered, to be replaced by education vouchers, private medical insurance and insurance-based pensions. There might be a transitional need for humanitarian relief for society's casualties, but these would become fewer and even disappear as the market worked its magic of providing for all. Meanwhile, welfare should be concentrated on selective provision for the truly needy rather than squandered on universal schemes covering those who could provide for themselves. Even unemployment was seldom if ever involuntary: at *some* level of wages all labour markets would clear and all willing workers would find jobs. Only the few unfortunates, the mentally and physically handicapped, the widows and orphans whose deceased breadwinners had failed to make provision for them, and the elderly who had failed to provide for themselves, would require the aid of the state. All the rest would be able, with foresight and private saving and insurance, to stand on their own feet.

This heroic attempt to put the clock back to the Victorian values of the Manchester School and the Charity Organization Society, however attractive to the rich and fortunate, did not in fact commend itself to a wide public opinion until Britain's relative economic decline threatened in the 1970s to become absolute. The power of ideas is not, after all, totally independent of circumstances, and circumstances were not yet ripe for this particular bundle of ideas. It was not a question of their being right or wrong; it was simply one of waiting for the inevitable disillusion with a set of opposing ideas which had either been wrong all the time, as they thought, or, as their opponents thought, had been so right in the circumstances of post-war Britain that they had succeeded only too well and had achieved so much that some beneficiaries felt they could now do without them.

It was, indeed, now so long since the ideas of classical economics had reigned supreme that the reasons for abandoning them in their extreme form were now forgotten. Extreme *laissez-faire* is an oxymoron: to let things completely alone is to abandon not only state intervention but civil society altogether and to embrace Hobbes's state of nature, the war of all against all. Once allow that the state is necessary to the free market, as Hayek does, then there is no predetermined line between what the state may and what it may not do for the benefit of its citizens. It is a matter of judgment and compromise. Hayek's distinction between 'law' defined as the minimal rules necessary to allow competition to operate and legislative 'directions' which go beyond that minimum is logically untenable.[55] It is predicated on the naive assumption of negative freedom, that only the state, controlled by the tyranny of the majority, is a threat to individual liberty. Yet, as any 5-year-old in an unsupervised kindergarten playground knows, one person's freedom is another's coercion, and universal liberty is freedom for the bully, the cunning and the criminal. It is the *distribution* of freedom that matters, and the state is necessary not only to protect the weak from the strong but also, paradoxically, to protect the citizens from itself.

There is indeed a law of the conservation of freedom which states that there is always the same amount of freedom in a society; in a tyranny or an oligarchy it is exercised by one man or a few; in an ideal democracy (not Aristotle's tyrannous 'ochlocracy') it is distributed as broadly as possible. The state can create positive freedom, and may be just as necessary to protect its citizens from the economically powerful as from the physical bully. The same law that guards the possessions of the rich from the predatory strong must guard the poor from the predatory rich. Hayek's false distinction is merely special pleading for the 'haves' against the 'have nots': by means of it those with the greater bargaining power in the market are free to exploit it while being protected by the state they deride from the depredations of the poor. It is the classic demand of the privileged in all societies. The aristocracy in that pre-industrial society which the original classical economists attacked in the early nineteenth century demanded power without responsibility, protection without paying for it, to have their lovely cake and eat it. The free marketeers demanded the same for the managers of great corporations. Small wonder that Hayek derided the concept of 'social justice' as meaning anything more than what the market allots, since by this device he cleverly denied the right of the victim to question the system and, once his premise was accepted, it would provide an impregnable defence of the *status quo*.

Unfortunately for Hayek and his followers, it is a self-defeating system. Like Herbert Spencer's Social Darwinian survival of the fittest to which it harks back, it contains the seeds of its own destruction. Not only is the free market a near-sighted giant that consumes whatever is cheapest and within immediate reach with no thought for the morrow and no concern for the unforeseen consequences, either of future shock from oil crises, wars or other disasters or of the social costs imposed on the innocent by acid rain, holes in the ozone layer, the export of jobs, deindustrialization and the like. It is also a cannibal that devours its own children. Competition by definition leads to the elimination of competitors, as the increasing concentration of British industry in the last hundred years demonstrates. By 1978, as we have seen, the leading 100 firms produced 41 per cent of manufacturing output and employed about two-fifths of the workforce.[56] This meant that in most industries three to five companies dominated output and employment and were in a position, even without collusion, to administer prices, and to a lesser extent, wages. The chief enemy of the free market is neither the state nor even the trade unions but the corporations themselves. The free marketeers paid little attention to this flaw in their theory, except to brush it aside with remarks about the substitutability of commodities (such as plastic for metals or porcelain, or nuclear power for gas, oil or coal) and the competitiveness of international free trade, neither of which holds up in a world of increasingly diversified conglomerate and multinational corporations.

The essential truth is that the theory of the free market is a throwback to the Victorian world of many small producers, none of whom was capable (though some did try) of rigging the market in his own favour. This is not to deny that free competition, other things being equal, is desirable and should be allowed to operate wherever there are not overriding arguments of national security, environmental damage, or social equity against it, and there is endless scope for argument about what the proper limits of public and private enterprise should be. But it *is* to affirm that in a great many cases the much vaunted freedom to choose is only a choice between public monopoly, which is amenable to some measure of democratic control, and private monopoly, which is not.

No doubt all this is patently clear to the talented and perceptive authors of the free enterprise lobby, some of whom are experts in the evolution of industrial structure, but who fear the state more than they fear their friends in the corporations. What, then, is the real explanation for the *acceptance* of a theory more appropriate to the economic circumstances of the early nineteenth century than those of the late twentieth? It would appear that its appeal in an age of rising public expenditure, decelerating economic growth, and shrinking company profits is to the private sector professionals who run the corporations and to the taxpayers who fund the public sector. Both are victims of the false economic distinction perpetrated by both Ricardo and Marx and now revived in a modern context: the distinction between productive industry and unproductive services. In a heroic oversimplification this is

501

equated with the distinction between the service-producing public sector and goods-producing private industry – ignoring some of the most basic nationalized industries (e.g. coal and steel) and the flourishing private financial and commercial services of the City. The original distinction was always untenable, not only because any service which people want (health, education, transport) is as productive as manufacturing (lollipops, doll's eyes, juke boxes) but because, as both Marx and Ricardo agreed, goods themselves consist almost entirely of service (labour) embodied in concrete form. The notion expressed by so many corporate executives, that the private sector produces the wealth which the public sector squanders, is manifestly false. It is just as valid to claim that the public sector produces and maintains, through the education and health services, most of the skills on which the private sector depends. In a complex interdependent society such claims and counter-claims are as naive and unhelpful as the pot calling the kettle black.

The freedom that the private sector demands is in practice freedom for the managers of the great corporations. The latter would be less than human if they did not welcome and applaud this vote of confidence in their benevolent despotism. Even the managers of nationalized industries such as British Telecom and British Airways eagerly anticipated emancipation from the scrutiny of Cabinet and Parliament and the transfer of responsibility to a small, feeble and unrepresentative annual general meeting of shareholders. Who would not welcome the opportunity to operate where one's salary and fringe benefits are no longer a charge resented by the taxpayer but a symbol of the company's success, where the real competition is not in price and quality but in the battle to take over one's rivals, and where the highest reward is to sit at the head of the largest corporation in one's industry? If in the process high-quality goods are sometimes produced, first-class services rendered, and promising innovations introduced, these are bonuses which have little to do with the power game played at the top. The most predictable outcome of that game, played since the Ernest T. Hooleys and Harry J. Lawsons of the Victorian age, are the Ivan Boeskys and Ernest Saunderses, lords of the high financial world of 'paper entrepreneurialism' in which the main products are not goods and services but paper securities and paper profits, to be used for acquiring still larger paper empires. As Alan Fox said in 1974, the modern corporation is self-defeating: it is 'hoist with its own petard'.[57]

According to a leading professor of business and public policy at Harvard University's Kennedy School of Government, Robert B. Reich, 'paper entrepreneurialism is the bastard child of scientific management.' It has replaced technological innovation with paper transactions designed to produce short-term profits by imposing losses on others – other firms, other taxpayers, other shareholders – often for the sake of making or fighting off take-over bids for other firms. Competition reaches its apotheosis in the gigantic conglomerate, appearing at breakneck pace in America, Britain and all over the Western world.

> Conglomerate enterprises rarely, if ever, bring any relevant managerial, technical or marketing skills to the new enterprises they acquire. Their competence lies in law and finance. Their relationship to their far-flung subsidiaries is that of an investor. Indeed, many conglomerates function almost exactly like mutual funds. . . . Like the mutual fund, the conglomerate organization does not create new wealth or render production more efficient. It merely allocates capital, duplicating – though awkwardly – the function of the financial markets.

Thus, he goes on:

> modern conglomerates are economically sterile. Their only effects are to facilitate paper entrepreneurialism and to spare managers the need to stake their careers on anything so risky as a single firm trying to make products. The growth of conglomerates illustrates managers' discretionary power to serve their own goals, and reveals how far economic change since the end of the [mass production manufacturing] management era has separated managers' incentives from socially productive results.[58]

Far from lagging behind the American 'symbolic economy', Britain is out in front:

> The fate of the British industry over the past twenty-five years illustrates this new reality. Britain has consistently led the world in major technological breakthroughs, such as continu-

ous casting of steel, monoclonal anti-bodies, and CAT-scan devices. But because British businesses lacked the skills necessary to incorporate these inventions into production process quickly enough, the British have reaped no real competitive advantage from them. These inventions were commercialized in Japan and the United States.

While British manufacturing has been declining, British 'paper entrepreneurialism' has been expanding, most rapidly of all in the financial sector with its international ramifications and in the multinational conglomerates which pursue their paper profits throughout the world at the expense of domestic industry. As Reich sees it in the American context, the biggest barrier to active adjustment to the new flexible systems of 'high tech' production in a highly competitive international economy

> is not technical but ideological. For fifty years Americans have been embroiled in an endless debate over the merits of two artificial concepts: the 'free market' and 'national planning'. The real choice facing Americans is rather between evading the new global context and engaging it – between protecting the American economy from the international market while generating paper profits, and adapting it to meet international competition. Either way, government will be actively involved. And though the form of government involvement may be different, the fact of it will be nothing new.[59]

Substitute 'Britons' for 'Americans' and that analysis equally describes Britain in the last few decades.

Like Keynes and Hayek, Reich lays the blame at the door of defunct economists: 'The enduring myth of the unmanaged market illustrates the power of ideology over political reality.'[60] The market, in fact, has always been managed, consciously or unconsciously, by the state, which has set the terms, controlled access, defined the property to be exchanged, enforced contracts, and protected the rights of those involved. Civil society, in which the market is embedded, is only possible in partnership with the political authority, which alone can prevent it from collapsing into a Hobbesian state of nature. To deny that partnership, to restrict the role of the state to the enforcement of neutral 'rules of the game', is by a sleight of hand to 'freeze the frame' and perpetuate the advantages of the currently privileged players. It is a dangerous ploy, since it may incite the less privileged players to repudiate what they perceive to be an unfair game, to kick over the board and repudiate the privileged. Only if the rules are democratically negotiable can the game continue, to the mutual benefit of all the players. To inscribe the rules in stone when they happen to favour one's own side, far from guaranteeing freedom, is an invitation to resistance and revolution on the other side. It certainly does not liberate human energies and enterprise.

Reich's conclusion, that 'this false choice – the free market versus central planning, business culture versus civic culture – has prevented us from understanding the importance of human capital to America's future', applies equally to Britain.[61] In a complex, interdependent society in which we all look to one another's human capital for prosperity and survival, it is foolish to set one set of professions at war with the other. Conflict is inherent in human society but in the last resort co-operation must prevail if society is to continue. Just as in Victorian society the classes, however locked in combat, were forced to live together like unhappy spouses, so in professional society the career hierarchies, however fierce their competition for resources, must learn to accommodate to one another's needs. The only alternative is mutually assured destruction.

The resurgence of the free market ideology, paradoxically, was not so much a reaction against professional society as a perverse by-product of it. It was an integral part of that struggle for power and resources between the professional hierarchies which, by a gross oversimplification, had bifurcated into two rival groups attached respectively to the public sector and the private sector. The brilliant siren-song of Hayek and his followers seduced the professional corporate managers and their political admirers into believing that freedom for giant corporations was the precise equivalent of freedom for individual citizens, consumers and workers, and that the corporate managers, though as great a threat to the free market as the state itself, were the best defenders of individual liberty. It was a superb example of double-think worthy of Orwell's *1984*. By holding aloft the icon of Big Brother they distracted attention from the more insidious embrace of Big Sister, the giant corporation.

This may not of course have been the intention of the free marketeers, many of whom believed their own propaganda. But it was certainly the effect, particularly via the small group of right-wing politicians who in the mid-1970s, according to one Tory ex-minister, hijacked the Conservative party.[62] Their use of the state to increase the monopolistic size and power of the private corporations in the name of competition was one of the choicest ironies of modern history.

Both Keynes and Hayek believed that ideas, especially of defunct economists, were more powerful than vested interests. What neither of them addressed was the question of why some ideas were powerful at certain times rather than others, and what induced politicians and the public to listen to one defunct economist rather than his rival. Keynes was listened to when things went wrong between the wars and many people saw their vital interests threatened by a failed and self-defeating market. Hayek and the free marketeers were largely ignored as long as professional society 'delivered the goods' of prosperity and welfare, and were only listened to when things began to go wrong in the 1970s and many people saw their vital interests threatened by accelerating inflation and the elephantiasis of the state. Their opportunity arose out of Britain's economic decline which, with the onset of world recession, threatened to change from the merely relative to the absolute mode. To the rival explanations of that decline and its connection with the dilemma of British politics we must finally turn.

4 BRITAIN'S ECONOMIC DECLINE AND THE POLITICAL DILEMMA

In October 1973 in the course of the short, disastrous war against Israel, the Arab states discovered a weapon to pressurize Israel's Western friends which dramatically changed the balance of the world economy. The oil embargo and the subsequent ten- to fifteenfold rise in oil prices by OPEC, the Organization of Petroleum Exporting Countries, abruptly shifted the terms of trade against the industrial countries and in favour of the primary producers. Not all the primary producers: the non-oil producing Third World suffered more than the First and some of the poorer countries were close to bankruptcy. But the cheap energy on which the West, unthinkingly, had come to rely for the continuing economic boom was suddenly cut off. This was not the beginning of the West's troubles. The economic Pax Americana by which the free world economy had been managed ever since the Bretton Woods Conference of 1944 had been showing signs of strain for some time and had in effect been abandoned in 1971 when the Nixon Administration abandoned the fixed gold-dollar exchange rate and left the world's currencies to float against the dollar. For the British government Anthony Barber at the Exchequer floated the pound sterling in 1972. These were symptoms that the victorious Western allies of the Second World War could no longer maintain the economic and financial framework which had sustained the long secular boom, and its main beneficiaries, the rapidly growing economies of Western Europe and Japan, were not yet ready to take up the burden. The oil crisis dramatized the changing balance of world trade. It put great strain on the weakest of the major industrial economies, namely Britain.

Britain's economy, as we have seen, had been in relative decline throughout the twentieth century. Some economic historians dated it from the First World War, some from the 'climacteric of the 1890s', some from the 'Great Depression' of 1874–96, some even from the Great Exhibition of 1851 which marked the end of the Industrial Revolution. Most regarded a relative decline in Britain's monopolistic position as workshop, merchant, banker and insurer to the world as inevitable, but few, even when the European Economic Community overtook the British living standard during the 1960s, thought that it would ever become absolute. The oil crisis changed that optimism. It precipitated a massive inflation which not only wiped out all the gains of the wage explosion of the mid-1970s but almost priced British exports out of world markets and instigated a balance of payments crisis in 1976 requiring a gigantic loan from the International Monetary Fund. Britain was saved from bankruptcy only by the fortuitous discovery of North Sea oil, which came on stream in the later 1970s. This. however, had the unfortunate side-effect of enabling Britain to restore the balance of payments and pay its way in the world without any fundamental reform of the underlying economic structure. The oil revenues were squandered in a spending spree on consumer imports which did nothing to arrest the further decline of the domestic industrial base, and on the consequent bill for a trebling of unemployment.

The result was that Britain's economic growth in terms of Gross Domestic Product was negative in 1974 and 1975 for the first time since the Great Depression of the 1930s, and again in 1980 and 1981. Overall, GDP per head did manage to grow between 1975 and 1985 by an average of 1.5 per cent per annum, but this was less than any other country in the EEC except the Netherlands and Spain, and much less than Japan and the United States.[63] Inflation averaged 14.2 per cent in the 1970s and 7.2 per cent in 1980–85, reaching the alarming heights of 24 per cent in 1975 and 22 per cent in 1980. The pound of 1971 was worth 32 pence by 1979 and 21 pence by 1985. Unemployment, never more than 3 per cent (660,000) before 1971, rose in the late 1970s to 7 per cent (1.5 million) and doubled to 13 per cent (3.5 million) in the early 1980s (despite reductive changes in the mode of calculation).[64] Worse still was the decline of employment in manufacturing, which fell by 18 per cent in the 1970s and by a further 22 per cent between 1979 and 1984. By then manufacturing industry employed only 22 per cent of the British workforce.[65] Commentators began to talk about 'deindustrialization' and the destruction of the industrial base. Aubrey Jones, a Conservative ex-minister much involved with planning and incomes policy in the 1960s, wrote in 1985 that 'the relative decline may now be turning into an absolute one, so great has been the destruction of equipment and the demoralization of the workforce'.[66] Britain's share of world exports of manufactures, which had shrunk from 25.3 per cent in 1950 to 9.3 per cent in 1975, declined further in the 1980s.[67] To some extent this loss has been compensated by gains in employment in services, but most of these jobs were in low-paid non-manual work such as retailing and routine clerical work. The expanding financial sector was more related to the world economy and overseas investments, diverting jobs away from Britain, than to investment in domestic industry, and may have cost more in export earnings than it gained. According to a leading American economist, William J. Baumol of Princeton University, Britain with its low productivity has 'preserved its jobs and competitiveness by becoming an exporter of cheap labour.'[68] The 'economic miracle' of the mid-1980s, a 2.5 per cent growth in GDP in 1984 and 3.5 per cent in 1985, was simply recovery from the abnormally low output levels of 1982.[69]

The explanations for this sorry performance were as manifold as the vested interests trying to escape blame and transfer it to others. Devotees of economic planning blamed the lack of foresight which left Britain at the mercy of sudden shifts in world economic winds, and the failure to use the consequent windfall from North Sea oil to rebuild the industrial base by selective investment in high technology and the transport and other infrastructures. The free market lobby derided such planning and blamed Britain's lack of competitiveness on the inflation caused by the growth of public expenditure on welfare and subsidies to nationalized and 'lame duck' private industries and by the open-ended growth of the money supply to meet inflationary pay increases. Public expenditure in its widest sense did indeed grow from about 50 per cent of GDP in 1970 to about 60 per cent in 1975; but these, as Sir Alec Cairncross has pointed out, are very misleading figures, including transfer payments such as social security which go straight back into personal expenditure, and capital investment in commercial assets, such as public housing and the nationalized industries, in addition to the provision of public services like defence, health and education. Arguing that only the last are what people mean by public expenditure, Cairncross estimated that 'there was no increase in the relative size of the public sector in the twenty-five years after the Korean War' and that the rise from 1970 to 1975 was only from 21 to 25 per cent at current prices. At constant (1970) prices, allowing for the fact that 'the productivity of doctors, teachers, soldiers and others in the public sector is constant' while it rises with investment in the private sector, 'real' public expenditure actually fell, from 29 per cent in 1952 to 21 per cent in 1970, and rose only to 23 per cent in 1975.[70] The free market lobby, concerned not only with the net cost of government but with the extent of personal dependence on the state, naturally rejected so narrow a definition. In terms of the Treasury compromise definition of 1976, which deducted fixed capital investment but included both spending on goods and services and transfer payments, public expenditure rose after the oil crisis from 41 per cent in 1973–74 to 43 per cent in 1978–79, 46.5 per cent in 1982–83 and (ignoring the capital receipts from privatization) to about 48 per cent in 1985–86.[71] The last two figures are an ironical comment on the anti-public spending policies of the Thatcher government.

It was not surprising therefore that the free market lobby should have urged the merits of their single weapon of economic policy, control of the money supply and especially of the 'Public Sector Borrowing Requirement' which enabled governments to spend beyond their means. A monetarist policy was first adopted by Chancellor Dennis Healey and the Labour government in 1976, confronted by a balance of payments crisis and a demand from the International Monetary Fund, as the condition of a £4 billion loan, for a cutback in public spending. But the real turning point came with the take-over of the Conservative Party by Sir Keith Joseph and his friends and their replacement of Edward Heath as leader by Margaret Thatcher in 1975.[72] This enabled the radical right when they came to power in 1979 to try the experiment of pure monetarism as a cure for inflation and slow economic growth upon the British people. In an article in the *Observer* on 31 August 1980 the Canadian economist John Kenneth Galbraith asked, if there had to be an experiment in monetarism, what better people to inflict it on than the tolerant, phlegmatic British?

After a disastrous start, in which inflation rose to 22 per cent in 1980, largely due to the government's own policies of raising indirect taxes, meeting promised public sector pay increases, and accepting the cost of monetarist-induced unemployment, the revolution in policy did succeed in bringing down inflation to 4.6 per cent in 1983, though it rose again to 6.1 per cent in 1985.[73] But monetarism itself completely failed to fulfil its promises. This was because, as the Bank of England itself had warned, the quantity of money in the economy was almost impossible to define much less control, and the 'intermediate' definition (Sterling M3) used by the Treasury failed to take full account of all the other tributaries to the money supply, especially private credit in all its forms from bank loans to credit cards. It was bank credit, not the Public Sector Borrowing Requirement, which was the most significant factor in the growth of the money supply, and bank credit was increasingly beyond the control of the Treasury and the central bank. Ironically, this was because the very market policies pursued by government gave free reign to the financial institutions providing the credit. Monetarism as a concept was gradually abandoned by the Treasury and was in effect pronounced dead by the Governor of the Bank of England on 24 October 1986.[74] The partial conquest of inflation was entirely due to the government's severe deflationary policies, to high interest rates (forced up by the need to prop up the pound), cash limits on public spending, real expenditure cuts in higher education, the Health Service and local government and, paradoxically, the privatization of nationalized

510

industries which soaked up private funds that might otherwise have found their way into private industrial investment. The cost of this massive deflation, as we have seen, was the reduction by a fifth of the manufacturing base of the economy and a more than doubling of unemployment. Ironically, it did not even reduce public expenditure, which went on rising, principally to support the direct and indirect costs of the unemployed and, from 1982 onwards, the Falklands war and its aftermath of maintaining an expensive and useless base in the south Atlantic.

The real causes of inflation and of economic decline were much more fundamental than the superficial analysis of the monetarists allowed. The components of the inflation of the 1970s were not money supply but rising costs, primarily import prices, especially of oil and energy-related supplies, and also wages, which rose in response to accelerating inflation but rarely managed to get far ahead of it. All other causes, including taxation and public expenditure, played a minor and sometimes negative role. In the first year of the oil crisis, 1973–74, seven-tenths of the 16.1 per cent inflation was due to import prices and another six-tenths to wage increases, moderated by a *decrease* of three-tenths in the contribution of taxes and other causes. The following year's record inflation (23.1 per cent) saw the same contribution, six-tenths, by wages, a reduction to three-tenths in the contribution of import prices, and a now positive contribution of one-tenth by taxes and other causes.[75] The monetarist argument failed before the cost-push of imports, and it would have required a draconian control over both company prices and every avenue of credit to hold down wages, not to mention some foolproof and necessarily authoritarian method of preventing strikes.

So much for inflation, which was only the symptom of a deeper malaise. It would have been no problem if British productivity had kept pace with that of competitors in Western Europe and Japan. If rising prices, in part at least, resulted from 'paying ourselves too much', the remedy applied by Britain's more successful rivals, who suffered much less from the oil-generated inflation, was not to pay themselves less but to produce more goods and services at lower prices. The real cause of Britain's economic sluggishness was the abysmally slow growth of British productivity. Production per head, contrary to popular opinion, is not increased by working harder (though it may be increased by working *longer* while at work) but by working more efficiently, which requires better equipment and organization. The most obvious reason for Britain's poor performance on this front was lack of capital investment. According to Sidney Pollard, the 'one failure in the Western European success story since the war' was due firstly to lagging investment, caused by 'concentrating first and foremost on symbolic figures and quantities, like prices, exchange rates and balances of payments, to the neglect of real quantities of goods and services traded', and secondly to the Treasury's 'wastrel, spendthrift and unregenerate' policies of cutting long-term public investment to solve short-term crises. His remedy, anathema to the free marketeers, was 'a mixed system in which much of the steering and the initiative is taken on by the state, on the French or Japanese model'.[76]

Investment in Britain *was* lower than elsewhere, except perhaps in the United States, but not sufficiently lower to account for all the difference in growth rates. According to Cairncross, 'What was different in Britain was what happened to output per unit of new investment.' It was the low incremental capital-output ratio which was the heart of the problem: Britain in 1963–73 required nearly three times as much investment in manufacturing as West Germany to achieve a given increase in output (with a British ICOR of 2.5 compared with the Germans' 7.2).[77] Both management and trade unions were blamed for restricting the benefits of innovation. Trade unions, fearful of redundancy, insisted on old levels of manning on new machinery and spun out the work over tea breaks and overtime to maintain as much employment as before. Managers, discouraged from investment by these practices, winked at them for the sake of a quiet life, and allowed overmanning not only on the shop floor but amongst the 'overhead' staff in the offices. Because of this, Cliff Pratten of Cambridge University found in 1976 that output per employee was 50 per cent higher in Swedish than in comparable British firms. In a second survey of multinational companies operating in Britain, the United States, France and West Germany Pratten found that in eighty-five out of 109 cases productivity was lower in Britain than abroad. This was partly due to shorter hours of actual work on the job – according to Sir Michael Edwardes of Chloride, their Dagenham battery factory managed only twenty-eight hours out of a forty-hour week as against thirty-four in a similar American factory. It was partly due to demarcation disputes and different maintenance practices: in the British car industry it took six maintenance men to restart the assembly line after a breakdown, compared with two on the continent. (It was commonly said that when a British assembly line broke down, the maintenance men had to be fetched from the back room; in West Germany the maintenance men circulated round the line, looking for trouble; in Japan *all* the workers co-operated to get the line moving again.) Finally, it was partly due to the higher ratio of indirect to direct workers: one French components firm achieved 80 per cent of the output of its British subsidiary with only half the workforce. The British plant had six time as many overhead staff in the personnel department and four times as many in production engineering.[78] Despite the closing of so many inefficient plants, productivity rose by only 9.4 per cent between 1979 and 1983, while the more important measure, labour cost per unit of output, actually rose in 1980–84 by 20 per cent.[79]

Only good management and better industrial relations could solve that problem. British management, with some honourable and exceptional examples like Courtaulds and Jaguar, was notoriously bad. We have already noted what Martin Wiener has called the decline of the industrial spirit in Britain since 1850, and attributed it not to the survival of aristocratic values but to the rise of the professional ideal of public service in the public schools and older universities.[80] What British managers suffered from still more, *pace* the free marketeers, was a decline in the *competitive* spirit. First noted by Alfred Marshall in the 1890s, it was still in evidence, according to Sir Arthur (now Lord) Cockfield, chairman of Boots the Chemists, in 1978:

> We suffer in this country from market domination, price leadership, parallel pricing, the lack of effective competition, unwillingness to compete on price, which in many trades is regarded as disreputable or undesirable, and a 'cost plus' mentality under which the instinctive reaction to cost increases is to pass them on in price, rather than absorb them in greater efficiency, with the resulting erosion of resistance to cost increases, particularly unjustified increases in labour costs.... [I]t is not so much the active and deliberate abuse which is the problem as a general attitude of uncompetitiveness.[81]

That is why Britain continued to rely on old and declining industries much longer than other countries, to find privileged markets for them in the old empire and the emerging Third World, and to trade low-value, high-labour-cost manufactures in exchange for raw materials rather than compete in the 'high tech' world of the expanding economies.[82]

Beneath all the other problems lay the state of British industrial relations. It was not that there were more strikes and more days lost by industrial disputes in Britain – there were far more than in Germany, Holland, Scandinavia or Japan, but far fewer than in Italy, Canada, Australia, or the United States – but there was too often between strikes a sullen lack of co-operation between managers and workers. It showed itself in a questioning of managerial prerogatives, in a clinging to work routines and spheres of influence, an insistence on watertight demarcations between different jobs, a deep suspicion of any innovation which might increase profits at the supposed expense of wages, and a mutual suspicion that any change suggested by the other side was a ploy to 'get something for nothing'. As Ralf Dahrendorf has observed, British workers and managers perceived their relationship as a zero-sum game in which there was only a limited kitty to be played for and one side's gain was the other side's loss.[83] The result was Alan Fox's 'low-trust' industrial relations in which confrontation is the natural posture and co-operation is at a premium.[84] This was in stark contrast to the high-trust industrial relations of the Japanese, who regard both managers and workers as members of the same family, sharing the benefits of innovation and productivity and seeing high profits as the main guarantee of rising wages. It is significant that in Japanese companies in Britain, such as the Sony works at Bridgend, the management was able to win co-operation by treating both workers and managers alike.

This would seem to suggest that the main cause of the bloody-mindedness which besets British industry, and therefore of the inability of the economy to break out of the vicious circle of slow growth, low expectations, and fear of redundancy, is the persistence of class. Managers and workers come from opposite sides of the tracks, from different social backgrounds and educational experiences, speak with different accents, have different expectations of lifetime incomes and careers, and feel themselves locked into different slots in the social framework. Managers, like other middle-class professionals, have stable careers, some security of tenure, automatic pensions, and regularly rising incomes – though some of these advantages are now being jeopardized by the absolute decline of manufacturing industry. Workers are paid 'the rate for the job', expect little or no promotion, have smaller pensions or none, and after reaching their peak earnings early in life can thereafter only 'rise with their class, not out of it'. The secret of the Japanese industrial success may not lie in better education, superior management skills, quality control groups, or any of the other devices extolled in the West, but in two professional conditions of service for manual workers which the West has never tried, lifetime employment and rising pay scales.[85] British workers and managers still inhabit two different social worlds between which conflict is the norm and co-operation the exception.

Industrial confrontation in the workplace has been exacerbated at the national level by the politics of confrontation. Like monetarism, the attempt by government to 'tame the unions' began, as we have seen, with the Labour Party, with *In Place of Strife* and the unsuccessful industrial legislation of the late 1960s. A second attempt was passed into law by the Heath government in 1972 but was immediately repealed by the second Wilson government in 1974. The real 'politics of confrontation' – her own term – began with Margaret Thatcher's government after 1979 which, after a 'softly-softly' start under James Prior when rising unemployment was expected to discipline the unions, erupted into violent confrontation with the miners' strike of 1984–85. Renewed legislation was passed to enforce ballots before strikes, individual members' rights against unions, and the democratic election of officials. Confrontation works both ways and, with class warriors like Arthur Scargill of the National Union of Mineworkers on the battle lines, it looked as if industrial relations would lead Britain to become once more as 'ungovernable' as in the early 1970s. However, deflation, recession and unemployment did their work, trade union numbers fell from 55 to 43 per cent of the employed workforce, and trade union voters continued to desert Labour for other parties. At the 1987 election as many as 58 per cent of trade unionists voted for other parties, 30 per cent for the Conservatives.[86] In other words, for all the confrontation and the class rhetoric on either side, class, though still important in the workplace, was no longer the master spring of politics.

The underlying malaise of Britain's economy is rooted in the transitional state of British society. We have the worst of both worlds: all the bitterness and mutual hostility of an old and obsolescent class society which refuses to die and all the greedy scramble for resources between the professional interest groups, but few of the benefits of a more fully developed professional society as in West Germany or Japan. In industry professionalization has not reached down far enough to persuade the manual workers that they fully belong to the new society or to the same order of human beings as the managers. The professionalization of the workers, their merger into a single status along with the non-manual staff, with the same conditions of employment, paid sick leave and holidays, pension rights and the like, is far from complete and has not been pursued with enough sincerity to convince them that corporations distribute rewards fairly and without special privileges to the few. The vaunted principle of equality of opportunity operates increasingly outside industry, through the educational system, so that inside the firm upward mobility is increasingly blocked off for the majority, and the career hierarchies are effectively open only to the managerial trainees with the right educational qualifications. The old class feeling of 'Us versus Them' still prevails and perpetuates the zero-sum game in which neither side will willingly yield an inch. To prevent the other side's gain rather than to co-operate for mutual benefit becomes the aim of the game. Mutual frustration and resistance to innovation are the result.

The transition is reflected in the division of Britain into two nations, north and south, or rather into the north and west and the south-east. In the north and west, including Scotland and Wales, the old class society persists, clinging to old industries and old grievances. Pockets of the new society exist in the suburbs around the major northern cities but they include fewer of the bright, young, upwardly mobile corporate managers and more of the public sector professionals – teachers, college lecturers, local civil servants, local government officers, Health Service employees, and so on. The latter now form the backbone of the opposition parties, both Labour and Alliance. At the 1978 Labour Party Conference 70 per cent of the delegates were white-collar workers, and 60 per cent were in public sector occupations.[87] This helps to account for the strength of Labour, and also of the Liberals in Scotland, the north, the west and Wales. The public sector professionals are torn between their old loyalty to class-based politics, with its demand for equality for the underprivileged, and the pull of their professional interests, which seek equality of opportunity. The tension shows itself partly in the split between Alliance and Labour, much more in the division in the Labour Party between an egalitarian left and a more pragmatic, opportunist right wing.

The split between north and south is, in part at least, a split within the professional middle class, between the public sector professionals who, with the decline of private industry, dominate the politics of the north and west, and the private sector professionals, the upwardly mobile managers of the new service and 'high tech' industries, who dominate the politics of the Home Counties. The south-east is the kingdom of the young urban professionals, riding high on the resurgence of the free market ideology which promises them their heart's desire, power without responsibility, wealth without compassion, status without a second thought for the underprivileged (although the stock market plunge of 19 October 1987, with its echoes of 1929, may have disturbed their complacency). In short, they want to have their cake and eat it, all the benefits of professional society without its costs.

The transition is reflected too in the division, in the south as well as in the north, between the decaying inner cities and the prosperous suburbs. Not all coloured immigrants have gravitated to the slums, and some, especially the Asians, have become spectacularly successful entrepreneurs and upwardly mobile professionals. But race as well as class has aggravated the tensions of the inner-city slums where both coloured immigrants and white residents inhabit a nether world little touched by the new society. Unemployment, material deprivation, poor health, low-grade schools, and a wretched physical environment all conspire to fuel social conflict. The periodic riots, in Brixton (London), St Paul's (Bristol), Toxteth (Liverpool), Handsworth (Birmingham), and many other inner-city areas both north and south, are a protest against exclusion from the good life promised by professional society. A hundred years ago Joseph Chamberlain asked what ransom property was prepared to pay for the security which it enjoyed.[88] The Bourbon critics of modern welfare, most of them owners of vulnerable human capital, seem to have learned nothing and forgotten nothing since his time. It is only the other face of professional society, the caring concept of social citizenship, that prevents the total alienation of the inner cities and their complete degeneration into crime, violence, riots and chaos.

The structure of British politics and the decline of democracy have conspired to sharpen these tensions. At first sight the hijacking of the Conservative Party by the free marketeers and the near hijacking of the Labour Party by the extreme left in the 1970s look like a classic backlash against professional society, a return to the old class politics of former times, with class warriors as vehement as Arthur Scargill and Norman Tebbit fighting the old battles all over again. On closer analysis, however, the more significant division appears to be between the public sector professionals who, with the decline of private industry there, dominate the politics of the north and west, and the private sector professionals who have taken over the Tory Party, especially in the south-east. On either side they have nearly driven out the manual workers and the individual capitalists in whose name they so confidently speak. The main issue in politics is which version of the professional social ideal is to be applied to British society, the public sector ideal of an egalitarian, caring and compassionate state run by well-paid professionals or the private sector ideal of equal opportunity for those able to climb the corporate ladder of success and compete in the struggle for survival of the fittest corporations.

Both extremes have their dangers, which might drag down the rest of us. The first could lead, if not to *1984*, then to an authoritarian regime in which individual differences are discouraged and individual enterprise frustrated. The second could lead to a more decentralized authoritarianism, paradoxically backed by a powerful centralized government, in which the new 'overmighty subjects', the feudal lords of the giant corporations, manipulate their multinational estates with scant regard to national governments or the interests of the local inhabitants, whose prosperity and survival they decide without consultation or compunction.[89] Both sets of idealists would hotly deny any such objective, but it is the logic of their positions, not their well-meaning intentions, that will determine the unintended consequences. We are on the horns of a political dilemma created by the logic of professional society.

Is there no escape from that dilemma? Only if we reject the false antithesis proffered by the two extremes. It is rarely 'madmen in authority' but true believers convinced of the rightness of their own ideals who lead nations to perdition. The true believers on each side have been able to force a choice between two equally repellent alternatives only because the structural flaws of the British political system have enabled two extreme minorities to capture the vehicles of power. As Edmund Burke so admirably said 200 years ago, 'Government is a contrivance of human wisdom to provide for human *wants*. Men have a right that these wants should be provided for by this wisdom.'[90] It is not beyond the wisdom of men and women, in a society as potentially well-fitted for the provision of human wants as the new professional society of late twentieth-century Britain, so to contrive its government that we may enjoy its benefits without falling into the rival pits, of corporate neo-feudalism and the authoritarian state, which the extremists are so busily digging for us.

NOTES

CHAPTER 1 THE MEANING OF PROFESSIONAL SOCIETY

1 Ralph Waldo Emerson, 'Ode inscribed to W. H. Channing', in Mark Van Doren (ed.), *The Portable Emerson* (Viking Press, 1956), p. 323.
2 Cf. Harold Perkin, *The Origins of Modern English Society, 1780–1880* (Routledge & Kegan Paul, 1969), p. 29.
3 This model was first adumbrated in my Stenton Lecture, 1980: *Professionalism, Property and English Society since 1880* (University of Reading, 1981), pp. 10–12.
4 Cf. Larkin, *Property in the 18th Century, with Special Reference to England and Locke* (Cork, 1930); C. B. Macpherson, *The Political Theory of Possessive Individualism: Hobbes to Locke* (Oxford University Press, 1962); Perkin, *Origins of Modern English Society*, pp. 51–5.
5 Peter H. Lindert, 'Unequal English wealth since 1670', *Journal of Political Economy*, vol. 94, 1986, p. 1131.
6 Gary S. Becker, *Human Capital* (Columbia University Press, 1964); Pierre Bourdieu, *Reproduction in Education, Society and Culture* (Sage, 1977); Alvin Gouldner, *The Future of the Intellectuals and the Rise of the New Class* (Macmillan, 1979); Anthony Giddens, *The Class Structure of the Advanced Industrial Countries* (Hutchinson, 1973).
7 Sir Alex Cairncross, 'The post-war years, 1945–77', in Roderick Floud and Donald McCloskey, *The Economic History of Britain since 1700*, vol. 2, *1860 to the 1970s* (Cambridge University Press, 1981), pp. 409–11.
8 Leslie Hannah, *The Rise of the Corporate Economy* (Methuen, 1976), p. 216; *Economic Trends Supplement*, no. 12, 1987, p. 201.
9 Cf. Friedrich A. von Hayek's works, esp. *The Road to Serfdom* (Routledge & Kegan Paul, 1944), *The Constitution of Liberty* (Routledge & Kegan Paul, 1960), and *Law, Legislation and Liberty* (Routledge & Kegan Paul, 1982); and the many publications of the Institute of Economic Affairs and the Centre for Policy Studies.
10 Cf. Henry Pelling, 'The working class and the origins of the welfare state', in *Popular Politics and Society in Late Victorian Britain* (Macmillan, 1968); Bentley B. Gilbert, *The Evolution of National*

Insurance in Great Britain (Michael Joseph, 1966), p. 450; Perkin, *Origins of Modern English Society*, pp. 319-39.

11 Richard M. Titmuss, *The Irresponsible Society* (Fabian Society, 1960), pp. 10-12, 13-14, 20.

12 *The Independent*, 24 September 1987.

13 Richard M. Titmuss, *Essays on 'The Welfare State'* (Allen & Unwin, 1976), pp. 23-8; Paul Wilding, *Socialism and Professionalism* (Fabian Society, 1981) and *Professional Power and Social Welfare* (Routledge & Kegan Paul, 1982).

14 David Hume, *Essays Moral, Political, and Literary* (ed. T. H. Green and T. H. Grose; London, 1875), vol. 1, p. 125.

15 Cf. Perkin, *Origins of Modern English Society*, pp. 257-9, 389.

16 Ibid., pp. 3-4.

17 Cf. V. Gordon Childe, 'The birth of civilization', *Past and Present*, no. 2, 1952 and *Man Makes Himself* (Watts, 1965).

18 Phyllis Deane and W. A. Cole, *British Economic Growth, 1688-1959* (Cambridge University Press, 1962), p. 282.

19 *Social Trends*, 1986, table 1.3; A. H. Halsey (ed.), *Trends in British Society Since 1900* (Macmillan, 1972), p. 87.

20 *Parliamentary Papers*, 1872, XVI. 37 [c. 602], *Reports of Inspectors of Factories and Workshops*, pp. 82-4; *Annual Abstract of Statistics*, 1985, p. 123.

21 Hannah, op. cit., p. 216; Brian Murphy, *A History of the British Economy* (Longmans, 1973), p. 806.

22 Joseph Sykes, *The Amalgamation Movement of British Banking, 1825-1924* (King, 1926), p. 113; Murphy, op. cit., p. 703; Scotland has a further 'Big Two', the Bank of Scotland and the Clydesdale Bank.

23 P. E. Harris and R. Clarke, *Concentration in British Industry, 1935-75* (Cambridge University Press, 1980), p. 27.

24 David E. Butler and Jennifer Freeman, *British Political Facts, 1900-67* (Macmillan, 1968), pp. 211-19; *Annual Abstract of Statistics*, 1981, table 6.28.

25 David C. Marsh, *The Changing Social Structure of England and Wales, 1871-1951* (Routledge & Kegan Paul, 1958), p. 172; Hugh A. Clegg, *The System of Industrial Relations in Britain* (Blackwell, 1972), p. 143.

26 Geoffrey Millerson, *The Qualifying Associations* (Routledge & Kegan Paul, 1964), pp. 246-54; Monopolies Commission, *Professional Services: A Report on the General Effect on the Public Interest of Certain Restrictive Practices ...* (Cmnd. 4463, 1970), part II, pp. 83-5.

27 Clive Jenkins and Barrie Sherman, *White Collar Unionism: The Rebellious Salariat* (Routledge & Kegan Paul, 1979), pp. 31-2.

28 G. R. Porter, *The Progress of the Nation* (ed. F. W. Hirst; Methuen, 1912), p. 141; *Annual Abstract of Statistics*, 1987, table 14.1.

29 *Parliamentary Papers*, 1914-16, XIX, *Reports from University Colleges*, pp. 28-9, table 4; *Commonwealth Universities Yearbook, 1979* (Association of Commonwealth Universities); *Annual Abstract*

of Statistics, 1981, loc. cit.; *Social Trends*, 1983, table 3.12.

30 Census of England and Wales, 1881; *Annual Abstract of Statistics*, 1981, table 6.1.

31 Emmeline W. Cohen, *The Growth of the British Civil Service, 1780–1939* (Allen & Unwin, 1941), p. 164; *Annual Abstract of Statistics*, 1981, table 6.5; M. Abramowitz and V. F. Eliasberg, *The Growth of Public Employment in Great Britain* (Princeton University Press, 1957).

32 Calculated from *Annual Abstract of Statistics*, 1981, tables 14.1 and 14.5.

33 Daniel Bell, *The Coming of Post-Industrial Society* (Penguin, 1976), pp. 129–42: the population in service-producing occupations in the USA is there given as rising from 49 per cent in 1947 to 64 per cent in 1968, but if transport, distribution, utilities and private domestic workers are excluded the latter figure drops to 35 per cent.

34 Colin Clark, *The Conditions of Economic Progress* (Macmillan, 1940), pp. 176–7, and (1951 edn), pp. 395–6. The 1960 edn drops the term 'Petty's Law' and substitutes 'a wide, simple and far-reaching generalization', p. 492.

35 R. Campbell, *The London Tradesman* (Gardner, 1747).

36 Adam Smith, *The Wealth of Nations* (1776; ed. E. B. Bax; Bohn, 1905), vol. 1, pp. 49–50.

37 Sidney Pollard, *The Genesis of Modern Management* (Penguin, 1965), p. 159.

38 Cf. Frederick W. Taylor, *The Principles of Scientific Management* (1911; Harper & Row, 1947); John Child, *British Management Thought* (Allen & Unwin, 1969), ch. 2.

CHAPTER 2   THE ZENITH OF CLASS SOCIETY

1 Cf. Harold Perkin, *The Origins of Modern English Society, 1780–1880* (Routledge & Kegan Paul, 1969), pp. 428–37.

2 Cf. Harold Perkin, *The Age of the Railway* (Panther, 1970; David & Charles, 1972), ch. 9.

3 Cf. H. J. Dyos and Michael Wolff (eds), *The Victorian City: Images and Realities* (Routledge & Kegan Paul, 1973), pp. 339–42; Kathleen Chorley, *Manchester Made Them* (Faber, 1950); H. B. Rodgers, 'The suburban growth of Victorian Manchester', *Journal of Manchester Geographical Society*, vol. 58, 1962.

4 L. G. Chiozza Money, *Riches and Poverty* (Methuen, 1905), pp. 41–3; figures derived from Inland Revenue, including information about the division of taxpayers (over £160 p.a.), multiplied by 5 to include families of taxpayers; the 38 million 'in poverty' were simply the residual, non-taxpaying population.

5 A. L. Bowley, *The Change in the Distribution of the National Income, 1880–1913* (Clarendon Press, 1920); cf. H. J. Perkin, 'Middle-class education and employment in the 19th century', *Economic History Review*, vol. 14, 1961.

6 For references, see Perkin, *Origins of Modern English Society*, pp. 85, 122, 180, 257, 263–4, 399, 446–8.

7 Cf. T. S. and B. Simey, *Charles Booth, Social Scientist* (Oxford University Press, 1960); Cf. Perkin, *Origins of Modern English Society*, pp. 326–8.
8 Charles Booth, *Life and Labour of the People of London* (Macmillan, 1889–1903, esp. vols 1 and 2 published 1892).
9 B. Seebohm Rowntree, *Poverty: A Study of Town Life* (Longmans, 1901), pp. 111, 117–18.
10 Booth, op. cit., vol. 1, p. 165; Patrick Colquhoun, *A Treatise on Indigence* (Hatchard, 1806).
11 Booth, op. cit., vol. 1, pp. 131–2.
12 Ibid., vol. 1, pp. 35, 62; vol. 2, p. 21.
13 Rowntree, op. cit., pp. 115–18.
14 Interdepartmental Committee on Physical Deterioration (Chairman: Almeric W. FitzRoy), *Report* (Cd. 2175, 1904).
15 A. L. Bowley and A. R. Burnett-Hurst, *Livelihood and Poverty* (London School of Economics, 1915); a fifth town, Bolton, was surveyed in 1913, and the results published in 1915.
16 Rowntree, op. cit., pp. 120–1; Bowley and Burnett-Hurst, op. cit., p. 40.
17 B. S. Rowntree and May Kendall, *How the Labourer Lives* (Nelson, 1913), pp. 31–2.
18 Bowley and Burnett-Hurst, op. cit., pp. 42–3.
19 B. J. Oddy, 'The health of the people', in Theo Barker and Michael Drake (eds), *Population and Society in Britain, 1850–1980* (Batsford, 1982), p. 123 (derived from *British Medical Journal*, 1953).
20 Registrar General's *Second Report on Infant Mortality*, supplement to *42nd Annual Report of Local Government Board* (Cd. 6909, 1913), p. 73.
21 *Report upon the Physical Examination of Men of Military Age by National Service Medical Boards*, (Cmd. 504, 1917), p. 22.
22 S. B. Saul, *The Myth of the Great Depression, 1873–96* (Macmillan, 1969), p. 37.
23 Harold Perkin, *The Economic Worth of Elites in British Society, 1880–1970* (Report to SSRC, 1977, deposited in British Library Lending Division, Boston Spa), Appendix 5.3.
24 Saul, op. cit., pp. 28–30, who is 'careful not to give too much emphasis to this topic' but allows 'the sagging price of wheat' and (presumably) of other foods and raw materials.
25 Perkin, *Elites*, Appendix 5.1.
26 E. H. Phelps Brown and S. J. Handfield Jones, 'The climacteric of the 1890s', *Oxford Economic Papers*, 1952.
27 H. L. Beales, 'The Great Depression in industry and trade', *Economic History Review*, vol. 5, 1934; and Saul, op. cit.
28 T. W. Fletcher, 'The Great Depression of British agriculture, 1873–96', *Economic History Review*, vol. 13, p. 421; Saul, op. cit., p. 35.
29 Cf. Perkin, *Origins of Modern English Society*, pp. 343–5; steep inflation without corresponding rises in real wages, however, as in 1910–14 and the 1970s, tends to exacerbate industrial conflict.
30 Cf. Harold Perkin, 'Land reform and class conflict in Victorian Britain', in *The Structured Crowd: Essays in English Social History*

(Harvester and Barnes & Noble, 1981).

31 J. A. Thomas, *The House of Commons, 1832–1901* (University of Wales Press, 1939), pp. 14–17, tables 1–6, and *1906–11* (idem, 1958), pp. 28–31, 44–5. Thomas counts 'interests' rather than MPs but it is possible to distinguish landowners from business men, though of course they overlapped.

32 The 1892 Liberal Cabinet contained six landowners, one rentier and two business men, as against eight lawyers and professional men; that of 1906 eight landowners and business men as against nine lawyers and professional men and one trade union official; cf. H. J. Laski, *Studies in Law and Politics* (Allen & Unwin, 1932), ch. 8; W. L. Guttsman, *The British Political Elite* (MacGibbon & Kee, 1963), ch. 4.

33 Cf. Robert McKenzie and Alan Silver, *Angels in Marble: Working Class Conservatives in Urban England* (Heinemann, 1968).

34 Paul Smith (ed.), *Lord Salisbury on Politics* (Cambridge University Press, 1972), pp. 343–5.

35 R. C. K. Ensor, 'Some political and economic interactions in later Victorian England', *Transactions of the Royal Historical Society*, 4th series, vol. 31, 1949.

36 Paul Thompson, *Socialists, Liberals and Labour: The Struggle for London, 1885–1914* (Routledge & Kegan Paul, 1967), pp. 294–8.

37 R. E. Pumphrey, 'The introduction of industrialists into the British peerage', *American Historical Review*, vol. 65, 1959; F. M. L. Thompson, *English Landed Society in the 19th Century* (Routledge & Kegan Paul, 1963), pp. 292–9.

38 Cf. W. D. Rubinstein, *Men of Property: The Very Wealthy in Britain Since the Industrial Revolution* (Croom Helm, 1987), pp. 166–8.

39 Statistics and tables calculated from J. A. Thomas, opera cit. (see note 31 above), as explained in Perkin, 'Land reform', Appendix, in *Structured Crowd*, pp. 128–31.

40 Cf. Henry Pelling, *Political Geography of British Elections, 1885–1910* (Macmillan, 1967), pp. 41, 278, 388; J. M. Lee, *Social Leaders and Public Persons: A Study of County Government in Cheshire since 1888* (Clarendon Press, 1963), *passim*.

41 C. F. G. Masterman, *The Condition of England* (Methuen, 1909), p. 66.

42 Perkin, 'Land reform', loc. cit.

43 John Vincent, *The Formation of the Liberal Party, 1857–68* (Constable, 1966).

44 Speech at Dorchester, 16 January 1884, in J. L. Garvin, *Life of Joseph Chamberlain* (Macmillan, 1932), vol. 1, p. 462.

45 Cf. Perkin, 'Land reform', loc. cit. pp. 100, 111.

46 Garvin, *Chamberlain*, vol. 1, p. 169; Jesse Collings and J. L. Green, *Life of Jesse Collings* (Longmans, 1920).

47 Cf. Perkin, 'Land reform', loc. cit. p. 117.

48 S. D. Headlam, *The Socialist's Church* (George Allen, 1907), p. 60; idem, 'Guild of St Matthew', in *New Encyclopedia of Social Reform* (Funk & Wagnall, 1909); Norman and Jeanne MacKenzie, *The First*

Fabians (Quartet, 1977), pp. 91-2, 108-9.

49 Chushichi Tsuzuki, *H. M. Hyndman and British Socialism* (Oxford University Press, 1961); Yvonne Cloud, *Eleanor Marx* (Lawrence & Wishart, 1972); N. and J. MacKenzie, op. cit., pp. 43, 49.

50 N. and J. MacKenzie, op. cit., ch. 13.

51 Cf. Alan M. McBriar, *Fabian Socialism and British Politics, 1884-1918* (Cambridge University Press, 1966), ch. 12, esp. p. 349; 'No major political development can be attributed with certainty to Fabian influence; but few similar groups, so small and so much outside the established centres of power, can have exercised as great or as varied an influence in minor but not unimportant ways.'

52 Henry Pelling, *The Origins of the Labour Party* (Macmillan, 1954), pp. 112, 120, 210, 218.

53 H. M. Hyndman, *The Record of an Adventurous Life* (Macmillan, 1911); Tom Mann, *Memoirs* (Labour Publishing Co., 1923), esp. pp. 58-62; MacKenzie, op. cit., pp. 85-9, 90-2, 104-7.

54 H. A. Clegg, A. Fox and A. F. Thompson, *A History of British Trade Unions Since 1889* (Clarendon Press, 1964), vol. 1, ch. 2; Richard Price, 'Rethinking labour history: the importance of work', in James E. Cronin and Jonathan Schneer (eds), *Social Conflict and the Political Order in Modern Britain* (Croom Helm, 1982), pp. 186-8. A. E. Musson, *British Trade Unions, 1800-75* (Macmillan, 1972), p. 58; B. A. Mitchell and P. Deane, *Abstract of British Historical Statistics* (Cambridge University Press, 1962), p. 66.

55 Clegg, Fox and Thompson, op. cit., pp. 249-68.

56 William Stewart, *J. Keir Hardie* (Independent Labour Press, 1925); Pelling, *Origins of Labour Party*, pp. 121-9.

57 Clegg, Fox and Thompson, op. cit., ch. 8; John Saville, 'Trade unions and free labour: the background to the Taff Vale decision', in M. W. Flinn and T. C. Smout (eds), *Essays in Social History* (Clarendon Press, 1974).

58 Clegg, Fox and Thompson, op. cit., pp. 302-3; Pelling, *Origins of Labour Party*, pp. 218-19, 225-8, 230-3.

59 For Herbert Spencer and his version of Social Darwinism, see below, ch. 4, section 3.

60 C. F. G. Masterman, *The Heart of the Empire* (Fisher Unwin, 1901), p. 8, and *The Condition of England* (Methuen, 1909), p. 9.

61 Karl Pearson, 'Reproductive selection', pp. 78-80, and *The Groundwork of Eugenics* (Eugenics Laboratory Series, 1912), pp. 27-30; in Richard A. Soloway, *Birth Control and the Population Question, 1877-1930* (University of North Carolina Press, 1982), pp. 25, 37.

62 Karl Pearson, *Socialism and Natural Selection* (1904), in Bernard Semmel, *Imperialism and Social Reform, 1895-914* (Allen & Unwin, 1960), p. 13.

63 Soloway, op. cit., p. 4; M. Crackanthorpe, 'Population and progress', *Fortnightly Review*, December 1906.

64 'Miles' [Sir John Frederick Maurice], 'Where to get men', *Contemporary Review*, vol. 81, January 1902; Sir John Frederick

Maurice, 'National health: a soldier's study', idem, vol. 83, January 1903.
65 Samuel A. Barnett, 'A scheme for the unemployed', *Nineteenth Century*, 1888, pp. 753–4; William Booth, *In Darkest England and the Way Out* (Salvation Army International Headquarters, 1890), p. 93; Booth, op. cit., vol. 1, pp. 154, 66–8; A. Marshall, 'The housing of the London poor, I', *Contemporary Review*, February 1884; cf. Gareth Stedman Jones, *Outcast London* (Clarendon Press, 1971), esp. chs 15 and 16.
66 Booth, op. cit., vol. 1, pp. 39, 154; vol. 5, p. 73.
67 H. M. Hyndman, 'English workers as they are', *Contemporary Review*, July 1887.
68 Sidney Ball, *The Moral Aspects of Socialism* (Fabian Society, 1896), p. 5; Shaw and Wells quoted in B. B. Gilbert, *The Evolution of National Insurance in Great Britain* (Joseph, 1966), p. 92.
69 S. Smith, 'The industrial training of destitute children', *Contemporary Review*, January 1885.
70 Committee on Physical Deterioration, *Report*, p. 8.
71 Ibid., pp. 13–14, 15.
72 Ibid., pp. 38–9.
73 Ibid., p. 39.
74 Ibid., p. 85.
75 Sidney Webb, *The Decline in the Birth-Rate* (Fabian Society, 1907), pp. 6–7.
76 F. W. Galton, *Inquiries into Human Faculty and its Development* (Macmillan, 1907), pp. 24–5; Soloway, op. cit., pp. 35–6; Semmel, op. cit., pp. 44–7.
77 David Heron, *On the Relation of Fertility in Man to Social Status* (Drapers' Company Research Memoirs, 1906), pp. 11–16; A. F. Tredgold in *Eugenics Review*, vol. 3, 1911, pp. 109–11; Ethel Elderton, *Report on the English Birth Rate*, part I (Eugenics Laboratory Memoirs 19 and 20, 1914), p. 232; *The Times*, 14 February 1912; *Daily Telegraph*, 28 October 1913; Soloway, op. cit., chs 2 and 3, and Bibliography, pp. 365–84.

CHAPTER 3   A SEGREGATED SOCIETY

1 Frank Harris, *My Life and Loves* (1925; Grove, 1963), 730.
2 K. Marx, *Theories of Surplus Value* (Lawrence & Wishart, 1969), part 2, p. 573; Leonore Davidoff, *The Best Circles* (Croom Helm, 1973), p. 62 (*The Queen* magazine ran a regular column called 'The upper 10,000 at home and abroad'); W. D. Rubinstein, 'Education and social origins of British elites, 1880–1970', *Past and Present*, no. 112, 1986; John Scott, *The Upper Classes: Property and Privilege in Britain* (Macmillan, 1982).
3 Cf. Davidoff, op. cit., ch. 2.
4 Cf. F. M. L. Thompson, *English Landed Society in the 19th Century* (Routledge & Kegan Paul, 1963), ch. 10; G. D. Phillips, *The Diehards: Aristocratic Society and Politics in Edwardian England* (Harvard University Press, 1979), chs 2 and 3.

5 Harold Perkin, *The Origins of Modern English Society, 1780-1880* (Routledge & Kegan Paul, 1969), p. 431.
6 Cf. F. M. L. Thompson, op. cit., pp. 303-18.
7 W. D. Rubinstein, *Men of Property: The Very Wealthy in Britain Since the Industrial Revolution* (Croom Helm, 1981), pp. 59-69, esp. tables 3.1, 3.2, 3.3 and 3.4.
8 Beatrice Webb, *My Apprenticeship* (Longmans, 1926), pp. 48-9.
9 Beatrice Webb, *Our Partnership* (Cambridge University Press, 1948), p. 347.
10 G. W. E. Russell, *Seeing and Hearing* (Grant Richards, 1907), p. 355.
11 Ralph Nevill (ed.), *The Reminiscences of Lady Dorothy Nevill* (Arnold, 1906), p. 100.
12 Cf. Perkin, *Origins of Modern English Society*, pp. 85-9. My view has not been changed by Lawrence and Jeanne C. F. Stone, *An Open Elite? England 1540-1880* (Clarendon Press, 1984) – see my review in *Journal of British Studies*, vol. 24, October 1985, pp. 496-501.
13 Act I; Jack Worthing, whose income and source of wealth Lady Bracknell finds 'satisfactory' in a suitor for her daughter's hand, is a rentier with between £7,000 and £8,000 a year chiefly in investments: 'I have a country house with some land, of course, attached to it, about fifteen hundred acres, I believe; but I don't depend on that for my real income. In fact, as far as I can make out, the poachers are the only people who make anything out of it.' Lady Bracknell had in mind not only the decline in rents but the graduated death duties instituted by Sir William Harcourt the previous year.
14 F. M. L. Thompson, op. cit., pp. 310, 317-18.
15 W. T. Beastall, 'Landlords and tenants', in G. E. Mingay, *The Victorian Countryside* (Routledge & Kegan Paul, 1981), vol. 2, p. 435; Thompson, op. cit., p. 315.
16 F. M. L. Thompson, op. cit., pp. 303-6.
17 Phillips, op. cit., pp. 30, 44-5.
18 Ibid., p. 39.
19 F. M. L. Thompson, op. cit., p. 303.
20 Phillips, op. cit., p. 39.
21 Ibid., pp. 31-2.
22 Ibid., p. 40.
23 F. M. L. Thompson, op. cit., 306-7; Phillips, op. cit., p. 39.
24 F. M. L. Thompson, op. cit., p. 294.
25 Ibid., p. 299.
26 Nevill, op. cit., pp. 102-3.
27 F. M. L. Thompson, op. cit., p. 299.
28 G. W. E. Russell, 'Land and lodging houses (a colloquy with the Duke of Bedford),' *Nineteenth Century*, vol. 42, 1897, p. 384.
29 H. J. Perkin, *The Economic Worth of Elites in British Society Since 1880* (Report for SSRC, 1977, deposited in British Library Lending Division, Boston Spa).
30 Ibid.; Rubinstein, op. cit., pp. 59-69. Cf. also F. M. L. Thompson, 'English landed society in the 19th century', in Pat Thane, G.

Crossick and R. Floud (eds), *The Power of the Past* Cambridge University Press, 1984), who agrees with Rubinstein but cites as many rich industrialists as city men.

31 *Who was Who? Dictionary of National Biography*, GEC, *The Complete Peerage*, etc.

32 Rubinstein, op. cit., pp. 102-10, 166-7.

33 Ibid., p. 45; when Morrison's descendant 'played the game' he received a peerage in 1965, ibid., p. 170.

34 Ibid., p. 44; B. Webb, *Our Partnership*, pp. 412-13.

35 J. M. Bullock, 'Peers who have married Players', *Notes and Queries*, vol. 169, 1935; GEC, *The Complete Peerage*, under Rosslyn.

36 Lady Tweedsmuir, *The Lilac and the Rose* (Gerald Duckworth, 1952).

37 Norman and Jeanne MacKenzie (eds), *The Diary of Beatrice Webb* (Belknap Press of Harvard University, 1982-85), 8 July 1903; N. and J. MacKenzie, *The First Fabians* (Quartet Books, 1979), ch. 20, esp. pp. 303-4; F. M. L. Thompson, op. cit., p. 301.

38 *The Lady*, February 1893; Davidoff, op. cit., pp. 66-7.

39 Phillips, op. cit., pp. 20-1.

40 Advertisement quoted in *The Realm*, 8 March 1895; Davidoff, op. cit., p. 63.

41 T. H. S. Escott, *Social Transformations of the Victorian Age* (Seeley, 1897), p. 90.

42 Cf. Lee, op. cit., pp. 38-43.

43 Ibid., p. 79.

44 Ibid., ch. 2, esp. pp. 18-23 and 29-38.

45 Ibid., chs 2 and 3.

46 Phillips, op. cit., ch. 2, 'The lordliest life on earth' (all quotations in this paragraph are on p. 13, and references on p. 177, n. 1).

47 C. F. G. Masterman, *The Condition of England* (Methuen, 1909), p. 161.

48 Harold Perkin, *The Age of the Automobile* (Quartet, 1976), p. 53.

49 D. Lloyd George, Speech at Limehouse 30 July 1909, in Ely Halevy, *The Rule of Democracy, 1905-14* (Benn, 1952), part 1, p. 298.

50 F. M. L. Thompson, op. cit., pp. 321-33.

51 Ibid., p. 326.

52 L. G. Chiozza Money, *Riches and Poverty* (Methuen, 1905), pp. 41-2.

53 B. G. Orchard, *The Clerks of Liverpool* (J. Collinson, 1871), pp. 63-4; Booth, *Life and Labour of the People of London*, 2nd series, vol. 2, p. 189 and vol. 3, pp. 272-3, 449; Hugh McLeod, 'White collar values and the role of religion', in Geoffrey Crossick (ed.), *The Lower Middle Class in Britain, 1870-1914* (Macmillan, 1977), p. 63, n. 7.

54 Phyllis Deane and W. A. Cole, *British Economic Growth, 1688-1959* (Cambridge University Press, 1962), p. 142; W. H. Fraser, *The Coming of the Mass Market* (Macmillan, 1981), p. 21.

55 A. L. Bowley, *The Change in the Distribution of the National Income, 1880-1913* (Clarendon Press, 1920), p. 16; G. D. H. Cole, *Studies in Class Structure* (Routledge & Kegan Paul, 1955), pp. 55-7; see also T. W. Heyck, *The Transformation of Intellectual Life in Victorian England* (St Martin's Press, 1982), p. 28.

56 A. H. Halsey (ed.), *Trends in British Society Since 1900* (Macmillan, 1972), p. 113 (peak at 6.8 per cent in 1921); Deane and Cole, op. cit., p. 248, give only 4.6 per cent as employers in 1911, plus 8.2 per cent as workers on own account.

57 From H. J. Perkin, 'Middle-class education and employment in the 19th century: a critical note', *Economic History Review*, vol. 14, 1961.

58 Halsey, op. cit., pp. 114–17.

59 Katharine Chorley, *Manchester Made Them* (Faber, 1950), pp. 155–7.

60 Ibid., p. 157.

61 C. Stella Davies, *North-Country Bred: A Working-Class Family Chronicle* (Routledge & Kegan Paul, 1963), pp. 63–4.

62 K. Marx, *Theories of Surplus Value* (Lawrence & Wishart, 1969), part 2, p. 573.

63 Schools Inquiry Commission (Chairman: Lord Taunton), 1868, *Minutes of Evidence*, vol. 6, pp. 626–7. In *Culture and Anarchy* (Smith, Elder, 1869), however, Arnold still omitted the professional class in his tripartite division of society into 'barbarians, philistines and populace'.

64 Cf. Perkin, *Origins of Modern English Society*, pp. 273–5.

65 Henry B. Thompson, *The Choice of Profession* (London, 1857), p. 5.

66 Anthony Trollope, *The Bartrams* (1859).

67 Paul Thompson and Thea Vigne's oral history of Edwardian childhood interviews, nos 63 and 83, cited by McLeod, in Crossick, op. cit., p. 73.

68 Ibid., interview no. 450, in Thea Vigne and Alun Howkins, 'The small shopkeeper and market towns', in Crossick, op. cit., p. 203.

69 Rubinstein, op. cit., pp. 71–2; and 'The end of "Old Corruption" in Britain, 1780–1860', *Past and Present*, no. 101, 1983, p. 19.

70 Rubinstein, *Men of Property*, p. 45; Phillips, op. cit., p. 40.

71 F. M. L. Thompson, op. cit., p. 294.

72 Halsey, op. cit., p. 113, table 4.1; Deane and Cole, op. cit., p. 248, table 66.

73 Geoffrey Millerson, *The Qualifying Associations* (Routledge & Kegan Paul, 1964), pp. 246–58.

74 Cf. Christopher Lasch, *The New Radicalism in America: The Intellectual as a Social Type* (London: Chatto & Windus, 1966); p. xi; Edward Shils, *The Intellectuals and the Powers* (University of Chicago Press, 1972), pp. 3–22; and 'Intellectuals', in *International Encyclopaedia of the Social Sciences*, vol. 7 (Free Press, 1968), pp. 399–415; Heyck, op. cit., pp. 14–17.

75 Cf. Heyck, op. cit., pp. 24, 33.

76 O. J. R. Howarth, *The British Association for the Advancement of Science: A Retrospect, 1831–1921* (British Association for the Advancement of Science, 1922), chs. 1–7; L. P. Williams, 'The Royal Society and the founding of the BAAS', *Notes and Records of the Royal Society*, November, 1961; A. D. Orage, 'The origins of the BAAS', *British Journal for History of Science*, December 1972; Heyck, op. cit., pp. 60–2, 113.

77 Sheldon Rothblatt, *The Revolution of the Dons: Cambridge and Society in Victorian England* (Faber, 1968). Arthur Engel, *From Clergyman to Don: The Rise of the Academic Profession in 19th-century Oxford* (Clarendon Press, 1983).

78 Mark Pattison, 'A chapter of university history', *Macmillan's Magazine*, August 1875, p. 308.

79 Perkin, *Economic Worth of Elites*.

80 Rubinstein, op. cit., p. 95.

81 Booth, op. cit., vol. 4, pp. 10–25, 72–4, 80–3, 150–6, 191–4.

82 *Cornhill Magazine*, May, June, July and August 1901, articles by G. S. Layard, G. Colmore, Mrs Earle and Lady Agnew.

83 Cf. Geoffrey Crossick, 'The emergence of the lower middle class in Britain', and Thea Vigne and Alun Howkins, 'The small shopkeeper', in Crossick, op. cit.; J. B. Jeffreys, *Retail Trading in Britain, 1850–1950* (Cambridge University Press,1954), pp. 18–24.

84 Jeffreys, op. cit., p. 18.

85 Cf. J. A. Banks, *Prosperity and Parenthood: A Study of Family Planning Among the Victorian Middle Classes* (Routledge & Kegan Paul, 1954); J. A. and Olive Banks, *Feminism and Family Planning in Victorian England* (Liverpool University Press, 1964); though the Banks tend to take the supposed decline in money incomes at face value. For clear signs that the trend towards smaller families began in the higher classes as early as the 1850s, see *Census of England and Wales, 1911. Fertility of Marriage*, Part 1 (Cd. 8678, 1917) and Part 2, *Report* (Cd. 8491, 1923).

86 See *Cornhill Magazine* articles, above n. 82.

87 Vigne and Howkins, in Crossick, op. cit., pp. 187–8.

88 Vigne and Thompson, interview nos 135 and 183, quoted by McLeod in Crossick, op. cit., pp. 70–1, and local tradition.

89 Cf. McLeod, in ibid., pp. 68–79.

90 Quoted from Booth Collection, B267, by McLeod, ibid., p. 69.

91 Halsey, op. cit., p. 113, table 4.1.

92 Ibid.

93 P. H. J. H. Gosden, *The Evolution of a Profession: A Study of the Contribution of Teachers Associations . . .* (Blackwell, 1972), p. 2.

94 Cf. R. M. Hartwell, 'The service revolution', in C. M. Cipolla (ed.), *The Fontana Economic History of Europe*, vol. 3 (Fontana, 1973).

95 R. Church, *Over the Bridge* (Heinemann, 1955), pp. 134–5, 206–18.

96 Gregory Anderson, *Victorian Clerks* (Manchester University Press, 1976), and 'The social economy of Victorian clerks', in Crossick, op. cit.

97 F. Klingender, *The Condition of Clerical Labour in Britain* (Martin Lawrence, 1935), p. 20.

98 Anderson, *Victorian Clerks*, esp. pp. 74, 84, 108, 109–10, 115–16, 119.

99 Cf. Richard Price, *An Imperial War and the British Working Class* (Routledge & Kegan Paul, 1972), ch. 4.

100 Anderson, *Victorian Clerks*, chs 5 and 6.

101 This is not to say that opportunities for mobility out of, as well as into, the clerical class were increasing. Anderson, *Victorian Clerks*,

pp. 20–7, demonstrates that the chances of becoming a partner in the firm were decreasing, except for the well-connected or extremely able and lucky.

102 Anderson, *Victorian Clerks*, pp. 65–71; Crossick, 'The emergence of the lower middle class', in Crossick, op. cit., pp. 51–2.

103 Frederick Willis, *Peace and Dripping Toast* (Phoenix House, 1950), pp. 14–15.

104 Booth, op. cit., 3rd series, vol. 1, pp. 150–1.

105 C. F. G. Masterman, *The Condition of England* (Methuen, 1909), p. 66.

106 G. Stedman Jones, 'Working-class culture and working-class politics in London, 1870–1900: notes on the remaking of a working class', *Journal of Social History*, vol. 7, 1974, p. 498.

107 Booth, op. cit., 3rd series, vol. 7, p. 425.

108 Jones, op. cit., p. 499.

109 Ibid., p. 499.

110 Ibid., p. 500.

111 Andrew Mearns, *The Bitter Cry of Outcast London: An Enquiry into the Condition of the Abject Poor* (London Congregational Union, 1883); William Booth, *In Darkest England and the Way Out* (Salvation Army International Headquarters, 1890); Charles Booth, op. cit.; B. Seebohm Rowntree, *Poverty: A Study of Town Life* (Macmillan, 1908); A. L. Bowley and A. R. Burnett Hurst, *Livelihood and Poverty* (London School of Economics, 1915); Royal Commission on the Housing of the Working Classes, *Report* (C. 4402, 1884–85); Interdepartmental Committee on Physical Deterioration, *Report* (Cd. 2175, 1904); Royal Commission on the Poor Law and the Relief of Distress, *Report* (Cd. 4499, 4603 and 4922, 1909–13); Census of England and Wales, 1911, *Fertility of Marriage*, Part 1 (Cd. 8678, 1917) and Part 2, *Report* (Cd. 8491, 1923).

112 Paul Thompson, *The Edwardians: The Remaking of British Society* (Weidenfeld & Nicolson, 1975) and his journal *Oral History*; Raphael Samuel (ed.), *Village Life and Labour* (Routledge & Kegan Paul, 1975), and the journal *History Workshop*; Elizabeth Roberts, *A Woman's Place: An Oral History of Working-Class Women, 1890–1930* (Blackwell, 1984) and 'Working wives and their families', in Theo Barker and Michael Drake (eds), *Population and Society in Britain, 1850–1980* (Batsford, 1982); Flora Thompson, *Lark Rise to Candleford* (Oxford University Press, 1945); C. Stella Davies, *North Country-Bred: A Working-Class Family Chronicle* (Routledge & Kegan Paul, 1963); Robert Roberts, *The Classic Slum: Salford Life in the First Quarter of the Century* (Manchester University Press, 1971); M. K. Ashby, *Joseph Ashby of Tysoe* (Cambridge University Press, 1961).

113 Standish Meacham, *A Life Apart: The English Working Class, 1890–1914* (Thames & Hudson, 1977).

114 R. Roberts, op. cit., p. 1.

115 Ibid., p. 3.

116 Willis, op. cit., pp. 14–15.

117 R. A. Bray, 'The boy and the family', E. J. Urwick (ed.), *Studies of Boy Life in Our Cities* (Dent, 1904), pp. 19–20; J. C. Thresh, *Enquiry into the Causes of the Excessive Mortality in No. 1 District Ancoats* (Manchester, 1899), p. 31; Thompson and Vigne's interview no. 417, quoted in Meacham, op. cit., pp. 34, 35, 53.

118 Robert Tressell, *The Ragged Trousered Philanthropists* (*Monthly Review*, 1955 edn), p. 79.

119 B. S. Rowntree and May Kendall, *How the Labourer Lives: A Study of the Rural Labour Problem* (Nelson, 1913), pp. 315, 318, 320.

120 Thompson and Vigne's interview no. 185, quoted in Meacham, op. cit., p. 26.

121 Raymond Postgate, *The Builders' History* (National Federation of Building Trades Operatives, 1923), p. 243.

122 A. Morrison, in *Cornhill Magazine*, April 1901.

123 M. S. Pember Reeves, *Round About a Pound a Week* (Bell, 1913), ch. 6, 'Budgets', and ch. 16, 'The state as a guardian'.

124 Rowntree and Kendall, op. cit., ch. 3, 'Budgets', esp. table opp. p. 36, and pp. 303–4.

125 Thompson and Vigne's interview no. 206, in Meacham, op. cit., p. 26.

126 Elizabeth Roberts, *A Woman's Place*, ch. 4.

127 Thompson and Vigne interviews no. 312 and 253, in Meacham, op. cit., pp. 26–7.

128 Cf. Stephen Humphries, *Hooligans and Rebels: An Oral History of Working-Class Childhood and Youth, 1889–1939* (Blackwell, 1981).

129 E. Roberts, 'Working wives', in Barker and Drake, op. cit., p. 162.

130 P. H. J. H. Gosden, *Friendly Societies in England, 1815–75* (Manchester University Press, 1961), pp. 13–16.

131 G. D. H. Cole, *A History of Cooperation* (Cooperative Union, 1944), p. 371.

132 Price, *An Imperial War*, pp. 47–9. Solly broke with the Club and Institute Union in 1878 over his disputed criticism of the clubs' tied links with the brewers, ibid., pp. 49–54.

133 Ibid., pp. 66–80; quotations on pp. 72–3.

134 Ibid., pp. 82–9.

135 H. A. Clegg, A. Fox and A. F. Thompson, *A History of British Trade Unions Since 1889*, vol. 1 (Clarendon Press,1964), p. 1; B. R. Mitchell and Phyllis Deane, *Abstract of British Historical Statistics* (Cambridge University Press, 1962), p. 68.

136 Edward H. Hunt, *British Labour History, 1815–1914* (Humanities Press, 1981), pp. 304–6; Clegg, Fox and Thompson, op. cit., pp. 57–60; Hubert Llewellyn Smith and V. Nash, *The Story of the Dockers' Strike* (Fisher Unwin, n.d. [c. 1890]), pp. 32–3.

137 Clegg, Fox and Thompson, pp. 66–87; Hunt, op. cit., pp. 307–8.

138 Cf. Richard Price, 'Rethinking labour history: the importance of work', in J. E. Cronin and J. Schneer (ed.), *Social Conflict and Political Order in Modern Britain* (Rutgers University Press, 1982), pp. 185–90, 197–9. Cf. also Richard Price, *Labour in British Society* (Croom Helm, 1986), ch. 5.

139 Cf. Richard Price, 'The labour process and labour history', (unpublished paper presented at the Social History Society Conference at Chester, December 1980). I am grateful to Dr Price for a copy of this illuminating paper and its many useful references, including: James Samuelson, *Labour-Saving Machinery* (Kegan Paul, 1893), Carter Goodrich, *The Frontier of Control* (Bell, 1920), and W. F. Watson, *Machines and Men* (Allen & Unwin, 1935). See also Will Thorne, *My Life's Battles* (Newnes, 1925), pp. 47–8, Eric Hobsbawm, 'The British gas workers, 1873–1914', in *Labouring Men* (Weidenfeld & Nicolson, 1964); F. W. Taylor, *The Principles of Scientific Management* (Harper & Bros, 1911) and Richard Price, *Masters, Unions and Men: The Struggle for Work Control in Building and the Rise of Labour, 1830–1914* (Cambridge University Press, 1980).

140 Cf. John Saville, 'Trade unions and free labour: the background to the Taff Vale decision', in M. W. Flinn and T. C. Smout (eds), *Essays in Social History* (Clarendon Press, 1974).

141 Price, 'The labour process', cites *The Engineer*, 21 March 1902, condemning Taylorism as 'soulless', and Edward Cadbury, *Experiments in Industrial Organization* (Longmans, 1912), condemning the reduction of the worker to a living tool.

142 Cf. Charles More, *Skill and the English Working Class, 1870–1914* (St Martin's Press, 1980).

143 Saville, loc. cit.

144 Cf. Paul Adelman, *The Rise of the Labour Party, 1880–1945* (Longmans, 1972), ch. 2, and references there cited.

145 R. Roberts, op. cit., p. 109.

146 Jones, 'Working class culture', loc. cit., p. 500.

CHAPTER 4 CLASS SOCIETY AND THE PROFESSIONAL IDEAL

1 Harold Perkin, *The Origins of Modern English Society 1780–1880* (Routledge & Kegan Paul, 1969), pp. 252–70.

2 Ibid., pp. 257–60; Anton Menger, *The Right to the Whole Produce of Labour* (Macmillan, 1899).

3 For sources see Perkin, op. cit., pp. 257–60, nn.

4 Schools Enquiry Commission (Chairman: Lord Taunton), *Minutes of Evidence*, 1868, vol. 6, pp. 626–7.

5 Martin J. Wiener, *English Culture and the Decline of the Industrial Spirit, 1850–1980* (Cambridge University Press, 1981).

6 Quoted in ibid., p. 20.

7 Ibid., p. 18.

8 Ibid., p. 17.

9 Cf. Perkin, op. cit., p. 278.

10 A. C. Pigou (ed.), *Memorials of Alfred Marshall* (Macmillan, 1925), p. 103.

11 Edwin Chadwick, *On Unity* (1959), p. 99, quoted in S. E. Finer, *Life and Times of Sir Edwin Chadwick* (Methuen, 1952), p. 475; J. S. Mill, *The Principles of Political Economy* (Longmans, 1904 edn),

pp. 573, 590, and *Autobiography* (1873; Oxford University Press, 1924 edn), p. 196.

12 Cf. *inter alia* Thomas Carlyle, *Past and Present* (Chapman & Hall, 1843), book 3, ch. 2, 'The Gospel of Mammon'; F. D. Maurice, *On the Reformation of Society* (Southampton, 1851); John Ruskin, *Unto This Last* (1862) and *Munera Pulveris: Six Essays on Political Economy* (1862–63) in E. T. Cook and Alexander Wedderburn (eds), *Works of John Ruskin* (George Allen, 1905), vol. 17, pp. 12–114 and 129–293.

13 Ruskin, loc. cit., vol. 17, p. 40.

14 Beatrice Webb, *Our Partnership* (Longmans, 1948), p. 210; F. G. Bettany, *Stewart Headlam* (John Murray, 1926); E. P. Thompson, *William Morris* (Lawrence & Wishart, 1955).

15 Beatrice Webb, *My Apprenticeship* (Longmans, 1926), pp. 190, 194, 199.

16 Madeline Rooff, *A Hundred Years of Family Welfare* (Michael Joseph, 1972), pp. 13, 268.

17 Cf. Melvin Richter, *The Politics of Conscience: T. H. Green and his Age* (University Press of America, 1983); Craig Jenks, 'T. H. Green, the Oxford philosophy of duty and the English middle class', *British Journal of Sociology*, vol. 28, 1977.

18 Ibid., pp. 277–8; Cf. Alan Ryan, *Property and Political Theory* (Blackwell, 1984), chs 3 and 5.

19 S. T. Coleridge, 'Remarks on Sir Robert Peel's Bill', 18 April 1818, in Kathleen Cockburn, *Inquiring Spirit: A New Presentation of Coleridge* (University of Toronto Press, 1979), pp. 351–9.

20 R. L. Nettleship (ed.), *Works of T. H. Green* (Longmans, 1885–88), vol. 3, p. 372.

21 Ibid., p. 374.

22 Arnold Toynbee, *Progress and Poverty* (Kegan Paul, 1883), pp. 233–4.

23 Richter, op. cit., pp. 118–21.

24 Charles Gore in Stephen Paget (ed.), *Henry Scott Holland, Memoirs and Letters* (John Murray, 1921), p. 241.

25 Herbert Samuel, *Liberalism* (Grant Richards, 1902), quoted by Reba Soffer, *Ethics and Society in England: The Revolution in the Social Sciences, 1870–1914* (University of California Press, 1978), p. 188.

26 Mrs Humphry Ward, *A Writer's Recollections* (Collins, 1918), p. 252 and *passim*.

27 Stefan Collini, 'Political theory and the "science of society"', *Historical Journal*, vol. 23, 1980.

28 Jeremy Bentham, *Supply without Burthen, or Escheat vice Taxation* (1775), in Werner Stark (ed.), *Jeremy Bentham's Economic Writings* (Allen & Unwin, 1952), vol. 1, esp. pp. 283–8; James Mill, *The Elements of Political Economy* (Baldwin, Cradock & Joy, 1821), pp. 201–3; John S. Mill, *Explanatory Statement of the Land Tenure Association* (July 1870), in *Dissertations and Discussions* (Parker, 1859–75), vol. 4, p. 239.

29 Pigou, op. cit., pp. 333–4.

30 Ibid., p. 174.

31 Ibid., p. 102.

32 Ibid., pp. 282-3, 352.
33 Edward David, 'The New Liberalism of C. F. G. Masterman', in K. D. Brown (ed.), *Essays in Anti-Labour History* (Macmillan, 1974), pp. 17-41.
34 B. S. Rowntree and A. C. Pigou, *Lectures on Housing* (Manchester University Press, 1914), p. 36.
35 Beatrice and Sidney Webb, *Industrial Democracy* (Longmans, 1902), pp. 766-84.
36 Peter F. Clarke, *Liberals and Social Democrats* (Cambridge University Press, 1978), pp. 34-8; Eric Hobsbawm, 'The Fabians reconsidered', in *Labouring Men* (Weidenfeld & Nicolson, 1974), ch. 14.
37 Cf. Clarke, op. cit., p. 4 on 'bourgeois socialism' and the 'radical bourgeoisie', meaning the academics Graham Wallas, L. T. Hobhouse, J. A. Hobson, J. L. and Barbara Hammond, and Gilbert Murray.
38 Cf. George Bernard Shaw (ed.), *Fabian Essays on Socialism* (Fabian Society, 1889) and *Fabianism and the Empire* (Fabian Society, 1900); and the voluminous writings of the Webbs.
39 B. Webb, *My Apprenticeship*, Appendix E, pp. 431-6, 'Why the self-governing workshop has failed'.
40 George Lansbury, *My Life* (Constable, 1928), p. 105.
41 Sidney Webb, 'The rate of interest and the laws of distribution', *Quarterly Journal of Economics*, vol. 2, 1887-88.
42 Graham Wallas, MS review of E. R. Pease, *History of the Fabian Society* (1916), quoted in Clarke, op. cit., p. 32.
43 Graham Wallas, in *The Practical Socialist* (Fabian Society journal), vol. 1, p. 119, in Clarke, op. cit., p. 38.
44 H. G. Wells, *An Experiment in Autobiography* (Gollancz, 1934), p. 598.
45 Except of course for the property professions - cf. Avner Offer, *Property and Politics, 1870-1914* (Cambridge University Press, 1981), p. 82.
46 J. A. Hobson, *The Crisis of Liberalism: New Issues of Democracy* (King, 1909; ed. P. F. Clarke, Macmillan, 1974), p. 81.
47 Cf. Harold Perkin, 'Land reform and class conflict in Victorian England', in *The Structured Crowd: Essays in English Social History* (Harvester and Barnes & Noble, 1981).
48 *Parliamentary Debates*, 30 August 1880, 4th series, vol. 256, col. 619.
49 Ibid., 14 August 1894, 5th series, vol. 28, col. 962.
50 Stewart D. Headlam, *The Socialist's Church* (George Allen, 1907), p. 60.
51 Cf. MacKenzie, op. cit., pp. 37-41.
52 Offer, op. cit., pp. 223-4.
53 J. L. Garvin, *Life of Joseph Chamberlain* (Macmillan, 1932), vol. 1, p. 462.
54 Cf. Perkin, 'Land reform', loc. cit., pp. 117-18; Offer, op. cit., pp. 76-84.
55 Offer, op. cit., pp. 82-7.
56 The Solicitors Act, 1974 confirmed the lawyers' monopoly of conveyancing, though this has since been ended by the Thatcher government, but the replacement of title deeds by simple registration (outside London and Yorkshire, where registration of title is required) has still not been achieved.

57 *The Economist*, 10 January 1885.
58 *Parliamentary Debates*, 14 August 1894, 4th series, vol. 28, col. 962.
59 Edward Bristow, 'The Liberty and Property Defence League and industrialism', *Historical Journal*, vol. 18, 1975, pp. 765–7.
60 Cf. Perkin, 'Land reform', loc. cit., pp. 123–8.
61 Asa Briggs, *Victorian Cities* (Odhams, 1963), p. 48.
62 *London* (magazine), 16 July 1896, quoted in Offer, op. cit., p. 222.
63 Ibid., pp. 223–4.
64 Bristow, loc. cit., p. 783; Sidney Webb, *Socialism in England* (Swan Sonnenschein, 1890), p. 190.
65 Offer, op. cit., p. 301.
66 Bristow, loc. cit., p. 769; Offer, op. cit., pp. 235–6, 254, 301–8.
67 *Property Owners' Journal*, January 1909, in ibid., pp. 309–10.
68 George J. Head, 'The property market – retrospect and outlook', *Auctioneers' Institute*, 12 January 1910, in ibid., p. 310.
69 Offer, op. cit., p. 301.
70 Cf. Eli Halevy, *The Growth of Philosophical Radicalism* (Faber & Gwyer, 1928), pp. 15–18 for the distinction between 'natural' and 'artificial' individualism.
71 Herbert Spencer, *The Man Versus the State* (Williams & Norgate, 1884), pp. 88–92.
72 Herbert Spencer, *Social Statics* (Williams & Norgate, 1851), pp. 322–3.
73 Spencer, *Man versus State*, p. 19.
74 Ibid., p. 18.
75 Ibid., pp. 17, 34, 68.
76 Ibid., p. 39.
77 Ibid., p. 34.
78 Ibid., pp. 73–4.
79 N. Soldon, 'Laissez-faire as dogma: the Liberty and Property Defence League, 1882–1914', in Brown, op. cit., p. 210.
80 Bristow, loc. cit., pp. 763–7.
81 Ibid., p. 767.
82 Ibid., p. 776.
83 Ibid., pp. 776–8; Soldon, loc. cit., p. 218.
84 Soldon, loc. cit., pp. 210–12, 219–21; J. W. Mason, 'Thomas Mackay: the anti-socialist philosophy of the Charity Organisation Society', and D. J. Ford, 'W. H. Mallock and Socialism in England, 1880–1918', in Brown, op. cit., pp. 290f. and 317f.
85 Thomas Mackay (ed.), *A Plea for Liberty* (John Murray, 1891).
86 Soldon, loc. cit., pp. 222–7; Edward Bristow, 'Profit-sharing, socialism and labour unrest', in Brown, op. cit., pp. 276–9.
87 Spencer, *Man versus State*, pp. 327, 324n.; Liberty and Property Defence League, *Dangers of Municipal Trading* (LDPL, 1899), p. 27, in Offer, op. cit., pp. 234–5.
88 Bristow, 'The LDPL', *Historical Journal*, 1975, p. 785; Offer, op. cit., pp. 236–8.
89 Soldon, loc. cit., pp. 219, 231.
90 *The Times*, 3 April 1911.

91   W. H. Mallock, 'Conservatism and the diffusion of property',
     National Review, 1888, p. 402; Ford, loc. cit., pp. 326–7.
92   Bristow, in Brown, op. cit., pp. 262, 274–5.
93   Soldon, loc. cit., p. 233.
94   Bristow, in Brown, op. cit., p. 289.
95   *Parliamentary Debates*, 15 February 1912, 5h series, vol. 34, col. 53.
96   Keith Middlemas, *Politics in Industrial Society: The Experience of
     the British System since 1911* (Deutsch, 1980), pp. 58, 61–2.
97   Cf. Colin Crouch, *The Politics of Industrial Relations* (Fontana,
     1982), pp. 212–22.
98   Mason, loc. cit., pp. 300, 307.
99   Lord Salisbury, Speech at Exeter, *The Times*, 3 February 1892;
     Offer, op. cit., p. 354.
100 *Parliamentary Debates*, 26 January 1886, 3rd series, vol. 302, col. 457;
     Offer, op. cit., p. 353.
101 Arthur Balfour, Speech at Birmingham, *The Times*, 23 September
     1909; Offer, op. cit., p. 357.
102 Viscount Milner's Memo, 1913, in ibid., p. 380.
103 F. M. L. Thompson, *English Landed Society in the 19th Century*
     (Routledge & Kegan Paul, 1963), p. 326.
104 Offer, op. cit., p. 361.
105 F. M. L. Thompson, op. cit., pp. 332–3.
106 Ibid., p. 332.
107 Karl Marx, *German Ideology* (1845–46), in T. B. Bottomore and M.
     Rubel (eds), *Karl Marx: Selected Writings on Sociology and Social
     Philosophy* (Oxford University Press, 1983), p. 94.
108 F. M. L. Thompson, op. cit., p. 300.
109 Sydney Checkland, *British Public Policy, 1776–1939* (Cambridge
     University Press, 1983), p. 225.
110 Edwin Chadwick, *On the Different Principles of Legislation and
     Administration in Europe* (1859), in Finer, op. cit., p. 476.
111 Pigou, op. cit., p. 229.
112 D. P. Crook, *Benjamin Kidd: Portrait of a Social Darwinist*
     (Cambridge University Press, 1984); Bernard Semmel, *Imperialism
     and Social Reform, 1895–1914* (Allen & Unwin, 1960), pp. 31–5;
     C. R. Searle, *The Quest for National Efficiency* (Oxford University
     Press, 1971).
113 Benjamin Kidd, *Social Evolution* (Macmillan, 1894), pp. 163–4,
     227–8, 233–7.
114 Karl Pearson, *The Grammar of Science* (Black, 1900), pp. 367–8,
     and *The Ethic of Free Thought* (Black, 1901), pp. 325–8, 345–50.
115 Benjamin Kidd, *The Science of Power* (Methuen, 1918), pp. 73–4.
116 Cf. Semmel, op. cit., p. 58.
117 Sidney Webb, 'Lord Rosebery's escape from Houndsditch',
     Nineteenth Century, September 1901.
118 Lord Rosebery, Speech at Chesterfield, 16 December 1901;
     MacKenzie, op. cit., p. 287.
119 Ibid., pp. 287–8.

120 Ibid., pp. 290–1.
121 Bentley B. Gilbert, *The Evolution of National Insurance in Great Britain* (Michael Joseph, 1966), p. 450.
122 Henry Pelling, 'The working class and origins of the welfare state', in *Popular Politics and Society in Late Victorian Britain* (Macmillan, 1968), p. 18.
123 For splits in the Labour party and TUC over National Insurance see K. D. Brown, *Labour and Unemployment, 1900–14* (David & Charles, 1971), ch. 7.
124 W. L. Blackley, 'National Insurance: a cheap, practical and popular means of abolishing poor rates', *Nineteenth Century*, vol. 4, 1878.
125 Charles Booth, *Life and Labour of the People of London* (Macmillan, 17 vols, 1889–1903, vol. 1, p. 167.
126 Cf. Brian Simon, *Education and the Labour Movement, 1870–1920* (Lawrence & Wishart, 1965), pp. 133–7, 278–85; John Hurt, *Elementary Schooling and the Working Class, 1860–1918* (Routledge & Kegan Paul, 1979), ch. 5.
127 Margaret McMillan, *The Child and the State* (Socialist Library, 1911).
128 Lord Londonderry's Memo to Cabinet, 10 February 1905; Gilbert, op. cit., p. 96.
129 Simon, op. cit., pp. 283, 285.
130 Gilbert, op. cit., pp. 72, 88.
131 Simon, op. cit., pp. 136–7, 278–85.
132 Evidence of the Royal Colleges of Physicians and Surgeons to the Committee on Physical Deterioration (Chairman: Sir Almeric FitzRoy), *Minutes of Evidence* (Cd. 2210, 1904).
133 B. M. Allen, *Sir Robert Morant* (Macmillan, 1934), pp. 231–4; Simon, op. cit., pp. 286–7.
134 Violet Markham, *Friendship's Harvest* (Max Reinhardt, 1956), pp. 200–1.
135 Gilbert, op. cit., p. 154.
136 Ibid., p. 156.
137 B. Webb, *Our Partnership*, pp. 79–81; Simon, op. cit., chs 6 and 7.
138 Allen, op. cit., pp. 145–81.
139 Hartmut Kaelble, *Social Mobility in the 19th and 20th Centuries: Europe and America in Comparative Perspective* (Berg, 1985), p. 72.
140 Allen, op. cit., pp. 211–12.
141 Ibid., pp. 255–63.
142 Ibid., pp. 268–86; Sir Henry Bunbury (ed.), *Lloyd George's Ambulance Wagon: Being the Memoirs of W. J. Braithwaite, 1911–12* (Methuen, 1957).
143 B. S. Rowntree, *Poverty: A Study of Town Life* (Nelson, [1903]), p. 154.
144 Royal Commission on the Poor Laws and the Relief of Distress (Chairman: Lord George Hamilton), *Report* (Cd. 4499, 1909), vol. 1, pp. 560–5; *Minority Report*, idem, vol. 3, pp. 686–9.
145 Allen, op. cit., pp. 275–82, 288; Gilbert, op. cit., pp. 297–303, 317, 380–3, 401–13; David Cox, 'Seven years of National Health Insurance in England', *Journal of American Medical Association*, vol. 76, 1921.

146 Allen, op. cit., p. 284.
147 Cf. Jose Harris, *William Beveridge: A Biography* (Clarendon Press, 1977), pp. 136-8, and *Unemployment and Politics, 1886-1914* (Clarendon Press, 1972), pp. 75-7, 180-2, 260, 263.
148 W. H. Beveridge, *Unemployment: A Problem of Industry* (Longmans, 1909).
149 W. H. Beveridge, 'The problem of the unemployed', paper read to London School of Economics Sociological Society, April 1906, in Harris, *Beveridge*, p. 119.
150 Ibid., pp. 147, 150-5, 169-73, 178-9, 180-5.
151 Gilbert, op. cit., pp. 61-86.
152 W. H. Beveridge, 'The economics of socialism', paper read to Oxford University Social Sciences Club, February 1906, in Harris, *Beveridge*, pp. 87-8.
153 B. R. Mitchell and P. Deane, *Abstract of British Historical Statistics* (Cambridge University Press, 1962), p. 429.
154 Letter from W. S. Churchill to H. G. Wells, 17 November 1902, in Wells Collection, University of Illinois, Urbana-Champaign.

CHAPTER 5   THE CRISIS OF CLASS SOCIETY

1 Cf. Edward H. Hunt, *British Labour History, 1815-1914* (Weidenfeld & Nicolson, 1981), pp. 329-34; Henry Pelling, 'The labour unrest, 1911-14', in *Popular Politics and Society in Late Victorian Britain* (Macmillan, 1968).
2 George Dangerfield, *The Strange Death of Liberal England* (Constable, 1936).
3 Keith Middlemas, *Politics in Industrial Society: The Experience of the British System since 1911* (Deutsch, 1979), pp. 30, 140-1, 178-9, 209-13.
4 Cf. Claus Offe, 'Political authority and class structures', *International Journal of Sociology*, vol. 2, 1972.
5 A. H. Halsey, *Trends in British Society Since 1900* (Macmillan, 1972), p. 127.
6 Hunt, op. cit., p. 319.
7 Standish Meacham, '"The sense of an impending clash": English working-class unrest before the First World War', *American Historical Review*, vol. 77, 1972; E. H. Phelps Brown, *The Growth of Industrial Relations* (Macmillan, 1959), pp. 330-1. G. A. Phillips, 'The triple industrial alliance of 1914', *Economic History Review*, vol. 24, 1971, disagrees.
8 Dangerfield, op. cit., p. 400.
9 Meacham, loc. cit.
10 David Lloyd George, *War Memoirs* (Odhams, 1938), pp. 1141-2.
11 W. S. Hilton, *Foes to Tyranny: A History of the Amalgamated Union of Building Trade Workers* (AUBTW, 1963), pp. 200-9; Frank Matthews, 'The building guilds', in Asa Briggs and John Saville (eds), *Essays in Labour History* (Macmillan, 1971), vol. 2, pp. 288-90.

12 National Transport Workers' Federation, *Annual General Conference Report, 1914*, p. 32, in Phillips, loc. cit., p. 65.
13 Halsey, op. cit., p. 121-2.
14 Cf. Phelps Brown, op. cit., pp. 332-8; Hunt, op. cit., pp. 329-34.
15 Cf. Joe White, '1910-14 reconsidered', in James E. Cronin and J. Schneer (eds), *Social Conflict and the Political Order in Modern Britain* (Croom Helm, 1982); Richard Price, *Masters, Unions and Men: Work Control in the Building Industry and the Rise of Class* (Cambridge University Press, 1980), esp. chs 5-7; Bob Holton, *British Syndicalism, 1900-1914: Myths and Realities* (Pluto Press, 1976), pp. 20, 198-200.
16 G. R. Askwith, *Industrial Problems and Disputes* (John Murray, 1920), p. 177.
17 White, loc. cit., pp. 80-1, 92; Phelps Brown, op. cit., p. 321.
18 Phelps Brown, op. cit., pp. 322-3; Askwith, op. cit., p. 150.
19 Phelps Brown, op. cit., p. 323.
20 Walter Kendall, *The Revolutionary Movement in Britain, 1900-21: The Origins of British Communism* (Weidenfeld & Nicolson, 1969), chs 1 and 2.
21 Phelps Brown, op. cit., p. xxxiv; Hunt, op. cit., p. 285.
22 H. A. Turner, *Trade Union Growth and Structure: A Comparative Study of the Cotton Unions* (Allen & Unwin, 1962), pp. 357, 374-5; G. D. H. Cole, *Labour in the Coal-Mining Industry 1914-21* (Clarendon Press, 1923), pp. 13-14.
23 Sidney and Beatrice Webb, *Industrial Democracy* (Longmans, 1902), p. 842.
24 Beatrice Webb, *My Apprenticeship* (Longmans, 1926), p. 376.
25 Webb, *Industrial Democracy*, p. 846.
26 Ibid., pp. 843-4.
27 Beatrice Webb, *Diaries, 1912-24* (ed. Margaret Cole; Longmans, 1952), p. 146.
28 Sir Arthur Clay, *Syndicalism and Labour* (John Murray, 1911), pp. vi, 172-3.
29 Independent Labour Party, *Conference Report, 1914*, pp. 114-16, in Briggs and Saville, op. cit., p. 7.
30 Robert Williams, *The New Labour Outlook* (Leonard Parsons, 1921), pp. 139, 192; Phillip S. Bagwell, 'The triple industrial alliance, 1913-22', in Briggs and Saville, op. cit., p. 103.
31 Middlemas, op. cit., pp. 57-60, 66.
32 Phelps Brown, op. cit., pp. 341-2.
33 Middlemas, op. cit., p. 61.
34 Master of Elibank (Liberal Chief Whip) to the King, 18 August 1911, in ibid., p. 61.
35 Phelps Brown, op. cit., p. 328.
36 William Ashley, 'Profit-sharing', *Quarterly Review*, 1913, in Bernard Semmel, *Imperialism and Social Reform, 1895-1914* (Allen & Unwin, 1960), p. 214.
37 William Ashley, *The Economic Organization of England*

(Longmans, 1914; 1949 edn), pp. 190–1.

38 Askwith, op. cit., p. 356 (my emphasis).

39 William Stewart, *J. Keir Hardie* (Independent Labour Party, 1925), pp. 359–60.

40 Christopher Addison, *Four and a Half Years: A Personal Diary, 1914–19* (Hutchinson, 1934), vol. 1, p. 85.

41 Arthur Marwick, *The Deluge: British Society and the First World War* (Bodley Head, 1965), pp. 157–63, 169–79, 248–50.

42 Ibid., pp. 57, 84, 205.

43 War Emergency Workers' National Committee, *The Workers and the War* [August 1914], and Labour Party, *Annual Reports*.

44 Federation of British Industries, *The Elements of Reconstruction* (FBI, 1916), p. 38.

45 *Parliamentary Debates*, 16 November 1916, 5th series, vol. 87, col. 1107.

46 *Official History of the Ministry of Munitions* (HMSO, 1918–22), vol. 1, part 1, pp. 58–9.

47 Marwick, op. cit., p. 252.

48 Ibid., pp. 201–2; Middlemas, op. cit., pp. 113–14; P. K. Cline, 'Eric Geddes and "the experiment" with business men in government, 1915–22', in K. D. Brown (ed.), *Essays in Anti-Labour History* (Macmillan, 1974).

49 Lord Salter, *Memoirs of a Public Servant* (Oxford University Press, 1921; 1960 edn), p. 87.

50 According to the MacDonnell Commission on the Civil Service (4th Report, pp 1914, XVI, p. 44) there were only 450 administrative class civil servants in 1914 out of a total non-industrial staff of 282,420. If they had increased in proportion to the rest there would have been about 600 out of 380,963 in 1920.

51 *Bulletin of Federation of British Industries*, 12 October 1918.

52 *Report of War Cabinet for 1918* (Cmd. 325, 1919), pp. 214–15.

53 Conservatives, alone or in Conservative-dominated coalitions, were in power for fifty of the next seventy years (71 per cent of the time), Labour for only twenty-five years, ten of which were in minority or coalition governments.

54 Stanislaw Andrzejewski, *Military Organization and Society* (Routledge & Kegan Paul, 1954).

55 A. J. P. Taylor, *English History, 1914–45* (Clarendon Press, 1965), p. 120.

56 Richard M. Titmuss, *Essays on 'The Welfare State'* (Allen & Unwin, 1958), p. 86.

57 Philip Abrams, 'The failure of social reform, 1918–20', *Past and Present*, no. 24, April 1963.

58 The standard rate of income tax before the First World War was 1s. 2d. in the £; between the wars it ranged between 4s. and 6s., usually around 4s. 6d. – B. R. Mitchell and P. Deane, *Abstract of British Historical Statistics* (Cambridge University Press, 1962), p. 429.

59 *Parliamentary Debates*, 11 February 1919, 5th series, vol. 112, col. 49–50.

60 Lloyd George to Ben Tillett, 25 August 1914, in J. Schneer, 'The

war, the state and the workplace: British dockers during 1914–18', in Cronin and Schneer, op. cit., p. 101.

61 Royden Harrison, 'The War Emergency Workers' National Committee, 1914–18', in Briggs and Saville, op. cit., p. 219.

62 Keith Middlemas, *The Clydesiders: A Left-Wing Struggle for Parliamentary Power* (Hutchinson, 1965), pp. 73–4; James Hinton, 'The Clyde Workers' Committee and the dilution struggle', in Briggs and Saville, op. cit.; Kendall, op. cit., ch. 7.

63 Hinton, loc. cit., pp. 155–6, 165–6.

64 Ibid., p. 167.

65 *The Worker*, 29 January 1916, in Marwick, op. cit., p. 73.

66 Kendall, op. cit., p. 116.

67 Hinton, loc. cit., pp. 173–8; Kendall, op. cit., pp. 122–5; Marwick, op. cit., pp. 173–6.

68 Hinton, loc. cit., pp. 181–3; Kendall, op. cit., 125–8, 136–8; Christopher Addison, *Politics from Within, 1911–18* (Jenkins, 1924), pp. 191–2.

69 Hinton, loc. cit., p. 163 ('one of the hoariest legends about the CWC is that it led the Rent Strike of the autumn of 1915', based on the false claim of William Gallacher, *Revolt on the Clyde* (Lawrence & Wishart, 1936), pp. 54–5); Joseph Melling, *Rent Strikes: People's Struggle for Housing in West Scotland, 1890–1916* (Polygon Books, 1983), ch. 7.

70 Matthew B. Hammond, *British Labour Conditions and Legislation During the War* (Oxford University Press, 1919), pp. 321–4.

71 Askwith, op. cit., p. 395.

72 Thomas Bell, *Pioneering Days* (Lawrence & Wishart, 1941), pp. 119–28; Kendall, op. cit., ch. 8.

73 Cf. Marwick, op. cit., p. 84; Middlemas, op. cit., p. 87.

74 Kendall, op. cit., pp. 152–6.

75 John T. Murphy, *Preparing for Power: A Critical History of the British Working-Class Movement* (Cape, 1934), pp. 145–6.

76 Kendall, op. cit., pp. 157–9.

77 John T. Murphy, *New Horizons* (John Lane, 1941), p. 61.

78 Murphy, *Preparing for Power*, pp. 152–4; T. Bell, op. cit, pp. 149–51, 302–3; Kendall, op. cit., pp. 164–5.

79 *Solidarity* (organ of London Shop Stewards' Committee), February 1918, in Kendall, op. cit., p. 168.

80 Sir Basil Thomson, *The Scene Changes* (Collins, 1939), p. 410.

81 Manchester District Armaments Committee, December 1918, in Middlemas, *Politics in Industrial Society*, p. 112.

82 FBI, op. cit., pp. 47–8; Engineering Employers' Confederation, *Workshop Committees* (EEF, 1917), in Middlemas, op. cit., pp. 112, 225.

83 War Workers' Emergency National Committee [August 1914]; Harrison, loc. cit., pp. 212–25, 227–8.

84 WWENC, *Why Pay More Rent?* (leaflet, 1915); ibid., pp. 233, 250–1, 253–9.

85 Middlemas, *Politics in Industrial Society*, pp. 123, 134.
86 Master of Elibank to George V, 18 August 1918, in ibid., p. 61.
87 Ibid., p. 82.
88 Industrial Unrest Commission, *Report*, and G. N. Barnes's *Summary* (Cd. 8662, 8663, 1913).
89 Middlemas, op. cit., pp. 137–8, 143–4.
90 *Report of War Cabinet for 1917* (Cd. 9005, 1918), p. xix.
91 Taylor, op. cit., pp. 128–9.
92 A. Gleason, *What the Workers Want: A Study of British Labour* (Allen & Unwin, 1920); Middlemas, op. cit., pp. 118, 128.
93 Halsey, op. cit., p. 123; David E. Butler and Jennie Freeman, *British Political Facts* (Macmillan, 1968), p. 141.
94 *Labour Party Constitution* (1918); *Labour and the New Social Order* (1918).
95 David Lloyd George, final campaign speech, *The Times*, 14 December 1918.
96 Kendall, op. cit., ch. 10.
97 Cf. notes 7, 11, 15, 20 and 30, above.
98 *Bulletin of the FBI*, 12 October 1918, 16 January 1919; Marwick, op. cit., pp. 254, 279.
99 Engineering Employers' Confederation, *Brief*; Middlemas, op. cit., p. 147.
100 Cabinet papers, 2 January 1918, in ibid., p. 119.
101 Hinton, 'Clyde Workers' Committee', loc. cit., Kendall, op. cit., chs 7, 8 and 14.
102 Kendall, op. cit., pp. 244–53.
103 Middlemas, op. cit., p. 132.
104 Ibid., chs 5 and 6.
105 Gallacher, op. cit., pp. 217–42; David Kirkwood, *My Life of Revolt* (Harrap, 1935), pp. 171–4; *Annual Register*, 1919, pp. 9–10.
106 *The Worker*, 28 December 1918, in Kendall, op. cit., p. 364, n. 205.
107 Royal Commission on the Coal industry (Chairman: Sir John Sankey), *Reports I–III* (Cmd. 359–61, 1919); Cole, *Labour in the Coal Mining Industry*, chs 5 and 6; Mowat, op. cit., pp. 30–6.
108 W. S. Churchill, *The Aftermath* (Scribner, 1929), pp. 40–5; S. R. Graubard, 'Military demobilization in Great Britain following the First World War', *Journal of Modern History*, vol. 19, 1947; *Annual Register*, 1919, pp. 5–6, 11.
109 G. D. H. Cole, *History of the Labour Party from 1914* (Routledge & Kegan Paul, 1948), pp. 103–7; G. A. Hutt, *Post-War History of the British Working Class* (Gollancz, 1937), pp. 33–40; Mowat, op. cit., pp. 41–2.
110 Bagwell, loc. cit., pp. 106–8.
111 Ibid., pp. 109–10.
112 J. C. C. Davidson, *Memoirs of a Conservative, 1910–37* (ed. Robert Rhodes James; Weidenfeld & Nicolson, 1969), pp. 178, 228–34.
113 Bagwell, loc. cit., pp. 114, 117.
114 Ibid., pp. 117–25; Mowat, op. cit., pp. 119–24.

115 G. A. Phillips, *The General Strike* (Weidenfeld & Nicolson, 1976), chs 6–11; Alastair Reid and Steven Tolliday, 'The General Strike, 1926', *Historical Journal*, vol. 20, 1977, and works there critically reviewed.

116 Rodney Lowe, 'The erosion of state intervention in Britain, 1917–24', *Economic History Review*, vol. 31, 1978.

117 Middlemas, op. cit., pp. 137–41; Mowat, op. cit., pp. 37–8.

118 Ralf Dahrendorf, *Class and Class Conflict in Industrial Society* (Routledge & Kegan Paul, 1959), p. 306.

119 *Parliamentary Debates*, 13 May 1926, 5th series, vol. 195, col. 1048.

120 Middlemas, op. cit., p. 191; Mowat, op. cit., p. 336; Phillips, *General Strike*, pp. 277–9.

121 W. Milne-Bailey, *The Industrial Parliament Project* (TUC, 1926), p. 8.

122 G. W. MacDonald and H. F. Gospel, 'The Mond-Turner Talks, 1927–32', *Historical Journal*, vol. 16, 1973; Phillips, *General Strike*, pp. 289–93.

CHAPTER 6   A HALFWAY HOUSE: SOCIETY IN WAR AND PEACE

1 Derek H. Aldcroft, *The Inter-War Economy, 1919–39* (Batsford, 1970), p. 246.

2 Ibid., p. 80.

3 Ibid., pp. 20, 26–7, 364.

4 Arthur Marwick, *The Deluge: British Society and the First World War* (Bodley Head, 1965), p. 290.

5 A. J. P. Taylor, *England, 1914–45* (Oxford University Press, 1965), p. 124.

6 Alan T. Peacock and John Wiseman, *The Growth of Public Expenditure in the United Kingdom* (Allen & Unwin, 1967), p. 166.

7 A. H. Imlah, 'British balance of payments and export of capital', *Economic History Review*, vol. 5, 1952.

8 Taylor, op. cit., p. 123.

9 Phyllis Deane and W. A. Cole, *British Economic Growth, 1688–1959* (Cambridge University Press, 1962), p. 37.

10 Sidney Pollard, *The Development of the British Economy, 1914–50* (Arnold, 1962), p. 44.

11 Joel Hurstfield, 'The control of British raw material supplies, 1919–39', *Economic History Review*, vol. 14, 1944, p. 2.

12 Marwick, op. cit., pp. 167–9, 178, 192–3, 250.

13 Royal Commission on Coal Industry, *Report No. 1* (Cmd. 359, 1919), pp. vii–xxiii.

14 J. M. Keynes, *The End of Laissez-Faire* (Hogarth Press, 1926), p. 35.

15 C. L. Mowat, *Britain Between the Wars* (Methuen, 1955), p. 7.

16 R. H. Tawney, 'The abolition of economic controls, 1918–21', *Economic History Review*, vol. 13, 1943; Rodney Lowe, 'The

erosion of state intervention in Britain, 1917-24', *Economic History Review*, vol. 31, 1978.

17 Robert Roberts, *The Classic Slum* (Manchester University Press, 1971), p. 149.

18 Ibid., p. 160.

19 Aldcroft, op. cit., p. 363.

20 Quoted in John Stevenson, *British Society, 1914-45* (Penguin, 1984), p. 82.

21 A. L. Bowley and Margaret Hogg, *Has Poverty Diminished?* (King, 1925), p. 20.

22 Hubert Llewellyn Smith, *The New Survey of London Life and Labour* (London School of Economics, 1930-35); B. S. Rowntree, *Poverty and Progress: A Second Social Survey of York* (Longmans, 1941); H. Tout, *The Standard of Living in Bristol* (Bristol University Press, 1938).

23 A. L. Bowley and J. Stamp, *The National Income, 1924* (Oxford University Press, 1927), p. 50.

24 Stevenson, op. cit., p. 92.

25 Philip Abrams, 'The failure of social reform, 1918-20', *Past and Present*, no. 24, 1963, p. 61.

26 Ray Strachey, *The Cause: A Short History of the Women's Movement in Britain* (Bell, 1928), pp. 337-43.

27 Abrams, loc. cit., p. 60.

28 R. Roberts, op. cit., pp. 161-2.

29 Marwick, op. cit., pp. 91-2.

30 *New Statesman*, 23 June 1917; Marwick, op. cit., p. 94.

31 Anthony J. Coles, 'The moral economy of the crowd: some 20th century food riots' (unpublished paper, University of Lancaster, 1974); Joseph Melling, *Rent Strikes: The People's Struggle for Housing in West Scotland, 1890-1916* (Polygon Books, 1983).

32 A. M. Carr-Saunders and D. C. Jones, *A Survey of Social Conditions in England and Wales* (Clarendon Press, 1958), p. 25; the average number of children of (presumably skilled or semi-skilled) manual workers went down from 4 to 2.7, of agricultural workers from 3.9 to 2.7, and of labourers from 4.5 to 3.4, representing a rise in living standards (counting two parents per family) of 22, 20 and 20 per cent respectively.

33 Ibid., p. 25.

34 Royal Commission on Population, *Report* (Cmd. 7695, 1949); Richard A. Soloway, *Birth Control and the Population Problem in England 1877-1930* (University of North Carolina Press, 1982), p. 212.

35 Diana Gittins, 'Women's work and family size between the wars', *Oral History*, vol. 5, 1977, and *Fair Sex: Family Size and Structure, 1900-39* (Hutchinson, 1982), esp. ch. 6.

36 Doris M. Stenton, *The English Woman in History* (Allen & Unwin, 1957), ch. 1.

37 Marwick, op. cit., p. 107; A. H. Halsey, *Trends in British Society Since 1900* (Macmillan, 1972), p. 51.

38 Strachey, op. cit., p. 392.
39 *Parliamentary Debates*, 13 March 1918, 5th series, vol. 97, cols 795-6; Marwick, op. cit., p. 244.
40 Stevenson, op. cit., p. 65.
41 *Parliamentary Debates*, 26 February 1919, 5th series, vol. 112, col. 1829-30.
42 Marwick, op. cit., p. 244.
43 B. A. Waites, 'The effect of the First World War on class and status in England, 1910-20', *Journal of Contemporary History*, vol. 11, 1976, p. 30.
44 Ibid., p. 30.
45 Alan D.Gilbert, *The Making of Post-Christian Britain* (Longmans, 1980), pp. 76-7.
46 Rowntree, op. cit., pp. 417-20.
47 E. T[ownshend]., ed., *Keeling's Letters and Reminiscences* (Allen & Unwin, 1918), p. 238; Marwick, op. cit., p. 218.
48 Gilbert, op. cit., p. 77.
49 Robert Currie, Alan D. Gilbert and Lee Horsley, *Churches and Churchgoers: Patterns of Church Growth in the British Isles Since 1700* (Clarendon Press, 1977), p. 1.
50 Halsey, op. cit., p. 528; F. H. McClintock and N. H. Avison, *Crime in England and Wales* (Heinemann, 1968), p. 23.
51 Peter H. Lindert and Jeffrey Williamson, 'Revising England's social tables, 1688-1867', Dept of Economics, Working Paper Series no. 176, University of California, Davis, 1981 (kindly supplied by the authors), pp. 33-4.
52 Lee Soltow, 'Long-run changes in British economic inequality', *Economic History Review*, vol. 21, 1968.
53 Peter H. Lindert, forthcoming book on the distribution of private wealth in England since 1760, quoted in W. D. Rubinstein, *Wealth and Inequality in Britain* (Faber, 1986), p. 95.
54 Royal Commission on Distribution of Income and Wealth (Chairman: Lord Diamond), *Report No. 1* (Cmnd. 6171, 1975), p. 97.
55 Ibid., p. 92.
56 A. B. Atkinson, *Wealth, Income and Inequality* (Penguin, 1973), p. 23.
57 George Polanyi and John B. Wood, *How Much Inequality?* (Institute of Economic Affairs, 1974), pp. 76-7.
58 Rubinstein, *Wealth and Inequality*, pp. 145-6.
59 Bowley and Stamp, op. cit., p. 160.
60 Peacock and Wiseman, op. cit., pp. 82, 86, 92.
61 John Hilton, *Rich Man, Poor Man* (Allen & Unwin, 1944), pp. 39-41.
62 Sidney Pollard and D. W. Crossley, *The Wealth of Britain* (Batsford, 1968), p. 263.
63 T. H. Marshall, *Citizenship and Social Class* (Cambridge University Press, 1950), reprinted in *Class, Citizenship and Social Development* (ed. S. M. Lipset; Doubleday, 1964), p. 116.
64 Hartmut Kaelble, *Social Mobility in the 19th and 20th Centuries: Europe and America in Comparative Perspective* (Berg, 1985), pp. 72, 76.

65 David V. Glass (ed.), *Social Mobility in Britain* (Routledge & Kegan Paul, 1954); A. H. Halsey *et al.*, *Origins and Destinations: Family, Class and Education in Modern Britain* (Clarendon Press, 1980); John H. Goldthorpe *et al.*, *Social Mobility and Class Structure in Modern Britain* (Clarendon Press, 1980).

66 Glass, op. cit., pp. 98, 106, 107.

67 Ibid., pp. 114, 120-1.

68 Ibid., pp. 114, 120-1, 122-3.

69 R. K. Kelsall, in ibid., p. 317.

70 Ibid., pp. 183, 186-7.

71 Harold Perkin, *Economic Worth of Elites* (SSRC report, 1977), tables 3.1-6, 5.1-6, 7.1-6, 7.2.1-6, 7.8.1-6.

72 F. M. L. Thompson, *English Landed Society in the 19th Century* (Routledge & Kegan Paul, 1963), pp. 329-32; *The Times*, 19 May 1920; C. F. G. Masterman, *England After the War* (Hodder & Stoughton, 1922), p. 32; W. L. Guttsman, *The English Ruling Class* (Weidenfeld & Nicolson, 1969), pp. 121-6.

73 F. M. L. Thompson, op. cit., pp. 333, 337.

74 6th Duke of Portland, *Men, Women and Things* (Faber, 1937), pp. 1-3.

75 F. M. L. Thompson, op. cit., p. 342.

76 Scott Committee on Land Utilisation in Rural Areas, *Report* (HMSO, Ministry of Works, 1942).

77 David Cannadine, *Lords and Landlords: The Aristocracy and the Towns, 1774-1967* (Leicester University Press, 1980), pp. 420-2.

78 Perkin, *Economic Worth of Elites*, tables 5.7-15, 10.7-15; W. D. Rubinstein, *Men of Property: The Very Wealthy in Britain Since the Industrial Revolution* (Croom Helm, 1981), pp. 60, 62-3, 228.

79 W. L. Guttsman, *The British Political Elite* (MacGibbon & Kee, 1963), pp. 95, 77n.

80 Ibid., pp. 105, 107.

81 Charles H. Wilson, *History of Unilever* (Cassell, 1968), vol. 1, p. 297; P. W. S. Andrews and Elizabeth Brunner, *Life of Lord Nuffield* (Blackwell, 1953), pp. 182-3; W. J. Reader, *Imperial Chemical Industries: A History* (Oxford University Press, 1975), vol. 2, p. 133.

82 Rubinstein, *Men of Property*, p. 185; Leslie Hannah, *The Rise of the Corporate Economy* (Methuen, 1976), p. 121.

83 W. D. Rubinstein, 'Wealth, elites and the class structure of modern Britain', *Past and Present*, no. 76, 1977 and *Men of Property*.

84 Deane and Cole, op. cit., pp. 142, 147.

85 Contrast Peter Mathias, *The Brewing Industry in England, 1700-1830* (Cambridge University Press, 1959).

86 Recalculated from Rubinstein, *Men of Property*, tables 3.3 and 3.6.

87 T. H. J. Bishop and R. Wilkinson, *Winchester and the Public School Elite* (Faber, 1967), pp. 98-101.

88 W. D. Rubinstein, 'Education and the social origins of British elites, 1880-1970', *Past and Present*, no. 112, 1986, pp. 168-9.

89 Cf. Perkin, *Economic Worth of Elites*, (SSRC report, 1977), 'The recruitment of elites in British society since 1880', *Journal of Social*

History, vol. 12, 1978, and *Essays in English Social History* (Harvester and Barnes & Noble, 1981), ch. 9; and Rubinstein, 'Wealth, elites and class structure', loc. cit., *Men of Property*, 'The end of "Old Corruption" in Britain, 1760-1850', *Past and Present*, no. 101, 1983, *Wealth and Inequality*, and 'Education and social origins', loc. cit. See also Hartmut Kaelble, *Historical Research on Social Mobility* (Columbia University Press, 1981) and *Social Mobility in the 19th and 20th Centuries* (Berg, 1985) where the British data were privately supplied by Perkin from the 1977 SSRC report.

90 Rubinstein, 'Education and social origins', loc. cit., pp. 175-7.

91 Harold E. Dale, *The Higher Civil Service of Great Britain* (Oxford University Press, 1944), p. 69; Rubinstein, 'Education and social origins', loc. cit., p. 185.

92 Ibid., p. 182.

93 Contrary to popular opinion that death duties are easily and frequently avoided and therefore tend to reduce the wealth measured by the probate returns, the amounts left by the really rich elites (landowners and millionaires) have not declined as much as expected if large-scale evasion were in operation; and the probate returns of most members of the other elites were not sufficiently large to attract high enough rates to be worth evading; cf. Perkin, *Economic Worth of Elites*, esp. tables 4.10.15, 10.10.15.

94 William Watson, 'Spiralism', in Max Gluckman (ed.), *Closed Systems and Open Minds* (Oliver & Boyd, 1962); cf. A. H. Birch, *Small Town Politics* (Oxford University Press, 1959), esp. ch. 2, 'The development of modern Glossop'.

95 J. B. Priestley, *English Journey* (Heinemann, 1934), pp. 300-1.

96 Royal Commission on Distribution of Income and Wealth (Chairman: Lord Diamond), *Report No. 7* (Cmnd. 7595, 1979), p. 150; Marian Bowley, *Housing and the State* (Allen & Unwin, 1945), p. 271.

97 Goldthorpe *et al.*, op. cit., pp. 60, 251: the reference is to the 1940s-70s, but the same principle applies to earlier decades.

98 Goldthorpe *et al.*, op. cit., p. 60, table 2.3; Guy Routh, *Occupation and Pay in Great Britain, 1906-60* (Cambridge University Press, 1965), p. 4.

99 Aldcroft, op. cit., pp. 352, 357; Routh, op. cit., pp. 4, 64-5, 70-1, 78, 104, 107.

100 Ibid., pp. 65, 70.

101 Ibid., pp. 147-54; cf. Elliott Jacques, 'An objective approach to pay differentials', *New Scientist*, 3 July 1958; Michael Fogarty, *The Just Wage* (Geoffrey Chapman, 1961), pp. 11-20.

102 Goldthorpe *et al.*, op. cit., p. 60; Routh, op. cit., p. 5.

103 Industrial Society, *Status and Benefits in Industry* (IS 1966), p. v.

104 Alan Fox, *Beyond Contract: Work, Power and Trust Relations* (Faber & Faber, 1974).

105 F. D. Klingender, *The Condition of Clerical Labour in Britain*

(Martin Lawrence, 1935), p. 61.

106 Clive Jenkins and Barrie Sherman, *White-Collar Unionism: The Rebellious Salariat* (Routledge & Kegan Paul, 1979), p. 29.

107 George Tomlinson, *Coal Miner* (Hutchinson, 1937), p. 10; George Orwell, *The Road to Wigan Pier* (Gollancz, 1937); Arthur Marwick, *Class: Image and Reality in Britain, France and the USA Since 1930* (Fontana, 1981), pp. 91–2.

108 Richard Hoggart, *The Uses of Literacy* (Penguin, 1958), pp. 72–3.

109 Tomlinson, op. cit., Marwick, *Class*, p. 85.

110 H. L. Beales and R. S. Lambert, *Memoirs of the Unemployed* (Gollancz, 1934); Marwick, *Class*, p. 81.

111 Aldcroft, op. cit., p. 80.

112 David Lockwood, 'The new working class in Europe', *European Journal of Sociology*, vol. 1, 1960.

113 C. Chisholm (ed.), *Marketing Survey of the UK* (Business Publications, 1937); James E. Cronin, *Labour and Society in Britain, 1918–79* (Batsford, 1984), p. 89.

114 Aldcroft, op. cit., pp. 359, 364.

115 Assuming 3.7 persons per household; Aldcroft, op. cit., p. 371.

116 Ibid., pp. 357, 372–3; Pollard and Crossley, op. cit., p. 263.

117 Aldcroft, op. cit., p. 367; the Ministry of Labour's family budget inquiries suggested a 60–70 per cent increase in average real income in cash and kind, 1913–38.

118 Bowley and Hogg, op. cit., pp. 16–17.

119 Llewellyn Smith, op. cit.; Tout, op. cit.; Rowntree, *Poverty and Progress*.

120 B. S. Rowntree, *The Human Needs of Labour* (Longmans, 1937), and *Poverty and Progress*, pp. 456–7.

121 Brian Abel Smith and Peter Townsend, *The Poor and the Poorest* (Bell, 1965); Peter Townsend, *Poverty in the United Kingdom* (Penguin, 1979).

122 Sir John Boyd Orr, *Food, Health and Income* (Macmillan, 1936), and Sir John Boyd Orr and David Lubbock, *Feeding the People in Wartime* (Macmillan, 1940), p. 1.

123 Ministry of Health, *Report on Overcrowding in England and Wales* (HMSO, 1936); Political & Economic Planning, *British Health Services* (PEP, 1937), pp. 35–6.

124 G. C. M. M'Gonigle and J. Kirby, *Poverty and Public Health* (Gollancz, 1937).

125 Mary Spring Rice, *Working Class Wives* (Penguin, 1939), pp. 28, 37–40, 155, 188.

126 Richard M. Titmuss, *Birth, Poverty and Wealth* (Hamilton, 1943), p. 31.

127 Halsey, op. cit., p. 339.

128 Stevenson, op. cit., p. 204.

129 Compare, for example, two photographs of boys at the same school in East London in 1894 and 1924 in E. H. Phelps Brown, *The Growth of British Industrial Relations* (Macmillan, 1959), facing p. 42.

130 Rowntree, *Poverty and Progress*, p. 363–4.
131 Stevenson, op. cit., p. 383.
132 Mass Observation, *The Pub and the People* (MO, 1943), p. 334.
133 Richard Stone and D. A. Rowe, *The Measurement of Consumers' Expenditure and Behaviour in the United Kingdom, 1920–38* (Cambridge University Press, 1966), pp. 80–1, 91; James Walvin, *The People's Game* (Allen Lane, 1975), p. 119.
134 Halsey, op. cit., pp. 120, 564–5; Harold Perkin, *The Age of the Automobile* (Quartet, 1976), pp. 136–7.
135 J. A. R. Pimlott, *The Englishman's Holiday* (Faber, 1947; Harvester, 1976), pp. 214–22.
136 Halsey, op. cit., p. 299; Stone and Rowe, op. cit., pp. 17, 21, 25.
137 Hoggart, op. cit.; Michael Young and Peter Willmott, *Family and Kinship in East London* (Penguin, 1957).
138 Cronin, op. cit., p. 71.
139 Rice, op. cit., p. 17.
140 Terence Young, *Becontree and Dagenham* (Becontree Social Survey Committee, 1934).
141 Ruth Durant, *Watling: A Survey of Social Life on a New Housing Estate* (King, 1939), p. 253.
142 Mass Observation, *People's Homes* (MO, 1943).

CHAPTER 7   TOWARDS A CORPORATE SOCIETY

1 Ray Pahl and John Winkler, 'The coming corporatism', *New Society*, 9 October 1974; Colin Crouch, *The Politics of Industrial Relations* (Penguin, 1979), pp. 188–96. Cf. also Benito Mussolini, *Speeches on the Corporate State* (Vallecchi, 1936).
2 Philippe Schmitter, 'Still the century of corporatism?', *Review of Politics*, vol. 36, 1974, reprinted in P. Schmitter and G. Lembroke (eds), *Trends Towards Corporatist Intermediation* (Sage, 1979).
3 Colin Crouch, 'Research on corporatism in Britain: an interim report', Discussion Paper at the Conference on Organizational Participation and Public Policy, Princeton University, September 1981.
4 Pahl and Winkler, loc. cit.
5 Keith Middlemas, *Politics in Industrial Society: The British Experience Since 1911* (Deutsch, 1979), ch. 13.
6 Cf. Harold Perkin, *The Origins of Modern English Society, 1780–1880* (Routledge & Kegan Paul, 1969), p. 29.
7 Evan Davis and Andrew Dilnot, *The Institute of Fiscal Studies Tax and Benefit Mode* (IFS Working Paper no. 58, 1985), reported in the *Guardian*, 18 July 1985: between fiscal years 1978/9 and 1985/6 personal taxation, including both direct and indirect taxes, increased such that only the richest 6 per cent of taxpayers paid less while the lowest 87 per cent suffered an up to 5 per cent loss of real income.
8 Cf. Perkin, *Origins of Modern English Society*, pp. 107–24.

9 Karl Marx and Friedrich Engels, *The Manifesto of the Communist Party* (1848; reprinted in *Marx and Engels: Collected Works*, Lawrence & Wishart, 1975–), vol. 6, p. 489.
10 Alfred Marshall, *Industry and Trade: A Study of Industrial Technique and Business Organization* (Macmillan, 1920), pp. 315–16; he added: 'except in so far as it was closed by tarif [sic] barriers'. So far 'no firm ever had a sufficiently long life of unabated energy and power of initiative for the purpose,' but 'a large joint stock company has special advantages, which do not materially dwindle with age.'
11 Leslie Hannah, *The Rise of the Corporate Economy* (Methuen, 1976), p. 13.
12 Ibid., table A2, p. 216.
13 Ibid., tables 8.1, 8.2 and A5, pp. 118–21 and 225.
14 Leslie Hannah and J. A. Kay, *Concentration in British Industry* (Macmillan, 1977), pp. 85, 96 and table 6.2, pp. 89–91.
15 *Observer*, 20 July 1985.
16 S. J. Prais, *The Evolution of Giant Firms: A Study of the Growth of Concentration in Manufacturing Industry in Britain, 1909–70* (Cambridge University Press, 1976), pp. 10, 13.
17 Derek F. Channon, 'Corporate evolution in the service industries', in Leslie Hannah (ed.), *Management Strategy and Business Development* (Macmillan, 1976).
18 Charles Wilson, *The History of Unilever* (Cassell, 1954), vol. 1, pp. 73–88; W. J. Reader, *Imperial Chemical Industries: A History* (Oxford University Press, 1970), vol. 1, ch. 19 and cartoon facing p. 449.
19 Reader, op. cit., vol. 1, esp. pp. 208–11 and ch. 19.
20 Liberal Industrial Inquiry, *Britain's Industrial Future* (Liberal Party, 1928), p. 100; Adolf A. Berle, Jr and Gardner C. Means, *The Modern Corporation and Private Property* (Macmillan, 1932), p. 4; A. A. Berle, Jr, *The 20th Century Capitalist Revolution* (Harcourt, Brace, 1954), p. 39.
21 Royal Commission on the Distribution of Income and Wealth (Chairman: Lord Diamond), *Report No. 1* (Cmnd. 6171, 1975), p. 97; Balfour Committee on Industry and Trade, *Factors in Industrial and Commercial Efficiency* (HMSO, 1927), p. 128.
22 Graham Bannock, *The Juggernauts* (Penguin, 1973), p. 5.
23 *The Sunday Times*, 10 January 1982.
24 Arthur Marwick, *The Deluge: British Society and the First World War* (Bodley Head, 1965), pp. 192–93, 201; W. J. Reader, *Architect of Air Power: The Life of Viscount Weir* (Collins, 1968), ch. 2.
25 John Maynard Keynes, *The Economic Consequences of the Peace* (Macmillan, 1919), and *Collected Writings* (Macmillan, 1971), vol. 2, p. 150.
26 Hannah, *Corporate Economy*, p. 33.
27 Ibid., p. 36.
28 Lyndall Urwick, 'The pure theory of organization with special refer-

ence to business enterprise' (British Association typescript, 1930), p. 10, quoted in John Child, *British Management Thought* (Allen & Unwin, 1969).

29 *The Economist*, 9 February 1924, quoted in Hannah, *Corporate Economy*, p. 45.

30 Arthur E. Cutforth, *Methods of Amalgamation and the Valuation of Businesses for Amalgamation and Other Purposes* (Bell, 1926), p. 17.

31 P. Sargant Florence, 'Problems of Rationalization', *Economic Journal*, vol. 40, 1930, p. 365.

32 Derek F. Channon, *The Strategy and Structure of British Enterprise* (Macmillan, 1973), ch. 9.

33 Ibid., p. 239.

34 Ibid., pp. 64, 67.

35 John H. Dunning, *The Role of American Investment in the British Economy* (Political & Economic Planning, 1969), pp. 135-6.

36 Robert Heller, 'Britain's top directors' and 'Britain's boardroom anatomy', *Management Today*, March 1967, pp. 62-5, and September 1970, pp. 82-5.

37 Martin J. Wiener, *English Culture and the Decline of the Industrial Spirit, 1850-1980* (Cambridge University Press, 1981).

38 Harold Perkin, *The Economic Worth of Elites in British Society, 1880-1970*, Report to the Social Science Research Council, 1977 (deposited in the British Library Lending Division, Boston Spa), tables 5.13, 5.14, 7.13, 7.14.

39 Child, op. cit., p. 40.

40 Edward Cadbury, *Experiment in Industrial Organization* (Longmans, 1912), p. xvii.

41 John Lee, *Management: A Study of Industrial Organization* (Pitman, 1921), in Child, op. cit., pp. 59-63.

42 John Lee, *The Social Implications of Christianity* (Student Christian Movement, 1922), pp. 114-15.

43 Child, op. cit., pp. 72-3, 80-3.

44 Ibid., pp. 88-97.

45 Note also the many other management professional bodies emerging at this time: the Sales Managers' Association, the Office Managers' Association, the Institute of Cost Accountants, etc.; cf. Geoffrey Millerson, *The Qualifying Professions* (Routledge & Kegan Paul, 1964), pp. 246-54.

46 Child, op. cit., pp. 113-14.

47 Tom Lupton, *Management and the Social Sciences* (Penguin, 1972), p. 9.

48 C. A. R. Crosland, 'The transition to socialism', in R. H. S. Crossman (ed.), *New Fabian Essays* (Turnstile Press, 1953), p. 42; Labour Party, *Industry and Society* (Labour Party, 1957), p. 16.

49 Quoted by David Lockwood, *The Black Coated Worker* (Allen & Unwin, 1958), p. 40.

50 Alice Russell, 'The quest for security: the changing working

conditions and status of the British working class in the twentieth century' (unpublished PhD thesis, University of Lancaster, 1982) – to which much of this section is indebted – p. 52. For holidays with pay generally, see ch. 2; also J. A. R. Pimlott, *The Englishman's Holiday* (Faber, 1947; Harvester, 1976), chs 8 and 13; Departmental Committee on Holidays with Pay (Chairman: Lord Amulree), *Report* (Cmd. 5724, 1938) and G. C. Cameron, 'The growth of holidays with pay in Britain', in Graham L. Reid and Donald J. Robertson (eds), *Fringe Benefits, Labour Costs and Social Security* (Allen & Unwin, 1965).

51 Russell, op. cit., pp. 71, 84, 96; Pimlott, op. cit., p. 221.

52 *Social Trends*, 1986, p. 71.

53 Russell, op. cit., pp. 155, 184, 210-11, 235. For occupational pensions generally, see ch. 3, and Committee of Inquiry into the Economic and Financial Problems of the Provision for Old Age (Chairman: Sir Thomas Phillips), *Report* (Cmd. 9333, 1954); A Group of Trade Unionists, *Plan for Industrial Pensions* (Fabian Society, 1956); Government Actuary, *Occupational Pension Schemes: A Survey* (HMSO, 1958) and his Second to Fifth Surveys (HMSO, 1966, 1968, 1972 and 1975); Jack Wiseman, 'Occupational pension schemes', in Reid and Robertson, op. cit.; British Institute of Management, *Pensions Today: A Survey of Current Practice* (BIM, 1972); The Industrial Society, *Employee Involvement in Occupational Pension Schemes: Survey and Report* (Industrial Society, 1975); K. Kekelm, A. E. G. Round and T. G. Arthur, *Hoskings' Pension Schemes and Retirement Benefits* (Sweet & Maxwell, 4th edn, 1977); and H. Lucas, *Pensions and Industrial Relations: A Practical Guide* (Pergamon, 1977).

54 Cf. *inter alia* Trades Union Congress, *Conference Report, 1975* and *Occupational Pension Schemes: A TUC Guide* (TUC, 1971).

55 Stanley D. Chapman, *The Early Factory Masters* (David & Charles, 1967), p. 161; Eric Roll, *An Early Experiment in Industrial Organization: Boulton and Watt, 1775-1805* (Longmans, 1930), p. 225; *Parliamentary Debates*, 28 May 1816. For sick pay schemes generally, see Russell, op. cit., ch. 4; The Industrial Welfare Society, *Works Sickness and Benevolent Schemes* (IWS, 1934), *Employee Benefit Schemes* (IWS, 1949), and *Sick Pay Schemes and Benevolent Schemes Among Hourly Paid Employees* (IWS, 1957); Institute of Personnel Management, *Company Sick Pay Schemes* (IPM, 1959) and *Sick Pay Schemes* (IPM, 1971); Ministry of Labour, *Sick Pay Schemes* (HMSO, 1964).

56 Ministry of Labour, *Sick Pay Schemes*, p. 7; Russell, op. cit., pp. 305, 319.

57 Russell, op. cit., pp. 355-73; Geoffrey Goodman, *Redundancy in the Affluent Society* (Fabian Society, 1962), pp. 15-20. For security of earnings and employment generally, see Russell, op. cit., ch. 5; Goodman, op. cit.; Acton Society Trust, *Redundancy: A Survey of Problems and Practice* (AST, 1958); Ministry of Labour, *Security*

and Change (HMSO, 1961); Donald J. Robertson, 'Redundancy in Great Britain', in Reid and Robertson, op. cit.; Cyril Grunfield, *The Law of Redundancy* (Sweet & Maxwell, 1971); S. R. Parker, *et al.*, *Effects of the Redundancy Payments Act* (HMSO, 1971); Department of Employment, *Code of Industrial Practice* (HMSO, 1972); S. Mukherjee, *Through No Fault of Their Own: Systems for Handling Redundancy in Britain, France and Germany* (Macdonald, 1973); The Industrial Society, *Security of Earnings and Employment* (IS, 1973); J. Henderson, *Guide to the Employment Protection Act, 1975* (IS, 1975); J. Jackson, *Employment Protection: The New Law* (Brehon, 1976); H. A. Clegg, *The Changing System of Industrial Relations in Great Britain* (Blackwell, 1979), pp. 488–90.

58 Roy A. Church, *Kenricks in Hardware* (David & Charles, 1969), pp. 291–2; *Ministry of Labour Gazette*, 1931, p. 9; Russell, op. cit., pp. 355–6.

59 *Ministry of Labour Gazette*, 1963, pp. 50–5, quoted in Russell, op. cit., pp. 385–6.

60 Parker *et al.*, op. cit., p. 3.

61 Cf. British Institute of Management, *Towards Single Status* (BIM, 1975). For single status, i.e. equal treatment for manual and non-manual workers alike, see Russell, op. cit., ch. 6; Industrial Society, *Status and Benefits in Industry* (IS, 1966) and *Status Differences and Moves Towards Single Status* (IS, 1970); T. Robinson, *Staff Status for Manual Workers* (Kogan Page, 1972); British Institute of Management, *Employee Benefits Today* (BIM, 1974) and *Employee Benefits* (BIM, 1978).

62 Cf. Clive Jenkins and Barry Sherman, *White-Collar Unionism: The Rebellious Salariat* (Routledge & Kegal Paul, 1979), pp. 84, 88; J. Bugler, 'The shopfloor struggle for status', *New Society*, 25 November 1965.

63 Industrial Society, *Status and Benefits*; BIM, opera cit., 1974 and 1978.

64 Russell, op. cit., p. 490.

65 *Code of Industrial Practice* (HMSO, 1972).

66 Industrial Society, *Status and Benefits*, p. 30; Alan Fox, *Beyond Contract: Work, Power and Trust Relations* (Faber & Faber, 1974).

67 Reid and Robertson, op. cit., p. 30.

68 Robinson, op. cit., pp. 84–5.

69 Hannah and Kay, op. cit., p. 112; Sir Alec Cairncross, 'The postwar years', in Roderick Floud and Donald McCloskey (eds), *The Economic History of Britain Since 1700* (Cambridge University Press, 1981), vol. 2, p. 409.

70 *Economic Trends Supplement*, no. 12, 1987, p. 201; Hannah and Kay, op. cit., p. 112. In 1985 the public sector still employed 27 per cent – *Social Trends*, 1987, p. 73.

71 David Butler and Anne Sloman, *British Political Facts, 1900–79* (Macmillan, 1980), pp. 348–9.

72 *Guardian*, 18 July 1985.

73 Sir Leo G. Chiozza Money, *Riches and Poverty* (Methuen, 1906),

pp. 41–3; *Social Trends*, 1984, p. 78.
74 Samuel H. Beer, *Modern British Politics: A Study of Parties and Pressure Groups* (Faber & Faber, 1965), p. 337.
75 Richard M. Titmuss, *The Irresponsible Society* (Fabian Society, 1960), p. 20.
76 Middlemas, op. cit., pp. 207–9.
77 Walter M. Citrine, *Men and Work: An Autobiography* (Hutchinson, 1964), p. 250.
78 L. P. Carpenter, 'Corporatism in Britain, 1930–45', *Journal of Contemporary History*, vol. 11, 1976, pp. 3–8. See also Sir Basil Blackett, 'The era of planning', in G. R. Stirling Taylor (ed.), *Great Events in History* (Cassell, 1934); Sir Arthur Salter, *The Framework of an Ordered Society* (Cambridge University Press, 1933); Leo S. Amery, *The Framework of the Future* (Oxford University Press, 1944); Hugh Sellon, *Democracy and Dictatorship* (Lovat Dickson, 1934); Lord Eustace Percy, *Government in Transition* (Methuen, 1934); Roy G. Glenday, *The Economic Consequences of Progress* (George Routledge, 1934) and *The Future of Economic Society* (Macmillan, 1944).
79 Carpenter, loc. cit., p. 13.
80 Robert Boothby, Harold Macmillan, Oliver Stanley and John Loder, *Industry and the State* (Macmillan, 1927); 'A National Plan for Great Britain', *Weekend Review*; 14 February 1931; Harold Macmillan, *Reconstruction* (Macmillan, 1933), *The Next Five Years* (Macmillan, 1935) and *The Middle Way: A Study of the Problem of Economic and Social Progress in a Free and Democratic Society* (Macmillan, 1938).
81 Macmillan, *The Next Five Years*; G. D. H. Cole, *Guild Socialism: A Plan for Economic Democracy* (Fabian Society, 1920); Carpenter, op. cit., p. 12.
82 Trades Union Congress, 'The public control and regulation of industry and trade', *Conference Report* (TUC, 1932); Carpenter, loc. cit., pp. 16–19.
83 Sir Robert Hacking to Colin Brooks, Colin Brooks's Diary, quoted in Middlemas, op. cit., p. 258.
84 TUC, *Special Conference Report* (TUC, 1940), p. 18.
85 Middlemas, op. cit., pp. 276–7.
86 H. M. D. Parker, *Manpower; A Study of Wartime Policy and Administration* (HMSO, 1954), pp. 95–6.
87 Middlemas, op. cit., pp. 278–89.
88 Henry M. Pelling, *A History of British Trade Unionism* (Macmillan, 1976 edn), p. 219; Middlemas, op. cit., p. 286.
89 Middlemas, op. cit., p. 296.
90 Butler and Sloman, op. cit., pp. 208–10.
91 Ibid., pp. 42, 82.
92 W. L. Guttsman, *The British Political Elite* (MacGibbon & Kee, 1963), pp. 237–9; P. G. J. Pulzer, *Political Representation and Elections in Britain* (Allen & Unwin, 1967), pp. 67–72; David

Coombes, *Representative Government and Economic Power* (Heinemann, 1982), pp. 46-7.

93 Walter Milne-Bailey, *The Industrial Parliament Project* (TUC Research Department, December 1926), and *Trade Union Documents* (Bell, 1929), pp. 24-5; Middlemas, op. cit., pp. 176, 178.

94 For lists of Reports of Royal Commissions and Departmental Committees, most of which entailed taking evidence from 'corporatist' representatives, see Butler and Sloman, op. cit., pp. 268-71 and 274-6.

95 Beer, op. cit., pp. 337-8.

96 Andrew Shonfield, *Modern Capitalism: The Changing Balance of Public and Private Power* (Oxford University Press, 1965), pp. 153, 161; Middlemas, op. cit., p. 20.

97 See, *inter alia*, Reports of the Council on Pay, Productivity, and Incomes (Chairman: Lords Cohen and Heyworth), 1957-61; the National Incomes Commission (Chairman: Sir G. Lawrence), 1961-64; the Prices and Incomes Board (Chairman: Aubrey Jones), 1965-70; the Pay Board (Chairman: Sir F. Figgures), 1973-74; the Commission on Pay Comparability (Chairman: Hugh A. Clegg), 1979.

98 Ralf Dahrendorf, *Class and Class Conflict in Industrial Society* (Routledge & Kegan Paul, 1959), p. 306.

99 *Annual Register*, 1974 (Longmans, 1975), pp. 21, 41-2.

100 Pelling, op. cit., chs 13 and 14.

101 Cf. A. L. Beier, *The Death of the Body Politic: English Society 1640-1760* (Routledge, forthcoming).

102 Adam Smith, *The Wealth of Nations* (1776; University of Chicago Press, 1976), vol. 1, p. 487.

103 T. H. Marshall, *Citizenship and Social Class* (Cambridge University Press, 1950), pp. 10-21.

104 Ibid., p. 34.

105 Sir Henry Maine, *Ancient Law* (Murray, 1874), p. 170.

106 T. H. Marshall, op. cit., p. 32.

107 Ibid., p. 81.

108 Ibid., pp. 83-4; Lionel Robbins, *The Economic Problem in Peace and War* (Macmillan, 1947), pp. 9, 16.

109 For 'National Efficiency', Liberal imperialism and the Fabians, see ch. 4 above.

110 R. C. Birch, *The Shaping of the Welfare State* (Longmans, 1984), p. 3.

111 Ross Terrill, *R. H. Tawney and his Times* (Deutsch, 1973), ch. 1.

112 R. H. Tawney, *Equality* (Allen & Unwin, 1931; 1938 ed), pp. 108-15.

113 Ibid., pp. 115-16, 144, 150, 127, 164-9, 176-7, 180-1.

114 Ibid., pp. 222-46.

115 R. H. Tawney, *The Acquisitive Society* (Harcourt, Brace & Howe, 1920), p. 180.

116 Cf. Norman and Jeanne MacKenzie, *The First Fabians* (Weidenfeld & Nicolson, 1977), pp. 117-18, 375-6; B. S. Rowntree and A. C. Pigou, *Lectures on Housing* (Manchester University Press, 1914), p. 36.

117 N. and J. MacKenzie, op. cit., *passim*; W. H. Beveridge, *Insurance*

for All and Everything (Liberal Party, 1924), for Beveridge's doubts about 'the national minimum' beyond the insurance cover, see José Harris, *William Beveridge: A Biography* (Clarendon Press, 1977), pp. 322-3; J. M. Keynes, *The Means to Prosperity* (The Times, 1924), which begins his interest in full employment through deficit finance - cf. Harrod, op. cit., pp. 441-2; Macmillan *et al.*, opera cit.

118 Cf. N. and J. MacKenzie, op. cit., pp. 375-6.
119 The phrase is Churchill's in a Cabinet minute of 14 February 1943, Birch, op. cit., p. 114.
120 Harris, op. cit., chs 1-3.
121 Cf. ibid., pp. 87-8, 165, 314.
122 Beveridge, *Insurance for All*; Harris, op. cit., pp. 349-52.
123 Sir William Beveridge, *Social Insurance and Allied Services* (Cmd. 6404, 1942); Harris, op. cit., chs 16 and 17.
124 Ibid., p. 353.
125 W. H. Beveridge, *The Causes and Cure of Unemployment* (Longmans, 1931), pp. 64-6.
126 Harris, op. cit., pp. 462-3.
127 Beveridge, *Social Insurance and Allied Services*, pp. 6-7.
128 Harrod, op. cit., chs 1-4.
129 Ibid., ch. 7.
130 Ibid., p. 332.
131 J. M. Keynes, article in *The Nation*, 7 June 1924; Harrod, op. cit., p. 348.
132 J. M. Keynes, *The End of Laissez-Faire* (Sidney Ball Lecture, Oxford University, 1924; Hogarth Press, 1926), pp. 52-3.
133 Harrod, op. cit., p. 462.
134 J. M. Keynes, *The General Theory of Employment, Interest and Money* (Macmillan, 1936).
135 John Eatwell, *Whatever Happened to Britain? The Economics of Decline* (Oxford University Press, 1984), esp. ch. 4; J. F. Wright, *Britain in an Age of Economic Management* (Oxford University Press, 1979), pp. 140-5, 170.
136 Harrod, op. cit., pp. 575-85.
137 Harold Macmillan, *Winds of Change 1914-39* (Macmillan, 1966), p. 285.
138 Friedrich A. von Hayek, *Collectivist Economic Planning: Critical Studies on the Possibilities of Socialism* (George Routledge, 1935), p. 1; for the 'white emigration' [sic] see Perry Anderson, 'Components of the national culture', in Alexander Cockburn and Robin Blackburn, (eds), *Student Power* (Penguin, 1969), pp. 229-34.
139 Birch, op. cit., p. 40.
140 Clement Attlee to Harold Laski, 1 May 1944, quoted in Kingsley Martin, *Harold Laski, 1893-1950; A Biographical Memoir* (Gollancz, 1953), p. 161.
141 Harry Eckstein, *The English Health Service: Its Origins, Structure and Achievements* (Harvard University Press, 1985), p. ix.
142 N. and J. MacKenzie, op. cit., pp. 290-91; H. G. Wells, *A Modern*

Utopia (Chapman & Hall, 1905); George Bernard Shaw, *Man and Superman* (1903); Harris, op. cit., p. 87.

143 Titmuss, *Welfare State*, pp. 24-5.

144 Ibid., p. 27.

145 Bentley B. Gilbert, *The Evolution of National Insurance in Britain: The Origins of the Welfare State* (Michael Joseph, 1966), pp. 401-16. Gilbert thinks that the BMA were defeated, but they had gained a larger capitation fee and the predominant share in the running of the panel doctor system, and according to Dr Alfred Cox, a BMA official and critic of the BMA leadership's tactics, they had 'won on points'.

146 Cf. Charles Webster, 'Designing a National Health Service, 1918-42' (unpublished paper presented at the SSRC conference on 'The Roots of welfare', University of Lancaster, 1983). I am grateful to Dr Webster for access to this paper, on which much of the next three paragraphs is based.

147 Sir Bertram Dawson, 'Medicine and the state', *The Medical Officer*, vol. 23, 5 June 1920, pp. 223-4.

148 Consultative Council on Medical and Allied Services (Chairman: Sir Bertrand Dawson), *Interim Report on the Future Provision of Medical and Allied Services* (Cmd. 693, 1920).

149 Ibid., para. 3.

150 British Medical Association, *A General Medical Service for the Nation* (BMA, 1938).

151 Sir Arthur S. MacNalty, *The Reform of the Public Health Services* (Nuffield College, Oxford, 1943), pp. 30-1; Nuffield Provincial Hospitals Trust, *A National Hospitals Service* (NPHT, 1941); Webster, op. cit., pp. 13-17.

152 British Medical Association, Medical Planning Commission, 'Draft Interim Report', *British Medical Journal*, vol. 1, 1942, pp. 743-53; Webster, op. cit., pp. 20-1.

153 Webster, op. cit., pp. 23-4.

154 Eckstein, op. cit., p. 3.

155 Ibid., pp. 155-60. Again, the leadership of the BMA did not get all it wanted, but the outcome was a substantial victory for the rank and file doctors.

156 Ibid., pp. 229-31.

157 Harry Eckstein, *Pressure Group Politics* (Allen & Unwin, 1960), pp. 101-2.

158 Brian Abel Smith, *A History of Nursing* (Heinemann, 1975), p. 248.

159 Paul Wilding, *Professional Power and Social Welfare* (Routledge & Kegan Paul, 1982), pp. 27-8, 44-5, 50-1.

160 Committee of Inquiry into the Regulation of the Medical Profession, *Report* (Cmnd. 6018, 1975), para. 11.

161 A. Cartwright and R. Anderson, *Patients and Their Doctors, 1977* (Institute for Social Studies in Medical Care, 1979); British Medical Association, General Practitioner Charter Working Group Report, *British Medical Journal*, 24 February 1979; Wilding, op. cit., p. 110.

162 Ivan Illich, *Medical Nemesis* (Boyars, 1975).

163 Ivan Illich *et al.*, *Disabling Professions* (Boyars, 1977); Joseph K. Lieberman, *The Tyranny of the Expert* (Walker, 1970).

164 Lewis Yablonsky, *The Tunnel Back: Syanon* (Macmillan, 1965), p. 368.

165 Charles L. Mowat, *The Charity Organization Society, 1869–1913* (Methuen, 1961), esp. ch. 5; Titmuss, *Welfare State*, p. 15; Elizabeth Wilson, *Women and the Welfare State* (Tavistock, 1977), p. 111.

166 Richard M. Titmuss, *Commitment to Welfare* (Allen & Unwin, 1968), p. 85.

167 Committee on Local Authority and Allied Personal Services (Chairman: Lord F. Seebohm), *Report* (Cmnd. 3703, 1968).

168 A. Sinfield, *Which Way for Social Work?* (Fabian Society, 1969), p. 2.

169 Quoted in Kathleen Jones (ed.), *Year Book of Social Policy in Britain, 1971* (Routledge & Kegan Paul, 1972), p. 46.

170 Asher Tropp, *The School Teachers: The Growth of the Teaching Profession in England and Wales from 1800 to the Present Day* (Heinemann, 1957), esp. chs 8, 9 and 14; Harold Perkin, 'The teaching profession and the game of life', in Peter Gordon (ed.), *Is Teaching a Profession?* (Heinemann, 1983).

171 Cf. Harold Perkin, *Key Profession: The History of the Association of University Teachers* (Routledge & Kegan Paul, 1969), p. 222.

172 Caroline Benn and Brian Simon, *Halfway There: Report on the British Comprehensive School Reform* (Penguin, 1972), ch. 10, found that, despite a considerable swing away from streaming, more than half the schools in their survey still taught in streams or broad bands of ability and no less than 70 per cent by some sort of streaming or setting.

173 Maurice Kogan and W. van der Eyken, *County Hall* (Penguin, 1973), p. 54.

174 Lady Plowden, *Children and their Primary Schools* (HMSO, 1967), vol. 1, p. 123.

175 Idem, and A. H. Halsey, *A New Partnership for Our Schools* (HMSO, 1977); Wilding, op. cit., pp. 24–5.

176 Maurice Kogan, *Educational Policy Making: A Study of Interest Groups and Parliament* (Allen & Unwin, 1975), pp. 37, 108–9.

177 Cf. Perkin, 'Teaching profession'.

178 Cf. D. H. MacKay and A. W. Cox, *The Politics of Urban Change* (Croom Helm, 1979); cf. Harold Perkin, 'Public participation in government decision-making', *Town and Country Planning School: Report of Proceedings* (Royal Town Planning Institute, 1973).

179 Norman Dennis, *Public Participation and Planners' Blight* (Faber & Faber, 1972).

180 Wilding, op. cit., p. 18.

181 Gilbert, op. cit., p. 450.

182 Friedrich A. von Hayek, *The Road to Serfdom* (Routledge & Kegan Paul, 1944) and *Law: Legislation and Liberty*, vol. 2, *The Mirage of Social Justice* (Routledge & Kegan Paul, 1976); Milton and Rose Friedman, *Free to Choose* (Penguin, 1980).

183　Claus Offe, *Contradictions of the Welfare State* (ed. John Keane, MIT Press, 1984), p. 263.

CHAPTER 8　THE TRIUMPH OF THE PROFESSIONAL IDEAL

1　Harold Perkin, *The Origins of Modern English Society* (Routledge & Kegan Paul, 1969), pp. 218-21.

2　Ibid., pp. 252-70.

3　'A' [J. S. Mill], 'On Miss Martineau's summary of political economy', *Monthly Repository*, vol. 8, 1834, p. 320.

4　Thomas Carlyle, *Past and Present* (1843; Chapman & Hall, 1893 edn), p. 56; F. D. Maurice, *On the Reformation of Society* (Forbes & Knibb, 1851), pp. 10-13; Karl Marx, *Capital* (Chicago, 1909 edn), vol. 3, pp. 1031-2; Matthew Arnold, *Culture and Anarchy* (Smith, Elder, 1869), ch. 3.

5　Matthew Arnold, *Schools and Universities on the Continent* (1868; ed. R. H. Super, University of Michigan, 1964), pp. 308-9.

6　James Mill, *Essay on Government* (1820); S. T. Coleridge, *On the Constitution of Church and State* (1852 edn), pp. 54-5; J. S. Mill, *Principles of Political Economy* (1848; Longmans, 1904 edn), pp. 589-90; Carlyle, *Past and Present*, pp. 23-4; Norman and Jeanne MacKenzie, *The First Fabians* (Weidenfeld & Nicolson, 1977), pp. 290-1; H. G. Wells, *A Modern Utopia* (Chapman & Hall, 1905); José Harris, *William Beveridge: A Biography* (Clarendon Press, 1977), p. 87.

7　Cf. Perkin, *Origins*, pp. 267-9.

8　Martin Wiener, *English Culture and the Decline of the Industrial Spirit, 1850-1980* (Cambridge University Press, 1981).

9　William Morris, *The Earthly Paradise: A Poem* (F. S. Ellis, 1868-70).

10　Wiener, op. cit., jacket summary.

11　Samuel Courtauld, Address to the Engineers' Club, Manchester, 1942, and John Child, *British Management Thought* (Routledge & Kegan Paul, 1969), p. 121; quoted in Wiener, op. cit., pp. 127 and 144.

12　Cf. D. C. Coleman, 'Gentlemen and players', *Economic History Review*, vol. 26, 1973.

13　Wiener deals with the major contributions to the controversy over the deceleration of British economic growth in the Appendix, op. cit., pp. 167-70, including Charles Kindleberger, *Economic Growth in Britain and France, 1851-1950* (Harvard University Press, 1964); H. J. Habakkuk, *American and British Technology in the 19th Century* (Cambridge University Press, 1964); Peter Mathias, *The First Industrial Nation* (Methuen, 1969); David Landes, *The Unbound Prometheus: Technological Change and Industrial Development in Western Europe from 1750 to the Present* (Cambridge University Press, 1969), pp. 331-58; D. H. Aldcroft, 'The entrepreneur and the British economy, 1870-1914', *Economic History Review*, vol. 17, 1964-65; A. L. Levine, *Industrial Retardation in Britain, 1880-1914*

(New York, 1967); E. J. Hobsbawm, *Industry and Empire: An Economic History of Britain Since 1750* (Penguin, 1969); Donald McCloskey (ed.), *Essays on a Mature Economy: Britain Since 1840* (Methuen, 1971) and 'Did Victorian Britain fail?', *Economic History Review*, vol. 23, 1970; N. F. R. Crafts, 'Victorian Britain did fail', idem, vol. 32, 1979; Michael Fores, 'Britain's economic growth and the 1870 watershed', *Lloyd's Bank Review*, no. 99, January 1971; Wilfred Beckerman (ed.), *Slow Growth in Britain: Causes and Consequences* (Oxford University Press, 1979); and John Saville, 'The development of British industry and foreign competition, 1875-1914', *Business History*, vol. 12, 1970. See also Donald Coleman and Christine Macleod, 'Attitudes to new techniques: British businessmen, 1800-1950', *Economic History Review*, vol. 39, 1986. Like the last, the reviews of Wiener's book by economic as distinct from political, social and cultural historians have been almost uniformly critical of a cultural explanation of economic phenomena.

14 See, *inter alia*, Michael Sanderson, *The Universities and British Industry, 1950-1970* (Routledge & Kegan Paul, 1972), T. J. H. Bishop and R. Wilkinson, *Winchester and the Public School Elite* (Faber & Faber, 1967), and John Rae, *The Public School Revolution: Britain's Independent Schools, 1964-79* (Faber & Faber, 1981).

15 For references, see Perkin, *Origins*, pp. 73-8.

16 Cf. ibid., pp. 428-37.

17 F. M. L. Thompson, *English Landed Society in the 19th Century* (Routledge & Kegan Paul, 1964), p. 307.

18 See above, ch. 3, section 1.

19 Cf. John Chandos, *Boys Together: English Public Schools, 1800-64* (Hutchinson, 1984), and Lawrence Stone, 'The size and composition of the Oxford student body, 1580-1909', in L. Stone (ed.), *The University in Society* (Oxford University Press and Princeton University Press, 1975), esp. vol. 1, part 3, pp. 37-58.

20 Cf. Perkin, *Origins*, pp. 272-8.

21 Quoted by Wiener, op. cit., p. 13.

22 J. J. Findlay (ed.), *Arnold of Rugby* (Cambridge University Press, 1897), p. 65. For a reassessment of Arnold's contribution see T. W. Bamford, *Thomas Arnold on Education, with a Selection from his Writing* (Cambridge University Press, 1970), and J. A. Mangan, *Athleticism in the Victorian and Edwardian Public School* (Cambridge University Press, 1981), pp. 15-18.

23 Bishop and Wilkinson, op. cit., pp. 104-8.

24 Ibid., pp. 64-9.

25 Sheldon Rothblatt, *The Revolution of the Dons: Cambridge and Society in Victorian England* (Faber & Faber, 1968 and Cambridge University Press, 1981); Arthur Engel, 'The emerging concept of the academic profession at Oxford, 1800-54', in Stone, op. cit., vol. 1, and *From Clergyman to Don: The Rise of the Academic Profession in 19th-Century Oxford* (Clarendon Press, 1983).

26 Rothblatt, op. cit., Appendix IIA, p. 280; Edward Hilliard (ed.), *The*

Balliol College Register, 1832-1914 (Oxford University Press, 1914), p. vii.

27 T. W. Heyck, *The Transformation of Intellectual Life in Victorian England* (Croom Helm, 1982), p. 21.

28 Margery Perham, *Lugard*, vol. 1, *The Years of Adventure* (Collins, 1956), p. 35; Wiener, op. cit., p. 130.

29 Letter to J. A. Mangan, quoted in *The Games Ethic and Imperialism* (Viking Penguin, 1986), p. 86.

30 C. A. Anderson and Miriam Schnaper, *School and Society: Social Backgrounds of Oxford and Cambridge Students* (Public Affairs Press, 1952), pp. 6-7.

31 Bishop and Wilkinson, op. cit., pp. 64-9 and 104-8.

32 Sanderson, op. cit., pp. 52-4.

33 Bishop and Wilkinson, op. cit., pp. 68-9 and 107.

34 Sir Ernest Barker, *Age and Youth: Memories of Three Universities* (Oxford University Press, 1953), p. 125; Sanderson, op. cit., pp. 306-8.

35 Royal Commission on Public Schools (Chairman: Sir John Newson), *First Report* (HMSO, 1968), vol. 1, p. 56 (the footnote reference is to Appendix 6, vol. 2, p. 95, which shows only 84 per cent of the pupils from professional and managerial families, though 10 per cent from the armed forces, presumably mainly officers' children, and only 5 per cent from the manual and non-manual working classes III and IV.)

36 Ibid., vol. 1, p. 58 and vol. 2, Appendix 8, p. 236.

37 Rae, op. cit., esp. ch. 6.

38 Anthony Sampson, *The New Anatomy of Britain* (Hodder & Stoughton, 1962), p. 609; Graham Turner, *Business in Britain* (Eyre & Spottiswoode, 1969), p. 141; W. J. Reader, *Imperial Chemical Industries: A History* (Oxford University Press, 1970, 1975), vol. 1, pp. 218-19, vol. 2, pp. 91-2; quoted in Wiener, op. cit., pp. 148, 149, 150.

39 Acton Society Trust, *Management Succession* (AST, 1956), p. 91. Another study of 646 managers in 1954-55 by R. V. Clements, *Managers: A Study of their Careers in Industry* (Allen & Unwin, 1958) showed that 26.2 per cent came from public schools, and 35 per cent from universities, of whom 19.6 per cent were from Oxford and Cambridge (p. 174). Clements comments:

> . . . so influential and deeply felt are social origins that they have tended to reproduce a sort of class system in the management hierarchy. In a sense top jobs have been filled by men, usually of higher social origins, expecting and sometimes even trained for top management, and inferior posts by men expecting and trained for no more than lower management jobs. (p. 95)

40 *Directory of National Biography* under Morris; *Who's Who?* under Robinson and Wolfson.

41 Noel Annan, 'The possessed', *New York Review of Books*, 5 February 1976; Wiener, op. cit., p. 131; see also Noel Annan, 'The intellectual aristocracy of Victorian England', in J. H. Plumb (ed.),

Studies in Social History (Longmans, 1955).

42 Much of the argument of this section is anticipated by my Stenton Lecture, *Professionalism, Property and English Society Since 1880* (University of Reading, 1981).

43 Cf. 'Land reform and class conflict in Victorian Britain', in Harold Perkin, *The Structured Crowd: Essays in English Social History* (Harvester and Barnes & Noble, 1981).

44 Cf. Gary S. Becker, *Human Capital* (Columbia University Press, 1964).

45 Joseph Melling, *Rent Strikes: People's Struggle for Housing in West Scotland, 1890–1916* (Polygon Books, 1983); F. H. Lawson, *Introduction to the Law of Property* (Clarendon Press, 1977 edn), pp. 125–6; T. M. Aldridge, *Rent Control and Leasehold Enfranchisement* (Oyez, 1977), chs 1–12; Lloyd Evans, *The Law of Landlord and Tenant* (Butterworths, 1974), chs 14–17; R. Jarmain, *Housing Subsidies and Rents* (Stevens, 1948), pp. 16–18; Adela A. Nevitt, *Housing Taxation and Subsidies* (Nelson, 1966), ch. 8; Christina M. E. Whitehead, *The United Kingdom Housing Market* (Saxon House, 1974), pp. 44–6; and Bruce Headey, *Housing Policy in the Development Economy* (St Martin's Press, 1978), ch. 6.

46 Cf. Murray Forsyth, *Property and Property Distribution Policy* (PEP, 1971), p. 38.

47 *Social Trends*, 1986, p. 133.

48 *Shorthold Tenancies* (Department of the Environment, Housing Booklet no. 8, HMSO, 1985).

49 Cf. Aldridge, op. cit., chs 16–18; Evans, op. cit., ch. 18.

50 Cf. William Ashworth, *The Genesis of Modern British Town Planning* (Routledge & Kegan Paul, 1954), ch. 8; Lewis B. Keeble, *Town Planning at the Crossroads* (Estates Gazette, 1961), esp. ch. 12; Gordon E. Cherry, *The Evolution of British Town Planning* (Halstead Press, 1974).

51 Andrew Cox, *Adversary Politics and Land: The Conflict over Land and Property Policy in Post-War Britain* (Cambridge University Press, 1954), *passim*.

52 Cf. Perkin, 'Land reform and class conflict', loc. cit., pp. 122–31.

53 Cox, op. cit., esp. part C.

54 Cf. Ashworth, Keeble & Cherry, opera cit.

55 B. B. Gilbert, *The Evolution of National Insurance in Great Britain* (Michael Joseph, 1966), esp. chs 5, 6 and 7, and *British Social Policy* (Batsford, 1970), esp. chs 4, 5 and 6; Pat Thane, *The Foundations of the Welfare State* (Longmans, 1982), chs 3, 6 and 7.

56 Cf. A. B. Atkinson, *Unequal Shares: Wealth in Britain* (Penguin, 1974), pp. 103–5.

57 H. A. Clegg, *The Changing System of Industrial Relations in Great Britain* (Oxford University Press, 1979), pp. 306–13; C. Saunders *et al.*, *Winners and Losers: Pay Patterns in the 1970s* (PEP, 1977).

58 Henry George, *Progress and Poverty* (Appleton, 1880); J. Hyder, *The Case for Land Nationalization* (Simkin & Marshall, 1913).

59 *Burke's Landed Gentry* (Burke's Peerage, 1956 edn), Preface; Harold

Perkin, *The Economic Worth of Elites in British Society Since 1880* (Report to SSRC, 1977, deposited in British Library Lending Division, Boston Spa), table 10.1 (male millionaires' own probate returns).

60 Royal Commission on the Distribution of Income and Wealth (Chairman: Lord Diamond), *Report No. 1* (Cmnd. 6171, 1975), ch. 5, esp. tables 41 and 45.

61 Cyril Grunfield, *The Law of Redundancy* (Sweet & Maxwell, 1980), pp. 3, 5 and *passim*; Peter Wallington (ed.), *Butterworths Employment Law Handbook* (Butterworths, 1979), pp. 140, 151, 157–264; W. W. Daniel and Elizabeth Stilgoe, *The Impact of Employment Protection Laws* (Policy Studies Institute, 1978). Cf. also Audrey Hunt, *Management Attitudes and Practices Towards Women Workers* (HMSO, 1975).

62 *Report of the (Bullock) Committee of Inquiry on Industrial Democracy* (Cmnd. 6706, 1977); White Paper on *Industrial Democracy* (Cmnd. 6810, 1978). Cf. also Clegg, op. cit., pp. 438–43; Stephen Bubb, 'The industrial democracy White Paper', *Industrial Law Journal*, vol. 7, 1978; Sir Otto Kahn-Freud, 'Industrial democracy', ibid., vol. 6, 1977; and Paul Davies and Lord Wedderburn, 'The law of industrial democracy', ibid., vol. 7, 1977.

63 Ralf Dahrendorf, *Class and Class Conflict in Industrial Society* (Stanford University Press, 1959), p. 51; A. A. Berle, Jr and G. C. Means, *The Modern Corporation and Private Property* (Macmillan, 1932); R. H. Tawney, *The Acquisitive Society* (Harcourt, Brace & Howe, 1920), p. 180.

64 Graham Bannock, *The Juggernauts* (Penguin, 1973), p. 5.

65 *The Sunday Times*, 10 January 1982, citing a Stock Exchange survey; this proportion has now been increased substantially by the privatization of nationalized industries but is still a small minority of the population.

66 Cf. the increase in alleged 'insider trading' on the London and New York Stock Exchanges, associated with, amongst others, Ivan Boesky, Dennis Levine, Sir Ernest Saunders, etc. in 1986.

67 Cf. Franklin L. Baumer, *Modern European Thought: Continuity and Change in Ideas, 1660–1950* (Collier Macmillan, 1977), p. 7. Cf. also Perkin, *Origins of Modern English Society*, pp. 252–70; and T. W. Heyck, op. cit., pp. 13–14.

68 Cf. Leon Edel, *Bloomsbury: A House of Lions* (J. B. Lippincott, 1979); Quentin Bell, *Virginia Woolf: A Biography* (Harcourt Brace Jovanovich, 1972).

69 Margaret Llewellyn Davies (ed.), *Life As We Have Known It, By Cooperative Working Women* (Hogarth Press, 1931; Virago 1977), Introductory Letter by Virginia Woolf, pp. xxi, xxx.

70 J. M. Keynes, *Essays in Persuasion* (Macmillan, 1931), p. 324.

71 Clive Bell, *Civilization* (1928; Penguin, 1947), p. 1.

72 T. S. Eliot, *The Idea of a Christian University* (Faber, 1938).

73 T. S. Eliot, 'On the place and function of the clerisy', Appendix to
    Roger Kojecky, *T. S. Eliot's Social Criticism* (Farras, Strous &
    Giroux, 1971), pp. 241–8.
74 A. Wade (ed.), *Letters of W. B. Yeats* (Hart-Davis, 1954), pp. 811–12;
    D. H. Lawrence, Introduction to F. M. Dostoievsky, *The Grand
    Inquisitor*, reprinted in E. D. McDonald (ed.), *Phoenix: The
    Posthumous Papers of D. H. Lawrence* (Heinemann, 1936).
75 Percy Wyndham Lewis, *Rude Assignment* (Hutchinson, 1950),
    p. 184, and *The Art of Being Ruled* (Chatto & Windus, 1926), p. 199.
76 Bertrand Russell, *Education and the Social Order* (Union Press,
    1970), p. 49.
77 Aldous Huxley, *Brave New World* (Chatto & Windus, 1932).
78 Christopher Caudwell, *Studies in a Dying Culture* (Monthly Review
    Press, 1972), p. 9; John Strachey, *What Are We to Do?* (Gollancz,
    1938), p. 83; Stephen Spender, *Forward from Liberalism* (Gollancz,
    1937), p. 70.
79 George Orwell, *The Road to Wigan Pier* (Gollancz, 1937), and *Keep
    the Aspidistra Flying* (Gollancz, 1936), p. 98.
80 L. Abercrombie *et al.*, *The Next Five Years: An Essay in Political
    Agreement* (London, 1935); Douglas Jay, *The Socialist Case* (Faber,
    1937); Barbara Wootton, *Freedom under Planning* (Allen & Unwin,
    1945).
81 Harold J. Laski, *A Grammar of Politics* (Allen & Unwin, 1925),
    pp. 17, 43.
82 Tawney, *Acquisitive Society*, p. 176.
83 Perry Anderson, 'Components of the national culture', in Alexander
    Cockburn and Robin Blackburn (eds), *Student Power* (Penguin,
    1969), pp. 229–34.
84 Eliot, Appendix, in Kojecky, op. cit., pp. 246–7.
85 Cf. John W. Saunders, *The Profession of English Letters* (Routledge
    & Kegan Paul, 1967).
86 Cf. Harold Perkin, *Key Profession: The History of the Association of
    University Teachers* (Routledge & Kegan Paul, 1969).
87 F. R. Leavis and Denys Thompson, *Culture and the Environment*
    (Chatto & Windus, 1960); F. R. Leavis, *Education and the University*
    (Chatto & Windus, 1961).
88 Q. D. Leavis, *Fiction and the Reading Public* (Chatto & Windus,
    1965); Richard Hoggart, *The Uses of Literacy* (Penguin, 1958).
89 F. R. Leavis, *Nor Shall My Sword* (Chatto & Windus, 1972), p. 169;
    Culture and the Environment, p. 82; *Education and the University*,
    p. 143; and 'The responsible critic: or the function of criticism at any
    time', *Scrutiny*, vol. 19, 1952, p. 179.
90 Peter Scott, *The Crisis of the University* (Croom Helm, 1984).
91 The titles of two influential books of the 1930s, Julien Benda, *La
    Trahison des Clercs* (Paris, 1927) and José Ortega y Gasset, *The
    Revolt of the Masses* (Norton, 1932), both concerned with the increas-
    ing isolation of the intelligentsia or clerisy.

CHAPTER 9   THE PLATEAU OF PROFESSIONAL SOCIETY

1 *Britain: A Reference Book* (HMSO, 1949), p. 100.
2 *Statistical Digest of the War* (HMSO, 1951), p. 195; A. S. Milward, *War, Economy and Society, 1939–45* (Allen Lane, 1977), p. 211; see also Angus Calder, *The People's War* (Panther, 1971) for much of the detail in this section.
3 John Stevenson, *British Society, 1914–45* (Penguin, 1984), pp. 449–50.
4 W. K. Hancock and Margaret Gowing, *The British War Economy* (HMSO, 1949); M. M. Postan, *British War Production* (HMSO, 1952); H. M. D. Parker, *Manpower* (HMSO, 1957); E. L. Hargreaves and Margaret Gowing, *Civil Industry and Trade* (HMSO, 1952).
5 Sir Keith Murray, *Agriculture* (HMSO, 1955); Ministry of Information, *Land at War* (HMSO, 1945); Victoria Sackville-West, *The Women's Land Army* (HMSO, 1944); Calder, op. cit., pp. 482–93.
6 Ministry of Food, *How Britain Was Fed in Wartime* (HMSO, 1946); R. J. Hammond, *Food and Agriculture in Britain, 1939–45* (Stanford University Press, 1954); Lord Woolton, *Memoirs* (Cassell, 1959); Calder, op. cit., pp. 438–47.
7 Parker, op. cit., pp. 309–10; Calder, op. cit., pp. 124, 271–2, 308–11, 383–5, 505–6.
8 R. M. Titmuss, *Problems of Social Policy* (HMSO, 1950), pp. 101–95; Arthur Marwick, *The Home Front: The British and the Second World War* (Thomas & Hudson, 1976), pp. 23–38; Calder, op. cit., pp. 40–58.
9 Marwick, *Home Front*, pp. 132–8; Calder, op. cit., pp. 382–6.
10 Basil Dean, *The Theatre at War: A History of the Entertainments National Service Association* (Harrap, 1956); Calder, op. cit., pp. 429–37.
11 W. S. Churchill, *The War Speeches* (Cassell, 1963–65), vol. 2, pp. 425–37.
12 John Wheeler Bennett, *King George VI* (Macmillan, 1958), p. 470.
13 A. J. P. Taylor, *England, 1914–45* (Oxford University Press, 1965), pp. 437–8.
14 Titmuss, *Problems of Social Policy*, p. 506.
15 Harold J. Laski, *Where Do We Go from Here?* (Penguin, 1940).
16 Calder, op. cit., p. 284.
17 *Picture Post*, 4 January 1941 (reprinted by Morrison & Gibb, 1974).
18 Marwick, *Home Front*, p. 128.
19 Sir William Beveridge, *Social Insurance and Allied Services* (Cmd. 6404, 1942), esp. pp. 6–11, 120–1, 137–40, 153–70; for the report's provenance and reception see Janet Beveridge, *Beveridge and his Plan* (Hodder & Stoughton, 1954); British Institute of Public Opinion, *The Beveridge Report and the Public* (BIPO, 1943); Calder, op. cit., pp. 607–14.
20 W. S. Churchill, *The Hinge of Fate* (Houghton Mifflin, 1950), p. 603.
21 Maurice Bruce, *The Coming of the Welfare State* (Batsford, 1961), p. ix, citing William Temple, *Citizen and Churchman* (Eyre & Spottiswoode, 1941).

22 Quintin Hogg, *One Year's Work* (Hurst & Blackett, 1944), p. 53.
23 Alan Bullock, *The Life and Times of Ernest Bevin* (Heinemann, 1967), vol. 2, pp. 224–31.
24 G. S. Bain and Richard Price, *Profiles of Union Growth* (Oxford University Press, 1980), pp. 46–7.
25 Richard Croucher, *Engineers at War, 1939–45* (Merlin Press, 1982), pp. 162–7; James E. Cronin, *Labour and Society in Britain, 1918–79* (Batsford, 1984), pp. 117–20.
26 Cronin, op. cit., p. 125.
27 John Eatwell, *Whatever Happened to Britain? The Economics of Decline* (Oxford University Press, 1984), p. 11.
28 Bernard Levin, *The Pendulum Years: Britain and the Sixties* (Cape, 1970), p. 210.
29 J. F. Wright, *Britain in the Age of Economic Management* (Oxford University Press, 1979), p. 21.
30 Cf. P. N. S. Mansergh, *The Commonwealth Experience* (Weidenfeld & Nicolson, 1969); *Cambridge History of the British Empire*, vol. 3, *The Empire Commonwealth* (Cambridge University Press, 1959); Colin Cross, *The Fall of the British Empire* (Hodder & Stoughton, 1968); Bernard Porter, *The Lion's Share: A Short History of the British Empire* (Longmans, 1984), chs 9 and 10.
31 Cf., *inter alia*, Sheila Patterson, *Immigration and Race Relations, 1960–67* (Oxford University Press, 1969); Nicolas Deakin, *Colour, Citizenship and British Society* (Panther Books, 1970); Thomas J. Cottle, *Black Testimony: The Voices of British West Indians* (Wildwood House, 1978); Colin Holmes (ed.), *Immigrants and Minorities in British Society* (Allen & Unwin, 1978); Charles Husband, *'Race' in Britain* (Hutchinson, 1982).
32 Sir Ian Fraser, letter to Miss Stanley, 11 May 1938, in BBC Archives, quoted by Arthur Marwick, *Class: Image and Reality in Britain, France and the USA Since 1930* (Fontana, 1981), p. 159.
33 *Social Trends*, 1972, pp. 78, 103; ibid., 1973, p. 96.
34 Ibid., 1986, p. 168.
35 J. H. Goldthorpe *et al.*, *Social Mobility and Class Structure in Modern Britain* (Clarendon Press, 1980), pp. 60–1; A. H. Halsey (ed.), *Trends in British Society Since 1900* (Macmillan, 1972), p. 118; *Social Trends*, 1973, p. 88.
36 Goldthorpe *et al.*, *Social Mobility*, pp. 60–1.
37 Ibid., chs 2, 3 and 9.
38 A. H. Halsey *et al.*, *Origins and Destinations: Family, Class and Education in Modern Britain* (Clarendon Press, 1980), chs 10 and 11.
39 Royal Commission on the Distribution of Income and Wealth (Chairman: Lord Diamond), *Report No. 1* (Cmnd. 6171, 1975), p. 36.
40 Peter Townsend, *Poverty in the United Kingdom* (Penguin, 1979), pp. 344, 348.
41 Calculated from *Social Trends*, 972, p. 87.
42 Cf., *inter alia*, Mark Abrams and Richard Rose, *Must Labour Lose?* (Penguin, 1960), and David E. Butler and Richard Rose, *The*

British General Election of 1959 (Macmillan, 1960).

43 J. H. Goldthorpe *et al.*, *The Affluent Worker: 1. Industrial Attitudes and Behaviour; 2. Political Attitudes and Behaviour; 3. The Affluent Worker in the Class Structure* (Cambridge University Press, 1968–69).

44 B. S. Rowntree and G. R. Lavers, *Poverty and the Welfare State: A Third Social Survey of York* (Longmans, 1951), pp. 30–1.

45 Brian Abel Smith and Peter Townsend, *The Poor and the Poorest* (Bell, 1965), p. 36.

46 Cf., *inter alia*, Peter Townsend (ed.), *The Concept of Poverty* (Heinemann, 1970); W. G. Runciman, *Relative Deprivation and Social Justice* (Routledge & Kegan Paul, 1966); A. B. Atkinson, *Unequal Shares* (Penguin, 1972); Dorothy Wedderburn (ed.), *Poverty, Inequality and Class Structure* (Cambridge University Press, 1974); Peter Willmott (ed.), *The Poverty Report 1976* (Temple Smith, 1976); Frank Field, Michael Meacher and Clive Pond, *To Him that Hath* (Penguin, 1977); Frank Field (ed.), *The Wealth Report* (Routledge & Kegan Paul, 1979); and Peter Townsend, *Poverty in UK* (Penguin, 1979).

47 Townsend, *Poverty in UK*, pp. 88, 160–6, 207–71, 273.

48 Diamond Commission, *Report No. 1*, p. 102; Townsend, *Poverty in UK*, p. 344.

49 Calculated from Townsend, *Poverty in UK*, pp. 243 and 344 by the following method: add differences between mean non-asset income of each of bottom four deciles and general mean ($£777$) = $£11,322$; calculate as percentage of mean of top 1 per cent ($£6,053$) = 187 per cent and of top 10 per cent ($£27,424$) = 41.3 per cent. The non-asset income is taken because that is accessible to taxation; Townsend's 'final income' of the richest 1 per cent in kind and imputed benefits from assets ($£12,331$) would not be realizable but if it were it would have required 92 per cent of it to raise those below $£777$ to 79 per cent of the mean.

50 Peter H. Lindert, 'Unequal English wealth since 1670', *Journal of Political Economy*, vol. 94, 1986, pp. 1131, 1154–6.

51 Diamond Commission, *Report No. 1*, pp. 92, 97, 102; Townsend, *Poverty in UK*, p. 345.

52 Lindert, op. cit., p. 1150.

53 *Social Trends*, 1972, p. 94; 1973, p. 107; 1986, pp. 14, 17.

54 Michael Young and Peter Willmott, *The Symmetrical Family* (Penguin, 1973), esp. ch. 4; the term has a longer history and can be found in Geoffrey Gorer, *Exploring English Character* (Cresset, 1955), p. 301.

55 Most of the pioneers of the women's movement in the post-war period were, like many of their Victorian predecessors, professional women, chiefly academics and journalists: e.g. Germaine Greer, *The Female Eunuch* (MacGibbon & Kee, 1970); Eva Figes, *Patriarchal Attitudes* (Faber & Faber, 1970); Juliet Mitchell, *Women's Estate* (Penguin, 1971); Sheila Rowbotham, *Woman's*

Consciousness, Man's World (Penguin, 1973); Ann Oakley and Juliet Mitchell (eds), *The Rights and Wrongs of Women* (Penguin, 1976).

56 Cf., *inter alia*, Stuart Hall and Tony Jefferson (eds), *Resistance Through Rituals: Youth Subcultures in Post-War Britain* (Hutchinson, 1975); Mark Abrams, *The Teenage Consumer* (London Press Exchange, 1959); Robin Blackburn and Alexander Cockburn (eds), *Student Power* (Penguin, 1969); Timothy Raison (ed.), *Youth in the New Society* (Hart-Davis, 1966); Peter Willmott, *Adolescent Boys of East London* (Penguin, 1969); Kenneth Leech, *Youthquake: The Growth of a Counter-Culture Through Two Decades* (Sheldon Press, 1973).

57 Young and Willmott, *Symmetrical Family*, pp. 19–26.

58 Gorer, op. cit., p. 96.

59 George Mikes, *How to Be an Alien* (Allan Wingate, 1946).

60 *Social Trends*, 1973, p. 76; *The Economist*, 10 January 1987. Cf. Christie Davies, *Permissive Britain: Social Change in the Sixties and Seventies* (Pitman, 1975); Geoffrey Gorer, *Sex and Marriage in England Today* (Nelson, 1971).

61 Arthur Marwick, *British Society Since 1945* (Penguin, 1982), p. 152.

62 *Britain: An Official Handbook* (HMSO, 1972), pp. 23–4.

63 Alan D. Gilbert, *The Making of Post-Christian Britain* (Longmans, 1980), pp. 95–6; Halsey, *Trends*, pp. 448–9; Gorer, *Exploring English Character*, ch. 14.

64 John A. T. Robinson, *Honest to God* (Student Christian Movement, 1963); David Jenkins, *The Contradiction of Christianity* (Student Christian Movement, 1976); Don Cupitt, *The Sea of Faith* (BBC, 1984).

65 Leslie Hannah, *The Rise of the Corporate Economy* (Methuen, 1976), p. 166; M. Abramowitz and V. F. Eliasberg, *The Growth of Public Employment in Great Britain* (Princeton University Press, 1957), and *Economic Trends* (HMSO, June 1972).

66 Perkin, *Modern English Society*, pp. 220–1, 252–4.

67 Geoffrey Millerson, *The Qualifying Professions* (Routledge & Kegan Paul, 1964), pp. 246–54; Monopolies Commission, *Professional Services: A Report on the General Effect on the Public Interest of Certain Restrictive Practices . . .* (Cmnd. 4463, 1970), part 2, pp. 83–5.

68 Clive Jenkins and Barrie Sherman, *White-Collar Unionism: The Rebellious Salariat* (Routledge & Kegan Paul, 1979), pp. 31, 34; George S. Bain and Richard Price, 'Union growth and employment trends in the United Kingdom, 1964–70', *British Journal of Industrial Relations*, November 1972.

69 Jenkins and Sherman, op. cit., pp. 31, 148–9.

70 Cf. John Hughes, *Nationalized Industries in the Mixed Economy* (Fabian Society, 1960).

71 Clive Jenkins, 'Occupational backgrounds of principal public corporation boards', in John Urry and John Wakeford (eds), *Power*

in Britain (Heinemann, 1973), pp. 154–6.

72 Tom Lupton and C. Shirley Wilson, 'The social background of top decision makers', *Manchester School*, January 1959.

73 Michael Barratt Brown, 'The controllers of British industry', in Ken Coates, *Can the Workers Run Industry?* (Sphere, 1968).

74 Cf. Leslie Hannah, *The Rise of the Corporate Economy* (Methuen, 1976), ch. 10.

75 David E. Butler, *The British General Election of 1951* (Macmillan, 1952); and David E. Butler and D. Kavanagh, *The British General Election of 1979* (Macmillan, 1980).

76 Quintin Hogg, *The Case for Conservatism* (Penguin, 1947), p. 13.

77 Iain Macleod, 'The political divide', in *The Future of the Welfare State* (Conservative Political Centre, 1958).

78 Timothy Raison, *Why Conservative?* (Penguin, 1964), pp. 24, 26.

79 R. H. Tawney, *Equality* (Allen & Unwin, 1938 edn), pp. 108–15.

80 Aneurin Bevan, *In Place of Fear* (Heinemann, 1952), pp. 127–8.

81 P. H. M. Williams, *Hugh Gaitskell: A Political Biography* (Oxford University Press, 1979), p. 554.

82 C. A. R. Crosland, *The Future of Socialism* (Cape, 1956), p. 103; R. H. S. Crossman, *Labour in the Affluent Society* (Fabian Society, 1960), pp. 22–4; Jim Northcott, *Why Labour?* (Penguin, 1964), pp. 162–3.

83 Anthony Crosland, *Social Democracy in Europe* (Fabian Society, 1975), p. 2.

84 Townsend, *Poverty in UK*, p. 633.

85 Beveridge, *Social Insurance*, p. 7.

86 Townsend, *Poverty in UK*, pp. 828–9.

87 R. M. Titmuss, *The Irresponsible Society* (Fabian Society, 1960), pp. 3, 10–12, 13–14, 20.

88 Geoffrey Howe, 'The reform of the social services', in *Bow Group Essays* (Conservative Party, 1964), quoted in Michael Shanks, *The Stagnant Society* (Penguin, 1961).

89 Cf. Townsend, *Poverty in UK*, pp. 922–6; and *inter alia*, Julian LeGrand, *The Strategy of Equality* (Allen & Unwin, 1982).

90 Cf. Shanks, op. cit., pp. 166–74, 184–92.

91 Robin Pedley, *Comprehensive Education: A New Approach* (1957; Penguin, 1969); John Vaisey, *Education in a Class Society* (Fabian Society, 1962).

92 Michael Young, *The Rise of the Meritocracy, 1870–2033* (Penguin, 1961).

93 Shanks, op. cit., p. 167.

94 Crosland, *Future of Socialism*, pp. 260–1.

95 Vaisey, op. cit., pp. 15–17.

96 Royal Commission on the Public Schools (Chairmen: Sir John Newson, David Donnison), *First* and *Second Reports* (HMSO, 1968, 1970).

97 Halsey *et al.*, *Origins and Destinations*, pp. 211–12.

98 Ibid., p. 180.

99 *Social Trends*, 1976, p. 215; E. G. Edwards, *Higher Education for Everyone* (Spokesman Press, 1982), esp. ch. 12.

100 Ibid., pp. 50-65, 95-96; UNESCO, *Conference of Ministers of Education of European Member States on Access to Higher Education, Vienna, 20-25 November 1967: Background Document No. 3.*

101 University Grants Committee, *University Development, 1947-52* (HMSO, 1953), p. 11; *Social Trends*, 1972, p. 132.

102 University Grants Committee, *University Development, 1957-62* (HMSO, 1963), pp. 96, 100-1. For the origins and development of the 1960s expansion of higher education and the binary system see H. J. Perkin, *Innovation in Higher Education: New Universities in the United Kingdom* (OECD, 1969).

103 Committee on Higher Education (Chairman: Lord Robbins), *Report* (HMSO, Cmnd. 2154, 1963), pp. 160, 277.

104 *Social Trends*, 1986, p. 53.

105 Labour Party, *Labour and the Scientific Revolution* (Labour Party, 1963).

106 Cf. Perkin, *Innovation in Higher Education*, pp. 35-45.

107 *Social Trends*, 1972, p. 168.

108 Cf. Perkin, *Key Profession*, pp. 223-5.

109 National Opinion Poll, *Bulletin No. 109*, 1972, pp. 14, 17.

110 Margaret Stacey *et al.*, *Power, Persistence and Change: A Second Study of Banbury* (Routledge & Kegan Paul, 1975), p. 121.

111 A. S. C. Ross, *et al.*, *Noblesse Oblige: An Enquiry into the Identifiable Characteristics of the English Aristocracy* (ed. Nancy Mitford, Penguin, 1956); Basil Bernstein (ed.), *Language, Primary Socialization and Education* (Routledge & Kegan Paul, 1970) and *Class, Codes and Control: Theoretical Studies Towards a Sociology of Language* (Routledge & Kegan Paul, 1971).

112 Jilly Cooper, *Class: A View from Middle England* (Eyre Methuen, 1979).

113 Crosland, *Future of Socialism*, pp. 178, 186, 259.

114 Ronald P. Dore, *British Factory, Japanese Factory: The Origins of Diversity in Industrial Relations* (Allen & Unwin, 1973), pp. 31-41, 98-108. With the trade recession and unemployment now at 3.2 per cent Japanese corporations are now finding ingenious ways of shedding labour, by transfers to folding subsidiaries and the like – *Observer*, 2 August 1987 (*Magazine* section, pp. 23-7).

115 Cf. John Westergaard and Henrietta Resler, *Class in a Capitalist Society* (Penguin, 1976), pp. 80-4.

116 Central Statistical Office, 'Social commentary; social class', *Social Trends*, 1975, pp. 10-32.

117 Cf. Townsend, *Poverty in UK*, pp. 285, 414-16; Committee on One-Parent Families (Chairman: S. E. Finer), *Report* (Cmnd. 5629, 1974), p. 22 and Appendix 4.

118 R. H. S. Crossman, *Diaries of a Cabinet Minister* (Cape, 1976-77), vol. 2, p. 190.

119 W. D. Rubinstein, *Men of Property: The Very Wealthy in Britain Since the Industrial Revolution* (Croom Helm, 1981), pp. 228-9; industrialists outnumbered financiers by twelve to three.

120 Ibid., p. 237.
121 *The Sunday Times*, 7 October 1984.
122 Harold Perkin, *The Economic Worth of Elites in British Society, 1880–1970* (Reort to SSRC, 1977, deposited in British Library Lending Division, Boston Spa), tables 4.14, 10.14.
123 *Who's Who? Who Was Who?* and *The Sunday Times*, 28 October 1984.
124 Harold Macmillan, *Pointing the Way, 1959–61* (Macmillan, 1972), p. 18.
125 Goldthorpe *et al.*, *Social Mobility*, pp. 60–1.
126 *Department of Employment Gazette*, December 1971.
127 J. M. and R. E. Pahl, *Managers and Their Wives* (Penguin, 1972), pp. 47–8.
128 Cf., *inter alia*, Cronin, *Labour and Society*, Richard Price, *Labour in British Society* (Croom Helm, 1986); David Coates, *The Labour Party and the Struggle for Socialism* (Cambridge University Press, 1975).
129 Ferdinand Zweig, *Productivity and the Trade Unions* (Oxford University Press, 1951); Price, op. cit., pp. 215–18; Hugh A. Clegg, *The Changing System of Industrial Relations in Great Britain* (Blackwell, 1979), pp. 215–20.
130 James E. Cronin, *Industrial Conflict in Modern Britain* (Croom Helm, 1979), p. 141.
131 Price, op. cit., pp. 214–27.
132 H. A. Turner, Garfield Clack and Geoffrey Roberts, *Labour Relations in the Motor Industry* (Allen & Unwin, 1967), pp. 115, 334–6.
133 Cronin, *Industrial Conflict*, pp. 141–4.
134 Monopolies Commission, *Professional Services* (Cmnd. 4463, 1970).
135 Sir Otto Kahn-Freund, *Labour Relations: Heritage and Adjustment* (Oxford University Press, 1979), pp. 48–52.
136 *Aldington-Jones Report* (Joint Special Committee of Employers and Unions, 1972); Committee of Inquiry into ... the Port Transport Industry (Chairman: Lord Devlin), *First Report* (Cmnd. 2523, 1964) and *Final Report* (Cmnd. 2734, 1965); David Wilson, *Dockers: The Impact of Industrial Change* (Fontana, 1972), pp. 215–17; Price, op. cit., pp. 224–7.
137 Clegg, op. cit., pp. 472–3; Alan Fox, *History and Heritage: The Social Origins of the British Industrial Relations System* (Allen & Unwin, 1985), p. 393.
138 An excellent example of Mancur Olson's *Logic of Collective Action* (Harvard University Press, 1971) and the role of 'special interest groups'; cf. also his *The Rise and Decline of Nations* (Yale University Press, 1982).
139 Cf. Colin Crouch, 'The intensification of industrial conflict in the United Kingdom', in C. Crouch and A. Pizzorno, *The Resurgence of Class Conflict in Europe Since 1968* (Holmes & Meier, 1979), vol. 1, pp. 228–9.
140 National Opinion Polls, *Bulletin*, August 1969, pp. 5–6;

Goldthorpe *et al.*, *Affluent Worker*, vol. 1, pp. 112–14.

141 Ivor Crewe *et al.*, 'Class dealignment in Britain, 1964–74', *British Journal of Political Science*, vol. 7, 1977; Richard Rose, 'Class does not equal party: the decline of a model of British voting', *Studies in Public Policy*, no. 74 (University of Strathclyde, 1980).

142 Ivor Crewe, 'The electorate: class dealignment ten years on', *West European Politics*, 1984, p. 194.

143 Clegg, op. cit., ch. 12, 'The crisis in British industrial relations'; Anthony King, *Why Is Britain Becoming Harder to Govern?* (BBC, 1976).

CHAPTER 10 THE BACKLASH AGAINST PROFESSIONAL SOCIETY

1 Ivan Illich, *Deschooling Society* (Penguin, 1973), *Medical Nemesis: The Expropriation of Health* (Calder & Boyars, 1975), *Disabling Professions* (Boyars, 1975), and *The Right to Useful Employment and its Professional Enemies* (Boyars, 1978). Cf. also Jethro K. Lieberman, *The Tyranny of the Experts* (Walker, 1970).

2 Magali S. Larson, *The Rise of Professionalism* (University of California Press, 1977), esp. pp. 51–2.

3 Cf. Margaret Thatcher's speech to Lobby correspondents, *The Times*, 19 January 1984.

4 Richard M. Titmuss, *The Irresponsible Society* (Fabian Society, 1960), pp. 10–11, 13–14, 20.

5 Paul Wilding, *Professional Power and Social Welfare* (Routledge & Kegan Paul, 1982), and *Socialism and Professionalism* (Fabian Society, 1981); see also Tim Robinson, *In Worlds Apart: Professionals and Their Clients in the Welfare State* (Bedford Square Press, 1978).

6 *The Times*, 19 January 1984.

7 *Guardian*, 21 April 1979; *Observer*, 27 May 1979; see also John Mortimer's defence of the binary legal profession and Lord Goodman's rejoinder, *Guardian*, 30 July and 1 August 1979.

8 *The Sunday Times*, 16 October 1983.

9 Sir Leslie Scarman *et al.*, *English Law and Social Policy* (A Symposium on his Hamlyn Lectures, 1974, Centre for Studies in Social Policy, 1976); Peter Jenkins, 'A sorry state for justice in Britain', *Guardian*, 21 November 1984.

10 Law Commission, *Codification of the Criminal Law* (Law Commission no. 143, HMSO, 1985); Robert Maclennan in *The Independent*, 8 January 1987. For further criticism of the Law Commission and the legal profession see Philip A. Thomas (ed.), *Law in the Balance: Legal Services in the Eighties* (Martin Robertson, 1982).

11 *Guardian*, 17 September 1984.

12 Cf. two widely publicized cases of medical negligence: (1) of a woman who had both breasts removed on a mistaken diagnosis of cancer; (2)

of 'catastrophic brain damage' arising from a cyst operation on a young man – *The Sunday Telegraph*, 19 July 1987.

13 *Guardian*, 16 April 1979.

14 Katharine Whitehorn in the *Observer*, 6 May 1979.

15 John A. T. Robinson, *Honest to God* (Student Christian Movement, 1963); Don Cupitt, *The Sea of Faith* (BBC, 1984); David Jenkins, *The Contradiction of Christianity* (Student Christian Movement, 1976). Cf. Franklin L. Baumer, *Modern European Thought, 1660–1950* (Collier Macmillan, 1977), part 5, ch. 3, 'The eclipse of God'.

16 Dennis Kavanagh, *Thatcherism and British Politics* (Oxford University Press, 1987), pp. 85, 252, 289.

17 Monopolies Commission, *Professional Services: A Report on the General Effect on the Public Interest of Certain Restrictive Practices*, Part II (Cmnd. 4463, 1970).

18 Sir Gordon Borrie, Hamptons Lecture to the Incorporated Society of Valuers and Auctioneers, *The Times*, 15 November 1983.

19 *Observer*, 18 January 1976, 29 March 1987.

20 James Lovelock, *Gaia: A New Look at Life on Earth* (Oxford University Press, 1979).

21 Cf., *inter alia*, Christopher Driver, *The Disarmers: A Study in Social Protest* (Hodder & Stoughton, 1964); Frank Parkin, *Middle-Class Radicalism: The Social Bases of the British Campaign for Nuclear Disarmament* (Manchester University Press, 1968); John Minnion and Philip Bolsover (eds), *The CND Story: The First 25 Years in the Words of the People Involved* (Allison & Busby, 1983); Meredith Veldman, 'Romantic and religious protest in a secular society: fantasy literature, the Campaign for Nuclear Disarmanent, and eco-activism in Britain, 1945–80' (unpublished PhD dissertation, Northwestern University, 1988), part 2.

22 John Kenneth Galbraith, *The Affluent Society* (Houghton Mifflin, 1958); E. J. Mishan, 'Review of *The Economics of Underdevelopment*', *Economica*, vol. 27, 1960; *Technology and Growth: The Price We Pay* (Praeger, 1973); and 'Whatever happened to progress?', *Journal of Economic Issues*, vol. 12, 1978, p. 412.

23 Rachel Carson, *Silent Spring* (Houghton Mifflin, 1962); Paul Ehrlich, *The Population Bomb* (Ballantine, 1968); D. H. Meadows *et al.*, *The Limits to Growth: A Report for the Club of Rome on the Predicament of Mankind* (Potomac Association, 1972); Edward Goldsmith *et al.*, *A Blueprint for Survival* (Penguin, 1972); E. F. Schumacher, *Small Is Beautiful: Economics as if People Mattered* (Blond & Briggs, 1973). See also Edward M. Nicholson, *The Environmental Revolution* (Penguin, 1972); Richard Kimber and J. J. Richardson, *Campaigning for the Environment* (Routledge & Kegan Paul, 1974); Stephen Cotgrove, *Catastrophe or Cornucopia: The Environment, Politics and the Future* (Wiley, 1982); Veldman, op. cit., part 3.

24 Cf., *inter alia*, Robert Bacon and Walter Eltis, *Britain's Economic Problem: Too Few Producers* (Macmillan, 1978).

25 Cf. *Guardian*, 9 August 1979.

26 *Observer*, 6 May 1979.

27 Cf., among other Institute of Economic Affairs publications: Arthur Seldon, *Wither the Welfare State* (1981); David G. Green, *The Welfare State: For Rich or Poor?* (1982); Hermione Parker, *The Moral Hazard of State Benefits* (1982); David Green, *Which Doctor? A Critical Analysis of the Professional Barriers to Competition in the Health Service* (1985) and *Challenge to the NHS* (1986); Arthur Seldon, *The Riddle of the Voucher ... Obstacles to Choice and Competition in State Schools* (1986).

28 Peter Townsend, *The Concept of Poverty* (Heinemann, 1970), p. 275.

29 Nick Bosanquet and Peter Townsend, *Labour and Equality* (Heinemann, 1980), p. 229.

30 Julian Le Grand, *The Strategy of Equality: Redistribution and the Social Services* (Allen & Unwin, 1982), p. 32.

31 Andrew Glyn and Bob Sutcliffe, *British Capitalism, Workers and the Profits Squeeze* (Penguin, 1972); J. O'Connor, *The Fiscal Crisis of the Capitalist State* (St Martin's Press, 1973); David Coates and John Hilliard (eds), *The Economic Decline of Modern Britain* (Harvester, 1986), part 4, 'Marxist views of economic decline'.

32 Ralph Harris, *No, Minister! A Radical Challenge on Economic and Social Policies* (Institute of Economic Affairs, 1985), pp. 57, 63.

33 Calculated from Richard Rose, *Politics in England* (Faber & Faber, 1985), p. 395.

34 *Government Expenditure Plans, 1986-7 and 1988-9* (Cmnd. 9702, 1986), vol. 2, pp. 6-7.

35 Kavanagh, op. cit., p. 294.

36 Margaret Thatcher, Speech at Newcastle-on-Tyne, 23 March 1985, in ibid., p. 291.

37 *Guardian*, 19 July 1985.

38 Anthony Heath *et al.*, *How Britain Votes* (Pergamon, 1985), p. 132.

39 Kavanagh, op. cit., p. 222.

40 *Observer*, 5 July 1987.

41 *Economic Trends Supplement*, no. 12 (HMSO, 1987), p. 201.

42 Kavanagh, op. cit., pp. 308-9.

43 Friedrich A. von Hayek, *A Tiger by the Tail: The Keynesian Legacy of Inflation* (Institute of Economic Affairs, 1972), pp. 107-8, 117.

44 Harris, op. cit., p. 26.

45 Adam Smith, *The Wealth of Nations* (1776; Bell, 1905 edn), vol. 1, p. 134.

46 *OECD Economic Outlook*, no. 41, June 1987; *Observer*, 21 June 1987; cf. also *The Sunday Times*, 9 October 1983.

47 Evan Davis and Andrew Dilnot, *The IFS Tax and Benefit Model* (Institute of Fiscal Studies, 1985).

48 *Paying for Local Government* (Cmnd. 9714, 1986).

49 See esp. Friedrich A. von Hayek, *The Road to Serfdom* (Routledge & Kegan Paul, 1944), *The Constitution of Liberty* (Routledge & Kegan Paul, 1960) and *Law, Legislation and Liberty* (Routledge & Kegan

Paul, 1982 edn).

50 Hayek, *A Tiger by the Tail*, pp. 99–100, 104–5.

51 Ibid., p. 111.

52 J. M. Keynes, *The General Theory of Employment, Interest and Money* (Macmillan, 1936), pp. 383–4.

53 John B. Wood, 'How it all began', in Arthur Seldon (ed.), *The Emerging Consensus?* (Institute of Economic Affairs, 1981).

54 James B. Buchanan and Gordon Tulloch, 'An American perspective', in idem, pp. 82–3.

55 Cf. Hayek, *Law, Legislation and Liberty*, and 'Will the democratic ideal prevail?', in Arthur Seldon (ed.), *Confrontation: Will the Open Society Survive to 1989?* (Institute of Economic Affairs, 1978).

56 Leslie Hannah, *The Rise of the Corporate Economy* (Methuen, 2nd edn, 1983), p. 180.

57 Alan Fox, *Beyond Contract: Work, Power and Trust Relations* (Faber & Faber, 1974), p. 336.

58 Robert B. Reich, 'The new American frontier', in *Atlantic Monthly*, March (pp. 43–58) and April (pp. 97–107, 1983), pp. 52, 55; see also his book, *The Next American Frontier* (Times Books, 1984).

59 Ibid., pp. 47, 108.

60 Ibid., p. 108.

61 Ibid., p. 108.

62 William Keegan, *Mrs Thatcher's Economic Experiment* (Allen Lane, 1984), p. 33.

63 *Social Trends*, 1987, pp. 103, 104.

64 *Social Trends*, 1979, p. 163; 1987, p. 80.

65 *Economic Trends Supplement*, no. 12 (HMSO, 1987), p. 123.

66 Aubrey Jones, *Britain's Economy: The Roots of Stagnation* (Cambridge University Press, 1985), p. 133.

67 Sir Alec Cairncross, 'The post-war years, 1945–77', in Roderick Floud and Donald McCloskey (eds), *The Economic History of Britain Since 1700*, vol. 2, *1860 to the 1970s* (Cambridge University Press, 1981), p. 388; M. A. Utton and A. D. Morgan, *Concentration and Foreign Trade* (Cambridge University Press, 1983), p. 72.

68 *New York Times*, 15 February 1987.

69 *OECD Economic Outlook*, no. 41, June 1987, p. 92.

70 Cairncross, loc. cit., pp. 409–11.

71 *The Economist*, 18 January 1986.

72 Keegan, op. cit., ch. 2.

73 *Social Trends*, 1987, p. 104.

74 *Observer*, 28 October 1986.

75 Cairncross, loc. cit., p. 394.

76 Sidney Pollard, *The Wasting of the British Economy* (Croom Helm, 1982), pp. 14, 73, 90, 189.

77 Cairncross, loc. cit., p. 380.

78 Cf. C. F. Pratten, *A Comparison of Swedish and UK Companies* (esp. ch. 14), and *Labour Productivity Differentials Within International Companies* (both Cambridge University Press, 1976); and Frances

Cairncross in the *Guardian*, 19 February 1977.

79 Jones, op. cit., pp. 139, 147.

80 Cf. above, ch. 8, section 1.

81 Sir Arthur Cockfield, 'The Price Commission and price control', *Three Banks Review*; March 1978.

82 M. W. Kirkby, *The Decline of British Economic Power* (Allen & Unwin, 1981); cf. Sir Henry Phelps Brown, 'What is the British predicament?', *Three Banks Review*; December 1977. See also Coates and Hilliard, op. cit., *passim*.

83 Ralf Dahrendorf, *On Britain* (BBC, 1982), pp. 84–5.

84 Fox, op. cit., *passim*.

85 Cf. Ronald P. Dore, *British Factory, Japanese Factory* (Allen & Unwin, 1973), pp. 31–41, 98–108. Even the Japanese are finding it difficult to maintain lifelong employment in the current recession, in which unemployment has risen to 3.2 per cent, and are finding 'familial' ways of laying off some workers, by offloading them to subsidiary companies, and so on – *Observer*, 2 August 1987 (*Magazine* section, pp. 23–7).

86 Robert Taylor in the *Observer*, 28 June 1987.

87 P. Whiteley and I. Gordon, in the *New Statesman*, 11 January 1980.

88 J. L. Garvin, *Life of Joseph Chamberlain* (Macmillan, 1932), vol. 1, p. 549.

89 Cf. J. H. Hexter, 'A new framework for social history', *Journal of Economic History*, vol. 15, 1955 on 'overmighty subjects'.

90 Edmund Burke, *Reflections on the Revolution in France (1790)*.

INDEX